T0219869

Lecture Notes in Computer Science 11115

Commenced Publication in 1973
Founding and Former Series Editors:
Gerhard Goos, Juris Hartmanis, and Jan van Leeuwen

Editorial Board

More information about this series at http://www.springer.com/series/7407

Giancarlo Mauri · Samira El Yacoubi
Alberto Dennunzio · Katsuhiro Nishinari
Luca Manzoni (Eds.)

Cellular Automata

13th International Conference on Cellular Automata
for Research and Industry, ACRI 2018
Como, Italy, September 17–21, 2018
Proceedings

 Springer

Editors
Giancarlo Mauri 🆔
University of Milano-Bicocca
Milan
Italy

Samira El Yacoubi 🆔
University of Perpignan
Perpignan
France

Alberto Dennunzio 🆔
University of Milano-Bicocca
Milan
Italy

Katsuhiro Nishinari
University of Tokyo
Tokyo
Japan

Luca Manzoni 🆔
University of Milano-Bicocca
Milan
Italy

ISSN 0302-9743   ISSN 1611-3349 (electronic)
Lecture Notes in Computer Science
ISBN 978-3-319-99812-1   ISBN 978-3-319-99813-8   (eBook)
https://doi.org/10.1007/978-3-319-99813-8

Library of Congress Control Number: 2018952243

LNCS Sublibrary: SL1 – Theoretical Computer Science and General Issues

This Springer imprint is published by the registered company Springer Nature Switzerland AG
The registered company address is: Gewerbestrasse 11, 6330 Cham, Switzerland

Preface

This volume contains a collection of original papers covering both applications and theoretical results on cellular automata, that were selected for presentation at the 13th International Conference on Cellular Automata for Research and Industry, ACRI 2018, held in Como, Italy, during September 17–21, 2018. The event was organized by the Department of Informatics, Systems, and Communication of the University of Milano-Bicocca.

The primary goal of the conference was to bring together researchers coming from many different scientific fields in order to foster international collaborations on cellular automata and to spread scientific knowledge among the experts in several scientific areas: computer science, pure and applied mathematics, physics, biology, and systems theory.

Cellular automata are a powerful computational model that can be applied to the study of complex phenomena characterized by the presence of many simple local interactions. Cellular automata are a discrete model (in both time and space) that have been successfully applied as a simplified representation of complex non-linear dynamics and as a general model of complexity. Starting from their discovery in the middle of the 20th century, cellular automata have generated more and more interest in both the theoretical aspects and the practical applications.

The ACRI conference series was first organized in Italy, namely, ACRI 1994 in Rende, ACRI 1996 in Milan, ACRI 1998 in Trieste and followed by ACRI 2000 in Karlsruhe (Germany), ACRI 2002 in Geneva (Switzerland), ACRI 2004 in Amsterdam (The Netherlands), ACRI 2006 in Perpignan (France), ACRI 2008 in Yokohama (Japan), ACRI 2010 in Ascoli Piceno (Italy), ACRI 2012 on Santorini (Greece), ACRI 2014 in Kraków (Poland), and ACRI 2016 in Fez (Morocco).

This 13th edition of ACRI aimed at expanding the classic topics to include other areas related to or extending cellular automata. This allowed a larger community to have the opportunity to discuss their work in various related fields like, for example, complex networks, bio-inspired computing, cryptography, biological network modelling, multiagent models, etc.

This volume contains the accepted papers from the main track and from the three organized workshops. We would first like to take this opportunity to express our sincere thanks to the invited speakers, Raul Rechtman and Andreas Deutsch, who kindly accepted our invitation to give plenary lectures at ACRI 2018. The whole book is divided into eight parts:

The part "Biological Systems Modeling" contains papers that deal directly with biological problems by using cellular automata. It is followed by the part "Simulation and Other Applications of CA," where cellular automata are applied in the study of other real-world phenomena.

The part "Multi-agent Systems" contains papers dealing more with the multi-agent view of cellular automata and, in the part "Pedestrian and Traffic Dynamics" this view is further explored in the specific cases of traffic and pedestrian dynamics.

The more theoretical papers are collected in the two parts "Synchronization and Control" and "Theory and Cryptography," where the results vary from the classic theory of control, to the solution of classic problems in cellular automata, like the firing squad synchronization problem, to the study of the dynamical properties of cellular automata, and to their application to cryptography.

The part titled "Asynchronous Cellular Automata" collects the papers accepted the workshop Asynchronous Cellular Automata (ACA). We want to thank the chairs of the workshop's Program Committee, Alberto Dennunzio and Enrico Formenti, together with all the members of the workshop's Program Committee for their work in selecting the papers.

The part "Crowds, Traffic, and Cellular Automata" contains the papers accepted for the workshops Crowds and Cellular Automata (C&CA) and Traffic and Cellular Automata (T&CA). We want to thank the Program Committee chairs of the two workshops: Giuseppe Vizzari, Jarosław Wąs, Katsuhiro Nishinari, and Andreas Schadschneider together with the members of the Program Committees for their work in selecting the papers.

We are grateful to the Program Committee and all the additional reviewers for their invaluable help in selecting the papers. We extend our thanks to the remaining members of the local Organizing Committee, Stefania Bandini and Luca Mariot. We are also grateful for the support by the Department of Informatics, Systems and Communication and the University of Milano-Bicocca. Finally, we acknowledge the excellent cooperation from the Lecture Notes in Computer Science team of Springer for their help in producing this volume in time for the conference.

July 2018

Giancarlo Mauri
Samira El Yacoubi
Alberto Dennunzio
Katsuhiro Nishinari
Luca Manzoni

Organization

Chairs

Giancarlo Mauri (Chair) University of Milano-Bicocca, Italy
Samira El Yacoubi University of Perpignan, France
(Co-chair)

Workshop Chair

Stefania Bandini University of Milano-Bicocca, Italy

Asynchronous Cellular Automata

Alberto Dennunzio University of Milano-Bicocca, Italy
Enrico Formenti Nice Sophia Antipolis University, France

Crowds and Cellular Automata

Giuseppe Vizzari University of Milano-Bicocca, Italy
Jarosław Wąs AGH University of Science and Technology, Poland

Traffic and Cellular Automata

Katsuhiro Nishinari RCAST, The University of Tokyo, Japan
Andreas Schadschneider Institute for Theoretical Physics, University of Cologne, Germany

Program Committee

Andy Adamatzky University of the West of England, UK
Jan Baetens Ghent University, Belgium
Franco Bagnoli University of Florence, Italy
Stefania Bandini University of Milano-Bicocca, Italy
Bernard De Baets Ghent University, Belgium
Pedro de Oliveira Universidade Presbiteriana Mackenzie, Brazil
Alberto Dennunzio University of Milano-Bicocca, Italy
Andreas Deutsch TU Dresden, Germany
Salvatore Di Gregorio University of Calabria, Italy
Witold Dzwinel AGH University of Science and Technology, Poland
Nazim Fates LORIA, Inria Nancy, France
Enrico Formenti Nice Sophia Antipolis University, France

Ioakeim Georgoudas	Democritus University of Thrace, Greece
Rolf Hoffmann	TU Darmstadt, Germany
Toshihiko Komatsuzaki	Kanazawa University, Japan
Krzysztof Kułakowski	AGH University of Science and Technology, Poland
Martin Kutrib	Institut für Informatik, Universität Giessen, Germany
Anna T. Lawniczak	University of Guelph, Canada
Laurent Lefevre	LCIS, University of Grenoble Alpes, France
Luca Manzoni	University of Milano-Bicocca, Italy
Sara Manzoni	University of Milano-Bicocca, Italy
Luca Mariot	University of Milano-Bicocca, Italy
Genaro J. Martínez	National Polytechnic Institute, Mexico
Giancarlo Mauri	University of Milano-Bicocca, Italy
Angelo B. Mingarelli	Carleton University, Canada
Shin Morishita	Yokohama National University, Japan
Katsuhiro Nishinari	RCAST, The University of Tokyo, Japan
Dipanwita Roy Chowdhury	IIT kharagpur, India
Biplab K. Sikdar	Indian Institute of Engineering Science and Technology, India
Georgios Ch. Sirakoulis	Democritus University of Thrace, Greece
Domenico Talia	University of Calabria, Italy
Marco Tomassini	University of Lausanne, Switzerland
Paweł Topa	AGH University of Science and Technology, Poland
Leen Torenvliet	University of Amsterdam, The Netherlands
Hiroshi Umeo	University of Osaka Electro-Communication, Japan
Giuseppe Vizzari	University of Milano-Bicocca, Italy
Gabriel Wainer	Carleton University, Canada
Jaroslaw Was	AGH University of Science and Technology, Poland
Thomas Worsch	Karlsruhe Institute of Technology, Germany
Radouane Yafia	Ibn Zohr University, Morocco

Workshops Program Committee

Asynchronous Cellular Automata

Alberto Dennunzio	University of Milano-Bicocca, Italy
Nazim Fates	Inria Nancy-Grand Est, France
Enrico Formenti	Nice Sophia Antipolis University, France
Maximilien Gadouleau	University of Durham, UK
Christophe Guyeux	University of Bourgogne Franche-Comté, France
Adrien Richard	CNRS and Nice Sophia Antipolis University, France

Crowds and Cellular Automata

Stefania Bandini	University of Milano-Bicocca, Italy
Mohcine Chraibi	Jülich Supercomputing Centre, Germany
Luca Crociani	University of Milano-Bicocca, Italy

Ioakeim Georgoudas	Democritus University of Thrace, Greece
Tomasz M. Gwizdalla	University of Lodz, Poland
Hubert Klüpfel	TraffGo GmbH – Duisburg, Germany
Gerta Köster	Munich University of Applied Sciences, Germany
Tobias Kretz	PTV AG, Germany
Shin Morishita	Yokohama National University, Japan
Katsuhiro Nishinari	The University of Tokyo, Japan
Andreas Schadschneider	University of Cologne, Germany
Armin Seyfried	Jülich Supercomputing Centre, Germany
Georgios Sirakoulis	Democritus University of Thrace, Greece
Weiguo Song	University of Science and Technology of China, Hefei, China
Kazuhiro Yamamoto	Nagoya University, Japan
Daichi Yanagisawa	The University of Tokyo, Japan

Traffic and Cellular Automata

Sven Maerivoet	Transport and Mobility Leuven, Belgium
Akiyasu Tomoeda	Musashino University, Japan
Antoine Tordeux	University of Jülich, Germany
Martin Treiber	University of Dresden, Germany
Peter Wagner	DLR Berlin, Germany
Shin-ichi Tadaki	Saga University, Japan
Tetsuji Tokihiro	The University of Tokyo, Japan
Stefania Bandini	University of Milano-Bicocca, Italy
Daichi Yanagisawa	The University of Tokyo, Japan
Rui Jiang	University of Science and Technology of China, China
Jun Sato	The University of Tokyo, Japan

Steering Committee

Stefania Bandini	University of Milano-Bicocca, Italy
Bastien Chopard	University of Geneva, Switzerland
Samira El Yacoubi	University of Perpignan, France
Giancarlo Mauri	University of Milano-Bicocca, Italy
Katsuhiro Nishinari	RCAST, The University of Tokyo, Japan
Georgios Ch. Sirakoulis	Democritus University of Thrace, Greece
Hiroshi Umeo	University of Osaka Electro-Communication, Japan
Thomas Worsch	Karlsruhe Institute of Technology, Germany

Organizing Committee

Giancarlo Mauri (Chair)	University of Milano-Bicocca, Italy
Stefania Bandini	University of Milano-Bicocca, Italy
Alberto Dennunzio	University of Milano-Bicocca, Italy
Luca Manzoni	University of Milano-Bicocca, Italy

Luca Mariot   University of Milano-Bicocca, Italy
Giuseppe Vizzari   University of Milano-Bicocca, Italy

Università degli Studi di Milano-Bicocca

Dipartimento di Informatica, Sistemistica e Comunicazione
Università degli Studi di Milano-Bicocca

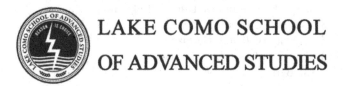

LAKE COMO SCHOOL
OF ADVANCED STUDIES

Contents

Multi-Agent Systems

Pedestrian and Traffic Dynamics

Biological Systems Modeling

Biological System Modeling

Cellular Automata Model for Proteomics and Its Application in Cancer Immunotherapy

Soumyabrata Ghosh[✉] and Parimal Pal Chaudhuri

CARLBio Pvt. Ltd., Kolkata, India
soumya@carlbio.com
https://carbio.com

Abstract. This paper presents our first version of Protein modeling Cellular Automata Machine (PCAM). The peptide chain of amino acid backbone of a protein having n number of amino acids is designed with an $8n$ cell uniform CA employing one of the 64 three neighborhood CA (3NCA) rules. Each amino acid of a protein chain is modeled by a group of eight CA cells. Variation of the interaction pattern of a protein backbone under different physical conditions is modeled with different sixty-four 3NCA rules. Another set of twenty 8-bit patterns are next designed to encode the molecular structure of side chains of twenty amino acids. The eight CA cells representing an amino acid in the chain is initialized with the 8 bit pattern of its side-chain. A set of features extracted from evolution of PCAM are mapped to real life experimental results. The PCAM model is validated from cancer immunotherapy experimental results for MAb-PD-L1 interaction on multiple MAbs (Monoclonal Antibodies) with the protein PD-L1 associated in human immunity.

Keywords: Cellular automata · Proteomics · Cancer immunotherapy

1 Background

On completion of the Human Genome project in 2003, the discipline of Proteomics got enriched with addition of large number of proteins displaying wide varieties of structure and function. This explosive growth of protein sequences demands high-throughput tools for rapidly identifying various attributes based on their sequence information alone. Machine Learning (ML) methodologies for modeling protein sequences [1,2] have attracted considerable attention in recent years. Such ML based tools have high dependency on voluminous experimental data. However, "the majority of data in biology are still atypical for Machine Learning; they are too sparse and incomplete, too biased and too noisy." rightly pointed out by Moreira et al. [3]. In this background, we propose a Cellular Automata (CA) model named as **Protein modeling CA Machine (PCAM)** which employs *information* content of bio-molecules and their building blocks.

© Springer Nature Switzerland AG 2018
G. Mauri et al. (Eds.): ACRI 2018, LNCS 11115, pp. 3–15, 2018.
https://doi.org/10.1007/978-3-319-99813-8_1

PCAM is designed with uniform 3-neighborhood CA (3NCA) to model protein interaction. PCAM evolution parameters are algorithmically mapped to the protein functions without extensive training procedures used in machine learning. To summarize, the PCAM employs (1) a relatively simple CA model for protein-protein interaction, uses (2) a new amino acid digital encoding based on physico-chemical properties and generates (3) CA output patterns which can be analyzed and mapped to the behaviors of interacting proteins.

Extensive study of CA rule evolution to analyze the behavior of complex systems is a well-researched area [4–7]. Xiao et al. [6,7] first introduced CA as the interaction modeling tool for proteomics. Most of the CA-based model for protein chain converts amino acid sequence as an array of binary CA cells. Thus, translating amino acid to binary code is a prerequisite for CA modeling. Many researchers have proposed different amino acid encoding based on its structure and codon degeneracy. Cristea [8] proposed a representation of genetic code, which converts the DNA sequences into digital signals and used a base four representation of the nucleotides. It leads to the conversion of the codons into numbers in the range 0 to 63 and the amino acids in the range 0 to 20. Cristea model reflects better amino acid structure and degeneracy. Pan et al. [9] also proposed another amino acid coding scheme. Though both the procedures can encode a protein sequence to a sequence of digital signals, the physico-chemical properties of the amino acids were ignored. Xiao et al. [6] proposed a model of digital coding for amino acids based on rule similarity, complementarity of rule, molecular recognition theory, and information theory. The model reflects better amino acid physico-chemical properties and degeneracy. The PCAM model, introduced next, employs a new amino acid encoding based on its molecular configuration.

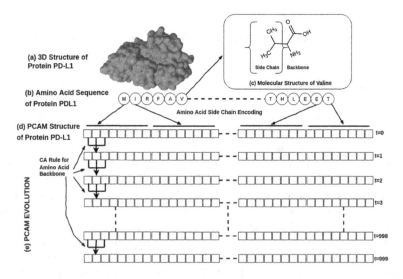

Fig. 1. PCAM Structure for a protein PD-L1 - (a) 3D structure of PD-L1, (b) amino acid chain of PD-L1, (c) molecular structure of amino acid Valine, (d) PCAM seed at time-step $t = 0$, and (e) PCAM evolution for time-steps $t = 999$

2 Design of Protein Modeling CA Machine (PCAM)

Cellular Automata is a discrete model consisting of a set of cells, which occupy some or all sites of a regular lattice [10]. These cells have one or more internal state variables and a set of rules specifying the evolution of their state. The change of a cell state depends on the current state of the cell and those of neighboring cells. The simplest type of cellular automata is one-dimensional, three neighborhood and two state per cell, referred as 3NCA [10].

Proteins are covalently bonded chain of amino acids, also known as peptide chain, which is folded to form a complex 3D structure having biological functions. There are 20 common amino acids found in proteins, having a similar backbone molecular structure with $-C_\alpha H(-NH_2) - COOH$. Amino acids differ in their respective side-chain. In a peptide chain, the common backbone of amino acids are interconnected with its neighbors through peptide bonds between carboxyl group $(-COOH)$ and amino group $(-NH_2)$ of two neighboring amino acids. In Fig. 1, an illustration of PCAM design for an example protein PD-L1 (Human Programmed cell death 1 ligand 1) is shown. PD-L1's 3D structure and the amino acid sequence are shown in Fig. 1(a) and (b) respectively. Figure 1(c) (top-right corner box) reports the molecular structure of amino acid Valine (V), with its backbone and side-chain marked. Figure 1(d) and (e) show PCAM structure and its evolution respectively, which will be discussed next.

To design a PCAM for an input protein sequence, the backbone and side-chain of each amino acid are represented by a uniform 3NCA rule and a 8 bit binary string respectively. The connected array of side-chains' 8 bit binary strings represents the CA seed (initiation step at time-step $t = 0$) of the PCAM structure (Fig. 1(d)). Thus a protein chain with n amino acid residues is represented by an $8n$ cell uniform 3NCA. Next, the PCAM is evolved by backbone 3NCA rule for $t = 999$ time-steps to generate a binary evolution matrix of $(1000, 8n)$ dimension (Fig. 1(e)). The assignment of backbone rule is discussed next, followed by the discussion on side-chain encoding.

2.1 Modeling Amino Acid Backbone

To design the CA rules for interconnected amino acid backbone $(-C_\alpha H(-NH)-CO)$ in a peptide chain, we consider only heavy atoms (C, N, O) and exclude hydrogen atom (H). Thus, the molecular structure of the common uniform backbone $(-C\alpha(-N) - CO)$ of all amino acid residues has 4 atoms - one O, one N, and two Cs. Next, the 8 bit pattern of uniform 3NCA rules for backbone is designed as follows borrowing the concept of "switching function". A 3 variable switching function has 8 Min Terms from 000 to 111. A 3NCA rule implements a three variable switching function. The eight min terms of a 3NCA rule are referred to as Rule Min Terms (Rule Min Terms):

- Step 1: Rule Mean Term (RMT) [10], the 3-bit binary string of CA Rule input state, is classified into two classes:
  1. 1-Major RMTs having two 1's $(111, 110, 101, 011)$.

2. 0-Major RMTs having two 0's (000, 001, 010, 100).
- Step 2: Two 1's are assigned to represent O and N atoms in the next state values of 1-Major RMTs.
- Step 3: Two 1's are assigned to represent two C atoms in the next state value of 0-Major RMTs.

In the process, the following sixty-four non-trivial balanced 3NCA rules are designed to model different variants of amino acid backbone:

[141, 197, 177, 163, 75, 89, 210, 154, 45, 101, 180, 166, 58, 114, 92, 78, 139, 209, 153, 195, 57, 99, 156, 198, 46, 116, 60, 102, 77, 178, 90, 165, 135, 149, 225, 169, 27, 83, 216, 202, 39, 53, 228, 172, 30, 86, 120, 106, 147, 201, 150, 105, 15, 85, 240, 170, 29, 71, 184, 226, 51, 204, 54, 108].

This sixty-four 3NCA rules model sixty-four different variations of an amino acid backbone, which means, for an input protein chain, we have sixty-four PCAMs. While only heavy atoms are included in the modeling and all atoms are treated equally, the variety of sixty-four rules essentially models the effect of various molecular configurations. The diversity of derived PCAMs represents the diverse functionality of a protein. The amino acid side-chain encoding is discussed next.

2.2   Modeling Amino Acid Sidechain

Similar to the amino acid backbone, the digital encoding of side-chain proceeds on considering only non-H atoms in the side-chains. We consider an 8 bit pattern to be assigned to side-chains as 1-Major and 0-Major format discussed earlier. The side-chain encoding is based on the assignment of atoms as 1's to the next state of Palindromic RMT (PRMT): 7(111), 5(101), 2(010), 0(000), which remain unaltered on reversal of its sequence, and other non-palindromic RMT pairs called CoP (Conjugate Pair): (6(110), 3(011)) and (4(100), 1(001)), where one RMT is derived out of the other on reversing the three bit string.

Atoms are assigned as 1's to the next state of different RMTs based on the following conditions:

CONDITIONS FOR SIDE-CHAIN ENCODING

1. Only non-H atoms C, N, O, S of the side-chain are considered in the design process.
2. The 6-carbon ring (Aromatic ring) is considered as a single entity and it is placed as the next state of the RMT 7(111) for the residues having ring in the side-chain.
3. The design ensures that the covalent bond between a pair of side-chain atoms are mapped while assigning atoms as 1's to next states of RMTs maintaining following rules:
   - A covalent bond is implicit between atoms placed on CoP RMT pairs (6, 3) and (4, 1).
   - An atom placed on a PRMT (7, 5, 2, 0), whenever necessary, is assumed to make a covalent bond with any atom placed as the next state of any other RMT.

– C atoms, in general, are placed as the next state of 0-Major, while O, N, S atoms are mapped to the next state of 1-Major RMTs. In case, the number of C atoms is more than 2, it is placed as the next state of a 1-Major RMT, and marked as an exception.

It is possible to assign atoms differently while maintaining the above conditions. Thus the amino acid encoding used here is one of such possible configurations. This is an open area of discussion and development to find the best configuration to be used. For the current study, we are using the encoding reported in Table 1 showing RMTs as < 7 6 5 4 3 2 1 0 > with marking of 1-Major RMTs in grey background and 0-Major RMTS in white background.

The first two columns of Table 1 show the name and abbreviation of 20 amino acids. The 8 bit binary patterns for each amino acid side-chain are reported in 3rd column. The 1-Major RMTs <7 6 5 3> are marked in grey background. While next state value of each RMT from 0 to 6 represent an individual non-H atom, the RMT 7 represents the 6-Carbon Aromatic Ring (R) – all amino acids

Table 1. Amino acid Side-chain Encoding. 1-Major RMTs are marked in grey background; total non-H atoms and compositions are shown – R = six carbon aromatic ring, C = Carbon, O = Oxygen, N = Nitrogen, and S = Sulfur.; Exception * represents exception in Condition 3.

Amino acids	Abbreviations	RMTs 7 6 5 4 3 2 1 0	Total non-H atom	Exception
Glycine	G (Gly)	0 0 0 0 0 0 0 0	0	
Alanine	A (Ala)	0 0 0 0 0 1 0 0	1 (1C)	
Proline	P (Pro)	0 0 1 0 0 1 1 0	3 (3C)	*
Valine	V (Val)	0 0 0 1 0 1 1 0	3 (3C)	
Methionine	M (Met)	0 0 1 1 0 1 1 0	4 (3C + 1S)	
Tryptophan	W (Trp)	1 0 1 1 0 1 1 0	R + 4 (R + 3C + 1N)	
Phenylalanine	F (Phe)	1 0 0 0 0 1 0 0	R + 1 (R + 1C)	
Isoleucine	I (Ile)	0 0 0 1 1 1 1 0	4 (4C)	*
Leucine	L (Leu)	0 0 0 1 0 1 1 1	4 (4C)	
Serine	S (Ser)	0 0 1 0 0 1 0 0	2 (1C + 1O)	
Cysteine	C (Cys)	0 1 0 0 0 1 0 0	2 (1C + 1S)	
Threonine	T (Thr)	0 0 1 1 0 1 0 0	3 (2C + 1O)	
Asparagine	N (Asn)	0 0 1 0 1 1 1 0	4 (2C + 1N + 1O)	
Glutamine	Q (Gln)	0 0 1 0 1 1 1 1	5 (3C + 1N + 1O)	
Tyrosine	Y (Tyr)	1 0 1 0 0 1 0 0	R + 2 (R + 1C + 1O)	
Histidine	H (His)	0 1 1 1 1 1 1 0	6 (4C + 2N)	*
Lysine	K (Lys)	0 0 1 1 0 1 1 1	5 (4C + 1N)	
Arginine	R (Arg)	0 1 1 1 1 1 1 1	7 (4C + 3N)	
Aspartic Acid	D (Asp)	0 1 1 1 0 1 0 0	4 (2C + 2O)	
Glutamic Acid	E (Glu)	0 1 1 1 0 1 1 0	5 (3C + 2O)	

containing such ring structure will have 1 in RMT 7 (Condition 1). The 4th column shows the count of non-H atoms and their compositions.

For example, amino acid Asparagine (Asn) has total 4 non-H atoms – 2 Cs, 1 N, and 1 O. It's encoding is $< 0\ 0\ 1\ 0\ 1\ 1\ 1\ 0 >$. There are two 1's in 1-Major RMTs representing 1 N and 1 O, while two C atoms are placed in 0-Major RMTs, maintaining Condition 3 representing covalent bond structures.

For seventeen out of twenty amino acids, all conditions are maintained. For three amino acids, Pro, Ile and His, Condition 3 is not maintained to implement the covalent bonds (marked * in Table 1 last column). The side-chain encoding of amino acid Valine (Val) is illustrated next.

An Illustration of Amino Acid Sidechain Encoding for Valine. In Fig. 2, the encoding of amino acid Valine is shown in the 4th row along with the decimal values and binary patterns of RMTs in 1st and 2nd row respectively. The 3rd row shows the class of RMT - PRMT or CoP. The side-chain of Valine has three non-hydrogen atoms, all are Carbon (C). There are two $C-C$ covalent bonds in the side-chain. One C atom (C_β) is connected to other two C atoms - C_γ and C_δ by these bonds. The encoding of Valine in 4th row shows three 1's representing three C atoms – CoP RMT 4 and 1 are assigned to C_β and C_γ respectively, while PRMT 2 is assigned to C_δ. Thus, under Condition 3, CoP RMT 1 and 4 are connected by covalent bond ($C_\gamma - C_\beta$), and PRMT 2 is connected to CoP RMT 4 by covalent bond ($C_\delta - C_\beta$). In Fig. 2, the atom assignment and covalent bonds are shown in 5th and 6th rows respectively. This atom assignment is interchangeable between C_δ and C_γ, similar to the configuration change among L/R isomers.

RMT	7	6	5	4	3	2	1	0
Binary	111	110	101	100	011	010	001	000
Class	PRMT	CoP(3)	PMRT	CoP(1)	CoP(6)	PRMT	CoP(4)	PRMT
Valine	0	0	0	1	0	1	1	0
Atom				C_β		C_δ	C_γ	
Bond								

Fig. 2. Amino acid side-chain encoding. The decimal value and binary pattern of RMTs and their class (PRMT or CoP) are shown. y = CoP(x) means RMT y is the Conjugate Pair (CoP) of RMT x. An example side-chain encoding for amino acid Valine is also shown with the assigned atoms and covalent bonds.

To summarize, we now have the sixty-four 3NCA rules for the amino acid backbone and twenty 8-bit binary code for amino acid side-chain. The PCAM evolution and feature extraction from PCAM output are discussed next.

2.3 PCAM Evolution

As discussed earlier, a PCAM model of a protein has two components - (1) a uniform 3NCA rule modeled by amino acid backbone and (2) a 3NCA seed modeled by amino acid side-chain. The choice of backbone 3NCA rule depend on the protein functions to be modeled. This means that we need to choose the backbone rule depending on what we want to model and predict. For example, the rule for analyzing localization of a protein will be different from the rule for predicting its binding affinity with a ligand.

PCAM evolution is illustrated in Fig. 1(e) for a 3NCA rule. For each sixty-four backbone rule, PCAM of a n-length protein is evolved for time-steps $t = 999$ to generate **PCAM Evolution Matrix (PEM)** - a binary matrix of $(1000, 8n)$ dimension. The resulting PCAM Evolution Matrix (PEM), also known as CA-image, are stored for further texture analysis. The PCAM program steps are discussed next.

Program: PCAM Module

Input: Amino acid sequence of n-length in Fasta format and sixty-four 3NCA rules designed for backbone

Output: PCAM Evolution Matrices (PEM) for sixty-four backbone 3NCA rules

Steps:

1. Parse the input amino acid sequence. Check for any symbol other than 20 common amino acids. If passed, proceed to Step 2.
2. Encode the amino acid string using amino acid side-chain encoding Table 1. This $8n$ length encoded binary string will be used as the CA seed.
3. For each of the sixty-four backbone 3NCA rules,
   (a) Create a PEM matrix of ($8n$ columns × 1000 rows).
   (b) Store the CA seed as the first row in the PEM matrix.
   (c) Evolve the next-state as null-boundary 3-neighborhood CA and repeat the step for 999 times. Store the binary-output of each step in consecutive row in the PEM matrix.

For sixty-four backbone rules, sixty-four PEM matrices are generated.

The PCAM is implemented as an in-house Python module. To make it faster, the Python code is translated into C++ code by Shed Skin utility, an experimental (restricted-Python)-to-C++ compiler. The compiled module is used as a Python extension in larger complex code. Many open source Python libraries, including MatPlotLib for graphics, Scikit-Learn for data analysis and SKImage for texture analysis are also used.

PCAM is designed to be a platform to experiment with proteins of any length and origin. Single or multiple mutation at any amino acid residue can be modeled through PCAM. The effect of the mutation is modeled from the comparison of the Mutant and Wild PEM matrices. From the known data, we can map a PCAM with a specific backbone rule, for which the PEM matrices can efficiently model the experimental findings in respect of difference observed between wild and mutant proteins. Those rules can be used for the prediction of the unknown or test-cases.

The sixty-four PEM matrices, generated by sixty-four backbone rules are analyzed to extract features for the model. The feature extraction method is discussed next.

2.4   Feature Extraction

We employ a statistical method of examining texture that considers the spatial relationship of pixels known as Gray-Level Co-occurrence Matrix (GLCM) scheme [7] on the binary PEM matrices generated from PCAM evolution. Image texture represents the information in respect of the spatial arrangement of binary data in the PEM matrix. The GLCM functions characterize the texture of an image by calculating how often pairs of pixel with specific values and in a specified spatial relationship occur in an image, creating a GLCM, and then extracting statistical measures from this matrix.

GLCM matrix can be derived row-wise or column wise. Row-wise GLCM (rGLCM) is sequence length independent, which means any length of protein sequence will form a $(t, 4)$ rGLCM matrix with the time-step of t. Further, rGLCM captures the spatial nature of CA evolution. For our PCAM texture analysis purpose, we have used rGLCM exclusively.

Four features extracted from GLCM - Angular Second Momentum (ASM), Contrast, Correlation, and Entropy are commonly used in texture analysis [11]. In our applications, Angular Second Moment (ASM) values from GLCM analysis found to be the most useful parameter. ASM for a GLCM matrix is derived as a four element array.

For analyzing the effect of mutation on a specific residue position of a protein, we substitute the amino acid side-chain code at that position with Alanine's side-chain code. This process is known as *in silico* Ala-mutagenesis. Subsequently, we run PCAM on both Wild and Mutant (with Ala-mutagenesis) sequences to generate Wild and Mutant rGLCM matrices. Next, the ASM values (four element array) are derived from both GLCMs. The **Difference Score (DS)** of a Mutant is the Mahalanobis Distance [12] between Wild and Mutant ASM arrays. Higher DS value signifies higher effect of mutation at that position.

Next section reports the application of PCAM in the study of monoclonal antibodies (MAbs), clinically used in cancer immunotherapy.

3   Study of Monoclonal Antibodies (MAb) for Cancer Immunotherapy

Cancer immunotherapy utilizing Monoclonal Antibodies (MAb) to mask the inhibitory receptor PD-L1 have drawn considerable attention in recent years. Blockage of PD-L1 binding is an attractive strategy for restoring tumor-specific T-cell immunity in patients with several forms of cancer [13–15]. It has been shown that many residues are often involved in a protein binding interface between MAbs and PD-L1, but only a few of them make critical contributions towards formation of the complex. These key residues are called the **hot-spots** and they are general targets for rational drug design in blocking protein interactions.

Although MAb based immunotherapy has achieved great successes in recent years, some basic questions yet exist. What are the hot-spots in the PD-L1-MAb interaction surface for checkpoint blockade MAb targeting? Can we predict the possible mutational escapes on PD-L1 under the immune selective pressure of the MAbs during immune checkpoint blockade therapy? We've employed our PCAM based model to understand PD-L1-MAb interaction and answer these questions in next two sub-sections.

3.1 PCAM Model for Hot-Spot Detection on MAbs

To design more specific MAbs for PD-L1, the knowledge of hot-spot residues of the MAbs is a necessity. A computational model for hot-spot detection on MAbs will decrease the time and cost of actual trial.

Recent structural studies of clinically used MAbs reports the high resolution complex structure of Avelumab [13], Atezolizumab [14], and Durvalumab [15] with PD-L1. The amino acid sequences of the heavy and light chain of these MAbs are available on Drugbank [16].

PCAMs for each of the MAbs, for both heavy and light chain, are evolved for time-steps $t = 999$. Next we have introduced in silico ALA mutagenesis in each of residue positions of these MAbs, and evolved the PCAM. The derived PEM (PCAM Evolution Matrix) data is analyzed by GLCM method and DS (Difference Score) is calculated for each residue positions as reported in Subsect. 2.4.

DS shows an interesting pattern among all the MAbs. For Rule 197 CA evolution, the DS values can be grouped into a small number of clusters (1 to 3) for each of the twenty amino acids irrespective of its position except a few positions, which do not fall in any clusters. We mark these non-clustered residue positions as the probable hot-spots. The experimental and structural data [13–15] of PDL1-MAb binding confirms that the majority of hot-spot residues necessary for the binding are present in our predicted hot-spot list.

The detailed result of PD-L1 binding MAbs - Avelumab and Atezolizumab are reported in Table 2. Each MAb has two chains - Heavy Chain and Light Chain. For each chain, the known hotspots positions with amino acid are shown in second column. Third column reports our prediction where HS means Hot-spot and NS means Non-hot-spot. The Prediction quality and accuracy are reported in last two columns.

The PCAM based hot-spot identification method shows prediction accuracy more than 90%. Due to its highly variable regions in amino acid sequence, the de facto homology based schemes are not suitable for MAb analysis. PCAM model is next extended to analyze the effect of PD-L1 mutation on PD-L1-MAb binding.

3.2 PCAM Model for Prediction of Mutational Effect on PD-L1-MAb Binding

The aim of this study is to compare the binding affinity of wild and mutant PD-L1 with two MAbs. To analyze the effect of mutation on PD-L1, the PCAM is generated from the PD-L1 sequence. This study establishes the modeling capability of the PCAM on a case study recently reported [14]. Further, the 3NCA

Table 2. PCAM based hot-spot prediction of MAbs (Avelumab and Atezolizumab) for PD-L1-MAb binding

Chain	Known hotspot	Predicted hotspot	Prediction quality	Accuracy
Avelumab heavy chain	F27	HS	Total residue: 450 TP: 8 TN: 427 FP: 11 FN: 4	96.6%
	T28	HS		
	S31	HS		
	I33	HS		
	Y52	NS		
	P53	HS		
	S54	HS		
	G55	HS		
	I57	NS		
	F59	HS		
	L101	NS		
	G102	NS		
Avelumab light chain	Y32	NS	Total residue: 216 TP: 4 TN: 193 FP: 17 FN: 2	91.2%
	Y34	NS		
	Y93	HS		
	S95	HS		
	S97	HS		
	R99	HS		
Atezolizumab heavy chain	G55	HS	Total residue: 448 TP: 6 TN: 412 FP: 28 FN: 2	93.9%
	S57	HS		
	T54	HS		
	T58	NS		
	D31	HS		
	R99	HS		
	W101	NS		
	S30	HS		
Atezolizumab light chain	Y93	HS	Total residue: 214 TP: 1 TN: 194 FP: 19 FN: 0	91.1%

rule to be employed for the study of any mutant of PD-L1 with a specific MAb gets identified from this study. A recent study [14] reported the crystal structure of an anti-PD-L1 molecule KN035 and analyzed the contribution of each PD-L1 residue of the interface towards binding through mutagenesis and affinity measurement. The hot-spot residues of PD-L1 surface identified are I54, Y56, E58, Q66 and R113 [14].

Table 3. PCAM based prediction of the effect of mutation on PDL1 - the known K_d values of PD-L1 variants for KN035 and Atezolizumab and Difference Scores (DS) calculated from PCAM with Rule 99 and Rule 201. Significantly higher changes of K_d and DS values are marked in bold.

1	2	3	4	5	6	7
PD-L1 Mutants	K_d of KN035	$\frac{K_d^{Wild}}{K_d^{Mutant}}$	DS Rule 201	K_d of Atezolizumab	$\frac{K_d^{Wild}}{K_d^{Mutant}}$	DS Rule 99
Wild	3.0E-09	1	0	9.96E-09	1	0
I54A	2.42E-07	80.7	0	3.23E-08	3.2	1.42
Y56A	1.24E-06	413.3	**2441.32**	2.68E-08	2.7	0.57
E58A	1.49E-07	49.7	1	1.81E-07	**18.2**	**334.43**
D61A	1.99E-08	6.6	0	9.99E-09	1.0	0.35
N63A	2.30E-08	7.7	1	1.73E-08	1.7	12.55
Q66A	4.88E-07	**162.7**	**998**	2.46E-09	0.25	**335.32**
R113A	5.34E-07	**178**	0	8.52E-08	8.6	0.18
M115A	5.51E-08	18.4	1	4.57E-08	4.6	0.36
Y123A	4.24E-08	14.1	1	4.66E-08	4.7	**374.78**
R125A	2.97E-08	9.9	**998**	5.89E-08	6.0	0.51

In Table 3, the K_d values for KN035 and Atezolizumab are shown for ten mutants and Wild Type (WT) of PD-L1 protein. Smaller the K_d value, higher is the binding affinity of the ligand for its target. Column 1 of Table 3 reports the ten mutants analyzed under this case study with wild. K_d value and ratio of K_d^{Mutant} with K_d^{Wild} are reported on columns 2, 3, (for KN035) and columns 5, 6 (for Atezolizumab). These 10 mutants are analyzed through PCAM model. The 4th and 7th columns (grey colored) report the Difference Score (DS) calculated from the GLCM analysis of PCAM model from Rule 201 and Rule 99 respectively.

For KN035-PD-L1 interaction, PCAM with Rule 201 generates high DS values for mutants Y56A, Q66A and R125A respectively (4th column of Table 3). Among these, Y56A, and Q66A are known mutants having high K_d value changes towards KN035 reported in [14]. For Atezolizumab, the K_d values do not vary as much as that for KN035. DS values estimated by PCAM model using Rule 99, reported in the 7th column in Table 3), show high value for three mutants E58A, Q66A, and Y123A. Among these, E58A is a known mutant having high K_d value change towards Atezolizumab [14]. Thus Rule 201 and Rule 99 model the behavior of KN035-PD-L1 and Atezolizumab-PD-L1 binding. For any other mutational study on KN035-PD-L1 and Atezolizumab-PD-L1 interactions, the backbone 3NCA rule for PCAM will be Rule 201 and Rule 99 respectively.

4   Conclusion

The first version of our PCAM model lays the foundation on - how real life problems of Bioinformatics can be addressed with Cellular Automata model employing simple CA rules. Two key issues of this model are – (i) design of CA rules that should represent the relevant information of physical domain features including peptide backbone, its interaction with other bi-molecules, side chain molecular structure; and (ii) unambiguous mapping of features extracted out of CA evolution to real life experimental results. This generic approach, in our view, should be followed for design of CA model to address any application of real-life problems in any field.

The proposed PCAM framework provides a novel approach to model protein interaction with other bio-molecules. The model encodes amino acid backbone and side-chain with sixty-four 3NCA rules based on their molecular configuration. Parameters extracted out of sixty-four PCAM evolutions represent features of diverse protein interactions. Based on limited experimental data, PCAM models the specific interaction with a bio-molecule and identifies the specific 3NCA rule out of available sixty-four rules. Prediction of interaction with any mutated version of the interacting bio-molecule employs this 3NCA rule.

The current version of PCAM considers only heavy atoms. The next version of PCAM design, which takes into account all types of atoms including "hydrogen", is under rapid development.

References

1. Min, S., Lee, B., Yoon, S.: Deep learning in bioinformatics. Brief. Bioinform. **18**(5), 851–869 (2017)
2. Libbrecht, M.W., Noble, W.S.: Machine learning applications in genetics and genomics. Nat. Rev. Genet. **16**(6), 321 (2015)
3. Moreira, I.S., et al.: SpotOn: high accuracy identification of protein-protein interface hot-spots. Sci. Rep. **7**(1), 8007 (2017)
4. Burks, C., Farmer, D.: Towards modeling DNA sequences as automata. Physica 10D **10**(1–2), 157–167 (1984)
5. Sirakoulis, G., Karafyllidis, I., Mizas, C., Mardiris, V., Thanailakis, A., Tsalides, P.: A cellular automaton model for the study of DNA sequence evolution. Comput. Biol. Med. **33**(5), 439–453 (2003)
6. Xiao, X., Shao, S., Ding, Y., Chen, X.: Digital coding for amino acid based on cellular automata. In: 2004 IEEE International Conference on Systems, Man and Cybernetics, vol. 5, pp. 4593–4598, October 2004
7. Xiao, X., Wang, P., Chou, K.-C.: Cellular automata and its applications in protein bioinformatics. Curr. Protein Pept. Sci. **12**(6), 508–519 (2011)
8. Cristea, P.: Independent component analysis for genetic signals. In: SPIE Conference BIOS 2001-International Biomedical Optics Symposium, San Jose, pp. 20–26, January 2001
9. Pan, Y.-X., et al.: Application of pseudo amino acid composition for predicting protein subcellular location: stochastic signal processing approach. J. Protein Chem. **22**(4), 395–402 (2003)
10. Ghosh, S., et al.: On invertible three neighborhood null-boundary uniform cellular automata. Complex Syst. **20**(1), 47 (2011)
11. Haralick, R.M., Shanmugam, K.: Textural features for image classification. IEEE Trans. Syst. Man, Cybern. **3**(6), 610–621 (1973)
12. De Maesschalck, R., Jouan-Rimbaud, D., Massart, D.L.: The mahalanobis distance. Chemom. Intell. Lab. Syst. **50**(1), 1–18 (2000)
13. Tan, S., Zhang, C.W.H., Gao, G.F.: Seeing is believing: anti-PD-1/PD-L1 monoclonal antibodies in action for checkpoint blockade tumor immunotherapy. Sig. Transduct. Target. Ther. **1**, 16029 (2016)

14. Zhang, F., et al.: Structural basis of the therapeutic anti-PD-L1 antibody atezolizumab. Oncotarget **8**(52), 90215–90224 (2017). PMC.Web. 12 March 2018
15. Tan, S., et al.: Distinct PD-L1 binding characteristics of therapeutic monoclonal antibody durvalumab. Protein Cell **9**(1), 135–139 (2018)
16. Wishart, D.S., et al.: DrugBank 5.0: a major update to the DrugBank database for 2018. Nucleic Acids Res. **46**(D1), D1074–D1082 (2017)

Modeling Spatio-Temporal Dynamics of Metabolic Networks with Cellular Automata and Constraint-Based Methods

Alex Graudenzi[1], Davide Maspero[2], and Chiara Damiani[1,3](✉)

[1] Department of Informatics, Systems and Communication,
University of Milan-Bicocca, Milan, Italy
chiara.damiani@unimib.it
[2] Department of Biotechnology and Bioscience,
University of Milan-Bicocca, Milan, Italy
[3] SYSBIO Centre of Systems Biology, Milan, Italy

Abstract. Increasing experimental evidence suggests that the behaviour of multi-cellular systems, such as tissues and organs, might be largely driven by the complex interplay occurring among metabolic networks. Computational approaches are required to unravel this complexity. However, they currently deal with either the simulation of the spatial dynamics of cell populations or with the simulation of metabolism of individual cells. In order to integrate the modeling of these two key biological processes, we here introduce FBCA (Flux Balance Cellular Automata) a new multi-scale modeling framework that combines a cellular automaton representation of the (higher-level) spatial/morphological dynamics of multi-cellular systems, i.e., the Cellular Potts Model, with a model of the (lower-level) metabolic activity of individual cells, as modeled via Flux Balance Analysis. The representation via cellular automata allows to identify and analyze complex emergent properties and patterns of real-world multi-cellular systems, in a variety of distinct experimental settings. We here present preliminary tests on a simplified model of intestinal crypt, in which cell populations with distinct metabolic properties compete for space and nutrients. The results may allow to cast a new light on the mechanisms linking metabolic properties to clonal dynamics in tissues.

Keywords: Cellular Potts Model · Metabolic networks
Flux Balance Analysis · Population dynamics · Multi-cellular systems

1 Introduction

Computational models are increasingly used to investigate the properties of complex biological systems, and especially those of multi-cellular systems, such as

A. Graudenzi, D. Maspero and C. Damiani—Equal contributors.

© Springer Nature Switzerland AG 2018
G. Mauri et al. (Eds.): ACRI 2018, LNCS 11115, pp. 16–29, 2018.
https://doi.org/10.1007/978-3-319-99813-8_2

tissues and organs [9,26]. Compartmental models, for instance, analyze population dynamics by employing mean-field approaches [1,2], whereas more recent *off*- and *in-lattice* models explicitly account for the spatial and mechanical properties [3,12,15,18,20,23,28]. Cellular automata, in particular, are widely used to represent in a very efficient way cell displacement, movement and interactions, and are often employed in multi-scale models, which describe processes and phenomena occurring at different space/time scales [16,27]. For example, in [12] the relation between the spatial behaviour of cells on a tissue and that of the underlying gene regulatory networks was investigated, allowing to identify the necessary conditions for homeostasis in intestinal crypts, whereas in [20] the spatial dynamics of cell populations during colorectal cancer development was analyzed with a multi-scale cellular automaton modeling framework.

Conversely, current approaches to metabolic network modeling typically simulate the steady state behavior of an individual (or average) cell, or the interaction of several networks, via exchange of nutrients, while disregarding the cell population dynamics in time, as well as the biophysical properties of cells and their interactions, e.g., within tissues and organs. For instance, in [14] a steady state condition is assumed for the population composition, while in [6] a single snapshot of the composition of a population in time is depicted.

In this work, we aim at investigating the relation among high-level spatial properties of a generic multi-cellular systems and the metabolism of its constituting cells. In fact, increasing experimental evidences suggest that complex biological phenomena, such as cancer emergence and development, might be ruled by the complex metabolic interplay and its possible deregulation or rearrangement, one of the key hallmarks of cancer [13]. To this end, we exploit Flux Balance Analysis (FBA), which is by far the most used approach to simulate the dynamics of individual metabolic networks [4]. FBA relies on Linear Programming to determine a metabolic flux distribution (i.e. the rate of each reaction) that maximizes/minimizes a predefined objective function, given constraints on: (i) the stoichiometry of reactions; (ii) the steady state assumption for internal metabolites; (iii) constraints on the domain of the metabolic fluxes, as derived from experimental measurements or from reaction thermodynamics.

We here introduce FBCA (Flux Balance Cellular Automata), a new multiscale modeling framework, which includes two distinct and interacting levels:

(1) A spatial/morphological level, modeled via the Cellular Potts Model (CPM) [11], in which biological cells are represented by sets of contiguous cells over a lattice, and the overall dynamics is probabilistically driven according to an energy minimization criterion, as provided by an Hamiltonian function. In CPM framework cells can expand, move, undergo mitosis, die and interact with each other. CPM has been used in several works and proved to reproduce complex emergent properties of real multi-cellular systems (see, e.g., [22]).

(2) A metabolic network level, in which the metabolic activity of each individual cell is represented via Flux Balance Analysis.

The growth rate at the spatial level (and consequently the cell replication pace) is determined as a function of the biomass increase, computed for each cell via FBA computation. Conversely, the emergent spatial dynamics at the spatial level influence the distribution of nutrients among cells, which is essential for cell survival and growth.

Our modeling approach is rooted in statistical physics and complex systems, as we aim at designing the simplest possible model (with fewer parameters) able to reproduce complex phenomena of multicellular systems, which might be experimentally validated. Therefore, we keep the *a priori* assumptions at a minimum and we investigate the *emergent* dynamical properties of the system, taking advantage of extensive simulations in different experimental settings, as proposed for instance in [7,19], where the dynamical interaction of simplified models of gene regulatory networks was investigated by employing a cellular automata-based representation of space.

To our knowledge, this is the first attempt to connect the dynamical behavior of metabolic networks to biophysically realistic spatial and morphological properties of real multi-cellular systems. Notice that in [25] the authors introduce a multi-scale model of colonic carbohydrate metabolism and bacterial population dynamics, with a simplified geometrical representation of the gut. The authors model bacteria metabolism via FBA and assume metabolites diffusion via PDEs over a grid, in which bacteria populations can move and divide according to the variations of biomass. There are major differences with our approach: most importantly, in [25] no biophysical properties of the cells are taken into account, as each point of the grid can contain different bacteria populations, therefore no morphological dynamics, nor competition for space is considered. In our finer-coarse model, cells and their spatial interactions are represented in a physically plausible way, e.g., cells own individual area (volume), shape, rigidity and velocity. Furthermore, cell growth rate, movement and division dynamics are influenced by the underlying metabolic network dynamics, i.e., the biomass production rate, but also by the available space, the composition of the neighborhood and the biomechanical properties of the cells and the tissue, in addition to the diffusion of metabolites.

We here focused on the representation of a generic intestinal crypt, as this particular biological structure has been largely characterized and is supposed to be the locus in which colorectal cancers originate. Furthermore, the geometrical structure of crypts, which are single-layer one-side open cylinders, allows to employ simplified representation of space.

The goal of this preliminary work is to provide a proof of principle of the potentialities of our methodology in increasing the informative power of constraint-based modeling of metabolic networks. In particular, FBA does predict the biomass production rate, at steady-state, of an individual (or average) cell, but it does not predict its proliferation rate. The division rate of cells does not necessarily correlate linearly with biomass, as many other factors come into play, such as cell size, which is affected, among others, by competition for space. To assess how competition for space affects cellular proliferation rates, as a first approximation, we performed simulations in which the interaction among cells is limited to the competition for space and nutrients, whereas the interaction among cells, via explicit exchange of metabolites is not taken into account.

2   Methods

2.1   Cellular-Automata Representation of Tissue Morphology

FBCA employs a simplified geometrical representation of a general tissue, based on the CPM [11], a cellular-automaton modeling framework often used to model energy-driven spatial pattern formation [22] (Fig. 1).

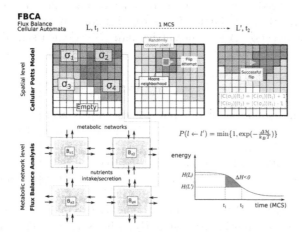

Fig. 1. FBCA scheme. In FBCA, biological cells (σ_1, σ_2, σ_3 and σ_4) are represented as sets of contiguous lattice sites over a lattice L with periodic boundary condition and opened at the lower side. Each cell includes an individual metabolic network, which is used in FBA computation to determine the biomass gain at each time step, according to the nutrients distributed over the lattice, which will be used to compute the Hamiltonian function in Eq. 3. An example MCS step is shown: at time t_1 a random lattice site in L is chosen, belonging to cell σ_1; a flip attempt is attempted with a randomly chosen lattice site in its Moore neighborhood and evaluated via the Hamiltonian function. In this case the flip is accepted and the lattice site is transferred from cell σ_2 to cell σ_1 at time t_2.

In this specific case we use a 2D representation of space, which is suitable to model single-layer tissues, yet the model could be easily extended to the 3D scenario. More in detail, the space is a rigid 2D grid with square lattice sites, opened and rolled out onto a rectangular $h \times w$ lattice L through periodic boundary condition, to mimic the morphology of intestinal crypts (i.e., approximately a lower-side opened cylinder constituted of single-layer epithelial cells).

A *biological* cell, identified with σ_i, is delimited by connected domains: the space occupied by cell σ_i is denoted as $\mathcal{C}(\sigma_i)$ and consists of all lattice sites $l \in L$ with value σ_i:

$$\mathcal{C}(\sigma_i) = \{l = \sigma_i | l \in L\} \tag{1}$$

For every disposition of cells, an Hamiltonian energy function $\mathcal{H}$ is evaluated, to account for the energy required for each mutual interaction, as well as other physical quantities. The dynamics of the system is driven by a discrete-time stochastic process (time unit: *Monte-Carlo Step* - MCS), in which cells are rearranged in order to minimize the Hamiltonian energy of the whole lattice. To this end, lattice sites of a given cell are probabilistically chosen to be *flipped* in favor of another cell in its neighborhood, and this allows cells to move over the lattice.

The update procedure can be summarized as follows: a lattice site l is selected with uniform probability in lattice L; another random lattice site l' is chosen in its Moore neighborhood $\mathcal{N}(l)$; the lattice site l' is then assigned to the cell including l with probability:

$$P(l \leftarrow l') = \min\{1, \exp(\frac{-\Delta\mathcal{H}}{k_b T})\} \tag{2}$$

where $\Delta\mathcal{H}$ is the Hamiltonian difference if the flip is accepted. A $h \times w \times k$ number of flips is attempted at each MCS (the parameters of the simulations are provided in Table 1).

In Eq. 2 the Boltzmann distribution is used to drive cells to the configuration with minimum energy, whereas the factor $k_b T$ accounts for the amplitude of the cell membrane fluctuations.

In our framework, the Hamiltonian function has two main components, which subsume: (*i*) the Differential Adhesion Hypothesis (DAH) [24], and (*ii*) the growth tendency of each cell. In order to account for the DAH, according to which cells of different types tend to segregate and form distinct compartments, we include in our model two abstract cell types, i.e., standard cells and empty space, along the lines of [12,28]. Cells will tend to fill the empty space, if available in their surroundings.

Cell growth is defined as a function of the biomass $\mathcal{B}_{\sigma_i}$ produced and accumulated by each cell, and computed via Flux Balance Analysis at each MCS (see below). In particular, at each MCS, cell σ_i will tend to grow toward an objective area $A_{target}(\mathcal{B}_{\sigma_i})$.

To link the biomass growth, which is measured in pico grams (pg), to the target area, which is measured in lattice sites (1 lattice site is equal to $1\,\mu m$), a conversion factor is needed and defined (see Table 1). This defines the multiscale link between the spatial and the metabolic levels.

The Hamiltonian function is then defined as:

$$\mathcal{H}(L) = \frac{1}{2} \sum_{\sigma_i, \sigma_j \in \mathcal{N}} J(\tau(\sigma_i), \tau(\sigma_j))(1 - \delta(\sigma_i, \sigma_j)) + \lambda \sum_i [|\mathcal{C}(\sigma_i)| - A_{target}(\mathcal{B}_{\sigma_i})]^2 \tag{3}$$

where i and j are lattice sites $\in L$, σ_i is the cell at site i, δ is the Kronecker delta, $\tau(\sigma_i)$ is the cell type of cell σ_i, $J(\tau(\sigma_i), \tau(\sigma_j))$ is the amount of energy required to stick tied cells σ_i and σ_j according to the DAH (which depends on cell types and, in our case, will favor the migration toward empty space), $|\mathcal{C}(\sigma_i)|$ is the current area of cell σ_i in lattice sites, and $\lambda > 0$ is a Lagrange multiplier that accounts for the capacity to deform a cell membrane.

Cells grow via the accumulation of biomass, as for Eq. 3, up to an objective area $A_{mitosis}$, which is initially set as double than the area of cells in the initial lattice configuration; when $|\mathcal{C}(\sigma_i)| = A_{mitosis}$, cell σ_i is divided in two daughter cells, by splitting its space along a randomly chosen direction (either horizontal or vertical), thus modeling *symmetric* cell division. Daughter cells will initially have area (approximately) equal to $\frac{A_{mitosis}}{2}$ and will inherit the metabolic network of the parent cell.

As we are modeling intestinal crypts, we recall that the lower boundary of the lattice is open: the expulsion of cells in the intestinal lumen is modeled by deleting the cells that reach the lower boundary from the lattice. Therefore, cell migration toward the open boundary is expected, due to cell growth and duplication dynamics.

2.2   Metabolic Networks Dynamics

The metabolic network of a generic cell σ is defined as a set $\mathcal{M} = \{m_1, \ldots, m_N\}$ of metabolites in the system and the set $\mathcal{R} = \{r_1, \ldots, r_M\}$ of chemical reactions taking place among them. Reactions are be defined as:

$$R_j : \sum_{i=1}^{N} \alpha_{ji} M_i \longleftrightarrow \sum_{i=1}^{N} \beta_{ji} M_i, \tag{4}$$

where $\alpha_{ji}, \beta_{ji} \in \mathbb{N}$ are stoichiometric coefficients associated, respectively, with the i-th reactant and the i-th product of the j-th reaction, with $i = 1, \ldots, N$, $j = 1, \ldots, M$. Let $[M_i]$ be the abundance of reactant M_i and v_j the flux of reaction R_j, i.e., the net value between forward and backward reaction rate.

Because a steady state is assumed for the abundance each metabolite, i.e., $d[M_i]/dt = 0 \; \forall i$, Linear Programming is applied to identify the flux distribution $v = (v_1, \ldots, v_M)$ that maximizes (or minimizes) the objective $Z = \sum_{j=1}^{M} w_j v_j$, where w_j is a coefficient that represents the contribution of flux j in vector v to the objective function Z.

In our simulations, we typically set the maximization of the rate of biomass production as objective function. It is standard practice in FBA computations [17] to approximate this rate with the flux of a pseudo-reaction, representing the conversion of biomass precursors into biomass.

Given a $N \times M$ stoichiometric matrix S, whose element s_{ji} takes value: (*i*) $-\alpha_{ji}$ if metabolite M_i is a reactant of reaction R_j, (*ii*) $+\beta_{ji}$ if metabolite M_i is a product of reaction R_j, and (*iii*) 0 otherwise.

In order to determine the biomass $\mathcal{B}_\sigma$ produced (and then accumulated) by cell σ in the unit of time (MCS), we solve the following Linear Programming Problem.

$$\text{maximize } \mathcal{B}_\sigma$$
$$\text{subject to } Sv = 0, \ \ v_L \leq v \leq v_U \tag{5}$$

where v_L and v_U are two vectors specifying, respectively, the lower and upper bounds of the admitted interval of each flux v_j. A negative lower bound indicates that flux is allowed in the backward reaction. The exchange of matter with the environment is represented as a set of exchange reactions, in the form $M_i \longleftrightarrow \emptyset$, enabling a predefined set of species to be inserted in or removed from the network.

2.3 Simulation Settings

The parameter settings are reported in Table 1. In all initial configurations (i.e., MCS $= 0$) cells are drawn as squares of 5×5 lattice sites, and fill the whole lattice. Example of initial configurations of the lattice are shown in Fig. 2[A]. It is clear that the square shape is a strong simplification, yet the energy minimization criterion that underlies the CPM simulation ensures that cells reach a rounded and more physically sound shape in a few MCSs (despite some possible and expected defects in cell boundaries). We assume a constant supply of nutrients: at each MCS, each cell is supplied with an amount of nutrients (i.e., upper bound of intake flux) that is proportional to the area of the cell. $|C(\sigma_i)|$ is the number of lattice sites occupied by cell σ_i; let $[M_j^l]$ be the abundance assumed for metabolite j in site $l \in C(\sigma_i)$; the upper bound $U_j^{\sigma_i}$ of the exchange reaction of metabolite j for cell σ_i is set as: $U_j^{\sigma_i} = \sum_{l=1}^{|C(\sigma_i)|} [M_j^l]$.

In all the analyses presented in this work, we used as metabolic network model associated to each cell the model of central carbon metabolism HMRCORE introduced in [10] and used in [6], composed of 240 metabolites and 272 reactions.

In this preliminary work, we simulated the dynamics of two populations of cells, each characterized by a different metabolism. A specific metabolism is modeled by assigning a specific objective function and specific constraints on flux bounds, which are both inherited by cell offsprings. We evaluated three scenarios:

[**SC 1**] A control scenario in which two kinds of cell populations are modeled: one mimicking the metabolism of cancer cells, in which biomass maximization is assumed, and the other mimicking normal cell metabolism, in which maximization of energy (ATP) production is assumed. In this setting, we assume that food is uniformly distributed and thus $[M_j^l] = k, \forall l \in L$. The constant values assumed for each nutrient are set in a way to mimic a well-oxygenated environment [5] and are reported in Table 1.

[**SC 2**] A scenario in which two slightly different cancer metabolic populations are simulated: one which is allowed to intake lactate, but not to secrete it and the other viceversa. We refer to these two populations respectively as "type 1" and "type 2". Also in this case, we assume a uniform distribution of nutrients.

[SC 3] A scenario in which the aforementioned cell populations of "type 1" and "type 2" are simulated in a non-uniform environment: two areas of 3875 lattice sites, positioned at the left/right sides of the lattice, are characterized by limited oxygen abundance ($[O_2] = 0.5$ fmol/lattice site), thus mimicking an hypoxic area.

For each scenario, we executed 20 distinct simulations with random initial configurations. At the initial condition ($MCS = 0$), 620 cells with an individual area of 25 lattice sites (5×5) and a biomass of 1250 pg are disposed on the lattice. Half of the cells are assigned to type 1 and the other half to type 2, and are alternatively disposed on the lattice (i.e., both the left and the right neighbours of a cell are of a distinct type).

Implementation. This preliminary version of FBCA has been implemented in MATLAB, so to exploit both the COBRA Toolbox [21] for FBA computation and matrix calculus for CPM computations. The computation time for a single MSC in a standard simulation setting is ~5 s (ASUS NOTEBOOK; CPU: Intel(R) Core(TM) i7-4710HQ CPU @ 2.50 GHz, 2501 Mhz, 4 core; RAM: 16.0 GB; WINDOWS 10 pro 64-bit).

Table 1. FBCA parameters. Most parameters have been chosen in accordance with existing literature and allow for a biophysically plausible representation of intestinal crypts (see, e.g., [12, 20, 28])

Symbol	Value	Description
-	1 lattice site = 1μm	Conversion of space unit
-	1 MCS = 1/10 h	Conversion of time unit
h	155 lattice sites	Height of the lattice
w	100 lattice sites	Width of the lattice
k	4	Number of lattice spin attempts per lattice site per MCS
$\mathcal{N}$	1	Moore neighborhood size
λ	1	Area rigidity constraint
$k_B T$	3	Temperature and Boltzmann constant
$A_{mitosis}$	50 lattice sites	Mitosis area for all cells
$J_{Normal-Normal}$	4	Hamiltonian adhesion factor among normal cells
$J_{Normal-Empty}$	0.5	Hamiltonian adhesion factor among normal cells and empty space
$\mathcal{F}$	0.02	Area/biomass conversion factor
$[O_2]$	6 fmol/lattice site	Oxygen abundance per lattice site l
$[Glc]$ and $[Lact]$	0.5 fmol/lattice site	Glucose and lactate abundance per lattice site l
$[Gln]$ and $[Arg]$	20 fmol/lattice site	Glutamine and arginine abundance per cell l

3   Results

3.1   Competition for Space in Homogenous Nutrients Environments

[SC 1] Proliferating Cells Colonize Space. With respect to the first scenario, we analyzed the dynamics of the model for a total time of 1000 MCS
(= 100 h). In Fig. 2[A–D], the screenshots of the population composition are
displayed in four distinct moments of an example simulation, i.e., MCS = 1,
MCS = 120, MCS = 160 and at the end of the simulation (MCS = 1000). Cancer cells, i.e., those maximizing the biomass, are represented with red tonalities,
whereas normal cells, i.e., those maximizing the ATP production, in blue tonalities. All the daughter cells maintain the same color of the parent, so each clone
is characterized by a unique and identifiable color.

A first visible result is that CPM simulation ensures that cells reach a cell-like
shape in a few MCSs. As expected, cancer cells quickly colonize the whole space.
It is also apparent that a few clones tend to colonize space in vertical stripes,
and such pattern remarkably reproduces the complex phenomenon of vertical
cell migration in real-world intestinal crypts [12].

In Fig. 2[F–I] the average volume and biomass of all the cells present on the
lattice as a function of time for each run is displayed (each run corresponds
to a different curve on the plot). It can be noticed that normal cells (blue
curves) always disappear from the system within 200 MCSs, and that, despite
the stochasticity, the dynamics of cancer cell population is conserved across the
different runs. As expected, cell division is synchronized, as it can be observed
also from the variation of the number of cells at each MCS (Fig. 2[E]), because
all cells start from the very same biomass and volume value at time $MCS = 0$.
This is reflected also in the observed oscillations in the values of volume and
biomass.

As opposed to standard FBA analysis, our model allows to compute the
duplication time, i.e., the number of MCSs passed before mitosis for a given
cell. The histogram in Fig. 2[H] shows the distribution of the duplication times
recorded for any cells in the lattice over 1000 MCSs, for the example simulation
run displayed in panels A–D.

With FBCA it is possible to analyze the variation of the distribution of the
clonal population size (i.e., the number of cells generated from a unique ances-
tor cell) in time. For instance, in Fig. 2[G] one can see that larger clones are
expectedly emerging during the example simulation displayed in panel A–D, yet
reaching a median value around 35/40 at the end of the simulation: starting from
the initial condition, in which 620 clones of size 1 are present on the lattice, at
the end of the simulation (MCS = 1000) around 15 distinct clones (on average)
composed by 35/40 cells are left.

[SC 2] Proliferative Cells with Fermentative Metabolism Colonize
Space. Type 1 (red) and type 2 (blue) cancer cells are both highly proliferative, but at slightly different rates (type 1 produces 11% more biomass than
type 2).

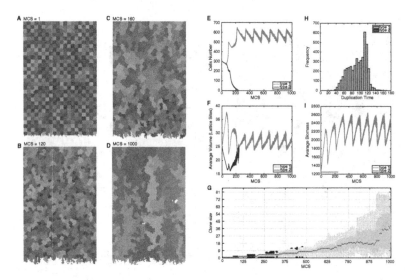

Fig. 2. [SC 1]. (A–D) Snapshots of FBCA dynamics respectively at 1, 120, 160 and 1000 Montecarlo time steps of an example simulation; shapes with red tonalities indicate type 1 cells, shapes with blue tonalities indicate type 2 cells; identical color refers to the same clonal population. (E) Total number of cells of each type as a function of time; one curve for each of the 20 simulations. (F) Average cell volume for each cell type as a function of time; one curve for each of the 20 simulations. (G) Box-plot of the distribution of clonal populations size for $MCS \in [0, 5, 10, \ldots, 1000]$ with respect to the example simulation in panels A–D. (H) Distribution of cell duplication time in the example simulation displayed in panels A–D; red rectangles correspond to type 1, notice that no type 2 cell duplicates during the simulation. (I) Average cell biomass for each cell type as a function of time; one curve for each of the 20 simulations. (Color figure online)

Surprisingly, although in this scenario nutrients are homogeneously distributed, and in spite of the minor advantage of type 1 in terms of biomass growth rate, type 2 cells tend to colonize all space after a period of time, in all simulation runs. It can indeed be observed in Fig. 3[E] that the number of cells of type 1 constantly decrease, in all 20 runs, approaching values close to zero after 1500 MCSs. This phenomenon, which may depend on the properties of the tissue and on the competition for limited space, deserves further investigations.

3.2 [SC 3] Competition for Space in Heterogenous Nutrients Environments

In this scenario, the population dynamics becomes more complex, as an heterogenous distribution of nutrients is mimicked by introducing the hypoxic areas depicted in Fig. 4[A].

In Fig. 4[A–D], one can see that type 1 cells (red) tend to migrate towards and occupy the highly-oxygenated area, whereas type 2 cells (blue), which are

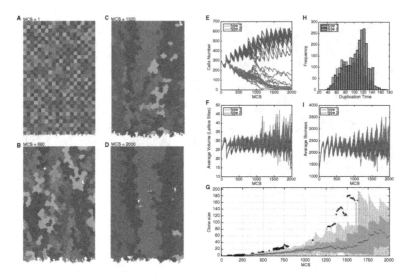

Fig. 3. [SC 2]. (A–D) Snapshots of FBCA dynamics respectively at 1, 660, 1320 and 2000 MCSs of an example simulation; shapes with red tonalities indicate type 1 cells, shapes with blue tonalities indicate type 2 cells; identical color refers to the same clonal population. (E) Total number of cells of each type as a function of time; one curve for each of the 20 simulations. (F) Average cell volume for each cell type as a function of time; one curve for each of the 20 simulations. (G) Box-plot of the distribution of clonal populations size for $MCS \in [0, 10, 20, \ldots, 2000]$ with respect to the example simulation in panels A–D. (H) Distribution of cell duplication time in the example simulation displayed in panels A–D; red histograms correspond to type 1, blue histograms correspond to type 2. Transparency is used to make both series visible: when bars overlap a darker color is displayed. (I) Average cell biomass for each cell type as a function of time; one curve for each of the 20 simulations. (Color figure online)

allowed to have a fermentative metabolism succeed to proliferate in hypoxic areas.

Two distinct dynamical behaviours emerge in different simulation runs: (i) colonization by one cell type, (ii) coexistence of both cell types (homeostasis). In the former case, one cell type ends up in colonizing the lattice; as one can see from Fig. 4[E], in most cases type 1 cells dominate, but in a relevant number of cases type 2 tend to colonize the space. We never observed complete extinction of a cell type, but this is most likely due to the limited simulation time. More interestingly, in a certain number of cases the two cell populations reach a dynamical equilibrium (i.e., homeostasis), in which they both coexist in a stable proportion during the simulation time, despite distinct metabolic properties, different growth rates and the heterogeneous distribution of nutrients.

Notice also that the distribution of the observed duplication time displays a long right tail, likely due to the non-homogeneity of nutrients, i.e., cells in hypoxic areas tend to grow at a slower pace.

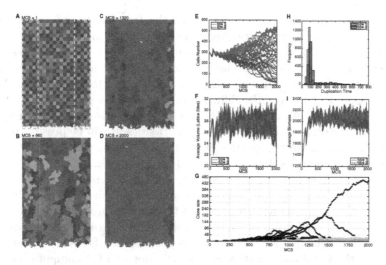

Fig. 4. [SC 3]. (A–D) Snapshots of FBCA dynamics respectively at 1, 660, 1320 and 2000 MCSs of an example simulation; shapes with red tonalities indicate type 1 cells, shapes with blue tonalities indicate type 2 cells; identical color refers to the same clonal population. The yellow dashed boxes at the left/right sides of the lattice indicates the hypoxic areas. (E) Total number of cells of each type as a function of time; one curve for each of the 20 simulations. (F) Average cell volume for each cell type as a function of time; one curve for each of the 20 simulations. (G) Box-plot of the distribution of clonal populations size for $MCS \in [0, 10, 20, \ldots, 2000]$ with respect to the example simulation in panels A–D. (H) Distribution of cell duplication time in the example simulation displayed in panels A–D; red histograms correspond to type 1, blue histograms correspond to type 2. Transparency is used to make both series visible: when bars overlap a darker color is displayed. (I) Average cell biomass for each cell type as a function of time; one curve for each of the 20 simulations. (Color figure online)

Finally, it is interesting to notice from Fig. 4[G] that in the simulation displayed in panels A–D certain clones tend to cyclically dominate the lattice (outliers in the boxplots), until a huge clone consisting of around 430 cells emerges at the end of the simulation.

4 Discussion

We have here introduced FBCA, a new multiscale modeling framework that combines a biophysically plausible representation of cell morphology and interactions, via Cellular Potts Model, and a model of cellular metabolic activity, via Flux Balance Analysis.

Despite the abstractions underlying both modeling approaches, we proved that FBCA can reproduce complex phenomena observed in real world biological systems, such as cell migration, tissue colonization and homeostasis, allowing to perform in-depth quantitative analyses of key properties of cell populations in a variety of simulated experimental settings.

The aim of this work was to introduce the framework and present some preliminary analyses to prove its effectiveness and reliability. Yet, many extensions are underway in order to model more biologically realistic processes and phenomena. For instance, metabolic communication among cells can be easily modeled with FBCA, by allowing the metabolites secreted by cells to diffuse over the tissue. In addition, the diffusion of nutrients via spacial gradients can be introduced in FBCA, and this will allow to explore scenarios that might be experimentally validated, e.g., in cell culture. Besides, it will be possible to characterize the features and properties of each cell by employing the increasingly available single-cell-omics data, as proposed for instance in [8].

The overall approach has a remarkable potential in several distinct application domains, ranging from cancer research to metabolic engineering. For instance, FBCA might be used to simulate the impact on tissue morphology of mutations in metabolic genes accumulating through successive clonal expansions.

Efforts to speed up the execution time are ongoing, focused on the parallelization of the CPM computation and distribution of FBA computation.

Acknowledgments. The institutional financial support to SYSBIO - within the Italian Roadmap for ESFRI Research Infrastructures - is gratefully acknowledged. CD received funding from FLAG-ERA grant ITFoC.

References

1. Bjerknes, M.: Expansion of mutant stem cell populations in the human colon. J. Theor. Biol. **178**(4), 381–385 (1996)
2. Bruce, M.B., Fields, J.Z., Bonham-Carter, O., Runquist, O.A.: Computer modeling implicates stem cell overproduction in colon cancer initiation. Cancer Res. **61**(23), 8408–8411 (2001)
3. Buske, P., Galle, J., Barker, N., Aust, G., Clevers, H., Loeffler, M.: A comprehensive model of the spatio-temporal stem cell and tissue organisation in the intestinal crypt. PLoS Comput. Biol. **7**(1), e1001045 (2011)
4. Cazzaniga, P., et al.: Computational strategies for a system-level understanding of metabolism. Metabolites **4**(4), 1034–1087 (2014)
5. Damiani, C., et al.: A metabolic core model elucidates how enhanced utilization of glucose and glutamine, with enhanced glutamine-dependent lactate production, promotes cancer cell growth: the WarburQ effect. PLOS Comput. Biol. **13**(9), e1005758 (2017)
6. Damiani, C., Di Filippo, M., Pescini, D., Maspero, D., Colombo, R., Mauri, G.: popFBA: tackling intratumour heterogeneity with flux balance analysis. Bioinformatics **33**(14), i311–i318 (2017)
7. Damiani, C., Kauffman, S.A., Serra, R., Villani, M., Colacci, A.: Information transfer among coupled random boolean networks. In: Bandini, S., Manzoni, S., Umeo, H., Vizzari, G. (eds.) ACRI 2010. LNCS, vol. 6350, pp. 1–11. Springer, Heidelberg (2010). https://doi.org/10.1007/978-3-642-15979-4_1
8. Chiara, D., et al.: Integration of single-cell RNA-seq data into metabolic models to characterize tumour cell populations. bioRxiv, 256644 (2018)
9. De Matteis, G., Graudenzi, A., Antoniotti, M.: A review of spatial computational models for multi-cellular systems, with regard to intestinal crypts and colorectal cancer development. J. Math. Biol. **66**(7), 1409–1462 (2013)

10. Di Filippo, M., et al.: Zooming-in on cancer metabolic rewiring with tissue specific constraint-based models. Comput. Biol. Chem. **62**, 60–69 (2016)
11. Graner, F., Glazier, J.A.: Simulation of biological cell sorting using a two-dimensional extended Potts model. Phys. Rev. Lett. **69**(13), 2013 (1992)
12. Graudenzi, A., Caravagna, G., De Matteis, G., Antoniotti, M.: Investigating the relation between stochastic differentiation, homeostasis and clonal expansion in intestinal crypts via multiscale modeling. PLoS One **9**(5), e97272 (2014)
13. Hanahan, D., Weinberg, R.A.: Hallmarks of cancer: the next generation. Cell **144**(5), 646–674 (2011)
14. Khandelwal, R.A., Olivier, B.G., Röling, W.F.M., Teusink, B., Bruggeman, F.J.: Community flux balance analysis for microbial consortia at balanced growth. Plos One **8**(5), e64567 (2013)
15. Murray, P.J., Walter, A., Fletcher, A.G., Edwards, C.M., Tindall, M.J., Maini, P.K.: Comparing a discrete and continuum model of the intestinal crypt. Phys. Biol. **8**(2), 026011 (2011)
16. Noble, D.: Modeling the heart-from genes to cells to the whole organ. Science **295**(5560), 1678–1682 (2002)
17. Orth, J.D., Thiele, I., Palsson, B.Ø.: What is flux balance analysis? Nat. Biotech. **28**(3), 245 (2010)
18. Pitt-Francis, J., et al.: Chaste: a test-driven approach to software development for biological modelling. Comput. Phys. Commun. **180**(12), 2452–2471 (2009)
19. Serra, R., Villani, M., Damiani, C., Graudenzi, A., Colacci, A.: The diffusion of perturbations in a model of coupled random boolean networks. In: Umeo, H., Morishita, S., Nishinari, K., Komatsuzaki, T., Bandini, S. (eds.) ACRI 2008. LNCS, vol. 5191, pp. 315–322. Springer, Heidelberg (2008). https://doi.org/10.1007/978-3-540-79992-4_40
20. Rubinacci, S., et al.: CoGNaC: a chaste plugin for the multiscale simulation of gene regulatory networks driving the spatial dynamics of tissues and cancer. Cancer Inform. **14**, 53–65 (2015). CIN–S19965
21. Schellenberger, J., et al.: Quantitative prediction of cellular metabolism with constraint-based models: the COBRA Toolbox v2. 0. Nat. Protoc. **6**(9), 1290–1307 (2011)
22. Scianna, M., Preziosi, L.: Cellular Potts Models: Multiscale Extensions and Biological Applications. CRC Press, Boca Raton (2013)
23. Shirinifard, A., Gens, J.S., Zaitlen, B.L., Popławski, N.J., Swat, M., Glazier, J.A.: 3D multi-cell simulation of tumor growth and angiogenesis. PloS One **4**(10), e7190 (2009)
24. Steinberg, M.S.: On the mechanism of tissue reconstruction by dissociated cells. I. population kinetics, differential adhesiveness, and the absence of directed migration. Proc. Natl. Acad. Sci. **48**(9), 1577–1582 (1962)
25. Van Hoek, M.J.A., Merks, R.M.H.: Emergence of microbial diversity due to cross-feeding interactions in a spatial model of gut microbial metabolism. BMC Syst. Biol. **11**(1), 56 (2017)
26. Van Leeuwen, I.M.M., Byrne, H.M., Jensen, O.E., King, J.R.: Crypt dynamics and colorectal cancer: advances in mathematical modelling. Cell Prolif. **39**(3), 157–181 (2006)
27. Walpole, J., Papin, J.A., Peirce, S.M.: Multiscale computational models of complex biological systems. Annu. Rev. Biomed. Eng. **15**, 137–154 (2013)
28. Wong, S.Y., Chiam, K.-H., Lim, C.T., Matsudaira, P.: Computational model of cell positioning: directed and collective migration in the intestinal crypt epithelium. J. Roy. Soc. Interface **7**(Suppl. 3), S351–S363 (2010)

A Novel Cellular Automata Modelling Framework for Micro-environmental Interaction and Co-invasion

Arran Hodgkinson[1,2](✉) (iD)

[1] DIMNP, Université de Montpellier, 34095 Montpellier, France
[2] Institut de Recherche en Cancérologie de Montpellier, 34298 Montpellier, France
arran.hodgkinson@umontpellier.fr

Abstract. Modern biological paradigms of invasion in tumour cells cannot be fully explained or described by existing modelling techniques. We present a novel cellular automata model which represents both the nucleus of a cell and its membrane, allowing one to capture the interaction of a cell with its environment, as well as selected theorems for the efficient computation of solutions to such systems. We use this technique to simulate cell-cell binding, single-cellular micro track invasion, and co-injection of $MITF^{HIGH}$(proliferative) and $MITF^{LOW}$(invasive) tumour cells into heterogeneous environments. Results shed new light on emergent phenomena of cellular elongation, filopodial protrusion, and the co-invasion of the local stroma by classically non-invasive cells. We also provide a new modelling framework in which the cellular automaton exhibits non-local interaction within its context.

Keywords: Cellular automata · Mathematical modelling
Cellular biology · Coöperation · Numerical analysis

1 Introduction

Biological paradigms involving mixtures of heterogeneous subpopulations of cells have become the subject of increased scrutiny in recent years. Beginning from problems of cell sorting [5], cellular interactions now have a field of automata devoted to their exploration. One problem of significance is the change in behaviour of ordinarily non-invading proliferative cells ($MITF^{HIGH}$) in the presence of highly invasive, non-proliferative cells ($MITF^{LOW}$). Injection of these cellular populations, *in vivo*, in isolation yielded ordinary pathological behaviour whereas co-injection of disparate species led to the co-invasion of the local stroma by $MITF^{HIGH}$cells, on a substrate altered by leading $MITF^{LOW}$cells [4].

This also gives rise to more general problems in invasion. One methodology of cellular invasion involves the utilisation of 'microtracks', or spaces of reduced ECM concentration, by cells in order to gain a competitive advantage, travelling

Supported by l'École Doctorale I2S de l'Université de Montpellier.

G. Mauri et al. (Eds.): ACRI 2018, LNCS 11115, pp. 30–41, 2018.
https://doi.org/10.1007/978-3-319-99813-8_3

at increased speeds by direct comparison with those cells forced to travel through the dense ECM [2]. This increase in migration through native microtracks was shown, using time-lapse photography, to occur within the 3D collagen matrix. These microtracks have further been shown to have varying mean width and variance [8] which may be as a result of underlying matrix structuring and varying collagen densities across a given region. Importantly, the cells were shown to exhibit patterns of actin recruitment that were not discernible from those found in migratory cells out with microtracks [8].

The discrete Cellular Potts models which have been proposed model the cell moving through a grid-like structure, however fine, guided by a mechanistic, stochastic function [5]. Indeed, these have great power in reproducing qualitatively realistic results and can model even relatively complex systems [10]. These models exist in a discrete space where the implementation of behaviours is dependent on a delta probability function rather than the continuous machinery of the cell. This means that they lack the ability to, for example, explain or describe microtrack motility or to fully explain any emergent phenomena due to the model's reliance on stochastic dynamics.

One particular model which does not study the cell mechanics themselves, demonstrates that one can take a more physical interpretation of the tumour and its environment [11]. This model, again, chooses to describe a cellular population as a non-autonomous series of ball-like structures in arbitrary space acting under the standard forces (drag, traction, *et cetera*). The complexity of membrane-dependent biological interactions requires the creation of a novel cellular automata model who describes not only the position of the cells but endows them with some physical form which mediates its interaction with its environment.

In Sect. 2 of this paper, we begin to build the novel framework necessary to accurately capture these phenomena and the field equations which biologically contextualise the automata. We then provide, in Sect. 3, numerical analysis of approximations, necessary for the fast computation of results, to the modelling scheme in order to bound the errors for these approximations. Finally, in Sect. 4, we present the result of simulations for a small system of cellular automata in order to demonstrate their ability to elucidate biological cell invasion in heterogeneous colonies and environments.

2   A Novel Modelling Framework

Firstly, we choose to express the environmental system in standard Cartesian coordinates and the radial equations for the distance of the membrane from the nucleus in polar coordinates. We then have that the standard coordinate conversion from polar to Cartesian is given by $x = \mathbf{r}\cos\theta$, $y = \mathbf{r}\sin\theta$ and we write $\mathbf{x} := [x, y]^T$. Therefore, let $\mathcal{I} = [0, T)$ be the time domain on which the system exists and $\mathcal{D} \subseteq \mathbb{R}^2$ be the spatial domain.

Secondly, let $\mathbf{r}(t, \theta)$, be a 2π periodic function such that $\mathbf{r}(t, \theta + 2n\pi) = \mathbf{r}(t, \theta)$, $\forall n \in \mathbb{N}$, and let it further define the perimeter of a cell with the brief notation $\mathbf{r} := \mathbf{r}(\theta) := \mathbf{r}(t, \theta)$. Let $\Theta = [0, 2\pi)$ be the domain for the nucleus-centred radius and let $\mathcal{R} \subseteq \mathbb{R}$ be the domain for the radius of the cell such that $\mathbf{r} : \mathcal{I} \times \Theta \to \mathcal{R}$. For cell i, we denote the radius $\mathbf{r}_i$. Finally, let $v : \mathcal{I} \times \mathcal{D} \to \mathbb{R}$ define the extracellular matrix (ECM) density and let $\mathbf{m} : \mathcal{I} \times \mathcal{D} \to \mathbb{R}^q$ define the q molecular species densities on the domain.

2.1   On Cell-Cell Bonding and Associated Field Equations

We begin by reposing every cell-cell interaction problem as a generic problem between two cells situated a given distance d from one another and with both of their respective centres at $y = 0$. First, let the vector $\mathbf{p}(c_i, c_j)$ be the vector in polar coordinates such that

$$||\mathbf{p}|| := \sqrt{(\bar{c}_{i,x} - \bar{c}_{j,x})^2 + (\bar{c}_{i,x} + \bar{c}_{j,x})^2}, \qquad \mathbf{p}_\theta := \tan^{-1}\left(\frac{\bar{c}_{j,y} - \bar{c}_{i,y}}{\bar{c}_{j,x} - \bar{c}_{i,x}}\right) \quad (1)$$

where $\bar{c}_i$ denotes the centre of mass for the cell c_i, then call this the pointing vector and perform the transforms $(r_j, \theta_j) \to \left(r_j, \theta_j - \mathbf{p}_\theta + \frac{\pi}{2}\right)$ and $(\bar{c}_{j,x}, \bar{c}_{j,y}) \to (0, ||\mathbf{p}||)$, in order to move cell j onto the x-axis and to rotate the cell such that the same points are aligned as was the case prior to the coordinate transform.

Then, from simple algebraic reasoning, one has that the distance between any two points on the membranes of these cells, with respect to θ, is given by

$$d(\theta) = \sqrt{(c_{i,r}\cos(\theta) - c_{j,r}\cos(\theta))^2 + (c_{i,r}\sin(\theta) - c_{j,r}\sin(-\theta) + ||\mathbf{p}||)^2} \quad (2)$$

and this means that the contribution to a given radius can be calculated by the force at that point, multiplied by the appropriate elongation factor which is given by the trigonometric relation $\bar{d} = d\cos\left(\theta - \frac{\pi}{2}\right)$, where $\frac{\pi}{2}$ is a factor which accounts for the reorientation of the cells.

Let us now look at the attractive intercellular force, $F_A(d)$. There is evidence to suggest that, below some limiting distance, the negative charges on repeat 3 of α-actinin and positive charges on intercellular adhesion molecule (ICAM)-1 dominate the interaction. Above this distance, the contribution of the positive-positive interaction is increased between the acidic centre of the α-actinin domain and Lys acids on ICAM1 [3,9]. We model this by introducing some constant imaginary distance, i, between the two membranes.

The repulsive Coulomb force, $F_R(d)$, emanates from the addition of pressure to the membrane reducing the spacing between membranous lipids, producing a restorative force. Therefore, we calculate the distance at which the centre of charge of the membrane sits, with respect to the cell radius. For a circle of uniform radius $r(\theta) = r$, the radial centre of charge is approximated by $\bar{r} \approx \frac{4}{3\pi}r$, which shall serve as a positioning of the internal charge.

We can then write the overall field equation as

$$F(d) = \frac{1}{(d - d_A)^2 + 1} - \frac{1}{\left(d + \frac{4}{3\pi}\right)^2 + \frac{1}{Q_s}} \quad (3)$$

where Q_s gives the ratio of charge separation for the protein complex, with respect to the separation of the charges in the lipid bilayer of the melanoma cells themselves. Biological precedents for this force distribution exists, with physical measurement being taken between staphylococcus aureus cells and biofilms [6].

2.2 On Cell-ECM Bonding and Associated Field Equations

The dissociation rate of one protein from another is widely considered [1,7] to have the form $k = k_0 \exp\left(fx/k_bT\right)$, where k_0 is the zero rate of dissociation, f is the force applied in separating the proteins, x is the distance of separation, and k_BT gives the thermal energy of the system. Now, consider an arbitrary force that brings the proteins of the cell and the ECM together, then their normalised association rate, $\bar{k}$, would be given by $\bar{k} = [1 - (k_0/K) \exp\left(-fx/k_bT\right)]$ where the maximal rate of dissociation is given by K.

The force on the cell from the ECM is proportional to the density of the ECM itself and therefore we write $|F_c^+| = \bar{k}v$. We also have that the direction of association is from lower to higher densities of protein, which follows directly from their proportionality. As for the force equation for pressure, we assume the field generated scales with the square of the ECM density, and acts in the opposite direction. Therefore, we can write the entirety of the force equation as

$$|F| = \left[1 - \frac{k_0}{K} \exp\left(-\frac{fx}{k_bT}\right)\right] v - k_p v^2, \qquad \hat{F} = \tan^{-1}\left(\frac{\partial v}{\partial y}\frac{\partial x}{\partial v}\right). \qquad (4)$$

2.3 Molecular Species on the Boundary — Chemotaxis

The chemotaxis of a cell is dependent on the molecular species concentration $m(t,x)$ on the immediate boundary of the cell, since it is not endocytosis but simply sensory response that is necessary for this stimulus.

Using the standard definition of a line integral, we can write the line integral of the molecular species concentration $m_i(x,y)$ over the boundary of the cell and with surface element σ as

$$I = \int_{\partial\Omega_i} m_i(\bar{x})\,d\sigma, \qquad d\sigma = \sqrt{\mathbf{r}(\theta)^2 \sin^2\theta + \mathbf{r}(\theta)^2 \cos^2\theta}\,d\theta = \mathbf{r}(\theta)\,d\theta. \qquad (5)$$

It is then trivial to rewrite the line integral with respect to the individual cell and a specific molecular species, $m_j(t,x)$, to obtain the overall molecular species concentration on the boundary, and the bias of such a concentration.

Taking the biased molecular concentrations and extract from them the optimal direction, in terms of chemical attractants, the mean biased chemotaxis is given by

$$\overset{\circ}{\chi} = \frac{1}{\sum\limits_{j=1}^{q} \chi_{m_j}} \begin{pmatrix} \chi_{m_1} \\ \vdots \\ \chi_{m_q} \end{pmatrix} \cdot \begin{pmatrix} \tan^{-1}\left(\dfrac{\int_\Theta m_1(\mathbf{r}(\theta)\cos\theta, \mathbf{r}(\theta)\sin\theta)\cos\theta\,d\theta}{\int_\Theta m_1(\mathbf{r}(\theta)\cos\theta, \mathbf{r}(\theta)\sin\theta)\sin\theta\,d\theta}\right) \\ \vdots \\ \tan^{-1}\left(\dfrac{\int_\Theta m_q(\mathbf{r}(\theta)\cos\theta, \mathbf{r}(\theta)\sin\theta)\cos\theta\,d\theta}{\int_\Theta m_q(\mathbf{r}(\theta)\cos\theta, \mathbf{r}(\theta)\sin\theta)\sin\theta\,d\theta}\right) \end{pmatrix} \qquad (6)$$

where the chemotactic constant for any given molecular species $m_j(t, x)$ is given by χ_{m_j}.

2.4   Temporal Changes in Intracellular Properties

We must, further, have a means by which the cell's interior can reposition itself with respect to the environment. A sensible candidate for this movement can simply be taken as a result of the net forces which move the membrane of the cell having direct and proportionate effect on the position of the nucleus such that we can write

$$\tfrac{\partial}{\partial t}x_1 = \int\limits_{[0,2\pi)} \tfrac{\partial}{\partial t}\mathbf{r}(\tilde{\theta}) \cdot \cos\tilde{\theta}\, d\tilde{\theta}\,, \qquad \tfrac{\partial}{\partial t}x_2 = \int\limits_{[0,2\pi)} \tfrac{\partial}{\partial t}\mathbf{r}(\tilde{\theta}) \cdot \sin\tilde{\theta}\, d\tilde{\theta}\,, \qquad (7)$$

reflecting a mechanical movement of the nucleus with the membrane.

Consider the overall change in the polarisation, ϕ, of the cell and that the cell is capable of rearranging its internal infrastructure in response to the attraction of chemicals and in order to maximise its potential for utilising the byproducts of this infrastructure. Then we assume that the cell will attempt to reorient itself to the optimal direction

$$\bar{\phi} = \frac{1}{\omega_F + \omega_\chi}\left(\omega_F \tan^{-1}\left(\frac{\partial x_2}{\partial t}\frac{\partial t}{\partial x_1}\right) + \omega_\chi \overset{\circ}{\chi}\right), \qquad (8)$$

given the weightings ω_F, ω_χ for the force and chemotactically mediated polarity preferences, respectively.

Then consider that the cell will have more success in achieving small angular reorientation than in large angular reorientations. Therefore, we make the assumption that the polarisation may only change through small changes around the perimeter of the cell and that $\ln(\partial\phi/\partial t) \propto -\left(\bar{\phi} - \phi\right)^2$. We write that the change in polarisation can be given by

$$\frac{\partial\phi}{\partial t} = \exp\left[-\left(\left(\frac{\partial x_1}{\partial t}\right)^2 + \left(\frac{\partial x_2}{\partial t}\right)^2\right)^{-\frac{1}{2}} \cdot \left(\bar{\phi} - \phi\right)^2\right]. \qquad (9)$$

3   Numerical Approach

3.1   Movement of the Nucleus: A Simple Translation Method

The current methodology for reassignment, or mathematical translation, of the position of a radial function $\mathbf{r}(\theta)$ to a differing position is given as follows

$$\mathbf{r}_1 = \sqrt{\mathbf{r}^2 + \mathbf{r}_0^2 + 2\mathbf{r}\mathbf{r}_0\cos(\theta_0 - \theta)}\,, \qquad \theta_1 = \cos^{-1}\left(\frac{\mathbf{r}\cos\theta + \mathbf{r}_0\cos\theta_0}{\mathbf{r}_1}\right), \qquad (10)$$

where $(\mathbf{r}, \theta)$ gives the original solution in polar coordinates; $(\mathbf{r}_0, \theta_0)$ gives the magnitude and direction of the translation; and $(\mathbf{r}_1, \theta_1)$ gives the translated set of solutions. Then observe the following simplification:

Theorem 1. *Let the space $\mathcal{N} \subseteq \mathbb{R}^2$ define the Cartesian plane on which the nucleus of a given 2-dimensional cell is defined, and the space $\mathcal{Q} \subseteq \mathbb{R} \times [0, 2\pi)$ define the polar domain centred at $(x, y) \in \mathcal{N}$ on which the membrane of the cell is defined. Then we can define a cell as some $[(x_0, y_0), (\mathbf{r}_0(\theta_0), \theta_0)] \in \mathcal{N} \times \mathcal{Q}$, where $\mathbf{r}(\theta) : [0, 2\pi) \to \mathbb{R}$ is the radial membrane distance as measured from the centre of the cell. Define further a formula for translation of the nucleus of this cell, given by $(x, y) \to (x + \xi, y)$, where the membrane of the cell retains its position in the cartesian space and dependence on θ_0, given by*

$$\mathbf{r}_1(\theta_0) = \mathbf{r}_0(\theta_0) - \xi \cos(\theta_0).$$

Then the error for this translation is given by

$$E_r \leq \left(1 - \sin\left(\frac{1}{2} \cos^{-1}\left(\frac{-\mathbf{r}(\hat{\theta}) + \sqrt{\mathbf{r}(\hat{\theta})^2 + 8\xi^2}}{4\xi} \right) \right) \right) \left(\frac{-\mathbf{r}(\hat{\theta}) + \sqrt{\mathbf{r}(\hat{\theta})^2 + 8\xi^2}}{4\xi} \right) \xi,$$

where $\mathbf{r}(\hat{\theta}) = \max\limits_{\theta \in [0, 2\pi)} \mathbf{r}(\theta)$.

Proof. Recall the coordinate relations given by $x_0 = \mathbf{r}(\theta) \cos \theta$, $y_0 = \mathbf{r}(\theta) \sin \theta$ and the counter-relation $\mathbf{r}(\theta)^2 = x^2 + y^2$. Consider, further, the translation in only the cartesian x-direction, of magnitude ξ, corresponding to a linear progression in an aligned set of polar axes given by $x_1 = \mathbf{r}(\theta) \cos \theta - \xi$, $y_1 = \mathbf{r}(\theta) \sin \theta$.

Using the translation approximation $\mathbf{r}_1(\theta_0) = \mathbf{r}_0(\theta_0) - \xi \cos(\theta_0)$ and allowing that the maximal error for this approximation is given at $\theta_0 = \hat{\theta}$, defined by $\mathbf{r}(\hat{\theta}) := \max\limits_{\theta \in [0, 2\pi)} \mathbf{r}(\theta)$, the maximal error is given by

$$\bar{E} = \underbrace{(\mathbf{r}(\hat{\theta}) + \xi \cos \hat{\theta}) \sin \hat{\theta}}_{\text{approximation}} - \underbrace{(\mathbf{r}(\hat{\theta})^2 - (\mathbf{r}(\hat{\theta}) \sin \hat{\theta} - \xi)^2)^{\frac{1}{2}}}_{\text{absolute calculation}}. \tag{11}$$

We can then find this maximum at $\hat{\theta}$ by considering the derivative of the term for the translation approximation, which simplifies to

$$\tilde{E}' = \mathbf{r}(\hat{\theta}) \cos \hat{\theta} + \xi \cos 2\hat{\theta} = 0 \tag{12}$$

and by further using the trigonometric relation $\cos 2\theta = 2\cos^2 \theta - 1$ we can write

$$\mathbf{r}(\hat{\theta}) \cos \hat{\theta} + 2\xi \cos^2 \hat{\theta} - \xi = 0 \tag{13}$$

who is a quadratic in $\cos \hat{\theta}$, such that the solution for $\hat{\theta}$ is given by

$$\cos \hat{\theta} = \frac{-\mathbf{r}(\hat{\theta}) \pm \sqrt{\mathbf{r}(\hat{\theta})^2 + 8\xi^2}}{4\xi} \implies \hat{\theta} = \cos^{-1}\left(\frac{-\mathbf{r}(\hat{\theta}) + \sqrt{\mathbf{r}(\hat{\theta})^2 + 8\xi^2}}{4\xi} \right). \tag{14}$$

Substituting this into the original equation, and recognising that the negative term in the error is minimised at $x = \xi$, one has that the maximal error is written

$$\bar{E} = \mathbf{r}\left(\cos^{-1}\left(\frac{-\mathbf{r}(\hat{\theta}) + \sqrt{\mathbf{r}(\hat{\theta})^2 + 8\xi^2}}{4\xi}\right)\right) + \left(\frac{-\mathbf{r}(\hat{\theta}) + \sqrt{\mathbf{r}(\hat{\theta})^2 + 8\xi^2}}{4\xi}\right)\xi - \mathbf{r}(\hat{\theta}).$$

(15)

Then the precise value of $y(\hat{\hat{\theta}})$ is given at $y(\hat{\hat{\theta}}) = \mathbf{r}(\frac{1}{2}\hat{\theta})\sin(\frac{1}{2}\hat{\theta})$, such that the maximal error can be given precisely by

$$\bar{E} = \left(1 - \sin\left(\frac{1}{2}\cos^{-1}\left(\frac{-\mathbf{r}(\hat{\theta}) + \sqrt{\mathbf{r}(\hat{\theta})^2 + 8\xi^2}}{4\xi}\right)\right)\right)\left(\frac{-\mathbf{r}(\hat{\theta}) + \sqrt{\mathbf{r}(\hat{\theta})^2 + 8\xi^2}}{4\xi}\right)\xi.$$

(16)

In this case, using Theorem 1, the error for values of $\xi \leq 0.1$ is such that $E_r < \frac{1}{2}\xi^2$ and ξ is proportional with the time step such that $\xi \propto \delta\tau$. Thus, for sufficiently small time steps one is able to discern that the error is sufficiently small, and non-cumulative, and that this may be acceptable within the bounds of expected numerical error.

3.2   Numerical Approximations of Line Integrals

We begin by recalling that the analytic, single-variable line integral for a radial function is given by $I = \int_S r(\theta)\,d\sigma$, where S is used to denote the surface of the cell and σ is some surface element on S. Discretisation of this system leads us to derive a metric on the basis of maximal efficacy on the discrete radial interval, $(\tilde{\theta}, \tilde{\theta} + \delta\theta)$. Begin by considering the true arc length in this portion of the radius of a given cell and notice that this can be approximated by sketching a line between the two extreme radii, $r(\tilde{\theta}), r(\tilde{\theta} + \delta\theta)$.

Theorem 2. *Let Ω be the internal cell space of a cell whose radius is is given by $\mathbf{r} : \mathcal{I} \times \Theta \to \mathcal{R}$. Further, let the perimeter length of the cell be given by $I_c = \int_{\partial\Omega} \mathbf{r}(t, \theta)\,d\sigma_{\partial\Omega}$, where $\sigma_{\partial\Omega}$ is a surface element on $\partial\Omega$, and let $\tilde{I}_c$ be given by the numerical approximation*

$$\tilde{I} = \sum_{\tilde{\theta}\in\{0,\delta\theta,...,2\pi-\delta\theta\}} \delta\theta \cdot \left(\left(\min(r(\tilde{\theta}), r(\tilde{\theta}+\delta\theta))\delta\theta\right)^2 + \left|r(\tilde{\theta}) - r(\tilde{\theta}+\delta\theta)\right|^2\right)^{\frac{1}{2}}.$$

Then, for a discrete step length, h, the error, E_L, for this approximation is of order $\mathcal{O}(h^2)$ and is given explicitly by

$$E_L \leq \int_{\partial\Omega} \left[\frac{h^2}{2}\frac{\partial^2}{\partial\theta^2}\mathbf{r}(\theta_i + \eta) + \mathcal{O}(h^3)\right] d\sigma_{\partial\Omega}$$

Proof. Begin by noticing that our approximation is given precisely by the length of the line connecting the points $\mathbf{r}(\theta_i)$ and $\mathbf{r}(\theta_i + h)$ such that

$$\tilde{\mathbf{r}}(\eta) = \frac{\mathbf{r}(\theta_i + h) - \mathbf{r}(\theta_i)}{h}\eta + \mathbf{r}(\theta_i) \tag{17}$$

for $\eta \in (0, h)$ and centred around the point θ_i and where we are interested in values in the interval $(\theta_i, \theta_i + h)$.

Further, write the analytic function as the Taylor series

$$I_c(\theta_i + \eta) \approx \mathbf{r}(\theta_i + \eta) + \eta\frac{\partial}{\partial\theta}\mathbf{r}(\theta_i + \eta) + \frac{\eta^2}{2}\frac{\partial^2}{\partial\theta^2}\mathbf{r}(\theta_i + \eta) + \mathcal{O}(\eta^3) \tag{18}$$

then from the intermediate value theorem, we can choose η such that it satisfies

$$\frac{\partial}{\partial\theta}\mathbf{r}(\theta_i + \eta) = \frac{\mathbf{r}(\theta_i + h) - \mathbf{r}(\theta_i)}{h}. \tag{19}$$

Next, we take the difference between the two line integrals to find the analytic error in our approximation

$$E_L = \int_{\partial\Omega} \left[\mathbf{r}(\theta_i + \eta) + \eta\frac{\partial}{\partial\theta}\mathbf{r}(\theta_i + \eta) + \frac{\eta^2}{2}\frac{\partial^2}{\partial\theta^2}\mathbf{r}(\theta_i + \eta) + \mathcal{O}(h^3) \right] d\sigma_{\partial\Omega}$$
$$- \int_{\partial\Omega} \left[\frac{\mathbf{r}(\theta_i + h) - \mathbf{r}(\theta_i)}{h}\eta + \mathbf{r}(\theta_i) \right] d\sigma_{\partial\Omega} \tag{20}$$

and since the linear terms for the Taylor expansion and the approximation (19) describes straight lines between two equidistant points, their magnitudes are equal. Therefore, considering that we have $h \geq \eta$, we obtain the maximal error bound

$$E_L \leq \int_{\partial\Omega} \left[\frac{h^2}{2}\frac{\partial^2}{\partial\theta^2}\mathbf{r}(\theta_i + \eta) + \mathcal{O}(h^3) \right] d\sigma_{\partial\Omega}. \tag{21}$$

4   Results and Conclusions

In order to attempt the sorting experiment, we began with high affinity cells as the outer cells of a cellular Bravais lattice and low affinity cells in the centre, repeating the results of Graner *et al.* [5] (*data not shown*), which provided some base validation of the model. Counterintuitively, cells who have high cell-cell binding coefficients quickly separate into a web like structure whereas low binding constant scenarios tend to instead form a 2-dimensional hexagonal lattice.

In our second experiment we wanted a testable scenario to measure the migration of simulated cancerous cells through the ECM. For this we chose the scenario of microtracks since this presents 2 unique and measurably distinguishable scenarios in which to place our cells. We endow each with a polarisation of $\theta_p = 0$ and with the initial conditions $r^0(\theta) = $ const. such that they are represented as circular cells in the 2D domain. Working with a normalised 2D domain

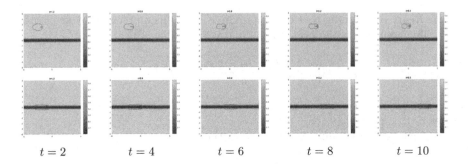

$t = 2$ $t = 4$ $t = 6$ $t = 8$ $t = 10$

Fig. 1. Snapshots of simulated cells migrating through the ECM for the initial condition for the nucleus of the cell given within the ECM itself (*top*) or within an artificial microtrack (*bottom*) at times $t' \in \{2, 4, 6, 8, 10\}$.

$\mathcal{D} = [0,1]^2$, parameter values were estimated and rescaled from experimental data [7] or approximated, in the case of cell-cell adhesion.

The first thing to notice is that although the membranes of cells within the microtracks start partially submerged in the ECM, they retract their membranes and conform entirely to the width of the microtrack (Fig. 1 *bottom*), as in the biological case [2]. Moreover, elongation in the microtrack cell is marked compared with those who remain within the ECM (Fig. 1).

Travel through the ECM also appears to be more conducive to the extension of lamellipodia (Fig. 1 *top*), whereas travel through the microtrack appears to be more conducive to the extension of longer, thinner, and more directive filopodia (Fig. 1 *bottom*). Not only this but the heterogeneity of the environment, alone, is sufficient to give rise to differing rates of travel within or without microtracks. Moreover, for increasing ECM density, one observes a decrease in velocity for cells within the ECM but no such changes in velocity for those within the microtrack (Fig. 2), which closely aligns with the results of *in vitro* experimentation [2].

Beyond the maximum time displayed ($t > 10$) these cells proceed to the right hand boundary and return to a more circular shape and lie dormant on this boundary *ad infinitum*. This is an artefact of the experiment, in that cells in this experiment have a fixed polarisation and are incapable of travelling in their assigned directions. In the following experiment we lifted this constraint.

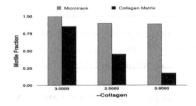

Fig. 2. Results of *in silico* microtrack experiments from the numerical simulations (*right*) and corresponding to those exemplar experiments in Fig. 1.

Our final experiment involves the interaction between two different metabolic phenotypes of cell: Highly proliferative, non-invasive ($\text{MITF}^{\text{HIGH}}$) cells and highly invasive, non-proliferative (MITF^{LOW}) cells. We begin with a heterogeneous distribution of v_1 and $v_2(t, x) = 0$. $\text{MITF}^{\text{HIGH}}$ cells are attracted to v_2 but not v_1 and MITF^{LOW} cells are attracted to v_1 but not v_2 and convert $v_1 \rightarrow v_2$ [4]. Furthermore, to begin the experiment, we generated a random polarisation for each cell.

Injection of $\text{MITF}^{\text{HIGH}}$ cells, alone (and in the absence of mitosis), reveals an extremely non-invasive behaviour with dominating cell-cell adhesive dynamics (Fig. 3 *top*). Injection of MITF^{LOW} cells, alone, one observes a highly invasive dynamic (Fig. 3 *middle*). Co-injection of the two disparate populations displays a mixture of behaviours between cell-cell binding and cell-ECM motility and one observes a co-invasion of $\text{MITF}^{\text{HIGH}}$ cells in the wake of invading MITF^{LOW} cells (Fig. 3 *bottom*). Again, one can identify the production of filopodia by cells who have elongated upon the heterogeneous substrate for invasion (Fig. 3).

The qualitative results of this experiment were not significantly effected by the random initial polarisations of the cells. In the short term ($t \leq 200$) cellular automata mimic the behaviour of *in vivo* cells [4], with $\text{MITF}^{\text{HIGH}}$ cells clustering and MITF^{LOW} cells dispersing, in isolation, and some intermediate behaviour, otherwise. These times were chosen to be indicative of the overall behaviour as, in the long term ($t > 200$), those cells who have not yet dispersed at $t = 200$ will continue to cluster, whilst those who have dispersed will find some steady state position at the boundary of the domain $t \rightarrow \infty$. Again, these behaviours show close conformity with *in vivo* experiments [4], assuming that those on the boundary of the domain would otherwise continue to invade.

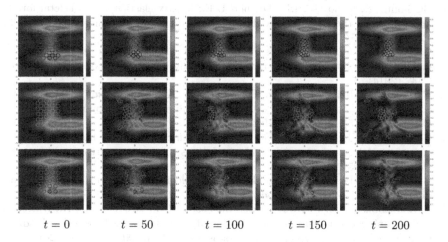

| $t = 0$ | $t = 50$ | $t = 100$ | $t = 150$ | $t = 200$ |

Fig. 3. Experimental *in silico* injection of *red* $\text{MITF}^{\text{HIGH}}$ cells (*top*); *green* MITF^{LOW} cells (*middle*); or both cell types (*bottom*) onto a heterogeneous density function for v_1 coloured *blue* through *yellow*, at time points $t \in \{0, 50, 100, 150, 200\}$. (Color figure online)

We have derived a modelling framework to solve problems which previous frameworks [5,10] were unable to approach. Errors for the numerical implementation of estimates for these models are small and, as such, allow one to be confident in their predictive power. Moreover, the introduction of low-error approximations to this framework allow for a fast model execution time. This novel modelling framework has also shown practical promise; recreating the cell sorting experiment before predicting the outcomes of biological microtrack [2] and co-invasion [4] experiments. Moreover, this model may explain emergent phenomena, such as cellular elongation and filo- or lamellipodia extension, which could be explained through simple physical interactions between the cellular membrane and the homo- or heterogeneous ECM. Future work should aim to extend this model through the addition of microscale boundary interactions and look to explore more complex biological phenomena.

This cellular automata model could also be useful in other environments where one requires a nuanced interaction between automata and their contexts. This can be achieved either through the method of implementation employed above, for entirely nonlocal interactions, or through treating the cellular membrane as a domain boundary and utilising a kernel to vary the impact across the domain, allowing diverse interactions between automata and their contexts. Obvious applications of this framework arise in cellular biology but one can also envisage application in game theory and financial markets, where individuals (automata) will or must take into account their environment (the context) to varying degrees.

References

1. Buxboim, A., Ivanovska, I.L., Discher, D.E.: Matrix elasticity, cytoskeletal forces and physics of the nucleus: how deeply do cells 'feel' outside and in? J. Cell Sci. **123**(Pt 3), 297–308 (2010)
2. Carey, S.P., et al.: Comparative mechanisms of cancer cell migration through 3D matrix and physiological microtracks. Am. J. Physiol. Cell Physiol. **308**(6), C436–C447 (2014)
3. Carpen, O., Pallai, P., Staunton, D.E., Springer, A.T.: Association of intercellular adhesion molecule-1 (ICAM-1) with actin-containing cytoskeleton and -actinin. J. Cell Biol. **118**(5), 1223–1234 (1992)
4. Chapman, A., del Ama, L.F., Ferguson, J., Kamarashev, J., Wellbrock, C., Hurlstone, A.: Heterogeneous tumor subpopulations cooperate to drive invasion. Cell Rep. **8**, 688–695 (2014)
5. Graner, F., Glazier, J.A.: Simulation of biological cell sorting using a two-dimensional extended Potts model. Phys. Rev. Lett. **69**(13), 2013–2016 (1992)
6. Herman-Bausier, P., El-Kirat-Chatel, S., Foster, T.J., Geoghegan, J.A., Dufrêne, Y.F.: Staphylococcus aureus fibronectin-binding protein a mediates cell-cell adhesion through low-affinity homophilic bonds. mBio **6**(3), e00413–e00415 (2015)
7. Johnson, C.P., Tang, H.Y., Carag, C., Speicher, D.W., Discher, D.E.: Forced unfolding of proteins within cells. Science **317**(5838), 663–666 (2007)
8. Kraning-Rush, C.M., Carey, S.P., Lampi, M.C., Reinhart-King, C.A.: Microfabricated collagen tracks facilitate single cell metastatic invasion in 3D. Integr. Biol. **5**(3), 606–616 (2013)

9. Nyman-Huttunen, H., Tian, L., Ning, L., Gahmberg, C.G.: α-Actinin-dependent cytoskeletal anchorage is important for ICAM-5-mediated neuritic outgrowth. J. Cell Sci. **119**(Pt 15), 3057–3066 (2006)
10. Turner, S., Sherratt, J.A.: Intercellular adhesion and cancer invasion: a discrete simulation using the extended Potts model. J. Theor. Biol. **216**, 85–100 (2002)
11. Zaman, M.H., Kamm, R.D., Matsudaira, P., Lauffenburger, D.A.: Computational model for cell migration in three-dimensional matrices. Biophys. J. **89**(2), 1389–1397 (2005)

PAM: Discrete 3-D Model of Tumor Dynamics in the Presence of Anti-tumor Treatment

Marta Panuszewska$^{(\boxtimes)}$, Bartosz Minch, Rafał Wcisło, and Witold Dzwinel

Department of Computer Science, AGH University of Science and Technology,
Krakow, Poland
panuszewska@agh.edu.pl

Abstract. Existing computer models of cancer focus mostly on disease progression rather than its remission/recurrence caused by anti-cancer therapy. Herein, we present a discrete model of tumor evolution in 3D, based on the Particle Automata Model (PAM) that allows for following the spatio-temporal dynamics of a small neoplasm (millimeters in diameter) under treatment. We confront the 3D model with its simplified 0D version. We demonstrate that the spatial factors such as the vascularization density, absent in the structureless 0D cancer models, can critically influence the results of treatment. We discuss briefly the role of computer simulations in personalized anti-cancer therapy.

Keywords: Tumor dynamics
3-D particle automata computer model
Anti-tumor treatment simulation

1 Introduction

Even though the mortality rate of cancer is slowly decreasing, it is still one of the main fatality factors worldwide. Approximately 40 percent of people will be diagnosed with some type of cancer at one point during their lifetime [1]. Development of an effective general anti-cancer treatment strategy is vastly restricted because the neoplasms greatly differ between each other. Moreover, the microenvironment of tumor evolution defined by bio-mechanical properties of a tissue and its vascularization can be completely different not only for various cancer types but also for various patients and even parts of attacked tissue. Computer model of a tumor that mimics its evolution before and after treatment for a specific patient, can help in control of principal tumor progression/recession mechanisms and in predicting possible scenarios of its dynamics, thus in development of optimal personalized anti-cancer therapy.

Tumor growth, regression/recession and recurrence are complex, multi-scale phenomena, influenced by countless mutually coupled microscopic and macroscopic factors (see e.g. [24]). The taxonomy of cancer models includes broad spectrum of homogeneous (discrete, stochastic, continuous: single-phase and multiphase) and heterogeneous (discrete-continuous) computational paradigms. They

© Springer Nature Switzerland AG 2018
G. Mauri et al. (Eds.): ACRI 2018, LNCS 11115, pp. 42–54, 2018.
https://doi.org/10.1007/978-3-319-99813-8_4

are employed for modeling both very detailed processes of oncogenesis occurring in a single spatio-temporal scale (in molecular, tissue or organism level) and complex multiscale systems. Diversity of existing tumor models are described in comprehensive books from computational oncology (e.g. [6,18,24]) and hundreds of papers.

Cancer dynamics can be simulated by means of both very simple 0D models described by ODEs (ordinary differential equations) and more complicated, computationally demanding spatio-temporal 3D systems (realized numerically by using finite element methods FEM, agent-based discrete models etc.) [21,23,24]. The latter ones are focused mostly on tumor progression. Meanwhile, its remission/recurrence caused by anti-cancer therapy is rather modeled by using simpler ODEs based codes [20,25]. This is understandable because the 3D tumor models are usually over-parametrized. Taking into account the processes responsible for the anti-cancer therapy may result in additional excessive increase of their complexity. Consequently, this can considerably lower the quality of predictions of cancer dynamics due to overfitting, ill-conditioning and high computational complexity of the models.

Therefore, simple 0D computer models of cancer, adapted to real data representing tumor dynamics [21], which exploits prediction/correction scheme (such as in [7]), could seem to be more useful in predictive diagnosis systems. On the other hand, because the variability of their parameters is prohibitively high and depends strongly on the microenvironment of cancer dynamics, the elaborated prognoses are too often inconclusive [21]. That is why, employing advanced image diagnostics of the future as input data, 3D models could be extremely helpful both in recognizing the most critical regression and recurrence factors and in the process of detailed analysis of various scenarios of tumor evolution. Especially, in respect to the specific tumor environment such as bio-mechanical properties of tissue and its vascularization topology. We expect that balanced use of tumor models of various complexity together with the new opportunities of the computational and diagnostic technologies will decide about usefulness of predictive oncology in personalized anti-cancer therapy in the future.

The main contribution of this paper is the application of 3D PAM modeling paradigm [8] in simulating cancer dynamics, assuming treatment. The 3D model considers the most important factors influencing cancer remission caused by the anti-tumor therapy. The PAM model allows for simulating the tumor evolution in the mesoscopic scale (a millimeter in diameter, i.e., $N = 10^5 - 10^6$ cells) in a reasonable CPU time on a laptop computer. Simulation time for a greater systems, scales up linearly with N. We also developed the method for generating realistic vascular network structure, which can be easily adapted to various tissues. Additionally, by assuming different types of interactions between cells, the extended PAM model reflects more realistic bio-mechanical properties of cancerous tissue in which the rheological properties of "healthy" and tumor cells are distinctly different. We aim to demonstrate that our model constitutes an important complement to approximate 0D tumor models, which are currently of clinical use [3,19,21]. Our goal is to show that the 3D model is sensitive to a specific tumor micro-environment defined by the density of tissue vascularization, which is a crucial factor determining the result of anti-cancer therapy.

In the following section we present a simple structureless 0D model of tumor dynamics, which was applied in clinical practice and is a good approximation of our 3D solution. Next, we briefly describe the 3D PAM model of cancer evolution under treatment and the computational layout, which mimics realistic tissue vascularization. We describe some computer experiments showing the influence of the tissue vascularization density on the tumor evolution under treatment. Finally, we discuss the conclusions.

2   Simplified 0D Cancer Model

The 0D tumor model [21] is presented schematically in Fig. 1. It is assumed that there are three basic types of tumor cells: proliferative P, quiescent Q and mutated quiescent Q_P. We assume also that only the proliferative cells are able to reproduce. The proliferative tumor cells, which stay some time in a very hostile environment (e.g. low concentration of oxygen and nutrients, high pressure etc.) become quiescent. In case of anti-tumor treatment, the proliferative cells die and the damaged (mutated) quiescent cells appear, which can either die, stay dormant or revert (after some time) to proliferative state, becoming "the seeds" of even more voracious cancer. The model is defined by the set of four ODEs. Each of them describes the dynamics of the population of a specific cell type. The equations are as follows [21]:

$$\frac{dC}{dt} = -T_c C, \text{ (1)} \qquad\qquad\qquad \frac{dQ}{dt} = k_{PQ}P - \gamma_Q CT_C Q, \text{ (2)}$$

$$\frac{dQ_P}{dt} = \gamma_Q CT_C Q - k_{QPP}Q_P - \delta_{QP}Q_P, \text{ (3)} \qquad P^* = P + Q + Q_P, \text{ (4)}$$

$$\frac{dP}{dt} = \lambda_P P(1 - \frac{P^*}{K}) + k_{QPP}Q_P - k_{PQ}P - \gamma_P CT_C P. \text{ (5)}$$

where: P - the total volume of proliferative cells; Q - the total volume of quiescent cells; Q_P - the total volume of mutated quiescent cells; C - anti-cancer drug concentration; T_C - a constant used for calculating decrease of anti-cancer drug concentration; λ_P - a rate of growth for P; k_{PQ} - a rate the cells change their states from P to Q; k_{QPP} - a rate the cells change their states from Q_P to P; γ_Q, γ_P - damage rates in proliferative and quiescent tissue, respectively.

In [21], the model parameters were adapted to real data - glioma cancer evolution - which were taken from many (more than 300) patients for three types of anti-cancer therapies. In Fig. 2 we can see two examples of tumor size dynamics for two different (averaged) "patients", obtained by solving the model equations. Herein, we have chosen the averaged set of model parameters obtained for PCV chemotherapy and trained additionally by using Bayesian adaptation technique (ABC) [5]. Despite apparent differences, we can remark that the tumor evolution

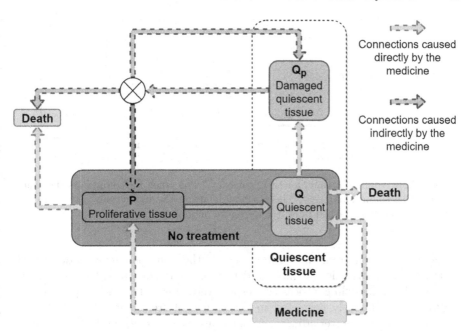

Fig. 1. Block diagram of the 0-D cancer model.

is very similar in both cases. The tumor increases in size at the beginning of the simulation, then rapidly shrinks due to treatment and, finally, some time after treatment it re-grows again. This simple model applies to rather big tumors, i.e., up to 8 cm of mean tumor diameter (MTD) [21]. Our 3-D model is able to simulate tumor of much more modest size - up to a millimeter in diameter (on a laptop computer). Thus, we expect the tumor evolution type such as that for the "first patient" with early tumor symptoms (see Fig. 2). As shown in [21], for the majority of cases, typical not optimistic result is observed - an inevitable and very quick re-growth of tumor mass. We demonstrate in Fig. 2 that a wrong choice of treatment plan, or its abrupt discontinuation, can result in a rapid tumor recurrence. For example, as shown in Fig. 2, the tumors of the two "patients" may be similar in size after 50 months of their appearance, despite the patients started their therapies in very different stages of tumor development. In the ideal case presented in Fig. 2, i.e., when the size of real tumor evolution follows exactly the model (1–5), we are able to predict tumor size dynamics not only after but also before treatment. The predictions were made by training the model (i.e., adapt its parameters from data) by using the Bayesian adaptation technique (ABC) [5] employing continually "measured" tumor volume in a relatively short time interval Fig. 2. On the other hand, as shown in [21], due to rather scarce and not accurate data, and most of all, incompatibility between the 0-D model and the reality, the quality of model predictions is definitely worse. Therefore, even though the 0D model can be very useful, it cannot extrapolate long term changes

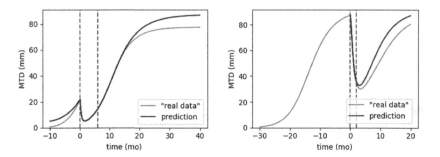

Fig. 2. Tumor volume in time, for two "patients". The green line represents the exact solution of the equations (1–5). The red line delineate the predictions based on data located between blue dashed lines. (Color figure online)

in the tumor spatial dynamics stimulated by the non-homogeneous density of tissue and vascularization, e.g., caused by occurrence of voids due to necrosis and vascular remodeling processes, respectively. Thus, the model parameters should be continuously corrected in the course of treatment. The 3D tumor model could help in better adjustment of the approximate 0D model to real data. Assuming that in the future we will be able not only to measure the tumor size in real time but also to observe its shape and biological structure of its growth environment, we can think about application of more sophisticated 3-D tumor models in predictive oncology. Knowing the real initial tumor layout, we would be able to predict spatial scenarios of its evolution taking into account that a specific tissue structure (its mechanical properties and/or density of vasculature) could block or accelerate its dynamics. Particularly, it might be possible to see if the cancer does not start to re-grow in a location where the access to the anti-cancer drug is restricted (for example, in a small tissue fragment which is away from blood vessels). This information plays a key role in choosing a therapy plan and decide about the way of its application, e.g., the dose and frequency of drug administration.

3 3D Tumor Model

3.1 Particle Automata Model

We extended the 0D model of tumor with treatment to three dimensions. To this end we adapted the PAM heterogeneous discrete-continuous modeling paradigm [8,23] to the framework from Fig. 1. The basic properties of 3D PAM model are described below.

As shown in Fig. 3a, the system consisting of tumor and healthy tissue can be represented by interacting cells (particles) with a few variable states. The particle system is bounded by a computational box under a constant external pressure. Each particle i (cell) is defined as a tuple $(\boldsymbol{x}_i, \boldsymbol{v}_i, \boldsymbol{a}_i)$, where: i - particle index and $(i = 1, ..., N)$, $\boldsymbol{r}_i$ - its position, $\boldsymbol{v}_i$ - velocity, $\boldsymbol{a}_i$ - attributes (states).

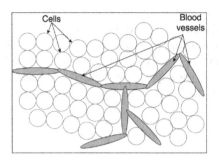 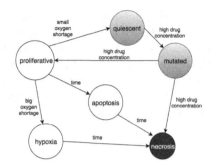

Fig. 3. The scheme of main components of the Particle Automata Model and cell states. (a) Particles representing tissue cells and blood vessels. (b) Life cycle of a cell. We mark in gray the states possible only for tumor cells.

Each particle represents a tissue cell while two particles create a single segment of a blood vessel. The blood vessels are made of connected segments. The vector of particle attributes a_i includes information on: the cell type (tumor: {proliferative, quiescent, mutated}, healthy, blood vessel}, a phase of the cell life-cycle (see Fig. 3b), cell size, cell age, hypoxia time, concentrations of O_2, TAF (tumor angiogenic factor) and anti-tumor drug, and total pressure exerted on a particle from the rest of the tissue. The spring-like forces [8] between particles mimic mechanical repulsion and attraction between cells. The total force acting on a particle i is the sum of all forces from other surrounding particles in a given cut-off radius. The particles of all types move according to the ODE system of the Newtonian equations of motion, while their states follow automata rules (defining, e.g., cell life-cycle from Fig. 3b, thresholding rules, chemical interactions between neighboring cells etc.). The blood pressure in the vessels is approximated by the Kirchhoff law. Spatio-temporal evolution of each cell is highly dependent on the concentrations of oxygen (and TAF in angiogenic phase) and anti-tumor drugs calculated in a cell position by solving continuous reaction-diffusion PDEs. The concentrations define internal state of each cell. The blood vessel network Ω releases in each time step a constant amount of oxygen and anti-tumor drugs (sources), which diffuse inside the tumor mass. Simultaneously, the diffusive oxygen and drugs are consumed in a given constant rate by the tissue cells (sinks).

3.2   The Layout and Blood Vessel Network

We have developed a simple algorithm that allows us to generate a realistic, non-deterministic vessel network being the approximation of more sophisticated approaches presented in [17,22]. We assumed that all the vessels consist of a series of line segments of the length equal to *"vessel_length"*. Starting and ending points of the vessels are chosen at the left and right sides of bounding box. Their radii are defined by *"max_thickness"* parameter. Then, the subsequent layers of vessel segments are added towards the center of the computational box with randomly chosen curvature from 0 to *"max_curvature"* interval. Each vessel segment has a chance to split into two vessels with a probability *"chance_of_split"*. The thickness of a blood vessel segment is inversely proportional to its distance to the center of the computational box. The number of layers of vessel segments is defined by *"levels"* parameter. When all the layers are created, we connect each blood vessel to the nearest neighbor. In Fig. 4, we present the layouts we used in our experiments.

Fig. 4. The layouts of the tissue model with dense (left) and poor vasculature (right). Healthy cells are hidden for visualization purposes.

Finally, the tissue cells surrounding the vessels are added. All of the cells are arranged in densely packed layers. The initial cluster of tumor cells is situated at the center of the computational box.

3.3 Viscosity of the Tissue

In the PAM model we have introduced a new model of interparticle forces. The healthy and cancerous tissues are represented by viscous SPH particles. Then, the whole particle ensemble simulates the dynamics of a multiphase Navier-Stokes fluid. The main reason for this assumption is the possibility to mimic real differences between rheological properties of tumor and healthy tissues (the healthy cells are more "viscous"). For smaller tumors, this difference in viscosity makes tumor cells much more flexible what is demonstrated in Fig. 5.

Fig. 5. Comparison of PAM simulations with and without SPH properties of viscosity force. Left: with viscosity force. Right: without viscosity force.

For larger tumors this difference in viscosity does not reveal in observed growth patterns. The pressure exerted on the tumor and its fluctuations are too small to trigger tumor surface instability effects. Therefore, the avascular tumors can evenly grow in all directions. We anticipate that, the surface instabilities can be visible for larger tumors (over 1 cm in diameter), for which the fingering instability can be expected, as it is in large ensembles of DPD (dissipative) particles in [9].

3.4 Anti-cancer Treatment

The PAM model of the tumor behavior after treatment is based on the same assumptions as the 0-D model [21]. We assume that all the tumor cells start their life cycle as the proliferative ones. If the oxygen concentration drops below a given threshold the proliferative cells become quiescent, i.e., they will no longer have the capability to replicate. If the medicine concentration is above a certain level, the proliferative cells die and the mutated quiescent cells appear [4]. If the medicine concentration will stay high, the mutated quiescent cells will either stay mutated (but dormant), die or become proliferative once again [14,18] being the sources of cancer re-growth. The tumor transforms from homogeneous to heterogeneous one.

Changes in drug concentration are governed by the mechanisms of medicine impact, transport&redistribution (diffusion and advection) and elimination (decay and cellular uptake), similar as in [15]. We assume, that drugs are secreted by the functional and permeable (destructed by vascular remodeling process) blood vessels at a constant rate. The cells also consume the medicine at a constant rate, depending on a tissue type. The medicine diffusion is governed by the diffusion-reaction equation:

$$\frac{\partial C}{\partial t} = D_c \cdot \Delta C - N_r C - T_c C + c \cdot h(\Omega, T - t), \tag{1}$$

where: N_r - drug consumption rate, D_c - medicine diffusion constant, C - drug concentration, T_C - a constant used for calculating decrease of anti-cancer drug concentration, c - medicine source rate in the blood network Ω during time T. For the sake of simplicity, constant drug secretion c and its absorption $T_c C$ rates by the tissue are assumed. The function $h(x,t) = 1$, for $t > 0$ and $h(x,t) = 0$, for $t < 0$. Our assumptions are consistent with the simple model described in Sect. 2 [21]. Comparing to the fully continuous drug diffusion model [15], the advection of drug in PAM is realized by moving particles. Therefore, the advection term $v \cdot \nabla C$ is lacking in (6).

4   Results of Simulation

The size of a fragment of tissue modeled was limited to $3.0 \cdot 10^5$ cells in total. This bound is defined mostly by the computational power we dispose for simulations. They have been run on a single core of the CPU specified in Table 1. One

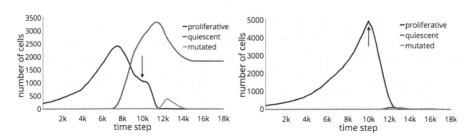

Fig. 6. Tumor evolution for the setups with (a) poor and (b) dense vasculature. The treatment was administered on the step marked with a black arrow.

simulation needs around 24 h CPU time for simulating $1.6 \cdot 10^4$ time steps. The initial setup of the simulations (Fig. 4) assumes around 200 cancer cells placed in the middle of the layout. In Table 2 we collected the most important parameters influencing tumor dynamics.

Table 1. Specification of the machine running the simulations.

CPU	Intel®Core™i7-5960X @ 4.2 GHz (8 cores, 16 threads, 20 MB of L3 cache)
RAM	DDR4 2666 MHz 32 GB (4 × 8 GB Quad-Channel)
Disk	Samsung NVMe SSD 960 Pro
GPU	nVidia GeForce GTX 1080

As shown in the previous section, the tumor evolves in a fragment of tissue composed of healthy cells and blood vessels. The proliferative and quiescent cells, being the components of the cancerous tissue, have different properties than the healthy cells and the vessels. The letter are more resistant to pressure and low oxygen concentration. The proliferative cells consume more oxygen and are very susceptible to anti-cancer drugs. These properties allow them, on the one hand, for rapid reproduction under favorable conditions and, on the other, fast necrosis (death) due to devastating effects of treatment. The quiescent cells are more resistant on the anti-cancer drugs and need extremely little oxygen to stay alive.

To show how the spatial topology of tissue exploits these cell properties and influences cancer evolution during and after treatment, we have compared tumor dynamics for two different layouts (see Fig. 4). In the first one, the tumor is well oxygenated by a dense vasculature, while in the other it is situated in a poorly vascularized tissue. As we can see in Fig. 6, after growth phase, the tumors collapse due to treatment (see also Figs. 7 and 8).

However, the results from Figs. 6 and 7 show that eradication of the tumor in the layout with poorer vasculature can fail. The tumor shrinks down during

Table 2. The most important parameters of the simulation (concerning tumor growth).

Name	Description	Value	Units
force_r_cut	Cut-off radius in forces calculations	10	μm
p_o2	O2 threshold to change state proliferative cells	0.7	norm.
q_o2	O2 threshold to change state for quiescent cells	0.35	norm.
diff_O2	Diffusion coefficient for O2	2000	p.u.
diff_med	Diffusion coefficient for medicine	4000	p.u.
time_apop	Time to apoptosis	3600	p.u
min_inter_time	Minimum interphase time	600	p.u
max_pressure_h	Max pressure in healthy cells	$1 * 10^{-16}$	p.u
max_pressure_t	Max pressure in tumor cells	$1 * 10^{-15}$	p.u
cons_rate_h	Medicine consumption rate in healthy cells	$2 * 10^{-12}$	$p.uh^{-1}$
cons_rate_t	Medicine consumption rate in tumor cells	$2 * 10^{-11}$	p.u
o2_cons_h	O2 consumption rate in healthy cells	$5 * 10^{-11}$	p.u
o2_cons_t	O2 consumption rate in proliferative cells	$1 * 10^{-10}$	p.u
o2_cons_q	O2 consumption rate in quiescent cells	$2 * 10^{-11}$	p.u
o2_hypoxia	O2 threshold for entering hypoxia state	0.01	p.u

*p.u. - program units, norm. - normalized

Fig. 7. Remission of the tumor in poor vasculature. The cross-section of the tumor is shown. Brown - proliferative cells, red - quiescent cells and blue - mutated. (Color figure online)

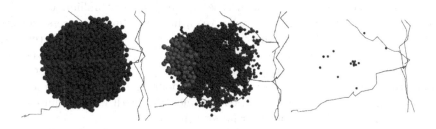

Fig. 8. Remission of the tumor in the tissue with dense vasculature.

treatment, but it can start to re-grow when the quiescent cells from tumor rem-
nants become mutated and will convert into tumor cells. On the other hand, one
can observe a dramatic decline in the number of proliferative tumor cells during
treatment for the second layout. As shown in Fig. 8, for denser vasculature, due
to good oxygenation, also the number of quiescent cells can be marginal. Consequently, as shown in Fig. 8 almost all cancer cell can be exterminated during
treatment. These results demonstrate that the choice of the right concentration
of anti-tumor drugs and the type of treatment is highly dependent on the tumor
vasculature what is in full agreement with observations (see, e.g., [11]. It also
shows that anti-angiogenic therapy - which inhibits tumor vascularization - in
the incipient stages of tumor grow may be very risky [11]. One can expect that if
anti-angiogenic therapy fails, more demanding chemotherapy need to be applied,
what leads to worse side effects and poor prognoses. If we compare the tumor
dynamics from Fig. 6 to the tumor evolution simulated by 0-D model from Fig. 2,
we can see that the results are fairly consistent. The initial growth stage and
rapid decline during treatment look similar to the tumor model with a dense
vasculature. The tumor regrowth is not observed due to insufficient number of
quiescent cells and the death of all proliferative ones. In the second case of poor
vascularization, many quiescent cells survive the treatment. Some of them, which
become mutated, can be the source of further cancer recurrence. This is particularly dangerous in case of cancers with scattered consolidation (e.g. in lung
cancer), i.e., evolving in the form of the cluster consisting of large number of
tiny tumors. After not sufficiently destructive chemotherapy, though the most
of small tumors will die, the cancer recurrence can be still feasible starting from
tumor blobs such as in Figs. 6a and 7.

5   Concluding Remarks

In this paper we present the 3-D model of a small (mesoscopic) tumor simulating various phases of its evolution, particularly, remission/recurrence stimulated by anti-cancer therapy. We demonstrate that our extended PAM model
reveals a strong dependence of the cancer dynamics under treatment on its
spatial environment, such as the tumor vascularization. The size of simulated
tumor is constrained by the high computational complexity of the PAM model
and the processing power of available computer systems. However, the modeling of anti-cancer treatment even in case of the tumors of millimeters size is
also very rational. Some types of cancer (e.g., lung and breast cancers) consist
of many scattered clusters of tumor cells. Moreover, the increasing effectiveness
of diagnostics enables us to discover minuscule tumors in very early stages of
their development. Consequently, due to different size and structure of small
tumors than large ones, what reveals in smaller population of mutated quiescent
cells, one can expect different scenarios of tumor re-growth which require other
therapy plans than those applied for larger tumors.

Although, we did not try to match the parameters of PAM model to the
0-D model (in fact, the two models presented here represent completely different

tumors) one can see that in the context of both their spatial scales and types, they behave very similarly for small tumor sizes. Thus, we believe that the calibration of the two is possible. So, afterwards, the 3-D model of tumor could be used as a "ground truth" for learning the parameters and normalization of approximated 0-D cancer model and to mimic a broad range of tumor evolution scenarios depending on its spatial structure and the environment.

Summarizing, nowadays, the 3-D model of tumor can be used as an extension and support for simpler 0-D models in personalized anti-cancer therapy. Its main disadvantage is the large number of parameters, what can make it useless (overfitting) when adapted to small and poor (e.g., only tumor MTD measurements) real data sets. However, in the future, having in mind, on the one hand, the fast development of medical imaging tools which soon will provide us with the realistic 3-D images of the environment of cancer evolution, and, on the other, the expected radical increase of computational power, the 3-D tumor models can soon become independent and precise tools in predictive oncology.

Acknowledgments. The work has been supported by the Polish National Science Center (NCN), in the scope of two projects: 2013/10/M/ST6/00531 (RW and BM) and 2016/21/B /ST6/01539 (MP and WD). We thank Piotr Pedrycz, (MSc student), for providing us with the results of parameters adaptation for 0-D tumor model.

References

1. American Cancer Society: Lifetime Risk of Developing or Dying From Cancer (2018). https://www.cancer.org/cancer/cancer-basics/lifetime-probability-of-developing-or-dying-from-cancer.html
2. Bender, J., Koschier, D.: Divergence-free smoothed particle hydrodynamics. In: Proceedings of ACM SIGGRAPH/EUROGRAPHICS Symposium on Computer Animation (SCA) (2015)
3. Benzekry, S., Lamont, C., Beheshti, A., Tracz, A., Ebos, J.M.L., Hlatky, L.: Classical mathematical models for description and prediction of experimental tumor growth. PLoS Comput. Biol. **10**(8), e1003800 (2014)
4. Chabner, B.A., Longo, D.L.: Cancer Chemotherapy and Biotherapy: Principles and Practice. Lippincott Williams and Wilkins, Philadelphia (2011)
5. Csilléry, K., Blum, M.G., Gaggiotti, O.E., François, O.: Approximate Bayesian computation (ABC) in practice. Trends Ecol. Evol. **25**(7), 410–418 (2010)
6. Cristini, V., Lowengrub, J.: Multiscale Modeling of Cancer: An Integrated Experimental and Mathematical Modeling Approach, p. 278. Cambridge University Press, Cambridge (2010)
7. Dzwinel, W., Kłusek, A., Wcisło, R., Panuszewska, M., Topa, P.: Continuous and discrete models of melanoma progression simulated in multi-GPU environment. In: Wyrzykowski, R., Dongarra, J., Deelman, E., Karczewski, K. (eds.) PPAM 2017. LNCS, vol. 10777, pp. 505–518. Springer, Cham (2018). https://doi.org/10.1007/978-3-319-78024-5_44
8. Dzwinel, W., Wcisło, R., Yuen, D.A., Miller, S.: PAM: particle automata in modeling of multi-scale biological systems. ACM Trans. Model. Comput. Simul. **26**(3), 1–21 (2016). Article no. 20

9. Dzwinel, W., Yuen, D.A.: Rayleigh-Taylor instability in the mesoscale modeled by dissipative particle dynamics. Int. J. Mod. Phys. C **12**(1), 91–118 (2001)
10. Gerlee, P., Anderson, A.R.A.: Diffusion-limited tumour growth: simulations and analysis. Math. Biosci. Eng. **7**(2), 385–400 (2010)
11. Huang, D., et al.: Anti-angiogenesis or pro-angiogenesis for cancer treatment: focus on drug distribution. Int. J. Clin. Exp. Med. **8**(6), 8369 (2015)
12. Iwasa, Y., Michor, F.: Evolutionary dynamics of intratumor heterogeneity. PLoS ONE **6**(3), e17866 (2011)
13. Jagiella, N., Rickert, D., Theis, F.J., Hasenauer, J.: Parallelization and high-performance computing enables automated statistical inference of multi-scale models. Cell Syst. **4**(2), 194–206 (2017)
14. Kaina, B.: DNA damage-triggered apoptosis: critical role of DNA repair, double-strand breaks, cell proliferation and signaling. Biochem. Pharmacol. **66**(8), 1547–1554 (2003)
15. Kim, M., Gillies, R.J., Rejniak, K.A.: Current advances in mathematical modeling of anti-cancer drug penetration into tumor tissues. Front. Oncol. **3**, 278 (2013)
16. Louzoun, Y., Xue, C., Lesinski, G.B., Friedman, A.: A mathematical model for pancreatic cancer growth and treatments. J. Theor. Biol. **351**, 74–82 (2014)
17. Łazarz, R.: Graph-based framework for 3-D vascular dynamics simulation. Procedia Comput. Sci. **101**, 415–423 (2016)
18. Masunaga, S.I., Ono, K., Hori, H., Suzuki, M., Kinashi, Y., Takagaki, M.: Potentially lethal damage repair by total and quiescent tumor cells following various DNA-damaging treatments. Radiat. Med. **17**(4), 259–264 (1999)
19. Ribba, B., Holford, N.H., Magni, P.: A review of mixed-effects models of tumor growth and effects of anticancer drug treatment used in population analysis. CPT Pharmacomet. Syst. Pharmacol. **3**, e113 (2014)
20. Ribba, B., Holford, N.H., Magni, P., Trocóniz, I., Gueorguieva, I., Girard, P.: A review of mixed-effects models of tumor growth and effects of anticancer drug treatment used in population analysis. CPT: Pharmacomet. Syst. Pharmacol. **3**(5), 1–10 (2014)
21. Ribba, B., et al.: A tumor growth inhibition model for low-grade glioma treated with chemotherapy or radiotherapy. Clin. Cancer Res. **18**(18), 5071–5080 (2012)
22. Rieger, H., Fredrich, T., Welter, M.: Eur. Phys. J. **131**, 31 (2016)
23. Wcisło, R., Dzwinel, W., Yuen, D.A., Dudek, A.Z.: A 3-D model of tumor progression based on complex automata driven by particle dynamics. J. Mol. Model. **15**(12), 1517 (2009)
24. Wodarz, D., Komarova, N.L.: Dynamics of Cancer: Mathematical Foundations of Oncology, p. 532. World Scientific, Singapore (2014)
25. Xie, H., Jiao, Y., Fan, Q., Hai, M., Yang, J., Hu, Z., et al.: Modeling Three-dimensional Invasive Solid Tumor Growth in Heterogeneous Microenvironment under Chemotherapy (2018). arXiv preprint arXiv:1803.02953

Simulation and Other Applications
of CA

Modeling of Electrical and Thermal Behaviors of Photovoltaic Panels Using Cellular Automata Approach

Iliasse Abdennour[1(✉)], Mustapha Ouardouz[1], and Abdes Samed Bernoussi[2]

[1] MMC Team, Abdelmalek-Essaadi University, B.P. 416, Tangier, Morocco
iliasseabdennour@gmail.com, ouardouz@gmail.com
[2] GAT Team, Abdelmalek-Essaadi University, B.P. 416, Tangier, Morocco
a.samed.bernoussi@gmail.com

Abstract. In this paper we propose a new approach to evaluate electrical performances and temperature field for standard photovoltaic (PV) panels. The model is based on two-component cellular automata (CA) that describe the dynamics and behavior of a solar cell. The first component represents the evolution and distribution of the temperature in PV panels and the second consists of the electrical output characteristics of the solar cells. The coupling of these two-components allows us to simulate numerically the operation mode of solar cells according to four defined states: direct mode, inverse mode, hot spot mode and failure mode in order to compute the generated electrical power. This model is adapted to the case of uniform and non-uniform irradiation. Some simulations and experimental results illustrate our approach.

Keywords: Cellular automata · Photovoltaic cell · Temperature field

1 Introduction

Nowadays, photovoltaic systems are some of the most widely used renewable energy sources in the world. They have a particular interest for governments, and industries because they are green and sustainable. As a result of their importance, multiple countries have inaugurated huge photovoltaic parks. However, because of the high initial capital required for this technology, the exploitation of solar energy produced must be optimized; this requires the use of reliable simulation and relevant modeling of PV system that takes into account the thermal behaviors in PV modules.

There are numerous published papers that describe the thermal behaviors in PV modules. In [1] a simple method have been considered to determine temperature of solar cells based on linear relationship between basic environmental variables; ambient temperature, humidity and wind speed, this method is still poor because the electrical operating points of the PV module are not taken into account. In [2] the thermal mechanism used is based on correlation of electrical

© Springer Nature Switzerland AG 2018
G. Mauri et al. (Eds.): ACRI 2018, LNCS 11115, pp. 57–67, 2018.
https://doi.org/10.1007/978-3-319-99813-8_5

Resistance and Capacitance (RC circuit) to Thermal Resistance and Thermal Capacitance (R_{th}, C_{th}), C_{th} concern the conductive heat transfer in the PV layers and R_{th} is defined as the index of a materials resistance.

Recently an important work on this subject has been provided by Pierre-Luc [3]; the method presented in this paper consists in combining an optical model with a five parameter PV electrical model and a 2-D heat conduction equation. Other papers have been proposed for modeling thermal and electrical behaviors of PV panel in the case of partial shading [4–6].

In this paper we propose a new approach for modeling the electrical and thermal behaviors of the PV panels. The model is based on two-component cellular automata (CA) through which a 2-D heat conduction equation is combined with a PV electrical model of five parameters for every time step of simulation. Our CA allows describing in a simple mathematical formalism the dynamics and behavior of a solar cell in a PV panel. Moreover, it is to be noted that this is the first time that the dynamic behavior of photovoltaic (PV) panels are simulated using CA.

2   Problem Statement

Several representative models of the PV cell are found in the literature, which differs from each other in the procedure and the number of parameters involved in the calculation of the voltage and current. The model proposed by Bishop [7] is the most representative to the actual behavior of the solar cell, because it takes into account the reverse bias polarity (see Fig. 1a).

Figure 1b shows solar cell current-voltage characteristics in two zones operation

- Zone 1: corresponds to forward mode. In this mode the cell works in a generator and delivers the power as shown in the rightn part of the vertical axis in Fig. 1b.
- Zone 2: corresponds to bias reverse polarity mode. The cell works in reception and dissipates the power in the form of heat which will cause overheating of the solar cell. This can provoke what is then called as a hot spot [8]. In general, the solar cell is polarized in reverse when it is shadowed.

The main purpose of this paper is that of modeling the thermal and electrical behavior of the solar cell in its two modes of operation.

3   Problem Approach

Because the cellular automaton (CA) is a powerful tool for modeling dynamics of systems, we have exploited it as an approach to achieve our purpose.
Let us recall the definition of the cellular automaton.

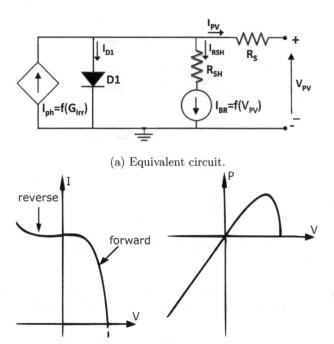

(a) Equivalent circuit.

(b) Electrical output and mode operation.

Fig. 1. Principles of solar cell operation.

3.1   CA Definition

A cellular automaton is a mathematical object, also studied in theoretical computer science. It was introduced by J. von Neumann in 1948. It consists of a grid of cells arranged in n-dimensional space, each cell bearing finite discrete states which can evolve over time depending on the state of its neighborhood. The simplest application is the Game of Life, proposed in 1970 by the British mathematician John Horton Conway. A cellular automaton is defined by the quadruplet $\mathcal{A}$, plus the boundary and initial condition [10].

$$\mathcal{A} = (\mathcal{L}, \mathcal{N}, \mathcal{S}, \mathcal{F}) \tag{1}$$

Where $\mathcal{L}$ is called lattice, $\mathcal{N}$ is a neighborhood, $\mathcal{S}$ is a set of states and $\mathcal{F}$ is a function of transition, as can be seen in Fig. 2.

3.2   Description of the Proposed CA

We present briefly the proposed cellular automaton model.

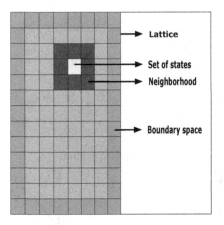

Fig. 2. Principle of cellular automata.

Lattice: The lattice consists of solar cells wired in series or parallels and arranged in a two-dimensional square grid to form a PV model as illustrated in Fig. 3:

$$\mathcal{L} = \{C_{ij}; \, i, j \in \mathbb{N}; \, i = 1, 2.., n_i \, and \, j = 1, 2.., n_j\} \tag{2}$$

with n_i and n_j are the numbers of solar cells along vertical and horizontal axis respectively.

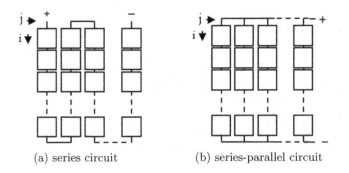

(a) series circuit   (b) series-parallel circuit

Fig. 3. Lattice considered in the approach.

Neighborhood: The neighborhood is adjusted according to the transition rules of the solar cell (current and temperature):

– To determine the maximum operating point current, the choice of the neighborhood depends mainly on the interconnection circuit of the PV panel. If the cells are wired in series, the neighborhood is the entire lattice as shown

in Fig. 4a, and if they are wired in series-parallel circuit, the neighborhood is the cells connected to the same string as illustrated in Fig. 4b.
– To compute the temperature, we consider a von Neumann neighborhood as in Fig. 4c and d.

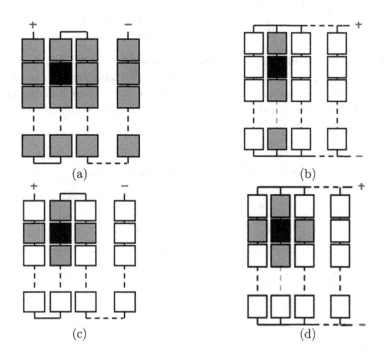

Fig. 4. Cellular automaton neighborhood considered in the approach in the case of a series circuit and series-parallel circuit; (a) and (b) for operating point current , (c) and (d) for temperature (the objective cell is shown in black and neighborhood in gray).

Set of States: The state of each cell corresponds to the mode operation of the PV cell, which is a coupling between the temperature $T_c\,(i,j)$ and the electrical characteristics of the solar cell $I_{opc}\,(i,j)$. There are four possible states as:

$$\mathcal{S} = \{1, 2, 3, 4\} \tag{3}$$

with

$$1 : Direct\ mode,$$
$$2 : Inverse\ mode,$$
$$3 : Hotspot\ mode,$$
$$4 : Failure\ mode.$$

The solar cell is characterized on several physico-chemical intrinsic attributes as illustrated in Fig. 5. Then, with these data, the proposed CA State is given as:

$$
\mathcal{S}(c_{ij}, t) : \begin{cases} 1 & if & I_s^t(i,j) \geq I_{opc}^t(i,j) \\ 2 & if & I_s^t(i,j) < I_{opc}^t(i,j) & and & T_c^t(i,j) < T_{hs} \\ 3 & if & I_s^t(i,j) < I_{opc}^t(i,j) & and & T_{hs} \leq T_c^t(i,j) < T_{cri} \\ 4 & if & I_s^t(i,j) < I_{opc}^t(i,j) & and & T_c^t(i,j) \geq T_{cri} \end{cases}
\tag{4}
$$

where I_s is solar cell short-circuit current at arbitrary conditions, I_{opc} is solar cell maximum operating point current at arbitrary conditions, T_c is solar cell temperature, T_{hs} is minimum temperature of hot spot phenomenon equal to $90\,°C$, and T_{cri} is the critical temperature value that can damage the solar cell (according to [9] $T_{cri} = 150\,°C$).

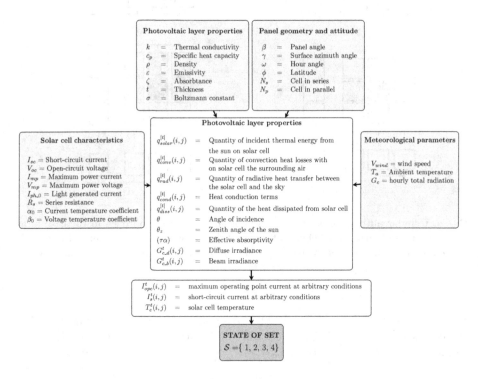

Fig. 5. The data considered in the approach (dynamic factors are shown in red and intrinsic attributes in blue). (Color figure online)

Transition Rules: According to Eq. 4, the evolution of the state between t_i and t_{i+1} depends on the evolution of the temperature $T_c^t(i,j)$ and the operating point current $I_{opc}^t(i,j)$. We have for:

– **Temperature:** The two-dimensional diffusion equation in Cartesian coordinates (x, y), is used to compute the temperature of solar cells:

$$\rho c_p \frac{\partial T\left(x,y\right)}{\partial t} = k\Delta T\left(x,y,t\right) + \xi(x,y,t) \tag{5}$$

where ρ, cp, k and ξ stand respectively for density, heat capacity, thermal conductivity and source term.

To solve Eq. 5 we use the iterative method formulation such as that proposed by Patankar [11]. The expression of temperature cell at instant $t+1$ is obtained by adding the heat generation term and the temperatures values of the four neighbor's cells as expressed in Eq. 6:

$$T_c^{t+1}\left(i,j\right) = F_0\left[T_c^t\left(i,j\right) + T_c^t\left(i+1,j\right) + T_c^t\left(i-1,j\right) + T_c^t\left(i,j+1\right) + \right.$$
$$\left. T_c^t\left(i,j-1\right)\right] + (1 - 4F_0) \times T_c^t\left(i,j\right) + \frac{\Delta t}{\rho c_p} \times \xi^{[t]}\left(i,j\right) \tag{6}$$

with

$$\xi^{[t]}\left(i,j\right) = q_{solar}^{[t]}\left(i,j\right) + q_{diss}^{[t]}\left(i,j\right) + q_{rad}^{[t]}\left(i,j\right) + q_{conv}^{[t]}\left(i,j\right) \tag{7}$$

$\xi^{[t]}$ is the source term rate per unit volume, corresponds to; incident thermal energy from the sun ($q_{solar}^{[t]}$), the heat dissipated from solar cell ($q_{diss}^{[t]}$), the heat transfer by radiation between the solar cell and the sky ($q_{rad}^{[t]}$) and the energy transfer between a cell surface and surrounding air ($q_{conv}^{[t]}$). A detailed description of each of these parameters is available in [3].

– **Operating Point Current:** The operating point current I_{opc} consist the current owing through each of the cell at instant t. If all cells are wired in series they all carry the same current I_{opc} equal to the minimum current (I_m) provided by the bad cell (shaded one) of the PV panel as expressed by Eq. 8. If the cells are wired in a series-parallel circuit, the operating point current is equal to the minimum current provided by the bad cell connected in the string, as expressed by Eq. 9:

$$I_{opc}^t\left(i,j\right) = min\left\{I_m^t\left(i,j\right); i = 1,2..n_i \, and \, j = 1,2..n_j\right\} \tag{8}$$

$$I_{opc}^t\left(i,j\right) = min\left\{I_m^t\left(k,j\right); k = 1,2..n_i\right\} \tag{9}$$

The diagram shown in Fig. 6 explains all of the possible scenarios that can arise for each cell and that explain the operation mode evolution of the solar cell.

Initial and Boundary Conditions: The initial condition is the solar cell temperature at the beginning of the experiment, also it's assumed to be equal to the ambient temperature :

$$T_c^{t=0}\left(i,j\right) = T_a \tag{10}$$

The boundary condition corresponds to convection heat transfer flux between ambient air and the solar cells.

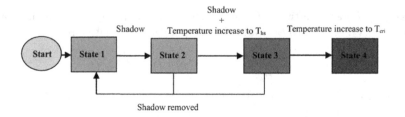

Fig. 6. Diagram of state.

4   Experimental Test and Simulation Result

The methodology for modeling the PV panel using CA method is described in the flowchart of Fig. 7.

The experimental setup for the proposed model is shown in Fig. 8. The setup consists of a Computer Controlled Photovoltaic Solar Energy Unit (EESFC). The EESFC is a scaled laboratory system which includes equipment that is used for the study of the transformation of solar power into electrical power [12]. It is installed in the laboratory of green energy of Abdelmalek- Essaadi University. At each step of simulation the sensors connected to EESFC unit measure respectively the ambient temperature (T_a), irradiation (E) and wind speed (V_v), which were used as inputs values to the numerical model to simulate the transient PV panel temperature field and the associated electrical power generated.

In Table 1 the measured data and simulation results of electrical power generation are summarized. The results are obtained every 5 min step for one continuous hour of simulation. Thus to compare between the measured and simulation results we have calculated the average relative error given by Eq. 11:

$$E_r = abs \left| \frac{(P_{mpS} - P_{mpM})}{P_{mpM}} \right| \times 100 \tag{11}$$

where P_{mpS} and P_{mpM} are simulated and measured values of maximum power. The simulation has been carried out for the situations described below:

- uniform irradiation during the time horizon.
- partial shading, created by an object in the cell C_{43} at time t = 35min.

It is readily apparent from results shown in Table 1 that the simulation results are in good agreement with measurement data in most of the time, the average relative error is low, and does not exceed 10%. These results indicate the capability of our model to evaluate electrical performances of PV panel.

The validation of temperature distribution is done through the use of thermal imaging by an infrared camera as shown in Fig. 9. The distribution of temperature varies between 18 °C (ambient temperature) and 150°C (critical value of temperature) as shows the color bar in Fig. 9e. The temperature ranges from 8 °C at step 1 which corresponds to ambient temperature, to 45 °C at step 3 (after

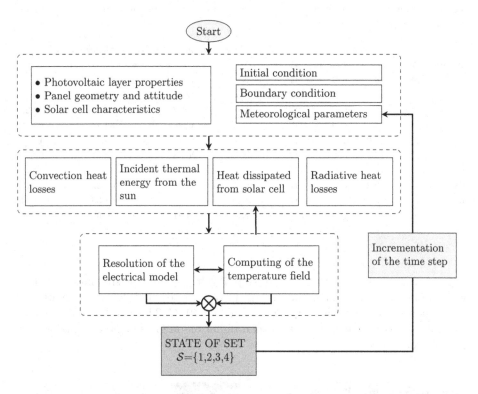

Fig. 7. Methodology for the proposed model.

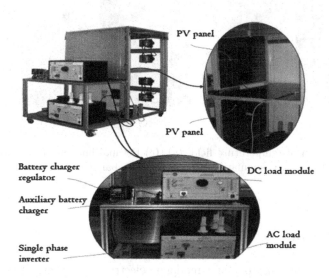

Fig. 8. Experimental setup elements. (Color figure online)

Table 1. Comparison of measured data and simulation result of electrical power generation

Time		Meteorological parameters			Shadowing	Simulation result	Measured data	
Iteration	Minute	$T_a(°C)$	$E(w/m^2)$	$V_v(km/h)$	Yes/No	$P_{mpS}(w)$	$P_{mpM}(w)$	$Er(\%)$
01	00	18.7	633	17	No	32.13	29.22	09.96
02	05	18.7	640	17	No	32.89	31.15	05.59
03	10	18.8	650	17	No	35.14	32.76	07.26
04	15	18.8	660	17	No	35.98	34.15	05.36
05	20	19.0	200	17	Yes	10.12	09.12	10.96
06	25	19.1	660	17	No	36.88	34.65	06.44
07	30	19.1	670	17	No	38.87	37.21	04.46
08	35	19.2	680	17	Yes	04.90	05.22	06.13
09	45	19.3	680	17	No	41.91	38.33	09.34
10	50	19.3	700	17	No	44.41	40.05	10.89
11	55	19.3	750	17	No	45.65	41.87	09.03

10 min of simulation) and 55 °C at step 7 (after 30 min of simulation). Also, we can observe that the simulation results (Fig. 9b, d) slightly overestimate the experiments data (Fig. 9a, c) by approximately 10 °C. This can be attributed to the influence of the reflection of thermal radiation on glass layer as explained by Krenzinger in [13].

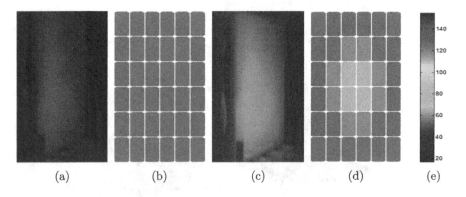

(a)   (b)   (c)   (d)   (e)

Fig. 9. Validation of temperature field: (a), (c) thermal imaging at iteration 02 and 06, respectively; (b), (d) simulation results; (e) color bar (Color figure online)

5   Conclusion

A cellular automata approach for modeling electrical and thermal behaviors of PV panels has been presented in this paper. The model has been validated by measurements of electrical characteristics and temperature distributions of

PV panel. Finally, this model can be developed to be adaptable to other types of collectors that exclude the technologies of the heat exchanger as a thermal absorber plate and amorche panel, in order to detect possible malfunctions.

Acknowledgments. This work has been supported by MESRSFC and CNRST under the project PPR2-OGI-Env, reference PPR2/2016/79.

References

1. Skoplaki, E., Scrofani, J.A.: On the temperature dependence of photovoltaic module electrical performance: a review of efficiency/power correlations. Sol. Energy **83**, 614–624 (2009)
2. Armstrong, S., Hurley, W.G.: A thermal model for photovoltaic panels under varying atmospheric conditions. Appl. Therm. Eng. **30**, 1488–1495 (2010)
3. Paradis, P., Rousse, D.R., Nesreddine, H.: A 2-D transient numerical heat transfer model of the solar absorber plate to improve PV/T solar collector systems. Sol. Energy **153**, 366–378 (2017)
4. Ko, S.W.: Electric and thermal characteristics of photovoltaic modules under partial shading and with a damaged bypass diode. Energy **128**, 232–243 (2017)
5. Carla, M., Vincenzo, D., Infield, D.: Detailed PV array model for non-uniform irradiance and its validation against experimental data. Energy **97**, 314–331 (2013)
6. Batzelis, E.I., Georgilakis, P.S., Papathanassiou, S.A.: Energy models for photovoltaic systems under partial shading conditions: a comprehensive review. Renew. Power Gener. **9**, 340–349 (2015)
7. Bishop, J.W.: Computer simulation of the effects of electrical mismatches in photovoltaic cell interconnection circuits. Sol. Cells **25**, 73–89 (1988)
8. Deng, S., Zhen, Z., Ju, C., Dong, J., Xia, Z.: Research on hot spot risk for high-efficiency solar module. Energy Procedia **130**, 77–86 (2017)
9. Alonso Garcia, M.C., Herrmann, W., Bohmer, W., Prois, B.: Thermal and electrical effects caused by outdoor hot-spot testing in associations of photovoltaics cells. Prog. Photovolt. Res. Appl. **307**, 293–307 (2003)
10. Yacoubi, S.E.L., Jai, A.E.L.: Cellular automata modelling and spreadability. Math. Comput. Model. **7177**, 1059–1074 (2002)
11. Patankar, S.: Numerical Heat Transfer and Fluid Flow. CRC Press, Boca Raton (1980)
12. Engineering and Technical Teaching Equipment, EESFC. http://www.edibon.com/en/equipment/computer-controlled-photovoltaic-solar-energy-unit
13. Krenzinger, A., Andrade, A.C.: Accurate outdoor glass thermographic thermometry applied to solar energy devices. Sol. Energy **81**, 1025–1034 (2007)

Hidden Costs of Modelling Post-fire Plant Community Assembly Using Cellular Automata

Juan García-Duro[1], Luca Manzoni[2], Iria Arias[1], Mercedes Casal[1], Oscar Cruz[1], Xosé Manoel Pesqueira[1], Ana Muñoz[1], Rebeca Álvarez[1], Luca Mariot[2(✉)], Stefania Bandini[2], and Otilia Reyes[1]

[1] Área de Ecoloxía, Departamento de Bioloxía Funcional, Facultade de Bioloxía, Universidade de Santiago de Compostela, Campus Vida, 15782 Santiago de Compostela, Spain
[2] Dipartimento di Informatica, Sistemistica e Comunicazione, Università degli Studi di Milano-Bicocca, Viale Sarca 336/14, 20126 Milano, Italy
{luca.manzoni,luca.mariot,bandini}@disco.unimib.it

Abstract. Cellular Automata (CA) models have been applied to different fields of knowledge, from cryptography, arts, to the modelling and simulation of complex systems. In the latter area, however, sometimes the ability to properly represent complex interacting but distinct dynamics taking place within a given area is limited by the need of calibrating models in which the number of necessary parameters grows. Hidden costs related to the identification of specific values or plausible ranges for parameters can become overwhelming.

Here we model the assembly process of plant communities after fire. The number of elements of plant communities (plants of different species) and processes involved (seed dispersal, plant recruitment, competence, etc.) require a high degree of parameterization because all those processes have great relevance on the evolution of the system, for instance during post-fire recovery.

The fire, aside negative effects, releases a number of resources (space, nutrients, ...) making them easily available for plants, which promptly use those resources so they are no longer available to other plants after a period of time which usually ranges from months to years. In the meantime, the plasticity of species in relation to fire and environment and the interactions among species determine the direction of changes to occur.

In this work we present a novel approach to the assembly of plant communities after fire using CA. In particular we gather the preliminary results of their application and give a feasible way to optimize the parameterization of the model.

1 Introduction

Plant Community Assembly After Fire. The vegetation is the base in the functioning of the majority of terrestrial ecosystems as it captures the energy from

© Springer Nature Switzerland AG 2018
G. Mauri et al. (Eds.): ACRI 2018, LNCS 11115, pp. 68–79, 2018.
https://doi.org/10.1007/978-3-319-99813-8_6

sunlight and makes it available to the other elements of the ecosystem. Despite the vegetation being primarily dependent on the environment, as it grows complex, it modifies the environment to such a degree that it takes control of certain processes in the ecosystem.

However, plant communities are continuously changing along time following a patch pattern, where the death of plants creates gaps, so that the temporary increase of resources (light, space, water, nutrients, ...) promotes the growth of neighbouring plants and the recruitment of new ones until the majority of those resources are retained, or occupied, by plants or leaked out of the system [18]. These changes are usually slow; however, disturbances trigger large changes in plant community structure and functioning [15]. Disturbances often produce a large increase in the availability of resources through plant mortality [26], and fire is one of the most widespread disturbances [13]. The recovery of vegetation after fire depends on the regenerative strategies of the species [12, 26], that should be interpreted as a measure of the resistance and resilience of communities and ecosystems. Indeed, this measure has been used in this way by other authors, for instance in [25]. Nonetheless, the assembly of plant communities after fire depend on interactions among species, which have a primary importance but that, up to now, have barely been considered due to their complexity [16]. In any case the general trend of vegetation assembly after fire and the involved process have been outlined in some types of vegetation such as Atlantic ecosystems [2, 26].

Plant Communities and Cellular Automata Models: State of the Art. CA models incorporate both spatial and temporal dynamics [1, 7], making them suitable tools to model space-oriented ecological processes [9, 10, 17]. The plasticity of CA models has encouraged researchers tackling new challenges in ecology and their application has increased during the last decades [8, 10, 29]. They have been used for methodological purposes [7, 19, 21], for modelling vegetation dynamics [3, 5, 9, 10, 14] and the impact of disturbances [1]. Despite their strong dependence on parameterization, the main advantage of such models is that they are less laborious and they can be used for simulating complex systems with only a few rules. However, the sampling effort and computation requirements have prevented CA becoming an ordinary tool in ecological research. In this regard, CA models are not usually intended to reproduce the spatio-temporal patterns of vegetation; they are just a loose approach to the structure of vegetation, for instance [7], or to any process.

Objectives. The objective of this work is the development of CA models that reproduce the assembly of plant communities after fire and shortly discuss a possible way of optimizing their parameterization.

2   Background Data

The information for the cellular automaton has been recorded by the Fire Ecology Group of the University of Santiago de Compostela in a high number of locations in the north-west of the Iberian Peninsula for the last 18 years. Some of those data have been previously published in scientific journals, for instance [4,16,23,24,26–28]. Other data still remain unpublished.

The burnt areas studied cover a wide range of conditions. The main environmental sources of variation in our database are topography and climate, which ranges from Atlantic to transition climates to Mediterranean. The information used to build the model covers a broad scope of biological processes along the biological cycle of plants, from seed production and dispersal, plant regeneration strategies after fire, plant structure and vegetation structure and assembly. However, the largest set of information and the main input in the model is species cover, recorded in burnt shrublands during the first years after fire.

3   The Cellular Automaton Model

The probabilistic CA herein developed is defined by the tuple $\langle L, H, Q, f, I \rangle$ where L is the lattice structure of the CA, H is the neighbourhood, Q the set of states, $f : Q \times Q^{|H|} \to Q$ the local rule, and I is the initial configuration of the CA. Notice that, differently from traditional probabilistic CA, where the probabilities of the possible transitions are constant with time, in this case they can change to better reflect the empirical observations. We are now going to define in detail each one of this components of the CA model developed.

Lattice L. The post-fire recovery of vegetation is simulated in a bidimensional square lattice intended to reproduce a $30\,\text{m} \times 30\,\text{m}$ field plot, so that each cell represents a $0.1\,\text{m} \times 0.1\,\text{m}$ square. Thus, the lattice is defined as $L = \{(i,j): 1 \leq i \leq N, 1 \leq j \leq M\}$ where $N = 300 \times M = 300$. The sizes of lattice and of the cells were chosen according to field studies and computation requirements, because the probability of finding new species is directly related to the size of the plot [11,30] and the cell size determines the relationships that can be detected among species [16]. However, a high number of cells increases the number of computations needed to simulate the whole model.

Neighbourhood H. The growth of plants across the plot was implemented in the CA model through the transition functions which use the Moore neighbourhood of radius 1. We assumed that the cells in the neighbourhood are not equidistant from the central cell. Namely, the cells reachable via a diagonal step are farther away from the central cell than the other ones. Since this distance has an influence in the real world, we have considered it when implementing the model.

Cell Values Q. The CA was designed to reproduce the dynamics of aboveground vegetation; accordingly, belowground characteristics are part of the initial configuration of the model and cell values are only concerned by changes aboveground. In the following, we will use the notation $Q_{i,j,t}$ to denote the state of the cell in position (i,j) at time t.

Each plant in the CA model, no matter the species or the way it was recruited, needs to be tracked through the entire simulation in order to display its spreading and interactions with other plants. In particular, every plant in the CA model has its own ID. In particular, for each $1 \leq v \leq V$ where V the maximum number of species, the set of possible plants is defined as follows:

$$Sp_{v,rs} = \{Sp_{v,rs,i}\}_{i=1}^{Z_v^{rs}} \qquad\qquad Sp_{v,sd} = \{Sp_{v,sd,i}\}_{j=1}^{Z_v^{sd}}$$

$$\text{Community} = \bigcup_{v=1}^{V} (Sp_{v,rs} \cup Sp_{v,sd})$$

where Z_v^{rs} is the number of plants recruited by resprouting and Z_v^{sd} is the number of plants recruited by seed germination; these two values depend on the particular species v under consideration. Community is the set that includes all plants in the CA, recruited by resprouting ($Sp_{v,rs}$) of by seed germination ($Sp_{v,sd}$). Accordingly, the state of a cell is either Bare ground, which means that is empty of vegetation, or the ID(s) of the plant(s) that occupy the cell. This means that $Q_{i,j,t} \subset \text{Community}$, where $Q_{i,j,t} = \varnothing$ designates Bare ground. With this representation the state of each cell can represent the presence of zero, one, or more than one plant in the physical space that the cell denotes.

Initial Configuration I. Initially $Q_{i,j,0} = \varnothing$ for $(i, j) \in L$. The recovery of vegetation strongly depends on the pre-fire situation and fire damages, and thus the statements which govern the initial configuration of the CA were carefully conceived.

1. The pre-fire plant community of v species with cover cv_v, randomly picked up from field data, is the target community assuming auto-succession.
2. The pre-fire plants are randomly placed in the plot according to the cover of each species.
3. The plot is environmentally homogeneous and empty of aboveground vegetation immediately after fire.
4. A proportion of plants of each species survives and are recruited following a temporal distribution obtained via field recruitment data. Post-fire resprouting mortality is not considered.
5. A number of plants of each species are recruited by seed germination following a temporal distribution that follows field recruitment data. The distribution of seeds is randomly uniform across the plot before fire. The number of seeds is not a limiting factor, and post-fire seedling mortality is not considered.

Thus, for all $1 \leq v \leq V$, the spatio-temporal location of new plants

$$S^{sd} = \{x_\ell, y_\ell, T_\ell\}_{\ell=1}^{Sp_{v,sd}} \qquad\qquad S^{rs} = \{x_\ell, y_\ell, T_\ell\}_{\ell=1}^{Sp_{v,rs}}$$

follows the following distribution:

$$S^{sd}, S^{rs} \sim (U(1, N), U(1, M), f_1(t))$$

where S^{sd} is the total amount of seedlings in the community, S^{rs} the set of resprouted plants, and $f_1(t)$ probability distribution of plant recruitment along time, taken from field data (Fig. 1). That is, a new plant is placed in the CA in a spatial position selected uniformly at random at a time determined by function f_1.

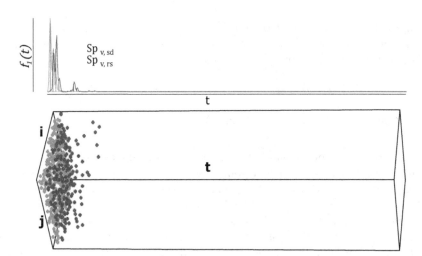

Fig. 1. Temporal distribution $(f_1(t))$ of recruitment events for seedling (red) and resprout (green) at the top and the their distribution across the lattice and time at the bottom. (Color figure online)

Rules of the Automaton. The transition rules to update the CA model in the context of the Moore neighbourhood are as follow:

1. A plant j of a species v spreads to neighbouring cells at time t with different probabilities depending on its origin: with probability $p_{v,rs,i}$ for resprouted plants $(Sp_{v,rs,i})$ and probability $p_{v,sd,j}$ for plants $(Sp_{v,sd,j})$ recruited by seed germination.
2. Any cell that is occupied by a plant j remains occupied by that plant till the end of the simulation. This means that mortality and pruning are not considered in the model.
3. The probabilities $p_{v,rs,i}$ and $p_{v,sd,j}$ depend on the age of the plant, the biological type and the way the plant was recruited after fire. Since the simulations run in a square lattice using the Moore neighbourhood, the distance from the central cell of the neighbourhood was also taken into account as a correction factor. Thus,

$$Q_{i,j,t+1} = F\left(Q_{i,j,t}, W_t, Q_{i,j,t}^{|H|}, S_t^{sd}, S_t^{rs}\right) \qquad \text{for } (i,j) \in L \text{ and } t \in \mathbb{N}$$

where W_t is the matrix containing the relationships and transition probabilities of elements in $Q_{i,j,t}$ and $Q_{i,j,t}^{|H|}$ at time t and the growth of plants through time follow the functions $d^{Sp_{v,rs,i}} = f_2(t)^{Sp_{v,rs,i}}$ and $d^{Sp_{v,rs,j}} = f_2(t)^{Sp_{v,rs,j}}$, where the family of functions $f_2^{Sp_{v,rs,i}}$ and $f_2^{Sp_{v,rs,j}}$ provide a time-dependant value obtained via field data.
4. Any cell occupied by a plant A can be occupied by another plant B in the neighbourhood with probability p_B if $t > 36$ and $B_B > B_A$ and with probability βp_B otherwise, where t is a time span (years after fire), B_A is the

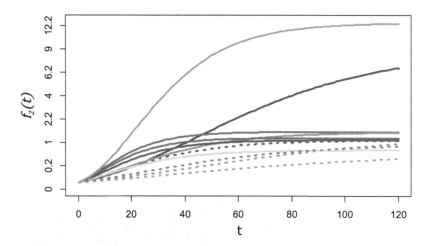

Fig. 2. Mean plant diameter of species and regenerative traits in the CA along time, fitted from field data. Species were coded with different colours; solid lines indicate plant growth of resprouts and dotted lines the growth of plants recruited by seed germination. (Color figure online)

biological type of plant A and B_B the type of plant B, and β is a correction factor.

Parametrization. The whole CA was parameterized by measuring the error with respect to field data values. The growth along time of each species and the regenerative trait in the CA were parameterized using a sigmoid distribution with the aim that one loop in the CA equals one month (Fig. 2); then, the whole community was simulated.

The cellular automata model can potentially reproduce the post-fire dynamics of any plant community because it gathers the main ecological processes in the post-fire recovery; it only requires some information about the species in that community. However, the availability of data limited the scope of plant communities to be modelled, being heathlands, broomlands and gorselands the best represented communities. The average number of woody species in those communities was relatively high ($\bar{x} = 10.6$, $\sigma^{\bar{x}} = 0.4$) and the majority of the woody species involved (33 out of 37) are able to regenerate through resprouting and seed germination. Thus, about 20 parameters (one for each species and regenerative trait) would be required in an average simulation, if independent growth among species was considered. Nevertheless, overlayering among species in nature is common and the competence among species usually decreases the rate of spreading of plants, indicating a non-independent growth and occurrence of species. Within this new context, having just two species coexisting in a single cell would already increase the mean number of parameters up to $2'^2 = 400$. Even though the number of species in a $0.1\,\text{m} \times 0.1\,\text{m}$ cell is usually low in nature, it has been reported to be greater than 5 in some cases. As a result, a highly

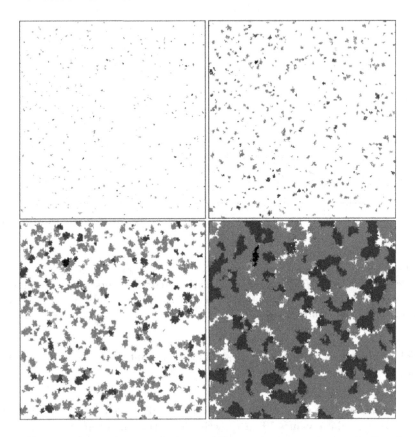

Fig. 3. Outputs of a random simulation at different time steps during the first 5 years after fire. Colours represent different cell states, that is plants or combination of plants. The background colour represents bare soil. (Color figure online)

complex parameterization should be used in order to fit real data. In order to reach a compromise among the number of parameters, data, and computation requirements, instead of parameterizing all the interactions among species, we decided to parameterize each species and regenerative trait in isolation and to use a one-off correction factor to fit the spreading rate in presence of any other species, as indicated in the rules of the automaton.

The squared error of the overall cover of woody species in the pre-fire community and the post-fire communities was used to validate the model because the model assumes autosuccession. We have chosen field data around 3 years after fire to validate the community model because it is a critical period in the post-fire recovery and has a high impact on the overall recovery of the vegetation. Afterwards, the increase in cover of woody species tends to decrease and changes tend to occur slowly. Furthermore, it is a suitable subset of data for validation since a high percentage of field data focuses on the development of plant communities around the first three years after fire.

4   Results and Discussion

The average value of pre-fire community around 3 years after fire in the validation subset was 88.1 ± 2.7 (*mean* ± *SEM*) and the average cost of the simulations, i.e., the squared error, was 5.16. The error of validation simulations was relatively low having into account the large variation of field data [4, 16, 23, 24], particularly, around 3 years after fire.

From an ecological point of view, the CA based model matches the objective of reproducing the main patterns of the plant community assembly after fire. There are strong differences in the occupation of available space among species and biological traits. In this regard, the growth of plants along time changes in the same way as field data do. As a result, CA models can be very useful for hypothesis testing and for exploring different scenarios, but it reproduces an idealized and oversimplified community, not in terms of the number of elements (plants and populations) but in terms of their interactions. Despite the high quality of data, the huge variation of ecosystems drives to the impossibility of sampling all the possible situations, resulting in missing information. Thus, some factors and processes have been simplified in order to get a good compromise among model performance and computing requirements. One useful performance for the model has been finding a good correspondence between plant growth and growth probability for each loop in the CA. In our model one month equals one loop, which makes it worthy in terms of computing resources requirements and ecological interpretation of the results. A relatively low number of loops is recommended due to the high number of parameters and the extent and number of cells in the lattice, which is predefined in this work. The size of plot and cells successfully fit our purpose of reproducing the vegetation recovery. Too small plots would produce results that are due to the specific vegetation patterns [30], not to ecological processes; instead, large cells would not reproduce plant competition for resources, following other studies [16], and would result in unreal morphologies. Hence, the spatial scale have a crucial role in the interpretation of interactions among the plants, and species, in the community [16]. Furthermore, the spatial structure cannot be neglected when an analysis of their sensitivity with respect to their inputs and parameters is performed [6]. The number of processes, parameters and data required by the model would increase exponentially, when considering the influence of other processes or even the environment, which is often the hidden force modulating biological processes and interactions, and has multiple feedbacks with the biological component.

4.1   Proposal for Parameter Optimization

As it is possible to observe, there are multiple parameters that are necessary for the model to provide a realistic simulation of real world phenomena. In particular, the functions that regulates the rates of spreading of the plants are an essential part of the model and should be estimated accurately. While field data provide some values for those functions, it is necessary to provide them for all possible input values (i.e., time, in this case).

Machine Learning Methods. Genetic Algorithms (GA) [22] are a well-known nature-inspired optimization method where a collection (called population) of solutions (called individuals) to an optimization problems is represented as fixed length vectors of bits. An initial random population is iteratively evolved using operators inspired by the Darwinian theory of evolution: first of all, a subsection of the population is selected via a *selection* process that mimics natural selection, where better solutions have better survival probabilities. This sampled individuals are then combined via the operations of *crossover*, which mimics reproduction, and *mutation* that, similarly to natural occurring mutations in DNA, changes bits in the individuals. This process is repeated until one of the termination criteria is met, for example once a good enough solution has been found.

Genetic Programming (GP) was introduced by Koza [20] as a mean to evolve not only arrays of bits, as in traditional GA, but entire programs. In GP a program is usually represented by a tree, by its parsing tree. As in GA, a population of is evolved by mean of selection, crossover, and mutation, where the last two operators, depending on the actual representation used, are specific to GP.

Parameter Optimization Architecture. To perform the parameter optimization process, a two-level method has been devised. Initially, for each species GP is employed to provide a function estimating the rate of spreading *in isolation*. That is, for each species we are estimating functions that provide a realistic spreading rate when no competition is present. While this is not a sufficient condition to obtain realistic solutions when other species are present, it is, nevertheless, a necessary condition. This first step is performed to limit the computational costs: the evaluation of the solutions can be performed by running a smaller and simpler simulation (since only one species is involved).

Once a large enough number m of solutions has been obtained for each species, we consider the following matrix:

$$\begin{bmatrix} f_{1,1} & f_{1,2} & \cdots & f_{1,V} \\ f_{2,1} & f_{2,2} & \cdots & f_{2,V} \\ \vdots & \vdots & & \vdots \\ f_{m,1} & f_{m,2} & \cdots & f_{m,V} \end{bmatrix}$$

where the i-th column represents the collection of m solutions for the i-th species that were found in the previous step. Now, it is possible to select via GA an element for each column to provide a solution to the problem of optimizing the spreading rates of the different species. For example, for 3 species the vector $(1, 3, 3)$ will represent the three functions $f_{1,1}, f_{3,2}, f_{3,3}$, one for each species. This second phase does not require to re-compute the spreading rates of the different species in isolation, but only to find a subset of them that produces a realistic simulation when they are combined. This two phase process should help reduce the computational burden of finding the correct parameters.

Field data will be separated into training, testing, and validation sets in the proportions 70%, 20% and 10% to deal with data dependence. Plant level data, particularly plant dimensions along time, will be used in the first phase to fit species spreading, while species abundance (cover data) will be used in the second phase. Furthermore, the cover of each woody species and their combined occurrence will be used to compute the cost of the parameters for the simulations unlike the current model, which only uses overall cover.

5 Conclusions

Ecosystems are highly complex systems that can be successfully simulated using cellular automata models. However there are two limiting factors: the availability of information about biological processes and the optimization of a high number of parameters. The balance between both of them (sampling effort and computational requirements) has to be met in order to make CA valuable for ecological research.

In the future we plan to apply the proposed two-level optimization procedure to correctly set the parameters. We think that this procedure can be generalised to other kinds of CA models where there are multiple distinct processes interacting in complex ways.

References

1. Alexandridis, A., Vakalis, D., Siettos, C.I., Bafas, G.V.: A cellular automata model for forest fire spread prediction: the case of the wildfire that swept through spetses island in 1990. Appl. Math. Comput. **204**(1), 191–201 (2008)
2. Allen, K.A., Harris, M.P., Marrs, R.H.: Matrix modelling of prescribed burning in calluna vulgaris-dominated moorland: short burning rotations minimize carbon loss at increased wildfire frequencies. J. Appl. Ecol. **50**(3), 614–624 (2013)
3. Altartouri, A., Nurminen, L., Jolma, A.: Spatial neighborhood effect and scale issues in the calibration and validation of a dynamic model of phragmites australis distribution-a cellular automata and machine learning approach. Environ. Model. Softw. **71**, 15–29 (2015)
4. Alvarez, R., Munoz, A., Pesqueira, X., Garcia-Duro, J., Reyes, O., Casal, M.: Spatial and temporal patterns in structure and diversity of mediterranean forest of quercus pyrenaica in relation to fire. For. Ecol. Manag. **257**(7), 1596–1602 (2009)
5. Anderson, T., Dragicevic, S.: A geosimulation approach for data scarce environments: modeling dynamics of forest insect infestation across different landscapes. ISPRS Int. J. Geo-Inf. **5**(2), 9 (2016)
6. Baetens, J.M., De Baets, B.: A Spatial sensitivity analysis of a spatially explicit model for myxomatosis in Belgium. In: El Yacoubi, S., Wąs, J., Bandini, S. (eds.) ACRI 2016. LNCS, vol. 9863, pp. 91–100. Springer, Cham (2016). https://doi.org/10.1007/978-3-319-44365-2_9
7. Baltzer, H., Braun, P., Köhler, W.: Modeling population dynamics with cellular automata. United States Department of Agriculture Forest Service, General Technical report RM, pp. 703–712 (1996)
8. Bandini, S., Manzoni, S., Redaelli, S., Vanneschi, L.: Automatic detection of go–based patterns in CA model of vegetable populations: experiments on *Geta* pattern recognition. In: El Yacoubi, S., Chopard, B., Bandini, S. (eds.) ACRI 2006. LNCS, vol. 4173, pp. 427–435. Springer, Heidelberg (2006). https://doi.org/10.1007/11861201_50

9. Bandini, S., Pavesi, G.: Simulation of vegetable populations dynamics based on cellular automata. In: Bandini, S., Chopard, B., Tomassini, M. (eds.) ACRI 2002. LNCS, vol. 2493, pp. 202–209. Springer, Heidelberg (2002). https://doi.org/10.1007/3-540-45830-1_19

10. Bandini, S., Pavesi, G.: A model based on cellular automata for the simulation of the dynamics of plant populations. In: International Congress on Environmental Modelling and Software, vol. 160 (2004)

11. Beck, J., Holloway, J.D., Schwanghart, W.: Undersampling and the measurement of beta diversity. Methods Ecol. Evol. **4**(4), 370–382 (2013)

12. Bellingham, P.J., Sparrow, A.D.: Resprouting as a life history strategy in woody plant communities. Oikos **89**(2), 409–416 (2000)

13. Bond, W.J., Keeley, J.E.: Fire as a global 'herbivore': the ecology and evolution of flammable ecosystems. Trends Ecol. Evol. **20**(7), 387–394 (2005)

14. Colasanti, R., Hunt, R., Watrud, L.: A simple cellular automaton model for high-level vegetation dynamics. Ecol. Model. **203**(3–4), 363–374 (2007)

15. Davies, G.M., Gray, A., Rein, G., Legg, C.J.: Peat consumption and carbon loss due to smouldering wildfire in a temperate peatland. For. Ecol. Manag. **308**, 169–177 (2013)

16. García-Duro, J., Álvarez, R., Basanta, M., Casal, M.: Aplicación de redes bayesianas ás relacións entre especies vexetais despois de incendio forestal e a súa sensibilidade ó tamaño das unidades de mostraxe. In: BIOapps2016. Encontro Galaico-Portugués de Biometría, Con Aplicación Ás Ciencias Da Saúde, Á Ecoloxía E Ás Ciencias Do Medio AmbienteD (2016)

17. Hogeweg, P.: Cellular automata as a paradigm for ecological modeling. Appl. Math. Comput. **27**(1), 81–100 (1988)

18. Huntley, B., Baxter, R.: Vegetation ecology and global change. In: Vegetation Ecology, pp. 357–372 (2005)

19. Kowalewski, L.K., Chizinski, C.J., Powell, L.A., Pope, K.L., Pegg, M.A.: Accuracy or precision: implications of sample design and methodology on abundance estimation. Ecol. Model. **316**, 185–190 (2015)

20. Koza, J.R.: Genetic programming as a means for programming computers by natural selection. Stat. Comput. **4**(2), 87–112 (1994)

21. Lengyel, A., Csiky, J., Botta-Dukát, Z.: How do locally infrequent species influence numerical classification? A simulation study. Community Ecol. **13**(1), 64–71 (2012)

22. Mitchell, M.: An Introduction to Genetic Algorithms. MIT press, Cambridge (1998)

23. Muñoz, A., García-Duro, J., Álvarez, R., Pesqueira, X., Reyes, O., Casal, M.: Structure and diversity of Erica ciliaris and Erica tetralix heathlands at different successional stages after cutting. J. Env. Manag. **94**(1), 34–40 (2012)

24. Pesqueira, X.M., del Viejo, A.M., Álvarez, R., Duro, J.G., Reyes, O.: Estudio ecológico del matorral atlántico de interés para conservación. Respuesta estructural a usos tradicionales en galicia. Rev. Real Acad. Galega de Cienc. **24**, 41–60 (2005)

25. Proença, V., Pereira, H.M., Vicente, L.: Resistance to wildfire and early regeneration in natural broadleaved forest and pine plantation. Acta Oecol. **36**(6), 626–633 (2010)

26. Reyes, O., Casal, M.: Regeneration models and plant regenerative types related to the intensity of fire in atlantic shrubland and woodland species. J. Veg. Sci. **19**(4), 575–583 (2008)

27. Reyes, O., Casal, M., Rego, F.C.: Resprouting ability of six atlantic shrub species. Folia Geobot. **44**(1), 19–29 (2009)
28. Reyes, O., García-Duro, J., Salgado, J.: Fire affects soil organic matter and the emergence of pinus radiata seedlings. Ann. For. Sci. **72**(2), 267–275 (2015)
29. Sree, P.K., Babu, I.R., et al.: Cellular automata and its applications in bioinformatics: a review. Glob. Perspect. Artif. Intell. **2**, 16–22 (2014)
30. Stier, A.C., Bolker, B.M., Osenberg, C.W.: Using rarefaction to isolate the effects of patch size and sampling effort on beta diversity. Ecosphere **7**(12) (2016)

Hardware Implementation of a Biomimicking Hybrid CA

Menelaos Madikas[1], Michail-Antisthenis Tsompanas[2(✉)], Nikolaos Dourvas[1],
Georgios Ch. Sirakoulis[1], Jeff Jones[2], and Andrew Adamatzky[2]

[1] Department of Electrical and Computer Engineering,
Democritus University of Thrace, Xanthi, Greece
{mmadikas,ndourvas,gsirak}@ee.duth.gr
[2] Unconventional Computing Laboratory, University of the West of England,
Bristol BS16 1QY, UK
{antisthenis.tsompanas,andrew.adamatzky}@uwe.ac.uk
http://gsirak.ee.duth.gr

Abstract. A hybrid model, combining a Cellular Automaton (CA) and a multi-agent system, was proposed to mimic the computation abilities of the plasmodium of *Physarum polycephalum*. This model was implemented on software, as well as, on hardware, namely on a Field Programmable Gate Array (FPGA). The specific ability of the *P. polycephalum* simulated here is given in brief, also bringing attention to the approximation of a Kolmogorov-Uspensky machine (KUM), an alternative to the Turing machine. KUM represent data and program by a labeled indirected graphs and a computation is performed by adding/removing nodes/edges. The proposed model implementation is taking full advantage of the inherent parallel nature of automaton networks, and CA, as a result of the mapping of the local rule to a digital circuit. Consequently, the acceleration of the computation for the hardware implementation, compared to the software, is as high as 6 orders of magnitude.

Keywords: Slime mould · Cellular automata · Hardware
Agents · Kolmogorov machine

1 Introduction

Physarum polycephalum is widely used in the last decade as an unconventional computing substrate, because it demonstrates complex behavior, regardless of its apparent simplicity, easy culturing and very low-cost experimentation. *In vivo* experiments with that biological, massively parallel computing prototype were developed [1]. A plasmodium, the 'vegetative' stage of *P. polycephalum* life cycle, was persuaded to scout for nutrients in its vicinity and link all of them with a tubular network. The importance of the functionality of the tubular network to the survival of the plasmodium (transfer of nutrients, metabolites, and chemical

© Springer Nature Switzerland AG 2018
G. Mauri et al. (Eds.): ACRI 2018, LNCS 11115, pp. 80–91, 2018.
https://doi.org/10.1007/978-3-319-99813-8_7

and electrical messages) subjects its actual configuration in rounds of optimization by the actual plasmodium and the local conditions of the experiment. This is the reason why the plasmodium is such a successful paradigm of a biological substrate computer with inputs of geometrical configuration of nutrient sources (NSs) and an output of an interconnected graph [2].

Some examples of the vast range of problems tackled by *P. polycephalum* [3] are labyrinth solving [4,5], approximation of Voronoi diagrams and Delaunay triangulation [6], travelling salesman problem [7], simulation of Boolean logic [8] and evaluation of transport [9] and ancient road networks [10]. Nonetheless, the abilities of *P. polycephalum* inspired scientists to invest efforts towards the simulation of its behavior and its usage to solve complex problems, like designing routes in information networks [11]. Some examples of the computerized approximation of the behavior of the plasmodium are a mathematical model with feedback of the tube dynamics [12], agent–based particle models [13] and cellular automata (CA) [14–16] We propose a novel approach towards computerizing the abilities of the slime mould by designing a hybrid model, which combines CA and a multi–agent system is introduced.

Moreover, a rather interesting paradigm of in-vivo experiments utilizing *P. polycephalum* is the approximation of Kolmogorov–Uspensky machine [17,18]. Thus, here the results produced from these experiments were used as a control for the novel hybrid model proposed. Kolmogorov and Uspensky [19,20] proposed that a dynamically changing graph could represent an abstract computing machine. This graph has a finite amount of nodes and the edges between them are not directed. Each of the graph's nodes are alternatively labelled and only one of the nodes can be activated for a given time step. This structured was initially defined as the Kolmogorov complex and, then, was more commonly known as Kolmogorov-Upsensky machine (KUM). This term will be used hereafter.

KUM is an alternative to the Turing machine, with the main difference of the replacement of the tape of the Turing machine by a graph. Given this geometric substrate of the KUM (the graph), it can accurately mimic growth phenomena and computation influenced by structure in natural systems (like biological systems, chemical systems etc.). An additional meaningful distinction is that whereas the Turing machine was intended to replicate a human-executed computation, the KUM aims to portray "computation as a physical process" [21].

Despite their differences, Turing and KU machines belong the same classes of abstract mathematical machines. A physical implementation of a KUM is searched within biological substrates, like the plasmodium of *P. polycephalum* [17,18]. *P. polycephalum* is an ideal choice for this because of its capacity of exploring and growing in a graph-like configuration and dynamic reshaping of the edges and nodes in the graph.

Moreover, as the plasmodium is stimulated by chemoattractant nutrient sources, utilizing a vast distributed array of membrane–bound sensor proteins, distributed tools were chosen for its simulation, like CA and multi-agent models. In this paper, we focus on the hardware implementation of the proposed hybrid model of *P. polycephalum* to mimic the physical implementation of a KUM in the plasmodium of *P. polycephalum*.

2   Description of the CA-Multiagent Model

A new model of CA was developed, in order to combine CA [15,16], and multi-agent modeling [22]. This new model integrates the parallel nature of CA along with the dynamic behavior in space and time of the multi-agent system without, however, increasing the complexity of the system. The model is computationally simple by using distributed local sensory behaviors, although approaching some of the complex phenomena observed in Physarum. In order to configure Physarum's adaptive motif, the selected mechanism must be able to adjust its pattern over time, i.e. the pattern must be more flexible to show the emerging properties, which are extensible and can be calculated.

In this model, the inherent flow of the colloidal solution is provided by agent-to-cell mediation, and gel matrix resistance is provided by the agent-agent collisions. The consistency of this set of "crowd" is ensured by the fact that there is mutual attraction to the stimuli deposited by the population of the agents. The directional orientation and movement of the activated plasmodium front is created by coupling the emerging mass behaviors by dragging local source stimuli. Changing the value of cell identities is equivalent to secreting a quantity of chemoattractant during their successful motion and detecting the largest amount in the cell's neighborhood by three sensors. As a result, they adjust the cell's angle, so the behavior of other agents can also affect their behavior.

The area of the experiment is divided into a grid of identical square cells, with the side of length equal to α and represented by a CA assuming that each square element of the surface is a cell of a CA. The width of the neighborhood of (i, j) cell is assumed to be equal to one on both sides, meaning that, we have a Moore neighborhood. The state of the new CA model at time t is:

$$C_{i,j}^t = \{griddata_{i,j}^t, trail_{i,j}^t, particle\_ids_{i,j}^t, angle_{i,j}^t\} \tag{1}$$

Parameter $griddata_{i,j}^t$ can get values at time t that indicate whether the cell is a wall or a food stimulus. Referring to $trail_{i,j}^t$, is the value derived from the food diffusion equation and represents the strength of the smell of the food stimuli at time t in the (i, j) cell. Additionally, $particle\_ids_{i,j}^t$ is the value of the agent's (i, j) identity at time t. When there is no agent in the cell, then, as normal, its value is equal to zero. Finally, $angle_{i,j}^t$ is a variable that shows the angle of the agent in a cell.

Some program variables are specified at the initialization of the model. The main parameters are the amount of agents in the population, grid size, consumption of food value ($diffdamp$) and the variable that indicates how large the value of the data nodes are. This is displayed as $griddata_{i,j}^t$ to $trail_{i,j}^t$ and can get two values, the *projectvalue* (when there is no agent nearby or on the central cell) or the *suppressvalue* (when there is at least one agent in the neighborhood of the central cell on which the food is placed).

Subsequently, the agents are placed in random positions within the CA grid with their velocity vectors oriented at random angle values. When a CA neighborhood contains one agent or is fully occupied of agents then the value of the trail value is generated by the equation:

$$trail_{i,j}^{t+1} = trail_{i,j}^{t} + suppressvalue \tag{2}$$

Else, if the area is free from agents then it gets the value

$$trail_{i,j}^{t+1} = trail_{i,j}^{t} + projectvalue \tag{3}$$

During the evolution of the model, the cell motor behavior is activated to move the agents along their velocity vectors, thus renewing the values of the *particle_ids* and their velocity vectors. The new coordinates of an agent are calculated and an attempt is made to move by one cell in the Moore neighborhood of the central cell (where the agent is located).

$$tvi = i + \cos(angle(i,j)) \times speed \quad \text{and} \quad tvj = j + \sin(angle(i,j)) \times speed \tag{4}$$

If a cell is bound or wall and is selected by an agent to make a move towards it, then that agent will not move to that cell but the angle of the velocity vector will be renewed to a random value, i.e. $angle_{i,j}^{t+1} = random() \times 360$. However, if all the prerequisites are met in order to make a movement, the value of the agent's identifier of the given cell will be given to the new cell, as well as its angle, and the trail value will be renewed by increasing it by an amount *depT*. This will be an attractive means for other agents to move towards it in order to create a single structure as the biological organism.

$$particle\_ids_{i,j}^{t+1} = particle\_ids_{i+1,j+1}^{t}$$
$$angle_{i,j}^{t+1} = angle_{i+1,j+1}^{t} \tag{5}$$
$$trail_{i,j}^{t+1} = trail_{i,j}^{t} + depT$$

The algorithm proceeds by calculating the sensory inputs of the cells. Each cell containing an agent has 3 sensors that are located in the neighborhood of this cell in the direction of the agent's angle. The neighborhood could be larger, e.g. by integrating all the cells that are spaced $2, 3, \ldots$ cells away from the central one. Moreover, this would act as an escalation parameter in a large CA, a cell would receive values in its sensors from a more distant area and could direct its agent towards that direction (Fig. 1).

The sensors receive the trail values of neighboring cells in which they are located. Then those three variables are compared, in order to decide the highest food value from the trail of the neighboring cells. The prevailing sensor, will be the one who will also indicate which direction the agent should follow to reach the point of feeding.

If **f** sensor has the highest value, then the cell's angle retains the same value. If the value of **f** is less than the other two, then if **fl** is less than **f**, $angle_{i,j}^{t+1} =$

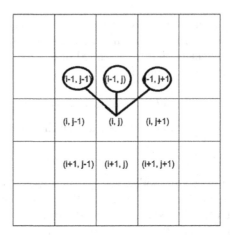

Fig. 1. Placement of 3 sensors in the Moore neighborhood of the cell according to its angle.

$angle_{i,j}^{t} + 45$, otherwise, if **fr** is less than **fl** then $angle_{i,j}^{t+1} = angle_{i,j}^{t} - 45$. Finally, if **f** is greater than **fl** and less than **fr** then $angle_{i,j}^{t+1} = angle_{i,j}^{t} + 45$, otherwise, if **f** is greater than **fr** and less than **fl** then $angle_{i,j}^{t+1} = angle_{i,j}^{t} - 45$.

The final step of the algorithm is to update the trail of each cell, where its value is given by the equation of food diffusion.

$$trail_{i,j}^{t+1} = \{(trail_{i-1,j-1}^{t} + trail_{i,j-1}^{t} + trail_{i+1,j-1}^{t} + trail_{i-1,j}^{t} + trail_{i,j}^{t} + trail_{i+1,j}^{t} + trail_{i-1,j+1}^{t} + trail_{i,j+1}^{t} + trail_{i+1,j+1}^{t})/9 * (1 - diffamp))\} \quad (6)$$

3   Hardware Implementation of the Proposed Model

The proposed hardware system is comprised of the same basic structure representing a CA cell. Each cell circuit (Fig. 2) is interconnected with other cells in its vicinity.

This circuit is equipped with 46 inputs and 19 outputs. As inputs we consider eight signals, 9 bits each, that indicate an integer from 0 to 511, representing the identifier number of the agents; eight signals, 9 bits each, that indicate an integer number with range from 0 to 511, which represents the food value; eight signals, 9 bits each, that indicate an integer number ranging from 0 to 360, representing the angle of agents in the CA; eight signals one bit each, needed to inform the cell that an agent is going to move in its direction.

Eight additional signals one bit each that inform the central cell that the agent cannot move to a neighboring cell; an 8-bit signal used to characterize the central cell ($food = 255$, $wall = 51$, $normalcell = 0$); two signals, 9 bits each that are used to initialize agents and angles in the grid and three signals, 1 bit each for clk, reset and initialize.

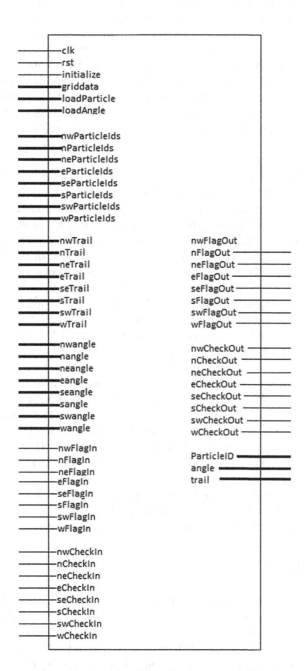

Fig. 2. Input and output signals of the circuit generated by the VHDL code.

As outputs there are eight signals, one bit each to inform neighbors that the agent will move in that direction; eight signals, one bit each indicating that the central cell is free to receive an agent and three signals, 9 bits each, which represent the identifier, the angle and the smell of the food in the central cell.

Firstly, `initialize` signal is set high, for cells to obtain random values needed. In the first stage, the cell in which the food stimuli is found, renews the trail value by noticing whether there is an agent in the neighborhood. The following stage is the motor behavior where each cell will signal if there is an agent to attempt to move in the direction which is indicated by the angle. If the agent cannot move, then the angle will be modified to a random value and the algorithm will continue.

However, if the agent can move, then the central cell will raise a flag to inform its neighbors. Two additional steps in relation to the software code are introduced to check whether two or more agents attempt to move to the central cell. In the next stage, if the previous prerequisites are met, the agent's identifier and angle of the neighboring cell will be transferred to the central cell and its trace value will be increased by $depT$. Afterwards, the sensory behavior of the food and the adjustment of the angle of each cell are followed. Direction is indicated by the higher smell of food detected by the sensors. Sensors f, fl and fr receive the trail of the neighboring cells and the front is impacted by the angle of the central cell. The final stage is the food diffusion equation.

A $n \times n$ grid of cells is designed and interconnected Then the grid circuit received the following input signals: $p + 1$ $(0 \leq p \leq 511)$ signals, 9 bits each, that indicate an integer with range from 0 to 511. These signals are used to load agents' identifiers into different cells within the grid. Another $p + 1$ signals are used to give angle values in the cells. An 8-bit signal set to zero, i.e. to the absence of food in a cell and another one 8-bit signal corresponding to the number 255 and given to the cells that we intend to have food stimulus. Three signals, one bit each corresponding to `clk`, `reset` and `initialize`. The outputs are $n \times n$ signals, 9 bits each representing the ID number of the agent in each cell of the grid.

In order to prove that the software program and the CA hardware circuit generated by the VHDL code have the same behavior, the following section presents the results of trying to create a Kolmogorov–Uspensky machine.

4 Simulation Results

In this section, the proposed CA–multiagent model will be used to reproduce functions Fuse and Mult. These functions are characteristic of the *Physarum* machine presented in [18], which mimics universal storage modification machines, like the Kolmogorov-Uspensky machine. The CA is selected to have a size of 20×20. The agents are placed in random locations and with random angles. The deposition value of the chemoattractant is equal to one for each successive transfer of the particle's identifier from one cell to another. The input signals given to the system designed with the VHDL code were: the period of the `clk`

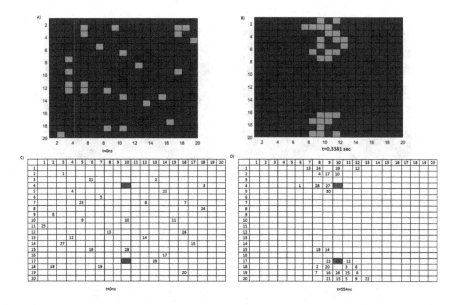

Fig. 3. Output of the model in software (a, b) and in hardware (c, d) with initial and final positions of agents.

signal is set to 1 ns, the rst signal for 9 ns equal to 1 and then 0, the initialize signal equal to one for 10 ns and then equal to 0.

The experimental operations with the active zones as recorded by Adamatzky and Jones [17,18] were used as verification of the model.

Initialization of the CA is illustrated in Fig. 3a for the software model and in Fig. 3c for the hardware model. It is noted that cell values that are closer to food sources will modify their status and will undergo changes in both identifiers and angles. As already mentioned the output signals are 400, so for convenience, all the changes noted in the cells are shown in a table. In the example of Fig. 3, each agent has a sensory behavior of a larger neighborhood (3 cells), so that it can detect the smell of the food of another cell on the grid without staying only around a constant food stimuli. The pieces of plasmodium are attracted by the food sources (red color) and plasmodium spots are created around these sources. The food stimuli are initially placed in the cells (4, 10) and (17, 10).

By comparing these two models, we observed that they present similar results. On the other hand, the time spent by the CA circuit to form the result (554 ns) is much less than the time spent in the software (0.3381 s).

In the following, a new stimulus is placed to attract the plasmodium in its location. The new food source is installed in cell (10, 10). The growing plasmodium is attracted by the inner source and the propagation continues inwards from each initial source (Fig. 4). These two active zones fuse and retain a structure spanning the array of nodes. After a few time steps, it is observed that the cells near the new food source are starting to change their ID values, which means

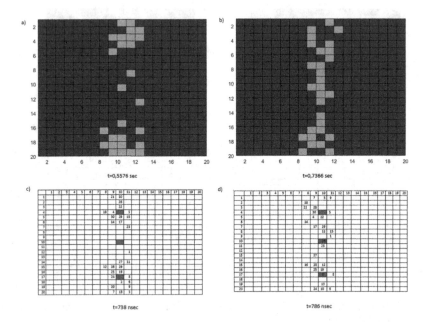

t=0,5576 sec   t=0,7366 sec

t=738 nsec   t=786 nsec

Fig. 4. The FUSE operation in software (a, b) and in hardware (c, d).

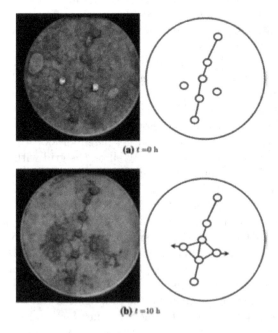

(a) $t = 0$ h

(b) $t = 10$ h

Fig. 5. The MULT operation of the Physarum machine (adopted from [18]).

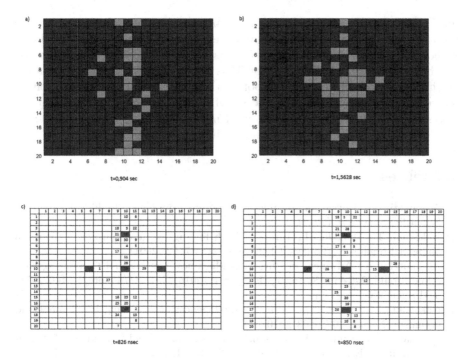

Fig. 6. (a, b, c, d). MULT operation of the virtual model. At the time of 1.5628 s the formation result for the software program (top) is produced, while for the program that is designed with hardware description language (below) the formation of the network is generated at 850 ns.

that the active zones migrate in these directions. In software the chain structure is formed at 0.7366 s (Fig. 4b), while in hardware at 786 ns (Fig. 4d).

An example is displayed in Fig. 5, given a food source chain where the plasmodium has formed protoplasmic tubes, two oat flakes can be added right and left and cause new active zones (Fig. 5a). After 10 h, 2 new active zones A1 and A2 are formed (Fig. 5b).

Using the chain structure created by the previous method (Fig. 4) two additional food sources are added to each side of the array, at points (10, 6) and (10, 14). Two active fronts were produced to engulf the sources (Fig. 6). In Fig. 6 is illustrated the function MULT of physarum machine, some agents will gradually become aware of the existence of new food stimuli and will start moving in that direction developing a diamond area.

5 Conclusions

A novel hybrid model was used to approximate the computing abilities of a (geometrically represented) biological substrate, namely the plasmodium of *P. polycephalum*. The model proposed here is a CA-based method incorporating a multi–agent system. The results of the computerized plasmodium were closely imitating the results obtained from in vivo experimental studies. The developed methodology was implemented in software as well as in hardware. The motivation was the fact that the parallel nature of CA is lost in the software implementation. The higher the complexity of the problem, the longer it will take to be resolved. Whereas, the circuit generated by the VHDL code uses the advantage of parallel processing and, therefore, solves the problem within a vast range of complexity, using the resources for a given amount of time.

References

1. Adamatzky, A.: Physarum Machines: Computers From Slime Mould, vol. 74. World Scientific, Singapore (2010)
2. Nakagaki, T., Yamada, H., Toth, A.: Path finding by tube morphogenesis in an amoeboid organism. Biophys. Chem. **92**(1–2), 47–52 (2001)
3. Adamatzky, A.: Advances in Physarum Machines: Sensing and Computing with Slime Mould, 1st edn. Springer, Heidelberg (2016). https://doi.org/10.1007/978-3-319-26662-6
4. Nakagaki, T., Yamada, H., Tóth, Á.: Intelligence: maze-solving by an amoeboid organism. Nature **407**(6803), 470 (2000)
5. Adamatzky, A.: Slime mold solves maze in one pass, assisted by gradient of chemo-attractants. IEEE Trans. Nanobiosci. **11**(2), 131–134 (2012)
6. Adamatzky, A.: Developing proximity graphs by physarum polycephalum: does the plasmodium follow the toussaint hierarchy? Parallel Process. Lett. **19**(01), 105–127 (2009)
7. Aono, M., Zhu, L., Hara, M.: Amoeba-based neurocomputing for 8-city traveling salesman problem. Int. J. Unconv. Comput. **7**(6), 463–480 (2011)
8. Tsuda, S., Aono, M., Gunji, Y.P.: Robust and emergent physarum logical-computing. BioSystems **73**(1), 45–55 (2004)
9. Adamatzky, A.: Bioevaluation of World Transport Networks. World Scientific, Singapore (2012)
10. Evangelidis, V., Tsompanas, M.A., Sirakoulis, G.C., Adamatzky, A.: Slime mould imitates development of Roman roads in the Balkans. J. Archaeol. Sci. Rep. **2**, 264–281 (2015)
11. Tsompanas, M.A.I., Mayne, R., Sirakoulis, G.C., Adamatzky, A.I.: A cellular automata bioinspired algorithm designing data trees in wireless sensor networks. Int. J. Distrib. Sens. Netw. **11**(6), 471045 (2015)
12. Tero, A., et al.: Rules for biologically inspired adaptive network design. Science **327**(5964), 439–442 (2010)
13. Jones, J.: From Pattern Formation to Material Computation: Multi-agent Modelling of Physarum Polycephalum, vol. 15. Springer, Heidelberg (2015). https://doi.org/10.1007/978-3-319-16823-4
14. Gunji, Y.P., Shirakawa, T., Niizato, T., Yamachiyo, M., Tani, I.: An adaptive and robust biological network based on the vacant-particle transportation model. J. Theor. Biol. **272**(1), 187–200 (2011)
15. Tsompanas, M.A.I., Sirakoulis, G.C.: Modeling and hardware implementation of an amoeba-like cellular automaton. Bioinspiration Biomim. **7**(3), 036013 (2012)

16. Tsompanas, M.-A.I., Sirakoulis, G.C., Adamatzky, A.: Cellular automata models simulating slime mould computing. In: Adamatzky, A. (ed.) Advances in Physarum Machines. ECC, vol. 21, pp. 563–594. Springer, Cham (2016). https://doi.org/10. 1007/978-3-319-26662-6_27

17. Adamatzky, A.: Physarum machine: implementation of a Kolmogorov-Uspensky machine on a biological substrate. Parallel Process. Lett. **17**(04), 455–467 (2007)

18. Adamatzky, A., Jones, J.: Programmable reconfiguration of physarum machines. Nat. Comput. **9**(1), 219–237 (2010)

19. Kolmogorov, A.N.: On the concept of algorithm. Uspekhi Mat. Nauk **8**(4), 175–176 (1953)

20. Kolmogorov, A.N., Uspenskii, V.A.: On the definition of an algorithm. Uspekhi Mat. Nauk **13**(4), 3–28 (1958)

21. Blass, A., Gurevich, Y.: Algorithms: a quest for absolute definitions. Bull. EATCS **81**, 195–225 (2003)

22. Jones, J.: Approximating the behaviours of *Physarum polycephalum* for the construction and minimisation of synthetic transport networks. In: Calude, C.S., Costa, J.F., Dershowitz, N., Freire, E., Rozenberg, G. (eds.) UC 2009. LNCS, vol. 5715, pp. 191–208. Springer, Heidelberg (2009). https://doi.org/10.1007/978-3-642-03745-0_23

Potential Oscillations in Cellular Automaton Based Model for Passivation of Metal Surface

Jan Stępień[1][✉] and Janusz Stafiej[2][✉]

[1] Department of Complex Systems and Chemical Information Processing,
Institute of Physical Chemistry, Polish Academy of Sciences,
ul. Kasprzaka 44/52, 01-224 Warsaw, Poland
jstepien@ichf.edu.pl
[2] Department of Mathematics and Natural Sciences,
Cardinal Stefan Wyszyński University, ul. Wóycickiego 1/3, Warsaw, Poland
j.stafiej@uksw.edu.pl

Abstract. Cellular Automata based approach to modelling of the corrosion and passivation of metals in electrolytes is presented. We simulate the growth of the passive layer using an asynchronous CA, implemented for parallel processing on a GPU. In the present version of our model, the studied system is under galvanostatic control. The electric potential is adjusted to fix the current flow to a prescribed value. In the electrochemical experiments, this leads to potential oscillations for certain values of the current. This is related to the fact that for certain range of potentials our system displays a negative differential resistivity. We manage to obtain potential oscillations in our simulations. To our knowledge this is the first time that this peculiar feature of passivating system is reproduced by a computer simulation.

Keywords: Corrosion · Passivation · Diffusion · Oscillations
Modelling · Parallel computing · Block-synchronous automata
Asynchronous cellular automata · Stochastic cellular automata

1 Introduction

This paper is devoted to modelling of the corrosion and passivation of metals. Many metals tend to corrode via electrochemical oxidation, particularly when in contact with electrolytes. Depending on the conditions, such corrosion may lead to creation of a passive layer on the metal surface [20]. This layer can be composed of weakly soluble corrosion products, including metal oxides, hydroxides and salts. Passivation slows corrosion down by a large factor. As the experiments have shown [11,12,15–17], it is possible to control whether, and how fast passivation occurs. The passive layer thickness and morphology can also be regulated. Passivation is strongly influenced by a constant or time dependent electric potential applied to the piece of metal, passing electric current through the surface, or by modifying the composition of the solution.

© Springer Nature Switzerland AG 2018
G. Mauri et al. (Eds.): ACRI 2018, LNCS 11115, pp. 92–101, 2018.
https://doi.org/10.1007/978-3-319-99813-8_8

We have been studying passivation in electrolyte solutions for many years, by means of simulations with stochastic asynchronous cellular automata. Our research so far [5,6,19] was focused on passivation in potentiostatic conditions, that is – with constant electric potential applied to the metal. In this paper, some results for passivation in galvanostatic conditions are presented. Connecting the passivating metal to a galvanostat may induce oscillations of the potential, and our simulations manage to reproduce such oscillations.

The simulations can help us understand the physico-chemical mechanism of passivation better, than using only experiments. Besides, they allow us to regulate any parameters of the system at will, particularly those that are not amenable to experimental control. Thus we can separate some features that have to be unseparated in the real world experiments. Furthermore, they may provide us with advice on how to control the morphology of passive layers, possibly including formation of interesting nanostructures. One example is the emergence of nanopores on titania or alumina [3,4,21] – hypothetically it could be possible to obtain similarly regular patterns on valve metals.

We are using CA in our work for a few reasons. Firstly, they find their use as general (toy) models applicable to wide classes of systems that have common features. Further, CA are often adequate models for complex phenomena. This is largely for efficiency reasons. In many cases molecular-scale simulations or differential equations are associated with unreasonably high computational costs. Corrosion is one of those complex phenomena – it is an inhomogenous system, involving many components and an unobvious interaction between reaction and diffusion. Finally, CA can be translated to parallel algorithms in a straightforward manner, and those algorithms will typically make use of multiprocessor hardware with high efficiency. In our work, graphics processing units (GPUs) are used for computation. Note that parallelization becomes slightly less trivial in cases where the choice is taken to employ an asynchronous CA, instead of a classic, synchronous one. This is the case for the model described here. Still, the solutions for the problems that arise can be found in the literature, e.g. in [1,2].

The CA-based models have found many applications in physical chemistry and related fields – including electrochemistry [13], corrosion science [7], materials science and metallurgy [8–10,14].

The rest of this paper is structured as follows: The *Model* section presents the CA model used for the simulations. It is discussed in which ways the model accounts for the particular physico-chemical phenomena, and how is it implemented for parallel execution. The *Simulations, Results and Discussion* section describes for which parameter vectors the simulations were conducted, what data was collected and how was it processed. After that, the most important results are presented, along with discussion. The article is summarized in *Conclusions*.

2   Model

The model of passivation presented here is the same as in our publications on the passivation in potentiostatic conditions [5,6,19]. This is why only a short description is presented in this section. The reader can find more details elsewhere. The new aspect is the galvanostatic control over the system.

The model is kept as general and simple as possible. It contains only the ingredients that are essential for reproducing the salient features of passivation. Corrosion and passivation works in similar ways for many different metals. This model assumes a metal with chemical properties similar to those of iron or other valve metals.

2.1   Physicochemical Basis of the Model

The model includes three processes that are responsible for the passive layer formation. The first of them is electrochemical oxidation of metal at its surface, caused by a corrosive environment. The rate of oxidation of exposed metal is a function of electric potential applied to the metal. The overall rate of corrosion depends also on the degree of passivation (coverage by the products of corrosion) and it is directly proportional to the current flowing through the system. In this model, we assume that the metal is connected with a galvanostat, therefore the potential is continuously regulated in an effort to keep the current constant. It should be emphasized, that the current cannot be controlled directly. Even with the best galvanostat, the current will be subject to random fluctuations. What is more, the maximum current in the studied system is limited by passivation. If the desired current value is too high, it is not possible to maintain it by galvanostatic control. In such a situation, the galvanostat will eventually output the highest potential available. The condition, when increasing the potential leads to a decrease in the current, is called negative differential resistivity.

The second modelled process is the precipitation of insoluble corrosion products on the metal surface and formation of a compact passive layer. For the passivation to occur, the corrosion product has to be hardly soluble. It has to adhere to the metal surface, as well as to itself. This is modelled by the random walk with asymmetric exclusion that mimics diffusion of the oxide to solution and its surface rearrangement. Passivation is never perfect – even with the surface fully covered with the oxide, a small current keeps flowing. In our study, this is made possible by a symmetry of oxide and solution in asymmetric exclusion. If the oxide particles can enter the solution, then in the same way solution inclusions can move into the oxide layer. This sustains a growth of the layer even when it becomes compact. The solution inclusions behave in an analogous way as the ionic vacancies postulated by Macdonald [18].

If only those two processes are taken into account, infinite growth of the passive layer becomes possible, although the growth rate will converge to zero as the layer's thickness increases. To limit the oxide layer thickness, we have included a mechanism of irreversible dissolution of oxide. This enables the system to achieve a steady state (equilibrium), when the rate of the irreversible dissolution balances the oxide production.

2.2   Specification of the Automaton

The CA used for the simulations is stochastic and asynchronous. The lattice is three-dimensional, cubic, with periodic boundary conditions. The neighbourhood is that of von Neumann. There are three cell states postulated: metal (MET for short), aqueous solution SOL, and metal oxide OXI. In the initial state, the bottom 40% of the lattice is filled with metal, with the upper part containing solution. The transition rule is composed of three transitions:

1. Metal oxidation: MET + SOL $\rightarrow$ OXI + OXI
   It can occur for a MET cell which is in contact with the solution, i.e. has at least one SOL neighbour.
2. Oxide diffusion (random walk): OXI + SOL $\rightarrow$ SOL + OXI
   Possible for an OXI cell which is in contact with the solution.
3. Oxide dissolution: OXI $\rightarrow$ SOL
   Considered only for an OXI cell whose all neighbours are SOL.

The automaton is stochastic, which means that the transitions listed above occur with certain probabilities, discussed below. The model has four parameters: P_{break} influences the oxide diffusion by regulating its adhesion to itself and the metal, P_{die} regulates the oxide loss via dissolution, R_{dif} and I_{GS} characterize the operation of the galvanostat.

The probability P_{corr} of an oxidation event depends on the potential V via the function:

$$P_{corr} = \frac{\exp(V)}{1 + \exp(V)} \tag{1}$$

which is plotted in Fig. 1. The probability P_{swap} of a diffusion event is dependent on $-n_{broken}$, the change in the number of MET and OXI neighbours of the OXI cell being moved. If $n_{broken} \leq 0$, then $P_{swap} = 1$. Otherwise, $P_{swap} = P_{break}^{n_{broken}}$, where P_{break} is a model parameter. The probability P_{die} of oxide dissolution is another parameter. If a MET is considered for dissolution, and it is stochastically chosen not to occur, then diffusion is considered immediately.

Electric potential V is adjusted by the galvanostat after each time step, in order to keep the actual current as close as possible to the set value. This is done using the following formula:

$$V_t - V_{t-1} = -R_{dif}(I_{t-1} - I_{GS}) \tag{2}$$

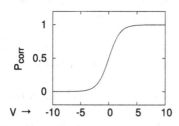

Fig. 1. Corrosion event probability P_{corr} as function of the potential V.

where V_t and I_t are respectively potential and current values during the time step number t, R_{dif} is the galvanostat's sensitivity factor, and I_{GS} is the desired current. Here, current is defined as the number of oxidation events per time step. Note that the state of the system is described by the states of the cells, and additionally a global variable V. Therefore, the initial V value also has to be specified.

2.3 Parallel Implementation

Due to the efficiency reasons, the lattice size has to be reasonable. In our case, it hardly ever exceeds $2048 \times 2048 \times 64$. We approximate studying a part of a much larger system by using periodic boundary conditions for the x and y directions. For z direction, it is assumed that the bulk solution extends to $+\infty$, and the bulk metal to $-\infty$. This condition is handled by introducing a scrolling mechanism. Every time when the corrosion consumes a metal volume corresponding to a single layer of cells, a monolayer is removed from the top of the lattice, and a monolayer of metal is appended to the bottom. When an oxide particle would diffuse past the z-extent of the lattice, it is annihilated (turned to SOL) instead. This method makes it possible to run a simulation for an arbitrarily long time.

Employment of a traditional, synchronous CA with the transition rule given is not possible without substantial changes to the model, because oxidation and diffusion transitions affect not just one cell, but also a randomly chosen neighbour. Therefore, as it has been mentioned, we decide to use an asynchronous automaton. In this case, an order of considering the cells for updating has to be given. To efficiently use the parallel processing capability of the GPUs, we have implemented our algorithm as a block-synchronous automaton, similar to those described in [1]. The only difference is that sampling with replacement is used in our case. The block size is set to 4^3.

The algorithm for the simulation, therefore, is as follows:
Until the desired simulation time is reached, do:

- for 64 times (block size):
  - Randomly choose a position in the unit block;
  - For the cell in that position, in every block: (the parallel part)
    - Choose a random neighbour (relevant for an oxidation or diffusion event);
    - Choose a transition based on the cell and selected neighbour's states – oxidation for MET and SOL, dissolution for OXI with only SOL neighbours, do nothing for SOL;
    - Randomly (with given probability) decide, whether the transition happens;
    - If the cell is OXI and dissolution has not been performed, consider diffusion next;
    - If a transition is chosen to be performed, update the cell(s) affected;
- If an equivalent of a monolayer of metal has been oxidized since last scrolling: Scroll by removing the top monolayer of the lattice and adding a monolayer of MET at the bottom;

– Compute the potential V for the next step (Galvanostat)

3 Simulations, Results and Discussion

The simulations are conducted to check the influence of all parameters. The sets of values for every parameter are selected based on initial test simulations, the earlier results presented in [19], and on the authors' intuition.

Instead of bare I_{GS} (current setting) and R_{dif} (galvanostat sensitivity), we used respectively I_{GS}/A and $R_{dif} \cdot A$ as parameters, where A is the area of the horizontal section of the lattice, $dim_x \cdot dim_y$ (all dimensions are in cells). Adopting this convention makes the system's behavior independent of the lattice size, if it is sufficiently large. To determine the appropriate size for further simulations, the impact of the lattice size was examined. First, the horizontal (dim_x and dim_y) dimensions from range 96–4096 were checked, with the lattice height (dim_z) = 96. Next, $dim_x = dim_y = 1024$ were assumed and dim_z was varied from 8 to 144. The other parameters were: $P_{break} = 0.15$, $P_{die} = 0.01$, $I_{GS}/A =$ 0.0002 and $R_{dif}A = 200$. Those values had been found to cause nice potential oscillations (see Fig. 2, discussed later). The simulation time was 40000 steps. We found that for most of the following simulations, $dim_x = dim_y = 1536$ and $dim_z = 64$ are sufficient. For the cases when very small I_{GS}/A values were chosen, we extended dim_x and dim_y to 2048. This was meant to reduce the content of the random noise in the observed current.

The impact of P_{die} was also examined, assuming its values of 0–1. The other parameters were as given in the preceding paragraph. For the next simulations, we decided to keep $P_{die} = 0.01$, like in the previous work [19].

The influence of $R_{dif}A$ and initial V was checked for several I_{GS}/A and P_{break} values. This influence is nontrivial and deserves more attention in a future work. For the presented simulations, we assumed $R_{dif}A = 200$ and $V = 0$ as the initial value. The focus is on the role of the two other parameters. Preliminary simulations were conducted for P_{break} in range 0.1–0.3, and $I_{GS}/A = 5 \cdot 10^{-5} - -6 \cdot 10^{-4}$. Having gained some experience, for further simulations we select the parameter values that seem most likely to produce interesting behavior.

Data collected from the simulations are mainly V and I values as functions of time. For selected simulations, surface morphologies at chosen moments of time are rendered as snapshots, mainly in order to analyse the connection between the layer morphology and the potential oscillation stage. This connection is shown in Fig. 2 on an example of a system's evolution at $P_{break} = 0.15$ and $I_{GS}/A = 2 \cdot 10^{-4}$. Here, we can notice that high potential corresponds to high coverage of metal by the oxide.

3.1 Impact of Current and Adhesive Forces

The plots in Fig. 3 show how the overall behavior of the system depends on P_{break} and I_{GS}/A. Observed current is shown in the units of I_{GS}, so if it remains close to one, then it can be said that the galvanostat serves its purpose well. The plots

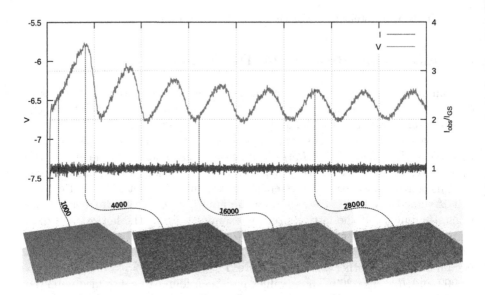

Fig. 2. Plot of time evolution of I (in purple) and V (green). observed current is divided by I_{GS}. Below the plot, shown are images of the metal surface at time $t \in \{1000, 4000, 16000, 28000\}$. Metal is rendered in light gray, oxide – in dark brown. (Color figure online)

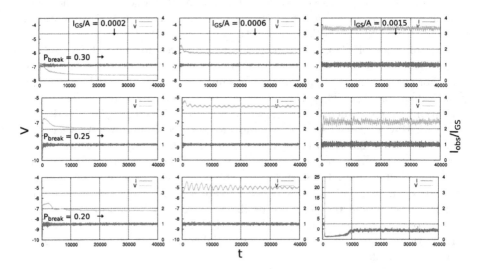

Fig. 3. Comparison of I and V evolution in time, for $I_{GS}/A \in \{2 \cdot 10^{-4}, 6 \cdot 10^{-4}, 1.5 \cdot 10^{-3}\}$ (left to right), $P_{break} \in \{0.3, 0.25, 0.2\}$ (top to bottom). Observed modes of behavior include: convergence to a steady state (left), stable oscillations of V (esp. central plot), damped oscillations (bottom central), chaotic oscillations (middle right) and passivation (bottom right plot).

show smooth convergence to a steady state, then damped, stable and chaotic oscillations, and passivation (saturation), when the potential grows rapidly, but no longer has any influence on the current, which stays below the target value. Those regimes occur approximately in the order of rising I_{GS}/A or falling P_{break}.

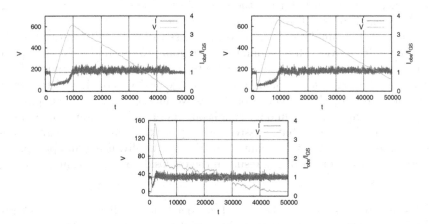

Fig. 4. Examples of I and V evolution in time, showing depassivation. Top: P_{break} = 0.2, with $I_{GS}/A = 7.75 \cdot 10^{-4}$ (left) and $8 \cdot 10^{-4}$ (right). Bottom: P_{break} = 0.25 and $I_{GS}/A = 1.8 \cdot 10^{-3}$. Depassivation occurs about t = 10000 (top) and 2000 (bottom).

Another phenomenon that can be observed in the simulations is the depassivation, when after a period of passivity the oxide layer becomes less compact and the current as set or greater starts flowing again. This can be seen in the I and V versus time plots, in Fig. 4. As we can see, the most interesting nonlinear behavior of the system occurs when the I_{GS} value is close to I_{max} – the maximum current that can be maintained for an arbitrarily long time. I_{max} obviously depends on all of the other parameters. It is difficult to calculate its value precisely, mostly due to the stochasticity of the model. When $I_{GS} \lesssim I_{max}$, we observe chaotic potential oscillations or passivation with subsequent depassivation.

4   Conclusions

We simulate passivation of metal in an electrolyte solution using a three-dimensional asynchronous stochastic cellular automaton as model. The model is taken from our earlier work, and coupled with a simple galvanostat, which changes the electric potential with a rate that is directly proportional to the difference between the desired and observed current. In the beginning of the research it was not obvious whether the oscillations could be obtained in our simulations. It could have been speculated, for example, that the time scale of the oscillations is too small related to the automaton's time step. Such doubts, however, appear to be unfounded. In fact, no modifications to the originally assumed model are required. All of the results are obtained just by varying the values of the parameters – mostly the galvanostat current setting and the oxide adhesion strength, expressed in terms of P_{break}. To our knowledge, at the time of writing this paper, the presented model is the only one that mimics the salient features of passivation in so much detail. The simulated oscillatory patterns are still simpler and less varied, than those seen in the experiments – compare e.g. [15,17]. Thus, there is still room for improvement.

In general, the simulation studies on the passivation in galvanostatic conditions are far from over. More simulations are going to be conducted to explore the influence of the parameters in more detail, especially the sensitivity of the galvanostat. Future research includes also topological description of the oxide layers, modelling of the influence of aggressive anions (Cl^-, F^-) on passivation, and the influence of boundary conditions (periodic conditions are assumed in this paper). Following that, passivation in potentiodynamic and galvanodynamic conditions is going to be simulated. Hypothetically, using an appropriate potential or current protocol can result in the corrosion product forming curious nanostructures.

Acknowledgements. The authors need to thank the National Science Centre (Poland) for funding – OPUS Project: Numerical simulations of passive layer morphology at the metal electrode, grant number *UMO-2015/19/B/ST4/03753*.

References

1. Bandman, O.: Parallel simulation of asynchronous cellular automata evolution. In: El Yacoubi, S., Chopard, B., Bandini, S. (eds.) ACRI 2006. LNCS, vol. 4173, pp. 41–47. Springer, Heidelberg (2006). https://doi.org/10.1007/11861201_8

2. Bandman, O.: Coarse-grained parallelization of cellular-automata simulation algorithms. In: Malyshkin, V. (ed.) PaCT 2007. LNCS, vol. 4671, pp. 370–384. Springer, Heidelberg (2007). https://doi.org/10.1007/978-3-540-73940-1_38

3. Bartosik, Ł.: Simulation of nanostructured surfaces obtained by passivity and growth. Ph.D. thesis, Institute of Physical Chemistry, Polish Academy of Sciences, Warsaw, Poland (2014)

4. Bartosik, Ł., Stafiej, J., di Caprio, D.: 3D simulations of ordered nanopore growth in alumina. Electrochim. Acta **188**, 218–221 (2016). https://doi.org/10.1016/j.electacta.2015.08.164

5. di Caprio, D., Stafiej, J.: Simulations of passivation phenomena based on discrete lattice gas automata. Electrochim. Acta **55**, 3884–3890 (2010). https://doi.org/10.1016/j.electacta.2010.01.106

6. di Caprio, D., Stafiej, J.: The role of adsorption in passivation phenomena modelled by discrete lattice gas automata. Electrochim. Acta **56**, 3963–3968 (2011). https://doi.org/10.1016/j.electacta.2011.02.018

7. di Caprio, D., Stafiej, J., Luciano, G., Arurault, L.: 3D cellular automata simulations of intra and intergranular corrosion. Corros. Sci. **112**, 438–450 (2016). https://doi.org/10.1016/j.corsci.2016.07.028

8. Chen, S., Guillemot, G., Gandin, C.A.: Three-dimensional cellular automaton-finite element modeling of solidification grain structures for arc-welding processes. Acta Mater. **115**, 448–467 (2016). https://doi.org/10.1016/j.actamat.2016.05.011

9. Lhuissier, P., de Formanoir, C., Martin, G., Dendievel, R., Godet, S.: Geometrical control of lattice structures produced by EBM through chemical etching: investigations at the scale of individual struts. Mater. Des. **110**, 485–493 (2016). https:// doi.org/10.1016/j.matdes.2016.08.029
10. Li, H., Sun, X., Yang, H.: A three-dimensional cellular automata-crystal plasticity finite element model for predicting the multiscale interaction among heterogeneous deformation, DRX microstructural evolution and mechanical responses in titanium alloys. Int. J. Plast. **87**, 154–180 (2016). https://doi.org/10.1016/j.ijplas.2016.09. 008
11. Pagitsas, M., Pavlidou, M., Sazou, D.: Localized passivity breakdown of iron in chlorate- and perchlorate-containing sulphuric acid solutions: a study based on current oscillations and a point defect model. Electrochim. Acta **53**, 4784–4795 (2008). https://doi.org/10.1016/j.electacta.2008.01.065
12. Pavlidou, M., Pagitsas, M., Sazou, D.: Potential oscillations induced by the local breakdown of passive iron in sulfuric acid media. An evaluation of the inhibiting effect of nitrates on iron corrosion. J. Solid State Electrochem. **19**(11), 3207–3217 (2015). https://doi.org/10.1007/s10008-015-2812-0
13. Pérez-Brokate, C.F., di Caprio, D., Mahé, E., Féron, D., de Lamare, J.: Cyclic voltammetry simulations with cellular automata. J. Comput. Sci. **11**, 269–278 (2015). https://doi.org/10.1016/j.jocs.2015.08.005
14. Popova, E., Staraselski, Y., Brahme, A., Mishra, R., Inal, K.: Coupled crystal plasticity - probabilistic cellular automata approach to model dynamic recrystallization in magnesium alloys. Int. J. Plast. **66**, 85–102 (2015). https://doi.org/10.1016/j. ijplas.2014.04.008
15. Sazou, D., Kominia, A., Pagitsas, M.: Corrosion processes of iron in acidic solutions associated with potential oscillations induced by chlorates and perchlorates. J. Solid State Electrochem. **18**, 347–360 (2014). https://doi.org/10.1007/s10008-013-2244-7
16. Sazou, D., Michael, K., Pagitsas, M.: Intrinsic coherence resonance in the chloride-induced temporal dynamics of the iron electrodissolution-passivation in sulfuric acid solutions. Electrochim. Acta **119**, 175–183 (2014). https://doi.org/10.1016/j. electacta.2013.12.029
17. Sazou, D., Pavlidou, M., Pagitsas, M.: Potential oscillations induced by localized corrosion of the passivity on iron in halide-containing sulfuric acid media as a probe for a comparative study of the halide effect. J. Electroanal. Chem. **675**, 54–67 (2012). https://doi.org/10.1016/j.jelechem.2012.04.012
18. Sikora, E., Macdonald, D.D.: Defining the passive state. Solid State Ionics **94**, 141–150 (1997)
19. Stępień, J., di Caprio, D., Stafiej, J.: 3D simulation studies of the metal passivation process. Electrochim. Acta (submitted)
20. Uhlig, H.H.: Passivity in metals and alloys. Corros. Sci. **19**(7), 777–791 (1979). https://doi.org/10.1016/S0010-938X(79)80075-X
21. Yang, F., Huang, L., Guo, T., Wang, C., Wang, L., Zhang, P.: The precise preparation of anodic aluminum oxide template based on the current-controlled method. Ferroelectrics **523**, 50–60 (2018). https://doi.org/10.1080/00150193.2018.1391540

Motion Detection and Characterization in Videos with Cellular Automata

Antonio Carrieri, Luca Crociani, Giuseppe Vizzari$^{(\boxtimes)}$, and Stefania Bandini

Dipartimento di Informatica, Sistemistica e Comunicazione (DISCo), Universitá degli studi di Milano Bicocca, Milan, Italy
a.carrieri4@campus.unimib.it
{luca.crociani,giuseppe.vizzari,bandini}@disco.unimib.it

Abstract. In this paper we present a method for motion detection and characterization using Cellular Automata. The original approach employs results of the application of the Sobel operator to individual frames, that are translated to CA configurations that are processed with the aim of detecting and characterizing moving entities to support collision avoidance from the perspective of the viewer. The paper formally describes the adopted approach as well as its experimentation videos representing plausible situations.

Keywords: Cellular Automata · Motion detection · Video analysis

1 Introduction

Motion detection and object tracking are both tasks of great interest in Computer Vision (CV). They are part of studies, for example, in medical imaging, surveillance methods [22] and (of more recent interest) driver assistance [2] and many other applications. The aim of this paper is to present a method for motion detection and characterization using Cellular Automata. The approach has the aim of detecting and characterizing moving entities to support collision avoidance from the perspective of the viewer.

In order to pursue this goal we identified in the edge detection, more specifically in the Sobel operator [19], an algorithm that performs an efficient transformation of an image in its edge-based counterpart with satisfactory effectiveness. This image transformation, leading to a gray-scale representation, can be easily translated in a cellular automaton configuration [21]. Considering that edge detection [3,5,15,17] is a very specific field of computer vision technique, it is nonetheless possible to find some peculiarities that fit well in the cellular automaton approach.

Likewise, intrinsic features of cellular automata make them naturally suited to parallelization [20] and efficient hardware implementation [7], with the support of ad-hoc devices, they could bear the development and usage of a real time system. We will now briefly discuss most relevant related works to this research, then the approach will be introduced. Discussion of achieved results and future research directions will end the paper.

© Springer Nature Switzerland AG 2018
G. Mauri et al. (Eds.): ACRI 2018, LNCS 11115, pp. 102–111, 2018.
https://doi.org/10.1007/978-3-319-99813-8_9

2   Related Works

Even though works related to motion detection using Sobel operator and CA are not present in the literature, Cellular Automata have recently been used for saliency detection [16]: the cited work, employing a stochastic CA approach, has been well received by the CV community being characterized, at the same time, by a good effectiveness and high efficiency, and it actually generated interest and further researches. Saliency detection analysis with CA, in fact, was later also investigated in [8], which also characterized it as one of the most relevant steps of the process of motion detection. CA approaches had been earlier used for other CV tasks, in particular to process edge detection [12,14] and to perform resizing operation preserving edges (and therefore quality of the image) [10], but also for segmentation of medical images [18].

3   The Introduced CA Approach

Our approach and the associated work-flow implies several steps in order to process a frame-by-frame object movement, as shown in Fig. 1. It involves Cellular Automata (CA) which is a mathematical idealization of physical systems in which space and time are discrete. It consists of a regular uniform lattice where, in each site, there is a discrete variable called "cell". Each individual cell is in a specific state and changes synchronously depending on the state of its neighbors, given a local update rule. The neighborhood at a certain site is typically taken to be the site itself and its immediate adjacent sites.

3.1   From a Frame to a Sobel-Filtered Frame

To transform an image into an instance of a CA, every frame of a video will be filtered using the Sobel operator. The latter applies two 3×3 kernels to the original image in order to calculate approximations of the derivatives, horizontal-axiswise and vertical-axiswise (see Fig. 2). Therefore the gradient $\mathbf{G}$ of the edge will be $G = \sqrt{G_x^2 + G_y^2}$. Because of its approximated nature, this filter helps in the process of discretization of an image. Applying this filter, colors are going to be removed, highlighting only edges in scales of gray. Edges are basically areas where contrast intensity $\gamma \in \varGamma$ is strong. Filtering an image with this operator, provides a new image which will be used to initialize a CA lattice.

The main reason for the usage of Sobel operator rather than other edge detectors can be found in the simplicity of the related algorithm. While other edge detectors (e.g. Canny edge detector) imply various steps to process the image and achieve its edge-based counterpart, as explained in [10], the Sobel operator edge detection method instead implies a shorter number of steps that are part of a much simpler algorithm.

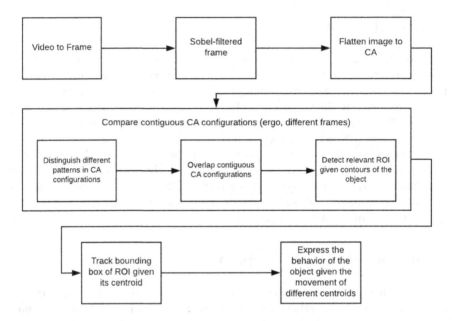

Fig. 1. The overall pipeline of the proposed approach for CA-based motion detection and characterization.

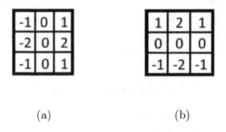

(a)   (b)

Fig. 2. (a) Matrix used on x axis (G_x); (b) Matrix used on y axis (G_y).

3.2   CA Initialization

Due to the intrinsic discrete nature of a CA, the actual set of contrasts Γ, processed by the Sobel filter, needs to be discretized in clusters. The cardinality of these clusters will be set as the highest value that a cell $c_i \in C$, where $i = 1 \ldots |C|$, in a lattice L can assume. The number of clusters is determined according to the content of the processed video with the aim of preserving the possibility to discriminate edges but also to keep limited the processing time. So once clustered, there will be a finite set of states $S = \{0, \ldots, K\}$ every cell can assume.

Therefore defining a frame $F^t = \{p_0^t, p_1^t, \ldots, p_{(n*m)-1}^t, p_{n*m}^t\}$, where n is the number of pixels on the x axis and m the number of pixels on the y axis, as the t_{th} frame in a video $V = \{F^0, F^1, \ldots, F^{max(t)}\}$, the flattening process will follow this method:

$$
S(c_i^t) = \begin{cases} k-1, & \text{if } min(\gamma_{K^n}) \leq \gamma_{p_i^t} \leq max(\gamma_{K^n}) \\ \vdots & \\ 1, & \text{if } 0 < min(\gamma_{K^1}) \leq \gamma_{p_i^t} \leq max(\gamma_{K^1}) \\ 0, & \text{otherwise} \end{cases}
\tag{1}
$$

At the end of this process there will be a fully initialized lattice L with cells assuming up to k different states which will be associated to a sobel-filtered video frame.

3.3   Frames Comparison

Having the lattice set, a process of frames comparison to elaborate movement within the considered video will start. In order to do this, we will use 2 different, but contiguous in time, lattices $L(F^t)$ and $L(F^{t+1})$; they will be overlapped to retrieve uncommon cells according to their position. As a result a new lattice $\Lambda(L(F^t), L(F^{t+1}))$ will be produced according to this method:

$$
S(c_i^{t,t+1}) = \begin{cases} 1, & \text{if } S(c_i^t) \neq S(c_i^{t+1}) \\ 0, & \text{otherwise} \end{cases}
\tag{2}
$$

In other words, lattice $\Lambda(L(F^t), L(F^{t+1}))$ will essentially show different pixels from each frame, which intuitively represent the focus of the movement detection process. More precisely, this new lattice presents edges that were present at time t and that changed at time $t+1$: it therefore includes edge pixels of both time t and $t+1$.

In order to determine more precisely the so called region of interest (ROI) of the distinct frames, we have to separate this information, to be then analyzed to characterize movement. More precisely, we would have to exclude from the lattice $\Lambda(L(F^t), L(F^{t+1}))$ cells that do not match their state value when compared to $L(F^t)$ cells and when compared to $L(F^{t+1})$ cells. Therefore, this process will bring to two new different lattices $ROI(L(F^t))$ and $ROI(L(F^{t+1}))$. Respectively, their cell states will be set according to this method:

$$
S(c_i^{ROI(L(F^t))}) = S(c_i^t) * S(c_i^{t,t+1})
\tag{3}
$$

and

$$
S(c_i^{ROI(L(F^{t+1}))}) = S(c_i^{t+1}) * S(c_i^{t,t+1})
\tag{4}
$$

(a)   (b)

Fig. 3. (a) Frame 104 of the video (b) Sobel-filtered frame 104.

3.4 Building a Bounding Box Around Salient Objects

Having reached this point of the pipeline, the expected output are 2 CA configurations showing salient objects meant to be evaluated in the process of motion detection. In order to do this, a bounding box will be constructed around the ROIs and thus we will be able to collect their centroids and process an approximate estimation of the frame-to-frame behavior of the salient object.

The effectiveness of the estimation will be calculated upon completion of the collection of salient objects' centroids. A trajectory of all of the bounding boxes will show the approximate behavior of the moving object in the whole video.

4   Experimental Results

To exemplify what has been explained so far, the whole pipeline has been developed in pure Python language, using SciPy (ndimage)[1] library for the Sobel filtering part along with OpenCV[2] for several tasks on the video processing.

4.1   Analyzed Videos and Achieved Results

For evaluating the effectiveness of the approach, we used a video[3] with no camera movement, whose frame resolution is 360×496 pixels; the background is therefore permanently motionless (unless for artifacts due to video compression, changes in the illumination, etc.). The video represents a cat entering the screen from the right side and moving towards the other end. It must be noted that we did not run benchmarking tests for the analysis of computational times yet: in this work we mainly focus on the effectiveness of the approach, and its potential regarding the parallelization aspect will be considered in future works.

---

[1] https://docs.scipy.org/doc/scipy/reference/ndimage.html.

[2] https://opencv.org/.

[3] https://www.youtube.com/watch?v=HDb9StNG8_Q.

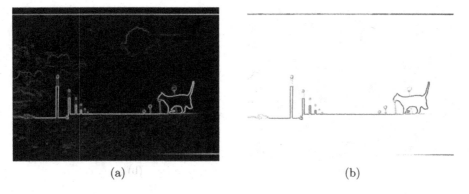

(a)   (b)

Fig. 4. (a) Sobel-filtered frame 104 (b) Flattened Sobel-filtered frame given as a CA configuration

From a Frame to a Sobel-Filtered Frame

In Fig. 3 it is shown how the Sobel operator works: given an image as input, it returns the most significant edges of that image based on their magnitude in terms of contrast.

CA Initialization

In Fig. 4 the Sobel-filtered frames was flattened to be better processed in the subsequent step of frames comparison. This step aims to remove superfluous edges, not so worth further evaluation.

Frames Comparison

In order to better evaluate the difference between frames, we propose, in Fig. 5, 2 examples of differences through overlapping frames

Bounding box of Regions of Interest and their trajectories

In an initial part of the video (frames *1* to *49*) there is no motion (the cat has not yet entered the screen) and consequently nothing is detected; starting at frame *50* and until frame *268* the system detects an object moving at a relatively constant speed from the right side of the frame to the left side. Finally, the sequence of frames between *269* and *293* depict the background since the cat has exited from the right side of the screen, and the system correctly does not report any movement. In Fig. 5d we show the positions of centroids of the bounding boxes built around ROIs.

In Fig. 6 we more briefly describe the results of another experiment, in which a video of a ball bouncing on screen[4], from the left side to the right side, was analyzed. Figure 6b shows the trajectory of centroids of ROIs of the video with a ball bouncing along the frame.

---

[4] https://www.youtube.com/watch?v=SW3rvS3wLqg from which we digitally removed the "Ball" text.

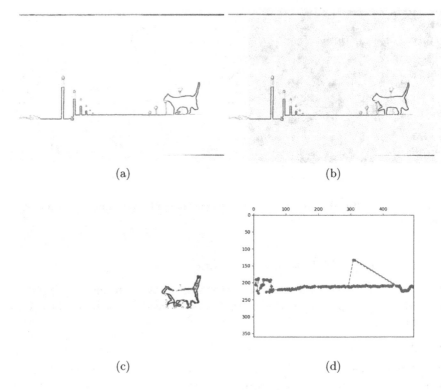

(a)   (b)

(c)   (d)

Fig. 5. (a) CA configuration of frame 104 (b) CA configuration of frame 106 (c) $\Lambda(L(F^{104}), L(F^{106}))$ (d) Trajectory of centroids of ROIs (markers identify centroids of bounding boxes of ROIs)

4.2   Discussion of Experiments

The heterogeneous movement of the cat and its tail provide a continuous although smooth change in the produced bounding box around the ROI, and this makes it quite dynamic and unstable. While the movement of the cat was basically homogeneous and predictable, the movement of its tail instead was fairly unpredictable. This lead to a continuous change of bounding boxes shapes. It is a matter of fact that this pointed out different movement directions between the cat and its own tail.

Moreover, the video presents some issues in terms of compression artifacts, leading to a slight change of colors of pixels in certain frames. On top of that, this method does not consider the problem of object classification, meaning that it does not consider the case of more objects moving in the same frame yet. Nevertheless, as it can be seen in Fig. 5, only 3 frames out of 219 show a clear discrepancy between the expected bounding box position and the one retrieved from the system: the points around the coordinates (300, 150) are due to the

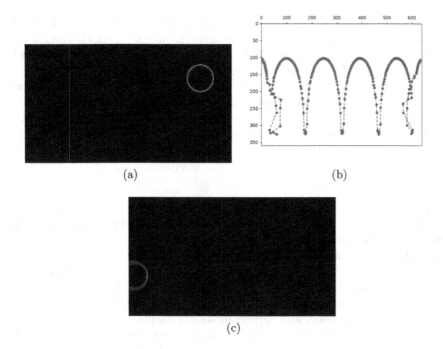

Fig. 6. (a) A frame taken from a video of a ball bouncing on screen (upper right part of the frame) (b) Trajectory of ROIs of video with a bouncing ball (markers identify centroids of bounding boxes of ROIs) (c) Frame where the left edge of the ball is not completely on screen (the ball is in the lower right part of the frame and it is much less visible than in the first frame).

recognition of noisy pixels in the top left part of the video as a possible moving object and part of the ROI.

The second test is proposed on another video that represents a ball with a black background bouncing at a static bouncing rate and moving from left to right at a constant speed. In this case, the object is fundamentally not changing from a morphological perspective, although it is constantly changing velocity, even with relatively significant displacements withing the frame. Results for this scenario are slightly more satisfactory than the previous experiment: even though the number of frames showing discrepancies between the expected bounding box position and the output one is 5 out of 295, the errors made in the estimated trajectory for those frames is very small (see the points at the borders of Fig. 6b). This is due to the fact that, in those frames, e.g. Fig. 6a, the ball speed is rather high and its edges become blurry. This makes the Sobel filter face some difficulties in processing the gradient of ball edges. Therefore only the right edge of the ball is detected and the bounding box built around it makes the centroid of the bounding box slightly shifted along the two axes.

With reference to the achieved results in both the experiments, even before moving in the direction of trying to classify the detected objects, simply considering some physical constraints characterizing the typically observed objects (or the movement capabilities of an autonomous robot on which the camera is positioned) supports the possibility of completely dismissing or significantly reducing this kind of error. For instance, in [11] the authors analyzed trajectories generated by pedestrians and they were able to reject as outliers tracks in which changes of direction were simply too sudden for a walking human, but analogous considerations could be done with respect to commonsense reasoning [4] on the morphology of the detected and tracked objects.

5   Future Works

The present paper fundamentally reports the current results of an ongoing work investigating a wider research challenge, that is, the possibility to transfer intuitions, approaches and concrete results from the field of insect sensory and motor system study to the area of autonomous robotics, in the vein of [1,13].

The present results show that CA can represent useful blocks within a more complex work-flow for the processing of videos, in particular with the aim of detecting and characterizing motion within the analyzed frame. Relationship between the present model and current biological results are still thin; nonetheless, there are results related to the functioning of individual photo-receptors [6] and the conjecture is that CA could be applied to explain the visual processing on the retina. Visual processing is basically composed of local interaction between nearby photo-receptor cells at receptor level and inter-neurons at higher levels.

With respect to the implementation aspect, due to the high level of parallelization of CA, we would like to focus our work on the classification of moving elements in an image, in order to process more objects within the CA. Regarding the classification problem, the greatest challenge is to reduce complexity computationwise.

An additional work that could be taken as inspiration for future implementations is also [9], describing a bio-inspired vehicle collision detection system using the neural network of a locust. While this work uses effectively cameras to process videos, our project would aim to do this with a CA abstracting the photo-receptor layer of the locust using a CA lattice.

References

1. Ando, N., Kanzaki, R.: Using insects to drive mobile robots–hybrid robots bridge the gap between biological and artificial systems. Arthropod Struct. Dev. 46(5), 723–735 (2017)
2. Avidan, S.: Support vector tracking. IEEE Trans. Pattern Anal. Mach. Intell. 26(8), 1064–1072 (2004)
3. Canny, J.: A computational approach to edge detection. In: Readings in Computer Vision, pp. 184–203. Elsevier (1987)
4. Davis, E., Marcus, G.: Commonsense reasoning and commonsense knowledge in artificial intelligence. Commun. ACM 58(9), 92–103 (2015)

5. Deriche, R.: Optimal edge detection using recursive filtering. Int. J. Comput. Vis. **2**, 167–187 (1987)

6. Frye, M.: Elementary motion detectors. Curr. Biol. **25**(6), R215–R217 (2015)

7. Georgoudas, I., Kyriakos, P., Sirakoulis, G., Andreadis, I.: An FPGA implemented cellular automaton crowd evacuation model inspired by the electrostatic-induced potential fields. Microprocess. Microsyst. **34**(7), 285–300 (2010)

8. Guo, J., Ren, T., Huang, L., Liu, X., Cheng, M.M., Wu, G.: Video salient object detection via cross-frame cellular automata. In: 2017 IEEE International Conference on Multimedia and Expo (ICME), pp. 325–330. IEEE (2017)

9. Hartbauer, M.: Simplified bionic solutions: a simple bio-inspired vehicle collision detection system. Bioinspiration Biomim. **12**(2), 026007 (2017)

10. Ioannidis, K., Andreadis, I., Sirakoulis, G.C.: An edge preserving image resizing method based on cellular automata. In: Sirakoulis, G.C., Bandini, S. (eds.) ACRI 2012. LNCS, vol. 7495, pp. 375–384. Springer, Heidelberg (2012). https://doi.org/10.1007/978-3-642-33350-7_39

11. Khan, S.D., Bandini, S., Basalamah, S.M., Vizzari, G.: Analyzing crowd behavior in naturalistic conditions: identifying sources and sinks and characterizing main flows. Neurocomputing **177**, 543–563 (2016)

12. Kumar, T., Sahoo, G.: A novel method of edge detection using cellular automata. Int. J. Comput. Appl. **9**(4), 38–44 (2010)

13. Linan-Cembrano, G., Carranza, L., Rind, C., Zarandy, A., Soininen, M., Rodriguez-Vazquez, A.: Insect-vision inspired collision warning vision processor for automobiles. IEEE Circ. Syst. Mag. **8**(2), 6–24 (2008)

14. Popovici, A., Popovici, D.: Cellular automata in image processing. In: Fifteenth International Symposium on Mathematical Theory of Networks and Systems, vol. 1, pp. 1–6 (2002)

15. Prewitt, J.M.: Object enhancement and extraction. Pict. Process. Psychopictorics **10**(1), 15–19 (1970)

16. Qin, Y., Lu, H., Xu, Y., Wang, H.: Saliency detection via cellular automata. In: 2015 IEEE Conference on Computer Vision and Pattern Recognition (CVPR), pp. 110–119. IEEE (2015)

17. Roberts, L.G.: Machine perception of three-dimensional solids. Ph.D. thesis, Massachusetts Institute of Technology (1963)

18. Rundo, L., et al.: Neuro-radiosurgery treatments: MRI brain tumor seeded image segmentation based on a cellular automata model. In: El Yacoubi, S., Wąs, J., Bandini, S. (eds.) ACRI 2016. LNCS, vol. 9863, pp. 323–333. Springer, Cham (2016). https://doi.org/10.1007/978-3-319-44365-2_32

19. Sobel, I.: An isotropic 3 × 3 image gradient operator. In: Machine Vision for Three-Dimensional Scenes, pp. 376–379 (1990)

20. Toffoli, T., Margolus, N.: Cellular Automata Machines: A New Environment for Modeling. MIT Press, Cambridge (1987)

21. Wolfram, S.: Cellular automata as models of complexity. Nature **311**(5985), 419–424 (1984)

22. Yilmaz, A., Javed, O., Shah, M.: Object tracking: a survey. ACM Comput. Surv. (CSUR) **38**(4), 13 (2006)

Multi-Agent Systems

Coexistence in Three-Species Cyclic Competition: Lattice-Based Versus Lattice-Free Individual-Based Models

Aisling J. Daly$^{(\boxtimes)}$, Ward Quaghebeur, Tim Depraetere, Jan M. Baetens, and Bernard De Baets

KERMIT, Department of Data Analysis and Mathematical Modelling, Ghent University, Ghent, Belgium
aisling.daly@ugent.be

Abstract. Individual-based modelling is an increasingly popular framework for modelling biological systems. Many of these models represent space as a lattice, imposing unrealistic limitations on the movement of the modelled individuals. We adapt existing models of three competing species by using a lattice-free approach, thereby improving the realism of the spatial dynamics. We retrieve the same qualitative dynamics as the lattice-based approach. However, by facilitating a higher spatial heterogeneity and allowing for small spatial refuges to form and persist, the maintenance of coexistence is promoted. This corresponds well with experimental results.

1 Background

Spatially explicit individual-based modelling is an increasingly popular framework for simulating a wide range of phenomena in various fields of research [13, 28,29], including racial segregation [4], microbial growth [17], pandemics [23], and multicellular self-organisation [27]. These models can reproduce a system's complex behaviour at the macroscopic level by modelling the characteristics and interactions of its individuals, whether these be cars, people, microbes, or other entities, through simple rules at the microscopic level. The emergent macroscopic dynamics can then be analysed to gain insight into the fundamental mechanisms underpinning the system, a key example being mechanisms that permit the coexistence of individuals of multiple types or species, even when these are engaged in competition. Determining whether this coexistence can be maintained, and under which conditions, is a major focus of modelling studies. In particular, a cyclic competition scheme has been used extensively in literature to investigate the mechanisms underlying coexistence of competing species, yielding valuable insights [25,30]. Such a competition scheme, where there is no strict hierarchy among the species, has been observed in natural systems of, among others, coral reefs, plant ecosystems, lizard mating strategies, and bacterial communities [8,15,16,32].

© Springer Nature Switzerland AG 2018
G. Mauri et al. (Eds.): ACRI 2018, LNCS 11115, pp. 115–124, 2018.
https://doi.org/10.1007/978-3-319-99813-8_10

Although their inherent flexibility allows individual-based models to be used in many different settings, this generality can however lead to oversimplifications, a very common example being the use of a lattice to represent space (e.g. [18,20,30,35]), thereby imposing an artificial restriction on the positioning of individuals, who typically occupy one lattice cell each. Although justified in applications where the geometry of the lattice cells has an actual meaning, such as urban planning modelling [31], the use of a lattice deviates significantly from reality when modelling biological systems [11]. Namely, the mobility of individuals in this lattice-based setting is restricted to displacement to one of their neighbouring lattice cells, uncharacteristic of the real movement of individuals [1], and precluding motile behaviour (the ability to move deliberately and actively). To mitigate these disadvantages, some lattice-free approaches have been developed [6,12], however these have focused on active matter rather than on species competition and coexistence.

2   Model Description

2.1   Model Versions

To investigate whether a lattice-free approach can enhance our understanding of coexistence mechanisms, we employ a spatially explicit individual-based model of a community of three species engaged in cyclic competition. To do so, we adapt the two-dimensional model proposed by [30] to account for (i) a lattice-free representation of space, and (ii) a continuous migration mechanism. We then assess the impact of these adaptations on the coexistence of the community by examining the respective extinction probabilities of the *in silico* species relative to those obtained using the less realistic lattice-based approach.

Benchmark Lattice-Based Model. The model proposed in [30] takes into account three key demographic processes at the individual level: reproduction, competition, and migration, which occur at rates μ, σ, and ϵ, respectively, identical for all species. For simplicity, we consider equal rates of reproduction and competition, and (without loss of generality) determine the time unit by fixing $\mu = \sigma = 1$. We consider two-dimensional space divided into a regular lattice of identical square cells, occupied by at most one individual. The system mobility M is proportional to the typical area explored by one individual per unit time, $M = 2\epsilon N^{-1}$, where N is the number of lattice cells in the system [30].

During each interaction event, a focal cell is randomly selected. If the focal cell is empty, another cell is chosen randomly. If the focal cell is occupied, then one of its four von Neumann neighbours (those sharing an edge) is randomly selected. Reproduction can occur if the neighbouring cell is empty. Competition can occur if the neighbouring cell is occupied by an individual of a different species than the focal individual, with the outcome determined by the cyclic competition scheme: species A beats species B, which beats species C, which beats species A. The defeated individual is removed and the lattice cell becomes empty. Migration can occur irrespective of the neighbouring cell's occupancy: if it is empty, the individual simply moves there, and if it is occupied then the two individuals exchange positions.

Simulations advance by iterating through the following procedure at every time step: an occupied focal cell and one of its neighbouring cells are randomly selected. A random number is drawn to determine which type of interaction will occur: a reproduction event occurs with probability $\frac{\mu}{s}$, a competition event with probability $\frac{\sigma}{s}$, and a migration event with probability $\frac{\epsilon}{s}$, where $s = \mu + \sigma + \epsilon$. The interaction outcome is determined as described above, and the lattice is updated accordingly. The time step is advanced and the procedure is repeated until the end of the simulation is reached. We define one generation as the number of interactions needed so that each cell had the chance to interact on average once, namely N^2.

Lattice-Free Approach. To assess the impact of continuous space on the maintenance of coexistence, we construct a model using the same framework as the benchmark model, except that individuals do not position themselves in lattice cells, but in continuous space. Each individual is represented by a circle of diameter of one unit length, equal to the length of a lattice cell, centred at a certain point (x, y). Two individuals i and j are considered to be neighbours if the Euclidean distance d_{ij} between their centres is less than or equal to one unit, so that they are either touching ($d_{ij} = 1$) or overlapping ($d_{ij} < 1$). We permit a certain maximal overlap between individuals, for reasons of both computational efficiency and biological realism, since the modelled individuals (e.g. bacteria) may slightly deform or cave into each other [33].

To minimize this overlap, thus permitting comparison with the benchmark lattice-based model (which assumes that individuals do not share space), we incorporate a repulsive force between overlapping individuals, modelled as soft spheres [21],

$$\mathbf{F}_{ij} = \begin{cases} \alpha\left(1 - d_{ij}\right)^{\frac{5}{2}}\mathbf{r}_{ij} & \text{, if } d_{ij} < 1, \\ \mathbf{0} & \text{, otherwise,} \end{cases} \tag{1}$$

where $\mathbf{F}_{ij}$ is the resulting repulsive force on individual i induced by individual j, α is a coefficient, d_{ij} is the distance between the centres of the individuals, $\mathbf{r}_{ij}$ is the vector defined by the centres of the two individuals, pointing outwards from the centre of individual i, and $\mathbf{0}$ is the zero vector. Hence, no repulsion occurs between individuals that are touching but not overlapping, or not touching at all.

When multiple individuals overlap with a given individual, vector addition of the individual forces applies. At the end of each generation, the repulsive force is computed for every individual, after which their positions are updated accordingly. Multiple iterations are executed until the minimum distance between the centres of neighbouring individuals exceeds a given threshold.

The distance travelled during one migration event is similar for the lattice-free and lattice-based models, since in the former case individuals can move a distance of one unit (the diameter of their body), analogous to the lattice-based displacement to a neighbouring cell (also having length one unit). Migration events may involve two neighbours exchanging their positions, again similar to the lattice-based model. Hence, we can consider the mobility $M = 2\epsilon N^{-1}$, analogous to the lattice-based model, thereby allowing us to compare the two approaches.

An individual positioned at (x, y) can reproduce by splitting itself into two daughter individuals of equal size, positioned at $(x + r \cos\theta, y + r \sin\theta)$ and $(x - r \cos\theta, y - r \sin\theta)$, where r is the radius of an individual (fixed as 0.5 units) and θ is a randomly chosen angle in $[0, \pi]$. Reproduction can occur when an individual's neighbourhood is not fully populated, i.e. it has less than six neighbours, the maximum number of neighbours in a hexagonal packing of circles.

3   *In Silico* Experiments

For the lattice-based approach, a 100×100 lattice is initialized with 10% empty lattice cells, and the remaining cells evenly and randomly distributed among the three species. Periodic boundary conditions are imposed to avoid boundary effects. Next, individual interactions are simulated as described in Sect. 2.1 for 10 000 generations.

The lattice-free approach is evolved in an analogous manner, with certain adaptations. A 100 unit $\times$ 100 unit space is initialized with 9000 individuals evenly and randomly distributed among the three species. At the start of each generation, a cell list [24] and Verlet list [34] are constructed to efficiently keep track of each individual's neighbours, as defined in Sect. 2.1. These two specialised data structures were initially developed for molecular dynamics simulations, and permit the practical simulation of large numbers of interacting individuals (particles). The cell list subdivides the continuous *in silico* domain into blocks and sorts the individuals into these blocks, so that interactions are computed between individuals in the same or neighbouring blocks. The Verlet list overcomes the need to determine an individual's neighbours at each interaction: by determining them only once, saving this information and updating it when needed, the simulation efficiency is also improved.

After an interaction event, the Verlet list and the *in silico* domain are updated accordingly. At the end of a generation, the repulsion mechanism described in Sect. 2.1 is executed, with $\alpha = 5$ and a threshold of 0.95 for the minimum distance between the centres of individuals, so that the repulsion mechanism converges rapidly (provided system carrying capacity is not reached).

At each time step, the identity and location of each individual are tracked. The probability of extinction P_{ext} is calculated at the end of the simulations as the fraction of simulations with at least one extinction event. Patchiness, a measure of spatial aggregation, is calculated as the average fraction of neighbours of the same species [22]. Similarly, the probability of interspecific encounter (PIE) is calculated as the average fraction of an individual's neighbours that are predator species [14]. A pressure distribution, visualizing the number of individuals within a certain distance, and thus spatial heterogeneity, is calculated from the position of the individuals, using the method described in [7].

The lattice-based approach is compared with the lattice-free approach to assess the impact of the latter on the probability of extinction. Both models are implemented in Mathematica (version 11.0, Wolfram Research, Champaign, IL, USA). For each model, the migration rate ϵ is varied in order to test different values of mobility M between 2×10^{-4} and 1.6×10^{-2}, while all other parameters are fixed. For each initial condition, 50 replicate simulations are conducted. Simulations are carried out using the High Performance Computing infrastructure at Ghent University.

4   Results and Discussion

Figure 1 shows an example of the spatial dynamics arising from the lattice-based and lattice-free approaches. Both approaches result in the same qualitative behaviour, with the individuals arranging themselves in stable spatial structures, thereby facilitating coexistence of all species. Moreover, these emerging spatial structures are of equal size for the same mobility, irrespective of the approach, thus resembling the results obtained with a similar lattice-free model [5]. However, the latter model considers a system where the total density of individuals is conserved, which is not always realistic.

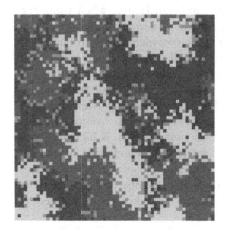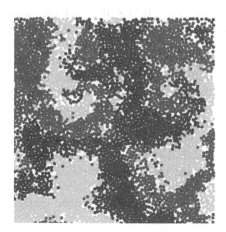

Fig. 1. Example of the spatial dynamics obtained for $M = 2 \times 10^{-4}$ with lattice-based approach (left) and lattice-free approach (right).

Figure 2 shows the extinction probability P_{ext} as a function of mobility M for both approaches. In both cases, we can observe a qualitative behaviour similar to the findings of [30], namely a higher probability of extinction P_{ext} for higher mobility M. However, the lattice-based P_{ext} is consistently higher than the lattice-free P_{ext} for the same mobility M. For the former, the transition from

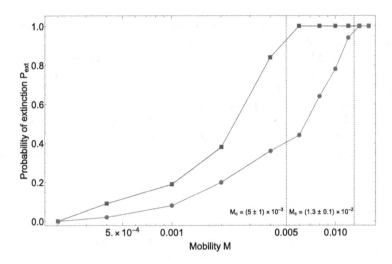

Fig. 2. Extinction probability P_{ext} (50 simulations, 10 000 generations) versus mobility M for the lattice-based (blue, square) and lattice-free approach (red, circle). (Color figure online)

stable coexistence ($P_{ext} = 0$) to extinction ($P_{ext} = 1$) sharpens at the critical mobility $M_c = (5 \pm 1) \times 10^{-3}$. In contrast, this happens at critical mobility $M_c = (1.3 \pm 0.1) \times 10^{-2}$ for the lattice-free approach. Hence, when using the latter approach coexistence is maintained for a wider parameter range than its lattice-based counterpart, and coexistence may be considered more robust.

By not constraining the individuals to lattice cells, the lattice-free approach permits individuals more freedom to position themselves. This influences the formation of spatial structures. In Fig. 3 we show an example of the pressure distribution, representing the number of individuals within a certain distance, therefore visualizing the spatial heterogeneity of the system. Comparing this plot with the spatial species distribution reveals that pressure is highest inside the spatial structures, and lowest along the borders between clusters of species, where interactions are manifold. This heterogeneity is in contrast to the lattice-based model, where the pressure is spatially homogeneous, and explains the more robust coexistence, since spatial heterogeneity is known to promote coexistence [26].

It is known that threatened species, when reduced to a few individuals, often retreat into small spatial structures called refuges [19]. Figure 4 shows an example of an *in silico* spatial refuge obtained with both approaches. When spatial refuges become surrounded by their predator, they are quickly destroyed [19]. However, inspection of the simulation results reveals that refuges tend to be more resilient in the lattice-free approach. Individuals can arrange themselves more compactly, since the highest density arrangement of circles in a continuous space (a hexagonal tessellation) leads to an area occupancy of $\pi/\sqrt{12}$, which is greater than the highest area occupancy that can be achieved with a

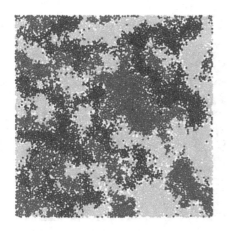 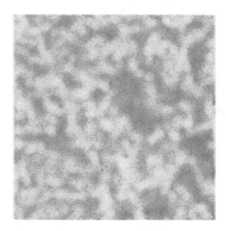

Fig. 3. Example of the spatial dynamics (left) obtained with the lattice-free approach for $M = 2 \times 10^{-4}$, and corresponding pressure distribution (right), representing the number of individuals within a certain distance (darker colour indicates higher density of individuals).

square lattice arrangement, namely $\pi/4$ [9]. This effect can be seen in Fig. 3, where species aggregations have clearly defined borders and permit fewer hostile intrusions. This increases their robustness in terms of maintaining coexistence, implying a lower extinction probability P_{ext} at the same mobility rate. This corresponds with experimental findings, where spatial refuges have been found to be important for maintaining diversity in predator-prey systems of, among others, crab-molluscs [2] and spider-bugs [10]. Furthermore, it reflects *in vivo* ecosystems, which are typically composed of a few dominant species and many rare species [3,36]. We can thus conclude that, by constraining individuals to a lattice, the lattice-based approach tends to underestimate the ability to maintain coexistence, compared to the more realistic lattice-free approach.

Thus, while the lattice-free approach produces qualitatively similar dynamics to the lattice-based approach, the maintenance of coexistence is affected by the more realistic spatial configurations that can arise from the former model. Furthermore, a lattice-free approach opens up many possibilities of extensions to study scenarios related to the fundamental persistence of biological systems. For example, we have also investigated a continuous mobility mechanism, whereby individuals no longer move in steps of length strictly equal to one unit, but instead may take steps of a random length less than a specified maximum of 1.5 units. While this is a more realistic implementation of individual movement, we found that it does not lead to significantly different results than those obtained with the implementation reported in this paper. Notably, the spatial dynamics and the relationship between the system's mobility and its probability of extinction are qualitatively very similar (results not shown).

The modelling framework outlined in this work would also permit various extensions to study motility (deliberate and active movement), an example being

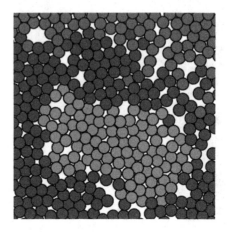

Fig. 4. Examples of spatial refuges retrieved with lattice-based (left) and lattice-free (right) approaches.

chasing and escaping behaviour. Such scenarios involving directed movement would also benefit from the additional spatial degrees of freedom offered by the lattice-free approach, and further studies on this topic are planned.

5   Conclusions

We have compared the lattice-based individual-based model for a three-species cyclic competition scheme proposed in [30] to a more realistic lattice-free model. By permitting more spatial heterogeneity and enhancing the formation and persistence of spatial refuges, the lattice-free approach tends to be more robust in terms of maintaining coexistence.

We have focused on the simplest possible lattice-free model so that we are able to make the most direct comparison with the lattice-based benchmark. Avoiding the restrictions and simplifications that are intrinsic to a lattice-based approach is of great importance for any future work seeking to understand the complex and inherently lattice-free phenomena found in real world biological systems, such as directed movement, the effect of variable body sizes, or biased movement. Overall, a lattice-free approach improves the realism of the individual-based model, and allows us to study more realistic scenarios related to the conditions under which coexistence is maintained in biological systems.

Acknowledgements. The authors gratefully acknowledge the financial support of the Belgian Science Policy Office (IUAP Contract No. P7/25). The computational resources (Stevin Supercomputer Infrastructure) and services used in this paper were provided by the VSC (Flemish Supercomputer Center), funded by Ghent University, the Hercules Foundation and the Flemish Government, department EWI.

References

1. Adamson, M.W., Morozov, A.Y.: Revising the role of species mobility in maintaining biodiversity in communities with cyclic competition. Bull. Math. Biol. **74**(9), 2004–2031 (2012)
2. Arsenault, D.J., Himmelman, J.H.: Size-related changes in vulnerability to predators and spatial refuge use by juvenile Iceland scallops Chlamys islandica. Mar. Ecol. Prog. Ser. **140**(1–3), 115–122 (1996)
3. Ashby, M.N., Rine, J., Mongodin, E.F., Nelson, K.E., Dimster-Denk, D.: Serial analysis of rRNA genes and the unexpected dominance of rare members of microbial communities. Appl. Environ. Microbiol. **73**(14), 4532–4542 (2007)
4. Auchincloss, A.H., Riolo, R.L., Brown, D.G., Cook, J., Diez Roux, A.V.: An agent-based model of income inequalities in diet in the context of residential segregation. Am. J. Prev. Med. **40**(3), 303–311 (2011)
5. Avelino, P.P., Bazeia, D., Losano, L., Menezes, J., de Oliveira, B.F.: Spiral patterns and biodiversity in lattice-free Lotka-Volterra models, pp. 1–5. arXiv preprint arXiv 1710 (2017)
6. Beppu, K., Izri, Z., Gohya, J., Eto, K., Ichikawa, M., Maeda, Y.T.: Geometry-driven collective ordering of bacterial vortices. Soft Matter **13**(29), 5038–5043 (2017)
7. Bernard, E.P., Krauth, W.: Two-step melting in two dimensions: first-order liquid-hexatic transition. Phys. Rev. Lett. **107**(15), 155704 (2011)
8. Buss, L.W.: Competitive networks: nontransitive competitive relationships in cryptic coral reef environments. Am. Nat. **113**(2), 223–234 (1979)
9. Chang, H.C., Wang, L.C.: A simple proof of Thue's theorem on circle packing, pp. 1–4. arXiv preprint arXiv 1708 (2010)
10. Finke, D.L., Denno, R.F.: Spatial refuge from intraguild predation: implications for prey suppression and trophic cascades. Oecologia **149**(2), 265–275 (2006)
11. Ginovart, M.: INDISIM, an individual-based discrete simulation model to study bacterial cultures. J. Theor. Biol. **214**(2), 305–319 (2002)
12. Gonnella, G., Lamura, A., Suma, A.: Phase segregation in a system of active dumbbells. Int. J. Mod. Phys. C **25**(12), 1441004 (2014)
13. Grimm, V., Berger, U., DeAngelis, D.L., Polhill, J.G., Giske, J., Railsback, S.F.: The ODD protocol: a review and first update. Ecol. Model. **221**(23), 2760–2768 (2010)
14. Hurlbert, S.H.: The measurement of niche overlap and some relatives. Ecology **59**(1), 67–77 (1978)
15. Kerr, B., Riley, M.A., Feldman, M.W., Bohannan, B.J.M.: Local dispersal promotes biodiversity in a real-life game of rock-paper-scissors. Nature **418**(6894), 171–174 (2002)
16. Kirkup, B.C., Riley, M.A.: Antibiotic-mediated antagonism leads to a bacterial game of rock-paper-scissors in vivo. Nature **428**(6981), 412–414 (2004)
17. Kreft, J.U., Booth, G., Wimpenny, J.W.T.: BacSim, a simulator for individual-based modelling of bacterial colony growth. Microbiology **144**(12), 3275–3287 (1998)
18. Kreft, J.U., Picioreanu, C., Wimpenny, J.W.T., van Loosdrecht, M.C.M.: Individual-based modelling of biofilms. Microbiology **147**(Pt 11), 2897–2912 (2001)
19. Laird, R.A., Schamp, B.S.: Does local competition increase the coexistence of species in intransitive networks? Ecology **89**(1), 237–247 (2008)

20. Laird, R.A., Schamp, B.S.: Species coexistence, intransitivity, and topological variation in competitive tournaments. J. Theor. Biol. **256**(1), 90–95 (2009)
21. Landau, L., Lifshitz, E.: EM Lifshitz Theory of Elasticity, 3rd edn. Pergamon Press, Oxford (1986)
22. Lloyd, M.: Mean crowding. J. Anim. Ecol. **36**(1), 1–30 (1967)
23. Luisa, M., et al.: Mitigation measures for pandemic influenza in Italy: an individual-based model considering different scenarios. PLOS One **3**(3), e1790 (2008)
24. Mattson, W., Rice, B.M.: Near-neighbor calculations using a modified cell-linked list method. Comput. Phys. Commun. **119**(2), 135–148 (1999)
25. May, R.M., Leonard, W.J.: Nonlinear aspects of competition between three species. Soc. Ind. Appl. Math. **29**(2), 243–253 (1975)
26. Neuhauser, C.: Mathematical challenges in spatial ecology. Not. AMS **48**(11), 1304–1314 (2001)
27. Osborne, J.M., Fletcher, A.G., Pitt-Francis, J.M., Maini, P.K., Gavaghan, D.J.: Comparing individual-based approaches to modelling the self-organization of multicellular tissues. PLOS Comput. Biol. **13**(2), 1–34 (2017)
28. Railsback, S.F., Grimm, V.: Agent-Based and Individual-Based Modeling: A Practical Introduction. Princeton University Press, Princeton (2011)
29. Railsback, S.F., Lytinen, S.L., Jackson, S.K.: Agent-based simulation platforms: review and development recommendations. Simulation **82**(9), 609–623 (2006)
30. Reichenbach, T., Mobilia, M., Frey, E.: Mobility promotes and jeopardizes biodiversity in rock-paper-scissors games. Nature **448**(7157), 1046–1049 (2007)
31. Schelling, T.C.: Dynamic models of segregation. J. Math. Sociol. **1**(2), 143–186 (1969)
32. Taylor, D.R., Aarssen, L.W.: Complex competitive relationships among genotypes of three perennial grasses: implications for species coexistence. Am. Nat. **136**(3), 305–327 (1990)
33. Touhami, A., Nysten, B., Dufrêne, Y.: Nanoscale mapping of the elasticity of microbial cells by atomic force microscopy. Microbiology **19**(11), 4539–4543 (2003)
34. Verlet, L.: Computer "experiments" on classical fluids. Phys. Rev. **159**(1), 98–103 (1967)
35. Vukov, J., Szolnoki, A., Szabó, G.: Diverging fluctuations in a spatial five-species cyclic dominance game. Phys. Rev. E - Statist. Nonlinear Soft Matter Phys. **88**(2), 1–8 (2013)
36. Wilsey, B.J.: Realistically low species evenness does not alter grassland species-richness - productivity relationships. Ecology **85**(10), 2693–2700 (2004)

Towards Self-organizing Sensor Networks: Game-Theoretic ε-Learning Automata-Based Approach

Jakub Gąsior[1]([✉]), Franciszek Seredyński[1], and Rolf Hoffmann[2]

[1] Department of Mathematics and Natural Sciences,
Cardinal Stefan Wyszyński University, Warsaw, Poland
{j.gasior,f.seredynski}@uksw.edu.pl
[2] Technische Universität Darmstadt, Darmstadt, Germany
hoffmann@ra.informatik.tu-darmstadt.de

Abstract. We consider a problem of lifetime optimization in Wireless Sensor Networks. The purpose of the system is to find a global activity schedule maximizing the lifetime of the Wireless Sensor Network while monitoring some area with a given measure of Quality of Service. The main idea of the proposed approach is to convert the problem of a global optimization into a problem of self-organization of a distributed multi-agent system, where agents take part in a game and search a solution in the form of a Nash equilibrium. We propose two game-theoretic models related to the problem of the lifetime optimization in Wireless Sensor Network and apply deterministic ε-Learning Automata as players in the games. We present results of an experimental study showing the ability of reaching optimal solutions in the course of Learning Automata self-organization by local interactions in an iterated game.

Keywords: Learning Automata · Non-cooperative games
Self-organization · Wireless Sensor Networks · Network lifetime

1 Introduction

Fast development of information and communication technologies opens new perspectives for creating Wireless Sensor Network (WSN)-based intelligent services oriented on collecting, sending and processing large amount of data. This idea is shortly termed as Ambient Intelligence and Internet of Things and is based in particular on different applications of Wireless Sensor Networks (WSNs). WSNs are networks of large number of tiny computer-communication devices called sensors deployed in some area, which sense a local environment, collect local data depending on an application and send them via a special node called a sink to an external world for processing and taking a decision.

In many applications, such as e.g., monitoring remote and difficult to access areas, sensors are equipped with single use batteries which can not be recharged.

© Springer Nature Switzerland AG 2018
G. Mauri et al. (Eds.): ACRI 2018, LNCS 11115, pp. 125–136, 2018.
https://doi.org/10.1007/978-3-319-99813-8_11

From the point of view of Quality of Service (QoS) of such a WSN, one of the most important issues is its operational lifetime. After a deployment (e.g., by an aircraft) of sensors at random locations of some area they should self-organize: to recognize their nearest neighbors to be able to communicate and start taking locally decisions in subsequent moments of time about turning on or off their batteries to monitor events. These decisions will directly influence the lifetime of the network and should be taken in such a way as to maximize it. The problem of lifetime maximization is closely related to the coverage problem. A group of sensors monitoring some area is usually redundant, i.e., usually more than one sensor cover monitored targets and forms of redundancy can be different. By solving the coverage problem one can indirectly also solve the problem of maximization of WSN lifetime.

There exists a number of algorithms to solve the problem of coverage/lifetime maximization. They are classified either as centralized and assume availability of entire information and a solution is delivered usually in the form of a schedule of activities of all sensors during the entire lifetime, or distributed, where a solution is found on the basis of only partial information about the network. Because these problems are known as NP-complete [4] centralized algorithms are oriented either on delivery of exact solutions for specific cases (see, e.g. [3]) or applying heuristics or metaheuristics to find approximate solutions (see, e.g. [7,14]). The main drawback of centralized algorithms is that a schedule of sensors' activities must be found outside the network and delivered to it before starting operation. Therefore distributed algorithms become more and more popular because they assume reactivity of sensors in real time, and they are scalable in contrast to centralized algorithms.

A number of such algorithms based on applying Learning Automata (LA) [6,11] or Cellular Automata (CA) [13] has been proposed recently. Each of these techniques taken separately has own advantages and disadvantages. The main disadvantage of classical CA is a lack of reactivity when they are applied to solve optimization problems. On the other hand, a distinctive feature of LA is the ability of interaction with an environment [1,2]. We believe that combining both techniques is a rational approach in an attempt to solve optimization problems. Some works to extend classical CA to the second order CA which are able to self-adopt have been also appeared recently [5] and they are based on multi-agent game-theoretic paradigm and we follow these both lines of research.

In this paper we propose a novel approach to the problem of coverage/lifetime optimization based on multi-agent interpretation of the problem and game-theoretic interaction between players participating in a non-cooperative game [10]. Each agent-player is oriented on the minimization of its level of redundant coverage of monitored targets shared with other agent-players. The functions of agent-players are performed by deterministic LA. We show that the agent-players are able to find in a fully distributed way a solution defined as a Nash equilibrium (NE) [8] corresponding to balanced coverage of (POIs) which reduces batteries expenditures and prolongs the lifetime of WSNs.

The structure of the paper is the following. Section 2 describes the problem of coverage/lifetime optimization in WSNs and the next section presents a multi-agent interpretation of the problem. In Sect. 4 two game-theoretic models related to the studied problem are proposed, and in Sect. 5 these games are experimentally studied with the use of deterministic LA as players. The last section contains conclusions.

2 Sensor Networks and Coverage and Lifetime Problems

It is assumed that a sensor network $S = \{s_1, s_2, ..., s_N\}$ consisting of N sensors is deployed over some area, where M POIs should be monitored. Sensors are distributed randomly, each sensor can monitor POIs in a sensing range R_s and has a non-rechargeable battery of capacity b. Each sensor can work in one of two modes: an *active* mode when battery is turned on and a unit of its energy is consumed and POIs in its sensing range are monitored; and a *sleep* mode when battery is turned off and POIs in its sensing range are not monitored.

It is assumed that decisions about turning on/off batteries are taken in discrete moments of time t. It is also assumed that there exists some QoS measure evaluating the performance of WSN. As such a measure one can accept a value of coverage defined as a ratio of POIs covered by active sensors to whole number M of POIs. At a given moment of time this ratio should not be lower than some predefined value of q $(0 < q \leq 1)$. Lifetime of WSN can be defined as a number of consecutive time steps in which the coverage is within the predefined value of q.

Figure 1(a) shows an example of a sensor network consisting of $N = 4$ sensors. One can notice that if a given sensor is active and some other neighbor sensors are also active than a number of POIs in the sensing ranges of these sensors are covered by more than one sensor. This possibly redundant coverage is related to extra use of sensors' batteries which has a negative impact on the lifetime of WSN. Figure 1(b) shows a graph of interaction depicting relations between sensors and POIs of exemplary WSN from Fig. 1(a).

One can notice that the graph has two types of vertices: black square vertices denote sensors and rectangle vertices denote POIs. A sensor s_i in an active mode covers m_i POIs which can be classified in the following way: POIs which can be covered only by sensor s_i (m_{i0} is a number of such POIs), POIs which are shared by sensors s_i and s_j and can be covered by part or all these sensors (m_{ij}), POIs which are shared by sensors s_i, s_j and s_k and can be covered by part or all these sensors (m_{ijk}), etc.

Sensors which share one or more types of POIs are immediate neighbors. One can see in Fig. 1(b) that e.g., sensors s_2 and s_4 are immediate neighbors because they share m_{24} POIs, and sensors s_1, s_2 and s_3 are immediate neighbors because they share m_{123} POIs.

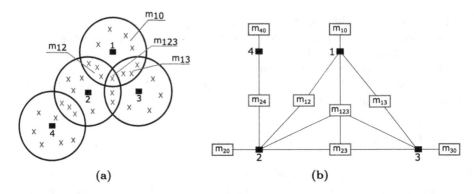

Fig. 1. Example of a sensor network: area view (a), corresponding interaction graph (b).

3   Multi-agent Approach to WSN Lifetime Optimization

Let us assume that each sensor s_i of WSN is controlled by an agent A_i of a multi-agent system consisting of N agents. Each agent has two alternative decisions (actions): $\alpha_i = 0$ (battery is turned off) and $\alpha_i = 1$ (battery is turned on) and neighbor relations between agents are defined by an interaction graph (see, Sect. 2). According to the interaction graph, an agent A_i has k_i immediate neighbors and will receive some reward $rev_i()$ which depends on its decision and decisions of its neighbors (see, Eq. (1)):

$$rev_i(\alpha_i, \alpha_{neigh_1}, \alpha_{neigh_2}, ..., \alpha_{neigh_{K_i}}) = \begin{cases} rev_i^{off} - pen_i^{off}(), & \text{if } \alpha_i = 0 \\ rev_i^{on} - tax_i^{bat}(), & \text{if } \alpha_i = 1, \end{cases} \quad (1)$$

where:

- $\alpha_i, \alpha_{neigh_1}, \alpha_{neigh_2}, \alpha_{neigh_{k_i}}$ – decisions of agent A_i and its neighbors;
- $neigh_{k_i}$ – a number of neighbors of sensor s_i;
- rev_i^{off} – a reward for covering by active neighbor sensors shared POIs while sensor s_i is inactive;
- pen_i^{off} – a penalty for not covering POIs which are in the range of sensing of inactive sensor s_i;
- rev_i^{on} – a reward for covering by active sensor s_i POIs which are in its range;
- tax_i^{bat} – tax for the use of battery by sensor s_i.

More detailed formulation of Eq. 1 (see, Sect. 4) shows that an agent A_i can receive some reward even if it is inactive ($\alpha_i = 0$) and saves its own battery. It happens when some neighbor sensors are active and shared POIs are covered by them, and when a number of not covered POIs does not exceed some threshold value related to a predefined coverage parameter q and penalty for that is lower that obtained reward.

On the other hand, agent A_i receives a reward when it spends energy of its battery, but this reward can be lowered when some other neighbor sensors are active and cover shared POIs. The purpose of each agent is to maximize its total reward which corresponds to finding a local trade-off between requested level of the coverage and expending battery power. This way of behavior of agents is in line with the main goal of this work: finding a global trade-off between requested level of QoS and minimization of battery expenditure to maximize the lifetime of WSN.

There exists many ways to organize the work of agents to realize this global goal. In this paper we propose a game-theoretic approach based on non-cooperative games where agent-players compete for achieving their own goals and a solution of the optimization problem is converted into a problem of searching for Nash equilibrium (NE) by players in a game. Similar game-theoretic approach has been recently successfully applied in the context of solar-powered WSN [9].

4   Game-Theoretic Approach to WSN Lifetime Optimization

One of the main sources of imbalance between the level of coverage of POIs and spending battery power are shared POIs. In particular, one can see from Fig. 1(b) two extreme patterns of sharing: the same number of POIs can be shared by some (perhaps huge) number of sensors (see, m_{123}), and on the other hand – different pairs of sensors can share different sets of POIs (see, m_{12}, m_{13}, m_{23}).

These situations correspond to two different models with different expected solutions, and they are shown in Figs. 2(left) and 3(right), respectively together with corresponding interaction graphs.

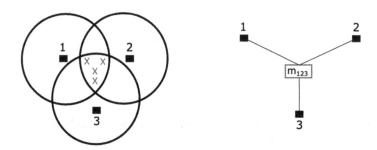

Fig. 2. Model 1: a sensor network (left), corresponding graph interaction (right).

4.1   Model 1: Leader Election Game

In this model (see, Fig. 2) it is assumed that a number of N sensors controlled by corresponding agents share a common set of POIs. A reward obtained by a single agent $rev_i(\alpha_1, \alpha_2, ..., \alpha_i, ..., \alpha_N)$ depends on actions of all agents and can be evaluated according to Eq. (2):

$$rev_i(\alpha_1, \alpha_2, ..., \alpha_i, ..., \alpha_N) = \begin{cases} rev_i^{off}(m_i^{shared\_on}), & \text{if } \alpha_i = 0 \\ rev_i^{on}(m_i), & \text{if } \alpha_i = 1, \end{cases} \quad (2)$$

where:

- $rev_i^{off}() = C_{rev}^{off} \times \frac{m_i^{shared\_on}}{M}$,
- $rev_i^{on}() = C_{rev}^{on} \times \frac{m_i}{M(N_{ij}^{on}+1)} = \frac{C_{rev}^{on}}{N_{ij}^{on}+1}$,

where:

- $m_i^{shared\_on}$ – a number of POIs which are in sensing range of inactive sensor s_i and shared with active neighbor sensors;
- m_i – a number of POIs which are in sensing range of sensor s_i;
- M – a total number of POIs;
- N_{ij}^{on} – a number of active neighbors of sensor s_i;
- $C_{rev}^{off}, C_{rev}^{on}$ – model constants.

In the NE of the game an expected rational behavior of players is such that only one agent-player selects action $\alpha_i = 1$ and remaining players select actions $\alpha_j = 0$ $(i \neq j)$. Therefore this game will be further referred to as the *Leader Election Game*. From definition of NE the following relations between payoffs of players selecting action $\alpha_i = 1$ and players selecting action $\alpha_j = 0$ $(i \neq j)$ should be fulfilled:

$$\frac{C_{rev}^{on}}{N_{ij}^{on}+1} > C_{rev}^{off} \times \frac{m_i^{shared\_on}}{M}, \text{ for } N_{ij}^{on} = 0,$$
$$C_{rev}^{off} \times \frac{m_i^{shared\_on}}{M} > \frac{C_{rev}^{on}}{N_{ij}^{on}+1}, \text{ for } N_{ij}^{on} > 0. \quad (3)$$

Thus, we obtain:

$$C_{rev}^{on} > C_{rev}^{off}, \text{ for } N_{ij}^{on} = 0,$$
$$C_{rev}^{off} > \frac{C_{rev}^{on}}{N_{ij}^{on}+1}, \text{ for } N_{ij}^{on} > 0. \quad (4)$$

Let us assume that:

$$a = C_{rev}^{off}, b = C_{rev}^{on}, c \leq 0, \quad (5)$$

so:

$$b > a, \quad \text{for } N_{ij}^{on} = 0,$$
$$a > \frac{b}{N_{ij}^{on}+1}, \text{ for } N_{ij}^{on} > 0. \quad (6)$$

Finally we can construct for Model 1 the following (see, Table 1) payoff function $u_i^1(\alpha_1, \alpha_2, ..., \alpha_N)$ of the game:

Table 1. Payoff function $u_i^1(\alpha_1, \alpha_2, ..., \alpha_N)$ for $i - th$ player.

	Number of opponents selecting action $\alpha = 1$				
	0	1	2	...	$N-1$
0 (off)	c	a	a	...	a
1 (on)	b	$b/2$	$b/3$	...	$b/(N-1)$

We will accept the following values for parameters of the game: $a = 1, b = 1.5$ and $c = 0$. The table shows a payoff of $i - th$ player selecting either the action "0" or the action "1" as a function of a number of remaining players selecting the action "1". If $i - th$ player selects "0" and 0 remaining players are "on" than the player receives the payoff equal to $c = 0$, while if at least one of remaining players is "on" the player receives the value of payoff equal to $a = 1$.

If $i - th$ player selects "1" and all remaining players are "off" the player receives the payoff equal to $b = 1.5$, but if more remaining players are "on" he receives lower value of the payoff which depends on the number of players being "on". Let us assume a two players $(N = 2)$ game. The following action profiles exist in the game: $(0, 0), (0, 1), (1, 0)$ and $(1, 1)$. Let us consider the action profile $(0, 1)$. Player 1 payoff $u_1^1(0, 1) = 1$ and player 2 payoff $u_2^1(0, 1) = 1.5$. If the player 1 changes its action it results in lowering its payoff to $u_1^1(1, 1) = 0.75$.

Similarly for the second player. It means that no player has a reason to change its action, and considered action profile is a NE point. This NE provides a perfect balance between coverage of POIs and spending battery power which maximizes lifetime of the considered network.

4.2   Model 2 - Synchronized Local Leader Election Game

In this model (see, Fig. 3) local sets of POIs are shared by neighbor sensors. The reward of agent A_i depends on its action α_i and the actions of its two nearest neighbors $rev_i(\alpha_{i\ominus 1}, \alpha_i, \alpha_{i\oplus 1})$ and can be calculated according to Eq. (7):

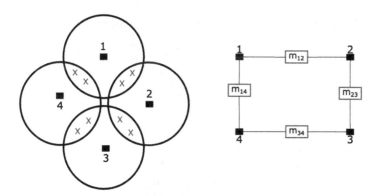

Fig. 3. Model 2: a sensor network (left), corresponding graph interaction (right).

$$rev_i(\alpha_{i\ominus 1}, \alpha_i, \alpha_{i\oplus 1}) = \begin{cases} rev_i^{off}() - pen_i^{off}(), & \text{if } \alpha_i = 0, \\ rev_i^{on}(), & \text{if } \alpha_i = 1, \end{cases} \qquad (7)$$

where:

$$- rev_i^{off}() = C_{rev}^{off} \times \frac{\sum_j m_{ij}^{shared\_on}}{M},$$

$$- pen_i^{off}() = \begin{cases} C_{pen}^{off} \times \frac{m_i - \sum_j m_{ij}^{shared\_on}}{M}, & \text{if } (m_i - \sum_j m_{ij}^{shared\_on}) \geq m_i(1-q), \\ 0, & \text{otherwise,} \end{cases}$$

$$- rev_i^{on}() = C_{rev}^{on} \times \left(\frac{m_i - \sum_j m_{ij}^{shared\_on}}{M} + \frac{\sum_j (m_{ij}^{shared\_on}/(N_{ij}^{on}+1))}{M}\right),$$

where:

- $rev_i^{off}()$ – a reward of inactive agent A_i for covering shared POIs by active neighbor sensors;
- $pen_i^{off}()$ – a penalty of inactive agent A_i for not covering its POIs when their number exceeds threshold value $m_i(1-q)$;
- $rev_i^{on}()$ – a reward of active agent A_i for covering its POIs and redundant covering by active neighbor sensors.

From the point of view of rational players each second player in a ring consisting of N player (N – even number) should select action "1" while remaining players should select action "0". It means that the following relations between rewards of a player i in the game should be fulfilled in order to achieve NE:

- $b = rev_i^{on}(0,1,0) > a = rev_i^{off}(1,0,1)$,
- $a = rev_i^{off}(1,0,1) > d_1 = rev_i^{off}(1,0,0) = rev_i^{off}(0,0,1) > c$,
- $a = rev_i^{off}(1,0,1) > d_2 = rev_i^{on}(1,1,0) = rev_i^{on}(0,1,1) > c$,
- $a = rev_i^{off}(1,0,1) > d_3 = rev_i^{on}(1,1,1) > c$,
- $d_2 = rev_i^{on}(0,1,1) > d_1 = rev_i^{off}(0,0,1) > c$.

The payoff function $u_i^2(\alpha_{i\ominus 1}, \alpha_i, \alpha_{i\oplus 1})$ (see, Table 2) fulfills these requirements.

Table 2. Payoff function $u_i^2(\alpha_{i\ominus 1}, \alpha_i, \alpha_{i\oplus 1})$ for $i - th$ player.

No.	$\alpha_{i\ominus 1}$	α_i	$\alpha_{i\oplus 1}$	$u_i^2(\alpha_{i\ominus 1}, \alpha_i, \alpha_{i\oplus 1})$
0	0	0	0	$c = 0$
1	0	0	1	$d_1 = 0.2$
2	0	1	0	$b = 1.5$
3	0	1	1	$d_2 = 0.5$
4	1	0	0	$d_1 = 0.2$
5	1	0	1	$a = 1.0$
6	1	1	0	$d_2 = 0.5$
7	1	1	1	$d_3 = 0.3$

5   Iterated Games of Learning Automata: Experimental Study

In this section we will study dynamic games of deterministic ϵ-LA [12,15] acting as players in iterated games presented in Sect. 4. ϵ-LA has d actions and acts in a deterministic environment $c = (c_1, c_2, ..., c_d)$, where c_k stands for a reward obtained for its action α_k. It has also a memory of the length H. Whenever an automaton generates an action, the environment sends it a payoff in a deterministic way. The objective of a reinforcement learning algorithm represented by ϵ-automaton is to maximize its payoff in an environment where it operates.

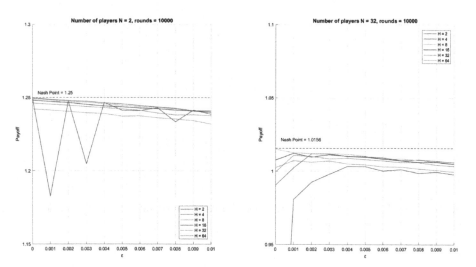

Fig. 4. Model 1: the average team payoff vs ϵ and H for $N = 2$ (left) and $N = 32$ (right).

The automaton remembers its last H actions and corresponding payoffs. As the next action ϵ-automaton chooses its the best action from the last H games (rounds) with the probability $1 - \epsilon$ $(0 < \epsilon \leq 1)$, and with probability ϵ/d any of its d actions. In our case $d = 2$ (*sleep* or *active*). The purpose of this study was to find out experimentally whether and under which conditions the team of players is able to find in a fully distributed way solutions of the games represented by NEs.

We start the overview of conducted experiments with results for Model 1. We studied the behavior of teams consisting of $N = 2, 4, 16$ and 32 players for different values of ϵ and H. Some results of this study are shown in Fig. 4. One can see (Fig. 4 (left)) that for $N = 2$ the ability to reach NE under given value of H depends on the value of ϵ. Lower value of ϵ results in higher average value of team payoff, which for NE is equal to 1.25. Increasing value of ϵ also increases the chance of disrupting NE. The figure shows also that this ability depends on the value of H. An optimal value of H is around 4–8. Too small values of H ($H = 2$) makes the team very unstable, while higher values of H reduce the ability to achieve NE.

For increasing values of N, the dependence on ϵ and H is similar (see, Fig. 4 (right)) like for small values of N, but the team of players is more stable for

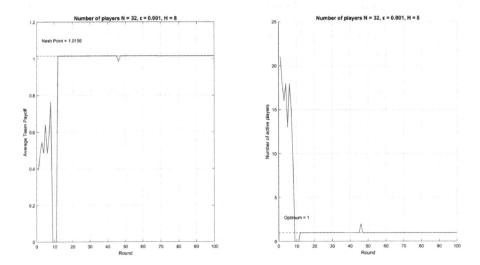

Fig. 5. Model 1: typical run ($N = 32$): the average team payoff (left) and a number of active players in the game (right).

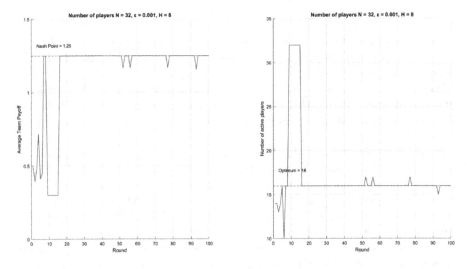

Fig. 6. Model 2: typical run ($N = 32$): the average team payoff (left) and a number of active players in the game (right).

a whole range of values of H. Figure 5 (left) shows a typical run ($N = 32$) of the game as a function of a number of rounds. One can see that the team of LA achieves NE after around 37 iterations. An optimal number of active player-sensors is equal to 1 (see, Fig. 5 (right)). One can see that while playing the game corresponding to NE there is a small probability that a player-leader can change suddenly and temporary its action.

Results of the experimental study of Model 2 are similar to Model 1. The ability to achieve NE by a team of LA depends in a similar way (not shown here) like for Model 1 on values of ϵ and H, except that only for small values of H and relatively large values of ϵ the system can lose its stability for any number of LA players. Figure 6 shows an example of the run of the game with a number of players $N = 32$ for values of $\epsilon = 0.001$ and $H = 8$. One can see (Fig. 6 (left)) that the team of LA is able to reach relatively fast the corresponding NE providing the highest average team payoff. Figure 6 (right) shows that an optimal number of active sensor-players in the NE is equal to 16. It may happen that a number of active players in the game may change suddenly and temporary.

6   Conclusion

We have proposed an approach to lifetime optimization in WSN which assumes replacing a problem of a global optimization by a problem of searching for NE by a team of players participating in a non-cooperative game. We analyzed relations between the coverage problem and the lifetime optimization problem, and selected two building blocks – basic sources of imbalance between the level of coverage of POIs and batteries expenditure and proposed game-theoretical models for their solutions.

We have shown that in iterated games a team of deterministic ϵ-LA was able to find in a fully distributed way global solutions presenting in this way the possibility of self-organization in WSN oriented on solving the lifetime optimization problem. We believe that combining this approach with CA will stimulate the development of second order CA able to solve optimization problems.

References

1. Abin, A.A., Fotouhi, M., Kasaei, S.: A new dynamic cellular learning automata-based skin detector. Multimed. Syst. **15**(5), 309–323 (2009). https://doi.org/10.1007/s00530-009-0165-1
2. Beigy, H., Meybodi, M.R.: A mathematical framework for cellular learning automata. Adv. Complex Syst. (ACS) **07**, 295–319 (2004). https://EconPapers.repec.org/RePEc:wsi:acsxxx:v:07:y:2004:i:03n04:n:s0219525904000202
3. Berman, P., Calinescu, G., Shah, C., Zelikovsky, A.: Power efficient monitoring management in sensor networks. In: 2004 IEEE Wireless Communications and Networking Conference (IEEE Cat. No. 04TH8733). vol. 4, pp. 2329–2334, March 2004

4. Cardei, M., Du, D.Z.: Improving wireless sensor network lifetime through power aware organization. Wirel. Netw. **11**(3), 333–340 (2005). https://doi.org/10.1007/s11276-005-6615-6

5. Katsumata, Y., Ishida, Y.: On a membrane formation in a spatio-temporally generalized prisoner's dilemma. In: Umeo, H., Morishita, S., Nishinari, K., Komatsuzaki, T., Bandini, S. (eds.) Cellular Automata, pp. 60–66. Springer, Berlin Heidelberg, Berlin, Heidelberg (2008). https://doi.org/10.1007/978-3-540-79992-4_8

6. Lin, Y., Wang, X., Hao, F., Wang, L., Zhang, L., Zhao, R.: An on-demand coverage based self-deployment algorithm for big data perception in mobile sensing networks. Future Gener. Comput. Syst. **82**, 220–234 (2018). http://www.science direct.com/science/article/pii/S0167739X17313262

7. Musilek, P., Krömer, P., Bartoň, T.: Review of nature-inspired methods for wake-up scheduling in wireless sensor networks. Swarm Evol. Comput. **25**, 100–118 (2015). sI: RAMONA. http://www.sciencedirect.com/science/article/pii/S2210650215000656

8. Nash, J.: Non-cooperative games. Ann. Math. **54**(2), 286–295 (1951). http://www.jstor.org/stable/1969529

9. Niyato, D., Hossain, E., Fallahi, A.: Sleep and wakeup strategies in solar-powered wireless sensor/mesh networks: performance analysis and optimization. IEEE Trans. Mob. Comput. **6**(2), 221–236 (2007)

10. Osborne, M.: An Introduction to Game Theory. Oxford University Press (2009). https://books.google.pl/books?id=_C8uRwAACAAJ

11. Razi, A., A. Hua, K., Majidi, A.: NQ-GPLS: N-queen inspired gateway placement and learning automata-based gateway selection in wireless mesh network. In: Proceedings of the 15th ACM International Symposium MobiWaC 2017, pp. 41–44, November 2017

12. Seredynski, F.: Competitive coevolutionary multi-agent systems: the application to mapping and scheduling problems. J. Parallel Distrib. Comput. **47**(1), 39–57 (1997). http://www.sciencedirect.com/science/article/pii/S0743731597913940

13. Tretyakova, A., Seredynski, F., Bouvry, P.: Cellular automata approach to maximum lifetime coverage problem in wireless sensor networks. In: Wąs, J., Sirakoulis, G.C., Bandini, S. (eds.) Cellular Automata, pp. 437–446. Springer, Cham (2014). https://doi.org/10.1007/978-3-319-11520-7_45

14. Tretyakova, A., Seredynski, F., Guinand, F.: Heuristic and meta-heuristic approaches for energy-efficient coverage-preserving protocols in wireless sensor networks. In: Proceedings of the 13th ACM Symposium on QoS and Security for Wireless and Mobile Networks, Q2SWinet 2017, pp. 51–58. ACM, New York (2017). http://doi.acm.org/10.1145/3132114.3132119

15. Warschawski, W.I.: Kollektives Verhalten von Automaten. Akademie-Verlag, Berlin (1978)

Termination and Stability Levels in Evolved CA Agents for the Black–Pattern Task

Rolf Hoffmann[1(✉)], Dominique Désérable[2], and Franciszek Seredyński[3]

[1] Technische Universität Darmstadt, Darmstadt, Germany
hoffmann@informatik.tu-darmstadt.de
[2] Institut National des Sciences Appliquées, Rennes, France
domidese@gmail.com
[3] Department of Mathematics and Natural Sciences,
Cardinal Stefan Wyszynski University, Warsaw, Poland
fseredynski@gmail.com

Abstract. Given a 2d Cellular Automaton (CA) with mobile agents controlled by a finite state automaton (algorithm). Initially the field is colored white and agents are randomly placed. They have the task to color the whole field into black in shortest time. The objective is to find algorithms that (1) can form the *black*–pattern, (2) keep it *stable* and then (3) change into a global state where all agents *stop* their activity. Four levels of stability are distinguished, depending on the grade of inactivity after having formed the pattern. For systems with up to four agents we found such algorithms by applying genetic algorithms (GA) and manual post fine tuning. Performances and simulations of these algorithms are presented.

Keywords: Termination in multi-agent systems · Stability
Cellular automata agents · Pattern formation · Genetic algorithm
Spatial computing

1 Introduction

The Problem. Initially all $N = n \times n$ cells of a square field with border are colored white, k agents are there randomly placed and their direction is also random. The CA multi-agent system ("CA–MAS") has to solve the *Black–Pattern* task with *Termination*, shortly the "BPT". That is, the agents must explore and *color* the whole cell field from white into black in shortest time and keep it stable, and then they must *stop* moving around and turning. This means that not only a stable output is required, but also a kind of termination for the entire multi-agent system. The agents shall be controlled by a finite state automaton with a minimal number of states. Actions and inputs must be very limited and local. Although this task sounds easy to accomplish, that is not the case, especially with more than one agent.

© Springer Nature Switzerland AG 2018
G. Mauri et al. (Eds.): ACRI 2018, LNCS 11115, pp. 137–145, 2018.
https://doi.org/10.1007/978-3-319-99813-8_12

The underlying general objective is to study the termination in CA–MAS and thereby to motivate further research thereon. For this purpose, and in order to keep the complexity as low as possible, we revisit an already studied very simple CA, the *Creature's Exploration Problem* [1], except that neither color (for indirect communication) nor termination were considered therein. Incidentally, the *basic* action of *blacking* a cell may also be interpreted as a *control* message – a primitive signal, a marker, a trace, a *stigma*. According to [2], *stigmergy* is "the process of indirect communication of behavioral messages with implicit signals" and where *indirect* means the "interaction through the environment". Thus, the cell color acts also as a very limited distributed communication memory. It is worth to emphasize the difference of nature between a *static* trace deposited in a cell and a *dynamic* message traveling through a channel in distributed computing. Stigmergy is now a feature widely highlighted in many environments [3].

Related Work to Termination. Termination detection is a fundamental problem in distributed computing. A set of processes execute a task and communicate through interprocess channels by messages. The computation is entering a quiescent state as soon as all processes are idle and all channels are empty. Since there is neither global clock nor a common memory, the detection of a global quiescence is impossible without an additional *control* mechanism which should not interfere with the *basic* computation. The pioneering works of Lamport, Dijkstra–Scholten, Francez, Misra–Chandy are well known and a lot of others in the eighties thereon. All those control schemes are categorized, at least until 1998, in an elegant taxonomy including eight classes [4]. Termination detection is also a fundamental problem in multi-agent "MAS" systems. As a matter of fact, there is a close relationship between distributed systems and multi-agent systems, although some dissimilarities can be highlighted [5,6]. We consider their differences as minor and thereby that MAS termination detection procedures could enter Matocha–Camp taxonomy [4], at least updated.

In Sect. 2, the termination problem is defined through the black–pattern task and four stability levels are proposed. In Sect. 3, the FSM–based multi–agent system is presented. Then k–agent algorithms are analyzed in Sect. 4 with $k = 1, 2, 4$ and various scenarios of stability and termination are studied as well as performances and robustness before Conclusion.

2   Termination and Stability Levels

The problem of termination in CA–MAS was already noticed in [7]. How can a multi-agent system be stopped in a decentralized way after having formed the required pattern? Like in [4], a simple way would be to flood the CA network with a *wave* at each time-step. This technique requires a lot of additional resources and is very time-consuming. Therefore we were looking for a more effective way. The idea is, that during the run (without a separate wave phase after each time-step), the agents themselves are able to detect that the pattern was formed (or will safely be formed in the near future) and then automatically stop their activities.

Thereby the energy consumption of the whole system stops or is minimized after the job is done. Another advantage is the following: when the agents recognize that the task is accomplished, they are able to trigger a new task. This is an important feature allowing to execute a sequence of subtasks in a decentralized way. Time is counted in discrete time steps $t = 0, 1, ...$, because CA agents are working in the synchronous CA model. We define four levels $\Lambda_0 \prec \Lambda_1 \prec \Lambda_2 \prec \Lambda_3$ of stability. The precedence means that Λ_j is stronger than Λ_i for $j > i$.

Λ_0 – *Unstable*: the aimed pattern is formed for the first time at $t = T_0$. After that, the pattern may change.

Λ_1 – *Stable*: the aimed pattern is formed and remains stable for time $t \geq T_1$ and at least one agent continues moving around.

Λ_2 – *Stable idle-stop*: the aimed pattern is formed and remains stable for time $t \geq T_2$, all agents have stopped moving around at time $T_2^{stop} \geq T_2$ and at least one agent continues turning. We call such algorithm *idle–stopping*.

Λ_3 – *Stable full-stop*: the aimed pattern is formed and remains stable for time $t \geq T_3$ and all agents have stopped moving around and turning at time $T_3^{stop} \geq T_3$. No activity is visible and we call such algorithm *full–stopping*.

Note that at level Λ_3 all agents become passive from the global observer's point of view. Nevertheless passive agents may change their internal state or may enter into in a special final dead-state. Note also that the agents need not to stop at the same time. If each agent wants to be informed about the termination, an additional *consensus* operation among the agents is necessary.

3   The Designed Multi-agent Cell Architecture

At first we have to design a cell architecture which is able to model agents, potentially can solve the problem, and is relatively simple in terms of "hardware" elements. It has to be tailored to a certain extent to the problem in order to solve it at all. Such an architecture consists in basic hardware elements, such as registers, memories, combinatorial logic and wires. We assume a synchronous

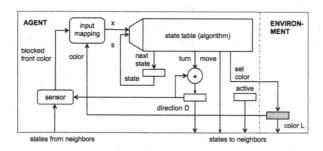

Fig. 1. The architecture of a cell. The state table defines the agent's next control state, its next direction, and whether to move or not. It defines also the setting of the color (0/1) as part of the environment.

working principle. One part of the architecture shall be fixed, and another part shall be configurable. The configurable part can be seen as a program, that allows to define the functionality within certain limits. For example a classical $1d$ CA cell consists of a 1–bit register (holding the state), a rule function (fixed, configurable or even variable logic or table), a feedback loop for the state, and wires in and between the cells. Such a classical cell corresponds to a simple Moore automaton.

Here we use a more complex cell, where the cell rule depends on the agent's current state (taking the history into account), and the rule is only executed on a site where an active agent is situated. The whole model is still fully compatible with the CA model, and therefore we use the term CA agent system. The designed cell architecture is depicted in Fig. 1. The whole *cell state* is stored in a composition of several registers:

$CellState = (Color, AgentState)$
　　$Color\ L \in \{0, 1\}$
　　$AgentState = (Active, Identifier, Direction, State)$
　　　　$Active \in \{\texttt{true}, \texttt{false}\}$
　　　　$Identifier\ ID \in \{0, 1, ..., k - 1\}$
　　　　$Direction\ D \in \{0, 1, 2, 3\} \equiv \{\texttt{toN}, \texttt{toE}, \texttt{toS}, \texttt{toW}\}$
　　　　$State\ S \in \{0, 1, ..., N_s - 1\}$. // control state, initially set to zero

Each cell contains a color (as part of the environment) and one agent, which is either active and visible, or passive and not visible. When an agent is moving from cell A to cell B, *AgentState* is copied from A to B and the *Active* bit of A is set to false. The first cell ahead (front cell) in the moving direction and the second cell ahead (in order to detect conflicts) are the neighbors.

An agent is controlled by a Mealy automaton, consisting of the state register s and the transition function, which here is defined by a state transition/output table, a *state table* for short. Table inputs are the control state s and defined input situations x, table outputs are the signals *nextstate, turn, move* and *setcolor*. The signal *nextstate* defines the next control state of the automaton. The *turn* signal triggers the change of the direction. The *move* signal is interpreted by the agent itself and is presented to the neighboring cells. The *setcolor* signal defines the setting of the color. The Mealy automaton realizes the "brain" or control unit of the agent. The state table can also be seen as a program or algorithm. Therefore we call the state table also *agent's algorithm* "AA". The state table corresponds to the genome (configurable part of the architecture) to be optimized by GA.

An agent has a moving direction D that also selects the cell in front as the actual neighbor. An agent can interpret the following conditions: *color*: cell color L, *front color*: front cell's color L_F, *blocked by border*: then the front color is defined as $L_F = -1$, *blocked by another agent*: either another agent is situated in front, or another agent with a higher priority wants to move to the same target cell in front. The *sensor* is responsible for the reduction of the neighboring states to the conditions *blocked* and *front color*, then further used by the input mapping.

Table 1. Input mapping function with $N_x = 10$ inputs.

	blocked	color	front color	x
blocked	1	0	-1	0
by border	1	1	-1	1
	0	0	0	2
free	0	0	1	3
	0	1	0	4
	0	1	1	5
	1	0	0	6
blocked	1	0	1	7
by agent	1	1	0	8
	1	1	1	9

Triggered by the state table output signals, the following actions are performed: **next state:** *state* ← *nextstate* ∈ $\{0, ..., N_s - 1\}$, **move:** *move* ∈ $\{0, 1\} \equiv \{wait, go\}$, **turn:** *turn* ∈ $\{0, 1, 2, 3\}$. The new direction is $D(t+1) \leftarrow (D(t) + turn) \bmod 4$, **set color:** *setcolor* ∈ $\{0, 1\} \equiv \{color0, color1\}$. The new color is $L(t+1) \leftarrow setcolor$.

All actions are performed in parallel. There is only one constraint: when the agent's action is *go* and the situation is *blocked*, then an agent cannot move and has to wait, but still it can turn and change the cell's color.

An input mapping function is used to limit the size of the state table memory. The *input mapping* reduces all possible input combinations to an index $x \in X = \{0, 1, \ldots, N_x - 1\}$ used in combination with the control state to select the actual line of the state table. The input mapping was defined as shown in Table 1.

Note that the hardware resources and capabilities (sensed situations, action set) are quite limited, which makes the given task with automatic termination difficult to solve. Moreover, the agents have not any knowledge about north–east–south–west orientation, that makes the task more complicated and more universal.

4 Multi-agent Algorithms

Algorithms for k-agent systems "k–AA" ($k = 1, 2, 4$) with different termination conditions were evolved by GA with manual improvement[1]. More details of the used GA method are given in [8]. Note that finite state algorithms were evolved, each represented as a state stable (the genome). The number of desired control states and the desired stability level were used as input parameters.

1–Agent Algorithm. A full-stopping algorithm was partly found by GA, and then manually improved. It needs only three states (Fig. 2). Zero is the initial

---

[1] The GA method was very time consuming (millions of multi-agent simulations) and took around 4 weeks of computation time on a state–of–the–art quad-core PC 3.5 GHz.

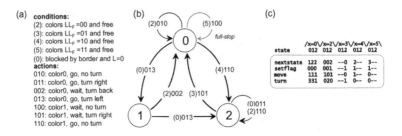

Fig. 2. The full-stopping 1-agent algorithm with 3 states. (a) Conditions and actions used in graph (b), (c) corresponding state table with don't cares (-).

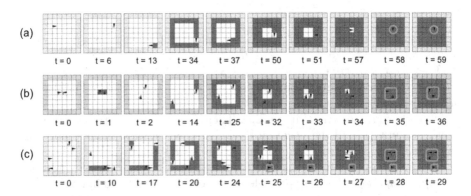

Fig. 3. (a) Simulation of the full-stopping 1–AA in a 6×6 field, $T_3^{stop} = 58$ (b) Simulation of the idle-stopping 2–AA, $T_2^{stop} = 35$ (c) Simulation of the full-stopping 4–AA, starting randomly, $T^{stop} = 28$.

and final state. The strategy can be understood by looking at a simulation (Fig. 3a). At first the agent searches for a corner, moving straight and turning right when detecting a border. After having found the corner, it starts to color the cells black, first moving along the borders and then moving inwards towards the center in a spiral-like trajectory. Then the agent stops moving and turning at $t \geq T_3^{stop}$. This full-stop corresponds to the self-loop in state 0 by Condition 5 (colors $LL_F = 11$) and Action 100 (color1, wait, no turn).

This full-stopping algorithm can easily be changed into an idle-stopping algorithm by changing the final actions from (color1, wait, no turn) into (color1, wait, turn). And it can be changed into a weaker algorithm (with stability level < 2) by changing actions into (color1, go, turn/no turn).

The number of needed time-steps is given in Table 2. Its time-complexity is linear in $O(N)$, an exact formula $t(n)$ could be derived by a simple analysis. The most time-consuming part is the coloring in a spiral-like way, in addition some steps are needed to detect borders, corners and already painted cells.

Table 2. Full-stopping 1–AA: number of time steps. Average is over 1000 fields.

Size	4×4	5×5	6×6	7×7	8×8	9×9	10×10
$T^{stop}_{3,mean}$	27.76	39.80	53.73	69.87	88.01	108.07	129.87
$T^{stop}_{3,min}$	24	35	48	63	80	99	120
$T^{stop}_{3,max}$	31	44	59	76	95	116	139
$T^{stop}_{3,mean}/N$	1.74	1.59	1.49	1.43	1.38	1.33	1.30

Table 3. Average time steps per cell T^{stop}/N. Full-stopping and idle-stopping 2–AA, evolved on 10×10 fields, simulated on 1000 fields for each field size.

	Size	4×4	5×5	6×6	7×7	8×8	9×9	10×10
FULL-STOP 2–AGENT SYSTEM	T^{stop}_3/N	1.22	1.09	1.01	0.96	0.72	0.90	0.87
IDLE-STOP 2–AGENT SYSTEM	T^{stop}_2/N	1.19	1.04	0.96	0.89	0.84	0.81	0.78
FULL-AND-IDLE-STOP 1-A. S.	T^{stop}/N	1.74	1.60	1.49	1.43	1.38	1.33	1.30

2–Agent Algorithm. The 2-agent algorithm was first evolved by GA on 6×6 fields. It turned out that the found algorithms were not working well on other field sizes. Therefore GA optimization was performed on one thousand 10×10 training fields with 4 states. Then the found idle-stopping algorithm was manually changed into a full-stopping algorithm.

A simulation sample is shown in Fig. 3b. At first, the agents search for corners. Then they start paint black in spiral-like way, with two active opposite coloring points. The agents in the idle-stopping algorithm continue turning after coloring whereas they fully stop in the full-stopping algorithm.

The performance for different field sizes is shown in Table 3. The 2-agent algorithm executed on 1-agent systems yields the same performance as the former 1–AA in Table 2. A full-stopping 10×10 system with 2 agents is 1.49 times faster $(1.30/0.87)$ than a system with 1 agent only. And a full-stopping 10×10 system with 2 agents is 1.12 times slower $(0.87/0.78)$ than an idle-stopping system. In order to compute T^{stop} average values, 1,000 random fields were simulated.

Table 4. Performance of 4–AA on 6×6 fields. Full-stopping (*left*), idle-stopping (*right*). Values are averaged over 1000 fields.

	T^{stop}	T^{stop}/N	cost per cell $k\,T^{stop}/N$	relative speedup		T^{stop}	T^{stop}/N	cost per cell $k\,T^{stop}/N$	relative speedup
4-agent system	30.46	0.85	3.38	2.07	4-agent system	26.53	0.74	2.95	1.87
2-agent system	43.95	1.22	2.44	1.50	2-agent system	38.96	1.08	2.16	1.37
1-agent system	58.73	1.63	1.63	1.00	1-agent system	56.73	1.58	1.58	1.00

4–Agent Algorithm. Many computer-time consuming attempts were made by GA to find a 4-agent algorithm with 6 states that can work successfully on any field size. Until now, no general algorithms were found. Nevertheless GA was able to find specialized algorithms that work on one thousand random fields of size 6×6 or 10×10.

If the agents start rotational symmetrically then they are first searching for corners and then they build the pattern using a counter-clock spiral trajectory. When the agents start randomly (Fig. 3c) then the pattern building is slower and not so symmetric, but still the tendency of building a counter-clock spiral can be observed.

The full-stopping 4-agent system is $30.46/26.53 = 1.15$ times slower than the idle-stopping system (Table 4). The cost per cell is the number k of agents multiplied with the number of needed time units per cell. So the 4-agent systems are about twice more costly than the 1-agent systems, while they are about two times faster.

5 Conclusion

In this paper four stability levels for the termination of CA multi-agent system were proposed. *Idle-stopping* and *full-stopping* algorithms were found for the *BPT* where the whole field has to be painted from white to black in shortest time. The general 1-AA need only 3 states and are relatively fast with time-complexity $O(N)$. The general full-stopping 2–AA needs 4 states and is about 50% faster than the 1–AA. Until now, no general 4–AA was found, but special ones for fields of size 6×6 and 10×10 were evolved by GA. They work about twice as fast as 1–AA. All found algorithms follow in principle the same strategy: first searching for corners, then follow a spiral-like trajectory until the midpoints are reached. Future work is directed to find general algorithms that can work successfully on any field size with any number of agents. Another topic is the efficient communication and synchronization of the stopping state between agents.

References

1. Halbach, M., Hoffmann, R., Both, L.: Optimal 6-state algorithms for the behavior of several moving creatures. In: El Yacoubi, S., Chopard, B., Bandini, S. (eds.) ACRI 2006. LNCS, vol. 4173, pp. 571–581. Springer, Heidelberg (2006). https://doi.org/10.1007/11861201_66
2. Tummolini, L., Castelfranchi, C.: Trace signals: the meanings of stigmergy. In: Weyns, D., Parunak, H.V.D., Michel, F. (eds.) E4MAS 2006. LNCS (LNAI), vol. 4389, pp. 141–156. Springer, Heidelberg (2007). https://doi.org/10.1007/978-3-540-71103-2_8
3. Weyns, D., Van Dyke Parunak, H., Michel, F., Holvoet, T., Ferber, J.: Environments for multiagent systems State-of-the-art and research challenges. In: Weyns, D., Van Dyke Parunak, H., Michel, F. (eds.) E4MAS 2004. LNCS (LNAI), vol. 3374, pp. 1–47. Springer, Heidelberg (2005). https://doi.org/10.1007/978-3-540-32259-7_1

4. Matocha, J., Camp, T.: A taxonomy of distributed termination detection algorithms. J. Syst. Softw. **43**(3), 207–221 (1998)
5. Wellman, M.P., Walsh, E.W.: Distributed quiescence detection in multiagent negotiation. In: Fourth International Conference on Multi-Agent Systems, ICMAS, pp. 317–324 (2000)
6. Lahlouhi, A.: MAS-td: an approach to termination detection of multi-agent systems. In: Gelbukh, A., Espinoza, F.C., Galicia-Haro, S.N. (eds.) MICAI 2014. LNCS (LNAI), vol. 8856, pp. 472–482. Springer, Cham (2014). https://doi.org/10.1007/978-3-319-13647-9_42
7. Hoffmann, R., Désérable, D.: Generating maximal domino patterns by cellular automata agents. In: Malyshkin, V. (ed.) PaCT 2017. LNCS, vol. 10421, pp. 18–31. Springer, Cham (2017). https://doi.org/10.1007/978-3-319-62932-2_2
8. Hoffmann, R.: How agents can form a specific pattern. In: Wąs, J., Sirakoulis, G.C., Bandini, S. (eds.) ACRI 2014. LNCS, vol. 8751, pp. 660–669. Springer, Cham (2014). https://doi.org/10.1007/978-3-319-11520-7_70

Size Effect in Cellular Automata Based Disease Spreading Model

Julianna Orzechowska, Dawid Fordon, and Tomasz M. Gwizdałła[✉]

Faculty of Physics and Applied Informatics, University of Łódź, Pomorska 149/153,
90-236 Łódź, Poland
tomgwizd@uni.lodz.pl

Abstract. In our paper we use the, recently proposed, model for simulating the process of disease spreading in the environment defined by the Cellular Automaton. The main effort goes to the analysis of the influence of cell size on the epidemic curves and other characteristics related to the studied process. We take into account some real data concerning the occupation in the city of Łódź, which has about 700000 inhabitants. The results show that by marshaling the parameters of simulation we can obtain explicitly different results. This comment applies to a lot of features like: the shape of epidemic curve, the total number of diseased or the amount of ill in particular areas/cells.

1 Introduction

The problem of modeling of the spreading of different illnesses in the populations is an interdisciplinary issue studied for many years and interesting due to the possibility of comparison of experimental and simulation results (see e.g. [1]). Basically, the majority of the proposed approaches base on the so-called **SEIR** model [2]. Its crucial part is the set of four first order differential equations describing the "velocity" of change of number of individuals in different groups, regarding to the state of illness. Some interesting versions of the use of **SEIR** model can be found in [3] where the seasonal increase of disease strength is studied in the frame of nonlinear transmission rate, [4] where the Principal Component Analysis is applied. We can mention also one of the review papers [5].

The Cellular Automata technique is also used to study the process of disease spreading. The main effort goes usually to model the transmission of disease through the boundaries of cells. The different approaches have been proposed by e.g.: Hoya White [6] where the slightly simplified **SIR** model with additional vaccination is studied on the system of equinumerous cells, Pfeifer et al. [7] who proposed a framework for study the different scenarios for Tyrol (Austria) conditions or quite new paper by Sharma et al. [8] where special attention is paid to the incubation process.

© Springer Nature Switzerland AG 2018
G. Mauri et al. (Eds.): ACRI 2018, LNCS 11115, pp. 146–153, 2018.
https://doi.org/10.1007/978-3-319-99813-8_13

2 Model

The model we use is based indeed on the one presented and accurately described in [9], therefore we do not pay special attention to present a lot of its details. We rather concentrate on the presentation of some basic ideas and formulas and later on weaknesses which can strongly influence the result.

The crucial observation following basic models devoted to study epidemics processes is the division of whole population into four groups defined as:

- Susceptible (**S**) - all people who can contract the disease
- Exposed (**E**) - people in the phase of incubation of illness
- Infectious (**I**) - individuals who are capable to transmit the disease
- Recovered (**R**) - individuals recovered who are permanently immune

In the model studied in the paper we do not use differential equations which correspond to some totalistic view on the problem but we adapt the Cellular Automata related approach [9]. As usually, we have to define the tuple containing the states, topology, neighborhood and the rule (transition function).

The set of states is certainly given by by 4-tuple $\{S, E, I, R\}$. In the original paper the topology is the result of the division of some geographical area into rectangular grid. Originally, as the considered one it was the territory of Poland divided into 36 rows and 36 columns. By combining these two factors we can obtain the mapping of number of individuals onto particular cells denoted by $\{S_{ij}, E_{ij}, I_{ij}, R_{ij}\}$, where $(i, j) \in C$ and C is the cellular space. The possibility of spreading of disease not only inside the cells but also into another ones is provided by the assumption about the possible transfers of individuals between different cells. In the paper we follow the original assumption that the transfer can take place only into cells in the Moore's neighborhood.

The transition function is based on some additional assumptions. When considering the particular disease we have to know the specific numbers defining the period when individual is in the exposed and infectious state. Following the original paper we denote then as a and b respectively and assume $a = 2$ and $b = 4$ [10] what corresponds to some statistical results of Infectious Period Distribution. The crucial problem is here the passage between states **S** and **E**, it means simply the chance to become ill. The probability of this process is given by the Eq. 1.

$$p_{ij}^t = \begin{cases} 0, & q_{ij}^t < 0 \\ 1, & q_{ij}^t > 1 \\ q_{ij}^t, & \text{elsewhere} \end{cases} \tag{1}$$

where the q_{ij}^t number is defined by:

$$q_{ij}^t = rnd\left(1 - exp\left(-\beta \frac{\sum_{k=1}^b l_{ij|k}^t + \sum_{(x,y) \in C} \sum_{k=1}^b I_{ij|k}^t (I_{x,y \to i,j|k}^t - I_{i,j \to x,y|k}^t)}{N_{ij}^t + \sum_{(x,y) \in C} (N_{x,y \to i,j}^t - N_{i,j \to x,y}^t)}\right), c_v\right) \tag{2}$$

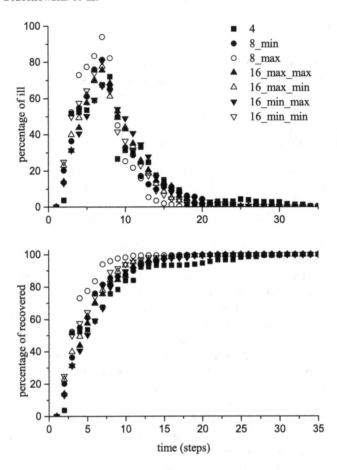

Fig. 1. Epidemic curves for parameters used in Holko [9] paper ($\beta = 0.6$, c_v = 0.5)

In the above equation *rnd* means sampling from the Gaussian distribution, β is called contact rate, pairs (i, j) and (x, y) describe he coordinates of cells on the rectangular grid, the vertical line in the subscript referring to the index of summation corresponds to the index of day, among the *b* in the infectious state, the individual stays in this state and *t* is the time index.

The model presented in [9] has several interesting features which need some discussion. We have e.g. to mention the large size of single cells (with edge of about 15 km) what leads to the fact that there are large differences between the occupation of particular cells. Also the division ratio of the studied area can be the property under consideration.

We select the smaller area, particularly the urban area of Łódź which shape is close to the square one. We are then able to easily find the amount of individuals in every cell. In order to do this we use the number of voters in the general election announced by the city council. Since this number is announced for irreg-

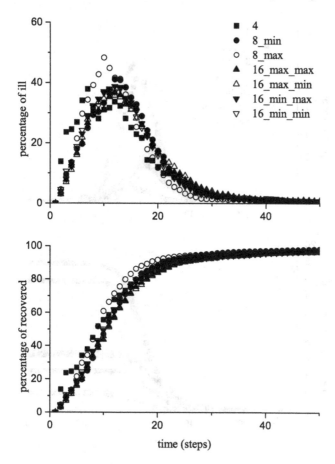

Fig. 2. Epidemic curves for lower c_v (c_v = 0.01)

ular parts of city called subdivision, by assuming that a distribution of people in every subdivision is uniform, we add to the given cell such a number of people which follows the surface percentage contribution of this cell in subdivision. Since the voters numbers is determined only for adults, the resulting numbers are then normalized in order to have in total 700 000 individuals. By using such an approximation we obtain for example from 1839 up to 106000 individuals in every cell of 4 × 4 grid.

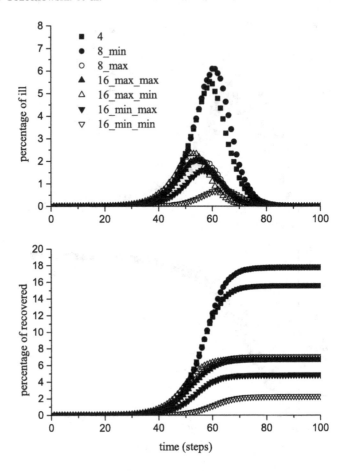

Fig. 3. Epidemic curves for variant c_v

3   Results and Conclusions

We decided to initialize the simulation with just one individual in the exposed state. The additional question we can try to answer is whether the location of "patient zero" influences the process of disease spread. These analysis we perform for more dense cells division. We decided to allocate "patient zero" in the cell $(1,1)$ in the 4×4 grid, where the cell $(0,0)$ is the westernmost and northernmost cell of grid. It means that our initial cell belongs to the group of cells with the relatively middle occupation however adjoining with the cells with low occupation as well as with the cell with the highest occupation in a system. When further dividing the cells into four smaller ones we consider the difference initializing the disease once in the cell with highest occupation among the subcells of cell $(1,1)$ then in the cell with the lowest occupation among them. In the pictures they are denoted as "8_max" and "8_min" respectively. The same procedure is then adapted for the divided cell in 8×8 grid, so "16_max_max" cell is the one with the highest occupation among four subcells of "8_max" while "16_max_min" is the one with lowest number of individuals among them. The same standard of notation is used for description of subcells of "8_min" cell.

Our first attempts are made for the parameters proposed in the original paper. Since the calculations were made for the set of values $\beta \in \{0.2, 0.4, 0.6\}$ we decided to use one of these pretested values and set $\beta = 0.6$. The selection of c_v value is also the effect of earlier suggestion and we choose the middle of the values used in the original paper and set $c_v = 0.5$. The results are presented in Fig. 1. It can be observed that there is no visible differences in the results of simulations performed for different sizes of grids. However, as opposed to the authors of original paper we present the epidemic curves on the percentage scale and not on the absolute one. This allow us to emphasize the fact that by using the model with given parameters we obtain the number of ill individuals encompassing whole population. It is well known that the typical local epidemy causes the illness of about 2–4% of population. Also the data concerning the most famous pandemy of 20th century [11–13] are not unambiguous. They show that the rate of ill was in the interval 10–30% and the mortality among the ill individuals was on the level of 10–30%. This leads to the conclusion that the numbers produced by the model are too high to describe the real case.

The first step we make is to decrease the c_v parameter. In the second attempt we use $c_v = 0.01$ which is close to the proposed $c_v = 0$ but introduces some dispersion of values. The Fig. 2 shows that this change does not lead to any substantial change. Certainly, the maximum of curves is shifted from about seventh to about tenth-twelfth day and the number of ill in the maximum declines from the totally unreal number of almost 100% to about 40–50% but the plot still do not correspond to the mentioned above features.

Finally we introduce the fundamental change into the model. We make c_v dependent on the average calculated as the first parameter of formula 2. The deviation is determined by simply multiplying the average by 0.1. Our idea is that the distribution can be ever wider when the number of ill is higher. We call ths case as "variant c_v" and present in Fig. 3. It can be observed that this change influences the results very strongly. We obtain the differences in the shape of epidemic curves as well the variable total number of ill. The crucial observation is that the decrease of cell size seems to decrease the epidemic curve. The points for 4×4 and 8×8 grids use to lay higher than for 16×16. The very interesting effect is the one that the height of epidemic curve peak is higher when starting the epidemy from the cell with lower occupation. This effect has to be explained by presenting the detailed curves for particular cells.

Some view on the run of simulation in particular groups is shown in Fig. 4. In the Figure, the number of people in particular phase of disease as well as the percentage in particular cell is presented for every cell and for the 7th day of simulation. The organization of rows and columns corresponds strictly to the organization of simulation and the cells number is 4×4. So, the upper row describes the northernmost part of the city and so on.

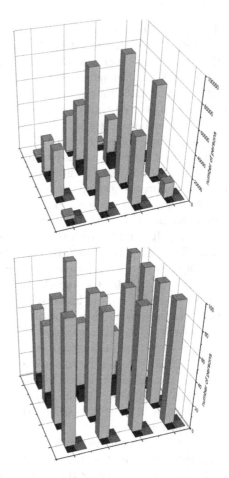

Fig. 4. The number of individuals in particular groups and cells in the same time - the 7th day. From up to down $c_v = 0.5$, $c_v = 0.01$, variant c_v From the lightest shade of grey: (S, R, E, I).

Only the results for variant c_v are presented. The results for absolute numbers shows clearly the high contribution of people in the **S** state for every cell in the simulation system. Especially when we compare it with the expected high number of individuals in the **E** and **I** states following the Figs. 1 and 2 for constant and larger c_v. Some more interesting information can be observed in the lower plot of Fig. 4 which shows the results for percentages. There are the lowest bars corresponding to the susceptible state in the northern part of the city, so the majority of ill concentrates in this region. Keeping in mind that a disease starts from the cell $(1, 1)$ so the cell second from up and second from left we can say that starting the illness in the sparsely populated part of the city we can rather easily limit it to rather confined area.

The presented results confirm that when using the Cellular Automata based model of disease spreading, even with the relatively simple mechanism of totalistic rules, we can generate different results corresponding to real process of the studied phenomena. In our opinion the next steps should be directed into several points, like: the further densifying of CA grid, the more realistic rules of disease transfer or the individualization of contacts between people what brings us closer to the mixed CA and agent oriented approach.

References

1. Guo, D., Li, K.C., Peters, T.R., Snively, B.M., Poehling, K.A., Zhou, X.: Multi-scale modeling for the transmission of influenza and the evaluation of interventions toward it. Sci. Rep. **5**, 8980 (2015)
2. Aron, J.L., Schwartz, I.B.: Seasonality and period-doubling bifurcations in an epidemic model. J. Theor. Biol. **110**, 665–679 (1984)
3. Yi, N., Zhang, Q., Mao, K., Yang, D., Li, Q.: Analysis and control of an seir epidemic system with nonlinear transmission rate. Math. Comput. Model. **50**, 1498–1513 (2009)
4. Schimit, P., Pereira, F.: Disease spreading in complex networks: a numerical study with principal component analysis. Expert Syst. Appl. **97**, 41–50 (2018)
5. Keeling, M., Eames, K.T.D.: Networks and epidemic models. J. Roy. Soc. Interface **2**, 295–307 (2005)
6. Hoya White, S., Martin del Rey, A., Rodriguez Sanchez, G.: Modeling epidemics using cellular automata. Appl. Math. Comput. **186**, 193–202 (2007)
7. Pfeifer, B., et al.: A cellular automaton framework for infectious disease spread simulation. Open Med. Inform. J. **2**, 70–81 (2008)
8. Sharma, N., Gupta, A.K.: Impact of time delay on the dynamics of SEIR epidemic model using cellular automata. Phys. A: Stat. Mech. Appl. **471**, 114–125 (2017)
9. Holko, A., Medrek, M., Pastuszak, Z., Phusavat, K.: Epidemiological modeling with a population density map-based cellular automata simulation system. Expert Syst. Appl. **48**, 1–8 (2016)
10. Lloyd, A.L.: Realistic distributions of infectious periods in epidemic models: changing patterns of persistence and dynamics. Theor. Popul. Biol. **60**, 59–71 (2001)
11. Cartwright, F.F., Biddiss, M.D.: Disease and History, 2nd edn. Sutton Publishing, Stroud (2000)
12. Johnson, N., Mueller, J.: Updating the accounts: global mortality of the 1918–1920 spanish influenza pandemic. Bull. Hist. Med. **76**, 105–115 (2002)
13. Knobler, S., Mack, A., Mahmoud, A. (eds.): The Threat of Pandemic Influenza: Are We Ready? Workshop Summary. Institute of Medicine (US) Forum on Microbial Threats, National Academies Press (US) (2005)

Pheromone Interactions in a Cellular Automata-Based Model for Surveillance Robots

Claudiney R. Tinoco[✉] and Gina M. B. Oliveira

Uberlândia Federal University, Uberlândia, MG, Brazil
{claudineyrt,gina}@ufu.br, claudineyrt@gmail.com

Abstract. This work investigates a coordination model based on a two-dimensional cellular automata applied to a team of surveillance robots. The synergy among the robots emerges from the indirect communication performed by repulsive pheromone interactions. Five strategies are evaluated for the decision-making related to the next-cell selection: three stochastic (pure, elitist and inertial), one random and one deterministic. The performance of the team performing surveillance are evaluated in respect to two aspects: the number of task cycles (visiting all the rooms) completed in a fixed interval of time and the homogeneity of the environment coverage. Experimental results corroborate the importance of the cooperative pheromone and shows that the decision-making strategies have different inherent skills that can be explored for distinct situations.

Keywords: Cellular automata · Inverted pheromone · Robotics

1 Introduction

Swarm robotics has been a popular topic among researchers [4]. Models for swarm robotics are characterized by decentralized coordination, mimicking the behaviour of social insects. Besides, they are characterized by the employment of simple robots with the emergence of a complex behaviour when they are working together to solve a cooperative task. Different methods have been investigated as the underlying model for the cooperative behaviour. A coordination mechanism based on the representation of the environment in graphs is proposed in [1]. Other works try to reproduce physical phenomena, such as fluid dynamics [9,17] and potential fields [14]. However, a large part of the works focus on the application of bioinspired strategies, such as ant pheromone-inspired models [2,5,15].

Cellular Automata (CA) are able to represent high complex phenomena and due to its massive decentralized structure based on local rules, they can be used for modelling the cooperative behaviour in robotics, providing high-distributed solutions. In [7], a review of several applications of CA models in robotics is presented. More recently, CA-based models for swarm robotics and multi-robot systems have been investigated for different robotics tasks, such as formation control [8], foraging [11–13], crowd evacuation [3] and surveillance [10,16].

© Springer Nature Switzerland AG 2018
G. Mauri et al. (Eds.): ACRI 2018, LNCS 11115, pp. 154–165, 2018.
https://doi.org/10.1007/978-3-319-99813-8_14

Five variations of a coordination model for a team of robots in surveillance are investigated here. The model is based on a two-dimensional cellular automata with Moore neighborhood, where the cells store a repulsive pheromone as a part of their states. The variations differ on the way the robot decides the next position at each time step. Previous work [10] proposed the basic model named IACA (Inverted Ant Cellular Automata), in which the next position decision is given by a probabilistic selection, where all the eight neighbors cells can be selected and their probabilities are inversely proportional to the pheromone amount in each cell. Later, this model was improved to IACA-DI (Inverted Ant Cellular Automata with Discrete pheromone diffusion), where the pheromone deposit based on a continuous function used in IACA was improved to reflect the discrete nature of CA modelling and achieving better results [16]. Besides, two variations of the next position decision was investigated, where the robots make decisions based on more elaborated stochastic rules. The first is an elitist probabilistic decision in which just a part of the neighbors can be selected. The second uses an inertial-elitist decision in which the maintenance of the robot's current direction of movement receives a higher probability. The cooperative model investigated here is based in IACA-DI and we introduce two variations for the next-step decision. The first is a deterministic selection, in which the neighbor with the smallest pheromone concentration is chosen (similar to the first-choice models used in crowd dynamics modelling [13]). In the second strategy, the next cell selection is made at random, without the pheromone influence.

Although previous works [10,16] have employed the pheromone interaction as a way to provide a good synergy among team members, it was not investigated the influence of the pheromone-sharing in the team performance. Therefore, here we also investigate two approaches: (i) the robots can make indirect communication based on the pheromone deposits in the floor or (ii) the pheromone can be used just as a model for decision based on its own past navigation. Each model variation is evaluated regarding both pheromone approaches (individual and combined) to evaluate the contribution of the indirect communication on team performance in the surveillance task, except for the random decision model since it does not use pheromone in its decision. The performance of the team in surveillance is analysed in two aspects: (i) the efficiency of the robots to make the higher number of cycles of visiting as possible, being that a cycle of visiting is completed when all the rooms of the environment receive at least one visit of one robot since the last cycle end; (ii) the efficiency of the team to make an homogeneous coverage of the environment, i.e., it is desirable that each cell in each room receives approximately the same number of visits.

This paper is organized as follows: Sect. 2 presents the coordination model with five variations in the movement strategy. Experimental results are discussed in Sect. 3. Section 4 presents the main conclusions and future works.

2   Model

The model is based on a two-dimensional CA with Moore neighbourhood. The CA lattice corresponds to the environment discretization in a grid composed of

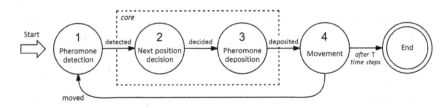

Fig. 1. Robot behavior controlled by a finite state machine (Adapted from [16]).

square cells of the same size. Each cell state is composed by two substates. The first represents the presence of robots, obstacles or free spaces, using the discrete set {R, O, F}. The second sub-state is continuous and stores the pheromone concentration: a real number belonging to the interval [0, 1]. This dual representation of states can also be seen as a CA lattice with two-layers [10].

The individual robot control is represented by a Finite State Machine (FSM) and it is illustrated in Fig. 1. It controls the robot behaviour at each time step and is composed by four states: Pheromone Detection, Next Position Decision, Pheromone Deposition and Movement. Pheromone detection is the state in which each robot of the swarm will read the pheromone values in the neighbourhood cells (within its vision radius r_v). In Next Position Decision, the robot will use the neighbourhood reading to decide which one of the cells will be the destination of its next move. In this work, five decision strategies are evaluated: (a) Random, (b) Deterministic, (c) Stochastic, (d) Elitist and (e) Inertial. Having made the choice of the next cell, the Pheromone Deposition is the state in which the robot deposits pheromone in its current position and in the neighbourhood. This deposition is a diffusion process given by Eq. 1:

$$\varpi_{ij}^t = \left[\alpha \cdot (\delta \cdot e)^{\eta \cdot \frac{r_p}{\pi}} \right] \tag{1}$$

where the constants α, δ and η represent, respectively, the maximum possible amount of deposited pheromone, the deposition pheromone rate and the environmental dispersion rate. Equation 1 represents the amount of pheromone deposited in each cell, by each robot in the swarm, at each time step t.

The pheromone diffusion has a pheromone radius (r_p) that can be different from the vision radius (r_v). Here, we use $r_v = r_p = 1$. The five decision strategies investigated here for the second state of the FSM are:

- **Random:** gives the same probability of being selected for all the cells in the neighbourhood. Therefore, no cell is discarded and there is the same probability to the robots move in any direction, even those recently visited. Thus, there is no influence of the pheromone concentration detected.
- **Deterministic:** takes into account the pheromone detected within the vision radius. It is used to carry out a deterministic choice, in which the neighbour cell with the lowest pheromone concentration is always chosen.

- **Stochastic:** takes into account the pheromone amount of all neighbourhood cells. The pheromone concentration in each cell x_{ij} is used to make a probabilistic selection. It is defined in such a way that the lower the pheromone concentration in the cell, the greater is the probability to be selected. The selection is given by Eq. 2, where ψ_{ij} represents the pheromone concentration of the cell x_{ij} and variables M, c, ψ_{max} and t are the set of cells belonging to the current neighbourhood, the index of a cell $\in M$, the maximum amount of pheromone in a cell and the current time step, respectively. This strategy was also investigated in [10,16].

$$P(x_{ij})^t = \frac{\psi_{max} - \psi_{ij}^t}{\sum\limits_{c \in M} (\psi_{max} - \psi_c^t)} \tag{2}$$

- **Elitist:** takes into account the pheromone of a limited number of neighboring cells. A percentage μ of these cells is selected in an elitist way (the lowest pheromone concentrations) and a percentage ν of them will be randomly selected, ensuring that all cells in the neighbourhood are selectable. This strategy was investigated in [16] and it was adapted from [6].
- **Inertial:** adds an inertial tendency in the robot movement jointly with an elitist selection. When identifying the percentage μ and ν of cells to be used in the elitist draw, it guarantees that the cell which represents a continuity on the robot moving direction belongs to this restricted set and it also amplifies the probability of this cell. As a consequence, the robot has a tendency to exhibit a smoother trajectory, as well as increases swarm performance, since turning moves require more effort and time. It was proposed in [16] and it returned the better results compared with elitist and stochastic strategies.

Regarding the model investigated here, it uses the same discrete pheromone adjustment scheme, compared to the IACA-DI model described in [16]. However, in addition to the three stochastic movement decision strategies (probabilistic, elitist, inertial) in the present work we also investigate the deterministic and purely random. The purpose of proposing the last one is to have a lower performance limit of the pheromone based model, since in the random decision this information is not taken into account. In addition, besides the shared use of the pheromone proposed in [16], in the present work we investigate the performance of the robots when they use, in the choice of movement, only the pheromone deposited by themselves. Thus, in this scenario, the robots do not take into account the pheromone of the other robots. Therefore, we investigate the influence of historical information sharing (stored in the pheromone) in the performance of the team. Another point to be highlighted is that, while in the previous work [16] the environmental cover was investigated from a more general point of view, in this work we deepen this analysis further, trying to understand how more specific regions of the environment are covered (walls, doors, room centers and intermediate regions).

3   Experiments

This section presents the results of experiments with the coordination model described in Sect. 2 and the five variations of the decision-making strategies. We can highlight as the main goal of the experiments reported here: (i) to investigate the emergence of synergy resulted by the sharing of the pheromone information among the robots, trying to characterized if any performance improvement could be associated with this synergy; (ii) to compare the five decision strategies taking in account the two desired characteristics of the surveillance task: a high number of visiting cycles and an homogeneous spreading over the environment.

Figure 2 shows the two environments used in the experiments. The Environment 1 is composed by seven rooms and the Environment 2 is composed by ten rooms. Figure 2c also shows the Environment 1 divided in regions of interest, which were defined to perform a more accurate analysis: the orange cells represent the doors, the blue cells represent the edge of the rooms, the white cells represent the centre of the room, and the green cells are related to an intermediate region between the centre and the edges (Environment 2b is also divided in an analogous way into regions of interest). All the experiments were performed using the same parameters defined in [16]: a team of $N = 3$ robots, $\beta = 0.5\%$, $r_v = 1$, maximum pheromone concentration in a cell $\psi_{max} = 1.0$, $\alpha = 0.5$, $\delta = 0.1$, $\eta = 2$, $\mu = \nu = 30\%$ of the neighbourhood cells (used in elitist and inertial strategies). All the simulations were executed using $T = 10,000$ time steps. When using the inertial strategy, the preferable cell (which keeps the movement direction) has its chance of being chosen doubled, after the pheromone detection.

Aiming to investigate the importance of the synergy resulted by the sharing of the pheromone information among the robots, we performed two experiments with each model variation: in the first one each robot accesses only the information about their own pheromone deposits and constructs its individual pheromone map, while in the second experiment all the robots are able to access the pheromone map resultant of the combined information of the pheromone deposits of the team. We called the first experiment as "Individual pheromone" and the second as "Combined pheromone". They were applied with four strategies, except for the random. Since the robots do not rely on the pheromone information to make their decisions at random, it does not matter if individual or combined pheromone map is used. Figure 3 shows the pheromone heatmaps taken after 10,000 time steps from two arbitrary executions of the individual and combined pheromone experiments using inertial strategy for the next cell decision. In these heatmaps, warm colors have high pheromone concentration whereas areas with cold colors have low concentration. Figures 3a, b and c shows the individual pheromone maps related to robots 1, 2 and 3, respectively. Figure 3d shows the combined pheromone map, which is shared by all the robots.

In order to evaluate the efficiency of each strategy in each pheromone approach (individual and combined) performing the surveillance task, the first analysis count the number of task points reached in each execution after 10,000 time steps. A task point is reached when all rooms have been visited by at least one member of the team, and then the count is restarted. Figure 4a illustrates the

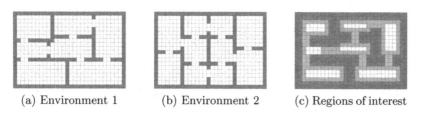

(a) Environment 1   (b) Environment 2   (c) Regions of interest

Fig. 2. Environments grids: (a) 7 rooms, (b) 10 rooms and (c) regions of interest. (Color figure online)

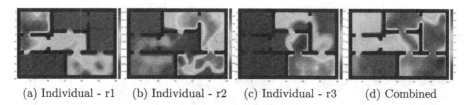

(a) Individual - r1   (b) Individual - r2   (c) Individual - r3   (d) Combined

Fig. 3. Pheromone heatmaps for individual and combined maps.

task point boxplots for the five strategies analysed, also considering both individual and the combined pheromone experiments, except for the random strategy. It results on 9 boxplots and each one represents the number of task points reached in 100 runs of $T = 10,000$ time steps, using the Environment 1. Some important points to highlight from this experiment: (i) the random strategy showed the worst performance (a mean of 13 task points in 10,000 time steps), as expected, showing that the pheromone information is important to spread the robots over the rooms and improving the team performance; (ii) the deterministic strategy showed the best performance in both experiments (individual and combined pheromone, a mean of 84 task points in the former and 110 task points in the later); (iii) among the stochastic strategies, the inertial decision returned the best performance as observed in [16]; (iv) an efficiency increase was observed in all the strategies based on pheromone detection when the information of the pheromones is combined, confirming that information sharing increases the synergy of the team, emerging a more coordinated behaviour: deterministic strategy (from 84 to 110 task points), stochastic (from 39 to 42), elitist (from 51 to 60) and inertial (from 55 to 63). Thus, the deterministic strategy was more efficient, showing a greater dynamism in the exchange of rooms, especially when using the combination of pheromone deposits information.

The second analysis about these experiments was performed considering the second desirable characteristic: an homogenous spreading of the robots visits over the entire environment. Firstly, this analysis was performed by means of a visual inspection of the number of visits to each free cell of the environment. Figure 5 illustrates the cellstep map obtained with each variation model using the Environment 1. In this figure we presented just the results of experiments with the combined pheromone approach. Each cell in the map represents the mean

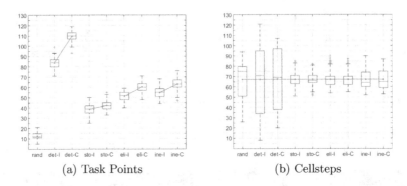

(a) Task Points   (b) Cellsteps

Fig. 4. Performance in surveillance task, using Environment 2a. (Color figure online)

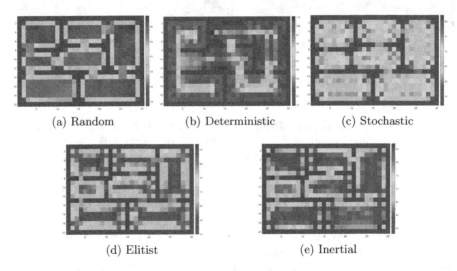

(a) Random   (b) Deterministic   (c) Stochastic

(d) Elitist   (e) Inertial

Fig. 5. Cellstep heatmaps for each model variation.

number of times that it has received a robot visit. For the mean calculation, each map has 100 runs of $T = 10,000$ time steps. Cold-colored cells represent a low mean of cellsteps, while warmer colors have a high mean of cellsteps. Each map in Fig. 5 represents an experiment with a different model variation: random strategy (Fig. 5a), deterministic strategy (Fig. 5b), stochastic strategy (Fig. 5c), elitist strategy (Fig. 5d) and inertial strategy (Fig. 5e).

When the random strategy was employed, it was possible to observe a high concentration of cellsteps in the intermediate and central regions and a low concentration of visits in the cells that are on the edges of the rooms. It shows a not good spreading of the team, although the random choice turns the team to walk with the same probability for any direction. This somehow unexpected behaviour is due to the fact that edge cells (specially corner cells) have lesser neighbours than central ones, therefore they will be chosen less often than the others. Aiming to clarify this point, suppose a single retangular room (without doors) with 5 cells of width and 5 cells of height and there is one robot inside this room. Suppose that there are free cells in positions (0, 0), (0, 3) and (3, 3). What is the possibilities of each free cell to receive a robot visit in the next time step? Considering the cell (0,0), there are 3 possibilities: if the current robot's position is (0, 1), (1, 0) or (1, 1). For the free cell (0, 3), there are 5 possibilities: if the current robot's position is (0, 2), (0, 4), (1, 2), (1, 3) or (1, 4). On the other hand, considering the free cell (3, 3) there are 8 possibilities: (2, 2), (2, 3), (2, 4), (3, 2), (3, 4), (4, 2), (4, 3) or (4, 4). Therefore, if a totally random choice is employed to make the robot to move, the central cells will receive more visits than the cells next to walls and even more compared to the corner cells.

It was possible to observe an opposite behaviour in Fig. 5b, when the deterministic strategy was employed: there are a concentration of cellsteps in the edges of the rooms, whereas the central regions have low concentration of visits. Besides, the movements of the robots are quite ordered, forming specific routes in the grid, concentrated in the edge cells. In general, the spreading is not homogeneous. The more homogeneous spreading was obtained by the three stochastic decision-based models, specially with the purely stochastic variation in Fig. 5c. It seems that the pheromone information pushes the team to occupy the edge cells although in a more random walk they tend to be avoided (except for the corner cells which have few visits). The other two variations (elitist and inertial) presented a good homogeneity in almost all regions of the rooms. However, the elitist presents a slightly higher concentration of visits on edge cells (with more visits in the corners than the purely stochastic), whereas the inertial variation presents a more significant concentration of visits on the edges.

Figure 4b presents results also related to the cellsteps, but using a more quantitative analysis. The boxplots in Fig. 4b represents the mean of cellsteps in the Environment 1. The boxplots were built using 100 runs of $T = 10,000$ time steps. Figure 4b illustrates the cellstep boxplots for each variation model, considering the cells of the entire environment. Here, we present the results for both approaches: individual and combined pheromone. The green line represents the mean cellsteps considering all the environment cells: 67.2 cellsteps. The boxplot dispersion helps us identify if the distribution of the cellsteps in the lattice is more homogeneous or heterogeneous. The boxplots show that random and deterministic decision strategies, both using individual and combined pheromones, present a great dispersion in the data. On the other hand, elitist, stochastic and inertial variations exhibited the smaller dispersions. It corresponds to the visual information given by the cellsteps heatmaps in Fig. 5. Thus, this analysis reinforce that the random and deterministic strategies implies a more heterogeneous coverage performed by the team, with respect to their scattering throughout the environment, while the stochastic, elitist and inertial strategies, imply a more homogeneous coverage. Moreover, we can verify that the homogeneous/heterogeneous behavior related to each variation does not change from experiments with individual to combined pheromones. One may conclude they are inherent to the decision strategy employed to choose the next robot position.

In order to confirm the results obtained in the previous experiments, the task point and cellsteps experiments were run again in Environment 2 (Fig. 2b), and are illustrated in Fig. 6. As in the experiment performed with Environment 1, Fig. 6a illustrates the task point boxplots considering all strategies analysed, using the individual and combined pheromone. The similarity with the same experiment performed with Environment 1 is remarkable, showing that, independent of the environment, the characteristics and particularities of each strategy are maintained. Of course, in this case since the environment has a larger number of rooms, the amount of task points reached by each strategy would be smaller, considering that the same 10,000 time steps were performed in the experiment. Again, pheromone-based strategies have been shown to have an efficiency greater than the lower limit we set (random strategy). The deterministic strategy presented a better dynamism and achieved the best results in this experiment. Followed by the inertial, elitist and stochastic strategies, respectively. In this case, the difference between the use of the individual pheromone and the combined pheromone was as follows: deterministic strategy (from 71 to 87 task points), stochastic (from 28 to 33), elitist (from 42 to 47) and inertial (from 44 to 49). This allows us to point out once again that the combination of the pheromones deposited by each robot increases the dynamism of the team, allowing better results.

Figure 6b shows the experiment with cellsteps. Similar to the previous experiment, 100 runs were done using Environment 2b with $T = 10,000$ time steps. Environment 2b has the same dimensions as Environment 2a, but with a different number of cells representing walls. Thus, for the Environment 2b, the mean of cellsteps, considering the entire set of free cells, is 68.9 cellsteps. This mean is represented by the green line in Fig. 6b. As seen in the experiment using the Environment 2a, the random and deterministic strategies showed a large dispersion of data, confirming the heterogeneity in the distribution of cellsteps by the environment. On the other hand, the stochastic, elitist and inertial strategies presented a more homogeneous distribution. Again, there was no significant difference between the boxplots using the individual pheromone and the combined pheromone in the same strategy. An interesting feature to highlight is the small increase in the dispersion of the number of cellsteps when the inertial strategy is applied, compared to the dispersion of the stochastic and elitist strategies. This increase can be observed both in the experiments performed, using the Environment 2a (Fig. 4b) and in the experiments using Environment 2b (Fig. 6b). This is due to the fact that the inertial strategy tends to keep the robots in their current direction, making them get in touch with the cells by the side of the walls more easily. Thus, increasing the amount of cellsteps in this area.

The same set of experiments presented in this section, was performed by doubling the dimensions of the two environments (Figs. 2a and b), resulting in environments with dimensions equal to (40×60). This was done to investigate the scalability of the model and the strategies. In both scenarios, the strategies allowed the swarm to exhibits similar behaviours to those observed in smaller environments.

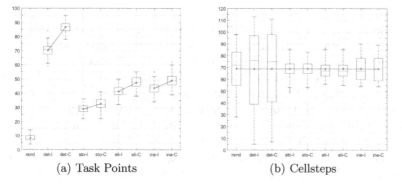

(a) Task Points   (b) Cellsteps

Fig. 6. Performance in surveillance task, using Environment 2b. (Color figure online)

4   Conclusion

A decentralized bio-inspired coordination model for a team of robots performing the surveillance task is investigated here. This model uses a two-dimensional cellular automata (CA) with Moore neighbourhood to support the navigation moves and the interaction between the robots. Cells store physical information about the environment using discrete states: walls, free cells and robot positions. Besides, they also store a real-coded information that enables the stigmergy among the team members: a repulsive pheromone that condenses the information about the recent paths navigated by the robots, helping the team to spread over the rooms. Five variations of the coordination model are investigated here, related to the next position decision performed at each time step. Three of them are stochastic and based on a probabilistic choice using the pheromone information. They were also investigated in [16]. The other two, although simple, have not been investigated with this model: a random decision is employed to compare its performance with the pheromone-based decisions and a deterministic strategy aims to investigate the importance of the probabilistic decision.

This work carried out an analysis of the influence of the indirect pheromone-based communication when the team performs the task of surveillance. For that, each model variation were executed with two approaches: in the first one, the robots make their decisions based on their own individual pheromone information and, in the second one, the pheromone information is shared among the robots.

Considering the experiments results, it was possible to conclude that (i) the pheromone information is very important for the team coordination, evidenced by the poor results obtained with the random strategy in terms of number of completed tasks points in a fixed interval of time; (ii) when the information about the pheromone deposited by each robot is combined, a cooperative behaviour emerges, allowing the team having a superior performance on the tasks, being that this behaviour was observed in all variations; (iii) the deterministic strategy returned the best performance considering its higher number of completed task points (even using the individual pheromone it overcame the other strategies);

(iv) on the other hand, the deterministic strategy does not spread the team in a homogeneous way, displaying a high predictable path close to the walls; (v) the elitist decision returned the most homogeneous coverage among all the analysed strategies, although it is the third strategy in terms of the number of completed tasks points; (vi) the inertial strategy exhibited the more balanced behaviour, both for the global scattering, searching for new areas, and locally, ensuring a homogeneous coverage through the environment; (vii) although not presented here due to the lack of space, experiments with larger environments have shown that the conclusions obtained here could be extended for other scenarios.

The most unexpected result for us was the good performance of the deterministic model in achieving an elevate number of task points. Previous investigations of CA models in other problems have shown that the deterministic choice can lead to jams and bottlenecks in the dynamics of robots, pedestrians and cars [13]. We believe that this difference is due to the fact that in the other problems, where jams and bottlenecks were observed, the information used to define the better choice at each next-move decision was fixed (or almost fixed). For example, in pedestrian models [12] typically the distance from a free cell to the door is used in a previously known environment. This information does not change along the time and the pedestrians tend to choose the same path to the door, with this, they collapse on the path. On our model for surveillance, on the other hand, the information that guides the next move – the pheromone – is changeable and once a robot decides to use a path because it has the lower value among neighbours, this value is incremented and the next robots will avoid the same path. Therefore, as the pheromone mapping is a dynamical environmental information, it seems that this problem was avoided and the use of the best choice turned the team to achieve the best walking close to the walls in the rooms. However, in the surveillance task, this predictable behaviour would be not appropriate, since intruders could anticipate robots trajectories. On the other hand, if the task is only for exploration, the deterministic strategy could be the most adequate.

Our analyses and conclusions allow us to characterize the model as being robust, scalable and flexible, the main desirable characteristics for a swarm robotics model [4]. However, here we present the results of experiments employing a team of 3 robots. We intend to continue this investigation towards swarms applications using teams with many robots. For future work, the authors also intend to investigate an automatic way to find the number of members of the swarm according to the variation in the sizes of the grid, ensuring that the model maintains the same efficiency independent of the environment. Furthermore, we intend to analyse new strategies, trying to get closer to the results of deterministic strategy without being predictable. The employment of mixed teams, where each robot can employ a different strategy, is also a hot topic of our future investigations.

Acknowledgment. GMBO is grateful to Fapemig, CNPq and CAPES financial support. CRT is grateful to CAPES for his scholarship.

References

1. Anisi, D.A., Ogren, P., Hu, X.: Cooperative minimum time surveillance with multiple ground vehicles. IEEE Trans. Autom. Control **55**(12), 2679–2691 (2010)
2. Bontzorlos, T., Sirakoulis, G.C.: Bioinspired algorithm for area surveillance using autonomous robots. Int. J. Parallel Emerg. Distrib. Syst. **32**(4), 368–385 (2017)
3. Boukas, E., Kostavelis, I., Gasteratos, A., Sirakoulis, G.C.: Robot guided crowd evacuation. IEEE Trans. Autom. Sci. Eng. **12**(2), 739–751 (2015)
4. Brambilla, M., Ferrante, E., Birattari, M., Dorigo, M.: Swarm robotics: a review from the swarm engineering perspective. Swarm Intell. **7**(1), 1–41 (2013)
5. Calvo, R., Constantino, A.A., Figueiredo, M.: Individual distinguishing pheromone in a multi-robot system for a balanced partitioned surveillance task. In: 2016 International Joint Conference on Neural Networks, pp. 4346–4353. IEEE (2016)
6. Calvo, R., de Oliveira, J.R., Romero, R.A., Figueiredo, M.: A bioinspired coordination strategy for controlling of multiple robots in surveillance tasks. Int. J. Adv. Softw. **5**(3 & 4), 2012 (2012)
7. Ferreira, G.B.S., Vargas, P.A., Oliveira, G.M.B.: An improved cellular automata-based model for robot path-planning. In: Mistry, M., Leonardis, A., Witkowski, M., Melhuish, C. (eds.) TAROS 2014. LNCS (LNAI), vol. 8717, pp. 25–36. Springer, Cham (2014). https://doi.org/10.1007/978-3-319-10401-0_3
8. Ioannidis, K., Sirakoulis, G.C., Andreadis, I.: Cellular ants: a method to create collision free trajectories for a cooperative robot team. Robot. Auton. Syst. **59**(2), 113–127 (2011)
9. Kerr, W., Spears, D.: Robotic simulation of gases for a surveillance task. In: 2005 IEEE/RSJ International Conference on Intelligent Robots and Systems, pp. 2905–2910. IEEE (2005)
10. Lima, D.A., Tinoco, C.R., Oliveira, G.M.B.: A cellular automata model with repulsive pheromone for swarm robotics in surveillance. In: El Yacoubi, S., Wąs, J., Bandini, S. (eds.) ACRI 2016. LNCS, vol. 9863, pp. 312–322. Springer, Cham (2016). https://doi.org/10.1007/978-3-319-44365-2_31
11. Lima, D.A., Oliveira, G.M.: New bio-inspired coordination strategies for multi-agent systems applied to foraging tasks. In: 28th International Conference on Tools with Artificial Intelligence, pp. 1–8. IEEE (2016)
12. Lima, D.A., Oliveira, G.M.: A probabilistic cellular automata ant memory model for a swarm of foraging robots. In: 2016 14th International Conference on Control, Automation, Robotics and Vision, pp. 1–6. IEEE (2016)
13. Lima, D.A., Oliveira, G.M.: A cellular automata ant memory model of foraging in a swarm of robots. Appl. Math. Model. **47**, 551–572 (2017)
14. Ludwig, L., Gini, M.: Robotic swarm dispersion using wireless intensity signals. In: Gini, M., Voyles, R. (eds.) Distributed Autonomous Robotic Systems 7, pp. 135–144. Springer, Tokyo (2006). https://doi.org/10.1007/4-431-35881-1_14
15. Sauter, J.A., Matthews, R., Van Dyke Parunak, H., Brueckner, S.A.: Performance of digital pheromones for swarming vehicle control. In: Proceedings of the Fourth International Joint Conference on Autonomous Agents and Multiagent Systems, pp. 903–910. ACM (2005)
16. Tinoco, C.R., Lima, D.A., Oliveira, G.M.B.: An improved model for swarm robotics in surveillance based on cellular automata and repulsive pheromone with discrete diffusion. Int. J. Parallel Emerg. Distrib. Syst., 1–25 (2017). https://doi.org/10.1080/17445760.2017.1334886
17. Zheng, Z., Tan, Y.: Group explosion strategy for searching multiple targets using swarm robotic. In: 2013 IEEE Congress on Evolutionary Computation, pp. 821–828. IEEE (2013)

Agent-Based Simulation of Information Spreading in VANET

Imre Varga$^{(\boxtimes)}$, Attila Némethy, and Gergely Kocsis

Department of Informatics Systems and Networks, University of Debrecen,
Egyetem tér 1, Debrecen 4032, Hungary
varga.imre@inf.unideb.hu

Abstract. A model of agent-based simulation of communicating vehicles is presented to study the information spreading in a vehicular ad hoc network (VANET). The agents are moving along the fastest paths between their starting points and their destinations on real urban topology. During the motion, they can exchange information by short-range wireless communication. The goal is to analyze the statistical properties of the information spreading in the system, e.g. the time evolution of the average awareness or the age distribution of information owned by separate vehicles.

Keywords: Agent-based simulation · Information spreading
VANET · Traffic simulation · City map

1 Introduction

Several smart city services are based on information dissemination in vehicular networks that is why the topic is in the focus of scientific research in the last couple of years. These applications try to make the urban traffic safer and our life even more comfortable. In order to increase the efficiency of these intelligent transportation systems the topological properties of urban road maps were analyzed [1,2], the traffic flow was measured and studied [3]. Different algorithms and methods were developed to simulate the motion of vehicles and generate traffic in urban or in highway environment [4–6]. Several communication protocols were introduced to ensure the communication of moving wireless devices using eighter Dedicated Short Range Communication (DSRC) or for example IEEE 802.11p standard [7–9]. In VANETs both the routing [10–12] and the broadcasting [4,13] is actively investigated fields.

Nevertheless, there are open questions still related to the statistical properties of the general spreading processes in VANETs. The goal of this research is to create a new framework in order to be able to answer some of the questions. What are the limits of the information spreading? Can we reach all actors of the traffic system based only on self-organization? Do all vehicles own up-to-date information? Similar questions have been appeared and already answered

© Springer Nature Switzerland AG 2018
G. Mauri et al. (Eds.): ACRI 2018, LNCS 11115, pp. 166–174, 2018.
https://doi.org/10.1007/978-3-319-99813-8_15

in social networks [14,15], but due to the continuously changing topology, the characteristics of spreading can be very different.

In Sect. 2 authors give some introduction how the realistic urban topology is built up. It is followed by the details of the simulation of vehicular motion in Sect. 3. The spreading of information based on carry-and-forward and multi-hop broadcast dissemination schemes is presented in Sect. 4 and then the first results of our investigation are shown in Sect. 5. This paper is closed by some conclusions.

2   Underlying Map Topology of Simulations

In order to reach realistic simulation environment, a real city map is applied as an underlying topology. The map of the authors' city was planned to apply. A very detailed dataset is available from the OpenStreetMap project [16]. For the later agent based simulation a much more simplified topology is needed, that is why the source was reduced keeping the topology of crossroad network and the distances between junctions, but losing the real geographical locations of road sections.

According to the original .osm format any crooked road can be build up from shorter straight segments and the geographical coordinates of their endpoints are given. In this way, a road section between crossroads can be described by a list of internal nodes with degree 2. In our traffic approach, the shape of a road section is negligible and only the length of the section is important. This was the base of our topology simplifying method. In case of any two road segments between nodes $A-B$ and nodes $B-C$, node B was eliminated if it has no other neighbors than A and C, merging the segments to only one longer segment between nodes $A - C$ with a distance equal to the sum of lengths of the previous segments (Fig. 1).

Fig. 1. Conversion of a street map to a simplified network. A small part of the map of Debrecen [16] is presented on the left. A visual representation of the corresponding graph is on the right, where crossroads are illustrated by circles. The thicker links represent road sections with higher average traffic speed. A possible route is highlighted.

Thus the map of Debrecen was reduced to a network of only 3422 nodes (junctions) connected by 4812 links (road sections). It was found that 84% of crossroads connects 3 or 4 roads. In the unit of linknumber (ignoring road length) the diameter of the network is 96. Taking into account the geographical distances the average distance between two crossroads is 121.5 m, however, the distribution is quite wide, there is almost 3 orders of magnitude difference between the shortest and the longest road section. (See the inset of Fig. 2.)

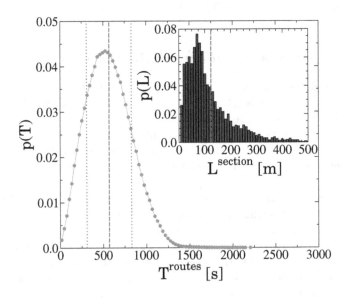

Fig. 2. Travel time distribution of routes. The vertical gray dashed line shows the average and the dotted lines indicate the standard deviation of the distribution. Inset: Length distribution of road sections (between crossroads).

3   Motion of Vehicles

It was assumed that vehicles proceed from their randomly chosen starting node toward their randomly chosen destination node along the fastest path because drivers usually use a route with the shortest travel time instead of the shortest distance route. The original dataset contains information about the rank of all road segments (for example: primary, secondary, residential, living street, etc.). The average speeds of cars depend on the rank of the road. Based on the speed prediction/offer of the Google Maps [17] different average velocity is applied in case of different road rank. Thus the shortest and the fastest route can be different.

Between two neighboring nodes, all vehicles proceed with constant velocity, at a crossroad they turn according to their route (and perhaps change speed). Traffic jams, traffic lights or the finite size of vehicles are not taken into account during the simulation because from the point of view of the later spreading process the short-term fluctuations of the speed of cars are negligible.

When a new vehicle is departed in the system it needs to get a route that is a node sequence to move along from the given location to the destination. Since the generation of shortest/fastest routes in a network of several thousand nodes is very time consuming, more than one million different random routes are generated and stored only once before the traffic simulation. In this way, the simulation itself can be fast because each vehicle just chooses a random route from the stored possibilities. However, the source and destination nodes are random the density of the traffic is really diversified due to the topology (connectivity, ranks).

It was assumed that the number of moving cars in the system at a given time can be constant because the simulated time interval is small compared to the daily life cycle of a city or the duration of rush-hours traffic. At the beginning of the simulation, the cardinality of vehicles is N. Later, when a vehicle arrives to its destination, it was removed and immediately a new one is initialized and started. At the beginning of the time evolution of the system, all the cars are just departed. In order to avoid artificial transient effects the measurement is started only later ($t = 0$) when the system become randomized, however, the simulation is started at $t = -T_0$. The length of the randomization time interval ($-T_0 \leq t < 0$) is longer then the most of trips ($T_0 = 750$ s, average travel time is 459 ± 261 s, see the main panel of Fig. 2), so when the scientific observation is started all the initial cars have been arrived and others are launched in different time moments.

The simulation is stopped at $t = T_{max}$. The time interval of the analysis ($0 \leq t \leq T_{max}$) is enough long to cover several generations of vehicles, so the total number of simulated cars (N_t) is at least five times greater the number of cars at a given moment ($N_t > 5N$). The time evolution of the system is discrete. The time step Δt is enough to move only a few meters, so it is tiny compared to the whole simulation time $\Delta t \ll T_0 + T_{max}$.

4   Spreading of Information

In this system, smart vehicles are represented by agents which can interact by short-range communication. If the distance of two vehicles at a given time moment is less than the range R of the wireless communication, they can exchange information. Based on this, in our model the agents can have two different states. On the one hand agent i can be uninformed, so it has not received any data (denoted by $S_i = 0$). On the other hand, it can be informed, so it has already got some data (denoted by $S_i = 1$). Beside this Inter-Vehicular Communication (IVC) there is Vehicle-to-Roadside Communication (VRC) as well. In the latter case the On Board Units (OBU) of smart vehicles can receive information from Road Side Units (RSU). In our first model initially all agents are in uninformed state and only one RSU is present, playing the role of an information source. When an agent passes by the RSU it receives a new up-to-date information (e.g. traffic or weather alert). The agent stores it together with the actual time stamp and later it shares with others within the communication range. If one of these neighboring agents is uninformed it becomes informed. If both agents in the contact have been already informed, the agent with older time stamp will update its knowledge storing the newer information with the given timestamp. Thus information can spread in this dynamically changing network from the RSU to any vehicle even if they have never passed by the RSU. In order to characterize agent i in detail we introduce the quantity τ_i which is the latest/newest time stamp of information owned by the informed agent i or $\tau_i = -1$, if agent i is uninformed. (So $\tau_i > 0$ is the simulation time when the given information entered into the system by the RSU.) The behavior of the system is shown in Fig. 3.

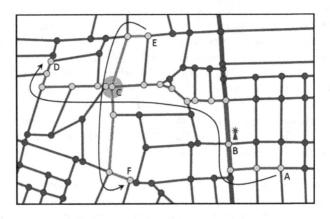

Fig. 3. The behavior of the system. A vehicle (agent i) proceeds from node A to node D. It goes by the RSU in node B receiving new information at $t = \tau$. An other vehicle (agent j) move from node E toward node F. Both of them are in the vicinity of the node C at the same time. Since they are within the range R, agent i can transmit the information to agent j. Between nodes A and B agent i is uninformed, but between C and D it is in an informed state, having timestamp τ. Agent j possesses also timestamp τ between nodes C and F.

At simulation time t an informed agent i have information with age $A_i = t - \tau_i$. The average age of information $\langle A \rangle$ owned by agents can be written as

$$\langle A \rangle = \frac{\sum_i \tau_i S_i}{N^i}, \tag{1}$$

where N^i is the number of informed agents, defined as $N^i = \sum_i S_i$. Large value of N^i indicate extensive information spreading. When the average age of information $\langle A \rangle$ is low, it means that our smart traffic system is in an up-to-date phase. Thus the number of informed agents N^i and the average age of information $\langle A \rangle$ are good measures of the effectiveness of information spreading in VANET.

5   Results

While an SI (Susceptible-Infected) model is applied more and more agents
become informed. Nevertheless, the system never reaches a fully informed state,
because of the continuously changing set of agents. Organically new, uninformed
agents appear in the system, while informed ones disappear. Investigating the
time evolution of the agents it was found that the system reaches a steady state
described by saturating functions. In Fig. 4 one can observe that at $t = 0$ (when
the RSU is just activated) there is no informed agents in the system, but soon
some agents pass by the information source of the infrastructure. Then the vehicles carry the information during their motion to different places of the city
meanwhile they also behave as information sources speeding up the spreading of
information so leading to increasing $N^i(t)/N$ function with a significant slope.

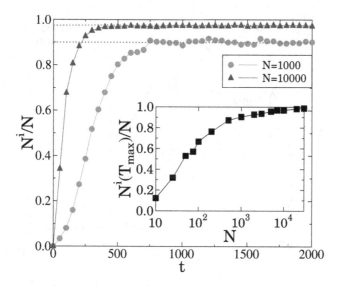

Fig. 4. Number of informed agents (vehicles) as a function of time for different numbers
of agents. After a short time period a saturation is achieved at a quite high value. Inset:
The saturation level depends on the number of vehicles in the system (of course more
smart vehicle leads to higher level of awareness).

After a quite short time period, a dominant proportion of agents are in the
informed state, spreading slows down resulting in saturation of the number of
informed agents. The average movement of vehicles during a simulation step
Δt is the half of the applied range of communication R. (Of course, increasing
range R speeds up the spreading.) Due to this, the propagation of information
can be faster then the motion of vehicles, so that is why we reach saturation
so quickly. The $N^i(t)/N$ curves never reach 1.0, the saturation level depends on
the number of agents (the density of smart vehicles in the city). It is illustrated
in the inset of Fig. 4. As we can observe the information coverage of VANET

can be effective only if the number of smart vehicles exceeds a given threshold (about few hundreds of vehicles in Debrecen).

The number of informed agents is proved to be relatively high in the system, but the really important questions are the follows. How old is the average information? Is the system in an up-to-date phase continuously? The average information age as a function of time $\langle A \rangle (t)$ can give the answers. It is illustrated in Fig. 5 the most of agents have relatively young information. Recent information from RSU overwrites the system very quickly without any outer control. Of course the level of $\langle A \rangle (t)$ (far from the opening time period) determined by the number of agents. More smart vehicles lead to a more up-to-date system. (See the inset of Fig. 5.) The average age of information is even less than the length of time period needed to reach the saturation of the number of informed agents.

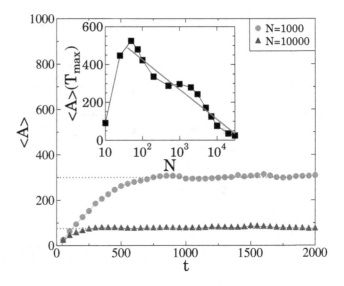

Fig. 5. The average age of information owned by the vehicles as a function of time. It shows saturation for different system size. Inset: The average age of information in the saturation phase decreases logarithmically with the number of vehicles, so denser vehicle park in the city results more up-to-date system.

6   Summary

An agent-based model of information spreading in VANET was presented. The time-dependent network topology of agents was based on the motion of smart vehicles. The changing set of vehicles (with constant cardinality) are following their routes based on shortest travel time between the randomly selected start and destination points of a real city. Due to the short-range communication moving vehicles can receive information from each other or from fix infrastructure unit(s). In this ad hoc network, the statistical properties of information spreading can be investigated. Above a threshold of smart vehicles information spreads in a very fast way, and a dominant part of the system can be in an up-to-date state. However this work is mainly focused on the implementation of the model, the some results of the computer simulation show that there are hidden potentials in the introduced complex system. In our further research, we try to find answers to essential, practical questions. What happens if the RSU is removed (turned off)? How does an old information die out? How to avoid the presence old (fake, not up-to-date) information? What is the effect of the introduction of an Susceptible-Infected-Susceptible (SIS) model (forgetting old information)? How to optimize spreading reducing the number of information exchanges (energy efficiency), but keeping system in an up-to-date phase? What is the topology of this ad hoc communication network?

Acknowledgments. Imre Varga is supported by the EFOP-3.6.1-16-2016-00022 project. The project is co-financed by the European Union and the European Social Fund.

Attila Némethy is supported by the EFOP-3.6.3-VEKOP-16-2017-00002 pro-ject. The project is co-financed by the European Union and the European Social Fund.

Map data copyrighted OpenStreetMap contributors and available from https://www.openstreetmap.org.

References

1. Porta, S., Crucitti, P., Latora, V.: The network analysis of urban streets: a dual approach. Phys. A **369**, 853–866 (2006)
2. Jiang, B.: A topological pattern of urban street networks: universality and peculiarity. Phys. A **384**, 647–655 (2007)
3. Yan, Y., Zhang, S., Tang, J., Wang, X.: Understanding characteristics in multivariate traffic flow time series from complex network structure. Phys. A **477**, 149–160 (2017)
4. Zeadally, S., Hunt, R., Chen, Y.S., Irwin, A., Hassan, A.: Vehicular ad hoc networks (VANETS): status, results, and challenges. Telecommun. Syst. **50**, 217–241 (2012)
5. Fiore, M., Härri, J., Filali, F., Bonnet, C.: Vehicular mobility simulation for VANETs. In: 40th Annual Simulation Symposium (ANSS 2007), Norfolk, pp. 301–309 (2007)
6. Bátfai, N., Besenczi, R., Mamenyák, A., Ispány, M.: Traffic simulation based on the robocar world championship initiative. Infocommun. J. **7**, 50–58 (2015)
7. Salvo, P., de Felice, M., Baiocchi, A., Cuomo, F., Rubin, I.: Timer-based distributed dissemination protocols for VANETs and their interaction with MAC layer. In: IEEE 77th Vehicular Technology Conference, Dresden, pp. 1–6 (2013)
8. Malla, A.M., Sahu, R.K.: A review on vehicle to vehicle communication protocols in VANETs. Int. J. Adv. Res. Comput. Sci. Softw. Eng. **3**, 409–414 (2013)
9. Xu, Q., Sengupta, R., Mak, T., Ko, J.: Vehicle-to-vehicle safety messaging in DSRC. In: Proceedings of the 1st ACM International Workshop on Vehicular Ad Hoc Networks, pp. 19–28 (2004)

10. Nishtha, D.M.: Vehicular ad hoc networks (VANET). Int. J. Adv. Res. Electron. Commun. Eng. **5**, 1003–1008 (2016)
11. Gong, J., Xu, C.Z., Holle, J.: Predictive directional greedy routing in vehicular ad hoc networks. In: 27th International Conference on Distributed Computing Systems Workshops (ICDCSW 2007), Toronto, p. 2 (2007)
12. Ramakrishna, M.: DBR: distance based routing protocol for VANETs. Int. J. Inf. Electron. Eng. **2**, 228–232 (2012)
13. Sanguesa, J.A., Fogue, M., Garrido, P., Martinez, F.J., Cano, J.C., Calafate, C.T.: A survey and comparative study of broadcast warning message dissemination schemes for VANETs. Mob. Inf. Syst. 1–18 (2016). Article no. 8714142
14. Varga, I.: Comparison of network topologies by simulation of advertising. In: Gusikhin, O., Méndez Muñoz, V., Firouzi, F., Mønster, D., Chang, C. (eds.) Proceedings of the 2nd International Conference on Complexity, Future Information Systems and Risk (COMPLEXIS 2017), pp. 17–22. SciTePress (2017)
15. Kocsis, G., Varga, I.: Agent based simulation of spreading in social-systems of temporarily active actors. In: Wąs, J., Sirakoulis, G.C., Bandini, S. (eds.) ACRI 2014. LNCS, vol. 8751, pp. 330–338. Springer, Cham (2014). https://doi.org/10.1007/978-3-319-11520-7_34
16. OpenStreetMap contributors (2017). https://www.openstreetmap.org
17. Google Maps (2017). https://maps.google.com

Pedestrian and Traffic Dynamics

Analysis of Rates of Agents' Decisions in Learning to Cross a Highway in Populations with Risk Takers and Risk Avoiders

Anna T. Lawniczak$^{(\boxtimes)}$ and Fei Yu

Department of Mathematics and Statistics, University of Guelph,
Guelph, ON, Canada
{alawnicz,fyu03}@uoguelph.ca

Abstract. The rates of cognitive agents' correct and incorrect crossing decisions, correct and incorrect waiting decisions in learning to cross cellular automaton based highway are studied. The effects of presence of risk takers and risk avoiders on these rates are investigated for agents using observational social learning strategies. One of these strategies is based on the assessment of agents crossing decisions, and another one is based on the assessment of agents crossing and waiting decisions. Also, the effects of transfer of agents' knowledge base built in one traffic environment to the agents in another one on the rates of agents' various decisions are investigated.

Keywords: Agents · Cognitive agents · Observational learning
Knowledge base · Decision-making · Autonomous robots

1 Introduction

The autonomous robots may be identified with cognitive agents. This permit studying, through modeling and simulation, how their learning performance depends on various parameters, [1]. We study performance of homogeneous and heterogeneous (i.e., containing risk takers and risk avoiders) populations of cognitive agents learning to cross a cellular automaton (CA) based highway under various traffic conditions. The agents use a simple *observational social learning strategy*, [2] in which they learn by observing the performance of other agents, mimicking what worked for them and avoiding what did not in the past. Our work focuses on simplicity of the learning algorithms and it is an extension of the previous research [3–5], in which the agents' decision formula was based only on the assessment of agents crossing decisions. In [6] we introduced a modified decision formula which incorporates the assessment of the agents both crossing and waiting decisions. We study how this modification improves agents' performance measured by the rates of agents four decision types: correct and incorrect crossing decisions, and correct and incorrect waiting decisions. We investigate the effects of the presence of risk takers and risk avoiders on these rates for various density of cars on the highway. We study how the transfer of agents' knowledge base, built by agents in one traffic environment to the agents learning to cross in a different traffic environment, affects the rates of their decisions.

© Springer Nature Switzerland AG 2018
G. Mauri et al. (Eds.): ACRI 2018, LNCS 11115, pp. 177–184, 2018.
https://doi.org/10.1007/978-3-319-99813-8_16

The paper is organized as follows: Sect. 2 describes the model focusing on agents' decision-making algorithms; Sect. 3 describes setup of simulation parameters, the resulting data, introduces the rate functions of agents' decisions and the considered agents' populations; Sect. 4 presents analysis of selected simulation results. Section 5 reports our conclusions and outlines future work.

2   Model of Agents Learning to Cross a Highway

For detailed description of the model the reader is referred to [3–6]. We assume that: (1) the environment is a single lane unidirectional highway, modelled by adopting the Nagel-Schreckenberg cellular automaton (CA) model [7]; (2) all agents want to learn how to cross the highway without being hit/killed by the oncoming vehicles and they witness what had happened to the agents that previously crossed the highway at a given crossing point (with exclusion of the first one). These allow each crossing point (CP) to build one knowledge base (KB) during an experiment that is available to all agents at that CP. An agent is generated only at the CPs set at the initialization step and is placed into the queue at this CP. Each generated agent falls with equal probability (0.25) into one of the four categories: (1) no Fear nor Desire; (2) only Fear; (3) only Desire; (4) both Fear and Desire. The agents' attributes/parameters of *Fear* and *Desire* play a role in their decision-making process of crossing the highway. The values of *Fear* reflect the agents' *aversion to risk taking* and the values of *Desire* reflect their *propensity to risk taking*. Agents attempt to cross the highway having a limited horizon of vision and they can perceive only *fuzzy* levels of speed (e.g., *slow, medium, fast, very fast*) and of distance (e.g., *close, medium, far*) of cars within this horizon. The distances and speeds that each agent can perceive are set in the configuration file. If an agent at some instance of time does not cross the highway, because it has become *afraid*, agents will build up in the queue until the agent at the top of the queue, called *active agent*, decides to cross, or moves to a different location from which to attempt crossing. If the simulation setup permits, an agent may move randomly right or left from its CP along the highway, [3–6].

Each active agent must make one of the following two decisions: Crossing Decision (CD) or Waiting Decision (WD). The CD is Correct Crossing Decision (CCD) if the active agent succeeds, if not then it is Incorrect Crossing Decision (ICD). The WD is: (1) Correct Waiting Decision (CWD), in the case when, if the agent did not wait and chose to cross, it would be hit; (2) Incorrect Waiting Decision (IWD), in the case when, the active agent chose to wait but it could have crossed the highway successfully. The assessment of each decision of an active agent, i.e. if the decision was CCD, ICD, CWD, or IWD, is recorded, respectively, as a count in the Knowledge-Based (KB) table of all agents waiting at the CP of the active agent. Thus, with each CP is associated its KB table.

Each KB table is organized as a matrix with an *extra row entry*. The columns names are *slow, medium, fast* and *very fast*. They stand for the car speeds perceived by the active agents. The rows names are *close, medium* and *far*. They stand for the car distances perceived by the active agents. Since the agents have limited horizon of vision, the *extra row entry* corresponds to agents' *out of range* vision, i.e. the situation in which an active agent cannot perceive if outside its horizon of vision there is a car and if it is, what is its velocity. Because of this the cells corresponding to the described fuzzy velocity levels are all merged together into the *extra row entry*. At each time t, each entry of the KB table (including the *extra row entry*) contains four numbers: number of CCDs, number of ICDs, number of CWDs and number of IWDs, i.e. of each of the decision type made by the active agents up to time $t-1$. The KB table is initialized as *tabula rasa*; i.e. a "blank slate", represented by "(0, 0, 0, 0)" at each table entry, for further details see [3–6]. After the initialization period the active agents make their decisions based on the outcomes of the implemented intelligence/decision-making algorithm, which for a given (distance, velocity) pair or *out of range* vision combines the *success ratio* of crossing the highway for the observed situation with the agent's *Fear* and/or *Desire* parameters' values.

The main simulation loop of the model consists of: (1) generating randomly cars using the Car Prob.; (2) generating agents at each CP with their attributes; (3) updating the car speeds according the Nagel-Schreckenberg model; (4) moving the agents from their CP queues into the highway (if the decision algorithm indicates this should occur); (5) updating locations of the cars on the highway, checking if any agent has been killed and updating the KB tables; (6) advancing of the current time step. After the simulation is completed, the results are written to output files using an output function.

The decision formula (DF) of [3–5] considers only the outcomes of agents' CDs, i.e. numbers of successful and killed agents for each fuzzy (distance, velocity) pair observation or for *out of range* vision at time t. Since the number of successful agents is equal to the number of CCDs, and the number of killed agents is equal to the number of ICDs, we call this formula Crossing Based Decision Formula (cDF).

After the initialization phase, at each time step t, each active agent, carries several tasks, namely: (1) determines if there is a car in its horizon of vision. If it is, then it determines the fuzzy (i^{th} distance, j^{th} velocity) values of the closest car; (2) from the KB table associated with its CP it gets information about the number of CCDs and the number of ICDs for the observed (i^{th} distance, j^{th} velocity) pair, or for the observed *out of range* vision situation, entry of which in the KB table is denoted by (0, 0) pair of indexes; (3) for the observed (i, j) situation it calculates the value of the cDF, i.e. the value $cDF_{ij}(t)$, corresponding to the (i, j) entry of the KB table (including the *extra row entry*). The expression $cDF_{ij}(t)$ is calculated as follows:

$$cDF_{ij}(t) = cSR_{ij}(t) + v(Desire) - v(Fear), \tag{1}$$

where $v(Desire)$ and $v(Fear)$ are the values of the active agent *Fear* and *Desire* attributes/parameters, and $cSR_{ij}(t)$ is the Crossing Based Success Ratio (cSR) corresponding to the ij^{th} entry of the KB table. The $cSR_{ij}(t)$ is calculated as follows:

$$cSR_{ij}(t) = \{CCD_{ij}(t-1) - ICD_{ij}(t-1)\} / CCD_{total}(t-1). \tag{2}$$

The terms $CCD_{ij}(t-1)$ and $ICD_{ij}(t-1)$ are, respectively, the numbers of CCDs and of ICDs recorded in the ij^{th} entry of the KB table up to time $t-1$. The term $CCD_{total}(t-1)$ is the number of all CCDs made by active agents up to time $t-1$, i.e. it is the sum of CCDs made up to time $t-1$ over all the entries of the KB table. The number $CCD_{total}(t-1)$ is equivalent to the total number of successful agents up to time $t-1$.

After the initialization period (for details see [6]), if $cDF_{ij}(t) \geq 0$, then an active agent decides to cross, if $cDF_{ij}(t) \geq 0$, then it decides to wait and additionally it may move to another crossing point, if simulation setup permits.

The modified decision formula, called Crossing-and-Waiting Based Decision Formula (cwDF) [6], is based on the assessment of both crossing and waiting decisions of the active agents. The formula cwDF is obtained from cDF formula by replacing the term $cSR_{ij}(t)$ by the term $cwSR_{ij}(t)$ in the cDF formula (1). The term $cwSR_{ij}(t)$, called Crossing-and-Waiting Based Success Ratio (cwSR), is defined for each ij entry of the KB table at time t as follows:

$$cwSR_{ij}(t) = \{CCD_{ij}(t-1) - ICD_{ij}(t-1) - CWD_{ij}(t-1) + IWD_{ij}(t-1)\}/S(t-1),$$
(3)

where $CCD_{ij}(t-1)$, $ICD_{ij}(t-1)$, $CWD_{ij}(t-1)$ and $IWD_{ij}(t-1)$, respectively, is the number of CCDs, ICDs, CWDs and IWDs, made by active agents up to time $t-1$, which is recorded in the entry ij of KB table. The term $S(t-1)$ is the sum of all the numbers of decisions made up to time $t-1$ over all the entries of the KB table, and it is given by

$$S(t-1) = \sum_{ij} \{CCD_{ij}(t-1) + ICD_{ij}(t-1) + CWD_{ij}(t-1) + IWD_{ij}(t-1)\}.$$
(4)

Thus, the formula cwDF can be written as follows

$$cwDF_{ij}(t) = cwSR_{ij}(t) + v(Desire) - v(Fear),$$
(5)

where the term $cwSR_{ij}(t)$ is defined in (3). As before $v(Desire)$, $v(Fear)$ are the values of an active agent *Desire* and *Fear* attributes/parameters and for an observed (i, j) situation an active agent decides to cross the highway only when $cwDF_{ij}(t) \geq 0$. Otherwise, the active agent will wait and additionally it may move to another crossing point, if the simulation setup allows this.

Depending on *Desire* and *Fear* parameters values the difference $v(Desire) - v(Fear)$ in the DFs (1) and (5) acts like a threshold and determines an agent "rationality", or "propensity to risk taking", or "aversion to risk taking". If the values of *Desire* and *Fear* are both 0.0, then all agents use cSR or cwSR in their decision-making process, i.e. the entire population of agents acts "rationally" alike in their decision-making process. However, if the values of Desire and Fear are different from 0.0, then no longer all agents act "rationally" alike, i.e. at least 25% of agents will have propensity to risk taking and at least 25% will have aversion to risk taking.

3 Simulation Data and Rate Functions of Agents Decisions

To study the effects of DF on agents performance data sets were generated, respectively, for cDF and cwDF, with the same setup of the other parameter values.

We consider the model parameters as factors with various levels in the sense of the experimental design paradigm [8]. Some parameters have constant values some other not. The detailed description of the parameters and their values is in [6]. We consider the same values of the parameters as in [6].

There are 6 parameters/factors values of which vary in the simulation setups of the software. These parameters are: (1) *car creation probability*, i.e. CCP; (2) *Fear* parameter; (3) *Desire* parameter; (4) the *KB transfer* parameter, i.e. KBT; (5) *random deceleration*, i.e. RD and (5) *horizontal movement* of an active agent, i.e. HM.

We measure the agents' performance by the *rate functions* of their CCDs, ICDs, CWDs and IWDs, i.e. by the time series $RCCD(t)$, $RICD(t)$, $RCWD(t)$ and $RIWD(t)$, where "*R*" stands for "rate". Each value of each of these times series at each time t is a mean calculated over many simulation runs. Consider $RCCD(t)$ as an example, then

$$RCCD(t) = \frac{1}{n}\sum_{k=1}^{n} \frac{CCD_k(t)}{t}, \qquad (6)$$

where $CCD_k(t)$ is the number of all CCDs up to time t in the simulation run k, where $k = 1, \ldots, n$, and n stands for the number of repeats. In our case $n = 30$. Thus, $CCD_k(t)$ is the sum of $CCD_{ij}(t)$ over all the entries of the KB table at time t in the simulation run k. The time series $RICD(t)$, $RCWD(t)$ and $RIWD(t)$ are calculated by replacing $CCD_k(t)$ in (6), respectively, by $ICD_k(t)$, $CWD_k(t)$ and $IWD_k(t)$, which are calculated similarly as $CCD_k(t)$. When HM = 0, i.e. when only one CP is allowed, then only one active agent makes decision per each time step. Thus, the values of each rate function are always between 0 and 1.

4 Simulation Results

We compare the rates of decision functions of the agents using cwDF with the rates of these functions when the agents use cDF instead. Also, we study how the values of *Fear* and *Desire* parameters and the transfer of KB affect the agents' rates of decisions. Let's recall that the values of *Fear* and *Desire* parameters determine the value of the threshold each agent uses in its decision-making process. Thus, they determine if an agent acts "rationally" or not (i.e., it makes its decision based on Success Ratio cSR or cwSR only), or if it is risk taker or risk avoider. To illustrate the effects of risk takers and risk avoiders on agents' populations performance we discuss the results for the following representative pairs of (*Desire, Fear*) parameters' values: (0.0, 0.0), (0.5, 0.5), (0.25, 0.75) and (0.75, 0.25). For (*Desire, Fear*) parameters' values (0.0, 0.0) each population of agents is homogeneous one, i.e. all agents act "rationally". For the other values of the parameters the populations of agents are heterogeneous ones. For (0.5, 0.5) they contain the same numbers of risk takers as risk avoiders, for (0.25, 0.75) smaller number, for (0.75, 0.25) larger number of risk takers than risk avoiders. The risk takers' and risk avoiders' subpopulations are homogeneous ones for (0.5, 0.5). However, the risk avoiders' subpopulations are heterogeneous ones for (0.25, 0.75) and the risk takers' subpopulations are heterogeneous ones for (0.75, 0.25), i.e. the agents in these subpopulations use different thresholds in their decisions.

The simulation results are organized as follows. The results are displayed for KBT = 0, RD = 0, HM = 0 in the first two columns and for KBT = 1, RD = 0, HM = 0 in the last two columns. The figure's first and third column display the decision rate functions for cDF and the second and fourth column display these functions for cwDF. On each inset of the figure the solid curves display the rate of decision functions, and the corresponding colour marker curves display one standard deviations of rate of decision functions. On each inset we display 5 graphs of the rate of decision functions, each one of them for different CCP value. We assign the colours to these graphs as follows: red to CCP = 0.1, blue to CCP = 0.3, green to CCP = 0.5, black to CCP = 0.7 and yellow to CCP = 0.9. The values of CWDs and ICDs rate functions are very small for both DF. Thus, we do not display them here.

Our simulations show that the values of rate functions of "rational" populations of agents (i.e., homogeneous ones) are alike for all CCP values and both DFs, and the transfer of KB does not improve significantly the agents' performance (results not display here). This is not the case for heterogeneous populations of agents, see Fig. 1, which displays CCDs and IWDs rate functions for (*Desire, Fear*) parameters' values (0.25, 0.75), (0.5, 0.5) and (0.75, 0.25). We notice that for heterogeneous populations of agents: (1) the performance depends on CCP vlaues and DF the agents use; (2) the performance degradation increases with the increase of *Fear* parameter values, i.e. with the increase of risk avoiders' numbers and their threshold values. For cwDF, after some transient times the agents' population overcome this and their decisions' rates are like those of homogeneous population of agents (except *RIWD* for (0.75, 0.25)), this is not the case for cDF; (3) variability in performance increases with the increase of *Desire* parameter values (i.e., with the increase of risk takers numbers and risk takers threshold values) significantly for cDF but not for cwDF. The transfer of KB reduces this variability for cwDF but not for cDF; (4) the transfer of KB improves significantly the performance of heterogeneous populations of agents for cwDF but does not for cDF. After the KB transfer the performance for cwDF becomes alike to the one of homogeneous population of agents but not for cDF.

Our simulations show that for the heterogeneous population of agents using cDF the values of IWDs rate functions are significantly higher than the respective values of the homogeneous populations, and with the increase of CCP values and as time progresses the values of IWDs rate functions monotonically increase causing decrease, to almost zero, in the values of CCDs rate functions. Thus, for cDF, the values of CCDs rate functions are significantly lower for the heterogeneous populations of agents than for the homogeneous ones. Also, these values are lower from those when the agents use cwDF instead. For cwDF and when KBT = 0, the values of CCDs rate functions, after some transient times, increase monotonically with the increase of CCP values and as time progresses they reach asymptotically almost the values like the ones of the homogeneous populations of agents. These monotonic increase is the result of the monotonic decrease in the values of IWDs rate functions. Thus, when the heterogeneous populations of agents use cwDF the values of CCDs and IWDs rate functions

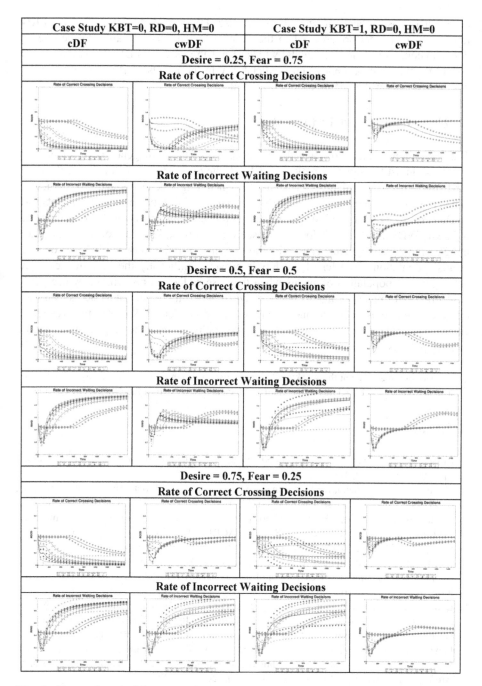

Fig. 1. Mean values (solid curves) of CCDs and IWDs rates and their one standard deviations (marker curves) for various *Desire, Fear* and CCP parameters values. (Color figure online)

behave in opposite way than when the agents use cDF instead. Also, transferring of KB improves agents' performance when they use cwDF, it becomes alike to the one of homogeneous population of agents, which is not the case for cDF. Thus, the use of cwDF guarantees consistency and predictability in the agents' performance, which is not the case when the agents use cDF instead.

5 Conclusions and Future Work

The simulation results show that the performance of the homogeneous population of agents is almost the same regardless which DF they use. However, this is not the case for heterogeneous populations of agents, i.e. including risk takers and risk avoiders. A heterogeneous population of agents' performance is much better when the agents use cwDF instead of cDF in their decision-making process. The inclusion of the assessment of agents WDs into their DF formula, based only on the assessment of their CDs, can mitigate the negative effects caused by the presence of risk takers and risk avoiders in agents' population. Transfer of the KB improves significantly the performance of a heterogeneous population of agents when they use cwDF but not when they use cDF. Also, the performance of agents using cwDF is much more consistent across various traffic environments, then the one when they use cDF instead. We plan to investigate agents' performance in learning to cross the highway for other types of decision-making process.

Acknowledgments. The authors acknowledge the useful discussions with B. Di Stefano, Leslie Ly and H. Wu. A. T. L. acknowledges partial financial support from the NSERC of Canada.

References

1. Russell, S., Norvig, P.: Artificial Intelligence, A Modern Approach. Pearson Education Limited, London (2014)
2. Nehavin, C., Dautenhahn, K.: Imitation and Social Learning in Robots, Humans and Animals. Cambridge University Press, Cambridge (2007)
3. Lawniczak, A.T., Ernst, J.B., Di Stefano, B.N.: Creature learning to cross a CA simulated road. In: Sirakoulis, G.C., Bandini, S. (eds.) ACRI 2012. LNCS, vol. 7495, pp. 425–433. Springer, Heidelberg (2012). https://doi.org/10.1007/978-3-642-33350-7_44
4. Lawniczak, A.T., Di Stefano, B.N., Ly, L., Xie, S.: Performance of population of naïve creatures with fear and desire capable of observational social learning. Acta Phys. Pol. Ser. B, Proc. Suppl. 9(1), 95–107 (2016)
5. Lawniczak, A.T., Ly, L., Yu, F., Xie, S.: Effects of model parameter interactions on Naïve creatures' success of learning to cross a highway. In: The 2016 IEEE Congress on Evolutionary Computation (IEEE CEC 2016) at IEEE WCCI 2016, 10 p. (2016)
6. Lawniczak, A.T., Yu, F.: Comparison of agent's performance in learning to cross a highway for two decisions formulas. In: Proceedings of the 9th International Conference on Agents and Artificial Intelligence, ICAART 2017, vol. 1, pp. 208–219 (2017)
7. Nagel, K., Schreckenberg, M.: A cellular automaton model for freeway traffic. J. Phys. I 2, 2221–2229 (1992)
8. Dean, A., Voss, D.: Design and Analysis of Experiments. Springer, New York (1999). https://doi.org/10.1007/b97673

The Automatic Generation of an Efficient Floor Field for CA Simulations in Crowd Management

Mohcine Chraibi$^{(\boxtimes)}$ and Bernhard Steffen

Jülich Supercomputing Centre – Forschungszentrum Jülich GmbH,
52425 Jülich, Germany
{m.chraibi,b.steffen,a.seyfried}@fz-juelich.de
http://www.fz-juelich.de/ias/jsc/cst

Abstract. The Hermes project [1] demonstrated the usefulness of on site predictive simulations of probable evacuation scenarios for security personnel. However, the hardware needed was prohibitively expensive [2]. For use in crowd management, the software has to run on available computers. The CA methods, which are fast enough, have well known problems with treating corners and turns. The present paper shows how a standard CA method can be modified to produce a realistic movement of people around bends and obstacles by changing the standard floor field. This can be done adaptively allowing for the momentary situation using simple predictions for the immediate future. The approach has one or two tuning parameter that have an obvious meaning and can therefore be set correctly by people not familiar with the inner process of a CA simulation. With this, a high end laptop can simulate more than 100 000 persons faster than real time, which should be enough for most occasions. It is intended to integrate the method into the tool JuPedSim [23].

Keywords: Cellular automata · Modeling · Pedestrian dynamics
Lanes at corners

1 Introduction

During the last few decades, the number and size of events that involve large crowds has increased considerably. At the same time, the safety requirements have increased also. Since about 1990, computer simulations have been established as a useful planning tool for the design of pedestrian facilities and are routinely applied in the design of large buildings, cruise ships, sports arenas or public transport facilities. However, the methods have not yet found their way into the steering of actual events, as the established systems for planning are too time consuming for steering of events, where simulation and display of results faster than real time is required. Faster and easier to use simulations can be helpful for crowd managers of large events, but also in the evacuation of facilities because of present danger (e.g. fire, bomb threat) where the preplanned

© Springer Nature Switzerland AG 2018
G. Mauri et al. (Eds.): ACRI 2018, LNCS 11115, pp. 185–195, 2018.
https://doi.org/10.1007/978-3-319-99813-8_17

evacuation routes may not be operational any more. The Hermes project demonstrated that on the site predictive simulations of probable crowd movement are feasible and useful for crowd management. However, the requirements in specific hardware were higher than facilities are willing to pay by a large margin.

Computer simulations of pedestrian facilities can be (and are) done on different scales. The coarsest scale uses a tree or network of pathways that take time, but have no active capacity restriction, and nodes (doors, junction of floors etc.), that do have active capacity restrictions [7]. These models are very fast, but there is no reliable way to include the highly nonlinear effects that appear in high density crowds. They may indicate that there is trouble ahead, but at that time (which is the time when information is needed most) they stop to make useful predictions. An intermediate scale is mostly handled by a cellular automata (CA) model where space and time are discrete and agents are moving from one space element to another according to some transition rules [11,15]. These methods are fast enough for on site real time simulations e.g. of a large sports stadium, and they can make predictions for high density crowds, but have in the established versions other deficiencies [16]. We will treat the details in the paper. The finest scale uses models in continuous space and time where agents are moved usually according to Newton's laws, by forces generated mostly internally as a reaction to the desired momentary destination and the local environment. Examples of this methods are [17,18]. It is possible to combine models on different scales [8–10], and this leads to a good combination of speed, resolution and reliability. Unfortunately, setting up the coupling is not automatic yet but requires expertise and time with predefined coupling zones, so this is at present not the way for crowd management.

In this paper we show how the most obvious problems of the standard CA can be removed by an automatic procedure with only a moderate increase in computing time. This modification is following the ideas of a manual changing of the floor field that the authors have implemented before [10,16] and demonstrated as reliable and useful. With this modification, a simple CA is able to simulate the movement of more than 100 000 persons faster than real time on an i7 quadcore for a large variety of floor plans. It still does not reach the flexibility and resolution of continuous models, and is not fully realistic in some aspects (more details below), but for a quick evaluation of the likely development of a situation over a few minutes it should be sufficiently accurate to be helpful.

2   General Properties of CA Models

Cellular automata are the most widely used approach. The commercial codes buildingEXODUS [12] and PedGo [13] are CA codes. They have demonstrated their ability to give good estimates of evacuation times of high rise buildings [19] or cruise ships, while details may still need improvement. While they differ in many aspects, the basics are identical.

2.1   Introduction to the General Theory

The principles of cellular automata for simulating pedestrians are explained in many places, e.g. [11,15]. For readability,we give a short sketch following [15]. The floor geometry is discretized into tiles, usually of 40 cm · 40 cm size. An initial distribution of persons on the tiles is defined. In every time step each person can move to another tile (or stay put) according to a probability depending on

- The availability of free space (only one person per tile at any time).
- A floor field describing the intended direction.
- Personal data, describing e.g. handicaps.

With a time step of ≈ 0.3 s this gives a reasonable speed of free movement of 1.3m/s.The movement is either done in parallel with subsequent conflict resolution or (simpler) in a random order sequentially. Non random orders have been used, but give strong artifacts. The floor field S is usually derived from the gradient of the distance to the destination (exit) in some metric, the Manhattan metric being the most common one because of its extreme simplicity.

Research codes may also use hexagonal tiles or smaller tiles with persons occupying more than one tile. They may also use more elaborate floor fields. These methods have somewhat different properties, but because they are not much in use they are not treated here.

2.2   Movement Properties of CA

The movement in simple CA grids is strongly non isotropic. Let us first consider the movement without interference from others towards a single cell goal. If for a person the direction to the goal is aligned with the grid, the movement probability is high (≈ 0.9) for that direction, small (≈ 0.03) for sidewards or no movement and almost nil for backward movement. If the direction is not aligned with the grid, the probability is ≈ 0.48 for the two grid directions that enclose the direction to the goal. For a grid aligned goal, this results in a very narrow path that is actually used. The probability to leave the direct path is low from the start, and when this has happened (on average once every 15 moves), the probability to get back to the direct path is almost $1/2$ for every move, so a deviation of more than one grid cell from the direct path is extremely rare.

Table 1. Probabilities to pass through a cell for a oblique goal - top left to bottom right. The sum along each diagonal from top right to bottom left is 1.

1	$1/2$	$1/4$	$1/8$	$1/16$	$1/32$
$1/2$	$2/4$	$3/8$	$4/16$	$5/32$	$7/64$
$1/4$	$3/8$	$6/16$	$10/32$	$15/64$	$29/128$
$1/8$	$5/16$	$16/32$	$42/64$	$99/128$	1

The situation is quite different for a direction not aligned with the grid. For simplicity, we will at first consider only forward movements. There is equal probability of ≈ 0.5 to move right or left of the actual direction. This results in a spreading out of the likely positions to a binomial distribution to the right and left of the diagonal of the grid. This carries on until a position is reached where the direction is grid aligned. From here on, the movement is again concentrating along the direct Table 1. The small probability of no or backward movement changes the spreading of the path by a tiny margin only, it mostly introduces a retardation, the person usually just reaches the same position using more moves.

When the forward movement is blocked by another person, the most probable reaction is moving sidewards or not at all. This leads to a spreading out of the plumes in front of a narrow pathway or exit. Backward movement is always improbable. This means that there is no automatic redirection from a jammed exit to a open one at some distance.

2.3   Natural Structuring of the Space

By simply counting the high probability routes leading in and out of a cell, we can distinguish different types of grid cells. There are the special cells - exits cells, which can be entered, but not left via the normal mechanism, because a person in an exit cell is taken out of the simulation either immediately or after completion of a move, and possibly entrance cells, which can be left but not entered with CA. Beside these, we have three kinds:

- The normal cells, where there are as many high probability passes leading in as there are leading out
- The convergence cells, where there are more high probability passes leading in than there are leading out
- The divergence cells, where there are less high probability passes leading in than there are leading out.

The divergence cells build lines that separate the grid into areas with minimal or no interaction, because people are striving away. Usually, unless there are entrance cells on such a line, after very few moves these lines are completely empty. The convergence cells build lines which are possible points of trouble because they can be fed easier than emptied. This is especially true for cells where two convergence lines meet. Whether there will be trouble depends on the densities further out. The normal cells can be fed and emptied at the same speed, so they may be critical only when there are convergence cells close ahead. Figure 3 right shows such a division for a building that could e.g. be an exhibition room, and Fig. 3 left the number of persons usage of the grid cells for a simulation where 1795 persons are randomly distributed on the floor and walk to the exit with an ordering and timing so that there is no interference. It shows clearly the severe concentration on the convergence lines and the preference for $\approx 45°$ to the grid when the direction is not aligned.

So there is a natural structure for the walking space: blocks defined by the convergence and divergence lines with a diagonal movement pattern inside, and

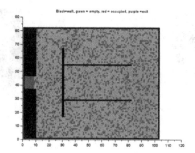

Fig. 1. Starting positions for all simulations. The size of the floor is 83 by 102 cells of $40 * 40 \, \text{cm}^2$

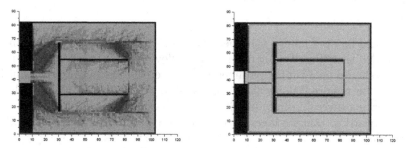

Fig. 2. Left: Utilization of tiles without conflicts (persons near exit start first, others wait till persons in front are out of reach), from pink–low (0-25) to green–high (>400) right: Exit (blue), walls (black) divergence lines (green) and convergence lines (purple) (Color figure online)

some blocks aligned with exits with parallel movement. The critical areas are near the crossing of two convergence lines. These are neighboring some of the corners or ends of the walls, other wall corners may be of no importance (Fig. 1).

3   Guiding People Around Corners

In actual walking, people are trying to cut corners only if that does not create conflicts with others. This results in the formation of lanes near the corner [14]. This can easily be modeled by changing the floor field near a corner in a way that not the shortest path is preferred but staying in lane [16]. The open questions are: How many lanes are needed, how long do they have to be and where exactly do they start and end. For use in crowd management, this needs an automatic procedure.

3.1   Getting the Required Number of Lanes

The number of lanes needed may be different for every corner and may change over simulation time. The easiest way to obtain the information is to run a simplified simulation - ignoring conflicts - and check the flow around each corner.

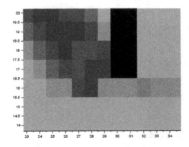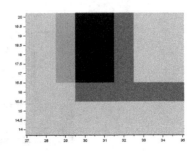

Fig. 3. Left: Utilization of tiles at corner of wall (black) without conflicts, from pink–low (0-25) to dark green – high (>600), right: divergence (green) and convergence (red/purple) lines. (Color figure online)

The maximal flow per lane is ≈ 1.5 persons/s, but this is modeling an uncomfortably crowded situation. Taking one lane for a flow of 1 p/s is usually better, but the factor should be a tuning parameter for the crowd manager to set. Multiple lanes may be required along walls and possibly (more below) along each side of an interior converging line. In the latter case, this line will often need to be moved outward so that its lanes do not end in a wall hugging lane that cannot take the flow.

With this, the computing time will be about twice the time for a simple CA simulation. In most cases, this is of no importance, CA is quite fast. For very large crowds, the time can be reduced by using the movement patterns described above. Any person can be moved to the next convergence line or along such a line to a corner in one action. This disregards the statistic spreading, but for the sum of many people moving, the spreading will cancel out to a large extent. The movement just along the most probable path will therefore be accurate enough to determine the expected flow, and reduce the computing time by a factor that depends on the distances between critical points. With this approximated simulation, the additional computing time will be dominated by the changing of the floor field.

It may be that the space available is not sufficient for the required number of lanes. This will result in an unavoidable jam in the final simulation, which will in all likelihood show up in reality just the same. The only thing that should be done is defining the lanes in a way that the load is approximately the same for all lanes, otherwise the simulation will perform worse than reality.

If the situation changes considerably over time, it may be advisable to gather and use information repeatedly. This will be treated below.

3.2   Placing the Lanes

At the forward end of a wall hugging convergence line the flux is expected the be largest in this critical area. This flux is used to determine the number of lanes required. Then we follow the convergence lines from the far end. As soon as the flux exceeds the capacity of the lanes placed there, we add one more lane. At the wall, it is obvious that new lanes will be added to the interior of the area. In the example, the wall hugging lane for the area where people move to the right will has receives its share at about the 45th cell to the right. From there on a second lane is defined, from which entering the first lane is no longer possible. This will be filled at about the 56th cell to the right, and so on until 5 lanes are defined.

At the inner convergence line, the situation is a little more complicated. Simply adding lanes to the side where people come from is not correct. These lanes would interfere with the lanes near the wall. In Fig. 3 we see that most people will reach the critical area following the inner convergence line, the flux along the wall does not require an additional line. What is needed is a change in the floor field in a block of cells such that the inner convergence line is moved away from the end of the wall and a gap a few cells wide is opened for the required number of lanes, see Fig. 4. Similarly, the floor field is changed in front of the exit and at the right end of the space within the inner walls, such that the convergence lines do not extend from the walls but from points a few cells away. With this, the cutting of corners will be reduced and the space actually used allows a passing with fairly high density, but without a jam.

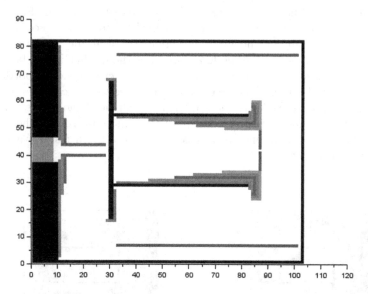

Fig. 4. Lanes (green/blue) and shifted inner convergence line (red) (Color figure online)

In many cases, it is not necessary to construct the lanes in the floor field, an opening two or three cells width will automatically be utilized quite well, because of the sideways movement if forward movement is blocked. For good performance on wider gaps, lanes at the new inner convergence line must be formed in the same way as near the walls. In the area concerned, the CA simulation is not fully realistic in all cases, the unisotropy of the grid gives unrealistic preferred individual pathways.

The lanes will end in a line leading out from the last cell of the convergence line. Test showed that small variations in the length of the lanes have no effect on performance, just on local pathways. What has to be avoided is a situation where the flux from the outer lane end tends inward as will happen with outer lanes that are too short.

Within the lanes, we redefine the floor field. The high probability step will be forward within the lane, and changing lanes will get a medium probability to get a local equilibration of usage. With these measures, the CA performance around corners will be fairly realistic.

3.3   Results

The procedure has been tested for a number of geometries, the one of Fig. 2 being the most complicated one. In all cases the results were satisfactory, while standard CA simulations showed unrealistic behaviors (jams) at all corners where our procedure estimated a need for more than two lanes. For the modified floor field, we can see that the number of cells heavily used at the corner is sufficient to give the required flow and the full width of the exit is utilized (Fig. 6). This is a big improvement over the standard floor field, where only two cells each are heavily used at the upper and lower corners of the wall and at the corners of the exit, with one more cell in moderate use. For the modified floor field, there are high densities near the corner, but they do not act as effective bottlenecks. The only effective bottleneck is the exit, which is used to capacity for almost the entire simulation time. What is not realistic is the shape of the plume of persons in the jam, they would in reality be accumulation more in front of the exit and not near the wall. This improvement also results in a much faster evacuation - 505 versus 764 time steps.

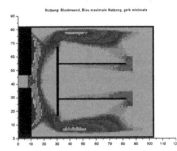 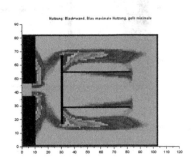

Fig. 5. Utilisation of tiles, colors and dimensions as above. left: modified floorfield, right: standard

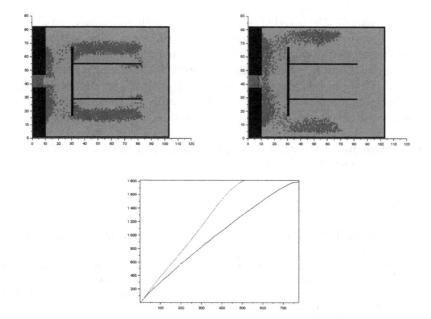

Fig. 6. Left: Positions at time step 200 for the standard floor field. right: for the modified floor field. bottom: People exited against time steps, black - standard, red - modified. (Color figure online)

3.4   Treating Variations in Time

The determination may either be done once for the entire simulation or repeatedly for a shorter period. In the latter case, the starting configuration for the predictive simulation should be taken from the final time step of the actual simulation, and the predictive simulation will run only for a limited time. The modified floor field will then be valid only for that time. This is useful if there are strong variations in the situation over time. The additional computing time needed for the predictive simulation is about the same for both cases, chopping the run into parts will not much change the required time. However, the time needed for setting up the new floor field will approximately be multiplied with the number of prediction runs. This can possibly be reduced by using incremental changes, but the present work does not include any tests in this direction (Fig. 5).

4   Conclusion and Outlook

CA methods still are very far from getting realistic individual trajectories or realistic distributions of people waiting in a jam, but with the proposed treatment of corners they can give realistic flows and evacuation times even for quite complicated buildings or sites. As long as large scale jams are avoided, the accuracy is sufficient to give e.g. a crowd manager an idea about what could be an upcoming situation. The speed of the simulation is high, available equipment will do for a faster than real time simulation. Constructing a floor field adaptively from monitoring the situation near the critical points can help, especially with the density distribution. A remaining problem of CA methods is the unisotropy introduced. This can be reduced by using hexagonal cells or Moore neighbourhood. The guidance near corners should be possible for these approaches, too, but has not yet been tried. Both approaches will be a topic of further research.

Acknowledgment. We thank the colleges in the CST division of the Jülich Supercomputing Centre for discussions and help.

References

1. Holl, S., Seyfried, A.: Hermes - an evacuation assistant for mass events. inSiDe **7**, 60–61 (2009)
2. Kemloh, U., Steffen, B., Seyfried, A., Chraibi, M.: Parallel real time computation of large scale pedestrian evacuations. Adv. Eng. Softw. **60–61**, 98–103 (2013)
3. Lämmel, G., Steffen, B.: A fast simulation approach for urban areas. Transp. Res. Board **93**, 84–98 (2014)
4. Dieckmann, D.: Die Feuersicherheit in Theatern. Jung, München (1911)
5. Fruin, J.J.: Pedestrian Planning and Design. Elevator World, New York (1971)
6. Predtetschenski, W.M., Milinski, A.I.: Personenströme in Gebäuden - Berechnungsmethoden für die Projektierung. Verlagsgesellschaft Rudolf Müller, Köln-Braunsfeld (1971)
7. Lämmel, G., Grether, D., Nagel, K.: The representation and implementation of time-dependent inundation in large-scale microscopic evacuation simulations. Transp. Res. C **18**, 84–98 (2010)
8. Lämmel, G., Steffen, B., Seyfried, A.: Large scale and microscopic: a fast simulation approach for urban areas Washington. Transportation Research Board Annual Meeting Online, 14–3890 (2014)
9. Lämmel, G., Chraibi, M., Kemloh Wagoum, A.U.: Hybrid multimodal and intermodal transport simulation: case study on large-scale evacuation planning. Transp. Res. Rec.: J. Transp. Res. Board **2561**, 1–8 (2016)
10. Chraibi, M., Steffen, B.: Multiscale simulation of pedestrians for efficient predictive modeling in large events. J. Cell. Autom. **11**(4), 299–310 (2016)
11. Blue, V.J., Adler, J.L.: Cellular automata microsimulation of bi-directional pedestrian flows. J. Transp. Res. B **1678**, 135–141 (2000)
12. Galea, E.R., Gwynne, S., Lawrence, P.J., Filippidis, L., Blackspields, D., Cooney, D.: buildingEXODUS V 4.0 - User Guide and Technical Manual (2004)
13. Klüpfel, H., et al.: Handbuch PedGo 2, PedGo Editor 2 (2005)
14. Zhang, J., Klinsch, W., Rupprecht, T., Schadschneider, A.: Empirical study of turning and merging of pedestrian streams in T-junction. In: Fourth International Symposium on Agent-Based Modeling and Simulation (ABModSim-4), Vienna, Austria (2012)
15. Kirchner, A., Schadschneider, A.: Simulation of evacuation processes using a bionics-inspired cellular automaton model for pedestrian dynamics. Phys. A **312**, 260–276 (2002)

16. Steffen, B., Seyfried, A.: Modelling of pedestrian movement around 90° and 180° bends. In: Advanced Research Workshop "Fire Protection and Life Safety in Buildings and Transportation Systems", pp. 243–253 (2009)
17. Molnár, P.: Modellierung und Simulation der Dynamik von Fußgängerströmen. Shaker, Aachen (1996)
18. Chraibi, M., Seyfried, A., Schadschneider, A.: Generalized centrifugal-force model for pedestrian dynamics. Phys. Rev. E **82**, 046111 (2010)
19. Rogsch, C., Klingsch, W., Seyfried, A., Weigel, H.: Prediction accuracy of evacuation times for high-rise buildings and simple geometries by using different software-tools. In: Appert-Rolland, C., Chevoir, F., Gondret, P., Lassarre, S., Lebacque, J.P., Schreckenberg, M. (eds.) Traffic and Granular Flow, pp. 395–400. Springer, Heidelberg (2007). https://doi.org/10.1007/978-3-540-77074-9_42
20. Seyfried, A., et al.: Enhanced empirical data for the fundamental diagram and the flow through bottlenecks. In: Klingsch, W., Rogsch, C., Schadschneider, A., Schreckenberg, M. (eds.) Pedestrian and Evacuation Dynamics, pp. 145–156. Springer, Heidelberg (2010). https://doi.org/10.1007/978-3-642-04504-2_11
21. Schadschneider, A., Eilhardt, C., Nowak, S., Will, R.: Towards a calibration of the floor field cellular automaton. In: Peacock, R., Kuligowski, E., Averill, J. (eds.) Pedestrian and Evacuation Dynamics, pp. 557–566. Springer, Heidelberg (2010). https://doi.org/10.1007/978-1-4419-9725-8_50. ein Artikel allgemein zu unseren Extraktionsmethoden ist
22. Boltes, M., Seyfried, A.: Collecting pedestrian trajectories. Neurocomputing **100**, 127–133 (2013). Special Issue on Behaviours in Video
23. Chraibi, M., Zhang, J.: JuPedSim: an open framework for simulating and analyzing the dynamics of pedestrians SUMO2016 - Traffic, Mobility, and Logistics. In: Proceedings SUMO Conference 2016, SUMO2016, Berlin, Germany, 23–25 May 2016, vol. 30, pp. 127–134. Deutsches Zentrum für Luft- und Raumfahrt e. V., Institut für Verkehrssystemtechnik, Berichte aus dem DLR-Institut für Verkehrssystemtechnik, Braunschweig (2016)

Traffic on Small Grids and the Ramp Problem

Jakub Wójtowicz, Igor Wadowski, Błażej Dyrda, and Tomasz M. Gwizdałła[✉]

Faculty of Physics and Applied Informatics, University of Łódź,
Pomorska 149/153, 90-236 Łódź, Poland
tomgwizd@uni.lodz.pl

Abstract. The problem of analysis of traffic jams performed by the Cellular Automata oriented techniques is widely studied since the beginning of 90th and the seminal paper of Nagel and Schreckenberg. The typical approach is based on the one to one relation between the sizes of cell and the particular vehicle. We propose to take into account the smaller size of cells what makes possible to consider more densely distributed values of typical features of vehicles like velocity or acceleration. On the other hand, the decrease of cell size can lead to the model which is very similar to the continuous one. We think that our approach does not exceed the limits sensible for CA.

1 Introduction

Since the pioneering work by Nagel and Schreckenberg [1] Cellular Automata was developed such that they now are one of the most important tools of modelling road traffic. Although the history of NaSch-based approaches is long and the number of models were used to study the traffic in a lot of different conditions, it seems that some new effects can still be presented.

In our paper we pay attention to the problem of small grids. In the seminal approach, the vehicle occupies one cell. This assumption causes a lot of effects. Such unified view of traffic is certainly easy to manage but disables to take into account many typical features describing the process. We can enlist here especially the diversity of vehicles, the abilities of drivers, the granularity of changes of physical quantities (velocity, acceleration, deceleration). The technique is certainly not new. Earlier for example Liu [2] shown the effect of small grid on the choice of optimal route between two points, in our earlier paper [3] some remarks concerning small grids were used to study the pedestrian motion. On the other hand we have to point out that a notion of "small grid" is often understood as an internal structure in the grid of grids (see e.g. [4]).

In the paper we present mainly some basic curves, like fundamental diagrams prepared for the selected features of system. This, very basic and simple, approach makes possible to study the effect itself and to distinguish it from a lot of features which can follow the proposed change and are mentioned in the previous paragraph.

G. Mauri et al. (Eds.): ACRI 2018, LNCS 11115, pp. 196–206, 2018.
https://doi.org/10.1007/978-3-319-99813-8_18

After some basic figures we show the effect of assumed changes on some practical problem. We choose very popular issue of "on-ramp" motion. The problem is a particular case of a study of vehicles motion on intersections [5, 6] and has been studied in different contexts almost from the beginning of NaSch model up today [7–10].

2   Model

Although all results presented in this paper are shown for the constant parameters of vehicles, the model is generalized in such a form that every vehicle is characterized by a set of properties. When enumerating them we can mention:

- position on a road - the number of the front cell (appropriate for the direction of vehicle) covered by a vehicle
- size ($size$) - the amount of cells covered by a vehicle
- velocity - the amount of cells, the vehicle will be moved during the next time step
- maximal velocity (v_{max}) - the maximal velocity achievable by the vehicle
- acceleration (acc) - the maximal positive change of vehicle's velocity during one time step
- deceleration (dec) - the maximal negative change of vehicle's velocity during one time step
- probability of random change velocity (p_{rnd}) - probability of random loss of velocity
- maximal value of random change velocity (v_{rnd}) - maximal value of random loss of velocity

The majority of features of model are the same as of the original one. The motion of vehicle is performed according to the current value of velocity, the random change of velocity is performed with respect to the above listed values. The only difference when taking into account the random change is that its value can be greater than 1, what characterized the seminal model [1].

The more important modifications concern the change of velocity. In the typical CA-related model the change is performed in the way that the increase (acceleration) takes value 1 and the decrease (deceleration) can be even infinite. The value of velocity can decline from some value to zero in one time step. When using the model with smaller cells we have to better consider the distance between the vehicle and the foregoing one. So, if the distance allows for acceleration, the value of velocity is increased and it reaches either the maximal defined for the particular type of vehicle or the maximal value following the physical restrictions on the road. Respectively, the process of deceleration is organized in the way that it is possible to adjust it taking the value of change from the interval $[0, deceleration]$.

The crucial parameters and results are presented as the same values as in the typical papers. However, due to changes introduced in the possibilities of different vehicles creation, we have to slightly redefine the well known formulas.

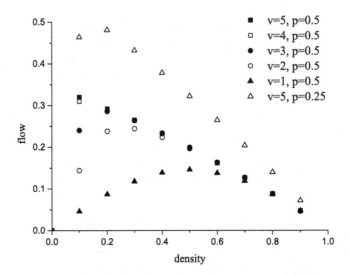

Fig. 1. Fundamental diagram for different maximal velocities in base model and different random velocity change probability.

The density, corresponding typically to a number of vehicles related to the length of the road averaged over the time of simulation:

$$\bar{\rho}^T = \frac{1}{T} \sum_T n_i(t) \tag{1}$$

is now understood as:

$$\bar{\rho} = \bar{\rho}^{TL} = \frac{1}{T \times L} \sum_T \sum_{road} size_i(t). \tag{2}$$

L means here the length of road (all roads) on which the density is determined. The formula 1 corresponds directly to the Nagel-Schreckenberg model and formulas, so $\bar{\rho}^T$ is the density on a fixed site i where n_i may be 0 or 1, dependently on the absence or presence of the vehicle at the ith position. In our approach we calculate the total density on the road by summing also all sizes of vehicles on the road. Such a formula makes it possible to generalize the model especially when taking into account different vehicles' sizes. The flow (also averaged) is defined:

$$\bar{q}^T = \frac{1}{T} \sum_T n_{i,i+1}(t) \tag{3}$$

with $n_{i,i+1}(t) = 1$ if the car motion is detected between cells numbered i and $i + 1$. We modify the formula 3 averaging over time as well as over the whole road:

$$\bar{q} = \bar{q}^{TL} = \frac{1}{T \times L} \sum_T \sum_{i \in road} n_{i,i+1}(t), \tag{4}$$

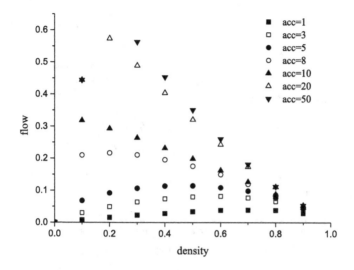

Fig. 2. Fundamental diagram for different accelerations

where i enumerates cells on road or on the passage between roads. This last concept will be in more detail described in the next section when some problems related to the motion on ramp will be studied.

In all simulations presented in the paper we simplify the model by introducing some assumptions. As the most important one it should be noticed that we do not take into account any distribution of different types of vehicles. During every simulation process we assume the same parameters of all vehicles. This makes it possible to analyze the effects which are related to the model itself and not to the variety of objects. The first set of results are shown for the simple construction of road with the length corresponding to about 5 km. We ensure that the density on the road is constant during the whole simulation run. For the second set of results we use the specially prepared organization of four roads which will be described later.

3   Results

In order to test the model we start from the simple simulation of base model which can be described by means of properties described as $\{size = 1, v_{max} \in \{1, 2, 3, 4, 5\}, acc = 1, dec = \infty, p_{rnd} \in \{0.25, 0.5\}, v_{rnd} = 1\}$. Certainly, the values of probabilities are relatively high but such values allow to distinguish the differences. The base model used as the maximal velocity value $v_{max} = 5$ which corresponds to the typical maximal velocity in highway conditions (about 130 km/h). The larger set of values makes it possible to try to use the model for different conditions. The similar approach was used e.g. in our earlier paper devoted to study the behavior of vehicles at different forms of intersections [5]. The results are shown in Fig. 1.

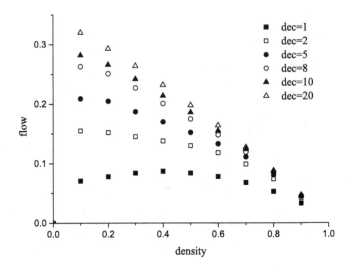

Fig. 3. Fundamental diagram for different decelerations (JW23/35)

Since the plot is well known we do not pay a lot of attention to the visible dependencies. We just want to notice that the effect of shift of position of maximal flow and the decrease of the value of maximal flow is observed with decreasing maximal velocity as well as the large decrease of maximal flow with the strengthening of random effects. This last effect can be even very strong. By using the two presented values of probabilities we can double the top value of flow.

The first case which shows the effects of the model presented in the paper on some fundamental characteristics concerns the process of acceleration. When preparing the Fig. 2 we use the model of vehicle with such tuple of features: $\{size = 10, v_{max} = 50, p_{rnd} = 0.5, v_{rnd} = 10\}$. When assuming the size of vehicle being the length of typical car and the length of time step equal $1\,s$ we can estimate the other values as: $\{v_{max} = 90\,km/h, v_{rnd} = -5\,m/s^2\}$. These values correspond to the typical single-track and to the very rapid sudden change of velocity which, applied to the full process of stopping, would lead to the little bit exaggerated value of braking distance of about $22.4\,m$ from the velocity of about 50 km/h. In the figure we use the values of acceleration from 1 up to 50. These highest values correspond to the parameters of such vehicles like those from formula 1. It means that taking these values into account is completely unrealistic for the typical traffic but allows to consider extremely high parameters.

For the typical cars the value of acceleration would be, in the conditions of current simulation, in the range about $[2, 6]$. So it corresponds to the three lower set of points in the figure. As we can see the highest flow is obtained for the similar for this range of accelerations values of densities around 0.6. This value means almost total occupation of the road with the separation between cars being unsafely small. The highest value is approximately proportional to the

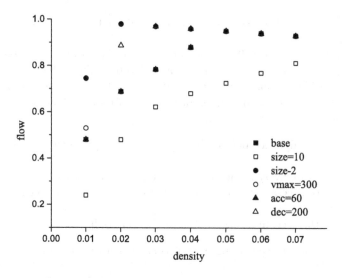

Fig. 4. Fundamental diagram for different vehicle properties (JW29/44)

value of acceleration. With increasing acceleration, the highest value increases but the dependence is not further proportional and the maximum point shifts to the lower densities.

The data presented in Fig. 3 are created from one of the plots of Fig. 2. We take the curve for $acc = 10$ and realign the value of deceleration. As it has been mentioned earlier the typical values for passenger cars are those less than $dec = 10$. By showing the values from $dec = 20$ down to $dec = 1$ allows to observe the change introduced by decreasing deceleration value. Certainly the differences are mainly the effect of the technique of slowing down when approaching the car in front. The crucial observation is that the change introduced does not influence strongly the value of density where maximal flow is observed. Indeed, just for $dec = 1$ the significant shift can be noticed.

Finally, we are going to show the influence of the single change of parameter. We select the initial parameters of cars as $\{size = 5, v_{max} = 24, acc = 4, dec = 10, p_{rnd} = 0.0, v_{rnd} = 0\}$. When taking into account that the cell size equals 0.5 m this parameters correspond to the very small car in city conditions. We try then to increase the size, maximal velocity, acceleration and deceleration. The results are shown in Fig. 4. We present the results for values of acceleration up to 50. It means that once more we have to mention the relatively unrealistic character of upper limit of assumed value. The value $acc = 50$ corresponds to the time of acceleration from 0 to 100 km/h lower than 2 s. An interesting information is that the shape of all dependencies is colinear above $\rho > 0.1$. The differences are visible only below this value. The change of velocity does not cause any significant change and while increasing the size we decrease the flow. We can however lead to the increase of flow by using smaller cars or by increasing the strength of brakes. All these results are certainly obtained when assuming the ideal driving technique.

In order to show the differences following the introduced changes in some practical case, we use the well known case of ramp. The vehicles try to enter the highway traffic through the special lane parallel to the lanes of highway. In our approach we distinguish 4 different sections of roads. They are labeled with numbers and understood as follows:

1. the section of highway before the common part, this section will be called "main"
2. the section of highway along the common part with ramp
3. the section of access road before the common part, this section will be called "approach"
4. the ramp - the section of access road along the highway.

The schematic view of the configuration is shown in Fig. 5.

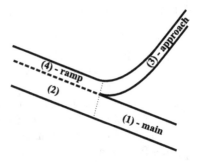

Fig. 5. The schematic view of different sections of ramp-type junction with the presentation of notation used in the paper.

The densities of vehicles at the roads will be defined according to the formula 2 on the main and approach section of both roads. We assume that the vehicles run on the main road with the maximal velocity permissible on the polish highways, i.e. 130 km/h and on the access road they run with the velocity 40 km/h. The difference between these velocities seems to be relatively large nevertheless it corresponds to the real conditions on polish roads.

The most important element of this part of model is certainly the existence of algorithms which ensure the save behavior of vehicles when changing the lane and entering the highway traffic. There are mainly two general aspects which are taken into account when analyzing this phase.

Firstly, we approximate the behavior of drivers in such a way that the driver with priority is not forced to dynamically brake the vehicle. This fact entrails that several options have to be included in the algorithm. There are certainly lot of factors influencing the characteristic of braking procedure: the type of vehicle, the type of tires, the time of driver's reaction, the road surface and weather conditions. We decided to set the deceleration value as the one corresponding to almost ideal case when the stopping of car running with velocity $\sim 15\,\text{m/s}$ takes place on the segment of $\sim 25\,\text{m}$. We consider the dynamic braking as the one when the vehicle slows down from the initial velocity by a factor of 10% in the three successive time steps. This limitation seems to make possible that driving would be relatively smooth. In our model we try to anticipate the behavior of drivers three time steps forward. The second factor is the analysis of different situations between the vehicles on neighboring lanes (ramp and the highway's lane). Here the numerous situations are taken into account and their detailed presentation exceeds the scope of this paper.

In the paper there are not considered the differences of sizes of vehicles. It is clear that by taking into account some distributions of properties of different road users, as it is in reality, we can force significant differences in obtained characteristics. We intentionally want to omit the confusion coming from the common consideration of different effects. Concerning the technique of driving we have also to mention that every driver aims to change the lane as quickly as possible even with the relatively small velocity.

We show two figures related to the problem, Fig. 6 shows the average velocity of vehicles moving from the ramp to the highway's lane, Fig. 7 - the flow of this process. The figures are prepared for 8 sets of possible pair of parameters determining the organization of road (ramp length $L_{ramp} \in \{200\,\text{m}, 300\,\text{m}, 400\,\text{m}, 500\,\text{m}\}$) as well as the organization of simulation (cell size, $size \in \{0.5\,\text{m}, 2\,\text{m}\}$). The simulations are performed for 400 different pairs of densities. The density of vehicles on the main as well as access road change in the interval $(0.01, 0.2)$ with the step 0.01. The selected range of densities can be easily related to the realistic values. Considering the typical size of vehicle as 5 m and assuming the maximal density 0.2 we obtain the spacing between vehicles as 20 m. It is certainly not safe in e,g, highway conditions but clearly sets the upper limit for the density value. Finally, for every configuration the simulation is 10000 time steps long.

The crucial effect we want to observe in the figures is the dependence of obtained surfaces on the parameters of simulation. Somehow helpful is the presentation of results for different ramp lengths. The plot for velocities (Fig. 6) shows that there exist the curve in the plane of densities where the transfer between ramp and highway starts. An interesting effect is that the transfer zeroes for large densities on access road and the value of threshold is larger for larger densities on main road. The crucial observation concerns however the differences between both plots. It is explicitly seen that the size of single cell has a decisive influence on the shape of surface. There are smaller differences following such features like the length of ramp than those caused by the some technical assumption.

We also have to point out that the scale of z-axis is different and this difference is not an effect of rescaled cell length. The velocities of transfer are higher for larger cells so the real velocities expressed in physical units are still more high. In order to show the presented relation in comparable scale we show also the transfer flows in Fig. 7. The figure confirms the dependence of the results on

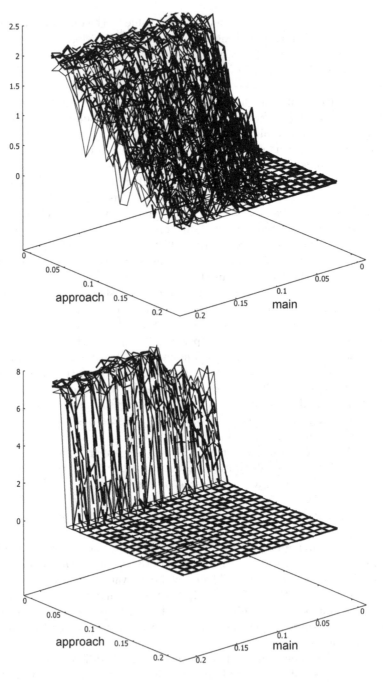

Fig. 6. The average velocity of vehicles changing lane between ramp and highway. The upper plot - cell size $0.5\,\mathrm{m}$, the lower one $2\,\mathrm{m}$. The line type corresponds to the length of ramp: thin solid line - $L_{ramp} = 200\,\mathrm{m}$, thick solid line - $L_{ramp} = 300\,\mathrm{m}$, thin dashed line - $L_{ramp} = 400\,\mathrm{m}$, thick dashed line - $L_{ramp} = 500\,\mathrm{m}$,

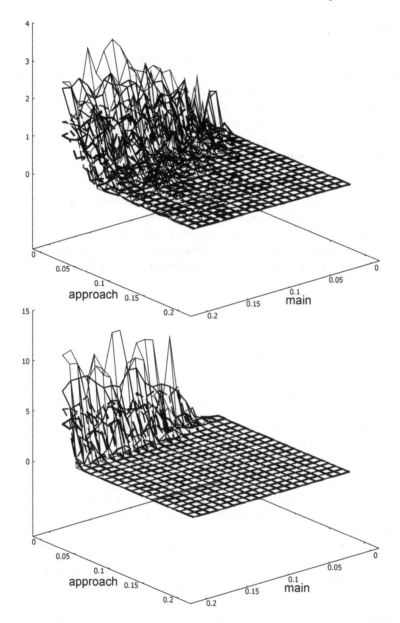

Fig. 7. The flow between ramp and highway. The organization of figure and the description of plots are the same as in Fig. 6

the size of cell. Although the characteristics are more similar one to another on both plots, the slope is once more significantly different. We must also emphasize the large deviations of particular measurements in the Figures. This is often due to jams rising at the end of ramp when driver was unable to change the lane.

4 Conclusions

In the paper we presented the model of traffic based on the small sizes of cells used to construct the roads. The figures, especially Figs. 6 and 7 shows explicitly that in the same road conditions, the choice of technical parameters of simulation plays a substantial role influencing the result. Considering the velocity of changing the lane as well as the flow we can observe different effects. The threshold by which the flow starts as well as the slope of characteristics depends on the size of cells. It means that we have to carefully study the effect in order to remove possible artifacts related to the parameters of modelling.

The future work can be lead in many directions. First of all we have to check the features just mentioned here in more detail. The surfaces shown in Figs. 6 and 7 were prepared for 10000 time steps what corresponds to relatively long time. But maybe some extend of simulation time will produce more smooth characteristics. The main direction is certainly the incorporation of real features of road motion, like the technique of driving of particular road user or the distribution of different vehicles.

References

1. Nagel, K., Schreckenberg, M.: A cellular automaton model for freeway traffic. J. Phys. I **2**, 2221–2229 (1992)
2. Liu, T., Huang, H.: Multi-agent simulation on day-to-day route choice behavior. In: Third International Conference on Natural Computation (ICNC 2007), vol. 5, pp. 492–498 (2007)
3. Gwizdałła, T.M.: Some properties of the floor field cellular automata evacuation model. Phys. A: Stat. Mech. Appl. **419**, 718–728 (2015)
4. Mallikarjuna, C., Ramachandra Rao, K.: Heterogeneous traffic flow modelling: a complete methodology. Transportmetrica **7**, 321–345 (2011)
5. Gwizdałła, T.M., Grzebielucha, S.: The traffic flow through different form of intersections. In: 2010 International Conference on Computer Information Systems and Industrial Management Applications (CISIM), pp. 299–304 (2010)
6. Malecki, K., Watrobski, J., Wolski, W.: A cellular automaton based system for traffic analyses on the roundabout. In: Nguyen, N.T., Papadopoulos, G.A., Jedrzejowicz, P., Trawinski, B., Vossen, G. (eds.) ICCCI 2017. LNCS (LNAI), vol. 10449, pp. 56–65. Springer, Cham (2017). https://doi.org/10.1007/978-3-319-67077-5_6
7. Campari, E.G., Levi, G.: A cellular automata model for highway traffic. Eur. Phys. J. B **17**, 159–166 (2000)
8. Belitsky, V., Maric, N., Schütz, G.M.: Phase transitions in a cellular automaton model of a highway on-ramp. J. Phys. A **40**, 11221–11243 (2007)
9. Echab, H., Lakouari, N., Ez-Zahraouy, H., Benyoussef, A.: Cellular automata model simulating traffic car accidents in the on-ramp system. Int. J. Mod. Phys. C **26**, 1550100 (2015)
10. Guzmán, H., Lárraga, M., Alvarez-Icaza, L., Huerta, F.: On-ramp traffic merging modeling based on cellular automata. In: 2015 IEEE European Modelling Symposium (EMS), pp. 103–109 (2015)

The Impact of Different Angle Paths on Discrete-Continuous Pedestrian Dynamics Model

Ekaterina Kirik[1,2](✉) ⓘ, Tatýana Vitova[1], Andrey Malyshev[1] ⓘ,
and Egor Popel[1] ⓘ

[1] Institute of Computational Modelling,
Russian Academy of Sciences, Siberian Branch, Akademgorodok 50/44,
Krasnoyarsk 660036, Russia
{kirik,vitova}@icm.krasn.ru
[2] Petroleum and Gas Engineering Department, Siberian Federal University,
pr. Svobodny 79, Krasnoyarsk 660041, Russia
http://3ksigma.ru

Abstract. In the article the influence of corners on the path on discrete-continuous pedestrian dynamics model have been discussed. Angles from classic 90° case study to "Z"-shaped geometry were considered. "Z"-shaped geometry is peculiar for modern shopping and entertainment centers, when we consider way from the stadium to outer perimeter.

Keywords: Pedestrian dynamics · Simulation · Turns on the path

1 Introduction

People movement around turns differs from movement along straight pathes. It is strongly dependent on local density. One can find variety of lengthes of trajectories, different velocities and not homogeneous density in the area around the corner (in front of a turn, just in the turn, and after the turn). Turns may shift laminar flow to turbulent depending on local density. But turns are inevitable parts of evacuation ways in every building. So it is very important to simulate movement around turns in a correct way to estimate travel/evacuation time correctly.

There are number of real experiments with investigation of movement around the turns. Real data is necessary to understand phenomenon and to calibrate and validate pedestrian movement mathematical models. In the project Hermes there were investigated movement around the 90° corner in a corridor 2.4 m in width, T-junction, movement from stadium tribunes [5–7,15]. Trajectories, full flow rate, speeds in front of a turn and after the turn were observed and

This study was partially supported by the Russian Foundation for Basic Research, Government of the Krasnoyarsk Territory, Krasnoyarsk Territorial Foundation for Support of Scientific and RD Activities, project no. 17-41-240947 p_a.

© Springer Nature Switzerland AG 2018
G. Mauri et al. (Eds.): ACRI 2018, LNCS 11115, pp. 207–217, 2018.
https://doi.org/10.1007/978-3-319-99813-8_19

connecting with density. In [8–11] a corridor 1.5 m in width and turns with angles 0°, 45°, 90° and 180° are considered. Movement trajectories, density and speed distribution over an investigation area, speed and flow rate for different initial densities were matter of investigation.

The following inferences come from real experiments. Flow rate and density after the turn is less then before. Speed is higher after the turn. Trajectories tend closer to inner angle. Geometries are proper for office buildings and similar ones and it gives restrictions for density which varies no higher then $3\,1/m^2$.

One approach to simulate pedestrian movement around turns correctly by cellular automata floor field (CA FF) models is to change a method to calculate the floor field S [13–15]. The field S give the shortest distance from each node. Such approach is justified for high densities. It allows to realize so called the shortest time [1,12]. But there are many situations when it does not work, and the strategy of the shortest path should be pronounced. Moreover a real sizes of the simulation area influence on flow dynamics, and it is pronounced for large facilities as stadiums.

Section 2 presents a discrete-continuous model which is realized in the computer module SigmaEva. Section 3 contains the description of tests, simulation experiments, and results obtained. Different angles from classic 90° case study to "Z"-shaped geometry were considered. We conclude with a summary.

2   Description of the Model

In this discrete-continuous model people (particles) move in a continuous space (in this sense model is continuous), but number of directions where particles may move is limited and predetermined by a user (in this sense model is discrete).

2.1   Space and Initial Conditions

A continuous modeling space $\Omega \in R^2$ and an infrastructure (obstacles) are known. People may move to (and on) free space only. To orient particles use the static floor field S [17]. A target point of each pedestrian is an assigned exit.

Shape of each particle is a disk with diameter d_i, initial positions of particles are given by coordinates of disks' centers $x_i(0) = (x_i^1(0), x_i^2(0))$, $i = \overline{1,N}$, N – number of particles (it is assumed that these are coordinates of body's mass center projection). Each particle is assigned with the free movement speed[1] v_i^0, square of projection, mobility group. It is also assumed that while moving the speed of any particular person does not exceed the maximal value (free movement speed), and speed of each person is controlled in accordance with local density.

Each time step t each particle i may move in one of the predetermined directions $e_i(t) \in \{e^\alpha(t), \alpha = i = \overline{1,q}\}$, q – the number of directions, model parameter (for example, a set of directions uniformly distributed around the circle will be considered here $\{e^\alpha(t), \alpha = \overline{1,q}\} = \{(\cos\frac{2\pi}{q}\alpha, \sin\frac{2\pi}{q}\alpha)\,\alpha = i = \overline{1,q}\}$). Particles that cross target line leave the modeling space.

---

[1] We assume that free movement speed is random normal distributed value with some mathematical expectation and dispersion [18,19].

2.2   Preliminary Calculations

To model directed movement a "map" that stores the information on the shortest distance to the nearest exit is used. The unit of this distance is meters, [m]. Such map is saved in static floor field S which is is imported from the FF CA model [17]. In our model this field increases radially from the exit; and it is zero in the exit(s) line(s). It does not change with time and is independent of the presence of the particles. Distance to the exit from arbitrary point is given by bidirectional interpolation among nearest nodes.

2.3   Movement Equation

For each time instant t, the coordinates of i-th particle are given by the formula:

$$x_i(t) = x_i(t - \Delta t) + v_i(t)e_i(t)\Delta t, \; i = \overline{1, N}, \tag{1}$$

where $x_i(t - \Delta t)$ denotes the particle's position at time $t - \Delta t$; $v_i(t)$ is the particle's current speed measures in m/s; $e_i(t)$ is the unit direction vector. The time shift $\Delta t = 0.25\,$s is assumed to be fixed, Fig. 1.

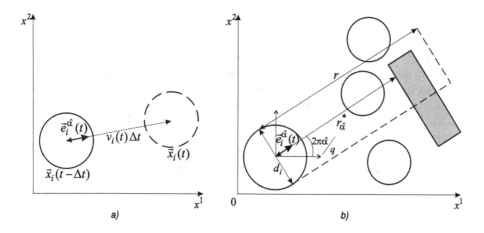

Fig. 1. Left: movement scheme. Right: visibility area.

Unknown values in (1) for every time step for each particle are the speed $v_i(t)$ and the direction $e_i(t)$. A probability approach is used to find direction for the next step. A procedure to calculate probabilities to move in each direction is adopted from previously presented stochastic CA FF model [1].

We propose to get the speed from experimental data (fundamental diagram), for example [18,19], according to the local density in the direction chosen.

2.4 Choosing Movement Direction

In this discrete-continuous model we took inspiration from our previously presented stochastic CA FF model [1,4]. All predetermined directions for every particle for each time step are assigned with some probability to move, and direction is chosen according to the probability distribution obtained.

Probabilities in the model are not static and vary dynamically and issued on the following basis. Pedestrians keep themselves at a certain distance from other people and obstacles. The tighter the people flow and the more in a hurry a pedestrian is, the smaller this distance. During movement, people follow at least two strategies: the shortest path and the shortest time. The highest probability is given to direction that has got most preferable conditions for movement.

Let i-th particle has current coordinate $x_i(t - \Delta t)$. The probability of movement from this position to the direction $e_i^\alpha(t), \alpha = \overline{1, q}$, during the next time step is:

$$p_\alpha^i(t) = \frac{\hat{p}_\alpha^i(t)}{Norm}$$
$$= \frac{\exp\left[k_S^i \Delta S_\alpha\right] \exp\left[-k_P^i F(r_\alpha^*)\right] \exp\left[-k_W^i (1 - \frac{r_\alpha^*}{r}) \, 1(\Delta S_\alpha)\right]}{Norm} W\left(r_\alpha^* - \frac{d_i}{2}\right),$$

where $Norm = \sum\limits_{\alpha=1}^{q} \hat{p}_\alpha^i(t)$.

Visibility radius r $(r \geq \max\{d_i/2\})$, [m], is model parameter representing the maximum distance at which people and obstacles influence on the probability in the given direction. It may be reduced to a value r_α^*, in Fig. 1 (right) grey area is obstacle, and visibility radius r is reduced up to r_α^* in this direction. People density $F(r_\alpha^*)$ is estimated in the visibility area. $1(\cdot)$ is the Heaviside unit step function.

The model parameter $k_S^i > 0$ is the field S-sensitive parameter, $k_W^i > 0$ is wall-sensitive parameter, $k_P^i > 0$ is density-sensitive parameter.

$\Delta S_\alpha = S(t - \Delta t) - S_\alpha$, where $S(t - \Delta t)$ is the static floor field in the coordinate $x_i(t - \Delta t)$, S_α is the static floor field in the coordinate $x = x_i(t - \Delta t) + 0.1 \, e_i^\alpha(t)$. With ΔS_α moving to the target point is controlled.

$W\left(r_\alpha^* - \frac{d_i}{2}\right) = \begin{cases} 1, & r_\alpha^* - \frac{d_i}{2} > w; \\ 0, & r_\alpha^* - \frac{d_i}{2} \leq w. \end{cases}$ The function $W(\cdot)$ controls approaching to obstacles, model parameter $w \in [0, 0.1]$, [m].

If $Norm = 0$ than particle does not leave present position. If $Norm \neq 0$ than required direction $e_i(t)$ is considered as discrete random value with distribution that is given by transition probabilities obtained. Exact direction $e_i(t) = e_i^{\hat{\alpha}}(t)$ is determined in accordance with standard procedure for discrete random values.

2.5 Speed Calculation

Person's speed is density dependent [18–21]. We assume that only conditions in front of the person influence on speed. It is motivated by the front line effect (that is well pronounced while flow moves in open boundary conditions) in a dense people mass. It results in the diffusion of the flow. Thus, only density $F_i(\hat{\alpha})$ in the direction chosen $e_i(t) = e_i^{\hat{\alpha}}(t)$ is required to determine the speed. The current speed of the particle may be calculated, for instance, in the way [18,19]:

$$v_i(t) = v_i^{\hat{\alpha}}(t) = \begin{cases} v_i^0(1 - a \ln \frac{F_i(\hat{\alpha})}{F^0}), & F_i(\hat{\alpha}) > F^0; \\ v_i^0, & F_i(\hat{\alpha}) \le F^0. \end{cases} \tag{2}$$

where F^0 is the limit people density under which free movement is possible; $a = 0,295$ is for horizontal way; $a = 0,4$, for down stairs; $a = 0,305$, for upstairs.

Numerical procedures which is used to estimate local density is presented in [3]. An area where density is determined is reduced by chosen direction and visibility area which is presented in Fig. 1.

2.6   Model Parameters

There are non-dimensional model parameters: k_S^i, k_W^i, k_P^i. The parameter $k_S^i > 0$ is field S-sensitive parameter which can be interpreted as knowledge of the shortest way to the target or a wish to move to the target. The equality $k_S^i = 0$ means that the pedestrian ignore the information from field S and move randomly. The higher k_S^i, the better directed the movement.

Parameter $k_W^i > 0$ is wall-sensitive parameter which determines the effect of walls and obstacles. We assume that people avoid obstacles only moving towards the target. When $\Delta S_{\hat{\alpha}} < 0$ approaching the obstacles is not excluded.

Parameter $k_P^i > 0$ is the density-sensitive parameter which determines the effect of the people density. The higher parameter k_P^i, the more pronounced the shortest time strategy for the person.

Note that probabilities are density adaptive; the low people density lowers the effect of density-sensitive term, and the probability of the shortest path strategy increases automatically. But this automatic property is not enough. Ideally a time-spatial adaptation for model parameters is required. There are time-spatial conditions when it is necessary to adapt values of k_S^i, k_P^i and k_W^i. Turns provide just such spatial conditions when density-dependant correction of the model parameters is required.

3   Case Studies

An aim of the section is to consider behaviour of the discrete-continuous model presented in special geometrical situations with turns. Angles of classic 90° ("L"-shaped geometry, Figs. 2, 4) and "Z"-shaped geometry (Figs. 3, 5) were considered. "Z"-shaped geometry is peculiar for modern shopping and entertainment centers, stadiums. There were considered similar geometries of two scales.

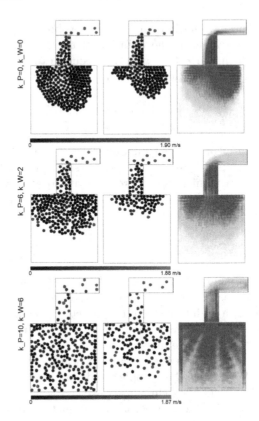

Fig. 2. "L"-geometry (small), $k_S = 40$. Position of the particles at $t = 30$ s and $t = 90$ s, and total intensity for three pairs of k_P, k_W.

3.1 Description of the Simulation Conditions

We considered "L"-shaped and "Z"-shaped corridors of two width 2 m (small) and 8 m (large) in sizes. Initially ($t = 0$) a set of initial numbers of people (particles) $N = 300$ and $N = 1200$ were placed in a square room. Square rooms played a role of a source of particles which move to the connected "L"-shaped and "Z"-shaped corridors.

Each person was assigned with a free movement speed of $v_1^0 = 1,66$ m/s. All persons were assigned with the same square of projection $0,125$ m^2.

There were considered a set of values of the model parameters[2]. They give an opportunity to vary dynamics of the model from only the shortest path strategy ($k_S = 40$, $r = 4$ m, $k_P = 0$, $k_W = 0$) to combination of the strategies – the shortest path and the shortest time ($k_S = 40$, $r = 4$ m, $k_P > 0$, $k_W > 0$), and investigate a force of parameters influence.

---

[2] All parameters were unified for all involved particles.

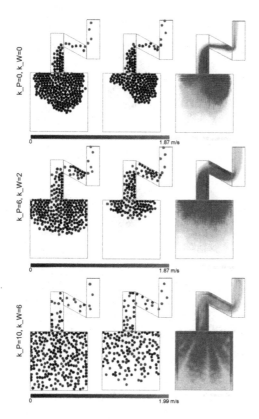

Fig. 3. "Z"-geometry (small), $k_S = 40$. Position of the particles at $t = 30\,$s and $t = 90\,$s, and total intensity for three pairs of k_P, k_W.

3.2 Simulation Results

The expected dynamics of people flow for geometries considered are the following. In "L"-geometry people tend to block those who move closer to inner angle. The tighter the flow, the more pronounced this effect. Thus people move faster along the outer perimeter of the turn trajectory. A congestion before turn is inevitable and density dependent. "Z"-geometry consists of three parts. Before the first turn the same effect is pronounced. And then there is a transformation of the flow because inner angle is changed. Those people who moved faster along the outer perimeter became blocked. Congestions before the both turns are inevitable and density dependent.

Qualitatively such description is independent on geometry linear sizes. But model dynamics is dependent and model parameters play important role.

For wide range of evacuation tasks which intend directed movement, $k_S = 40$ is normal and provides realisation of the shortest path strategy. A turn radius is the smallest. To have a goal not to disturb such strategy other parameter should be zero: $k_P = 0$, $k_W = 0$, see the first line of pictures in Figs. 2, 3, 4 and 5.

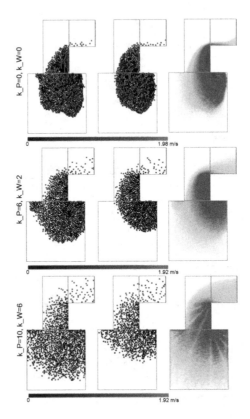

Fig. 4. "L"-geometry (large), $k_S = 40$. Position of the particles at $t = 30$ s and $t = 90$ s, and total intensity for three pairs of k_P, k_W.

The worthiest (not realistic) dynamics is in these pictures. Particle are colored according to local speed, black color is for zero value. Thus particles not move mainly and wait for the shortest path to became free.

Parameter $k_W^i > 0$ is wall-sensitive parameter which determines the effect of walls and obstacles. Making detours around the angle (moving along the outer trajectory) implies avoiding the walls. At the same time density perceptibility should be activated to avoid congestions. The way to do it is to "turn-on" the density-sensitive parameter $k_P^i > 0$.

One can observe influence of two pairs of parameters $k_P = 6$, $k_W = 2$ and $k_P = 10$, $k_W = 6$ and their manifestation for "L"-geometry and "Z"-geometry for small and large scales. See the second and the third lines of pictures in Figs. 2, 3, 4 and 5 correspondingly. The first pair ($k_P = 6$, $k_W = 2$) is good for small scale (Figs. 2 and 3) and the other pair ($k_P = 10$, $k_W = 6$) is good for the large scale (Figs. 4 and 5). It is pronounced in an expected spatial distribution of the particles over the simulation area and dynamics which is shown by speed colors.

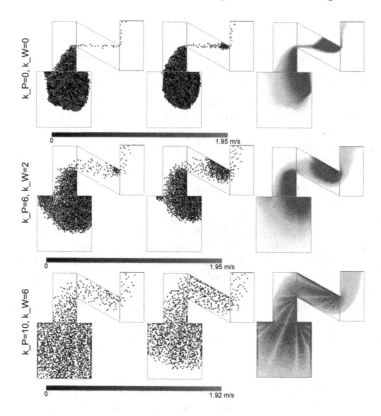

Fig. 5. "Z"-geometry (large), $k_S = 40$. Position of the particles at $t = 30$ s and $t = 90$ s, and total intensity for three pairs of k_P, k_W.

The opposite correspondences does not work due to unsuitable combination of linear sizes and values of model parameters.

4 Conclusion

Model parameters k_P and k_W allows to tune dynamics of the model. And movement along "L"-shaped geometry and "Z"-shaped geometry could be simulated in a proper way. But as it is now clear these parameters are not only density-dependent they are scale-dependant.

Very often model parameters are calibrated for one scale of geometry but they are not good for the larger ones. And there are still thing to be done to improve quality of the simulation of pedestrian dynamics. It is concern not only of the model presented but other models as well. A new point for investigation is to develop a scale-sensitive algorithms for self-adaptation of model parameters.

References

1. Kirik, E., Yurgel'yan, T., Krouglov, D.: On realizing the shortest time strategy in a CA FF pedestrian dynamics model. Cybern. Syst. **42**(1), 1–15 (2011)
2. Kirik, E., Yurgel'yan, T., Malyshev, A.: On discrete-continuous stochastic floor field pedestrian dynamics model SIgMA.DC. In: Proceedings of the International Conference "Emergency Evacuation of People from Buildings", pp. 155–161. Belstudio, Warsaw (2011)
3. Kirik, E., Malyshev, A., Popel, E.: Fundamental diagram as a model input - direct movement equation of pedestrian dynamics. In: Weidmann, U., Kirsch, U., Schreckenberg, M. (eds.) Pedestrian and Evacuation Dynamics 2012, pp. 691–703. Springer, Cham (2014). https://doi.org/10.1007/978-3-319-02447-9_58
4. Kirik, E., Vitova, T.: On formal presentation of update rules, density estimate and using floor fields in CA FF pedestrian dynamics model SIgMA.CA. In: El Yacoubi, S., Wąs, J., Bandini, S. (eds.) ACRI 2016. LNCS, vol. 9863, pp. 435–445. Springer, Cham (2016). https://doi.org/10.1007/978-3-319-44365-2_43
5. Zhang, J., Klingsch, W., Rupprecht, T., Schadschneider, A., Seyfried, A.: Empirical study of turning and merging of pedestrian streams in T-junction. https://arxiv.org/abs/1112.5299 (2011)
6. Boltes, M., Seyfried, A.: Collecting pedestrian trajectories. Neurocomputing **100**, 127–133 (2013)
7. Boltes, M., et al.: Experimentation, data collection, modeling and simulation of pedestrian dynamics. In: Statistics, Probability and Numerical Analysis, pp. 49–60. Tirana, Albania (2014)
8. Gorrini, A., Bandini, S., Sarvi, M., Dias, C., Shiwakoti, N.: An empirical study of crowd and pedestrian dynamics: the impact of different angle paths and grouping. In: Transportation Research Board, 92 Annual Meeting, p. 42. Washington, D.C. (2013)
9. Dias, C., Ejtemai, O., Sarvi, M., Burd, M.: Exploring pedestrian walking through angled corridors. Transp. Res. Procedia **2**, 19–25 (2014)
10. Dias, C., Sarvi, M., Ejtemai, O., Burd, M.: Elevated desired speed and change in desired direction effects on collective pedestrian flow characteristics. Transp. Res. Rec. **2490**, 65–75 (2015)
11. Dias, C., Sarvi, M.: Exploring the effect of turning manoeuvres on macroscopic properties of pedestrian flow. In: 38th Australasian Transport Research Forum, Melbourne, Australia (2016)
12. Kretz, T., Grosse, A., Hengst, S., Kautzsch, L., Pohlmann, A., Vortisch, P.: Quickest paths in simulations of pedestrians
13. Li, S., Li, X., Qu, Y., Jia, B.: Block-based floor field model for pedestrian's walking through corner. Phys. A **432**, 337–353 (2015)
14. Dias, C., Lovreglio, R.: Calibrating cellular automaton models for pedestrians walking through corners. Phys. Lett. A **382**, 1255–1261 (2018)
15. Steffen, B., Seyfried, A.: Modeling of pedestrian movement around 90 and 180 degree bends. https://arxiv.org/abs/0912.0610 (2009)
16. Hall, E.T.: The Hidden Dimension. Garden City, New York (1966)
17. Schadschneider, A., Seyfried, A.: Validation of CA models of pedestrian dynamics with fundamental diagrams. Cybern. Syst. **40**(5), 367–389 (2009)
18. Kholshevnikov, V., Samoshin, D.: Evacuation and human behavior in fire. Academy of State Fire Service, EMERCOM of Russia, Moscow (2009)

19. Kholshevnikov, V.: Forecast of human behavior during fire evacuation. In: Proceedings of the International Conference on Emergency Evacuation of People from Buildings - EMEVAC, pp. 139–153. Belstudio, Warsaw (2011)
20. Predtechenskii, V.M., Milinskii, A.I.: Planing for Foot Traffic Flow in Buildings. American Publishing, New Dehli (1978)
21. Schadschneider, A., Klingsch, W., Kluepfel, H., Kretz, T., Rogsch, C., Seyfried, A.: Evacuation dynamics: empirical results, modeling and applications. In: Meyers, R. (ed.) Encyclopedia of Complexity and System Science, vol. 3, pp. 3142–3192. Springer, New York (2009). https://doi.org/10.1007/978-1-4419-7695-6

Two-Way Road Cellular Automaton Model with Loading/Unloading Bays for Traffic Flow Simulation

Krzysztof Małecki[✉][iD]

West Pomeranian University of Technology, Żołnierska 52, 71-210 Szczecin, Poland
kmalecki@wi.zut.edu.pl

Abstract. The paper presents a model of a two-way one-lane road with loading/unloading bays. The developed model is based on the theory of cellular automata. The model reflects the real behaviour of drivers described in the literature and observed in reality. A micro-simulator was developed to present the measurement results. The model was compared with the one-way two-lane road with loading/unloading bays model described in the literature.

Keywords: Cellular automata (CA) · Computer simulation
Urban freight transport (UFT)

1 Introduction

Analysis of the effectiveness of freight deliveries in cities is particularly importance due to the number of interested parties, narrow areas for freight delivery or environmental problems like poor air quality, noise and greenhouse gas emissions. The analysis of the impact of urban freight transport (UFT) is the subject of research [1–4]. Particularly important is the fact that the attempt to improve the situation in the supply of goods often takes place at the expense of the inhabitants of a given area of the city [5]. For example, designating space for loading and unloading in city centres often results in narrowing the road or reducing the number of public parking spaces. Narrowing the road reduces the speed of vehicles which, in turn, leads to a smaller number of vehicles that will pass through the area. This aspect will be further referred to as reducing the capacity of the road.

Lack of data on traffic volumes, vehicle classifications, car routes and deliveries contributes to difficulties in analysing the effectiveness of the freight transport system and its impact on the urban environment [6]. Computer simulation can be helpful in this area of research. Many mathematical models for traffic modelling have been prepared and the investigation of behaviour of road users have been checked [7–10].

This article presents the model of unloading bays for two-way one-lane roads, which in city centres are much more common than one-way two-lane roads analysed in [11,12]. Additionally a comparison between both models has been done.

© Springer Nature Switzerland AG 2018
G. Mauri et al. (Eds.): ACRI 2018, LNCS 11115, pp. 218–229, 2018.
https://doi.org/10.1007/978-3-319-99813-8_20

2   Related Work

There are various simulation solutions related to traffic research [13–15]. Among the proposed models CA methods are used as simulation techniques for complex traffic. The ability to manage with various types of traffic and high computational efficiency made CA a widely used tool for simulation of traffic nature. Basic mathematical models of car traffic, based on CA, are presented in [16–21].

The simple and effective computational method of traffic modelling was proposed by Nagel and Schreckenberg [16]. The authors formulated a stochastic model (NaSch) of a cellular automaton for single-lane roads. In the developed model time and space are discretized, and due to the low computational complexity, the model can be used to model a large number of vehicles [22]. The model was extended and discussed in further studies [23–25]. The original assumptions of the NaSch model have been maintained. Additionally a second lane of road and the lane-changing possibility have been introduced. The symmetry and asymmetry of traffic flow were also studied.

A hybrid approach, a graph-based cellular automaton model has been done and the comparison to previous models has been presented [26]. Studies have shown that the computational complexity of such approach was much greater than the computational complexity of classic CA-based models.

The literature also includes articles analysing the use of loading/unloading bays. The most important benefit of loading/unloading bay is its impact on reducing traffic congestion, and consequently a perceptible reduction of pollutant emissions [12,27]. Gatta and Marcussi [28] investigate the impact of loading and unloading bays number, the probability of finding bays free and entrance fees and they conclude that these aspects have an influence on retailers' and transport providers' utilities.

3   Proposed Approach

The CA paradigm stems from the attempts made by scientists to develop seemingly complicated processes in the form of a series of simple local decisions [29]. The implementation of that paradigm consists in presenting the analysed space in the form of a homogeneous network of cells. The decision at the cell level is made on the basis of the transition function, which depends on the analysed cell and its surroundings (i.e. adjacent cells). Each cell takes one state from a finite set of states. Adjacent cells are cells connected to a specific cell and they do not change [30]. The time in the model is discreet. Due to the iterative application of the rules, the CA process coincides with the description of the global system behaviour [31]. Moreover, as Was and Sirakoulis indicate, CA can be considered as a mature computational system [32].

The proposed model is a discreet, non-deterministic model that extends the well-known NaSch model [16]. The model was adapted to the needs of parking analysis and departure from unloading bays located on the two-way one-lane road (Fig. 1). Elements describing the behaviour of truck drivers (willingness to

park in the unloading bay and a parameter describing the possibility of joining
the traffic) were introduced.

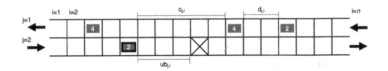

Fig. 1. Schematic sketch of the road segment.

The model includes the occurrence of two types of vehicles with different
characteristics - passenger vehicles and delivery vehicles. In Fig. 1 a rectangle
with a contour symbolizes a delivery vehicle, which has a lower maximum speed
compared to a passenger vehicle. The numbers on cars indicate the current vehicle speed, i - the cell number, j - the road number, $d_{j,i}$ - the distance to the
nearest preceding vehicle, $ub_{j,i}$ - the distance of the vehicle to the nearest unloading bay, $c_{j,i}$ - the distance of the vehicle located in the i-th cell of road numbered
j to the car before it on the adjacent road lane in the opposite direction.

The "2-way-road-ub" model simulates a situation in which the deliverer is
forced to stop the vehicle on the road lane in order to carry out the delivery.
The road fragment (the cell of the CA indicated as X) is the unloading bay
(Fig. 1). If the unloading bay is not occupied by another freight vehicle, the
remaining vehicles can pass through this part of the road without any restriction.
If, however, the vehicle has stopped in the loading/unloading bay, the remaining
vehicles must avoid this part of the road. The transition function of this CA
consists of six steps, pointed below.

Step 1 – Parking in the Unloading Bay. At this stage, a case that "the
unloading bay is free" is considered. If "the unloading bay is busy" then step 2
is realised. In addition, the following parameters have been defined whose values
may vary and allow observation of the simulated phenomenon:

- *desire* - desire (willingness) to stop the car in the unloading bay - value 1
  means that the driver wants to park in the bay (0 as the opposite). Individual
  vehicles will get a value of 1 with a certain probability, which symbolizes the
  fact that not every car is entitled to park in such place.
- *ub* - the distance from which the unloading bay is visible. This parameter,
  in addition, allows to enforce the vehicle to slow down systematically before
  stopping completely on the marked cell.

The parking process (Fig. 2) can be written as follows: if the driver wants to
park in the bay (the bay is within sight and is empty), he/she reduces the speed
(to a minimum of 1) and slowly drives up:

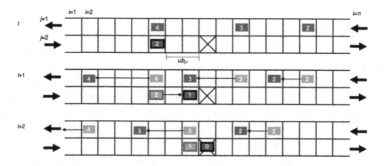

Fig. 2. Particular steps of the CA operation for parking in the unloading bay, $ub = 3$, $ub^t_{j,i} = 2$. Delivery vehicle is a vehicle with contour. The light gray rectangles show where vehicles have been in the previous iteration.

$$desire^t_{j,i} = 1 \quad \text{and} \quad ub^t_{j,i} <= ub \quad \text{and} \quad v^t_{j,i} > min - (d^t_{j,i}, ub^t_{j,i}),$$
$$\Rightarrow \quad v^{t+1}_{j,i} = min(d^t_{j,i}, ub^t_{j,i}), \tag{1}$$

$$desire^t_{j,i} = 1 \quad \text{and} \quad ub^t_{j,i} <= ub \quad \text{and} \quad v^t_{j,i} = 1 \quad \Rightarrow \quad v^{t+1}_{j,i} = 1, \tag{2}$$

When the vehicle approaches the bay area $(ub^t_{j,i} = 0)$, the vehicle stops:

$$desire^t_{j,i} = 1 \quad \text{and} \quad ub^t_{j,i} = 0 \quad \text{and} \quad v^t_{j,i} >= 1 \quad \Rightarrow \quad v^{t+1}_{j,i} = 0, \tag{3}$$

Stopping in the unloading bay area results in the *desire* parameter getting 0:

$$ub^t_{j,i} = 0 \quad \text{and} \quad v^t_{j,i} = 0 \quad \Rightarrow \quad desire^t_{j,i} = 0, \tag{4}$$

After a certain time (the unloading time), the vehicle leaves the unloading bay increasing its speed, according to the third step of the NaSch model – acceleration.

All parameter values are presented in Table 1.

If the vehicle approaches a loading/unloading bay occupied by another vehicle, it performs a maneuver to overtake the unloading bay (Step 2).

Step 2 – Overtaking the Unloading Bay. The unloading bay is overtaken when another vehicle is parked in it. If the unloading bay is free, vehicles can pass over this part of the road (ignoring this area). In the case the bay is occupied, the vehicle will change the road lane if it is possible to overtake the bay (there are enough free CA cells on the opposite lane - the driver has sufficient courage) and the unloading bay is visible for the vehicle:

$$ub^t_{j,i} <= ub \quad \text{and} \quad c + ub^t_{j,i} + v^t_{j,i} =< c^t_{j,i} \quad \text{and} \quad c + v^t_{j,i} =< c^{t+1}_{j,i}$$
$$\Rightarrow j^{t+1} = (j^t \bmod 2) + 1 \quad \text{and} \quad overtake^{t+1}_{j,i} = 1, \tag{5}$$

where: ub – the distance from which the unloading bay is visible, $ub_{j,i}^t$ – the distance of the vehicle located in the i-th cell of the road numbered j to the nearest unloading bay located on its lane, c – driver's courage parameter, $c_{j,i}^t$ – the distance of the vehicle located in the i-th cell of the road numbered j to the nearest vehicle located on opposite lane, $c_{j,i}^{t+1}$ – the predicted distance of a vehicle in the i-th cell of the road numbered j to the nearest vehicle located on opposite lane, $b_{j,i}$ - the distance between car which is overtaking the unloading bay and that bay, $overtake_{j,i}^t$ - the variable indicating that the car bypasses the unloading bay, t - the moment of time.

In the next iteration, when the car has passed the unloading bay, it has to change the road lane again:

$$overtake_{j,i}^t = 1 \quad and \quad b_{j,i}^t >= 0$$
$$\Rightarrow j^{t+1} = (j^t \ mod \ 2) + 1 \quad and \quad overtake_{j,i}^{t+1} = 0, \tag{6}$$

Figure 3 shows the case of this step.

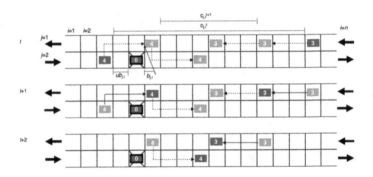

Fig. 3. Visualization of the step 2 – overtaking the unloading bay.

The next steps of the developed model are consistent with the NaSch model: acceleration, braking, random events and shifts.

Step 3 – Acceleration.

$$v_{j,i}^t < v_{max} \quad \Rightarrow \quad v_{j,i}^{t+1} = v_{j,i}^t + 1, \tag{7}$$

where: $v_{j,i}$ – velocity of the car in the i-th cell of the road numbered j, t - time.

Step 4 – Breaking.

$$v_{j,i}^t > min - (d_{j,i}^t, ub_{j,i}^t) \quad \Rightarrow \quad v_{j,i}^{t+1} = min - (d_{j,i}^t, ub_{j,i}^t), \tag{8}$$

where: $d_{j,i}$ – the distance between the cars on the same lane, $ub_{j,i}$ – the distance of the car in the i-th cell of the road numbered j to the nearest loading/unloading bay located on its lane.

Step 5 – Randomization. This step corresponds to the additional, random appearing lane obstructions and it is described as:

$$v_{j,i}^t > 0 \quad \text{and} \quad P < p \quad \Rightarrow \quad v_{j,i}^{t+1} = v_{j,i}^t - 1, \tag{9}$$

where: P – random value, p – the probability of the random event, t - time.

Step 6 – Car Motion. The last step concerns car motion on the lane and it is described as:

$$x_{j,i}^{t+1} = x_{j,i}^t + v_{j,i}^{t+1}, \tag{10}$$

where: $x_{j,i}$ - location of the car in the cell i of the road numbered j, $v_{j,i}$ – velocity of the car in the i-th cell of the road numbered j, t – the moment of time.

Table 1. Parameters used in the model.

Name of parameter	Possible values	Description
desire	0, 1	1 - the car is going to park in the unloading bay
		0 - the opposite
overtake	0, 1	1 - the car is going to overtake the occupied bay
		0 - the opposite
ub	1..15	Determines the distance from which the bay is visible
c	5..12	Determines the courage of driver who is going to overtake the occupied unloading bay
i	$i \in \mathbb{N}$	The number of CA cell
j	1, 2	The road number
$d_{j,i}$	$d \in \mathbb{N}$	The distance to the nearest preceding car
$ub_{j,i}$	$ub \in \mathbb{N}$	The distance to the nearest unloading bay
$c_{j,i}$	$c \in \mathbb{N}$	The distance between cars on opposite lanes
$b_{j,i}$	$b \in \mathbb{N}$	The distance between car which is overtaking the unloading bay and that bay
$v_{j,i}$	$v \in \mathbb{N}$	The car speed
v_{max}	$v_{max} \in \mathbb{N}$	The maximum speed
$x_{j,i}$	$x_{j,i} \in \mathbb{N}$	The location of the car

4   The System Developed for the Simulation

In order to carry out the simulation, the presented model has been implemented in the form of a computer application. The process of starting the simulation consists of two stages: defining the parameters' values of the simulated road section and the run of the simulation using the traffic parameters defined in the model.

As part of the first stage, it is possible to determine the length of the analysed road section, adding or removing unloading points, as well as adding or removing additional permanent road blocks, which allows to simulate restrictions in traffic, resulting from road works, as an example.

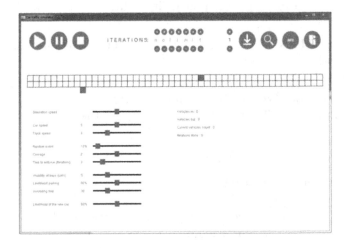

Fig. 4. The main window of the developed simulator.

After determining the parameters of the analysed road, the main simulator window is started (Fig. 4). The analysed road is visible in the centre of the screen. Cells marked in blue represent unloading bays located on the road lane or on side of the road (this type of unloading bays is not described in this article). At the bottom of the panel there are sliders, which are responsible for setting the parameters of the simulation: maximum passenger car speed, maximum delivery vehicle speed, probability of a random event, visibility of loading bays, delivery time, corresponding to the number of CA iterations and others. The developed system updates every 1 s.

5   Experimental Results

The main goal of this paper was to develop a CA model, aimed at investigating the impact of the unloading bays located at 2-way road on traffic flow.

In order to verify the proper operation of the model, several experiments have been done. A measure of the capacity of the road in all the presented experiments is the simulation time with the assumed number of 10.000 vehicles passing through a certain stretch of road. The simulation time is the average time of 10 simulations performed for the same settings. The greater the time is, the road capacity is smaller. The road length was set at 100 CA cells, which, under the premise of the NaSch model gives the actual length of 750 m.

The first simulation (Fig. 5) was carried out for the following input parameters:

- the maximum velocity of the passenger car: 5;
- the maximum velocity of the delivery vehicle: 3;
- the probability of random event: 0.1;
- the timidity of the driver: 2 (the higher the value is, the greater number of CA free cells is required to a vehicle parked in that bay could leave the unloading bay);
- the visibility of bays: 5 (the number of cells of CA - the distance from which the unloading bay can be seen);
- the probability of the new car appearance: 0.9;
- the unloading time: 20–100 iterations of CA;
- the number of unloading bays: 0–4;

Simulations were performed for a set number of vehicles that were to pass through the analysed road.

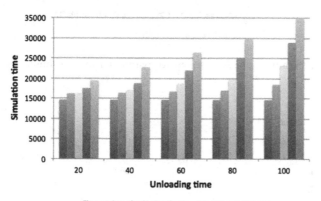

Fig. 5. The impact of the number of unloading bays and unloading time on the simulation time.

Analysis of the results leads to the conclusion that the time of unloading of goods has a significant impact on the capacity of the road with loading/unloading bays. This parameter becomes crucial when unloading bays are located in the lane of a road.

While the delivery vehicle occupies the unloading bay, the remaining vehicles are forced to bypass the place of unloading. This requires an overtaking maneuver. It is a maneuver depending on the courage of the driver ahead of the unloading bay. In the next experiment the courage parameter takes values – from 8 to 12. The smallest value means that the driver has a lot of courage (he/she needs only some space to overtake the vehicle in the unloading bay). The value of 12 means low courage, i.e. the driver needs a lot of free space to perform the overtaking maneuver. Analysis of the results of the experiment (Fig. 6) indicates that drivers who are courageous (they do not need a lot of free space between vehicles) generate a smaller slowdown in traffic, although sometimes they slow down vehicles approaching on the opposite lane of the road. The unloading time in this study has a constant value. With the increase in the number of unloading bays, the slowdown of traffic also increased.

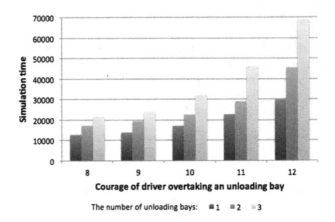

Fig. 6. The impact of driver's courage parameter on the simulation time.

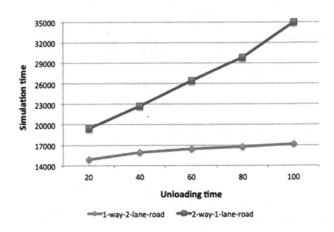

Fig. 7. The comparison of developed model and model presented in [11,12].

The results of comparison of the developed model with the model presented in [11,12] are shown in Fig. 7. In the case of unloading bays located on a two-lane one-way road, the problem of traffic slowdown is minimal. However, placing unloading bays on the two-way road results in an increase the local congestion, which is caused by the need to bypass the vehicle parked in the bay. If traffic flow is big, the phenomenon of avoiding the vehicle delivering the goods is more difficult and congestion is increasing. The solution may be such an organization that there are two road lanes at the unloading bay.

6   Conclusion

This paper focused on applying cellular automata in modelling a two-way road with loading/unloading bays. A model was developed and implemented in the form of a simulation system, which served to carry out the research study described herein.

The basic traffic CA model has been extended with the parking and leaving the unloading bay mechanism and the mechanism of bypassing the unloading bay which is occupied. Experimental research has shown that as the unloading time increases, the capacity of the road decreases, i.e. it takes more time for vehicles to overcome a given section of the road. In addition, the developed model was compared with another model taking into account unloading bays and conclusions were presented on figure. The developed model can be used to test traffic flow, air pollution generated by transport within the analysed road and other aspects oriented to the use of loading/unloading bays.

Further work will be aimed at extending the model with unloading bays placed off the road and performing tests based on field data.

References

1. Kijewska, K., Johansen, B.G., Iwan, S.: Analysis of freight transport demand at Szczecin and Oslo area. Transp. Res. Proc. **14**, 2900–2909 (2016)
2. Kijewska, K., Konicki, W., Iwan, S.: Freight transport pollution propagation at urban areas based on Szczecin example. Transp. Res. Proc. **14**, 1543–1552 (2016)
3. Macioszek, E., Staniek, M., Sierpiński, G.: Analysis of trends in development of freight transport logistics using the example of Silesian Province (Poland) - a case study. Transp. Res. Procedia **27**, 388–395 (2017)
4. Macioszek, E.: First and last mile delivery - problems and issues. In: Sierpiński, G. (ed.) AISC 631. Springer, Switzerland (2018). https://doi.org/10.1007/978-3-319-62316-0_12
5. Lapko, A., Hącia, E.: The importance of the transport accessibility of coastal areas in the development of the Western Pomeranian region. Sci. J. Maritime Univ. Szczecin **51**, 78–85 (2017)
6. Sierpiński, G., Celiński, I., Staniek, M.: The model of modal split organisation in wide urban areas using contemporary telematic systems. In: Proceedings of 3rd International Conference on Transportation Information and Safety. IEEE Explore Digital Library, pp. 277–283 (2015)
7. Sierpiński, G.: Model of incentives for changes of the modal split of traffic towards electric personal cars. In: Mikulski, J. (ed.) TST 2014. CCIS, vol. 471, pp. 450–460. Springer, Heidelberg (2014). https://doi.org/10.1007/978-3-662-45317-9_48
8. Macioszek, E.: The comparison of models for follow-up headway at roundabouts. In: Macioszek, E., Sierpiński, G. (eds.) Recent Advances in Traffic Engineering for Transport Networks and Systems. LNNS, vol. 21, pp. 16–26. Springer, Cham (2018). https://doi.org/10.1007/978-3-319-64084-6_2
9. Staniek, M., Sierpiński, G., Celiński, I.: Shaping environmental friendly behaviour in transport of goods - new tool and education. In: 8th ICERI 2015, Seville, Spain, pp. 118–123 (2015)

10. Małecki, K., Wątróbski, J.: Cellular automaton to study the impact of changes in traffic rules in a roundabout: a preliminary approach. Appl. Sci. **7**(7), 742 (2017)
11. Iwan, S., et al.: Analysis of the environmental impacts of unloading bays based on cellular automata simulation. Transp. Res. D: Transp. Env. **61**(A), 104–117 (2018)
12. Iwan, S., Małecki, K.: Utilization of cellular automata for analysis of the efficiency of urban freight transport measures based on loading/unloading bays example. Transp. Res. Proc. **25**, 1021–1035 (2017)
13. Fellendorf, M.: VISSIM: a microscopic simulation tool to evaluate actuated signal control including bus priority. In: Proceedings of the 64th Institute of Transportation Engineers Annual Meeting, Dallas, TX, USA, 16–19 October 1994, pp. 1–9, Technical Paper (1994)
14. Barcelo, J., Ferrer, J.L., Montero, L.: AIMSUN: advanced interactive microscopic simulator for urban networks. User's Manual, Departament d 'Estadística i Investigacio Operativa, UPC (1997)
15. Krajzewicz, D., Erdmann, J., Behrisch, M., Bieker, L.: Recent development and applications of SUMO-simulation of urban mobility. Int. J. Adv. Syst. Meas. **5**, 128–138 (2012)
16. Nagel, K., Schreckenberg, M.: A cellular automata model for freeway traffic. J. Phys. **I**(2), 2221–2229 (1992)
17. Biham, O., Middleton, A.A., Levine, D.: Self-organization and a dynamical transition in traffic-flow models. Phys. Rev. A **46**(10), 6124 (1992)
18. Nagel, K., Wolf, D.E., Wagner, P., Simon, P.M.: Two-lane traffic rules for cellular automata: a systematic approach. Phys. Rev. E **58**(2), 1425–1437 (1998)
19. Chowdhury, D., Schadschneider, A.: Self-organization of traffic jams in cities: effects of stochastic dynamics and signal periods. Phys. Rev. E **59**, 1311–1314 (1999)
20. Chowdhury, D., Santen, L., Schadschneider, A.: Statistical physics of vehicular traffic and some related systems. Phys. Rep. **329**, 199–329 (2000)
21. Małecki, K., Iwan, S.: Development of cellular automata for simulation of the crossroads model with a traffic detection system. In: Mikulski, J. (ed.) TST 2012. CCIS, vol. 329, pp. 276–283. Springer, Heidelberg (2012). https://doi.org/10.1007/978-3-642-34050-5_31
22. Hoogendoorn, S., Bovy, P.: State-of-the-art of vehicular traffic flow modelling. Proc. IMECH E Part I J. Syst Control Eng. **215**(4), 283–303 (2001)
23. Nagel, K., Paczuski, M.: Emergent traffic jams. Phys. Rev. E **51**(4), 2909–2918 (1995)
24. Schadschneider, A., Schreckenberg, M.: Traffic flow models with 'slow-to-start' rules. Ann. Phys. **509**(7), 541–551 (1997)
25. Chopard, B., Luthi, P.O., Queloz, P.: Cellular automata model of car traffic in a two-dimensional street network. J. Phys. A **29**(10), 2325–2336 (1996)
26. Małecki, K.: Graph cellular automata with relation-based neighbourhoods of cells for complex systems modelling: a case of traffic simulation. Symmetry **9**(12), 322 (2017)
27. Roche-Cerasi, I.: State of the art report. Urban logistics practices. Green Urban Distribution, Deliverable 2.1. SINTEF Teknologi og samfunn (2012)
28. Gatta, V., Marcucci, E.: Behavioural implications of non-linear effects on urban freight transport policies: the case of retailers and transport providers in Rome. Case Stud. Transp. Policy **4**(1), 22–28 (2016)
29. Wolfram, S.: A New Kind of Science. Wolfram Media, Champaign (2002)

30. Mamei, M., Roli, A., Zambonelli, F.: Emergence and control of macro-spatial structures in perturbed cellular automata, and implications for pervasive computing systems. IEEE Trans. Syst. Man Cybern.-Part A: Syst. Hum. **35**(3), 337–348 (2005)
31. Missoum, S., Gürdal, Z., Setoodeh, S.: Study of a new local update scheme for cellular automata in structural design. Struct. Multidiscip. Optim. **29**(2), 103–112 (2005)
32. Wąs, J., Sirakoulis, G.C.: Cellular automata applications for research and industry. J. Comput. Sci. **11**, 223–225 (2015)

A Microscopic CA Model of Traffic Flow?

Peter Wagner[1]([⊠])[iD] and Johannes Rummel[1,2][iD]

[1] DLR, Institute for Transport Systems, Rutherfordstrasse 2, 12489 Berlin, Germany
{peter.wagner,johannes.rummel}@dlr.de
[2] Technical University Berlin, Berlin, Germany

Abstract. Cellular automaton (CA) models of traffic flow are typically constructed to reproduce macroscopic features of traffic flow. Here, a few thoughts based on real car-following data are presented that show how to construct a discrete time/discrete space microscopic model of traffic flow. The question whether this can still be called a CA-model is left to the reader.

Keywords: CA models for traffic flow · Natural driving studies
Traffic simulation

1 Introduction

The title of this article seems strange, since a traffic flow model like the CA introduced in [9] (see e.g. [2,8] for reviews) may be called with right a microscopic model of traffic flow.

And the answer is: no, since CA models are created to reproduce macroscopic features of traffic flow, and not microscopic ones. Clearly, this boundary is fuzzy [5,7], especially when it comes to CA models with smaller spatial discretization δx than the paradigmatic $\delta x = 7.5$ m used in the original work of [3,9]. To make this boundary clearer, a microscopic model of traffic flow discrete in space and time will be constructed here which is based on real car-following data.

1.1 Notation, CA-Rules, Data-Set

The time, space, speed, and acceleration discretization (in real metric units) will be called $\delta t, \delta x, \delta v$ and δa, respectively. Each vehicle i at time-step t is described by a position x_i, a speed v_i, and the acceleration a_i. Sometimes, to write clearer equations, the index is dropped and instead capital letters X, V, A are used for the vehicle in front $i - 1$, while the follower is described by small letters (x, v, a), Then, the net space headway g is defined as

$$g = X - x - \ell \quad \text{or} \quad g_i = x_{i-1} - x_i - \ell$$

where ℓ is the length of the vehicle plus the distance when standing. Note, that this is correct only when working with homogeneous traffic, i.e. all vehicles have

G. Mauri et al. (Eds.): ACRI 2018, LNCS 11115, pp. 230–239, 2018.
https://doi.org/10.1007/978-3-319-99813-8_21

the same length. If not, then one must fix the co-ordinate system (front of the car, e.g.) and include the lengths of both vehicles.

Another useful short-hand notation is the speed difference Δv between the lead and the following vehicle:

$$\Delta v = V - v = \dot{g} \quad \text{or} \quad \Delta v_i = v_{i-1} - v_i$$

The CA model introduced in [9] is characterized by $\delta t = 1\,\text{s}$, $\delta x = 7.5\,\text{m}$, from which $\delta v = 7.5\,\text{m/s}$ and $\delta a = 7.5\,\text{m/s}^2$ follows. Its deterministic rule-set is defined, in a slightly different variant as in the original formulation as:

$$a = \min\{g - v, 1\} \tag{1}$$
$$v' = \max\{\min\{v + a, v_0\}, 0\} \tag{2}$$
$$x' = x + v' \tag{3}$$

The primed variables are the updated variables, and the stochastic term is left-out because an explicit white noise acceleration noise is a bad physical description of a heavy vehicle. The complicated looking second Eq. (2) simply restricts the speed to the interval $[0, v_0]$.

The data to be used in the following are an excerpt (from 3 August 2012) from a German project named simTD [1], which was a natural driving study although with the goal to do research on vehicle-to-vehicle communication. There, about 100 vehicles, most of them instrumented with sensors to measure position, speed, acceleration, distance, and speed-difference to the lead vehicles drove with about 1000 different drivers for three months in an area around Frankfurt/Main, Germany. A more detailed description of the data can be found else-where [12], here the data from the car-following episodes have been used. A first glimpse into the data can be gained from Fig. 1, where the distributions of the speed, the speed differences, the gaps, and the time headways are displayed.

2   From Scratch

To fix the spatial discretization at the vehicle length as done in [9] is definitely very elegant. Nevertheless, this is also creating the biggest problems for a truly microscopic model, since it makes acceleration way too big. To fix that, it is argued here that there is a kind of a minimum acceleration step δa, that is given by the acceleration noise (its standard deviation denoted σ_a) created by human drivers. This variable is difficult to measure, the following approach is used here to get hold of it, at least to a certain approximation.

2.1   Acceleration Noise

Acceleration noise will be defined as follows: in a deterministic world, the acceleration of a vehicle is determined by a function $a(v, g, \Delta v)$, and eventually additional variables which are difficult to measure or have not been measured. In

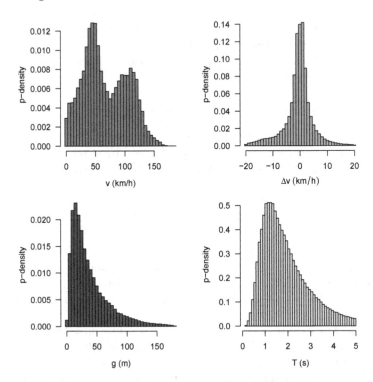

Fig. 1. The distribution of the variables speed (upper left), speed-difference (upper right), gap (lower left), and net time headway T (lower right). The headway data are filtered and contain only values where $v > 10$ km/h, $g > 5$ m, and $T \leq 5$.

a stochastic setting, even for the same set of variables, the acceleration at the same point is drawn from a distribution $p_{v,g,\Delta v}(a)$, and therefore it has a certain width, which can be quantified e.g. by the standard-deviation of the acceleration $\sigma_a(v, g, \Delta v)$. Neither the exact function $a(v, g, \Delta v)$, nor the distribution is known, and to make life even more complicated, it might be suspected that it depends on the state itself. However, both $a(v, g, \Delta v)$ and $\sigma_a(v, g, \Delta v)$ can be extracted from these data, to a rough approximation and within certain limits.

To do so, two sub-sets of the data are picked, a city and a freeway data-set. This is motivated by the two peaks in the speed distribution, so in a first step all speeds $v \in [40, 60]$ km/h (city) and $v \in [100, 120]$ km/h (freeway) will be selected. In addition, only data from close following situations will be used, which are defined by $\Delta v \leq 10$ km/h and $g \leq 80$ m. Then, the phase-space $(\Delta v, g)$ is partitioned into boxes whose width is chosen so that in each dimension the same number of points is in each box. Within each box, now, the mean value of the acceleration and the corresponding standard deviation can be computed. This yields the result in Fig. 2.

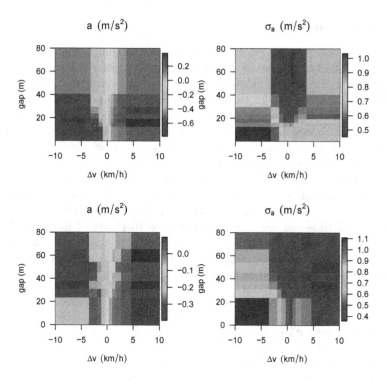

Fig. 2. $a(v = 50, \Delta v, g)$ (upper left) and $\sigma_a(v = 50, \Delta v, g)$ for city speeds, and for freeway speeds (lower row).

From Fig. 2, a minimum value of $\sigma_a \approx 0.4\,\mathrm{m/s}^2$ may be read out. This will be chosen in the following equal to the minimum acceleration step $\delta a = 0.4\,\mathrm{m/s}^2$.

2.2 Time Step Size δt

Having fixed $\delta a = 0.4\,\mathrm{m/s}^2$, the time-step size is the next. Here, either the minimum reaction time of humans, which is of the order of $0.3\,\mathrm{s}$ might be used. Interestingly, this value is also close to the minimum time headway found in empirical data, see Fig. 1. Using $\delta t = 0.25\,s$ gives an additional safety margin and it divides nicely by 1 (what is not really necessary).

Having fixed δa and δt, which also shows that this construction process is bottom up, the remaining discretization values are determined, too. Since

$$\delta a = \delta v / \delta t \quad \text{and} \quad \delta v = \delta x / \delta t,$$

the spatial discretization follows to be $\delta x = \delta a \delta t^2$ which gives $\delta x = 0.025\,\mathrm{m}$. This is of course way smaller than the value in [9]. For the speeds, this yields $\delta v = 0.1\,\mathrm{m/s}$. For maximum speeds larger than $25.5\,\mathrm{m/s}$, this will no longer fit into a 1 byte integer.

2.3   The Dynamics

There are two observations relevant here: the first is that human control is discrete. At so called action-points [10], the human controler changes acceleration (more precisely, the gas- and or brake-pedal position) quickly, and keeps it constant for 0.5...5 s, see [11] for the distribution of this times which may follow a gamma-distribution. This might have made another time-discretization δt, but it is more difficult to measure, since a small acceleration change is hard to discern from high-frequency acceleration noise. However, at least the size is similar to the 0.25 s that have been chosen above.

The second observation is that to model the car-following process (car-following is abbreviated CF in the following), at least the original model is too gross. Additionally, it mixes the car-following with a safety consideration, and since the small time-step size chosen above lead to plenty of modelling leeway, these two will be separated in the following. So, there is an emergency braking which happens if the normal car-following fails and that is with the typical Euler backward update formulated as follows:

$$\text{if } v > g/\delta t \text{ then } v = g/\delta t \tag{4}$$

Since in the discretization framework chosen here $\delta t = 1$, this is exactly the same as in the original formulation.

For the CF-process, a slightly more complex approach is chosen. Instead of the original dependence on distance g alone, the model acts as a linear controler with limited acceleration a_0, which is also pretty close to some of the adaptive cruise control of modern driver assistant systems. Furthermore, there is the need to introduce two pre-factors c_1, c_2 to the two terms in the equation, whose physical relevance will be discussed later on. Here, they simply scale the variables to a reasonable size (typically, $c_i < 1$).

$$a_0 = \min\left\{\max\left\{c_1\left(\frac{g}{T} - v\right) + c_2(V - v), -\beta\right\}, \alpha\right\} \tag{5}$$

and a_0 is bounded between $-\beta$ from below, and α from above, which again is written as the complicated min, max combination. This is however not the whole model. In addition, the action-points are included in the dynamics pretty much like in a Monte Carlo simulation. This acceleration a_0 is only made the new acceleration with a certain probability p_{AP}, so the additional step is needed:

$$a' = \begin{cases} a_0 \text{ with probability } p_{AP} \\ a \quad \text{else} \end{cases} \tag{6}$$

The rest, then, is just the same as in Eqs. (2), (3):

$$v' = \max\{\min\{v + a', v_0\}, 0\}$$
$$x' = x + v'$$

This is a simple linear controler, and it clearly has a stable fixed-point at $v = g/T$. The randomness injected by the action-point mechanism is too weak to change this. However, some randomness is needed, since it seems almost impossible to find car-following data where the lead vehicle's speed is constant. There are many ways how to do this, and the worst one (not to be followed here) is to add acceleration noise. Better is the approach of the so called 2D models [4]. There the preferred headway T is made stochastic. Here, we only allow three values of the headway $T = 3, 4, 5$ (in units of δt), and the driver switches between them each time a new AP is issued.

3 Phenomenology

Here, we simulate first the microscopic features, and then have a look at the macroscopic ones like the fundamental diagram.

3.1 Microscopic

For the microscopic description, it should be noticed that the behaviour, and especially the stability of the car-following process is strongly determined by the choice of the two parameters c_1, c_2. Clearly, they are inverse time-constants, named T_g and $T_{\Delta v}$. From the theory of linear controlers which is being used for adaptive driver assistant systems, it is well-known, that a platoon of those vehicles is only platoon-stable for a certain range of parameters, typically for small values. The model here is a little bit more complicate than a linear controler, since the acceleration is bounded, making it a non-linear controler. Therefore, for too small values of T_x, the acceleration distribution becomes bimodal with peaks at the limiting value a_0. Which is not realistic. Therefore, there is only a fairly small range of values for the T_x, where they are platoon stable and not bimodal. In the following, the parameters $T_1 = 26$ (6.5 s) and $T_2 = 6$ (1.5 s) are chosen, while $p_{AP} = 0.4$ is used. For a string of four vehicles, this yields then the results presented in Fig. 3.

The lower panel compares the distributions of Δv and of T with the empirical ones. While this fits well for the speed-differences, it does not so well for the headways. The simulation has used only three headway values $T = 3, 4, 5$ (0.75, 1, 1.25 s in real units), it seems that the distribution of real drivers is much wider than this three values.

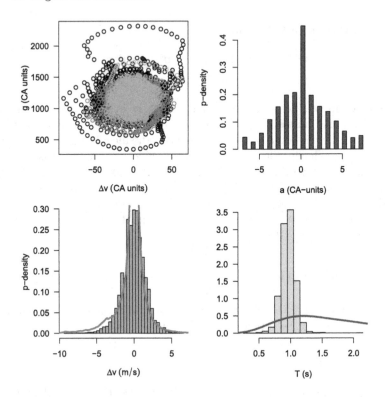

Fig. 3. The behaviour of the model in $(\Delta v, g)$-space, for the first follower (green), the second (red) and the third (black, upper left). The upper right displays the acceleration distribution in CA-units, still a slight peak at the boundary value is to be seen. The lower panel displays the speed-difference and headway distribution, and compares it directly with the empirical ones. (Color figure online)

3.2 Macroscopic

To compute a fundamental diagram, the simplest possible set-up is chosen. The vehicles run in a ring, which means that the density k is the control parameter of the fundamental diagram. Simulations are run for 1024 vehicles for 40 values of the scaled density $k/k_{\max}$ values ranging from 0.01 to 0.99. The system is started either in a homogeneous or in a jammed configuration, each simulation runs for 10^5 time-steps of which the first 25,000 time-steps are discarded. Only the speed distribution is sampled, where 40 simulation steps are left out between each sampling step to minimize correlations between subsequent states. The results shown in Fig. 4 the following: at small densities, only the free flow state exists. There is an intermediate range, where the system's state consists of a mixture of free flow and jams, and finally, for large densities, the system eventually becomes bistable.

No more detailed and exhaustive studies have been performed.

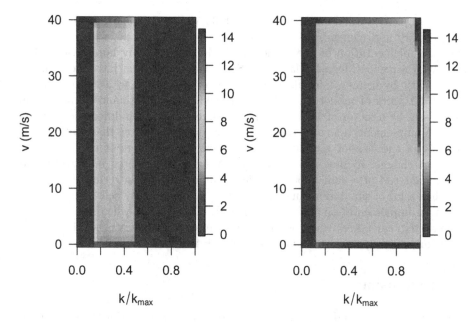

Fig. 4. The fundamental diagram of the model. Presented is the speed distribution $p(v)$ as function of the scaled density. The left plot is for homogeneous initial conditions, while the right plot for a system started in a jammed condition, the color scale is logarithmic to include more information about the distributions.

4 Execution Speed

There are a lot of science tales around the fantastic numerical performance of CA models. Partially, they stem from the time where the floating point units of computers were weak in comparison with the integer units, and therefore it was worth to look for integer-based models. With this model at hand that lingers between discrete and continuous, it is time to have a look into this issue. Note, that there is also a much more detailed contribution to this conference by Moreno Marzolla, which discusses in much detail what can be reached and which kind of tricks to apply in order to achieve good performance. Therefore, only a few short remarks to the issue of numerical performance may be added here.

One of the challenges with this problem is, that the performance depends very much on a lot of things that are difficult to control. Just for starters, when writing a program that implements the model in [9], and comparing it with a continuous one that implements SUMO's [6] default model, not much of a difference can be seen. This difference becomes even smaller, when real world things like copying data from the running simulation, or if the open system's simulations are needed. For some-one to dive into the depths of modern compilers and the tremendous possibilities of modern CPU's such as their SIMD (=Single Instruction Multiple Data) units, some differences can be found.

The implementation used here runs with 30 MUPS on a Pentium G4400 with Windows 10 and cygwin's g++ compiler in the version 6.4.0, which is on par with a implementation of the model of SUMO without any fancy tricks. The unit MUPS means Mega Updates Per Second and has been introduced in [9]. This is just by using a normal optimization setting of a year 2017 compiler. If the SIMD units of modern CPU's are utilized, this performance improves, in some cases by a factor of 10. Interestingly, there is not much difference between the CA implementation and the continuous one. But note, that this is only possible in the case of a closed system, where the numbers of particle (cars) does not change. It may also work, if the CA is implemented in a grid-based manner instead of a vehicle-based which is more efficient in terms of memory, but then a lot of simulation time is spent by updating empty cells. We have not found an implementation that can utilize SIMD or GPU's when simulating an open system car-based, which is the case for most applied settings. Then, those beautiful speed-ups vanish and one sticks with the 30 MUPS above.

5   Conclusions

In conclusion, the building blocks of a microscopic discrete space/discrete time CA model have been presented. When following the approach pursued here, this leads to a CA model with time-step size $\delta t = 0.25\,\mathrm{s}$ and spatial discretization $\Delta x = 0.025\,\mathrm{m}$. While still discrete, we think that such a model is not easy to discern from a continuous model, if this possible at all. When looking into the plots in this article only the acceleration is clearly discrete. It may be interesting to see what of the features included here can be left out to still have a valid description of microscopic driving. Another valid conclusion is also, that such simple models as the CA have their value, but should not be used when a really microscopic description of traffic flow is needed for the application at hand.

References

1. Safe and intelligent mobility - test field germany (2012). http://www.simtd.de/index.dhtml/enEN/index.html, http://www.simtd.de/index.dhtml/enEN/index.html. Accessed 7 Jul 2015
2. Chowdhury, D., Santen, L., Schadschneider, A.: Statistical physics of vehicular traffic and some related systems. Phys. Rep. **329**(4–6), 199–329 (2000)
3. Cremer, M., Ludwig, J.: A fast simulation model for traffic flow on the basis of boolean operations. Math. Comput. Simul. **28**, 297–303 (1986)
4. Jiang, R., et al.: Traffic experiment reveals the nature of car-following. PLoS One **9**(4), e94351 (2014). https://doi.org/10.1371/journal.pone.0094351. http://journals.plos.org/plosone/article?id=10.1371/journal.pone.0094351
5. Kerner, B.S., Klenov, S.L., Wolf, D.E.: Cellular automata approach to three-phase traffic theory. J. Phys. A Math. Gen. **35**, 9971–10013 (2002)
6. Krajzewicz, D., Erdmann, J., Behrisch, M., Bieker, L.: Recent development and applications of SUMO - Simulation of Urban MObility. Int. J. Adv. Syst. Meas. **5**(3&4), 128–138 (2012)

7. Lee, H.K., Barlovic, R., Schreckenberg, M., Kim, D.: Mechanical restriction versus human overreaction triggering congested states. Phys. Rev. Lett. **92**, 238702 (2004)
8. Maerivoet, S., Moor, B.D.: Cellular automata models of road traffic. Phys. Rep. **419**(1), 1–64 (2005). https://doi.org/10.1016/j.physrep.2005.08.005. http://www.sciencedirect.com/science/article/pii/S0370157305003315
9. Nagel, K., Schreckenberg, M.: A cellular automaton model for freeway traffic. Journal de Physique I France **2**, 2221–2229 (1992). https://doi.org/10.1051/jp1:1992277
10. Todosiev, E.P., Barbosa, L.C.: A proposed model for the driver-vehicle-system. Traffic Eng. **34**, 17–20 (1963/1964)
11. Wagner, P.: A time-discrete harmonic oscillator model of human car-following. Eur. Phys. J. B **84**(4), 713–718 (2011). https://doi.org/10.1140/epjb/e2011-20722-8
12. Wagner, P., Nippold, R., Gabloner, S., Margreiter, M.: Analyzing human driving data an approach motivated by data science methods. Chaos Solitons Fractals **90**, 37–45 (2016). https://doi.org/10.1016/j.chaos.2016.02.008. http://www.sciencedirect.com/science/article/pii/S096007791630039X

Synchronization and Control

Regional Control of Probabilistic Cellular Automata

Franco Bagnoli[1,2(✉)], Sara Dridi[3], Samira El Yacoubi[3], and Raúl Rechtman[4]

[1] Department of Physics and Astronomy and CSDC, University of Florence,
via G. Sansone 1, 50019 Sesto Fiorentino, Italy
franco.bagnoli@unifi.it
[2] INFN, sez. Firenze, Sesto Fiorentino, Italy
[3] Team Project IMAGES_ESPACE-Dev, UMR 228 Espace-Dev IRD UA UM UG
UR, University of Perpignan Via Domitia, 52, Avenue Paul Alduy,
66860 Perpignan Cedex, France
yacoubi@univ-perp.fr
[4] Instituto de Energías Renovables, Universidad Nacional Autónoma de México,
Apartado Postal 34, 62580 Temixco, Morelos, Mexico
rrs@ier.unam.mx

Abstract. Probabilistic Cellular Automata are extended stochastic systems, widely used for modelling phenomena in many disciplines. The possibility of controlling their behaviour is therefore an important topic. We shall present here an approach to the problem of controlling such systems by acting only on the boundary of a target region.

Keywords: Probabilistic cellular automata · Control theory
Boundary control · Reachability

1 Introduction

Cellular Automata (CA) are widely used for studying the mathematical properties of discrete systems and for modelling physical systems [1–6]. They come in two major "flavours": deterministic CA (DCA) [9–14] and probabilistic CA (PCA) [15,16].

DCA are the discrete equivalent of continuous dynamical systems (i.e., differential equations or maps) but are intrinsically extended, constituted by many elements, so they are in principle the discrete equivalent of system modelled by partial differential equations. DCA are defined by graph, a discrete set of states at the nodes of the graph, and a local transition function that gives the future state of a node as a function of the present state of the node connected to it, its so-called neighbourhood. This evolution rule is applied in parallel to all nodes. PCA can be thought as an extension of DCA where the transition function gives the probability that the target node goes in a certain state. If all these probabilities are either zero or one, that the PCA reduces to a DCA. In both cases, the state of the CA is the collection of states at the nodes of the graph and this state changes in time according to functions defined in every node of the graph.

© Springer Nature Switzerland AG 2018
G. Mauri et al. (Eds.): ACRI 2018, LNCS 11115, pp. 243–254, 2018.
https://doi.org/10.1007/978-3-319-99813-8_22

In analogy with continuous dynamical systems, it is important to develop methods for controlling the behaviour of DCA and PCA. In particular, the main control problems for extended systems are reachability and drivability. The first is related to the possibility of applying a suitable control able to make the system reach a given state or a set of states. For instance, assuming that the system under investigation represents a population of pests, the control problem could be that of bringing the population towards extinction at a given time or to keep the population under a certain threshold.

The drivability problem is somehow complementary to the reachability one; once that the system is driven to a desired state or collection of states, what kind of control may make it follow a given trajectory? For instance, one may want to stabilize a fixed point, or make the system follow a cycle, and so on.

As usual in control problems, one aims at achieving the desired goal with the optimal cost or smallest effort, and we speak of an optimal control problem. One may be interested not in controlling the whole space, but rather the state of a given region, for instance how to avoid that a pollutant reaches a certain area.

The techniques for controlling discrete systems are quite different from those used in continuous ones, since discrete systems are in general strongly non-linear and the usual linear approximations cannot be directly applied. What one can do is to change the state at a node or a set of chosen nodes. For Boolean CA the state is either 0 or 1, so a change is either 1 or 0. The "intensity" of the control therefore can be only associated to the average number of changes, and cannot be made arbitrary small. We are interested in regional control of PCA, that is, how to achieve a certain goal in a set of neighbouring nodes of a graph.

This problem is related to the so-called regional controllability introduced in Ref. [17], as a special case of output controllability [18–20]. The regional control problem consists in achieving an objective only in a subregion of the domain when some specific actions are exerted on the system, in its domain interior or on its boundaries. This concept has been studied by means of partial differential equations. Some results on the action properties (number, location, space distribution) based on the rank condition have been obtained depending on the target region and its geometry, see for example Ref. [17] and the references therein.

Regional controllability has also been studied using CA models. In Ref. [21], a numerical approach based on genetic algorithms has been developed for a class of additive CA in in one and two dimensions. In Ref. [22], an interesting theoretical study has been carried out for one dimensional additive CA where the effect of control is given through an evolving neighbourhood and a very sophisticated state transition function. However, these studies did not provide a real insight in the regional controllability problem.

Some results for control techniques applied to one dimensional DCA can be found in Refs. [23–27].

For DCA, once the states in the neighbouring nodes are known, the future state at the node under consideration is fixed and for PCA we have in general only the probability of reaching a certain state. One advantage of PCA vs. DCA is that their dynamics can be fine-tuned. PCA are summarized in Sect. 3.

The control problem of PCA is more subtle than of DCA. In general, it is impossible to exactly drive these systems towards a given configuration, but it is possible to increase the probability that the system will reach a target state in a collection of nodes, or, alternatively, to lower as much as possible the probability of the appearance of a given configuration, for instance the extinction of a species inside a given region.

The evolution of a PCA can be seen as a Markov chain, where the elements of the transition matrix are given by the product of the local transition probabilities (Sect. 3). In particular we shall study here a particular PCA (BBR model) with two absorbing states in Sect. 4.

A Markov chain is said to be ergodic if there is the possibility of going to any state in the graph to any other state in a finite number of steps. If this goal can be achieved for all pairs of states at a given time, the Markov chain is said to be regular. This consideration allows us to define the reachability problem in terms of the probability, once summed over all possible realizations of the control, of connecting any two sites. And since DCA can be considered as the extreme limit of PCA, this technique can be applied to them too, see Sect. 5.

Finally, one should remark that the problem of controllability (in particular that of drivability) is strictly related to that of synchronization (see Ref. [25] for instance). In this same issue the regional synchronization problem for the BBR model is addressed [28].

2   Definitions

Cellular Automata are defined on graph composed by N nodes identified by an index $i = 1, \ldots, N$, by an adjacency matrix a_{ij} that establishes the neighbourhood of each node with $a_{ij} = 1$ ($a_{ij} = 0$) if node j is (is not) in node i's neighbourhood, and by a transition function f_i that gives the new state at node i given the states in its neighbourhood. The connectivity of node i is $k_i = \sum_j a_{ij}$. We shall deal here with graphs having fixed connectivity $k_i = k$ and use the same transition function in all the nodes, $f_i = f$.

A lattice is a graph invariant by translation and the nodes are called sites. For a one dimensional lattice with N sites with connectivity $k = 2r + 1$, $r = 1, 2, \ldots$ and r the range, the neighbourhood of site i is the set $\{i - r, \ldots, i + r\}$. Periodic boundary conditions are generally imposed. The state at site i at time t, $x_i(t)$, is chosen from a finite set of values, for Boolean CA, $x_i(t) \in \{0, 1\}$. Then

$$x_i(t + 1) = f(x_{i-r}(t), \ldots, x_{i+r}(t))$$

We shall indicate with $x'_i = x_i(t + 1)$ its value at the following time step.

An ordered set of Boolean values like $x_1, x_2, \ldots, x_N$ can be read as a Boolean vector or as base-two number and we shall indicate it as $\boldsymbol{x}$, $0 \leq \boldsymbol{x} < 2^N$. We

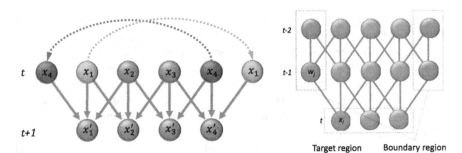

Fig. 1. Left: The space-time lattice of 1D CA with periodic boundary conditions. Right: CA boundary-value problem.

shall also indicate with v_i the state of all connected neighbours. The state of x_i' depends on the state of the neighbourhood v_i, and on some random number $r_i(t)$ for stochastic CA. In formulas (neglecting to indicate the random numbers) we have

$$x_i' = f(v_i).$$

The function f is applied in parallel to all sites. Therefore, we can define a vector function F such that

$$x' = F(x).$$

The sequence of states $\{x(t)\}_{t=0,...}$ is a trajectory of the system with $x(0)$ as the initial condition.

When f depends symmetrically on the states of neighbours, it can be shown that f actually depends on the sum $s_i = \sum_j a_{ij} x_j$. In this case we say that the cellular automaton is totalistic and write

$$x_i(t+1) = f_T(s_i(t)), \tag{1}$$

with $f_T : \{0, \ldots, k\} \rightarrow \{0, 1\}$. Totalistic cellular automata are generic, since they exhibit the whole variety of behaviour of general rules [12]. It is possible to visualize the evolution of the automata as happening on a space-time oriented graph or lattice, Fig. 1-left.

3   Probabilistic Cellular Automata

Probabilistic CA constitute an extension of DCA. Let us introduce the transition probability $\tau(1|v)$ that, given a certain configuration $v = v_i$ of the neighbourhood of site i, gives the probability of observing $x_i' = 1$ at next time step. Clearly $\tau(0|v) = 1 - \tau(1|v)$. DCA are such that $\tau(1|v)$ is either 0 or 1, while for PCA it can take any value in the middle. For a PCA with k inputs, there are 2^k independent transition probabilities, and for totalistic PCA there are $k + 1$ independent probabilities. If one associates each transition probability to a different axis, the

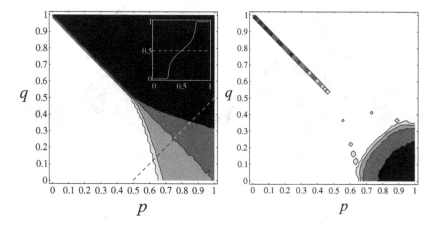

Fig. 2. Phase diagram of the BBR model. Left: Density phase diagram. Right: Damage phase diagram.

space of all possible PCA is an unit hypercube, with corners corresponding to DCA.

PCA can be also *partially* deterministic, i.e., the transition probability $\tau(1|\boldsymbol{v})$ can be zero or one for certain $\boldsymbol{v}$. This opens the possibility for the automata to have one or more absorbing state, i.e., configurations that always originate the same configuration (or give origin to a cyclic behaviour). The BBR model illustrated below has one or two absorbing states.

The evolution of all possible configurations $\boldsymbol{x}$ of a PCA can be written as a Markov chain. Let us define the probability $P(\boldsymbol{x},t)$, i.e., the probability of observing the configuration $\boldsymbol{x}$ at time t. Its evolution is given by

$$P(\boldsymbol{x},t+1) = \sum_{\boldsymbol{y}} M(\boldsymbol{x}|\boldsymbol{y})P(\boldsymbol{y},t), \tag{2}$$

where the matrix M is such that

$$M(\boldsymbol{x}|\boldsymbol{y}) = \prod_{i=1}^{N} \tau\left(x_i|\boldsymbol{v}_i(\boldsymbol{y})\right). \tag{3}$$

For a CA on a 1D lattice and $k = 3$ we have

$$M(\boldsymbol{x}|\boldsymbol{y}) = \prod_{i=1}^{N} \tau(x_i|y_{i-1}, y_i, y_{i+1}). \tag{4}$$

Phase transitions for PCA can be described as degeneration of eigenvalues in the limit $N \to \infty$ and (subsequently) $T \to \infty$ [29].

Notice that since DCA are limit cases of PCA, they also can be seen as particular Markov chains.

Fig. 3. Damage spreading; time runs downwards. Left: CA rule 150. Right: CA rule 126.

A Markov chain such that, for some t, $(M^t)_{ij} > 0$ for all i, j is said to be regular, and this implies that any configuration can be reached by any configuration in time t. A weaker condition (ergodicity) says that t may depend on the pair i, j (for instance, one may have an oscillating behaviour such that certain pairs can be connected only for even or odd values of t). Also for ergodic systems all configurations are connected.

4   The BBR Model

We shall use as a testbed model the one presented in Ref. [30], which is an extension of the Domany-Kinzel CA [15]. We shall refer to it as the BBR model from the name of its authors. It is a totalistic PCA defined on a one-dimensional lattice, with connectivity $k = 3$. The transition probabilities of the model are

$$\tau(1|0) = 0; \qquad \tau(1|1) = p; \qquad \tau(1|2) = q; \qquad \tau(1|3) = w. \qquad (5)$$

This model has one absorbing state, corresponding to configuration $\mathbf{0} = (0, 0, 0, \dots)$, For $w = 1$ also the configuration $\mathbf{1} = (1, 1, 1, \dots)$ is an absorbing state. This is the version studied in Ref. [30].

Notice that for $p = 1$, $q = 1$, $w = 0$ we have DCA rule 126 while for $p = 1$, $q = 0$, $w = 1$ we have DCA rule 150. In the following we shall use $w = 1$.

The implementation of a stochastic model makes use of one of more random numbers. For instance, the BBR model can be implemented using the function

$$x_i' = f(x_{i-1}, x_i, x_{i+1}; r_i) = [r_i < p](x_{i-1} \oplus x_i \oplus x_{i+1} \oplus x_{i-1}x_ix_{i+1})$$
$$\oplus [r_i < q](x_{i-1}x_i \oplus x_{i-1}x_{i+1} \oplus x_ix_{i+1} \oplus x_{i-1}x_ix_{i+1}) \quad (6)$$
$$\oplus x_{i-1}x_ix_{i+1},$$

where $[\cdot]$ is the truth function which takes value one if $\cdot$ is true and zero otherwise, and $\oplus$ is the sum modulo two. The $r_i = r_i(t)$ random numbers have to be extracted for each site and for each time. One can think of extracting them once and for all at the beginning of the simulation, i.e., running the simulation on a space-time lattice on which a random field $r_i(t)$, $i = 1, \dots, N$; $t = 0, \dots$ is defined. Notice that in this way one has a deterministic CA over a quenched random field.

The phase diagram of the BBR model is reported in Fig. 2-left. One can see three regions. The one marked in white, for $p < 0.65$, is where the only asymptotically stable configuration is the absorbing state formed by all zeros, i.e., the asymptotic probability distribution of configurations $P(x)$ is a delta on zero. The symmetric region marked in black, for $q > 0.35$ is where the only stable configuration is formed by all ones. Actually, in a region near the diagonal $q = 1 - p$, for $p < 0.5$ the two absorbing states are both stable, the transition line is fixed by the initial configuration, which in the figure is drawn at random with the same probability of extracting a zero and a one. These regions are denoted with the term "quiescent". The region marked in shades of grey, for $p > 0.65$ and $q < 0.35$ is a region where the two absorbing states are unstable, and the asymptotic probability distribution is distributed over many configurations, with average number of ones proportional to the shades of grey. In the insect it is reported the asymptotic average number of ones (the "density") computed along the dashed lines. This region is denoted with the term "active".

4.1 Damage Spreading

One possibility for controlling the evolution of a system with little efforts is offered by the sensitive dependence on initial conditions, i.e., when a small variation in the initial state propagates to the whole system. Indeed, this is also the main ingredient of chaos, which in general prevents a careful control. But in discrete systems the situation is somehow different. These systems are not affected by infinitesimal perturbations in the variables (assuming that they can be extended in the continuous sense), only to finite ones. The study of the propagation of a finite perturbation in CA goes under the name of "damage spreading", indicating how an initial disturbance (a "defect" or "damage") can spread in the system. A CA where a damage typically spreads is said to be chaotic.

Mathematically, one has two copies of the same system, say x and y, evolving with the same rule but starting from different initial conditions. We shall indicate with $z_i = x_i \oplus y_i$ the local difference at site i. Typical patterns of the spreading of a damage (i.e., the evolution of z) are reported in Fig. 3.

For PCA, the concept of damage spreading is meant "given the random field". The phase diagram of the damage z for the BBR model is shown in Fig. 2-right.

5 Reachability Problem

We shall mainly deal here with the problem of regional control via boundary actions, i.e., boundary reachability as illustrated in Fig. 1-right, however the techniques of analysis can be extended to other cases.

Let us now consider the problem of computing the probability $M_{xy}(a, b) = M(x|y; a, b)$ which is the probability of getting configuration x at time $t+1$ given the configuration y at time t, and boundaries a and b (for simplicity we refer here only to one-dimensional cases). The Markov matrix $M(a, b)$ is given by

$$M_{xy}(a, b) = \tau(x_1|a, y_1, y_2)\tau(x_2|y_1, y_2, y_3) \ldots \tau(x_n|y_{n-1}, y_n, b),$$

where n indicates the size of the target region.

For a given control sequence $a = a_1, \ldots, a_T$ and $b = b_1, \ldots, b_T$, the resulting Markov matrix for time T is

$$M(a, b) = \prod_{t=1}^{T} M(a_t, b_t).$$

We can define several control problems. A first one is about ergodicity: which is the best control sequence a and b so that $M_{xy}(a, b) > 0$ for all pairs x, y and minimum time T? Another is: given a certain time T and a pair x, y, which is the best control sequence a and b that maximises $M_{xy}(a, b) > 0$?

Clearly, one can also be interested in avoiding certain configurations, for instance, if $x_i = 1$ represents the presence of some animal or plant in position i at time t, one could be interested in devising a control that prevents the extinction of animals, i.e., avoid the state $x = 0$.

As we shall show in the following, so far we have not found algorithms for finding the best control but exhaustive search.

Beyond finding the actual sequence that maximises the observable, one could be rather interested in determining the *existence* of such a sequence, for a certain time interval T, or to find the minimum time T for which an optimal sequence exists.

In particular this latter problem can be faced with less computer efforts than finding the actual sequence for the best control. If one considers the matrix

$$C = \frac{1}{4} \sum_{a,b} M(a, b) = \frac{1}{4}(M(0, 0) + M(0, 1) + M(1, 0) + M(1, 1)),$$

and then computes its power C^T, all possible control sequences of length T are contained in such a power. Therefore, the problem of the existence of a control sequence for a given time T reduces to checking if $(C^T)_{xy} > 0$. One can also quantify the effective of the control by computing the ratio η between the minimum and maximum values of C. If this ratio is zero, it means that there are certain pairs of configurations that cannot be connected by any control sequence, while $\eta = 1$ means that all pairs of configurations can be connected with equal easiness.

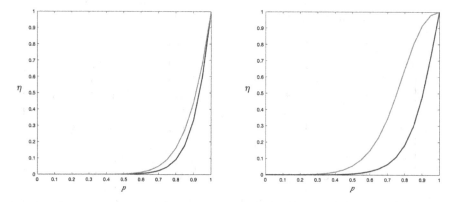

Fig. 4. The ratio $\eta = \min(C)/\max(C)$ for the BBR model with $n = 5$ for $T = 3$ (lower, blue curve) and $T = 5$ (upper, red curve). Left: $q = 0$, Right: $q = 1 - p$ (color figure online)

Let us illustrate some of these concepts for the BBR model, for $p = q$ and for $q = 0$. In Fig. 4 we show the easiness parameter η in function of p for $q = 0$ and $q = 1 - p$, for $n = 5$ and different values of T. One can see that in the "quiescent" phase $p < 0.5$ the control is almost impossible, and that on the line $q = 1 - p$, for $p > 0.5$, the easiness of the control rises with T faster that on the line $q = 0$. Indeed, referring to Fig. 2, one can see that this portion of the diagram corresponds to the "active" phase, where the BBR model is ergodic. One can also notice that the easiness of the control is not related to the damage spreading phase: considering for instance the line $q = p$, from Fig. 2-right one sees that the damage spreading phase starts for $p > 0.75$, while from Fig. 4-right one sees that the control is possible well before this threshold. The control properties are probably associated to the "chaoticity" of the associated deterministic CA over the random quenched field, a problem which will be faced in the future (for "chaotic" CA and the associated Boolean derivatives, see Refs. [31–33]).

Let us now turn to the problem of finding the best control. For compactness, let us consider the case $n = 3$, for which the minimum control time is $T = 2$. The highest probability for each pair of configurations $\boldsymbol{x}$ (row index in base two) and $\boldsymbol{y}$ (column index in base two) for $q = 1 - p$ and $p = 0.7$ is

$$
M = \begin{array}{c@{}c}
 & \begin{array}{cccccccc} 0 & \quad 1 & \quad 2 & \quad 3 & \quad 4 & \quad 5 & \quad 6 & \quad 7 \end{array} \\
\begin{array}{c} 0 \\ 1 \\ 2 \\ 3 \\ 4 \\ 5 \\ 6 \\ 7 \end{array} &
\left(\begin{array}{cccccccc}
1.000 & 0.262 & 0.213 & 0.396 & 0.262 & 0.396 & 0.396 & 0.240 \\
0.700 & 0.278 & 0.208 & 0.293 & 0.208 & 0.293 & 0.293 & 0.343 \\
0.343 & 0.221 & 0.221 & 0.253 & 0.221 & 0.195 & 0.253 & 0.490 \\
0.343 & 0.293 & 0.293 & 0.278 & 0.293 & 0.208 & 0.208 & 0.700 \\
0.700 & 0.208 & 0.208 & 0.293 & 0.278 & 0.293 & 0.293 & 0.343 \\
0.490 & 0.253 & 0.195 & 0.221 & 0.253 & 0.221 & 0.221 & 0.343 \\
0.343 & 0.293 & 0.293 & 0.208 & 0.293 & 0.208 & 0.278 & 0.700 \\
0.240 & 0.396 & 0.396 & 0.262 & 0.396 & 0.213 & 0.262 & 1.000
\end{array}\right)
\end{array} ,
$$

corresponding to controls a and b (again in base two)

$$a = \begin{array}{c} \\ 0 \\ 1 \\ 2 \\ 3 \\ 4 \\ 5 \\ 6 \\ 7 \end{array} \begin{array}{cccccccc} 0 & 1 & 2 & 3 & 4 & 5 & 6 & 7 \\ \left(\begin{array}{cccccccc} 0 & 1 & 1 & 0 & 0 & 1 & 1 & 1 \\ 2 & 2 & 2 & 2 & 3 & 3 & 3 & 3 \\ 0 & 0 & 0 & 3 & 1 & 1 & 1 & 1 \\ 1 & 2 & 2 & 1 & 3 & 0 & 0 & 3 \\ 0 & 3 & 3 & 0 & 2 & 1 & 1 & 2 \\ 2 & 2 & 1 & 2 & 0 & 3 & 3 & 0 \\ 0 & 0 & 0 & 0 & 1 & 1 & 1 & 1 \\ 1 & 2 & 2 & 3 & 3 & 2 & 2 & 3 \end{array}\right) \end{array} \qquad b = \begin{array}{c} \\ 0 \\ 1 \\ 2 \\ 3 \\ 4 \\ 5 \\ 6 \\ 7 \end{array} \begin{array}{cccccccc} 0 & 1 & 2 & 3 & 4 & 5 & 6 & 7 \\ \left(\begin{array}{cccccccc} 0 & 0 & 1 & 1 & 1 & 1 & 0 & 2 \\ 0 & 2 & 3 & 1 & 3 & 1 & 0 & 2 \\ 3 & 1 & 0 & 1 & 0 & 2 & 3 & 1 \\ 0 & 1 & 0 & 1 & 0 & 1 & 0 & 1 \\ 2 & 3 & 2 & 3 & 2 & 3 & 2 & 3 \\ 2 & 0 & 2 & 3 & 2 & 3 & 2 & 3 \\ 1 & 3 & 2 & 0 & 2 & 0 & 1 & 3 \\ 2 & 3 & 2 & 2 & 2 & 2 & 3 & 3 \end{array}\right) \end{array}.$$

These results should be read in this way. Let us consider for instance the initial configuration $y = 3 = 110|_2$ (numbers are coded in reverse order) and final configuration $x = 4 = 001|_2$. The best control is given by a sequence $a = 0 = 00|_2$ and $b = 3 = 11|_2$, which is reasonable since one is trying to force zeros on the left side of the configurations and ones on the right side.

Notice however that the entries for a and b are not always either 0 or 3, meaning that the best control is not a uniform one for all pairs. For instance, for going from $y = 3 = 110|_2$ to $x = 1 = 100|_2$ one has to apply $a = 2 = 01|_2$ and $b = 1 = 10|_2$, exploiting the fact that $q = \tau(1|3) = 1 - p = 0.3$ and therefore for forcing a zero in the presence of a neighbourhood already containing a one, it is better to insert another one than a zero.

6   Conclusions and Future Perspectives

We have introduced the problem of controlling probabilistic cellular automata by an action performed on the boundary of a target region (boundary control or boundary reachability problem). We have formulated the problem and presented the first results.

The field of control of cellular automata and discrete systems is extremely recent and only a handful of results are known [26,27]. In particular, the control of probabilistic cellular automata is still to be explored in depth, and more efficient algorithms for finding the best control sequence are needed if one wants to exert control on large regions, and in higher dimensions.

A promising possibility is that of exploring the relationship between the control and the "chaotic" properties of the associated deterministic CA over a quenched random field.

Acknowledgment. R.S. acknowledges partial financial support from PPA-DGAPA-UNAM.

References

1. See for instance the series of proceedings of the ACRI (Cellular Automata for Research and Industry) conferences Cellular Automata (Lectures Notes in Computer Science, Springer): ACRI2002, LNCS 2493, DOI: https://doi.org/10.1007/3-540-45830-1;ACRI2004, LNCS 3305, https://doi.org/10.1007/b102055; ACRI2006, LNCS 4173, https://doi.org/10.1007/11861201; ACRI2008, LNCS 5191, https://doi.org/10.1007/978-3-540-79992-4; ACRI2010, LNCS 6350, https://doi.org/10.1007/978-3-642-15979-4; ACRI2012, LNCS 7495, https://doi.org/10.1007/978-3-642-33350-7; ACRI2014, LNCS 8751, https://doi.org/10.1007/978-3-319-11520-7; ACRI2016, LNCS 9863, https://doi.org/10.1007/978-3-319-44365-2
2. Kauffman, S.A.: Metabolic stability and epigenesis in randomly constructed genetic nets. J. Theor. Biol. **22**, 437 (1969). https://doi.org/10.1016/0022-5193(69)90015-0
3. Damiani, C., Serra, R., Villani, M., Kauffman, S.A., Colacci, A.: Cell-cell interaction and diversity of emergent behaviours. IET Syst. Biol. **5**, 137 (2011). https://doi.org/10.1049/iet-syb.2010.0039
4. Deutsch, A., Dormann, S.: Cellular Automaton Modeling of Biological Pattern Formation: Characterization, Applications, and Analysis. Birkhäuser, Berlin (2005). https://doi.org/10.1007/b138451
5. Ermentrout, G., Edelstein-Keshet, L.: Cellular automata approaches to biological modeling. J. Theor. Biol. **160**, 97–133 (1993). https://doi.org/10.1006/jtbi.1993.1007
6. Boccara, N., Goles, E., Martínez, S., Picco, P. (eds.): Cellular Automata and Cooperative Systems. Nato Science Series C, vol. 396. Springer, Amsterdam (1983). https://doi.org/10.1007/978-94-011-1691-6
7. Chopard, B., Droz, M.: Cellular Automata Modeling of Physical Systems. Cambridge University Press, Cambridge (1998). https://doi.org/10.1007/978-1-4614-1800-9_27
8. Codd, E.F.: Cellular Automata. Academic Press, New York (1968). ISBN 0121788504
9. Burks, A.W.: Essays on Cellular Automata. University of Illinois Press, Champaign (1970)
10. Berlekamp, E.R., Conway, J.H., Guy, R.K.: Winning Ways for Your Mathematical Plays, vol. 2. Academic Press, New York (1982). EAN 9781568811420
11. Vichniac, G.: Simulating physics with cellular automata. Phys. D **10**, 96–115 (1984). https://doi.org/10.1016/0167-2789(84)90253-7
12. Wolfram, S.: Statistical mechanics of cellular automata. Rev. Mod. Phys. **55**, 601 (1983). https://doi.org/10.1103/RevModPhys.55.601
13. Wolfram, S.: Universality and complexity in cellular automata. Physica **10D**, 1 (1984). https://doi.org/10.1016/0167-2789(84)90245-8
14. Kari, J.: Theory of cellular automata: a survey. Theor. Comput. Sci. **334**, 3–33 (2005). https://doi.org/10.1016/j.tcs.2004.11.021
15. Domany, E., Kinzel, W.: Equivalence of cellular automata to Ising models and directed percolation. Phys. Rev. Lett. **53**, 311–314 (1984). https://doi.org/10.1103/PhysRevLett.53.311
16. Louis, P.-Y., Nardi, F. (eds.): Probabilistic Cellular Automata, Emergence, Complexity and Computation, vol. 27. Springer, Basel (2018). https://doi.org/10.1007/978-3-319-65558-1

17. Zerrik, E., Boutoulout, A., El Jai, A.: Actuators and regional boundary controllability for parabolic systems. Int. J. Syst. Sci. **31**, 73–82 (2000). https://doi.org/10.1080/002077200291479
18. Lions, J.: Controlabilité exacte des systèmes distribueés. CRAS, Série I(302), 471–475 (1986)
19. Lions, J.: Exact controllability for distributed systems. Some trends and some problems. In: Spigler, R. (ed.) Applied and Industrial Mathematics. MAIA, vol. 56, pp. 59–84. Springer, Dordrecht (1991). https://doi.org/10.1007/978-94-009-1908-2_7
20. Russell, D.: Controllability and stabilizability theory for linear partial differential equations. Recent progress and open questions. SIAM Rev. **20**, 639–739 (1978). https://doi.org/10.1137/1020095
21. El Yacoubi, S., El Jai, A., Ammor, N.: Regional controllability with cellular automata models. In: Bandini, S., Chopard, B., Tomassini, M. (eds.) ACRI 2002. LNCS, vol. 2493, pp. 357–367. Springer, Heidelberg (2002). https://doi.org/10.1007/3-540-45830-1_34
22. Fekih, A.B., El Jai, A.: Regional Analysis of a Class of Cellular Automata Models. In: El Yacoubi, S., Chopard, B., Bandini, S. (eds.) ACRI 2006. LNCS, vol. 4173, pp. 48–57. Springer, Heidelberg (2006). https://doi.org/10.1007/11861201_9
23. El Yacoubi, S.: Mathematical method for control problems on cellular automata models. Int. J. Syst. Sci. **39**(5), 529–538 (2008). https://doi.org/10.1080/00207720701847232
24. Bagnoli, F., El Yacoubi, S., Rechtman, R.: Synchronization and control of cellular automata. In: Bandini, S., Manzoni, S., Umeo, H., Vizzari, G. (eds.) ACRI 2010. LNCS, vol. 6350, pp. 188–197. Springer, Heidelberg (2010). https://doi.org/10.1007/978-3-642-15979-4_21
25. Bagnoli, F., Rechtman, R., El Yacoubi, S.: Control of cellular automata. Phys. Rev. E **86**, 066201 (2012). https://doi.org/10.1103/PhysRevE.86.066201
26. Bagnoli, F., El Yacoubi, S., Rechtman, R.: Toward a boundary regional control problem for Boolean cellular automata. Nat. Comput. (2017). https://doi.org/10.1007/s11047-017-9626-1
27. Bagnoli, F., El Yacoubi, S., Rechtman, R.: Control of cellular automata. In: Meyers, R.A. (ed.) Encyclopedia of Complexity and Systems Science. Springer, Heidelberg (2018). https://doi.org/10.1007/978-3-642-27737-5_710-1
28. Bagnoli, F., Rechtman, R.: Regional synchronization of a probabilistic cellular automaton. In: Mauri, G., et al. (eds.) ACRI 2018, LNCS, vol. 11115. pp. 255–263. Springer, Heidelberg (2018)
29. Bagnoli, F.: Cellular automata in dynamical modelling in biotechnologies. In: Bagnoli, F., Lió, P., Ruffo, S. (eds.) p. 3. World Scientific, Singapore, (1998). https://doi.org/10.1142/9789812813053_0001
30. Bagnoli, F., Boccara, B., Rechtman, R.: Nature of phase transitions in a probabilistic cellular automaton with two absorbing states. Phys. Rev. E **63**, 046116 (2001). https://doi.org/10.1103/PhysRevE.63.046116
31. Vichniac, G.: Boolean derivatives on cellular automata. Physica **10D**, 96 (1984). https://doi.org/10.1016/0167-2789(90)90174-N
32. Bagnoli, F.: Boolean derivatives and computation of cellular automata. Int. J. Mod. Phys. C. **3**, 307 (1992). https://doi.org/10.1142/S0129183192000257
33. Bagnoli, F., Rechtman, R.: Synchronization and maximum Lyapunov exponents of cellular automata. Phys. Rev. E **59**, R1307 (1999). https://doi.org/10.1103/PhysRevE.59.R1307

Regional Synchronization of a Probabilistic Cellular Automaton

Franco Bagnoli[1,2(✉)] and Raúl Rechtman[3]

[1] Dipartimento di Fisica e Astronomia and CSDC, Università di Firenze,
Via G. Sansone 1, 50019 Sesto Fiorentino, Italy
franco.bagnoli@unifi.it
[2] INFN, sez. Firenze, Sesto Fiorentino, Italy
[3] Instituto de Energías Renovables, Universidad Nacional Autónoma de México,
Apdo. Postal 34, 62580 Temixco, Morelos, Mexico
rrs@ier.unam.mx

Abstract. We study the regional master-slave synchronization of a one dimensional probabilistic cellular automaton with two absorbing states. The master acts on the boundary of an interval, the region, of a fixed size. For some values of the parameters, this is enough to achieve synchronization in the region. For other values, we extend the regional synchronization to include a fraction of sites inside the region of interest. We present four different ways of doing this and show which is the most effective one, in terms of the fraction of sites inside the region and the time needed for synchronization.

1 Introduction

Cellular Automata (CA) are spatially extended systems that are widely used for modelling various problems ranging from physics to biology, engineering, medicine, ecology and economics [1–8].

Cellular automata are discrete systems in time and space. The state at each node, here 0 or 1, changes in time according to the transition probabilities of assuming a certain state knowing the state of neighbouring nodes. When the transition probabilities are either zero or one, the automata is deterministic, otherwise it is probabilistic. Despite their simplicity, cellular automata may exhibit a large number of different features.

In particular, deterministic cellular automata may exhibit "chaotic" trajectories, in which a initial small disturbance (a "defect") amplifies or spreads, in average, over time. This is also called the "damage spreading" feature.

Deterministic cellular automata may be considered discrete dynamical systems, and one is interested in the problem of controlling the resulting trajectories. The control problem can be divided in two sub-problems: how to drive a system into a desired state (reachability problem) and how to make it follow a desired trajectory, which can be also a fixed point (drivability problem). We are

G. Mauri et al. (Eds.): ACRI 2018, LNCS 11115, pp. 255–263, 2018.
https://doi.org/10.1007/978-3-319-99813-8_23

interested here in the regional version of this problem, i.e., how to control just a given region of a system. Clearly, one has at least to act on the boundaries of such a region in order to promote this control, but this can be insufficient, especially for chaotic CA.

As shown in Refs. [9,10], while it is possible to make a system reach a desired state acting on the boundaries, it is in general not possible to impose a trajectory which is not "natural", i.e., a trajectory different from one that the system would follow if starting from a proper initial configuration and with proper boundary conditions. Except for simple states like fixed points or cycles, the identification of a "natural" trajectory is best done using a replica of the system, that evolves freely. The drivability problem is related to master-slave synchronization. The problem of regional control, that is, where the control is applied in on the boundary of a region with a fixed number of sites is discussed in Ref. [11].

One of the problems in studying discrete cellular automata is that it is not possible to continuously vary their dynamical properties, so that it is difficult to observe bifurcations and changes of behaviour. On the contrary, this is possible with probabilistic cellular automata which however are intrinsically stochastic, and therefore in principle impossible to synchronize. A review of phase transitions for probabilistic cellular automata may be found in Ref. [12].

However, it is possible to "convert" probabilistic cellular automata into deterministic ones, considering that the actual computation of a trajectory of such systems makes use of random numbers, used to choose, for each site and each time step, among the possible alternatives. One may assume that the set of all needed random numbers is extracted at the beginning of the simulation for all sites and all time steps, thus constituting a quenched random field. The evolution of the automata over such a random field becomes deterministic, and therefore it is possible to consider the problem of the divergence of initially similar trajectories (damage spreading) also for Probabilistic Cellular Automata (PCA). The advantage of such an approach is that the behaviour of PCA can be fine-tuned by means of their control parameters, and therefore it is possible to investigate in details the elements that contribute to chaoticity, control and synchronization, a task that is much more difficult with Deterministic Cellular Automata (DCA).

In principle the synchronization characteristics depend on the quenched random field, but in practice these systems are always self-averaging so that a large enough simulation already gives the same value of observables as if one performs an averaging over many realizations of the random field.

In Ref. [13], the problem of synchronization of DCA was addressed, showing that it is possible achieve this goals by randomly choose at each time step a large enough fraction of sites in which the state of sites in the slave system is imposed to be that of the corresponding sites in the master one and it was shown that the synchronization threshold is related to the chaotic properties of automata. In Ref. [9], a similar technique, called pinching synchronization, was applied to control problems, looking for the most efficient way of achieving the synchronization goal. In Ref. [10] this procedure was applied to the regional control problem of DCA. We want here to apply, and extend, this technique to PCA (see also Ref. [14]).

In what follows, we investigate different strategies of regional master-slave pinching synchronization of a one-dimensional three-state probabilistic cellular automaton with two absorbing states [15]. The state at any site in the lattice at time $t + 1$ depends probabilistically on the states of the site itself and its two next-nearest neighbours at time t, and two probabilities. The master and the slave are two realizations of the same PCA starting from different initial states and the slave is forced to follow the master at the boundary of a given region of width L. Since this is in general insufficient to synchronize the two systems, the slave is additionally forced to take the state of the master at certain sites inside the target region, at every time step.

In Sect. 2 we present this cellular automaton. In our first attempt, boundary regional synchronization, or simply L-synchronization, the master imposes his state on the border of a region of size L on the slave and we find that for some values of the probabilities, there is synchronization in the sense that the slave follows the master in the region of length L. This is discussed in Sect. 3. When there is no L-synchronization, we discuss in Sect. 4 four different pinching synchronization schemes at a fraction π of sites inside the region of size L and show which one is the most successful one in the sense that synchronization occurs with the smallest value of π and the shortest time. We finish with some conclusions in Sect. 5.

2   The Probabilistic Cellular Automaton

We recall the definition of the probabilistic cellular automaton with two absorbing states presented in Ref. [15]. The state at site i at time t, $x_i^{(t)}$, with $i = 0, \ldots, N - 1$ and $t = 0, 1, \ldots$, can take two values, $x_i^{(t)} = 0$, dry, or $x_i^{(t)} = 1$, wet. The state of the cellular automaton at time t is $\boldsymbol{x}^{(t)} = (x_0^{(t)}, \ldots, x_{N-1}^{(t)})$ and $x_i^{(t+1)}$ depends on the number of wet sites in its neighbourhood and four parameters or probabilities $p_0, \ldots, p_3$. With

$$\sigma_i^{(t)}(\boldsymbol{x}) = \sum_{j=-1}^{1} x_{i+j}^{(t)},$$

$\sigma_i^{(t)}(\boldsymbol{x}) = 0, \ldots, 3$, and the sum on the sub-indices taken modulo N to account for periodic boundary conditions,

$$x_i^{(t+1)} = \sum_{s=0}^{3} \left[r_i^{(t)} \leq p_s \right] \left[\sigma_i^{(t)}(\boldsymbol{x}) = s \right]. \tag{1}$$

In this expression $r_i^{(t)}$ is a random number uniformly distributed between 0 and 1 and $[\cdot] = 1$ if $\cdot$ is true and zero otherwise. In what follows $p_0 = 0$, and $p_3 = 1$, which means that if the neighbours are all dry (wet), the central site will be dry (wet) at the next time step. Then, the states $x = 0 = (0, \dots, 0)$ and $x = 1 = (1, \dots, 1)$ are absorbing. The activity $a(t)$ is defined by

$$a(t) = a(x^{(t)}) = \frac{1}{N} \sum_{i=0}^{N-1} x_i^{(t)}. \tag{2}$$

We indicate with a the asymptotic value of $a(t)$.

In Fig. 1(a) we show the phase diagram of the average activity $\bar{a}$ over M samples with random initial conditions with $a(0) \simeq 1/2$. In the bottom left part (in white), any random initial configuration will end in the absorbing state $x = 0$, and in the upper right part, (in black), any random initial configuration will end in the absorbing state $x = 1$. In the lower right part there is a region where $0 < \bar{a} < 1$.

We can also define the damage spreading problem for such a model. Two replicas, x and y, starting from different random initial conditions, evolve in time with the same random numbers $r_i^{(t)}$,

$$x_i^{(t+1)} = \sum_{s=0}^{3} \left[r_i^{(t)} \leq p_s \right] \left[\sigma_i^{(t)}(x) = s \right],$$

$$y_i^{(t+1)} = \sum_{s=0}^{3} \left[r_i^{(t)} \leq p_s \right] \left[\sigma_i^{(t)}(y) = s \right]. \tag{3}$$

The Hamming distance between the two replicas, in a region of width L, is defined as

$$h_L = \frac{1}{L} \sum_{i=1}^{L} x_i \oplus y_i \tag{4}$$

where $\oplus$ is the logical exclusive disjunction (sum modulo two).

In Fig. 1(b) we show the phase diagram of the average normalized regional Hamming distance $\overline{h_L}$, that takes values different from zero at the phase boundaries of the activity a, since in these cases it is possible that a replica goes into a state and the other into another state, and in the "chaotic" region for high values of p_1 and low values of p_2.

3   L-synchronization

Let us now consider the problem where the two replicas, x and y, evolve in time starting from different initial conditions chosen at random with the same random numbers $r_i^{(t)}$ but where at the fixed sites $i = 0$ and $i = L+1$, a distance L apart, $y_0^{(t)}$ and $y_{L+1}^{(t)}$ take the values of $x_0^{(t)}$ and $x_{L+1}^{(t)}$, respectively, before updating as in Eq. (1). In other words, the master, x imposes his state at two fixed sites on the slave y or x and y are pinched together at $i = 0$ and $i = L + 1$. The normalized regional damage h_L is still defined as in Eq. (4).

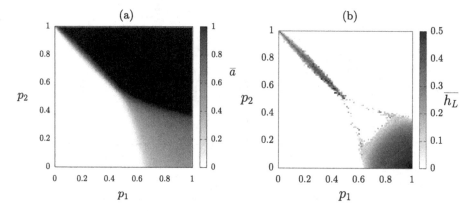

Fig. 1. (a) Phase diagram of the average activity $\bar{a}$ with $N = 1,000$ sites, after $T = 500$ time steps, and $M = 100$ samples with different random initial conditions $\boldsymbol{x}^{(0)}$ with $a(\boldsymbol{x}^{(0)}) \simeq 1/2$. (b) Phase diagram of the average normalized regional Hamming distance $\bar{h}_L$ as a function of p_1 and p_2 for the same values of N, T, and M as in (a) and $L = 100$ sites. (Color online)

If $h_L = 0$ at some time t we say there is L-synchronization. In Fig. 1(b) we show the phase diagram of the average $\bar{h}_L$ over M samples as functions of p_1 and p_2. The area where $h_L > 0$ with $L = N$ is known as the chaotic phase [16] but we prefer to call it the L-damage spreading phase for any value of L.

In Fig. 2(a) we show $\bar{h}_L$, as a function of p_1 on the diagonal $p_2 = 1 - p_1$. There are three different behaviors of $\bar{h}_L$, separated by $\xi_1 \simeq 0.5$ and $\xi_2 \simeq 0.75$. For $0 < p_1 \leq \xi_1$, $\bar{h}_L$ grows with L, with fixed T. For $\xi_1 < p_1 \leq \xi_2$, $\bar{h}_L = 0$ and for $\xi_2 < p_1 \leq 1$, $\bar{h}_L$ seems to become independent of L for large L. However, in the first interval of p_1, $\bar{h}_L$ goes to zero as T grows.

In Fig. 2(c) we show the average time for synchronization T_s as a function of p_1, $p_2 = 1 - p_1$, with $0 < p_1 < \xi_1$ for different values of L. This average time grows with L as expected.

In the third interval $\xi_2 < p_1 \leq 1$ the quantity $\bar{h}_L$ is practically independent of T. Clearly, since the automata is probabilistic and ergodic, and the synchronized state is absorbing, the asymptotic state is always the synchronized one, but the time required for achieving this result is so large, for large enough L, that it is practically unachievable. Indeed, the synchronization task is essentially the same of a percolation problem for defects [17].

In summary L-synchronization is successful for $0 < p_1 < \xi_1$ although it may take a long time T_s that grows with L. For $\xi_1 < p_1 \leq \xi_2$, L-synchronization is present and for $\xi_2 < p_1 < 1$ there is no L-synchronization. In the next section, we present four strategies that achieve regional synchronization when $\xi_2 < p_1 \leq 1$ by adding a fraction π of sites where $\boldsymbol{y}$ follows $\boldsymbol{x}$.

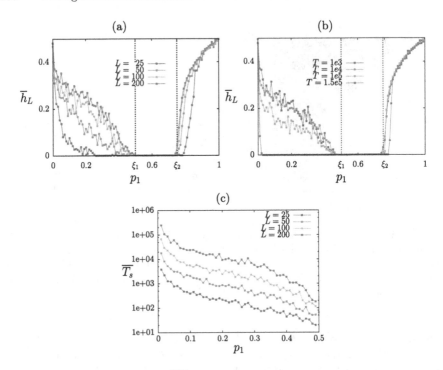

Fig. 2. (a) The average damage $\overline{h_L}$ for $L = 25, 50, 100, 200$ as a function of p_1 on the diagonal $p_2 = 1 - p_1$. We estimate that $\xi_1 \simeq 0.5$ and $\xi_2 \simeq 0.75$. The number of sites is $N = 1,000$ and the average is taken over $M = 100$ samples after a time $T = 1,000$. (b) The average damage $\overline{h_L}$ for $L = 100$ and different total times, $T = 1e3, 1e4, 1e5, 1.5e5$ as a function of p_1 with $p_2 = 1 - p_1$, $N = 1,000$ and $M = 100$. (c) The average synchronization time $\overline{T_s}$ for $L = 25, 50, 100, 200$ as a function of p_1, $0 \le p_1 \le \xi_1$, with $N = 1,000$ and $M = 100$. (Color online)

4 $L\pi$-synchronization

By $L\pi$-synchronization we mean that in the region of size L, besides the sites a distance L apart, a fraction π of sites, denoted by j, are chosen and at every time step the slave takes the values of the master, that is $y_j^{(t)} = x_j^{(t)}$.

In other words, $\boldsymbol{x}$ and $\boldsymbol{y}$ are pinched together at those sites. We propose four strategies of $L\pi$-synchronization, L-divide pinching synchronization, L-quenched pinching synchronization, L-annealed pinching synchronization and L-random walk pinching synchronization. In what follows we refer to them as LDP, LQP, LAP and LRWP synchronization respectively.

In the four strategies, a fraction πL, $0 < \pi \le 1/2$, of sites in the region of length L are chosen. In the first strategy, LDP, the sites j divide the region of length L into equally spaced intervals. In the second one LQP, the sites j are chosen at random in the region L while in the third one, LAP, the sites j are chosen at random at every time step. In the fourth strategy, LRWP, the fraction

πL of sites are the starting point of random walkers that at every time step can move one site to the right or left with the same probability.

Walkers do not know the others' position, cannot coordinate with them, and may cross each other. When they reach the border of the region at $i = 0$ or $i = L+1$, they bounce back. In Fig. 3 we show examples of the four strategies.

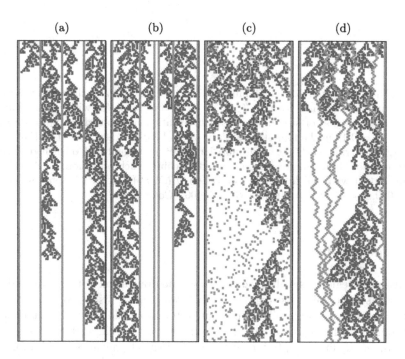

Fig. 3. Space-time diagrams of the four bulk synchronization schemes. (a) L-divide pinching synchronization. (b) L-quenched pinching synchronization. (c) L-annealed pinching quenched synchronization. (d) L-random walk pinching synchronization. In all cases, $L = 60$, $p_1 = 0.8$, $p_2 = 0.2$, $\pi = 0.1$ and the region of size $L = 60$ is shown during $T = 200$ time steps. (Color online)

In Fig. 4(a) and (b) we show $\overline{h_L}$ and $\overline{T_s}$ as functions of π with $p_1 = 0.85$ and $p_2 = 0.15$ respectively. The best strategy, in the sense of achieving synchronization for the smallest value of π in the shortest time, is LDP synchronization. This is valid for other values of p_1. To simplify our results, if $T_s > T$, that occurs for small p_1, we write $T_s = T$.

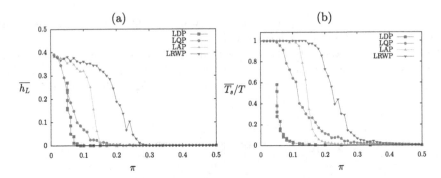

Fig. 4. The average normalized Hamming distance $\overline{h_L}$ in (a), and the average normalized synchronization time fraction $\overline{T_s}/T$ in (b) as functions of π with πL the fraction of sites in the region of size L where synchronization is imposed for $p_1 = 0.85$ and $p_2 = 1 - p_1 = 0.15$ in the four strategies. In (a) and (b) the data correspond, from left to right, to L divide pinching synchronization, LDP (in magenta), L quenched pinching synchronization, LQP (in green), L annealed pinching synchronization, LAP (in blue), and L random walk pinching synchronization, $LRWP$ (in red). The parameters are $N = 1,000$, $L = 100$, $M = 100$ and $T = 10,000$. (Color online).

5   Conclusions

We presented regional synchronization, the synchronization of two extended systems to a sub-domain, the region. As an example, we discussed some properties the three state probabilistic cellular automaton and showed that regional synchronization has three different behaviours on the diagonal $p_2 = 1 - p_1$ of Fig. 1(b). In the first one, $0 < p_1 < \xi_1 \simeq 0.5$, L-synchronization occurs for long times. In the second one, $\xi_1 < p_1 < \xi_2 \simeq 0.75$, L-synchronization is always present, and in the third one, $\xi_2 < p_1 < 1$, L-synchronization is not possible. If we insist on trying to synchronize y with x in this third case, we have to split the region in subregions and we presented four different strategies and show which one is the most effective. It might prove interesting to extend the analysis of $L\pi$-synchronization to the whole phase diagram of Fig. 1 and to other cellular automata.

Acknowledgments. We thank S. El Yacoubi for useful comments. R.S. acknowledges partial financial support from PPA-DGAPA-UNAM.

References

1. Bandini, S., Chopard, B., Tomassini, M. (eds.): ACRI 2002. LNCS, vol. 2493. Springer, Heidelberg (2002). https://doi.org/10.1007/3-540-45830-1
2. Sloot, P.M.A., Chopard, B., Hoekstra, A.G. (eds.): ACRI 2004. LNCS, vol. 3305. Springer, Heidelberg (2004). https://doi.org/10.1007/b102055

3. El Yacoubi, S., Chopard, B., Bandini, S. (eds.): ACRI 2006. LNCS, vol. 4173. Springer, Heidelberg (2006). https://doi.org/10.1007/11861201
4. Umeo, H., Morishita, S., Nishinari, K., Komatsuzaki, T., Bandini, S. (eds.): ACRI 2008. LNCS, vol. 5191. Springer, Heidelberg (2008). https://doi.org/10.1007/978-3-540-79992-4
5. Bandini, S., Manzoni, S., Umeo, H., Vizzari, G. (eds.): ACRI 2010. LNCS, vol. 6350. Springer, Heidelberg (2010). https://doi.org/10.1007/978-3-642-15979-4
6. Sirakoulis, G.C., Bandini, S. (eds.): ACRI 2012. LNCS, vol. 7495. Springer, Heidelberg (2012). https://doi.org/10.1007/978-3-642-33350-7
7. Wąs, J., Sirakoulis, G.C., Bandini, S. (eds.): ACRI 2014. LNCS, vol. 8751. Springer, Cham (2014). https://doi.org/10.1007/978-3-319-11520-7
8. El Yacoubi, S., Wąs, J., Bandini, S. (eds.): ACRI 2016. LNCS, vol. 9863. Springer, Cham (2016). https://doi.org/10.1007/978-3-319-44365-2
9. Bagnoli, F., Rechtman, R., El Yacoubi, S.: Control of cellular automata. Phys. Rev. E **86**, 066201 (2012). https://doi.org/10.1103/PhysRevE.86.066201
10. Bagnoli, F., El Yacoubi, S., Rechtman, R.: Toward a boundary regional control problem for Boolean cellular automata. Nat. Comput. (2017). https://doi.org/10.1007/s11047-017-9626-1
11. Bagnoli, F., Dridi, S., El Yacoubi, S., Rechtman, R.: Regional control of probabilistic cellular automata. In: Mauri, G., et al. (eds.) ACRI 2018. LNCS, vol. 11115, pp. 243–254. Springer, Heidelberg (2018)
12. Bagnoli, F., Rechtman, R.: Phase transitions of cellular automata. In: Louis, P.-Y., Nardi, F.R. (eds.) Probabilistic Cellular Automata. ECC, vol. 27, pp. 215–236. Springer, Cham (2018). https://doi.org/10.1007/978-3-319-65558-1_15
13. Bagnoli, F., Rechtman, R.: Synchronization and maximum Lyapunov exponent in cellular automata. Phys. Rev. E **59**, R1307 (1999). https://doi.org/10.1103/PhysRevE.59.R1307
14. Bagnoli, F., El Yacoubi, S., Rechtman, R.: Control of cellular automata. In: Robert, A.M. (ed.) Encyclopedia of Complexity and Systems Science. Springer, Heidelberg (2018). https://doi.org/10.1007/978-3-642-27737-5_710-1
15. Bagnoli, F., Boccara, N., Rechtman, R.: Nature of phase transitions in a probabilistic cellular automaton with two absorbing states. Phys. Rev. E **63**, 046116 (2001). https://doi.org/10.1103/PhysRevE.63.046116
16. Martins, M.L., Verona de Resende, H.F., Tsallis, C., Magalhães, A.C.N.: Evidence for a new phase in the Domany-Kinzel cellular automaton. Phys. Rev. Lett. **66**, 20145 (1991). https://doi.org/10.1103/PhysRevLett.66.2045
17. Grassberger, P.: Are damage spreading transitions generically in the universality class of directed percolation? J. Stat. Phys. **79**, 13 (1995). https://doi.org/10.1007/BF02179381

Firsts Steps in Cellular Fields Optimization: A FSSP Case Study

Tien Thao Nguyen[✉] and Luidnel Maignan[✉]

LACL, Université Paris-Est Créteil, Créteil, France
tien-thao.nguyen@lacl.fr, luidnel.maignan@u-pec.fr

Abstract. A large number of cellular automata have been given as a transition table constructed by hand. The methodology of "cellular fields" propose to give them by their modular design principles instead, and to generate the transition table in last step, as it is the case for high-level programming language source code and their binary executable file. In this paper, we check whether this generated tables can be optimized to be as small a their counterpart constructed by hand. This is done in the particular case of a cellular automaton solving the Firing Squad Synchronization Problem using cellular fields. We study the internal structure of this solution and study their reductions in the same vein as deterministic finite automata minimization. We also compare this solution with the 8-states solution of Noguchi and devise another notion of optimization.

Keywords: Cellular automata · Automata minimization
Program optimization · Firing Squad Synchronization Problem

1 Introduction

Since von Neumann's studies on auto-replication and synchronization of *Cellular Automata* (CA for short), a number of algorithmic problems have been considered. Their solutions have been developed by explicitly building the automata transition table "by hand". More recently, the works of Maignan and Yunès [2] put forward a high-level approach allowing to have a formal description closer to the design principle of a cellular automaton and to generate only in last step its transition table. It is achieved by the use of a concept of modularity and abstraction called "cellular field". However, the transition tables thus generated are currently not comparable in terms of size with those produced "by hand". This situation is like a recall of the period of the first compilers and the competition between assembly assembler "by hand" and that by compilation from a high-level program. In analogy with this story, the goal is to enrich the set of methods for generating transition tables and also to set up optimization processes to reduce the number of states.

To build these tools, the study of a particular case is useful as a first step in order to identify some strategies that can then be generalized in a second step. In this paper, we study the transition table generated by following the field-based

G. Mauri et al. (Eds.): ACRI 2018, LNCS 11115, pp. 264–273, 2018.
https://doi.org/10.1007/978-3-319-99813-8_24

approach described in [2] to solve the *Firing Squad Synchronization Problem* (FSSP for short). We study its internal structure to identify some possible optimizations and also compare it with a similar, but more efficient, pre-existing solution produced by hand by Noguchi [3] to identify more possibilities.

The paper is organized as follows. In Sect. 2, we compare our goal with classical deterministic finite automata minimization, then introduce the class of cellular automata at study and the FSSP. In Sect. 3, we present the CA at study and its generated transition table and study exhaustively all of its reductions, for a notion of reduction similar to that of deterministic finite automata minimization. In Sect. 4, we present the 8-states Noguchi's solution and compare it with the generated CA. This leads to a generalization of the definition of reduction formalizing the relation between the two CA. We then discuss, in Sect. 5 the results together with the other on-going works and future works as a conclusion. To allow reproducability of the results, we fully provided the transition tables.

2 Theoretical Grounds and Backgrounds

2.1 Relation with Deterministic Finite Automata Minimization

When talking about automata optimization, one immediately thinks about the minimization of *Deterministic Finite Automata* (DFA for short) and there are a number of well-known algorithms like the Moore algorithm, the Brzozowski algorithm and the Hopcroft algorithm. A DFA receives an input word $u_1 u_2 \ldots u_n$ build from its input alphabet, and transitions through a sequence $q_0 q_1 q_2 \ldots q_n$ of states according to a transition function. Each state produces a bit of information called "accepting" or "rejecting". The collection gathering for each possible input word its last outputted bit of information is taken as a complete specification of the input-output behavior of the DFA and is usually formalized by the notion of recognized language. To minimize a DFA means to merge together its states in a coherent way so that the input-output behavior stays unchanged. It is known that starting with any DFA recognizing a language, such a merging of states produces the best possible DFA that recognizes this language.

For CA, things are more intricate and such a strong minimization is impossible but we can start by approaching the problem in a similar way (although a departure from this approach in initiated in Sect. 4). Using the modular notion of cellular fields, it is possible to describe a CA-equivalent to the notion of input word (input field), output bit of information (output field) and cellular field respecting a specified input-output behavior as initiated in [2], but this is out of the scope of this short paper. We narrow the discussion to the particular case of the FSSP.

2.2 Cellular Automata Minimization and the FSSP Particular Case

CA and FSSP Informally. A cellular automaton is a set of rules describing the local, synchronous and homogenous evolution of any array of cells having a finite number of state. The Firing Squad Synchronization Problem was proposed by John Myhill in 1957. The goal is to find a single cellular automaton that synchronizes any one-dimensional horizontal array of an arbitrary number of cells. More precisely, one consider that at initial time, all cells are inactive (i.e. in the *quiescent state*) except for the leftmost cell which is in the general (i.e. in the *general state*). One wants the evolution of the cellular automaton to lead all cells to transition to a special state (i.e. the *synchronization* or *firing state*) *for the first time at the same time*. This time t_s is called the synchronization time and it is known that the minimal possible value for it is $2n - 2$ where n is the number of cells.

Here, its input-output behavior is mainly specified by the fact the quiescent state should act as an inactive state and, considering the firing state as the only accepting state, by the fact that no accepting state should appears before the transition $2n - 2$ and all states should be accepting at transition $t_s = 2n - 2$ for any length n.

CA Formally. We consider a definition of cellular automata that fits the purpose of this article. A *cellular automaton* α is specified by a finite set of states Σ_α, a set of *initial configurations* $I_\alpha \subseteq \bigcup_{n \in \mathbb{N}^+} \Sigma_\alpha{}^n$ and a partial function $T_\alpha : \Sigma_\alpha^\star \times \Sigma_\alpha \times \Sigma_\alpha^\star \rightharpoonup \Sigma_\alpha$ called the *local transition function* or *local transition table*. Here, we denote $\Sigma_\alpha^\star = \Sigma_\alpha \cup \{\star\}$ where $\star$ is a new element representing the absence of cell. The elements of $\Sigma_\alpha^\star \times \Sigma_\alpha \times \Sigma_\alpha^\star$ are called *local configurations* and are noted in the form $[a, b, c]$. A *local transition*, or *rule*, is denoted by $[a, b, c] \mapsto d$ with $a, c \in \Sigma^\star$ and $b, d \in \Sigma$. This partial function is required to respect a certain closure condition, namely that all space-time diagrams are totally defined. A cellular automaton associates any initial configuration $c \in I_\alpha$ of size n with a *space-time diagram* $D_\alpha(c) : \mathbb{N} \times [\![0, n+1]\!] \to \Sigma_\alpha^\star$ such that:

$$D_\alpha(c)(t, p) = \begin{cases} \star & \text{if } p = 0 \text{ or } p = n+1; \\ c_p & \text{if } t = 0 \text{ and } p \in [\![1, n]\!]; \\ T_\alpha(s(p-1), s(p), s(p+1)) & \text{if } t > 0 \text{ and } p \in [\![1, n]\!]; \\ & \text{with } s(p') = D_\alpha(c)(t-1, p'). \end{cases}$$

When we have $D_\alpha(c)(t, p) = s$, we say that, with the cellular automaton α and initial configuration c, the cell at position p has state s at time t.

FSSP Formally. A cellular automaton is a *minimal-time FSSP solution* if there are three special states $g_\alpha, q_\alpha, f_\alpha \in \Sigma_\alpha$ and if for any size n, $D_\alpha(\overline{n})(t, p) = f_\alpha$ if and only if $t \geq 2n - 2$ and $1 \leq p \leq n$. Here, $\overline{n}$ denotes the *FSSP initial configuration* of size n, i.e. $\overline{n}_1 = g_\alpha$ and $\overline{n}_p = q_\alpha$ for any $p \in [\![1, n]\!]$. Moreover, q_α must be a *quiescent state*, i.e. we must have $T_\alpha(s, q_\alpha, s') = q_\alpha$ whenever s and s' are either q_α or $\star$. We are only concerned with minimal-time solutions but sometimes simply write *FSSP solution*, or *solution* for short.

Family of Space-Time Diagrams. We have also the notion of a *family of space-time diagrams* $D \subseteq \bigcup_{n \in \mathbb{N}^+} (S \cup \{\star\})^{\mathbb{N} \times [\![0, n+1]\!]}$ on a set of states S. Such a family is said to be a *deterministic family* when for any two diagrams $d, d' \in D$ of respective sizes n and n', and for any $(t, p) \in \mathbb{N} \times [\![1, n]\!]$ and $(t', p') \in \mathbb{N} \times [\![1, n']\!]$ we have :

$$(\forall x \in \{-1, 0, 1\}, d(t, p + x) = d'(t', p' + x)) \Rightarrow d(t + 1, p) = d(t' + 1, p').$$

We forget here the details of the border cells. It is obvious that, for any cellular automaton α, the family $\{ D_\alpha(c) \mid c \in I_\alpha \}$ of all its space-time diagrams is deterministic. Conversely, when we have a deterministic family of space-time diagram D on a finite set of state S, we can construct a cellular automaton α such that $\Sigma_\alpha = S$ and $\{ D_\alpha(c) \mid c \in I_\alpha \} = D$, the local transition function T_α : $[d(t, p-1), d(t, p), d(t, p+1)] \mapsto d(t+1, p)$ for any $d \in D$ and $(t, p) \in \mathbb{N} \times [\![1, n]\!]$ being well defined because of the determinism of the family. Note that, since T_α has a finite domain, there are finite subsets of D that are enough to specify it completely.

3 Optimizations of a Field - Based FSSP Solution

3.1 The Cellular Automaton $\mathfrak{F}$

Maignan - Yunès have proposed a modular minimal-time FSSP solution. The modularization is to replace the traditional notion of "signals" by the concept of "cellular fields". A cellular field is a module that takes inputs from its environment and produces a result to its environment. The cellular fields can be composed to produce larger modules or be a complete cellular automaton. The FSSP solution is described in two steps: the first step is to describe the fields and to compose them into a cellular automaton with an unbounded number of states and the second step is to *reduce* the latter into a new finite state classical cellular automaton. The detailed procedure of this solution is described in [2]. This work has been done for the generalized FSSP where the general is not necessarily the leftmost cell.

Following the procedure, we re-implemented the unbounded solution and, to retrieve the transition table for the restricted case of classical FSSP, we generated a finite subpart of its family of space-time diagrams, i.e. the space-time diagrams associated with the FSSP initial configuration of size 2 to 1000. For each of space-time diagram, we transformed each state according to the prescribed reduction function to produce a new family of space-time diagram. We found that this family is deterministic (see Sect. 2.2) and extracted the local transition table of cellular automaton associated to it. In fact, the extraction was already complete with the FSSP initial configurations of size 2 to 105.

The result is a cellular automaton $\mathfrak{F}$ of 21 states and 486 local transition rules. Among these rules, there are 477 symmetric rules consisting of 23 self-symmetric rules and 227 pairs of symmetric rule. A rule $[a, b, c] \mapsto d \in T_\mathfrak{F}$ is self-symmetric if $a = c$ and symmetric if $[c, b, a] \mapsto d \in T_\mathfrak{F}$. In Fig. 3 in page 10

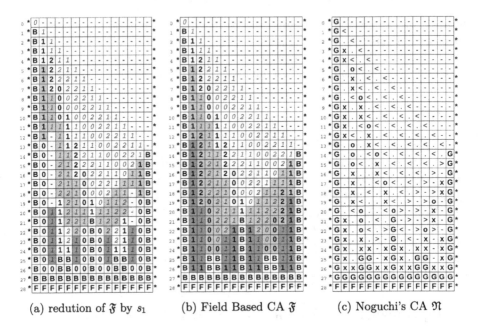

(a) redution of 𝔉 by s_1 (b) Field Based CA 𝔉   (c) Noguchi's CA 𝔑

Fig. 1. Space-time diagrams for the FSSP initial configuration of size 15

is depicted the 9 asymmetric rules firsts, and then the symmetric rules, keeping only one element of each pair of (non-self)-symmetric rules. The set of 21 states consists of the 3 states 🄱, ⬚ and 🄵. The other 18 states are composed of three informations: a number denoting the distance to a border modulo 3, a boolean the presenting the stability of the distance and represented by typesetting the number in bold or italics; and the level of division modulo 3 represented by have the background white, gray or dark gray. We have $g_{\mathfrak{F}} = \boxed{0}$, $q_{\mathfrak{F}} = \boxed{\cdot}$ and $f_{\mathfrak{F}} = \boxed{F}$. The space-time diagram $D_{\mathfrak{F}}(\overline{15})$ of the cellular automaton 𝔉 on the FSSP initial configuration of size 15 is shown in Fig. 1b.

3.2 Brute Force Exploration of All Reductions

As in the case of DFA minization, we want to merge as many states of 𝔉 as possible while preserving the fact that it is a minimal-time FSSP solution. The merging of many states can always be obtained by merging two states, then another two states, and so on so forth. Also, merging two states might be described simply as a substitution of one of them by the other. However, the resulting object might not be a CA in the strict sense. Indeed, we might have a cellular automaton α with two transitions $[a, b, c] \mapsto d, [e, f, g] \mapsto h \in T_\alpha$ with $d \neq h$ and the substitution renders $[a, b, c]$ equals to $[e, f, g]$ but keeps $d \neq h$. In this case, the transition table is not a partial function anymore and we have a non-deterministic CA. However, if we then substitute d by h, and so on so forth every time we obtain a non-deterministic CA, we will necessarily end up with a deterministic CA at some point.

More precisely, let α be a CA, $e_0 \in \Sigma_\alpha$ be a state and e_1 an arbitrary element, a *substitution* of e_0 by e_1 in α gives a new (maybe non-deterministic) CA $\beta = \rho(e_0, e_1, \alpha)$ with $\Sigma_\beta = (\Sigma_\alpha \backslash \{e_0\}) \cup \{e_1\}$, $I_\beta = \{c' \mid c \in I_\alpha\}$ and $T_\beta = \{[a', b', c'] \mapsto d' \mid [a, b, c] \mapsto d \in T_\alpha\}$ where

$$x' = \begin{cases} e_1 \text{ if } x = e_0 \\ x \text{ otherwise.} \end{cases}$$

As we are considering FSSP solutions, we also need to keep track of the three special states and have $g_\beta = g_\alpha'$, $q_\beta = q_\alpha'$ and $f_\beta = f_\alpha'$.

We also define $\gamma = \rho^+(e_0, e_1, \alpha)$ the closest deterministic CA obtained by first computing $\beta = \rho(e_0, e_1, \alpha)$, and then taking $\gamma = \beta$ if β is deterministic. If β is not deterministic, then there exists $a, b, c, e_2, e_3 \in \Sigma_\beta^\star$ such that $[a, b, c] \mapsto e_2 \in T_\beta$ and $[a, b, c] \mapsto e_3 \in T_\beta$ but $e_2 \neq e_3$. In this case, we recursively set $\gamma = \rho^+(e_2, e_3, \beta)$. This operation is well defined up to a state renaming. We use the following straightforward algorithm to explore all reductions by brute force. This algorithm is indeed exhaustive because once a CA is not an FSSP solution, none of its reductions can be. Indeed, if it is not a FSSP solution, it is necessarily because the firing state occurs too early, and more merging can only make the firing states occur in more places in the space-time diagrams.

```
AllReductions(α)
  res := {}
  for {e₁, e₂} ⊆ Σα with e1 ≠ e2 do
      β = ρ⁺(e₁, e₂, α)
      if β is an FSSP solution then
          res := res ∪ {β}
          res := res ∪ AllReductions(β)
      end
  end
  return res
```

3.3   A Brief Analysis of the Reductions

An execution of this algorithm on the CA $\mathfrak{F}$ does not produce a combinatorial explosion and stops after a few minutes. We found 3483 distinct reductions: 30 reductions appear at recursion depth 1, 294 reductions at depth 2, 1106 reductions of depth 3, 1466 reductions of depth 4, 530 reductions of depth 5, 56 reductions of depth 6, and 1 reduction of depth 7. We verified that the 3483 CA are minimal-time FSSP solution by checking their space-time diagram for all FSSP initial configuration of size 2 to 1000. All the other reductions that have been generated and declared non-solution merges the firing state with some other

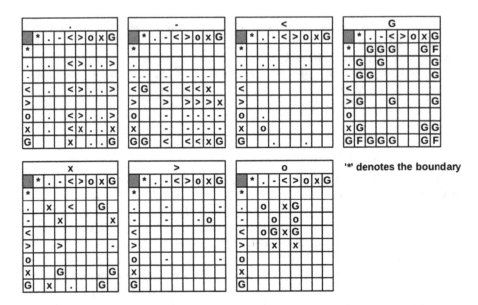

Fig. 2. Transition table of an 8-state and 119-rule Noguchi's CA $\mathfrak{N}$

state, and in fact merges almost all states together to become deterministic. Another interesting fact is that all of the valid reductions only merges states two by two. In other words, changing $\rho^+(e_1, e_2, \alpha)$ into $\rho(e_1, e_2, \alpha)$ and changing the test β *is an FSSP solution* by the test β *is a deterministic CA* in the algorithm lead to the same set of reductions. Figure 1a shows a space-time diagram of the CA reduction of 14-state. It has 480 rules and is obtained by merging the following set of substitutions: (⬛2, ⬜0), (⬜0, ⬛2), (⬛0, ⬛2), (⬛1, ⬜0), (⬛2, ⬜-), (⬜0, ⬜1), (⬜0,⬜1). Note that these pairs are all disjoints.

Organizing these reductions into a Hasse diagram under the finer-coarser partial order reveals some more interesting structure, but this is out of the scope of this paper. This 14-state symmetric FSSP solution should be compared with other symmetric solutions. However, there are hand-made solution with smaller number of state and we now jump to the subject of a comparison with $\mathfrak{F}$, which will lead to a generalization of the concept of reduction.

4   Comparison of $\mathfrak{F}$ with Noguchi's Solution

4.1   The Cellular Automaton $\mathfrak{N}$

Kenichiro Noguchi proposed an 8-state and 119-rule solution for the FSSP as described in [3]. The space-time diagrams of this solution have the same structure with those of the field-based solution. Figure 2 shows the transition table $T_{\mathfrak{N}}$ of this CA that we denote $\mathfrak{N}$. In each table, the first line presents the current state e_0, the second line présents the state of the right neighbour e_1, the first column presents the state of the left neighbour e_{-1}. Each other cell of the table shows the results $T_{\mathfrak{N}}(e_{-1}, e_0, e_1)$. A cell is empty to say there is no local transition for $[e_{-1}, e_0, e_1]$. Figure 1c shows the space-time diagram of this CA on an FSSP initial configuration of size 15. In Figs. 2 and 1c, G denotes the general $g_{\mathfrak{N}}$, – the quiescent state $q_{\mathfrak{N}}$ and F denotes the firing state $f_{\mathfrak{N}}$.

4.2   Generalized Reductions of $\mathfrak{F}$ into $\mathfrak{N}$

Although the space-time diagram of $\mathfrak{N}$ looks similar to the one of $\mathfrak{F}$, $\mathfrak{N}$ is not a reduction of $\mathfrak{F}$ since we did not obtained any 8-state reduction in the previous section. It is expectable since that transition table of $\mathfrak{N}$ is non symmetric, i.e. that are local configurations that gives a different results when reversed. However, looking only a local part of the space-time diagram of $\mathfrak{F}$ seemed enough to known a local part of the corresponding space-time diagram of $\mathfrak{N}$. More precisely, one can check on Fig. 1 that at any time t and any position p, the local configuration $[D_{\mathfrak{F}}(\overline{15})(t, p-1), D_{\mathfrak{F}}(\overline{15})(t, p), D_{\mathfrak{F}}(\overline{15})(t, p+1)]$ on the space-time diagram of $\mathfrak{F}$ determines the state $D_{\mathfrak{N}}(\overline{15})(t+1, p)$ on the space-time diagram of $\mathfrak{N}$, i.e. if this local configuration appears at some other place (t', p') on $\mathfrak{F}$, leads to the same states at $(t'+1, p)$ on $\mathfrak{N}$.

Formally, we therefore consider the generalized reduction function $f : \Sigma_{\mathfrak{F}}^{\star} \times \Sigma_{\mathfrak{F}} \times \Sigma_{\mathfrak{F}}^{\star} \to \Sigma_{\mathfrak{N}}$ defined as :

$$f = \{[D_{\mathfrak{F}}(\overline{n})(t, p-1), D_{\mathfrak{F}}(\overline{n})(t, p), D_{\mathfrak{F}}(\overline{n})(t, p+1)] \mapsto D_{\mathfrak{N}}(\overline{n})(t+1, p)\}$$

for any $n \in \mathbb{N}^{+}, t \in \mathbb{N}$ and $p \in [\![1, n]\!]$. We approximated it by taking it with $n \in [\![2, 1000]\!]$, i.e. we only considered the FSSP initial configuration of size 2 to 1000, but the function stayed unchanged above $n = 105$. This is indeed the size at which all local transition of $\mathfrak{F}$ appears. The check until $n = 1000$ was still necessary to check informally that the function is indeed well defined, and is not a mere non-functional relation.

4.3   A Brief Analysis of the Result

We have built the generalized reduction function which have the same number of elements with the local transition table $T_{\mathfrak{F}}$. Each element of f of the form $[a, b, c] \mapsto d$ with $a, c \in \Sigma_{\mathfrak{F}}^{\star}, b \in \Sigma_{\mathfrak{F}}, d \in \Sigma_{\mathfrak{N}}$ is indeed well-defined. This is indeed a notion of reduction because the CA $\mathfrak{N}$ can be recovered from the CA $\mathfrak{F}$ in the following way. From the CA $\mathfrak{F}$, we that consider its family of space-time diagram (up to a certain size). Using the generalized reduction function, we can transform of those space-time diagrams to obtain a new family of space-time diagram. This new family being deterministic, we can obtain $\mathfrak{N}$ as the CA associated to this deterministic family.

Moreover, this is indeed a generalization because the previous notion of reduction can always be described as a particular case of this new notion. Indeed, merging many states of a CA α transform each state $e \in \Sigma_{\alpha}$ to some state $g(e)$. The associated generalized reduction function f is simply defined as $f(a, b, c) = g(T_{\alpha}(a, b, c))$.

(a) Asymmetric rules

(b) Symmetric rules

Fig. 3. Transition table of Maignan - Yunès's solution

5   Conclusion

We found a 14-states reductions of a field-based solution to the FSSP. Note that the original solution is designed for the generalized FSSP where the general can be at any position. We also have shown in which sense the Noguchi's solution can be viewed as a particular reduction of the field-based solution. Other relations between FSSP solutions are currently under study. Indeed, the original unbounded field-based CA can be reduced in many different way, by consdering modulo 2 instead of modulo 3 for the level value, and more relation exists with Noguchi's solution, and certainly with other solutions. These study should allow to identify technics to optimized automatically other solutions designed using the field-based approach.

References

1. Balzer, R.: An 8-state minimal time solution to the firing squad synchronization problem. Inf. Control **10**, 22–42 (1967)
2. Maignan, L., Yunès, J.B.: Finitization of infinite field-based multi-general FSSP solution
3. Noguchi, K.: Simple 8-state minimal time solution to the firing squad synchronization problem. Theor. Comput. Sci. **314**(3), 303–334 (2004)
4. Mazoyer, J.: A six-state minimal time solution to the firing squad synchronization problem. Theor. Comput. Sci. **50**, 183–238 (1987)

Implementations of FSSP Algorithms on Fault-Tolerant Cellular Arrays

Hiroshi Umeo$^{(\boxtimes)}$, Naoki Kamikawa, Masashi Maeda, and Gen Fujita

University of Osaka Electro-Communication,
Hatsu-cho, 18-8, Neyagawa-shi, Osaka 572-8530, Japan
umeo@cyt.osakac.ac.jp

Abstract. The firing squad synchronization problem (FSSP, for short) on cellular automata has been studied extensively for more than fifty years, and a rich variety of FSSP algorithms has been proposed. Here we study the classical FSSP on a model of fault-tolerant cellular automata that might have possibly some defective cells and present the first state-efficient implementations of fault-tolerant FSSP algorithms for one-dimensional (1D) and two-dimensional (2D) arrays. It is shown that, under some constraints on the distribution and length of defective cells, any 1D cellular array of length n with p defective cell segments can be synchronized in $2n - 2 + p$ steps and the algorithm is realized on a 1D cellular automaton with 164 states and 4792 transition rules. In addition, we give a smaller implementation for the 2D FSSP that can synchronize any 2D rectangular array of size $m \times n$, including O(mn) rectangle-shaped isolated defective zones, exactly in $2(m + n) - 4$ steps on a cellular automaton with only 6 states and 939 transition rules.

1   Introduction

Synchronization of large-scale networks is an important and fundamental computing primitive in parallel and distributed systems. The synchronization in ultra-fine grained parallel computational model of cellular automata, known as the firing squad synchronization problem (FSSP), has been studied extensively for more than fifty years [5,8], and a rich variety of synchronization algorithms has been proposed. In the present paper, we consider the FSSP from a viewpoint of fault tolerance. Reliable and fault-tolerant computation on a large-scale cellular automaton is a key issue to be studied so far. Gács [2] constructed reliable cellular automata from unreliable ones that make errors with some constant probability. Fault tolerance in FSSP has been studied by Kutrib and Vollmar [3], Umeo [6], Yunès [9], and recently by Dimitriadis, Kutrib, and Sirakoulis [1]. One of the major open questions on fault-tolerant FSSP is: how many states would be required in their realizations on a finite state automaton? No full implementations were given in the past. In this paper, we present two state-efficient implementations of fault-tolerant FSSP algorithms for one-dimensional (1D) and two-dimensional (2D) arrays. It is shown that, under some constraints on the

© Springer Nature Switzerland AG 2018
G. Mauri et al. (Eds.): ACRI 2018, LNCS 11115, pp. 274–285, 2018.
https://doi.org/10.1007/978-3-319-99813-8_25

distribution and length of defective cells, any 1D cellular array of length n with p defective cell segments can be synchronized in nearly minimum $2n - 2 + p$ steps and the algorithm is realized on a 1D cellular automaton with 164 states and 4792 transition rules. In addition, we give a smaller implementation for the 2D FSSP that can synchronize any 2D rectangular array of size $m \times n$, including $O(mn)$ rectangle-shaped isolated defective zones, exactly in $2(m + n) - 4$ steps on a cellular automaton with only 6 states and 939 transition rules.

2   Fault-Tolerant FSSP Algorithm and Its Implementation on 1D Arrays

In this section we review a nearly minimum-time fault-tolerant FSSP algorithm in Umeo [6] and present an implementation of the algorithm on a 1D cellular automaton with 164 states and 4792 transition rules.

2.1   FSSP on Cellular Automata with Defective Cells

Consider a 1D array of cells, shown in Fig. 1, some of which are defective. Each cell has its own self-diagnosis circuit that diagnoses itself before its operation. The diagnosis result is stored as a flag in the special register augmented with each cell. We assume that new defections do not occur during the operational lifetime on any cell, thus the fault-tolerance we study is a static one. A consecutive defective (intact) cells are referred to as a *defective* (*intact*) segment, respectively. Figure 1 illustrates a 1D array with three defective and four intact segments. Any defective and intact cells can detect whether its neighbor cells are defective or not.

Fig. 1. A one-dimensional (1D) cellular array with three defective and four intact segments

We use the following notations. The array consists of p defective segments and $(p+1)$ intact segments, denoted by I_i and D_j, respectively and p be any positive integer, where $1 \leq p \leq n$. Let n_i and m_j be number of cells on the ith intact and jth defective segments, where $1 \leq i \leq p + 1$ and $1 \leq j \leq p$. Let n be the length of the array such that $n = (n_1 + m_1) + (n_2 + m_2) +, ..., + (n_p + m_p) + n_{p+1}$.

In our model we assume that any cell in defective segment can only transmit a signal to its right or left neighbor depending on the direction in which it comes to the defective segment. The speed of the signal in any defective segment is

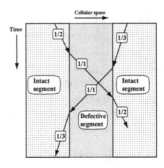

Fig. 2. In defective segments, any signal is transmitted at a constant speed 1/1

fixed to 1/1, that is, one cell per one step. In defective segments, both the information carried by the signal and the direction in which the signal is propagated are preserved without any modifications. Thus, we can see that any defective segment has two one-way pipelines that can transmit the state at 1/1 speed in either direction (Fig. 2).

The *fault-tolerant* FSSP for cellular automata with *defective* cells is to determine a description for cells that ensures all *intact* cells enter the *fire* state *at exactly the same time* and *for the first time*. The set of states and the next-state function must be independent of n.

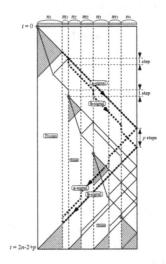

Fig. 3. A space-time diagram for the fault-tolerant FSSP algorithm operating on an array with three defective segments

2.2 Fault-Tolerant FSSP Algorithm and Its Implementation on 1D Arrays

First we introduce a *freezing-thawing* technique that yields a delayed synchronization developed in Umeo [6].

Theorem 1. Let t_1, t_2 and Δt be any integer such that $0 \leq t_1 \leq n - 1$, $t_1 \leq t_2$ and $\Delta t = t_2 - t_1$. We assume that the right end cell of the array of length n receives a special signal from outside at time $t = t_1$ and t_2. Then, there exists a CA that can fire at time $t = 2n - 2 + \Delta t$.

We can freeze the entire configuration on the array during Δt steps and delay the synchronization on the array for Δt steps.

Fault-Tolerant FSSP Algorithm

Let p be any positive integer and M be any cellular array of length n with p defective segments, where $n_i \geq m_i$ and $n_i + m_i \geq p - i$, for any i such that $1 \leq i \leq p$. A space-time diagram of the fault-tolerant FSSP algorithm is illustrated in Fig. 3. The algorithm is based on the freezing-thawing technique in Theorem 1. In order to thaw the intact segment, special thawing signals: a- and b-signals, are used and the initiation of synchronization process is delayed for one step at each intact segment. Precisely, the synchronization for the i-th segment is initiated at time $t_i = 2 \sum_{j=1}^{i-1}(n_j + m_j) + (i - 1)$. Whenever the fast signal arrives at each right end of intact segment, it splits into two signals. One is the freezing signal and the other is the a- and b-signals which propagate toward the right end of the array at 1/1-speed. The b-signal stays for one step at the left end of each intact segment that it encounters. Both a- and b-signals reflect at the right end of the array and proceed to the left direction at 1/1-speed. This time the reflected a-signal stops for one step at the left end of each defective segment that it encounters. When the conditions given above are satisfied, two reflected a- and b-signals meet at the right end of right intact segment just where the original a- and b-signals have been generated. Now the thawing operation for the configuration of the intact segment is started.

Let t_i^a and t_i^b be time steps at which the a- and b-signals emitted by the i-th segment hit the right end of the array, respectively. We have:

$$t_i^a = t_i + \sum_{j=i}^{p}(n_j + m_j) + n_{p+1}, t_i^b = t_i^a + p - i + 1.$$

The freezing and thawing operations for I_i are started, respectively, at time $t_{i_1} = t_i + n_i - 1$ and $t_{i_2} = t_{i_1} + 2m_i + 2\sum_{j=i+1}^{p}(n_j + m_j) + 2n_{p+1} + p - i + 1$. The condition: $t_{i+1}^a \geq t_i^b$ for any i such that $1 \leq i \leq p$ is necessary and sufficient for the configuration on I_i to be thawed by the thawing signal emitted by the i-th segment. The condition is satisfied for any i such that $1 \leq i \leq p$, since $t_{i+1}^a - t_i^b = n_i + m_i - p + i \geq 0$.

Thus the configuration on I_i is frozen during $\Delta t = t_{i_2} - t_{i_1} = 2m_i + 2\sum_{j=i+1}^{p}(n_j + m_j) + 2n_{p+1} + p - i + 1$ steps. Based on Theorem 1, the i-th intact segment I_i can be fired at time $t = t_i + 2n_i - 2 + \Delta t = 2n - 2 + p$. In

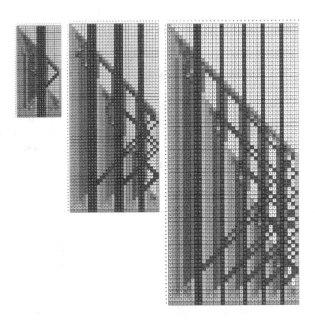

Fig. 4. Snapshots of the synchronization processes operating on a 1D array of length $n = 20$ with one defective segment (left), an array of length $n = 30$ with 3 defective segments (middle), and an array of length $n = 35$ with 5 defective segments (right), respectively

this way, the entire intact segments can be synchronized at time $t = 2n - 2 + p$. From the assumptions $n_i + m_i \geq p - i$, for any i, $1 \leq i \leq p$, it is seen that $p = O(\sqrt{n})$. Thus the time complexity of the algorithm is $2n + O(\sqrt{n})$. The algorithm is stated as follows.

Theorem 2. Let p be any positive integer and M be any cellular array of length n with p defective segments, where $n_i \geq m_i$ and $n_i + m_i \geq p - i$, for any i such that $1 \leq i \leq p$. Then, M can be synchronized in $2n - 2 + p$ steps.

We have implemented the algorithm on a 1D cellular automaton with 164 states and 4792 transition rules. In Fig. 4 we give several snapshots of the synchronization processes operating on a 1D array of length $n = 20$ with one defective segment (left), an array of length $n = 30$ with 3 defective segments (middle), and an array of length $n = 35$ with 5 defective segments (right), respectively.

3   Fault-Tolerant FSSP Algorithm and Its Implementation on 2D Arrays

A fault-tolerant FSSP on 2D arrays has never been discussed nor studied due to the difficulties in designing synchronization algorithms. Here we present a

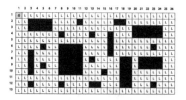

Fig. 5. A 2D rectangular array of size 13×26 with 20 isolated defective zones

6-state fault-tolerant FSSP algorithm on 2D arrays. The fault-tolerant model that we consider is slightly different from the 1D one in Sect. 2. Now we consider a 2D rectangular array of size $m \times n, m, n \geq 2$. Each cell is an identical (except the border and defective cells) finite-state automaton. The cell on the ith row, jth column is denoted by $C_{i,j}$, where $1 \leq i \leq m$ and $1 \leq j \leq n$. The array operates in lock-step mode in such a way that the next state of each cell (except border and defective cells) is determined by both its own present state and the present states of its north, south, east and west neighbors, thus assuming the von Neumann neighborhood. All cells (*soldiers*), except the general at the north-west corner and defective cells, are initially in the quiescent state at time $t = 0$ with the property that the next state of a quiescent cell with quiescent neighbors is the quiescent state again. At time $t = 0$, the general on $C_{1,1}$ is in the *fire-when-ready* state, which is the initiation signal for the array. The 2D rectangular array includes some defective regions, each consisting of defective cells that cannot transmit any information nor change their states. The defective regions can be regarded as obstacles or holes that cannot process any information in the array. We assume that no new defective cells appear after the initiation.

The fault-tolerant FSSP is to determine a description (state set and next-state function) for the intact cells that ensures all intact cells enter the *fire* state at exactly the same time and for the first time. The set of states and its transition function must be independent of m and n. A typical 2D rectangular array of size 13×26 with 20 isolated holes (obstacles) is shown in Fig. 5. Each defective region may be a rectangle, but must be isolated from each other and from the boundary of a given array. The readers can see that the initial general in yellow is on $C_{1,1}$, intact cells in white take the quiescent state L, and defective cells are illustrated as black cells in Fig. 5, respectively.

The fault-tolerant FSSP algorithm is based on a mapping developed in Umeo, Maeda, Hisaoka, and Teraoka [7], where any 1D FSSP algorithm can be embedded onto 2D arrays without introducing additional states. We consider a 2D array of size $m \times n$, where $m, n \geq 2$, shown in Fig. 6. The array is decomposed into $m + n - 1$ groups g_k, $1 \leq k \leq m + n - 1$, defined as follows.

$$g_k = \{C_{i,j} | i + j = k + 1\}, \text{i.e.,}$$

$g_1 = \{C_{1,1}\}, g_2 = \{C_{1,2}, C_{2,1}\}, g_3 = \{C_{1,3}, C_{2,2}, C_{3,1}\}, \ldots, g_{m+n-1} = \{C_{m,n}\}$.
Figure 6 shows the decomposition of the 2D array of size $m \times n$ into $m + n - 1$ groups.

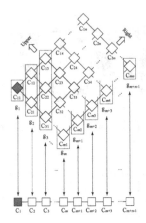

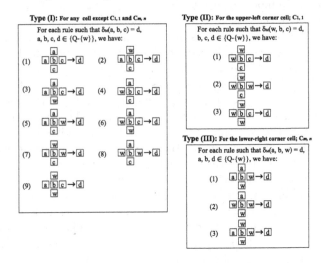

Fig. 6. Correspondence between 1D and 2D arrays

Fig. 7. Construction of transition rules for 2D fault-tolerant FSSP algorithm

Let $M = (Q, \delta_M, w)$ be any 1D array that fires ℓ cells in $T(\ell)$ steps, where Q is the finite state set of M, $\delta_M : Q^3 \to Q$ is the transition function, and $w \in Q$ is the state of the right and left ends. We assume that M has $m + n - 1$ cells, denoted by C_i, $1 \le i \le m+n-1$. For convenience, we assume that M has a left and right end cells of the array, denoted by C_0 and C_{m+n}, respectively. Both end cells C_0 and C_{m+n} always take the state $w \in Q$. We consider a one-to-one correspondence between the ith group g_i and the ith cell C_i on M such that $g_i \leftrightarrow C_i$, where $1 \le i \le m + n - 1$ (see Fig. 6). We can construct a 2D array $N = (Q, \delta_N, w)$ such that each cell in g_i simulates the ith cell C_i in real-time and N can fire any 2D $m \times n$ array at time $t = T(m+n-1)$ if and only if M fires the 1D array of length $m+n-1$ at time $t = T(m+n-1)$, where $\delta_N : Q^5 \to Q$ is the transition function, and $w \in Q$ is the border/defective state of the array. Note that the set of internal states of N is the same as M. The transition function δ_N is constructed as follows:

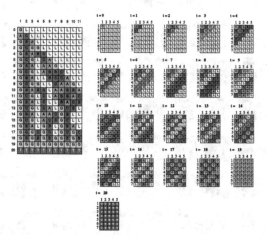

Fig. 8. Configurations of Mazoyer's 6-state FSSP algorithm on 11 cells (left) and snapshots of the synchronization processes on a 2D array of size 7×5 (right)

Let $\delta_M(a, b, c) = d$ be any transition rule of M, where $a, b, c, d \in \{Q - \{w\}\}$. Then, N has nine transition rules, as shown in Fig. 7, Type (I). The first rule (1) in Type (I) is used by an inner cell that does not include border/defective cells amongst its four neighbors. Rules (2)-(9) are used by an inner cell that has a border/defective cell as its upper, lower, left, right, lower left, and upper right neighbor, respectively. Here the terms *upper*, *right* etc. on the rectangular array are interpreted in a usual way, shown in Fig. 7, although the array is rotated by $45°$ in the counter-clockwise direction. When $a = w$, that is, $\delta_M(w, b, c) = d$, where $b, c, d \in \{Q - \{w\}\}$, then N has three rule, as shown in Type (II). These rules are used by the cell located in the upper left corner. When $c = w$, that is, $\delta_M(a, b, w) = d$, where $a, b, d \in \{Q - \{w\}\}$, then N has three rules, as shown in Type (III). These rules are used by the cell located in the lower right corner.

Now let M have $m + n - 1$ cells. We can show that the constructed 2D array N can generate the configuration of M in real-time. Specifically, for any i, $1 \leq i \leq m + n - 1$, the state of any cell in g_i at any step is the same and is identical to the state of C_i at the corresponding step. Let S_i^t, $S_{i,j}^t$ and $S_{g_i}^t$ denote the state of C_i, $C_{i,j}$ and the set of states of the cells in g_i at step t, respectively.

First we consider the case where a given 2D array of size $m \times n$ includes no defective zones. The following lemma holds.

Lemma 3. *Let i and t be any integer such that $1 \leq i \leq m + n - 1$, $0 \leq t \leq T(m + n - 1)$. Then, $S_{g_i}^t = \{S_i^t\}$.*

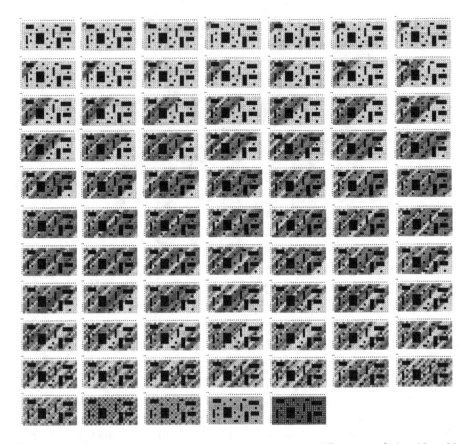

Fig. 9. Snapshots of the synchronization processes on a 2D array of size 13×26, containing 20 defective rectangle zones

We see that any configuration on a 1D array consisting of $m + n - 1$ cells can be mapped onto a 2D array of size $m \times n$. Therefore, if the embedded 1D array fires $m + n - 1$ cells in $T(m + n - 1)$ steps, then the corresponding 2D array of size $m \times n$ can be synchronized in $T(m + n - 1)$ steps. Thus, we can embed any 1D FSSP algorithm onto a 2D array without increasing the number of internal states. We complete the observation in the next theorem.

Theorem 4. Let M be any s-state FSSP algorithm operating in $T(\ell)$ steps on 1D arrays of length ℓ. Then, there exists a 2D s-state cellular automaton that can synchronize any rectangular array of size $m \times n$ in $T(m + n - 1)$ steps.

Here we can embed a 1D 6-state minimum-time FSSP algorithm developed in Mazoyer [4], synchronizing ℓ cells in $2\ell - 2$ steps. The next rectangle synchronization algorithm fires any $m \times n$ array in $2(m + n) - 4$ steps, since $T(m + n - 1) = 2(m + n - 1) - 2 = 2(m + n) - 4$.

Fig. 10. Snapshots of the synchronization processes on a 2D array of size 10×10, including 4 defective zones

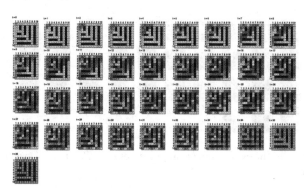

Fig. 11. Snapshots of the synchronization processes on a 2D array of size 10×10, including 7 defective rectangle zones

Theorem 5. There exists a 6-state 939-rule FSSP algorithm that can synchronize any $m \times n$ rectangular array in $2(m + n) - 4$ steps.

Figure 8 (left) illustrates snapshots of Mazoyer's 6-state FSSP algorithm on 11 cells. These configurations are mapped on a 2D array of size 7×5, shown in Fig. 8 (right).

We now consider a class of 2D arrays $\mathcal{A}$ of size $m \times n$, initially including intact and defective cells, which satisfies the following conditions:

1. The initial general is on the north-west corner cell $C_{1,1}$.
2. Any intact cell, except $C_{1,1}$, takes a quiescent state initially.
3. Any intact cell $C_{i,j}$, $1 \leq i \leq m, 1 \leq j \leq n$, except $C_{1,1}$ and $C_{m,n}$, must have at least one intact cell in $\{C_{i-1,j}, C_{i,j-1}\}$ and one intact cell in $\{C_{i+1,j}, C_{i,j+1}\}$ at time $t = 0$.
4. The defective cell, assuming the boundary state initially, keeps the state during operations.

Fig. 12. Snapshots of the synchronization processes on a 2D array of size 10×10, including 4 defective zones

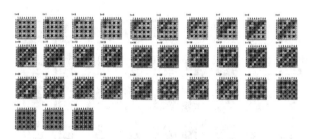

Fig. 13. Snapshots of the synchronization processes on a 2D array of size 9×9, including 16 defective cells

In the case where a given 2D array includes some defective zones satisfying the conditions above, the following lemma holds.

Lemma 6. *Let i and t be any integer such that $1 \leq i \leq m + n - 1$, $0 \leq t \leq T(m + n - 1)$. For any initial configuration in $\mathcal{A}$, we have:*

$$
S_{g_i}^t = \begin{cases} \{S_i^t, w\}, & \text{if } g_i \text{ includes some defective cells,} \\ \{S_i^t\}, & \text{otherwise.} \end{cases} \tag{1}
$$

The 6-state 2D FSSP algorithm stated in Theorem 5 can also synchronize any 2D array in $\mathcal{A}$. We have:

Theorem 7. *There exists a 6-state 939-rule fault-tolerant FSSP algorithm that can synchronize any $m \times n$ rectangular array in $\mathcal{A}$ in $2(m + n) - 4$ steps.*

Several snapshots of the 6-state fault-tolerant FSSP algorithm running on a rectangular array of size 13×26 including 20 holes (Fig. 5) are shown in Fig. 9. Figures 10, 11, 12 and 13 illustrate similar snapshots for some different initial configurations.

4   Conclusions

It has been shown that, under some constraints on the distribution of defective cells, any 1D cellular array of length n with p defective cell segments can be synchronized in $2n - 2 + p$ steps and the algorithm has been realized on a finite state automaton having 164 states and 4792 rules. We have also given a smaller implementation for the 2D FSSP that can synchronize any 2D rectangular array of size $m \times n$, including $O(mn)$ rectangle-shaped isolated defective zones, exactly in $2(m+n) - 4$ steps on a cellular automaton with only 6 states and 939 transition rules.

References

1. Dimitriadis, A., Kutrib, M., Sirakoulis, G.C.: Cutting the firing squad synchronization. In: El Yacoubi, S., Wąs, J., Bandini, S. (eds.) ACRI 2016. LNCS, vol. 9863, pp. 123–133. Springer, Cham (2016). https://doi.org/10.1007/978-3-319-44365-2_12
2. Gács, P.: Reliable computation with cellular automata. J. Comput. System Sci. **32**, 15–78 (1986)
3. Kutrib, M., Vollmar, R.: The firing squad synchronization problem in defective cellular automata. IEICE Trans. Inf. Syst. **E78–D**(7), 895–900 (1995)
4. Mazoyer, J.: A six-state minimal time solution to the firing squad synchronization problem. Theor. Comput. Sci. **50**, 183–238 (1987)
5. Moore, E.F.: The firing squad synchronization problem. In: Moore, E.F. (ed.) Sequential Machines, Selected Papers. Addison-Wesley, Reading, pp. 213–214 (1964)
6. Umeo, H.: A simple design of time-efficient firing squad synchronization algorithms with fault-tolerance. IEICE Trans. Inf. Syst. **E87–D**, 733–739 (2004)
7. Umeo, H., Maeda, M., Hisaoka, M., Teraoka, M.: A state-efficient mapping scheme for designing two-dimensional firing squad synchronization algorithms. Fundam. Inform. **74**, 603–623 (2006)
8. Umeo, H.: Firing squad synchronization problem in cellular automata. In: Meyers, R. (ed.) Encyclopedia of Complexity and System Science, vol. 4, pp. 3537–3574. Springer, New York (2009). https://doi.org/10.1007/978-0-387-30440-3
9. Yunès, J.-B.: Fault tolerant solutions to the firing squad synchronization problem in linear cellular automata. J. Cell. Autom. **1**(3), 253–268 (2006)

Theory and Cryptography

Do There Exist Non-linear Maximal Length Cellular Automata? A Study

Sumit Adak[1(✉)], Sukanya Mukherjee[2], and Sukanta Das[1]

[1] Department of Information Technology,
Indian Institute of Engineering Science and Technology, Shibpur 711103, India
{sumitadak,sukanta}@it.iiests.ac.in
[2] Department of Computer Science and Engineering,
Institute of Engineering and Management, Kolkata 700091, India
sukanya.mukherjee@iemcal.com

Abstract. An n-cell maximal length cellular automaton (CA) is a binary CA which is having a cycle of length $2^n - 1$. These CAs are linear and have been used in different applications, such as pseudo random number generation, VLSI design & test, cryptosystem etc. For some applications, however, it could be good if we can use non-linear maximal length CAs. In this paper, we arrange an experiment for the search of non-linear maximal length CAs. By experimentation, we have seen that there exists non-linear maximal length CAs.

Keywords: Non-linear cellular automata · Reversible
Maximal length · Configuration · Rule

1 Introduction

The cellular automata (CAs) that generate large cycles are highly useful in computational processes like pseudo random number generator (PRPG) [5,7], cryptosystem [3,6] etc. Prior works have considered the use of linear *maximal length* cellular automata [1,2] for such applications, where the cycle length is as large as $2^n - 1$ for an n-cell binary cellular automaton (CA). Linear maximal length CAs, however, suffer from some drawbacks. Firstly, the availability of n-degree primitive polynomial is limited. Besides, linear maximal length sequences are not secure. So, there is a necessity of a construction that can provide both non-linearity and maximal length sequence for optimized crypto-system (see [3,6] for details).

There have been some researches to introduce non-linearity in maximal length CAs [3,6]. The technique referred in [3] manipulates the number of clock cycles, based on inputs, in a maximum length additive CA. This method becomes unsynchronized for different inputs. An efficient technique [6] is devised for generating non-linear maximal length CA from linear maximal length CA by injecting non-linearity in different cell positions. The effect of the non-linearity can be propagated among multiple cells by shifting the non-linear function. However, it

© Springer Nature Switzerland AG 2018
G. Mauri et al. (Eds.): ACRI 2018, LNCS 11115, pp. 289–297, 2018.
https://doi.org/10.1007/978-3-319-99813-8_26

incurs increasing neighborhood dependency. For optimal design, the construction of non-linear maximal length CA limits upto 5 neighborhood. This motivates us to figure out if there exists a non-linear maximal length CA without exceeding the neighborhood dependency. In this paper we answer this question in an affirmative way.

2   Basics

2.1   Definitions

A 1-d finite CA of size n consists of an array of n cells. Each cell can be in either of two *states*, 0 or 1 as we use binary CA. Let x_i denote the state of cell i. Then, a configuration of the CA is $x = (x_0 x_1 \cdots x_{n-1})$ where $x_i \in \{0, 1\}$. In this work, we consider null boundary CA, which means $x_{-1} = x_n = 0$. Cell i of the CA changes its state at every time step following a next state function $f_i : \{0, 1\}^3 \mapsto \{0, 1\}$, which is defined over the present states of cell i and its left and right neighbors. Let us denote C as the set of all possible configurations of the CA. The CA thus can be interpreted as a function $F : C \to C$, which satisfies the following conditions: $y = F(x)$, $x, y \in C$, where $y = (y_i)_{0 \le i \le n-1}$ and $y_i = f_i(x_{i-1}, x_i, x_{i+1})$.

There can be eight possible combinations depending on the present states of a cell and its two neighbours. The next state for the cell for each of these combinations depends on the next state function. Thus there can be 2^8 distinct next state functions, and each next state function can be associated to a value between 0 and 255, which we call *rule*. The rule corresponding to a particular next state function is obtained as the decimal equivalent of next state generated for the eight combinations of the present states x_{i-1}, x_i and x_{i+1} (as shown in Table 1). For a particular rule $\mathcal{R}$, let $\mathcal{R}[x_{i-1} x_i x_{i+1}]$ denote the next state of cell i for the present states combination $x_{i-1} x_i x_{i+1}$ of cell i and its neighbours. For example, $30[011] = 1$. Thus a CA can alternatively be interpreted as a *rule vector* $\mathcal{R} = (\mathcal{R}_0, \mathcal{R}_1, \cdots, \mathcal{R}_i, \cdots, \mathcal{R}_{n-1})$, where each $\mathcal{R}_i$ is the rule to which f_i is associated. The uniform CA is a special case where $\mathcal{R}_0 = \mathcal{R}_1 = \cdots = \mathcal{R}_i = \cdots = \mathcal{R}_{n-1}$. If an $\mathcal{R}_i$ of an n-cell CA is said to be *linear* if its corresponding f_i follows XOR logic.

Definition 1 *If all the rules of a rule vector $\mathcal{R}$ are linear/additive, then the CA is linear/additive.*

Here, we consider only seven rules as linear – 60, 90, 102, 150, 170, 204 and 240. Another seven rules (15, 51, 85, 105, 153, 165 and 195) are complemented additive rules.

Definition 2. *If any $\mathcal{R}_i$ of $\mathcal{R}$ is not linear/ additive, then CA is non-linear.*

Definition 3. *A configuration $x \in C$ is said to be cyclic if $x = F^t(x)$ for some finite $t \in \mathbb{N}$.*

Definition 4. *A CA is reversible if all the configurations are cyclic.*

Table 1. Rules 90, 150, 54 and 30

Present state	111	110	101	100	011	010	001	000	Rule
(i) Next state	0	1	0	1	1	0	1	0	90
(ii) Next state	1	0	0	1	0	1	1	0	150
(iii) Next state	0	0	1	1	0	1	1	0	54
(iv) Next state	0	0	0	1	1	1	1	0	30

2.2   Synthesis of Reversible CAs

Synthesis of a reversible CA given in [4]. Here we briefly present the methodologies for sake of completeness.

Only 62 out of the 256 possible rules are used to form non-uniform reversible CAs. These rules can be classified into different classes as shown in Tables 2, 3 and 4. We now state how a reversible CA can be generated from these tables. The rule at the cell zero i.e., $\mathcal{R}_0$ is selected out of the rules given in first column of Table 2. Note that the first and last rules of a null boundary CA are to be chosen differently (see [4] for details). However, the selected rule at the cell zero defines the class (second column of Table 2) from which $\mathcal{R}_1$ has to be selected. For every i between 1 and $n-2$, the first column of Table 4 shows the probable classes of rule $\mathcal{R}_i$; the second column shows the possible rules for rule $\mathcal{R}_i$ from each class, while corresponding to a particular rule $\mathcal{R}_i$, the third column defines the class from which $\mathcal{R}_{i+1}$ has to be selected. Finally, depending on the class of the rule at the last cell, the rule $\mathcal{R}_{n-1}$ is selected from Table 3.

Example 1. Let us consider a 4-cell CA $(10, 150, 90, 20)$ which is reversible. It is obtained as follows: here, $\mathcal{R}_0$ is 10. The class of $\mathcal{R}_1$ is II (see Table 2). Thus the rule at cell 1 must be selected from the row corresponding to class II of Table 4. In particular, let $\mathcal{R}_1$ is selected to be 150. $\mathcal{R}_2$ should be selected from class I, as the class for selecting the next rule corresponding to rule 150 is class I (see last column of Table 4). Let $\mathcal{R}_2$ is selected as 90. Applying the same methodology, the class of rule $\mathcal{R}_3$ comes out to be class II. From Table 3, the rule $\mathcal{R}_3$ is selected from the row corresponding to class II, in particular $\mathcal{R}_3$ is selected to be 20.

Definition 5. *An n-cell CA is maximal length if, for a configuration $x \in \mathcal{C}$, $x = F^{2^n-1}(x)$, but $x \neq F^t(x)$ where $1 \leq t < 2^n - 1$.*

The CA $(10, 150, 90, 20)$ is equivalent to the CA $(90, 150, 90, 150)$ when the boundary condition is null. That is, this CA is linear. Further, it is a maximal length CA (see Fig. 1).

3   Cellular Automata with Large Cycles

Maximal length CAs are having the largest possible cycle length for given CA size n. In this section we develop a process to design CAs which are expected

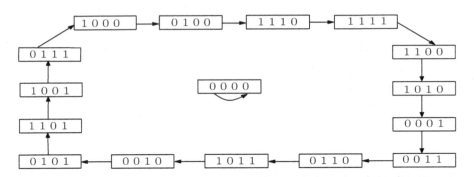

Fig. 1. Configuration transition diagram of the CA $(10, 150, 90, 20)$

Table 2. First rule table

Rules for $\mathcal{R}_0$	Class of $\mathcal{R}_1$
3, 12	I
5, 10	II
6, 9	III

Table 3. Last rule table

Rule class for $\mathcal{R}_{n-1}$	Rule set for $\mathcal{R}_{n-1}$
I	17, 20, 65, 68
II	5, 20, 65, 80
III	5, 17, 68, 80
IV	20, 65
V	17, 68
VI	5, 80

to have large cycles. If non-linear maximal length CAs really exist, we can get such CAs by repeatedly applying this process.

We first intuitively present the idea behind our approach. Clearly, a cell i changes its state in next time step depending on the present states of itself and its neighbours. If the cells of a CA does not depend on their neighbors, the CA cannot produce large cycles. For example, in the extreme case, if $f_i(x_{i-1}, x_i, x_{i+1}) = x_i$ for all i, then every cycle is of length one. Similarly, if $f_i(x_{i-1}, x_i, x_{i+1}) = 1 - x_i$ for all i, every cycle is of length two. Thus lower the dependency of the next state function on the present state of the neighbours of a cell, smaller will be the length of the cycles generated by the corresponding CA. Conversely, if the next state of a cell is more *influenced* by the state of its neighbours, greater is the chance of obtaining a large length cycle.

Let $(x_0 x_1 \cdots x_i \cdots x_{n-1})$ denote a configuration of the CA. Suppose $f_i(x_{i-1}, x_i, x_{i+1}) = f_i(x_{i-1}, x_i, 1 - x_{i+1})$, for all values of x_i and x_{i-1}. This implies that the next state of cell i is not influenced by the present state of cell $i + 1$; we say that cell i is *independent* of its right neighbor. In an analogous manner, if $f_i(x_{i-1}, x_i, x_{i+1}) = f_i(1 - x_{i-1}, x_i, x_{i+1})$ for all values of x_i and x_{i+1}, cell i is independent of its left neighbor.

We can define the degree of dependence on the neighbor of a cell as follows. Let $\alpha_{rd}(x_{i-1} = \mathbf{x}, x_i = \mathbf{y})$ denote the dependence of cell i on its right neighbor when the present states of x_{i-1} and x_i are respectively $\mathbf{x}$ and $\mathbf{y}$. Note that each of $\mathbf{x}$ and $\mathbf{y}$ can be either 0 or 1.

Table 4. Class relationship of R_i and R_{i+1}

Class of R_i	R_i	Class of R_{i+1}
I	51, 204, 60, 195	I
	85, 90, 165, 170	II
	102, 105, 150, 153	III
	53, 58, 83, 92, 163, 172, 197, 202	IV
	54, 57, 99, 108, 147, 156, 198, 201	V
	86, 89, 101, 106, 149, 154, 166, 169	VI
II	15, 30, 45, 60, 75, 90, 105, 120,	I
	135, 150, 165, 180, 195, 210, 225, 240	
III	51, 204, 15, 240	I
	85, 105, 150, 170	II
	90, 102, 153, 165	III
	23, 43, 77, 113, 142, 178, 212, 232	IV
	27, 39, 78, 114, 141, 177, 216, 228	V
	86, 89, 101, 106, 149, 154, 166, 169	VI
IV	60, 195	I
	90, 165	IV
	105, 150	V
V	51, 204	I
	85, 170	II
	102, 153	III
	86, 89, 90, 101, 105, 106,	VI
	149, 150, 154, 165, 166, 169	
VI	15, 240	I
	105, 150	IV
	90, 165	V

$$\alpha_{rd}(x_{i-1} = \mathbf{x}, x_i = \mathbf{y}) = \begin{cases} 1 & \text{if } f_i(\mathbf{x}, \mathbf{y}, x_{i+1}) \neq f_i(\mathbf{x}, \mathbf{y}, 1 - x_{i+1}) \\ 0 & \text{otherwise} \end{cases}$$

The degree of dependence of cell i on its right neighbor is the ratio of the number of combinations of values of x_i and x_{i-1} for which the next state function on x_i depends on x_{i-1}. This is called the *degree of right dependence* for rule $\mathcal{R}_i$ and denoted by $P_r(\mathcal{R}_i)$. Clearly, $P_r(\mathcal{R}_i)$ can take values 0, 0.5 or 1. Formally,

$$P_r(\mathcal{R}_i) = \frac{\sum_{\mathbf{x} \in \{0,1\}} \sum_{\mathbf{y} \in \{0,1\}} \alpha_{rd}(x_{i-1} = \mathbf{x}, x_i = \mathbf{y})}{4}$$

Similarly, let $\alpha_{ld}(x_i = \mathbf{x}, x_{i+1} = \mathbf{y})$ denote the dependence of cell i on its left neighbor when the present states of x_i and x_{i+1} are respectively $\mathbf{x}$ and $\mathbf{y}$.

$$\alpha_{ld}(x_i = \mathbf{x}, x_{i+1} = \mathbf{y}) = \begin{cases} 1 & \text{if } f_i(x_{i-1}, \mathbf{x}, \mathbf{y}) \neq f_i(1 - x_{i-1}, \mathbf{x}, \mathbf{y}) \\ 0 & \text{otherwise} \end{cases}$$

In an analogous way, we define the parameter P_1 which determines how much a cell i depends on its left neighbor. It is the ratio of the number of combinations of values of x_i and x_{i+1} for which the next state function on x_i depends on x_{i+1}. This is called the *degree of left dependence* for rule $\mathcal{R}_i$, and denoted by $P_1(\mathcal{R}_i)$.

$$P_1(\mathcal{R}_i) = \frac{\sum_{\mathbf{x} \in \{0,1\}} \sum_{\mathbf{y} \in \{0,1\}} \alpha_{ld}(x_i = \mathbf{x}, x_{i+1} = \mathbf{y})}{4}$$

Example 2. Let us consider rule 54. We observe that for the next state function corresponding to this rule, $\alpha_{rd}(x_{i-1} = 0, x_i = 0) = 1, \alpha_{rd}(x_{i-1} = 0, x_i = 1) = 1$, while $\alpha_{rd}(x_{i-1} = 1, x_i = 0) = 0, \alpha_{rd}(x_{i-1} = 1, x_i = 1) = 0$. Therefore, $P_r(54)$ is 0.5. On the other hand, $\alpha_{ld}(x_i = 0, x_{i+1} = 0) = 1, \alpha_{ld}(x_i = 1, x_{i+1} = 0) = 1$, while $\alpha_{ld}(x_i = 1, x_{i+1} = 1) = 0, \alpha_{ld}(x_i = 1, x_{i+1} = 0) = 0$. Therefore, $P_1(54)$ is 0.5. Similarly, for rules 90 and 60, $P_r(90) = 1$ and $P_r(60) = 0$. For rules 150 and 170, we get $P_1(150) = 1$ and $P_1(170) = 0$.

The rules of reversible CAs can be classified into three categories depending on P_r and P_1 parameter. The three categories are named as *completely right dependent*, *partially right dependent* and *right independent*, and they correspond respectively to right dependence degree values of 0, 0.5 and 1. In null boundary condition, all possible inputs to first and last rules are not valid. So, we need to classify first and last rules separately using the same process stated above.

In order to have a CA generates a cycle of $2^n - 1$ length, it is desirable to have the rules of the CA dependent on both the left and the right neighbours. The degree of dependence of a rule $\mathcal{R}_i$ on both of its neighbours can be determined by the product of $P_r(\mathcal{R}_i)$ and $P_1(\mathcal{R}_i)$, and we denote this by $P(\mathcal{R}_i)$.

$$P(\mathcal{R}_i) = P_r(\mathcal{R}_i) * P_1(\mathcal{R}_i).$$

Clearly, $P(\mathcal{R}_i)$ can take values 0, 0.25, 0.5 or 1. We can thus classify the rules here into four categories based on the P parameter. As shown in Table 5, any rule can correspond to either of the four categories *completely dependent*, *partially dependent*, *weakly dependent* and *independent* depending on the P values of 1, 0.5, 0.25 and 0 respectively. However, to obtain a large cycle, we generate the corresponding CA by selecting rules from Table 5 as follows.

The first and the last rules of every CA are selected uniformly at random from the class of *completely dependent*. For the remaining, we pick $n - 2$ rules randomly following Gaussian distribution in such a way that the maximum rules are selected from the category of *completely dependent*, some selected from the category of *partially dependent*, and a very few from the category of *weakly dependent*. Since most of the rules, selected in this manner, have high degree of dependence on both of their neighbours, it is highly likely that the corresponding CA will have a large cycle.

Table 5. Four categories of reversible CA rules on the parameter P

Category	$\mathcal{R}_i$	$\mathcal{R}_0$	$\mathcal{R}_{n-1}$
Completely dependent	90, 165, 150, 105	5, 6, 9, 10	5, 20, 65, 80
Partially dependent	30, 45, 75, 120, 135, 180, 210, 225, 86, 89, 101, 106, 149, 154, 166, 169		
Weakly dependent	53, 58, 83, 92, 163, 172, 197, 202, 54, 57, 99, 108, 147, 156, 198, 201, 23, 43, 77, 113, 142, 178, 212, 232, 27, 39, 78, 114, 141, 177, 216, 228,		
Independent	51, 204, 85, 170, 102, 153, 60, 195, 15, 240	3, 12	17, 68

Table 6. Cycles are close to $2^k - 1$ for k-cell CA (Here $k = 10$)

Cycle length	10-cell CA
1015	(9, 90, 43, 150, 166, 90, 165, 150, 90, 65)
923	(9, 166, 105, 105, 101, 150, 150, 105, 150, 20)
801	(9, 86, 90, 149, 105, 90, 165, 165, 90, 65)
1008	(10, 165, 86, 150, 165, 90, 105, 90, 150, 65)
1023	**(10, 90, 150, 169, 165, 101, 150, 90, 165, 20)**
1001	(10, 90, 53, 90, 90, 150, 89, 90, 105, 80)
1003	(10, 105, 90, 150, 57, 150, 90, 105, 150, 65)
761	(5, 90, 165, 180, 154, 165, 106, 165, 90, 80)
1000	(10, 165, 86, 90, 101, 165, 105, 105, 165, 65)
920	(10, 165, 90, 150, 86, 105, 105, 90, 150, 20)
1022	(9, 106, 150, 105, 90, 105, 150, 90, 150, 65)
827	(9, 43, 105, 154, 105, 165, 150, 90, 150, 20)
1017	(9, 90, 89, 150, 165, 150, 106, 90, 89, 80)
728	(10, 90, 57, 105, 165, 101, 150, 165, 90, 65)
1023	**(6, 150, 210, 53, 150, 150, 165, 105, 150, 20)**

4   Experimental Results

Using the above mentioned approach, we generate a number of CAs of different sizes. We observe that the cycles of the synthesized CAs are large, and most of the time, the largest cycle of such CAs are close to $2^n - 1$. Table 6 shows a sample result of our experiment. Bold faced rows are the non-linear maximal length CAs. This result proves that there exist non-linear maximal length CAs.

Let us now understand the percentage frequency distribution of different categories of rules which can generate non-linear maximal length by using the above process. For CA size 10, we generate 100 non-linear maximal length CAs and using these data, we observe that 83% of the rules belong to *completely dependent* category, 13.8% belong to the *partially dependent* class, while 3.02% belong to the *weakly dependent* class.

To understand the efficacy of the above mentioned approach, we conduct experiments. We generate random non-linear maximal length reversible CAs of size n extensively. Obviously, each CA follows a distribution for the rules being selected from the different categories based on P which mentioned already. By maintaining this distribution, we get CAs of length $2^n - 1$ of a fixed CA size n. We perform experiment for different values of n ranges from 4 to 20. Here, by experiments, we observe that there exists a non-linear maximal length CA for any n. In Table 7, we shows the CAs which contributes maximal length CA for sizes 4 to 20.

From the experimental results, however, we observe that *sixteen* rules from category *weakly dependent* have not participated in the maximal length CA generation. These rules are 92, 172, 197, 202, 108, 156, 198, 201, 77, 142, 212, 232, 78, 141, 216, 228.

Table 7. n-cell non-linear maximal length CAs

n (CA size)	$\mathcal{R}$ (CA)
4	$(6, 178, 90, 20)$
5	$(5, 150, 99, 165, 5)$
6	$(5, 90, 106, 90, 166, 5)$
7	$(6, 101, 90, 154, 105, 165, 65)$
8	$(9, 90, 105, 30, 54, 150, 105, 65)$
9	$(5, 180, 150, 105, 165, 149, 150, 90, 65)$
10	$(10, 105, 54, 154, 90, 166, 90, 86, 105, 65)$
11	$(5, 150, 165, 30, 58, 90, 150, 86, 105, 90, 65)$
12	$(6, 105, 165, 90, 180, 147, 165, 165, 105, 165, 150, 8)$
13	$(6, 86, 90, 169, 105, 150, 89, 90, 165, 150, 90, 90, 65)$
14	$(9, 177, 89, 90, 89, 90, 101, 105, 165, 90, 150, 90, 150, 65)$
15	$(10, 75, 90, 90, 166, 90, 86, 105, 90, 150, 166, 105, 90, 90, 20)$
16	$(6, 90, 178, 150, 154, 150, 105, 105, 90, 150, 150, 90, 165, 105, 90, 80)$
17	$(6, 165, 150, 165, 150, 150, 90, 101, 150, 165, 150, 105, 165, 169, 150, 165, 20)$
18	$(9, 165, 86, 150, 90, 90, 165, 150, 105, 150, 165, 150, 105, 105, 150, 149, 150, 20)$
19	$(10, 45, 58, 90, 165, 105, 165, 150, 165, 150, 149, 165, 90, 165, 90, 105, 105, 105, 5)$
20	$(10, 150, 165, 105, 149, 165, 165, 150, 150, 89, 90, 105, 105, 165, 105, 150, 150, 165, 165, 20)$

References

1. Cattel, K., Muzio, J.C.: Synthesis of one dimensional linear hybrid cellular automata. IEEE Trans. CAD **15**, 325–335 (1996)
2. Pal Chaudhuri, P., Roy Chowdhury, D., Nandi, S., Chatterjee, S.: Additive Cellular Automata - Theory and Applications, vol. 1. IEEE Computer Society Press, Los Alamitos (1997). ISBN 0-8186-7717-1

3. Das, S., Roy Chowdhury, D.: Generating cryptographically suitable non-linear maximum length cellular automata. In: Bandini, S., Manzoni, S., Umeo, H., Vizzari, G. (eds.) ACRI 2010. LNCS, vol. 6350, pp. 241–250. Springer, Heidelberg (2010). https://doi.org/10.1007/978-3-642-15979-4_26
4. Das, S.: Theory and applications of nonlinear cellular automata in VLSI design. Ph.D. thesis, Bengal Engineering and Science University, Shibpur, India (2007)
5. Das, S., Kundu, A., Sikdar, B.K.: Nonlinear CA based design of test set generator targeting pseudo-random pattern resistant faults. In: Proceedings of Asian Test Symposium, pp. 196–201 (2004)
6. Ghosh, S., Sengupta, A., Saha, D., Chowdhury, D.R.: A scalable method for constructing non-linear cellular automata with period $2^n - 1$. In: Wąs, J., Sirakoulis, G.C., Bandini, S. (eds.) ACRI 2014. LNCS, vol. 8751, pp. 65–74. Springer, Cham (2014). https://doi.org/10.1007/978-3-319-11520-7_8
7. Wolfram, S.: Random sequence generation by cellular automata. Adv. Appl. Math **7**, 123 (1984)

Polynomial Equations over Finite, Discrete-Time Dynamical Systems

Alberto Dennunzio[1], Valentina Dorigatti[1], Enrico Formenti[2],
Luca Manzoni[1(✉)], and Antonio E. Porreca[1]

[1] Dipartimento di Informatica, Sistemistica e Comunicazione,
Università degli Studi di Milano-Bicocca, Viale Sarca 336/14, 20126 Milan, Italy
{dennunzio,luca.manzoni,porreca}@disco.unimib.it,
v.dorigatti@campus.unimib.it
[2] Universite Côte d'Azur, CNRS, I3S, Sophia Antipolis, France
enrico.formenti@unice.fr

Abstract. We introduce an algebraic approach for the analysis and composition of finite, discrete-time dynamical systems based on the category-theoretical operations of product and sum (coproduct). This allows us to define a semiring structure over the set of dynamical systems (modulo isomorphism) and, consequently, to express many decomposition problems in terms of polynomial equations. We prove that these equations are, in general, algorithmically unsolvable, but we identify a solvable subclass. Finally, we describe an implementation of the semiring operations for the case of finite cellular automata.

1 Introduction

Discrete dynamical systems are a formal tool widely used in applications to model real phenomena. Even if this formalism provides very interesting results, the overall theory is still a hot research topic. In this paper, we are going to adopt an abstraction of the formalism of (finite) discrete dynamical systems in order to provide general results which are valid for all the systems. The underlying idea is that in the abstract view one can find patterns that are simpler to study and precisely define and, in a second step, these patterns can be assembled to help studying complex particular cases. For example, consider the finite dynamical systems which are bijective. Their dynamics is represented by a graph which is made of disjoint cycles and which coincides with the graph of a permutation. Assume that from experimental data one knows that the phenomenon being modelled has a certain number of periodic orbits. Then, it is natural to wonder whether the observed system is composed of smaller parts and the overall behaviour has some variables. In our setting this translates into the formulation of an equation on dynamical systems in which the unknowns multiply the

Enrico Formenti has been partially supported by PACA APEX FRI project. Luca Manzoni was partially supported by "Premio giovani talenti 2017" of Università degli Studi di Milano-Bicocca and Accademia dei Lincei.

© Springer Nature Switzerland AG 2018
G. Mauri et al. (Eds.): ACRI 2018, LNCS 11115, pp. 298–306, 2018.
https://doi.org/10.1007/978-3-319-99813-8_27

expected patterns. Unfortunately, we prove that solving equations over dynamical systems is algorithmically infeasible in the general case, even in the case of polynomial equations (Theorem 1). However, if one of the two sides of the equations is constant, then the problem of finding the roots turns out to be in **NP** (Theorem 2). We believe it to actually be complete, and we suspect that its weaker versions are good candidates for the class of **NP**-intermediate problems. As a concrete example, we show that (finite) cellular automata are a subsemiring of the semiring **D** of (finite) discrete dynamical system and that, indeed, they are isomorphic to the whole **D**.

The paper is structured as follows. The next section introduces the formalism and basic concepts. It also provides a first example of a subsemiring (Proposition 1). Section 3 introduces the concept of equations over dynamical systems and the main results of the paper. Cellular automata and their subsemiring are introduced in Sect. 4. In the last section we draw our conclusions and provide several research directions for further developments.

2   The Semiring of Dynamical Systems

In this paper, a *(finite, discrete-time) dynamical system* is any pair (D, f) where D is a finite set of *states* and $f\colon D \to D$ is the *next-state function* which maps each state to the next one. We sometimes refer to (D, f) simply as D when the function f is implied by the context. We also allow $D = \varnothing$ as a legitimate set of states; in that case, f is necessarily the empty function.

Given a dynamical system, one can consider the graph of its dynamics $G(D, f)$ having the states D as vertices, and those edges $(x, y) \in D^2$ such that $f(x) = y$. A graph represents the dynamics of a dynamical system if and only if it is *functional*, i.e., each vertex has outdegree exactly 1; since there is a bijection between dynamical systems and functional graphs, we sometimes refer interchangeably to a dynamical system and the graph of its dynamics.

Finite dynamical systems form a category **D** [3, p. 136], where arrows $(D, f) \to (E, g)$ are given by functions $\varphi\colon D \to E$ compatible with the two dynamics: $g \circ \varphi = \varphi \circ f$. This category has an initial object **0** (the empty dynamical system) and terminal objects **1** (any single-state dynamical system with the identity function). Furthermore, this category has products:

$$(D, f) \times (E, g) = (D \times E, f \times g) \qquad \text{where } (f \times g)(d, e) = (f(d), g(e))$$

which corresponds to the tensor product of the graphs of the dynamics, and coproducts (or sums):

$$(D, f) + (E, g) = (D \sqcup E, f + g) \quad \text{where } (f + g)(x) = \begin{cases} f(x) & \text{if } x \in D \\ g(x) & \text{if } x \in E \end{cases}$$

which corresponds to the disjoint union of the graphs of the dynamics.

The product $D \times E$ defined above consists in the parallel, synchronous execution of the two dynamical systems D and E. The sum $D + E$ is the mutually exclusive alternative between the behaviour of D and the behaviour of E; the resulting dynamical system behaves as one of the two terms, depending on its initial state.

In this paper we are only interested in the dynamics of dynamical systems, irrespective of the precise nature of their states and their next-state functions. In other words, we consider dynamical systems having isomorphic graphs of their dynamics as identical. With this convention, the objects of the category D of finite dynamical systems are a countable set rather than a proper class, and the operations of sum (coproduct) and product give it a *commutative semiring* structure *with zero and identity* [2]. Indeed, as can be easily checked from the definitions above:

- $(D, +)$ is a commutative monoid with neutral element $\mathbf{0}$,
- $(D, \times)$ is a commutative monoid with neutral element $\mathbf{1}$,
- products distribute over sums: $x \times (y + z) = x \times y + x \times z$.

Notice that this semiring is not a ring, since no element (besides the trivial case of $\mathbf{0}$) possesses an additive inverse; furthermore, the only element invertible with respect to the product is trivially $\mathbf{1}$. This follows immediately from the fact that sum and product are monotonic with respect to the sizes of the dynamical systems. On the other hand, this same property guarantees us that D is an integral semiring, *i.e.*, there are no zero divisors.

While the graphs of the dynamics of the sum of two dynamical systems simply consist of the juxtaposition of the graphs of the two terms, the product generates more interesting results, as shown in Fig. 1. Just by looking at the Cayley table of the monoid $(D, \times)$, we can already observe that the semiring D does not possess unique factorisations. Indeed, we have

$$\begin{matrix} \circ \\ \bullet \end{matrix} \times \begin{matrix} \bullet \rightarrow \bullet \end{matrix} = \left(\begin{matrix} \bullet \rightarrow \bullet \end{matrix} \right)^2$$

and both $\begin{matrix} \circ \\ \bullet \end{matrix}$ and $\begin{matrix} \bullet \rightarrow \bullet \end{matrix}$ are irreducible (any nontrivial factorisation would otherwise appear, due to its size, in the Cayley table of Fig. 1).

Another interesting property of D is that it contains the semiring of the natural numbers, which is initial in the category of commutative semirings.

Proposition 1. *The semiring D contains a subsemiring N isomorphic to the natural numbers.*

Proof. For each $n \in \mathbb{N}$, let $\varphi(n) \in D$ be the dynamical system consisting of exactly n fixed points (*i.e.*, the identity function over a set of n points), and let $N = \varphi(\mathbb{N})$. Clearly N contains both $\mathbf{0} = \varphi(0)$ and $\mathbf{1} = \varphi(1)$. Given $\varphi(m), \varphi(n) \in N$ we have $\varphi(m) + \varphi(n) = \varphi(m+n) \in N$ and $\varphi(m) \times \varphi(n) = \varphi(n \times m) \in N$. Finally, we have $\varphi(m) = \varphi(n)$ if and only if $m = n$. This means that φ is a semiring monomorphism, and that its image N is a subsemiring of D isomorphic to $\mathbb{N}$. □

Due to Proposition 1, in the following we will denote the subsemiring N of D simply by $\mathbb{N}$.

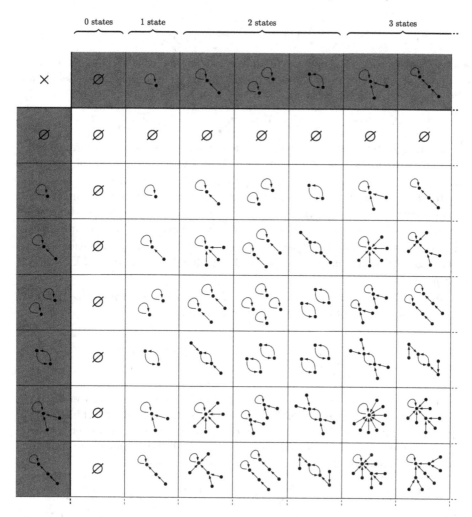

Fig. 1. A portion of the Cayley table of the commutative monoid $(\mathbf{D}, \times)$, including products of all dynamical systems with 0, 1, and 2 states, as well as some dynamical systems with 3 states, in increasing order of size (and arbitrary order among those with the same size).

3 Polynomial Equations

Having equipped the dynamical systems $\mathbf{D}$ with a semiring algebraic structure allows us to formulate a number of problems in terms of polynomial equations. Recall that the polynomials over a commutative semiring are themselves a commutative semiring; in our case, we deal with polynomials over several variables $\mathbf{D}[X_1, \ldots, X_k]$.

One basic problem is to analyse a given dynamical system D in terms of smaller, simpler components. For instance, a solution to an equation of the form

$$\bigcirc X + Y^2 = \bigcirc Z + \bigcirc$$

allows us to express the (parametric) behaviour on the right-hand side in terms of a possibly different set of components combined as described on the left-hand side. One possible solution is

$$X = \qquad\qquad Y = \qquad\qquad Z = \bigcirc$$

In a ring R, by moving all terms on the left-hand side, any polynomial equation can be expressed as $p(\vec{X}) = 0$ with $\vec{X} = (X_1, \ldots, X_k)$ a set of variables and $p \in R[\vec{X}]$ a polynomial. In a proper semiring this is generally impossible, due to the lack of additive inverses; in our case, due to the above-mentioned monotonicity of $+$ and $\times$ with respect to the sizes of dynamical systems, the equations of the form $p(\vec{X}) = \mathbf{0}$ are actually trivial, as they only admit the solution $\vec{X} = \vec{0}$ when the constant term of p is null, and no solution otherwise. A general polynomial equation in $\mathbf{D}$ will then have the form $p(\vec{X}) = q(\vec{X})$ with $p, q \in \mathbf{D}[\vec{X}]$.

Given a set of variables $\vec{X} = (X_1, \ldots, X_k)$, a polynomial $p \in \mathbf{D}[\vec{X}]$, where the maximum degree of each variable is d, can be denoted by

$$p = \sum_{\vec{i} \in [0,d]^k} a_{\vec{i}} \vec{X}^{\vec{i}} \qquad\qquad \text{with } \vec{X}^{\vec{i}} = \prod_{j=1}^{k} X_j^{i_j}$$

Unfortunately, the algorithmic solution of polynomial equations over $\mathbf{D}$ turns out to be impossible by reduction from Hilbert's tenth problem [4]. This is not an immediate corollary of Proposition 1, since a polynomial equation over $\mathbb{N}$ might admit non-natural solutions in the larger semiring $\mathbf{D}$ of dynamical systems[1]; for instance, the equation $2X^2 = 3Y$ has the non-natural solution

$$X = \bigcirc \qquad Y = 2\bigcirc \qquad \text{since} \left(\bigcirc\right)^2 = 3\bigcirc$$

However, this equation obviously also has the natural solution $X = 3, Y = 6$ (uncoincidentally, these are the sizes of the dynamical systems of the previous solution). As we are going to show, this is actually a general property of equations over $\mathbb{N}$: by moving to the larger semiring $\mathbf{D}$ we might be able to find extra solutions, but only if there already exists a natural one.

Given a dynamical system $D \in \mathbf{D}$, let $|D|$ denote the size of its set of states.

Lemma 1. *The function* $|\cdot| : \mathbf{D} \to \mathbb{N}$ *is a semiring homomorphism.*

Proof. Clearly $|\mathbf{0}| = 0$ and $|\mathbf{1}| = 1$. Since sums and products in $\mathbf{D}$ respectively involve the disjoint union and the Cartesian product of the sets of states, we have $|D_1 + D_2| = |D_1| + |D_2|$ and $|D_1 \times D_2| = |D_1| \times |D_2|$. $\qquad\square$

---

[1] While the existence of integer roots of a polynomial in $\mathbb{Z}[X]$ is undecidable, the existence of roots in the larger ring of real numbers is decidable, and the problem becomes even trivial for complex roots (due to the fundamental theorem of algebra).

Lemma 2. *Let $\vec{X} = (X_1, \ldots, X_k)$ be variables, let $p, q \in \mathbb{N}[\vec{X}]$ be polynomials, and suppose that $p(\vec{D}) = q(\vec{D})$ for some $\vec{D} \in \mathbf{D}^k$. Then, there exists $\vec{n} \in \mathbb{N}^k$ such that $p(\vec{n}) = q(\vec{n})$.*

Proof. Let $\vec{D} = (D_1, \ldots, D_k) \in \mathbf{D}^k$ and suppose

$$p = \sum_{\vec{i} \in [0,d]^k} a_{\vec{i}} \vec{X}^{\vec{i}} \qquad\qquad q = \sum_{\vec{i} \in [0,d]^k} b_{\vec{i}} \vec{X}^{\vec{i}}$$

Since $p(\vec{D}) = q(\vec{D})$, we also have $|p(\vec{D})| = |q(\vec{D})|$, and since $|\cdot|$ is a semiring homomorphism (Lemma 1), this means that

$$\sum_{\vec{i} \in [0,d]^k} a_{\vec{i}} |\vec{D}^{\vec{i}}| = \sum_{\vec{i} \in [0,d]^k} b_{\vec{i}} |\vec{D}^{\vec{i}}| \qquad \text{with } |\vec{D}^{\vec{i}}| = \prod_{j=1}^{k} |D_j|^{i_j}$$

or, in other words, that $p(|\vec{D}|) = q(|\vec{D}|)$, where $|\vec{D}| = (|D_1|, \ldots, |D_k|)$. By letting $\vec{n} = |\vec{D}|$, the thesis follows. □

Since, by Proposition 1, every natural solution to a polynomial equation over $\mathbb{N}$ is also a dynamical system, we obtain that each equation over $\mathbb{N}$ has a solution in $\mathbf{D}$ if and only if it has a solution in $\mathbb{N}$. The latter is a variant of Hilbert's tenth problem [4], proving our problem also algorithmically unsolvable.

Theorem 1. *The problem of deciding whether a general polynomial equation over $\mathbf{D}$ admits a solution (and, by implication, finding one such solution when it is the case) is undecidable.* □

Remark 1. Notice that, although polynomial equations over $\mathbb{N}$ with solutions in $\mathbf{D}$ always admit a natural solution, this is not always the case for equations with more general coefficients; for instance

$$X^2 = Y + \left(\begin{array}{c} \bullet \\ \bullet \end{array}\right) \qquad \text{has the solution } X = \left(\begin{array}{c} \bullet \\ \bullet \end{array}\right), Y = 2\left(\begin{array}{c} \bullet \\ \bullet \end{array}\right)$$

but cannot have a solution with natural X, since X^2 would also be natural, while the right-hand side of the equation is never natural.

The equations become algorithmically solvable if one side is a constant, *i.e.*, if the equation has the form $p(\vec{X}) = D$ with $p \in \mathbf{D}[\vec{X}]$ and $D \in \mathbf{D}$. Indeed, in that case the size $|D|$ of the right-hand side of the equation allows us to perform a bounded search: due to the monotonicity of $+$ and $\times$ with respect to the sizes of the dynamical system, each dynamical system of an assignment to $\vec{X}$ satisfying the equation (excluding any redundant variables which only appear with coefficient 0) has size at most $|D|$.

Assuming that the coefficients of the polynomials are given in input as explicit graphs, the value of each variable can be guessed in polynomial time by a non-deterministic Turing machine; the solution can then be checked by evaluating the polynomial on the left-hand side, with the caveat that we must halt and reject as soon as the partial result becomes larger than the right-hand side (this avoids a potentially exponential increase of the evaluated graph due to a polynomial of large degree). Finally, we need to check whether the evaluated left-hand side and the right-hand side of the equation are isomorphic, which can easily be performed by guessing an isomorphism between the two graphs. We can therefore conclude that

Theorem 2. *The problem of finding solutions of polynomial equations over* **D** *with a constant side is in* **NP**.

4   The Semiring of Cellular Automata

When dealing with a semiring, one interesting problem to tackle in order to understand its structure is to find its subsemirings. In the case of the semiring **D** specifically, it is also important to establish whether specific kinds of dynamical systems correspond to subsemirings or other subsets, such as ideals.

Let us consider finite, one-dimensional cellular automata (A, n, r, λ), where A is the alphabet of states, n the number of cells, r the radius and $\lambda \colon A^{2r+1} \to A$ the local rule; we also assume cyclic boundary conditions for simplicity.

The additive identity **0** of **D** has the empty graph as its dynamics; in terms of cellular automata this corresponds to length-0 automata. Notice that this is actually an equivalence class of automata, since any choice of A, r and λ generates this dynamics whenever $n = 0$.

The multiplicative identity **1** of **D** has a dynamics consisting of a single fixed point. This dynamics is generated exactly by the cellular automata having $|A| = 1$, *i.e.*, exactly one state a, with any length n and radius r, and with the constant local rule $\lambda(a, \dots, a) = a$.

Given two cellular automata $(A_1, n_1, r_1, \lambda_1)$ and $(A_2, n_2, r_2, \lambda_2)$ with global rule Λ_1 and Λ_2 respectively, their sum can be constructed as an automaton $(A_3, n_3, r_3, \lambda_3)$ with alphabet $A_3 = A_1^{n_1} \sqcup A_2^{n_2}$, i.e., the disjoint union of the global configurations of the two automata, length $n = 1$, radius $r = 0$ and local rule $\lambda_3 \colon A_3^1 \to A_3$ defined by

$$\lambda_3(c) = \begin{cases} \Lambda_1(c) & \text{if } c \in A_1^{n_1} \\ \Lambda_2(c) & \text{if } c \in A_2^{n_2} \end{cases}$$

Since $n = 1$, the local rule λ_3 is, in fact, identical to the global rule Λ_3, and this easily allows us to see that the dynamics of this automaton is the disjoint union of the dynamics of the terms of the sum, as required.

A configuration of the product of two cellular automata $(A_1, n_1, r_1, \lambda_1)$ and $(A_2, n_2, r_2, \lambda_2)$ is obtained by "laying side-by-side" the configurations of the two automata and grouping the cells together in order to obtain rectangular macro-cells:

The length of the product automaton is $n_3 = \gcd(n_1, n_2)$, with macro-cells consisting of $c_1 = n_1/n_3$ cells of the first automaton and $c_2 = n_2/n_3$ cells of the second; its alphabet is thus $A_3 = A_1^{n_1/n_3} \times A_2^{n_2/n_3}$. The radius can be computed by including the minimal number of macro-cells that suffices in order to include the neighbourhoods of the cells of the two automata being multiplied, as depicted in Fig. 2. A neighbourhood of the first automaton is contained within a radius of $\lceil r_1/c_1 \rceil = \lceil \frac{r_1 n_3}{n_1} \rceil$ macro-cells, and a neighbourhood of the second within a radius of $\lceil r_2/c_2 \rceil = \lceil \frac{r_1 n_3}{n_2} \rceil$; by taking the maximum, in order to account for both original automata, we obtain

$$r_3 = \max \left(\left\lceil \frac{r_1 n_3}{n_1} \right\rceil, \left\lceil \frac{r_1 n_3}{n_2} \right\rceil \right) = \left\lceil \gcd(n_1, n_2) \times \max \left(\frac{r_1}{n_1}, \frac{r_2}{n_2} \right) \right\rceil.$$

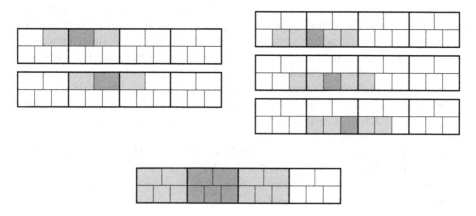

Fig. 2. If the two automata being multiplied have radius $r_1 = 1$ and $r_2 = 2$, respectively, then computing the next state of the dark grey micro-cell in the first (resp., second) row requires the states of the neighbouring cells in light grey, as shown in the top left (resp., top right) diagram. These are entirely contained in a neighbourhood of macro-cells of radius $r_3 = 1$ in the product automaton (bottom diagram).

Since finite cellular automata can generate the dynamics of the identity elements **0** and **1**, and are closed under sum and product, they constitute a sub-semiring of **D**. Notice that, since any finite dynamical system (D, f) can be implemented as a length-1, radius-0 cellular automaton over the alphabet D, this semiring actually coincides with the whole semiring **D**.

5   Conclusions

In this paper, we have presented a new abstract way of reasoning about finite discrete dynamical systems which is inspired by category theory. Introducing the natural operations of addition and multiplication over dynamical systems provides an algebraic structure of semiring to the set of dynamical systems. This allowed to introduce classical formalisms for semirings like polynomials and lead to polynomial equations. We stress the importance of polynomial equations as a tool for the analysis of the dynamics of a system. Indeed, their solutions (if any) provide useful decompositions to further analyse the overall behaviour of the system.

Although solving general polynomial equations is algorithmically impracticable (see Theorem 1), the same problem turn out to be in **NP** in the case of polynomial equations in which the right-hand side is constant (see Theorem 2). Of course, this might still prove infeasible (if the problem turns out to be **NP**-complete, as expected) but it has the merit of being decidable. However, remark that, the proof of Theorem 2 essentially consists of two parts: guessing potential candidates and then checking if the two members of the equation are isomorphic. Now, consider the subsemiring **B** of **D** made by the dynamical systems which have a bijective next-state function. These systems are indeed permutations and for them the graph isomorphism problem can be solved in polynomial time (see [1]). It is therefore natural to ask for a polynomial time algorithm for this subsemiring. This subsemiring might be a good candidate for targeting polynomial time solving algorithms.

Another research direction naturally arises along the same line of thoughts. It consists in finding more significant subsemirings and their practical implications.

The exploration of polynomial equations in the general case has just started and most of the questions are still open. For example, can the number of solutions to a polynomial equation be tightly bounded? Is there any interesting decomposition theorem into irreducibles? What is precisely the role played by irreducibles *w.r.t.* the dynamical behaviour? Are they just a base for the limit set or can we extract more information?

References

1. Colbourn, C.J.: On testing isomorphism of permutation graphs. Networks **11**(1), 13–21 (1981)
2. Hebisch, U., Weinert, H.J.: Semirings: Algebraic Theory and Applications in Computer Science. World Scientific, Singapore (1998)
3. Lawvere, F.W., Schanuel, S.H.: Conceptual Mathematics: A First Introduction to Categories, 2nd edn. Cambridge University Press, Cambridge (2009)
4. Matiyasevich, Y.: Hilbert's Tenth Problem. MIT Press, Cambridge (1993)

The Representation Role for Basic Operations Embodied in Cellular Automata: A Suitability Example for Addition in Redundant Numeral Systems vs Conventional Ones

Salvatore Di Gregorio[1,2(✉)]

[1] Department of Mathematics and Computer Science,
University of Calabria, 87036 Rende, CS, Italy
`salvatore.digregorio@unical.it`
[2] ISAC - CNR, Lamezia Terme Zona Industriale, 88046 Lamezia Terme, CZ, Italy

Abstract. Cellular Automata (CA) are both a parallel computational paradigm and an archetype for modelling complex systems, that evolve on the basis of local interactions. CA can embody different numeral representations and perform related basic arithmetical operations. However, conventional numeral representations are thought as intrinsically sequential in such operations, which implies that CA parallelism is underexploited when CA evolution mimics the sequentiality of calculation, while some redundant numeral representations could exalt the CA parallelism in a space/time trade-off, where the time complexity of some operations is constant on input length. The problem then arises when the result of an operation must be utilized in the conventional representation since, usually, the migration toward an advantageous redundant numeric representation is costless, but the inverse one implies necessarily a cost that cancels the benefits in terms of computation time. This paper explores the properties of the conventional binary positional representation embodied in a CA together with the addition operation and the corresponding ones of a redundant binary positional representation, the rules and time cost for the passage from conventional numeral system to redundant one and vice versa. The results permit to individuate the CA computation context, when redundancy could be exploited advantageously. It regards cases where a longest sequence of additions (or operations based on addition, e.g., fast Fourier transforms) has to be performed in well-defined short times as for the automatic control of mobile devices.

Keywords: Cellular Automata
Non-conventional positional numeral binary systems · Addition

1 Introduction

Cellular Automata (CA) were born with a paradox: von Neumann [1] embodied in a cellular space of finite states automata a modified Turing Machine in

© Springer Nature Switzerland AG 2018
G. Mauri et al. (Eds.): ACRI 2018, LNCS 11115, pp. 307–318, 2018.
https://doi.org/10.1007/978-3-319-99813-8_28

order to guarantee universal computation in the self-reproduction mechanisms. In such a way, a purely parallel computing device supports a purely sequential computation. CA are both a parallel computational paradigm and an archetype for modelling 'systems', that are extended in space and evolve on the basis of local interactions [2]. Using CA is suitable in such a type of context, even if a substantially sequential computational behavior could be easily hidden in many cases.

This question reveals distinctly itself for the case of the same numerical operations performed inside CA in numeral systems, that are related to the same set of numbers, but differ in their representation. Here another factor, the representation, comes into play, but the question cannot simply be treated in terms of time cost efficiency because in solving a particular problem, a type of representation could be mandatory for expressing solutions and/or the input data could be available only in a specific representation. Therefore it is necessary to investigate efficient translation methods in order to communicate between two or more worlds with different representations, but with the same basic operations. If we look at the single operation, e.g. the addition for the conventional vs redundant numeral systems, it is important to know if there is advantage in passing from a representation to another and returning to the previous one.

Nevertheless a criterion of computational cost effectiveness for a specific problem may be defined only if we consider the algorithmic features of the problem in terms of sequence of basic operations in the context of possible diverse representations and the eventual computational costs for passages from a representation to another one and vice versa. So the question does not regard the single operation but a specific problem, all having to be related for homogeneity to a single computational paradigm, that are in our case CA, where sequentiality can coexist with the structure parallelism.

In this paper, we consider the conventional binary representations vs a possible corresponding redundant binary representation for the addition operation on the set of natural numbers $\mathbb{N}$ and their implementation inside CA, furthermore opportune operations are evaluated in the same context for passing from a one representation to the other and vice versa.

The CA approach to 'fast' addition of binary numbers of Sheth et al. [3] is revisited as reference point for conventional representation of $\mathbb{N}$. This operation of binary addition was implemented on a Cellular Automata Machine (CAM-8 machine) [4]. A corresponding redundant representation, that is here presented together with the related addition operation, was studied and developed for basic arithmetic operations of integer numbers at the University of Calabria in some 'Laurea' theses and reports, e.g. [6], a similar representation for the set of integer numbers $\mathbb{Z}$ was adopted for addition implementation on the same CAM-8 by Clementi et al. in [5]. Mechanisms of translation between conventional and redundant representation of $\mathbb{N}$ on CA is investigated. Hardware implementations as in [7,8] are not here considered, but they can be deduced straightforwardly in manifold ways, FPGA integrated circuits, e.g. [9], could be more significant for using CA redundant arithmetic also in broader contexts. Anyway, the aim of this paper is a comparison between CA embodying two different numeral representations and efficient passage mechanisms from one to other and vice versa.

A CA performing the addition operations in the conventional binary representation for $\mathbb{N}$ (CBN) is presented in the next section, the third section introduces a CA, that performs addition operations in a redundant binary representation for $\mathbb{N}$ (RBN), RBN properties are defined, rules of passage between CBN CA and RBN CA are established. Conclusions and comments end the paper.

2   CA for Addition in the Conventional Binary Representation

Intuitively a homogeneous CA can be seen as a d-dimensional space, partitioned in cells of uniform size, each one embedding an identical finite states automaton, the elementary automaton (ea).

Input for each cell is given by the states of the neighboring cells, where the neighborhood conditions are determined by a pattern invariant in time and space.

At the time (step) $t = 0$, cells are in arbitrary states and the CA evolves changing the state at discrete times simultaneously, according to the transition function $\tau : S^r \rightarrow S$, where S is the finite set of the ea states and r is the number of the neighboring cells.

The following definition (partly from Di Gregorio and Trautteur [10]) for CA is adopted in this paper:

Definition 1. *A Cellular Automaton A is a quadruple* $A = \langle \mathbb{Z}^d, X, S, \tau \rangle$ *where:*

- $\mathbb{Z}^d$ *is the set of cells identified by points with integer co-ordinates in a Euclidean d-dimensions space; such a formal definition may be extended to different types of spaces (e.g., Riemannian spaces), different topologies (e.g., torus in 2-dimensions spaces), or different tessellations (e.g., hexagonal tessellation for 2-dimensions;*
- $X = \langle \xi_0, \xi_1, \ldots \xi_{r-1} \rangle$ *with* $\#X = r$ *is the neighborhood index, that is the ordered finite set of d-dimensional vectors, that defines for a generic cell* $i = \langle i_1, i_2, \ldots, i_d \rangle$ *the set* $N(X, i) = \langle i + \xi_0, i + \xi_1, \ldots, i + \xi_{r-1} \rangle$ *of the neighboring cells (usually* ξ_0 *is the null vector);*
- S *is the finite set of states of the elementary automaton. A specification of* S *as Cartesian product of sets of sub-states:* $S = S_1 \times S_2 \times \ldots \times S_s$ *is introduced.*
- $\tau : S^r \rightarrow S$ *is the deterministic transition function of the elementary automaton;*

furthermore:

- $C = \{c \, | \, c : \mathbb{Z}^d \rightarrow S\}$ *is the set of possible state assignment to the CA; it is called the CA configuration set;* $c(i)$ *is the state of the cell* i;
- $\gamma : C \rightarrow C \mapsto [\gamma(c)](i) = \tau(c(N(X, i)))$ *for* $c \in C$, *is the global transition function. A configuration* c *is stable if* $\gamma(c) = c$.

The following two CA embody the addends as sequence of sub-states in the configurations. So numbers may be so individuated and 'writing' and 'reading' for passage from one numeral representation to another one can be specified.

2.1 CA ADD Definition and Properties

A possible CA ADD for addition of two natural numbers m and n in the conventional binary representation CBN is here defined as a 1-dimension CA with ring topology of l cells with $l > max(\lceil \log_2 m \rceil), (\lceil \log_2 n \rceil)$:

Definition 2. $ADD = (Z_l, X, S, \tau)$ where:

- $Z_l = \langle l - 1, l - 2, \cdots, 1, 0 \rangle$ is the finite cellular space of length l with ring topology and reverse numeration of cells by formalization convenience;
- $X = \langle 0, -1 \rangle$ is the neighborhood: the cell itself and the 'right' one;
- $S = S_1 \times S_2$, the set of states with $S_1 = S_2 = 0, 1$, the four states are represented as $\{{0 \atop 0}, {0 \atop 1}, {1 \atop 0}, {1 \atop 1}\}$ where, for a configuration c, the former (upper) bit in the cell i is the ith bit of the former addend m specified as m_i and the latter (lower) bit in the cell i is the ith bit of the latter addend n specified as n_i, both with positional weight 2^i; m and n are respectively the upper and the lower addends of c (see Fig. 1).
- $\tau : S^2 \to S$ is the transition function so defined from the following equations, where two configurations c' and c'' are considered such that $c'' = \gamma(c')$:
  1. $m_i'' = m_{i-1}' \wedge n_{i-1}'$, $0 < i < l$; $m_0'' = m_{l-1}' \wedge n_{l-1}'$ by the ring topology;
  2. $n_i'' = m_i' \oplus n_i'$, $0 \le i < l$;

  being m' and n' respectively the former and latter addend of c', m'' and n'' respectively the upper and lower addend of c'', where m_i'' is the carry bit with positional weight 2^i of the sum $m_{i-1}' + n_{i-1}'$; n_i'' is the 'lesser' bit with positional weight 2^i of the sum $m_i' + n_i'$.

m (25)	$\to$	0	0	0	1	1	0	0	1
n (15)	$\to$	0	0	0	0	1	1	1	1
Positional weight	$\to$	2^7	2^6	2^5	2^4	2^3	2^2	2^1	2^0

Fig. 1. An example of ADD configuration c (highlighted) with $l = 8$; the upper sequence of bits is the former addend m, the lower sequence is the latter addend n; the positional weight of each cell is specified below, values in base 10 of m and n are on the left in brackets.

The ring topology of ADD (therefore a finite number of cells) involves that additions are performed properly, only if there is no overflow, i.e., significant length of numbers doesn't overcome $l - 1$ bits, because the last cell is neighbor to the first one; l may be large at will, so a sufficient length of bits may be always assumed (sufficient length condition). The ADD configuration example of Fig. 1 specifies the positional weight of the cells and values of m and n in the base 10 numeration.

Theorem 1. *Let c be a generic configuration of ADD with length l and m, n respectively the upper and lower addend of c; let $c' = \gamma(c)$, m' and n' respectively the former and latter addend of c', then $m' + n' = m + n$ (examples in Fig. 2).*

Proof. $m_{l-1} = 0$, $n_{l-1} = 0$ by the sufficient length condition, therefore $m'_0 = 0$, $n'_{l-1} = 0$ then:

$$m + n = \sum_{i=0}^{l-1} (m_i + n_i)2^i = m'_0 2^0 + \sum_{i=0}^{l-2} (m'_{i+1}2^{i+1} + n'_i 2^i) + n'_{l-1}2^{l-1}$$

$$= \sum_{i=0}^{l-1} (m'_i + n'_i)2^i = m' + n'$$

□

Theorem 2. *Let c be a configuration of ADD with m and n respectively the upper and lower addend of c; let $c' = \gamma(c)$ and m' and n' respectively the upper and lower addend of c', if $m_i = 0$ for $0 \leq i < k < l - 1$ then $m'_j = 0$ for $0 \leq j \leq k$.*

Proof. $m_{l-1} = 0$, $n_{l-1} = 0$ by the sufficient length condition, therefore it is always $m'_0 = 0$ and $m'_i = m_{i-1} \wedge n_{i-1} = 0$ for $1 \leq i \leq k$ by applying Eq. (1) of the τ specification of ADD. □

Corollary 1. *Let c be a configuration of ADD, $c' = \gamma(c)$ and $c'' = \gamma^{l-1}(c)$, with m, n, m', n', m'', n'', respectively the upper and lower addend of c, c' and c'', then always $m = 0$.*

Proof. $m_{l-1} = 0$, $n_{l-1} = 0$ by the sufficient length condition, therefore always $m_0' = 0$, then $m'' = 0$ by Theorem 2. □

Theorem 3. *Let c be a configuration of ADD with $m = 0$ and n respectively the upper and lower addend of c; let $c' = \gamma(c)$ and m' and n' respectively the upper and lower addend of c', $c' = c$ and c is a stable configuration (see example in Fig. 2).*

Proof. $m'_0 = m_{l-1} \wedge n_{l-1} = 0 \wedge n_{l-1} = 0$, $m'_i = m_{i-1} \wedge n_{i-1} = 0 \wedge n_{i-1} = 0$ for $1 \leq i \leq l-1$, by applying Eq. 1 of the τ specification of ADD; by applying Eq. 2 of the τ specification of ADD, $n_i' = m_i \oplus n_i = 0 \oplus n_i = n_i$ for $0 \leq i \leq l - 1$. □

Corollary 2. *Let c be a generic configuration of ADD of length l with m and n respectively the upper and lower addend of c, $c' = \gamma^{l-1}(c)$, with m', n', respectively the upper and lower addend of c', then it is always $m' = 0$ and $n' = m+n$ after $l - 1$ steps (see Fig. 2).*

Proof. $m' = 0$ from Corollary 2, $m + n = m' + n'$ from Theorem 1, therefore $n' = m + n$.   □

The addition is performed by ADD in $l - 1$ steps in the worst case, therefore the time cost is $\mathcal{O}(l)$. An example of ADD evolution with length $l = 8$ is presented in Fig. 2, where the stable configuration is obtained after 4 steps.

ADD parallelism speeds up addition in irregular way, it depends on how short is the longest sequence of consecutive carries 1 in the conventional arithmetic operation of addition.

An extension of ADD for integers according to the two complement representation could be developed in several ways; the most intuitive way is breaking the ring between cells 0 and $l - 1$ (cell $l - 1$ assumes a positional weight of -2^{l-1}) and considering that the state of the -1 neighbor of cell 0 (now such a neighbor no longer exists) is always acquired as $^0_0$. The operability holds for integers in the interval $[-2^{l-1}, 2^{l-1}]$.

Positional weight	→	2^7	2^6	2^5	2^4	2^3	2^2	2^1	2^0
m (25)		0	0	0	1	1	0	0	1
n (15)		0	0	0	0	1	1	1	1
	t=0								
m (18)		0	0	0	1	0	0	1	0
n (22)		0	0	0	1	0	1	1	0
	t=1								
m (36)		0	0	1	0	0	1	0	0
n (4)		0	0	0	0	0	1	0	0
	t=2								
m (8)		0	0	0	0	1	0	0	0
n (32)		0	0	1	0	0	0	0	0
	t=3								
m (0)		0	0	0	0	0	0	0	0
n (40)		0	0	1	0	1	0	0	0
	t=4								
m (0)		0	0	0	0	0	0	0	0
n (40)		0	0	1	0	1	0	0	0
	t=5								

Fig. 2. Evolution example of ADD with length 8 for 5 steps (t). Configurations are highlighted, the upper sequence of bit is the former addend m, the lower one is the latter addend n, their values in base 10 are on the left in brackets; the cell positional weight is specified on top.

3 CA for Addition in a Redundant Binary Representation

3.1 The Redundant Binary Representation RBN for $\mathbb{N}$

The proposed redundant binary representation RBN is very similar to those presented in [5,6]; it differs from CBN because the same positional weight is assigned to a couple of consecutive bits, this involves that there are more sequences of bits for the same value (except 0).

Definition 3. *RBN associates to a sequence of 2l bits: $b_{2l-1}, b_{2l-2}, \ldots, b_0$, the value:*

$$b = \sum_{i=0}^{2l-1} b_i 2^{\lfloor \frac{i}{2} \rfloor}$$

Examples:

- 1001 in RBN gives $1 \cdot 2^{\lfloor 3/2 \rfloor} + 0 \cdot 2^{\lfloor 2/2 \rfloor} + 0 \cdot 2^{\lfloor 1/2 \rfloor} + 1 \cdot 2^{\lfloor 0/2 \rfloor} = 3$
- 110 in RBN gives $1 \cdot 2^{\lfloor 2/2 \rfloor} + 1 \cdot 2^{\lfloor 1/2 \rfloor} + 0 \cdot 2^{\lfloor 0/2 \rfloor} = 3$

Definition 4. *A string of bits representing in RBN a natural number n is called canonical form $\alpha(\beta)$ of n if each even (odd) bit is 0.*

By the previous definition, if even (odd) 0 digits are removed from a canonical form $\alpha(\beta)$ of RBN, a binary string is obtained with the same value in CBN; if we put the 0 digit at the right (at the left) of each digit of a binary string representing a numerical value in CBN, a canonical form $\alpha(\beta)$ is obtained with the same value in RBN, an example is here given for $n = 13$:

$$\begin{array}{ccccc} 10100010 & \leftarrow & 1101 & \rightarrow & 01010001 \\ \text{RBN canonical form } \alpha & \leftarrow & \text{CBN} & \rightarrow & \text{RBN canonical form } \beta \end{array}$$

The passage from a canonical form $\alpha(\beta)$ of RBN to CBN and vice versa may be considered costless in the prospective of CA, as specified afterwards.

From now on, the length of strings of bits in RBN will be always taken even without loss of generality, the canonical form α is abbreviated in cfα.

3.2 CA ADDr Definition and Properties

A CA ADDr for addition of two natural numbers m and n in RBN is here defined as a 1-dimension CA of l cells with ring topology and $l > max(\lceil \log_2 m \rceil), (\lceil \log_2 n \rceil)$

Definition 5. $ADDr = (Z_l, X, S, \tau)$ *where:*

- $Z_l = \langle l-1, l-2, \cdots, 1, 0 \rangle$ *is the finite cellular space of length l with ring topology and reverse numeration of cells by formalization convenience;*
- $X = \langle 0, -1 \rangle$ *is the neighborhood: the cell itself and the 'right' one;*

- $S = \{ \begin{smallmatrix} 00 & 00 & 01 & 01 & 00 & 00 & 01 & 01 & 10 & 10 & 11 & 11 & 10 & 10 & 11 & 11 \\ 00 & 01 & 00 & 01 & 10 & 11 & 10 & 11 & 00 & 01 & 00 & 01 & 10 & 11 & 10 & 11 \end{smallmatrix} \}$ *is the set of states,*
  ($S = S_1 \times S_2$, with $S_1 = S_2 = \{00, 01, 10, 11\}$ the 4 couples of bits); the former
  (upper) couple of bits in the cell i are respectively the $(2i+1)^{th}$ and the $2i^{th}$
  bit of the former (upper) addend m and are specified as m_{2i+1}, m_{2i}, the latter
  (lower) couple of bits in the cell i are respectively the $(2i+1)^{th}$ and the $2i^{th}$
  bit of the latter addend n and are specified as n_{2i+1}, n_{2i}, all with positional
  weight 2^i (see Fig. 3).
- $\tau : S^2 \to S$ *is the transition function so defined from the following equations,*
  where two configurations c' and c'' are considered such that $c'' = \gamma(c')$:

1. $m''_{2i} = 0$, $0 \le i < l$;
2. $m''_{2i+1} = m'_{2i}$, $0 \le i < l$;
3. $n''_{2i} = (m'_{2i-1} \wedge n_{2i-1}{}') \vee (m'_{2i-1} \wedge n'_{2i-2}) \vee (n'_{2i-1} \wedge n'_{2i-2})$, $0 < i < l$;
   $n''_0 = (m'_{2l-1} \wedge n'_{2l-1}) \vee (m'_{2l-1} \wedge n'_{2l-2}) \vee (n'_{2l-1} \wedge n'_{2l-2})$
4. $n''_{2i+1} = m'_{2i+1} \oplus n'_{2i+1} \oplus n'_{2i}$, $0 \le i < l$;

m' and n' are respectively the former and latter addend of a configuration c',
m'' and n'' are respectively the former and latter addend of c'' where n''_{2i} is the
carry bit with positional weight 2^i of $m'_{2i-1} + n'_{2i-1} + n'_{2i-2}$; n''_{2i-1} is the 'lesser'
bit with positional weight 2^i of $m'_{2i+1} + n'_{2i} + n'_{2i+1}$ (see Fig. 4).

The ring topology of ADDr (therefore a finite number of cells) involves that
additions are performed properly, only if there is no overflow, i.e., significant
length of numbers doesn't overcome $l-1$ bits, because the last cell is the neighbor
to the first one; l may be large at will, so a sufficient length of cells may be always
assumed (sufficient length condition).

Theorem 4. *Let c' be a generic configuration of ADD with length l and m',*
n' respectively the upper and lower addend of c'; let $c'' = \gamma(c')$ and m'' and n''
respectively the upper and lower addend of c'', then $m' + n' = m'' + n''$ (see
Fig. 4).

Proof. $m'_{2l-1} = 0$, $n'_{2l-1} = 0$, $m'_{2l-2} = 0$, $n'_{2l-21} = 0$ by the sufficient length
condition. Therefore $m''_0 = 0$, $n''_{2l-1} = 0$, $m''_{2i} = 0$ for $0 \le i < l$ by Eq. 1 defining
τ:

m (37)	→	00	00	00	01	11	10	00	01
n (25)	→	00	00	00	00	11	01	11	10
Positional weight	→	2^7	2^6	2^5	2^4	2^3	2^2	2^1	2^0

Fig. 3. An example of ADDr configuration c (highlighted) with $l = 8$; the upper
sequence of bits is the former addend m, the lower sequence is the latter addend n; the
positional weight of each cell is specified below, values of m and n in base 10 are on
the left in brackets.

$$m' + n' = \sum_{i=0}^{l-1} (m'_{2i+1} + m'_{2i} + n'_{2i+1} + n'_{2i})2^i$$

$$= \sum_{i=0}^{l-2} (m'_{2i+1} + n'_{2i+1} + n'_{2i})2^i + (m'_{2l-1} + n'_{2l-1} + n'_{2l-2})2^{l-1} + \sum_{i=0}^{l-1} m'_{2i}2^i$$

$$= \sum_{i=0}^{l-2} (n''_{2i}2^{i+1} + n''_{2i+1}2^i) + (n''_0 2^0 + n''_{2l-1}2^{l-1}) + \sum_{i=0}^{l-1} m''_{2i+1}2^i + \sum_{i=0}^{l-1} m''_{2i}2^i$$

$$= \sum_{i=0}^{l-1} (m''_{2i+1} + m''_{2i} + n''_{2i+1} + n''_{2i})2^i = m'' + n''$$

$\square$

Theorem 5. *Let c be a generic configuration of ADDr with length l and m, n respectively the upper and lower addend of c; let $c' = \gamma(c)$ and $c'' = \gamma(c')$, m', n' and m'', n'', respectively the upper and lower addend of c' and c'', then m' is a cfa and $m'' = 0$.*

Proof. $m'_{2i} = 0, 0 \le i < l$ by ADDr definition (Eq. 1), then m' is a cfa (e.g., steps 1 and 2 in Fig. 4); $m''_{2i+1} = m'_{2i} = 0$ by ADDr definition (Eq. 2) and $m''_{2i} = 0$ by ADDr definition (Eq. 1), $0 \le i < l$; then $m'' = 0$ (e.g., steps 2 and 3 in Fig. 4).$\square$

Corollary 3. *Let c be a generic configuration of ADDr with length l and m, n respectively the upper and lower addend of c; let $c' = \gamma(c)$ and $c'' = \gamma(c')$, m', n' and m'', n'', respectively the upper and lower addend of c' and c'', $m + n = m' + n' = m'' + n'' = n''$.*

Proof. $m + n = m' + n' = m'' + n''$ by Theorem 4, m' is a cfa by Theorem 5, $m'' = 0$ by Theorem 5. $\square$

Therefore an addition in ADDr is exactly performed in two steps, the result is found in the latter addend, that is in RBN representation. If the former addend is in a cfa, such an addition is performed in one step (e.g., step 2 and 3 in Fig. 4).

Theorem 6. *Let c' be a configuration of ADDr of length l with m', n' respectively the upper and lower addend of c; let $c'' = \gamma(c')$, m'', n'', respectively the upper and lower addend of c'', if $m' = 0$, then $m'' = m' = 0$, $n'' = m' + n' = n'$. Furthermore, Eqs. 3 and 4 correspond to Eqs. 1 and 2 of the definition of ADD in Sect. 2.1.*

Proof. The configuration c' with the upper addend $m' = 0$ ($m'_{2i+1} = 0, m'_{2i} = 0$) evolves according to the following simplified equations:

1. $m''_{2i} = 0$
2. $m''_{2i+1} = m'_{2i} = 0$
3. $n''_{2i} = (m'_{2i-1} \wedge n'_{2i-1}) \vee (m'_{2i-1} \wedge n'_{2i-2}) \vee (n'_{2i-1} \wedge n'_{2i-2}) = (n'_{2i-1} \wedge n'_{2i-2})$
4. $n''_{2i+1} = m'_{2i+1} \oplus n'_{2i+1} \oplus n'_{2i} = n'_{2i+1} \oplus n'_{2i}$

$\square$

Note that by Theorem 6, Eqs. 1 and 2 ensure that if the upper addend of a configuration in ADDr is 0, the upper addend of the following configurations are 0; furthermore Eqs. 3 and 4 are the same of Eqs. 1 and 2 of ADD. Therefore, if the bits of lower addend of ADDr in even (odd) position match the bits of upper (lower) addend in a configuration of ADD, then the ADDr configurations evolve in a cfα after a maximum steps of $l+1$ (the first two steps obtain that the upper addend is 0, the following ones that the lower addend is a cfα) according to Corollary 3, therefore the following corollary holds:

Corollary 4. *Let c be a generic configuration of ADDr of length l with m, n respectively the upper and lower addend of c; let $c' = \gamma^2(c)$, $c'' = \gamma^{l-1}(c')$, being m', n', respectively the upper and lower addend of c', then $c'' = \gamma^{l+1}(c)$ implies that $n'' = m + n$ and n'' is a cfα.*

Proof. $m' = 0$ by Theorem 6, then $m' = 0$, $n' = m + n$, therefore n'' is a cfα. $\square$

Positional weight	$\rightarrow$	2^7	2^6	2^5	2^4	2^3	2^2	2^1	2^0
m (37)		00	00	00	01	11	10	00	01
n (25)		00	00	00	00	11	01	11	10
	t=0								
m (25)		00	00	00	10	10	00	00	10
n (37)		00	00	00	01	11	01	00	10
	t=1								
m (0)		00	00	00	00	00	00	00	00
n (62)		00	00	01	01	10	10	01	00
	t=2								
m (0)		00	00	00	00	00	00	00	00
n (62)		00	00	10	10	10	10	10	00
	t=3								
m (0)		00	00	00	00	00	00	00	00
n (62)		00	00	10	10	10	10	10	00
	t=4								

Fig. 4. Evolution example of ADDr with length $l = 8$ for 4 steps (t). Configurations are highlighted, the upper sequence of bit is the former addend m, the lower one is the latter addend n, their values in base 10 are on the left in brackets; the cell positional weight is specified on top.

An addend in CBN can be translated in RBN as a cfα costless, just adding in parallel 0's at right of each bit, vice versa an addend in cfα of RBN can be translated in CBN costless, just eliminating in parallel the even 0's, an addition in ADD takes $l - 1$ (l is the number of cells of ADD and ADDr) steps, while an addition in ADDr takes one step if the first addend is in cfα, but it takes $l - 1$ steps if the result of a such addition has to be obtained in cfα. So working in ADDr is convenient only if ADDR is fed by $p > 2l$ upper addends, if the calculation involves a sequence of additions of natural numbers.

An extension of ADDr for the integers according to the two's complement representation could be developed; an intuitive way is breaking the ring between cells 0 and $l - 1$ (cell $l - 1$ assumes a positional weight of -2^{l-1}) and considering that the state of the -1 neighbor of cell 0 is always acquired as $\begin{smallmatrix} 0 & 0 \\ 0 & 0 \end{smallmatrix}$.

4   Conclusions and Comments

The exemplary case of the addition operation on $\mathbb{N}$ within two CA ADD and ADDr with two different representations is here treated in order to investigate how CA can efficiently exploit their intrinsic parallelism. Natural numbers were considered in order that CA properties could emerge more clearly, even if a possible extension to $\mathbb{Z}$ (therefore to the elementary arithmetic) could be straightforward, but lengthy. A further investigation will be devoted to this problem.

The addition of two natural numbers can be surely operated by a CA in parallel way, but the carry problem in the usual numerical representation could make the parallel calculation a caricature of the sequential calculation, but, if we adopt an appropriate redundant numerical representation, then all the power of the parallelism discloses.

However to give an explicandum for a criterion of cost-effectiveness is not easy because situation is further complicated if a particular numeral representation is mandatory for the solution of a problem: e.g., sensors of automatic mobile systems could receive information only in a particular representation and utilize the elaborated solutions in that same representation. If a single operation (a single addition of two natural numbers in this case) is considered, there is no convenience in using a faster CA, because costs of translation from RBN to CBN annul any advantage, but not if a long sequence of consecutive additions is necessary.

This often elusive question has to move from the analysis of single operations over the whole of the operations, necessary for the problem solution. A notion of complexity that accounts for the relations operation/representation should possibly be investigated.

References

1. von Neumann, J.: Theory of Self-Reproducing Automata. University of Illinois Press, Urbana (1966)
2. Mitchell, M.: Computation in cellular automata: a selected review. In: Schuster, H.G., Gramms, T. (eds.) Nonconventional Computation, pp. 95–140. VCH Verlagsgesellschaft, Weinheim (1996)
3. Sheth, B., Nag, P., Hellwarth, R.W.: Binary addition on cellular automata. Complex Syst. **5**(5), 479–486 (1991)
4. Toffoli, T., Margolus, N.: Cellular Automata Machines: A New Environment for Modeling. MIT Press, Cambridge (1987)
5. Di Gregorio, S.: Una rappresentazione non univoca degli interi: basi per una nuova aritmetica degli elaboratori elettronici (in Italian). Quaderno del Progetto Nazionale Teoria degli Algoritmi, M.P.I., Università della Calabria (1984)
6. Clementi, A., De Biase, G.A., Massini, A.: Fast parallel arithmetic on cellular automata. Complex Syst. **8**(6), 435–442 (1994)
7. Clementi, A., De Biase, G.A., Massini, A.: Pipelined addition, accumulation and multiplication of binary numbers on cellular automata. Università della Sapienza, Roma (1995)
8. Choudhury, P.P., Sahoo, S., Chakraborty, M.: Implementation of basic arithmetic operations using cellular automaton. In: IEEE International Conference on Information Technology, ICIT 2008, pp. 79–80 (2008)
9. Vourkas I., Sirakoulis G.: FPGA based cellular automata for environmental modeling. In: 19th IEEE International Conference on Electronics, Circuits and Systems, ICECS 2012, pp. 93–96 (2012)
10. Di Gregorio, S., Trautteur, G.: On reversibility in cellular automata. J. Comput. Syst. Sci. **11**, 382–391 (1975)

Quantum Walks on Quantum Cellular Automata Lattices: Towards a New Model for Quantum Computation

Ioannis G. Karafyllidis[(⊠)] and Georgios Ch. Sirakoulis

Department of Electrical and Computer Engineering,
Democritus University of Thrace, 67100 Xanthi, Greece
ykar@ee.duth.gr

Abstract. Many physical problems cannot be easily formulated as quantum circuits, which are a successful universal model for quantum computation. Because of this, new models that are closer to the structure of physical systems must be developed. Discrete and continuous quantum walks have been proven to be a universal quantum computation model, but building quantum computing systems based on their structure is not straightforward. Although classical cellular automata are models of universal classical computation, this is not the case for their quantum counterpart, which is limited by the no-coning theorem and the no-go lemma. Here we combine quantum walks, which reproduce unitary evolution in space with quantum cellular automata, which reproduce unitary evolution in time, to form a new model of quantum computation. Our results show that such a model is possible.

Keywords: Quantum cellular automata · Quantum walks
Quantum computing

1 Introduction

Quantum circuits is the most known and most used quantum computation model [1]. In quantum circuits the quantum gates, which are unitary Hilbert space operators, act on the quantum bits (qubits) and evolve their state from the initial state, which is the input to the quantum computation, towards the final state, which is measured and produces the output of the quantum computation [2,3]. Most known quantum algorithms, such as Deutch [4], Grover [5] and Shor [6] quantum algorithms can be formulated as quantum circuits. Although quantum circuits are a powerful model, many physical problems and processes cannot be easily described as quantum circuits. This fact has initiated the quest for alternative models for quantum computation.

Quantum walks, first introduced in 1993, are quantum versions of classical random walks [7]. Since then, continuous and discrete quantum walks have been extensively studied and it has been proven that quantum walks are a universal model for quantum computation. Continuous quantum walks on graphs

© Springer Nature Switzerland AG 2018
G. Mauri et al. (Eds.): ACRI 2018, LNCS 11115, pp. 319–327, 2018.
https://doi.org/10.1007/978-3-319-99813-8_29

can reproduce quantum computations. In this model, quantum gates are implemented by scattering processes [8, 9]. On the other hand, discrete quantum walks have been proven to implement a universal quantum gate set and thus are able to execute any quantum computation [10]. Both continuous and discrete quantum walks on graphs are universal models for quantum computation, but building a physical quantum computing system based on the mathematical graph structures is not straightforward. In quantum walk models, graphs and wires do not represent qubits but basis states and cannot be mapped on a physical quantum computer architecture.

Feynman in 1982 introduced the concept of quantum cellular automata (QCAs) by examining the possibility of extending classical cellular automata (CAs) as models that can simulate quantum systems [11]. QCA evolution must be unitary, as is the evolution of all quantum systems. This fact causes several limitations on the use of QCAs as universal quantum computation models. The two most important limitations are imposed by the non-cloning theorem and the no-go lemma. The non-cloning theorem, that imposes the first limitation, forbids the cloning (copying) of an unknown quantum state [1]. Because of this, copies of the neighboring cell states are not available to the central cell, as is the case in classical CAs. Therefore, the evolution of the QCA cell states cannot be directly determined by the states of their neighbors. Several models have been proposed to circumvent this obstacle. Among them, a QCA with two qubits per cell has been introduced [12], and a relaxed unitary evolution has been proposed, in which probability is conserved and the evolution is linear, but the evolution is approximately unitary [13]. The second limitation is imposed by the no-go lemma, which states that except for the trivial case, unitary evolution of one-dimensional QCAs is impossible, i.e. in one dimension there exist no non-trivial homogeneous, local, linear QCA [14].

In QCAs one or more qubits are assigned to the QCA cells. The qubit states are quantum states and are described by wave functions, which are solutions to the Schrödinger equation. Quantum states should evolve both in space and time, whereas the states of qubits in the sites of the QCA have a trivial evolution. This is because their evolution in space is limited by the no-cloning theorem, which forbids the transfer of states between neighboring QCA cells. On the other hand, quantum walkers are quantum particles, the state of which evolves naturally in space. It is therefore possible that a model comprising quantum walks, which will reproduce quantum evolution in space, and QCAs, that will reproduce quantum evolution in time, can be developed so that it can serve as a universal model for quantum computation. Here we define the quantum walk on QCA lattices. The quantum particle (i.e. the quantum walker) is transferred between neighboring QCA sites and changes the quantum phase of the qubits according to a propagator, reproducing unitary space evolution. The QCA evolves in time reproducing unitary time evolution. Our results show that the development of a universal model of quantum computation based on quantum walks on the QCA lattice is possible.

2   Unitary Evolution of Quantum Walks on QCA Lattices

The most important characteristic of a quantum computing system is the reproduction of the solutions of the Schrödinger equation. The simplest solution is
the plane wave:

$$|\Psi(x,t)\rangle = Ae^{i(kx-\omega t)} = Ae^{i(px-Et)/\hbar} \tag{1}$$

Where Ψ is the wave function in Dirac notation, k is the wave vector and ω
the angular frequency. $E = \hbar\omega$ is the energy and $p = \hbar k$ is the momentum. The
one-dimensional, time dependent Schrödinger equation:

$$i\hbar\frac{\partial}{\partial t}|\Psi(x,t)\rangle = H|\Psi(x,t)\rangle \tag{2}$$

where H is the Hamiltonian operator:

$$H = \left(-\frac{\hbar^2}{2m}\frac{\partial^2}{\partial x^2} + V(x,t)\right) \tag{3}$$

has the following general solution:

$$|\Psi(x_b,t_b)\rangle = U(x,t)|\Psi(x_a,t_a)\rangle \tag{4}$$

where U is a unitary operator:

$$U(x,t) = e^{\frac{-iHt}{\hbar}} \tag{5}$$

Both the simplest solution of (1) and the general solution of (4) describe the
evolution of the wave function from an initial space-time point (x_a, t_a) to a final
space-time point (x_b, t_b), as shown in Fig. 1. In the quantum circuit model, space
is defined by an one-dimensional array of qubits and the computation proceeds
in time steps, in each of which a number of quantum gates act on the qubits. In
the proposed model we follow the same discretization scheme as in the quantum
circuit model, i.e. qubits form the QCA lattice and the computation evolves in
discrete time steps.

In the proposed model we consider one-dimensional QCAs in which the QCA
cells form a one-dimensional lattice. Three qubits are allocated at each QCA cell,
the a-qubit, which is the QCA qubit and a two-qubit quantum register, w, which
comprises the two qubits necessary for the quantum walk. The state of the ith
QCA cell at computation step t is written as: $|a_i^t w_i^t\rangle$. There are eight basis states
for each QCA cell. The global state of the QCA at the computation step t, $|Q^t\rangle$,
is the tensor product of the states of its cells and is written as:

$$|Q^t\rangle = |\cdots a_{i+1}^t w_{i+1}^t a_i^t w_i^t a_{i-1}^t w_{i-1}^t \cdots\rangle \tag{6}$$

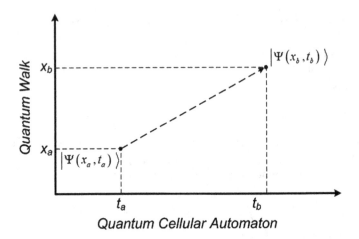

Fig. 1. Wave function evolution in space-time, from an initial space-time point (x_a, t_a) to a final space-time point (x_b, t_b). In the proposed model quantum walks evolve the wave function in space and QCAs in time.

The evolution of the global QCA state, from computation step t to computation step $t + 1$ is given by:

$$\left|Q^{t+1}\right\rangle = U(x, t)\left|Q^t\right\rangle = A(t)\, W(x)\left|Q^t\right\rangle \tag{7}$$

In our model the unitary operator $U(x, t)$ is decomposed in a product of two operators, $A(t)$, which describes the time evolution of the QCA and $W(x)$, which describes the space evolution of the QCA qubit states by the action of the quantum walk. Since only U has to be unitary, the unitarity criterion on both operators A and W could be relaxed, as long as their product is unitary. Nevertheless, we choose not to relax this criterion and in our model we demand both A and W to be unitary. We describe below the action of these two operators.

In the discrete quantum walk, a walker (which can be a particle or a quantum state) moves on the QCA lattice. The sites of this lattice are numbered by: $i = 0, \pm 1, \pm 2, \cdots \pm n$. The quantum walker tosses a quantum coin and moves to the right (towards $+n$) if the coin state is $|1\rangle$, and to the left (towards $-n$) if the coin state is $|0\rangle$. The state of the quantum walker found at location i is: $|w_i\rangle = |i, c_i\rangle$, where i indicates the location and c_i the coin state. The quantum walk operator W is given by: $W = S \cdot (I \otimes C)$, where I is the unit operator, and C is the coin operator, which can be any one-qubit unitary quantum operator, such as the Pauli, Hadamard or Phase-shift operators. The shift operator S that moves the quantum walker is given by:

$$S = \sum_{i=-n}^{n} |1\rangle\langle 1| \otimes |i+1\rangle\langle i| \; + \; |0\rangle\langle 0| \otimes |i-1\rangle\langle i| \tag{8}$$

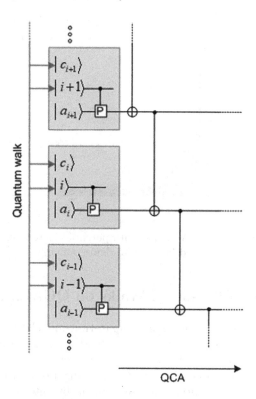

Fig. 2. The QCA structure and the W operator acting on qubits along with the A operator described by Eq. 10. Shaded rectangles represent QCA cells and the qubits connected with the arrowed (red) lines, are the qubits affected by the quantum walk. (Color figure online)

Figure 2 shows the QCA structure and the W operator acting on qubits. The global state of the QCA evolves according to evolution rules expressed by the operator A.

$$\left|Q^{t+1}\right\rangle = A \left|Q^t\right\rangle \tag{9}$$

This operator can be any two-qubit unitary quantum operator, for example it can comprise Controlled-NOT (CNOT) gates:

$$A = \cdots \otimes CN \otimes CN \otimes CN \otimes \cdots \tag{10}$$

Figure 2 shows the A operator in the case of Eq. 10. The phase of the QCA qubit, $|a_i\rangle$, is controlled by the location qubit of the quantum walk, $|i\rangle$. The qubits connected by the arrowed (red) line, i.e. $|c_i\rangle$ and $|i\rangle$ are the qubits affected by the quantum walk, which transfers information about the states of neighboring QCA qubits. The QCA evolves in time by interaction between its qubit states, which in the case of Fig. 2 is a concatenation of CNOT quantum gates.

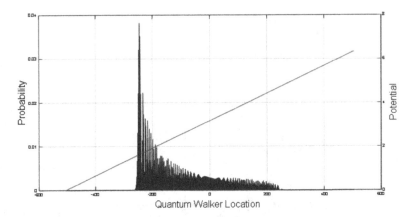

Fig. 3. Quantum walk on a QCA lattice, with potential increasing towards the right. The potential is shown by the red line. (Color figure online)

3   Simulation of Quantum Walks on QCA Lattices

We aim to develop a new quantum computation model that is closer to the structure of physical systems. We use our model to simulate the most basic quantum mechanical process: the motion of a particle (i.e. the quantum walker) in spaces where various potentials exist. Following Eq. 2, where the potential enters in the exponent, we formulate the problem by entering the values of the space potentials as phases of the QCA qubits and evolve the quantum walk in these spaces. It is well known that if the initial value of the quantum walker coin qubit is in state $|0\rangle$, the quantum walk is directed towards the left direction from the starting point and when the coin is in state $|1\rangle$ the quantum walk is directed towards the right. We start the evolution of the quantum walk with the initial coin state in superposition of the basis states $1/\sqrt{2}\,(|0\rangle + |1\rangle)$ which results in symmetric quantum walk evolution towards both directions.

Figure 3 shows the evolution of a quantum walk on a QCA lattice which encodes a potential that increases towards the right. The potential is shown by the red line. The quantum walk starts at location 0 with the initial coin state in the superposition described above. The red line shows the potential and the blue bars at lattice sites show the probability of the quantum walker to be found in the corresponding lattice sites. Our computation results reproduce the motion of the quantum walker towards the left, as expected.

We simulated a quantum walk on a QCA lattice encoding a potential that is mirror symmetric to the previous one and increases towards the left, shown by the red line. Again, the quantum walk starts at location 0 with the same initial coin state superposition. Figure 4 shows the evolution of this quantum walk, reproducing a mirror symmetric probability distribution, characteristic of the motion of the quantum walker towards the right, as expected.

We also simulated a quantum walk on a QCA lattice encoding a potential barrier shown in red in Fig. 5. The width of the potential barrier is small and

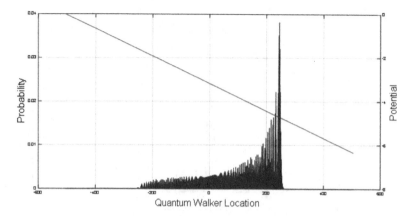

Fig. 4. Quantum walk on a QCA lattice, with potential increasing towards the left. The potential is shown by the red line. (Color figure online)

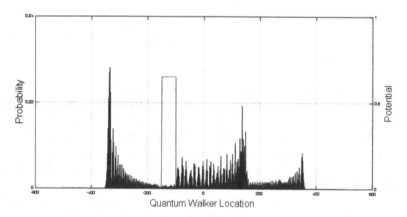

Fig. 5. Quantum walk on a QCA lattice, with a thin potential barrier. The barrier is shown by the red line. (Color figure online)

the barrier is relatively transparent to the quantum particle, with a large transmission coefficient. Our computation results, shown in Fig. 5, reproduced the tunneling through a barrier, characteristic of quantum particles. The quantum walk starts at lattice site 0. The probability distribution is near zero inside the potential barrier and the non-zero to the left of the barrier.

Figure 6 shows the evolution of a quantum walk on a QCA lattice encoding both a potential gradient and a potential barrier. The potential distribution is shown by the red line. In this case the width of the potential barrier is large, and its transmission coefficient is near zero. Although the potential gradient drives the quantum walk towards the left, the particle is not transmitted through the barrier and the probability distribution to the left of the barrier is almost zero, as expected.

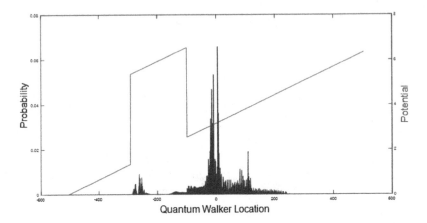

Fig. 6. Quantum walk on a QCA lattice, with a large potential barrier and with potential increasing towards the right. Potential and barrier are shown by the red line. (Color figure online)

4   Conclusions

We developed a new quantum computation model based on quantum walks on quantum cellular automata lattices. This new model is closer to the structure of many quantum mechanical systems and processes. We used this model to simulate the most basic quantum mechanical processes, i.e. the motion of a particle in a one-dimensional space in which potential distributions exist. Our model reproduced qualitatively the expected motions in spaces with potential gradients and potential barriers, which were encoded as phases of the quantum cellular automaton qubits. Our results show that the development of an accurate universal quantum computation model based on quantum walks on quantum cellular automata lattices is possible.

References

1. Nielsen, M.A., Chuang, I.L.: Quantum Computation and Quantum Information. Cambridge University Press, Cambridge (2000)
2. Cybenco, G.: Reducing quantum computations to elementary unitary operations. Comput. Sci. Eng. **3**, 27 (2001)
3. Karafyllidis, I.G.: Quantum computer simulator based on the circuit model of quantum computation. IEEE Trans. Circuits Syst. **I**(52), 1590–1596 (2005)
4. Deutsch, D.: Quantum theory, the church-turing principle and the universal quantum computer. Proc. R. Soc. Lond. A. **400**, 97–117 (1985)
5. Grover, L.K.: Quantum mechanics helps in searching for a needle in a haystack. Phys. Rev. Lett. **79**, 325–328 (1997)
6. Shor, P.: Algorithms for quantum computation: discrete logarithms and factoring. In: Proceedings of the 35th Annual Symposium on the Foundations of Computer Science, pp. 124–134 (1994)

7. Aharonov, Y., Davidovich, L., Zagury, N.: Quantum random walks. Phys. Rev. A **48**, 1687 (1993)
8. Childs, A.M.: Universal computation by quantum walk. Phys. Rev. Lett. **102**, 180501 (2009)
9. Lovett, N.B., Cooper, S., Everitt, M., Trevers, M., Kendon, V.: Universal quantum computation using the discrete-time quantum walk. Phys. Rev. Lett. **81**, 042330 (2010)
10. Childs, A.M., Gosset, D., Webb, S.: Universal computation by multiparticle quantum walk. Science **339**, 791–794 (2013)
11. Feynman, R.P.: Simulating physics with computers. Int. J. Theor. Phys. **21**, 467–488 (1982)
12. Karafyllidis, I.G.: Definition and evolution of quantum cellular automata with two qubits per cell. Phys. Rev. A **70**, 044301 (2004)
13. Grössing, G., Zeilinger, A.: Quantum cellular automata. Complex Syst. **2**, 197–208 (1988)
14. Meyer, D.: On the absence of homogeneous scalar unitary cellular automata. Phys. Lett. A **223**, 337–340 (1996)

Fractal Arrangement for 2D Cellular Automata and Its Implementation for Outer-Totalistic Rules

Yoshihiko Kayama$^{(\boxtimes)}$, Yuka Koda, and Ikumi Yazawa

Department of Media and Information, BAIKA Women's University,
2-19-5 Shukuno-sho, Osaka, Ibaraki 567-8578, Japan
y_kayama@ieee.org

Abstract. Cellular automata (CAs) have played a significant role in studies of complex systems. Recently, a recursive estimation of neighbors algorithm that distinguishes the perception area of each cell from the CA rule neighborhood was introduced to extend CA. This framework makes it possible to construct non-uniform CA models composed of cells with different sizes of the perception area, which can be interpreted as an individual attribute of each cell. For example, focusing primarily on one-dimensional (1D) elementary CA, fractal CAs composed of self-similarly arranged cells have been proposed and their characteristics have been investigated. In this paper, 2D fractal CAs are defined and implemented for outer-totalistic CA rules. Fractal CAs derived from a linear rule inherit that rule's features, including replicability and time reversibility, which indicate their applicability to various fields.

1 Introduction

Cellular automata (CAs), which were first introduced by von Neumann and Ulam to model biological self-reproduction [1], are discrete computational systems that have played a significant role in the study of complex systems. CAs comprise a set of cells arranged on a regular lattice where each cell in an initial state is taken from a finite set. The state is updated at each time step according to a local rule based on its own state and the states of a fixed set of neighboring cells. Such CAs are uniform and synchronous, i.e., all cells apply the same local rule and are updated synchronously, and are referred to as *standard* CAs. Various extended CA models that are of theoretical and practical interest have been investigated by relaxing the characteristics of standard CA. Recently, based on the *recursive estimation of neighbors* (REN) algorithm, a method to construct non-uniform CAs in which each cell is allowed to follow a different local rule has been proposed [2,3]. The REN algorithm, a framework inspired by that of Reynolds' Boids program [4], takes a standard CA rule with a unit rule radius and extends it to rules with larger radii other than the unit rule radius. The perception area of each cell, which is defined by the value of the extra radius, is no longer identical to the neighborhood specified by the standard CA rule.

© Springer Nature Switzerland AG 2018
G. Mauri et al. (Eds.): ACRI 2018, LNCS 11115, pp. 328–339, 2018.
https://doi.org/10.1007/978-3-319-99813-8_30

In the following, cells within the neighborhood of a cell defined by the standard CA rule are referred to as *neighbors*. The standard CA rule is used recursively to estimate the next states of the neighbors from the present states of cells within the perception area. Moreover, the extended rules form a sequence indexed by the value of the extra radius, which contains the standard CA rule, referred to as the *basic rule*, as its first term. Even though the rules in the sequence are obtained from the extension of a basic rule via REN, each extended rule corresponds to a standard CA rule with an equal value of the rule radius to its extra radius as a rule mapping cell configurations of the perception area of a target cell to its next state. In other words, extension using REN relates a standard CA rule with a unit radius to others with longer radius values.

A non-uniform CA can be constructed from cells that follow distinct extended rules that belong to the same sequence of extended rules. Among various possible cell arrangements, those with fractal geometries are particularly interesting because such geometries, such as Koch's curve and Sierpinski's gasket, have a property known as self-similarity. Fractal structures also play an important role in complex systems in nature, such as biological structures, Internet connections, and social networks. Such non-uniform CA that comprise fractally arranged cells, i.e., fractal CA (F-CA), have been proposed [5]. The attractive characteristics of basic rules, e.g., pattern replicability and reversibility in linear rules of 1D elementary CA (ECA), are carried over into their F-CA. Here we focus on F-CAs derived from 2D CA rules. A practical implementation is discussed in consideration of outer-totalistic rules. Similar to fractal ECA, some characteristics of linear basic rules in outer-totalistic CA are inherited by their F-CAs.

The remainder of this paper is organized as follows. Section 2 explains extension using REN. A practical extension of 2D outer-totalistic CA rules is described in Sect. 3. Section 4 describes the construction of 2D F-CA from the sequence of extended rules and implements the F-CA construction for outer-totalistic rules. In addition, as potential applications of F-CA derived from a multi-state linear outer-totalistic rule, a diffusion process of encryption systems and textile design samples are presented. Conclusions and suggestions for future work are given in Sect. 5.

2   Extension of CA Using REN

In case of Reynolds' Boids program, each boid acquires information regarding the positions and velocities of other boids within its perception area and determines its own movement to follow the representative values of the neighbors. The radius of the perception area can be treated as a parameter differentiating individual elements. To incorporate a similar scenario in a CA, the perception area of a cell should be separated from the neighborhood determined by the CA rule, so that the size of the area can be treated as an attribute of each cell. Under the standard CA framework, however, there is no scope for expanding the sensory area of a cell. For example, each cell of ECA acquires the states of the three cells within its radius-one neighborhood to determine its own state in the next time step. Such separation can be possible if the update process of each cell has an intermediate process of estimating next states of neighboring cells, given as follows:

$$\text{Acquire information about neighbors} \Rightarrow \text{estimate their next states}$$
$$\Rightarrow \text{determine its own nextstate} \quad (1)$$

Estimation and determination of states are assumed to be processed by only a basic CA rule because if other rules or mechanisms were introduced, the present framework would become complicated and finding a reasonable selection method would, therefore, be difficult. Moreover, it is assumed that all cells use the same update algorithm. Then, the basic rule will be used recursively as explained in the next subsection.

When a standard CA rule, i.e., the basic rule, is extended using REN, any extended rule is assumed to have a larger cell perception area than the neighborhood defined by the basic rule. The neighborhood and the perception area are parameterized by their respective radii, r and R, where r is the common radius of the neighborhoods of all cells defined by the basic rule, and R is the extra radius given by the perception area of each cell. As illustrated in Fig. 1, the neighbors in the neighborhood are included in the perception area. The value of the extra radius representing the size of the perception area of a target cell can now be recognized as its independent attribute.

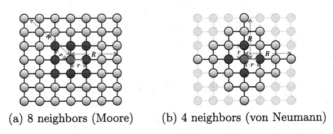

(a) 8 neighbors (Moore)   (b) 4 neighbors (von Neumann)

Fig. 1. Perception area of a target (yellow cell) including its neighbors (red cells) in 2D extended CAs with (a) Moore and (b) von Neumann neighborhoods. Each target cell has an extra radius $R = 3$ and the radius of the basic rule $r = 1$. (Color figure online)

The basic rule is used recursively in the REN process to estimate the *next states* of the neighbors of a target cell and to determine the next state of the target cell by applying it to the *estimated next states* of the neighbors and the *current state* of the target. The update process (1) is expressed by the following steps.

1. Perceive the current states of all cells within the perception area of a target.
2. Apply REN to estimate the next states of the neighbors.

3. Determine the next state of the target by applying the basic rule to the neighbors' estimated next states and to the target's current state.

In the second step, the next states of the target's neighbors are estimated as a set $\left\{\varphi_{neighbors}^{(t+1)}\right\}$ by applying REN to the information in the set of current states of the cells within the perception area $\left\{x_{p-area}^{(t)}\right\}$ (first step). Here, x and φ represent the actual and estimated states of a cell, respectively. { } indicates the set of states of cells within an area or a group. The next state of the target is estimated as $\varphi_{target}^{(t+1)}$ by applying the basic rule to $\left\{\varphi_{neighbors}^{(t+1)}\right\}$ together with its current state $x_{target}^{(t)}$. Finally, $\varphi_{target}^{(t+1)}$ is assigned to $x_{target}^{(t+1)}$, i.e., the next actual state of the target.

The estimated next states of the neighbors are not necessarily identical to their actual next states because the estimation requires information about the neighbors' extra radius values, and it is assumed that each cell cannot perceive such information. The REN algorithm includes an assumption about the estimation of the extra radius values of neighbors as mentioned in the next subsection. Given that we focus primarily on extending 2D eight-neighbor (or four-neighbor) CA rules, r is set to one in the following, where neighbors are adjacent to each cell. In the time evolution of a cell, only the basic rule is used recursively, regardless of the value of R. In that sense, R can be an attribute of each cell, thereby allowing the construction of non-uniform models containing cells with different R values. Note that this differs from standard CAs, which are always uniform.

2.1   Recursive Estimation of Neighbors

The recursive nature of REN comes from an assumption of self-similarity, i.e., the next state of each cell in a perception area is determined by the previously described three steps. A target cell's immediate neighbors estimate the states of their neighbors, which are denoted as $neighbors^{(1)}$. To describe REN more concretely, we set the radius R of the target to an integer k. As mentioned previously, the target can perceive the current states of its neighbors because they are all contained within its perception area (first step). However, the sizes of the neighbors' perception areas are assumed to be unperceivable by the target. Therefore, to estimate the neighbors' next states $\left\{\varphi_{neighbors}^{(t+1)}\right\}$, the target must evaluate their sizes. Here, we assume that the target cell estimates a perception area that is *as large as possible* for each neighbor within its own perception area. Thereafter, the radius value of the neighbor's perception area is assumed to be $k - 1$. The target cell then attempts to estimate the next state of each of its neighbors by assuming that a neighbor applies the same steps, i.e., the neighbor can be considered the next target, $target^{(1)}$, and its next state will be estimated by the next states of its neighbors (i.e., the neighbors' neighbors: $neighbors^{(1)}$) and its present state using REN. At this time, the size of the perception area of each of the $neighbors^{(1)}$ will be evaluated as $k - 2$. Next, if each of the $neighbors^{(1)}$ is considered the next target, i.e., $target^{(2)}$, the perception area size of its neighbors ($neighbors^{(2)}$) will be evaluated as $k - 3$. Similarly, each of the $neighbors^{(2)}$ can be considered the next target, i.e., $target^{(3)}$, and the perception area of its neighbors ($neighbors^{(3)}$) will be evaluated as $k - 4$. Eventually, the chain of neighbors will reach the edge of the perception area of the original target. Such a boundary cell, i.e., $target^{(k)}$, will have no neighbors; therefore, the basic rule cannot be applied. Here, we add the further assumption that the next state of the boundary cell will be estimated as being the same as the current state. Note that this is the REN algorithm's *termination condition*:

$$\varphi_{neighbor^{(k-1)}}^{(t+1)} = \varphi_{target^{(k)}}^{(t+1)} = x_{target^{(k)}}^{(t)}. \tag{2}$$

where $\varphi_{neighbor^{(k-1)}}^{(t+1)} \in \left\{ \varphi_{neighbors^{(k-1)}}^{(t+1)} \right\}$. Finally, the next states of all cells within the perception area are estimated recursively using the basic rule.

3   Extension of 2D Outer-Totalistic Rules

Outer-totalistic implies that the rule function depends on the sum of the states of the outer neighbors, i.e., all cells except the center cell within the neighborhood defined by a CA rule. When the state of the (i, j)-th cell at time step t and the CA rule function are denoted $x_{(i,j)}^{(t)}$ and f, respectively, the standard time evolution of the state is given as follows:

$$\text{Std.CA:} \, x_{(i,j)}^{(t+1)} = f(x_{(i,j)}^{(t)}, \sigma_8(i, j)), \, \sigma_8(i, j) = \sum_{nb(i,j)} x_{nb(i,j)}^{(t)} \tag{3}$$

where $\sigma_8(i, j)$ represents the sum of the states of the eight cells neighboring the target cell with the Moore neighborhood[1] (Fig. 1a), and $nb(i, j)$ represents each position of the target's immediate neighbors, such as the following.

$$nb(i, j) \in \{(i - 1, j - 1), (i, j - 1), (i + 1, j - 1), (i - 1, j),$$
$$(i + 1, j), (i - 1, j + 1), (i, j + 1), (i + 1, j + 1)\}. \tag{4}$$

Next, we demonstrate the time evolution process in extended 2D outer-totalistic CA. Here, an extended CA is assumed to be uniform such that all cells have the same value of $R = k$. The time evolution of the (i, j)-th cell requires the sum of the *estimated* states of its neighbors at $t + 1$ and its current state $x_{k,(i,j)}^{(t)}$, as mentioned in the third step discussed in the previous section. When the sum is denoted $\sigma_8(i, j; k - 1)$, Eq. (3) becomes:

$$\varphi_{k,(i,j)}^{(t+1)} = f(x_{k,(i,j)}^{(t)}, \sigma_8(i, j; k - 1)), \tag{5}$$

where $\varphi_{k,(i,j)}^{(t+1)}$ is the estimated state of the target, which is assigned as the actual next state $x_{k,(i,j)}^{(t+1)}$. The sum $\sigma_8(i, j; k - 1)$ can be expressed as follows:

---

[1] CAs with the von Neumann neighborhood (Fig. 1b) can be extended through similar steps.

$$\sigma_8(i,j;k-1) = \sum_{nb(i,j)} \varphi_{k-1,nb(i,j)}^{(t+1)} \tag{6}$$

where $\varphi_{k-1,nb(i,j)}^{(t+1)}$ is the estimated state of each neighbor at $t+1$ with an *assumed* radius R of $k-1$. This value comes from the assumptions of the REN algorithm because $k-1$ is the maximum value of the perception area for the immediate neighbors within the perception area of the target with $R = k$. However, each $\varphi_{k-1,nb(i,j)}^{(t+1)}$ is not necessarily equal to its respective actual state $x_{k,nb(i,j)}^{(t+1)}$ because the true value of R of the neighbors is not $k-1$ but k in this uniform case.

Following the procedure mentioned in Sect. 2.1, the REN algorithm produces the following recursive expressions for the estimated states of the m-th immediate neighbors ($neighbors^{(m)}$):

$$\varphi_{k-m,nb^{(m)}(i,j)}^{(t+1)} = f(x_{k,nb^{(m)}(i,j)}^{(t)}, \sigma_8(nb^{(m)}(i,j);k-m-1)) \tag{7}$$

$$\sigma_8(nb^{(m)}(i,j);k-m-1) = \sum_{nb^{(m+1)}(i,j)} \varphi_{k-m-1,nb^{(m+1)}(i,j)}^{(t+1)}, \tag{8}$$

where $nb^{(m)}(i,j) = \overbrace{nb(\cdots(nb(i,j))\cdots)}^{m}$, $m = 1,2,\cdots,k-1$. Given that $m = k$ implies that the estimated value of R will be equal to 0 ($< r = 1$), the following termination condition ends the recursion.

$$\varphi_{0,nb^{(k)}(i,j)}^{(t+1)} = x_{k,nb^{(k)}(i,j)}^{(t)}. \tag{9}$$

Once the next states of the k-th neighbors are determined, we can go back to Eq. (5) by using the above recursive expressions.

As a concrete demonstration, we begin by considering the case where $k = r = 1$. Equations (5) and (9) yield $x_{1,(i,j)}^{(t+1)} = f(x_{1,(i,j)}^{(t)}, \sigma_8(i,j;0))$ and $\varphi_{0,nb(i,j)}^{(t+1)} = x_{1,nb(i,j)}^{(t)} = x_{nb(i,j)}^{(t)}$ respectively. These mean that $\sigma_8(i,j;0) = \sigma_8(i,j)$ (Eq. (6)), such that the extended CA rule with $R = 1$ is identical to the basic rule (Eq. (3)). In the next case, where $R = 2$, Eq. (5) gives $x_{2,(i,j)}^{(t+1)} = f(x_{2,(i,j)}^{(t)}, \sigma_8(i,j;1))$ and the recursive expressions (Eqs. (7) and (8)) give the following:

$$\varphi_{1,nb(i,j)}^{(t+1)} = f(x_{nb(i,j)}^{(t)}, \sigma_8(nb(i,j);0)), \tag{10}$$

$$\sigma_8(nb(i,j);0) = \sum_{nb^{(2)}(i,j)} \varphi_{0,nb^{(2)}(i,j)}^{(t+1)}. \tag{11}$$

Owing to the termination condition $\varphi_{0,nb^{(2)}(i,j)}^{(t+1)} = x_{nb^{(2)}(i,j)}^{(t)}$ (Eq. (9)), the extended CA rule with $R = 2$ is expressed as follows:

$$x_{(i,j)}^{(t+1)} = f(x_{(i,j)}^{(t)}, \sum_{nb(i,j)} f(x_{nb(i,j)}^{(t)}, \sum_{nb^{(2)}(i,j)} x_{nb^{(2)}(i,j)}^{(t)})), \tag{12}$$

which can be considered a standard CA rule with $r = 2$. Considering that cases in which R takes larger values can be derived in the same manner, each extended rule is one of the standard CA rules with such large rule radius $r = R$. Eventually, the extended rules form a sequence indexed by the value of R, and the first term is identical to the basic rule.

Furthermore, if the rule function f of a basic rule is independent of the state of the (i, j) cell, i.e.,

$$\text{Std.CA:} \ x_i^{(t+1)} = f(\sigma_8(i,j)) = f(\sum_{nb(i,j)} x_{nb(i,j)}^{(t)}), \tag{13}$$

Equation (12) becomes

$$x_{(i,j)}^{(t+1)} = f(\sum_{nb(i,j)} f(\sum_{nb^{(2)}(i,j)} x_{nb^{(2)}(i,j)}^{(t)})). \tag{14}$$

The right hand side of Eq. (14) is identical to

$$\text{Std.CA:} \ x_i^{(t+2)} = f(\sum_{nb(i,j)} x_{nb(i,j)}^{(t+1)}) = f^{(2)} \bullet x_i^{(t)}, \tag{15}$$

thus indicating that the extended rule with $R = 2$ is identical to two evolutions of the basic rule. According to the similar discussion of cases with larger values of R, the sequences of extended rules derived from a basic rule independent of the state of the center cell are identical to the time evolutions of the basic rule.

When the basic rule is assigned the code $\mathcal{N}$, the sequence formed by its extended rules is represented as $[\mathcal{N}]$. If each rule in the sequence is identified, it is denoted by the code of the basic rule followed by the letter R, indicating the extra radius and its value k. Therefore, $[\mathcal{N}]$ can be enumerated as $\{\mathcal{N}R1, \mathcal{N}R2, \mathcal{N}R3, \cdots\}$, where $\mathcal{N}R1$ is identical to the basic rule, as discussed above. In the following, a cell with the value k for its attribute R or a cell that follows the rule $\mathcal{N}Rk$ is referred to as an Rk cell. For example, one of the most famous 2D CA, i.e., Conway's Game of Life (GoL) [6,7], can be specified as B3S23 in the Golly/RLE format [8,9]. The sequence of extended rules derived from the GoL rule is denoted $[B3S23] = \{B3S23R1, B3S23R2, B3S23R3, \cdots\}$, and the first term B3S23R1 is identical to the GoL rule.

4   2D Fractal CA

The extension of a basic rule enables the construction of non-uniform CAs in which cells take different values for the extra radius R or follow different extended rules that belong to the sequence originating from the basic rule. This allows CAs with self-similar fractal structures to be derived as a special arrangement of the cells using the classical initiator-generator method [10]. In Sect. 4.2, F-CAs for 2D outer-totalistic CA rules are discussed, whereas those for 1D elementary CA, or F-ECAs, have been studied in the literature [5].

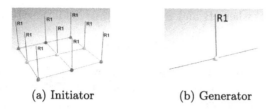

(a) Initiator   (b) Generator

Fig. 2. Initiator and generator of 2D F-CA. The white circles are cells, and the black lines are the links connecting them. The blue lines with an R1 sign represent the values of the extra radius R of the cells. In Fig. 2a, the four green cells at the corners are identical, and the two pairs of side cells (front and back (red) and left and right (yellow)) are also identical according to the periodic boundary conditions. (Color figure online)

4.1   2D Fractal Arrangement

To construct a self-similar fractal arrangement of cells that follows the extended rules in a sequence, an initiator and generator set must be defined. Given that the following discussion applies a periodic boundary condition (i.e., a torus), a F-CA with a Moore neighborhood begins with a 2×2 regular lattice, where the four R1 cells (green) at the corners are identical, and the two pairs of R1 cells (front and back (red) and left and right (yellow)) are also identical (Fig. 2a). Note that a generator can be adopted as two links with an R1 cell (Fig. 2b). Figure 3 shows that the level zero F-CA is identical to the initiator and that the level l F-CA is generated by the generator by replacing all links of the level $(l-1)$ F-CA. Eventually, the total number of independent cells becomes $2^{2(l+1)}$ at level l because the number of R2^l cells is four and that of R2^{l-m} cells is 3×2^{2m} ($m = 1 \ldots l$) due to the periodic boundary conditions (Fig. 3d).

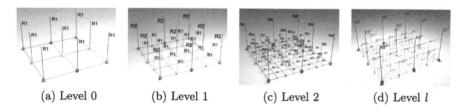

(a) Level 0   (b) Level 1   (c) Level 2   (d) Level l

Fig. 3. 2D F-CA with Moore neighborhood. The four green cells at the corners are identical, and the two pairs of side cells (front and back (red) and left and right (yellow)) are also identical due to the periodic boundary conditions. The level l F-CA is generated by replacing all links of the level $(l-1)$ F-CA (Fig. 2b). (Color figure online)

4.2   2D Fractal Outer-Totalistic CA

If we restrict examples to life-like CAs, which are outer-totalistic *binary* CAs (including the GoL), each rule can be denoted $Bb_1b_2 \cdots Ss_1s_2 \cdots$ in the

Golly/RLE format, where B and S mean "Born" and "Survival," respectively, and

$$b_1, b_2, \cdots, s_1, s_2, \cdots \in \{0, 1, 2, 3, 4, 5, 6, 7, 8\},$$

2D fractal life-like CAs can be constructed by arranging the cells presented above. As noteworthy examples, "Replicators" (B1357S02468 and B1357S1357 [11]) are expressed as follows:

$$f_{B1357S02468}(x_{(i,j)}^{(t)}) = \sum_{k=i-1}^{i+1} \sum_{l=j-1}^{j+1} \oplus x_{(k,l)}^{(t)}, \tag{16}$$

$$f_{B1357S1357}(x_{(i,j)}^{(t)}) = x_{(i,j)}^{(t)} \oplus \sum_{k=i-1}^{i+1} \sum_{l=j-1}^{j+1} \oplus x_{(k,l)}^{(t)}, \tag{17}$$

where $\oplus$ represents the exclusive-OR (XOR) operation. Because the latter function $f_{B1357S1357}$ is substantially independent of the current state of the center cell $x_{(i,j)}^{(t)}$ by the XOR between $x_{(i,j)}^{(t)}$ and $\sum\sum \oplus x_{(k,l)}^{(t)}$, the sequence [B1357S1357] is identical to the time evolution of a standard CA B1357S1357, as remarked in Sect. 3. As shown in Fig. 4, its F-CA, i.e., F-CA[B1357S1357] exhibits an interesting feature that every group of cells separated by the R value maintains an independent lifetime each: a group of cells with $R = 2^n$ has a lifetime of 2^n time steps, which means that all cell states of the group become zero from almost initial configurations after the lifetime and that each group evolves independently. The cause of the phenomena can be attributed to the coefficients of the extended rules in [B1357S1357] which form two-dimensional Sierpinski's gasket in the same manner that those of the extended rules in [#90] of ECA form one-dimensional Sierpinski's gasket [5].

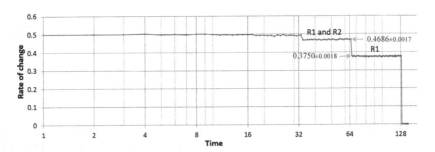

Fig. 4. A sample plot of rates of change of cell states in a level 7 F-CA[B1357S1357], starting from a pseudorandomly generated initial configuration. The red arrows indicate the averaged values for $time = 33 - 64$ and $65 - 128$, respectively. The values $0.4686 \pm 0.0017(std)$ and $0.3750 \pm 0.0018(std)$ correspond to the half values of the number rate of R1 and R2 cells $\frac{3 \times 2^{14}}{2^{16}} + \frac{3 \times 2^{12}}{2^{16}} = 0.9375$ and that of R1 cells $\frac{3 \times 2^{14}}{2^{16}} = 0.75$. (Color figure online)

As an attractive example among fractal ECAs, the time reversibility of linear rule #150 is inherited by its F-CA, denoted F-ECA[#150] [5]. Another linear rule B1357S02468 (Eq. 16) is also time reversible and leads to reversible F-CA[B1357S02468]. Although time reversibility for any level has not been proven mathematically, no counterexamples have been found to date[2]. The fractalization of the CA presented here is independent of the number of cell states; thus, multi-state CA rules can be adopted for the basic rules. If we assume linear 2^n-state (or modulo-2^n) CA [12], the above total sum is expressed by the modulo-2^n operation:

$$f_{modulo-2^n}(x_{(i,j)}^{(t)}) = (\sum_{k=i-1}^{i+1} \sum_{l=j-1}^{j+1} x_{(k,l)}^{(t)}) \bmod 2^n, \ (n = 1, 2, \cdots). \quad (18)$$

Note that the F-CA constructed from the above linear modulo-2^n rule also shows time reversibility. As a potential application, this may work as a diffusion algorithm for image encryption systems [13]. There are some possible advantages of such models, e.g., each cell can be used to handle an individual character or image pixel as is, and fewer time steps are required to fully scramble plain data. Specifically, from the above linear rule, the level l arrangement of the F-CA shows reversibility with a period 2^{l+n}. Table 1 illustrates the time reversibility of the uniform CA (R1 cells only) of the rule with $n = 4$ in Eq. (18) (16 colors) and the F-CA arrangement with level 7 (lattice size: 256 × 256). Figure 5a shows the changing averaged entropy of the cell-state frequencies of the process shown in Table 1. The rapid scrambling of the F-CA arrangement can be recognized by comparing the uniform CA and F-CA in Fig. 5b.

Table 1. Time reversibility of CA constructed from the 2D 16-state linear rule (Eq. (18)). The number of colors of the original Lenna image was reduced to $2^4 = 16$. The second and third rows show the time evolutions of the uniform CA (R1 cells only) and level 7 F-CA[modulo-2^4 linear], respectively. The period of the F-CA equals $2^{7+4} = 2048$ time steps.

Time	0: initial	1	2	⋯	2047	2048
Uniform CA				⋯		
Fractal CA				⋯		

As another example, fractally symmetric patterns generated from time advances of the F-CA can be used to design textiles. Table 2 shows sample pat-

---

[2] The time reversibility of F-CA[B1357S02468] was proved until level 2 by a round-robin check of all configurations.

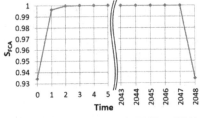
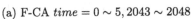
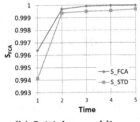

(a) F-CA *time* = 0 ∼ 5, 2043 ∼ 2048   (b) Initial scramblings

Fig. 5. Entropy changes of the cases in Table 1: (a) F-CA[modulo-2^4 linear] at *time* = $0 \sim 5$ and $2043 \sim 2048$, and (b) comparison of initial scramblings between the uniform CA (S_{STD}) and F-CA[modulo-2^4 linear] (S_{FCA}).

Table 2. Sample patterns of textile design using the level 8 F-CA[modulo-2^4 linear]. Each pattern appears from the respective initial state after the time steps. A color pallet showing the correspondence of cell states and colors is common to these three cases.

Initial State	Two $R=2^8$ cells at center and top-left	$R=2^8$ cell at center	Two $R=2^8$ cells at center and top-left
Time	4	5	30
F-CA level 8 16 colors			
Pallet	0 1 2 3 4 5 6 7 8 9 10 11 12 13 14 15		

terns generated from the F-CA of the linear modulo-2^n CA. Note that different initial configurations can reduce completely different patterns.

5   Conclusions and Discussion

The extension of standard CA rules using the REN algorithm allows the construction of non-uniform CA comprising cells with different sized perception areas. In this paper, we have proposed 2D F-CA by arranging such cells self-similarly and presented an implementation for outer-totalistic CA rules. By focusing on the extension of the linear CA rules, their features, such as replicability and reversibility, are carried over into their F-CA. In addition, image scrambling and textile design samples have been presented as specific application examples.

Note that the mathematical proof of the reversibility of F-CA[B1357S02468] should be provided, and its availability for encryption systems and the independent lifetimes of the cell groups of F-CA[B1357S1357] requires additional detailed discussion. Survey of F-CAs other than F-CA[modulo-2^n linear] is also the focus of our future work.

References

1. von Neumann, J.: The theory of self-reproducing automata. In: Burks, A.W. (ed.) Essays on Cellular Automata. University of Illinois Press (1966)
2. Kayama, Y.: Extension of cellular automata by introducing an algorithm of recursive estimation of neighbors. In: Proceedings of the 21st International Symposium on Artificial Life and Robotics, pp. 73–77 (2016)
3. Kayama, Y.: Expansion of perception area in cellular automata using recursive algorithm. In: Proceedings of the Fifteenth International Conference on the Simulation and Synthesis of Living Systems, pp. 92–99 (2016)
4. Reynolds, C.W.: Flocks, herds and schools: a distributed behavioral model. ACM SIGGRAPH Comput. Graph. **21**(4), 25–34 (1987)
5. Kayama, Y.: Cellular automata in fractal arrangement. In: Proceedings of the 23rd International Symposium on Artificial Life and Robotics (2018)
6. Gardner, M.: Mathematical games. Sci. Am. **223**, 102–123 (1970)
7. Berlekamp, E.R., Conway, J.H., Guy, R.K.: Winning Ways for Your Mathematical Plays. Academic, New York (1982)
8. Adamatzky, A. (ed.): Game of Life Cellular Automata. Springer, London (2010). https://doi.org/10.1007/978-1-84996-217-9
9. Eppstein, D.: Growth and decay in life-like cellular automata. In: Adamatzky, A. (ed.) Game of Life Cellular Automata, pp. 71–98. Springer, London (2010). https://doi.org/10.1007/978-1-84996-217-9_6
10. Mandelbrot, B.B., Pignoni, R.: The Fractal Geometry of Nature, vol. 173. WH Freeman, New York (1983)
11. Fredkin, E.: An informational process based on reversible universal cellular automata. Phys. D: Nonlinear Phenom. **45**(1–3), 254–270 (1990)
12. Willson, S.J.: Calculating growth rates and moments for additive cellular automata. Discrete Appl. Math. **35**(1), 47–65 (1992)
13. Wang, X., Luan, D.: A novel image encryption algorithm using chaos and reversible cellular automata. Commun. Nonlinear Sci. Numer. Simul. **18**(11), 3075–3085 (2013)

Self-verifying Cellular Automata

Martin Kutrib[1] and Thomas Worsch[2(⊠)]

[1] Institut für Informatik, Universität Giessen, Arndtstr. 2, 35392 Giessen, Germany
`kutrib@informatik.uni-giessen.de`
[2] Karlsruhe Institute of Technology, Karlsruhe, Germany
`worsch@kit.edu`

Abstract. We study the computational capacity of self-verifying cellular automata with an emphasis on one-way information flow (SVOCA). A self-verifying device is a nondeterministic device where each computation path can give one of the answers *yes*, *no*, or *do not know*. For every input word, at least one computation path must give either the answer *yes* or *no*, and the answers given must not be contradictory. Realtime SVOCA are strictly more powerful than realtime deterministic one-way cellular automata. They can be sped-up from lineartime to realtime and are capable to simulate any lineartime computation of deterministic two-way CA. Closure and decidability properties are considered as well.

1 Introduction

What is the power of nondeterminism in bounded-resource computations? Traditionally, nondeterministic devices have been viewed as having as many nondeterministic guesses as time steps. The studies of this concept of unlimited nondeterminism led, for example, to the famous open LBA-problem or the unsolved question whether or not P equals NP. In order to gain further understanding of the nature of nondeterminism, in for example [9] it has been viewed as an additional limited resource at the disposal of time or space bounded computations. We study the computational power of self-verifying cellular automata (SVCA). A self-verifying device is a nondeterministic device with symmetric conditions for acceptance/rejection. Each computation path can give one of the answers *yes*, *no*, or *do not know*. For every input word, at least one computation path must give either the answer *yes* or *no*, and the answers given must not be contradictory. So, if a computation path gives the answer *yes* or *no*, in both cases the answer is definitely correct. This justifies the notion *self-verifying* and is in contrast to general nondeterministic computations, where an answer that is not *yes* does not allow to conclude whether or not the input belongs to the language.

Self-verifying finite automata have been introduced and studied in [6,11,12] mainly in connection with randomized Las Vegas computations. Descriptional complexity issues for self-verifying finite automata have been studied in [14]. The computational and descriptional complexity of self-verifying pushdown automata has been studied in [8].

© Springer Nature Switzerland AG 2018
G. Mauri et al. (Eds.): ACRI 2018, LNCS 11115, pp. 340–351, 2018.
https://doi.org/10.1007/978-3-319-99813-8_31

The paper is organized as follows. In Sect. 2 we present the basic notation and the definitions of self-verifying (one-way) cellular automata as well as an introductory example. In Sect. 3 a strong speed-up result is derived that allows the conversion of lineartime SVOCA to realtime. Section 4 is devoted to explore the computational capacity of realtime SVOCA. It turns out that they are even capable to simulate any lineartime computation of a two-way CA. Moreover, the closure properties of the family of languages accepted by realtime SVOCA are studied. It is shown that the family is closed under the set-theoretic operations, reversal, concatenation, and inverse homomorphisms. Finally, decidability problems are considered. In particular, the property of being self-verifying turns out to be non-semidecidable.

Because of a page limit not all proofs are included in the version for the conference proceedings, but a research report with all details is available at [17].

2   Preliminaries

We denote the positive integers $\{1, 2, \dots\}$ by $\mathbb{N}$, the set $\mathbb{N} \cup \{0\}$ by $\mathbb{N}_0$, and the *powerset* of a set S by 2^S. We write $|S|$ for the *cardinality* of S. Let Σ denote a finite set of letters. Then we write Σ^* for the *set of all finite words* (strings) consisting of letters from Σ. The *empty word* is denoted by λ, and we set $\Sigma^+ = \Sigma^* \setminus \{\lambda\}$. For the *reversal of a word* w we write w^R and for its *length* we write $|w|$. A subset of Σ^* is called a *language* over Σ. The devices we will consider cannot accept the empty word. So, in order to avoid technical overloading in writing, two languages L and L' are considered to be equal, if they differ at most by the empty word, that is, if $L \setminus \{\lambda\} = L' \setminus \{\lambda\}$. Set *inclusion* is denoted by $\subseteq$ and *strict set inclusion* by $\subset$.

A two-way cellular automaton is a linear array of identical finite automata, called cells, numbered $1, \dots, n$. Except for border cells the state transition depends on the current state of a cell itself and those of its both nearest neighbors. Border cells receive a boundary symbol on their free input lines. Synchronous state changes take place at discrete time steps.

We first define *nondeterministic* cellular automata. The nondeterminism is restricted to the first step. All further transitions are deterministic [2, 16]. Although this is a very restricted case, we call such devices nondeterministic.

A *nondeterministic two-way cellular automaton* (NCA, for short) is a system $M = \langle S, \Sigma, F, \#, \delta_{nd}, \delta_d \rangle$, where

1. S is the finite, nonempty set of *cell states*,
2. $\Sigma \subseteq S$ is the nonempty set of *input symbols*,
3. $F \subseteq S$ is the set of *accepting states*,
4. $\# \notin S$ is the *boundary symbol*,
5. $\delta_{nd} \colon (S \cup \{\#\}) \times S \times (S \cup \{\#\}) \to (2^S \setminus \emptyset)$ is the *nondeterministic local transition function* applied in the first state transition,
6. $\delta_d \colon (S \cup \{\#\}) \times S \times (S \cup \{\#\}) \to S$ is the *deterministic local transition function* applied in all further state transitions.

In a *one-way* cellular automaton the next state of each cell only depends on the state of the cell itself and the state of its immediate neighbor to the right. So the domain of the transition functions is $S \times (S \cup \{\#\})$.

A *configuration* c_t of M at time $t \geq 0$ is a mapping $c_t : \{1, 2, \ldots, n\} \to S$, for $n \geq 1$, occasionally represented as a word over S. The *initial configuration* c_0 for an input $w = a_1 a_2 \cdots a_n \in \Sigma^+$ is defined by $c_0(i) = a_i$, for $1 \leq i \leq n$. For example, the initial configuration of an NOCA for w is represented by $a_1 a_2 \cdots a_n$. Successor configurations are computed according to the global transition function Δ mapping each configuration to a set of successor configurations.

For an NCA configuration c_t the set of its successors c_{t+1} is defined as:

$$c_{t+1} \in \Delta(c_t) \iff \begin{cases} c_{t+1}(1) \in \sigma(\#, c_t(1), c_t(2)) \\ c_{t+1}(i) \in \sigma(c_t(i-1), c_t(i), c_t(i+1)), i \in \{2, \ldots, n-1\} \\ c_{t+1}(n) \in \sigma(c_t(n-1), c_t(n), \#) \end{cases}$$

where $\sigma = \delta_{nd}$ if $t = 0$, and $\sigma = \delta_d$ if $t \geq 1$. For NOCA the global transition function is defined analogously. Thus, Δ is induced by δ_{nd} and δ_d. An NCA (NOCA) is *deterministic* if $\delta_{nd}(s_1, s_2, s_3)$ ($\delta_{nd}(s_1, s_2)$) is a singleton for all states $s_1, s_2, s_3 \in S \cup \{\#\}$. Deterministic cellular automata are denoted by CA and OCA.

An input w is *accepted* by a cellular automaton if at some time step during some computation the leftmost cell enters an accepting state. The *language accepted by* M is $L(M) = \{ w \in \Sigma^+ \mid w \text{ is accepted by } M \}$. Let $t : \mathbb{N} \to \mathbb{N}$ be a mapping. If all $w \in L(M)$ are accepted with at most $t(|w|)$ time steps, then M is said to be of time complexity t (see [15] for a more on this general treatment of time complexity functions). If $t(n) = n$ acceptance is said to be in *realtime*. If $t(n) = k \cdot n$ for a rational number $k \geq 1$, then acceptance is in *lineartime*. The set of all languages accepted by devices X with time complexity t is denoted by $\mathscr{L}_t(X)$. We write $\mathscr{L}_{rt}(X)$ for real time and $\mathscr{L}_{lt}(X)$ for linear time.

Now we turn to *self-verifying* (one-way) cellular automata (SV(O)CA). As for NCA during the first step cells may choose between several new states. But the definition of acceptance is different from nondeterministic CA.

There are now three disjoint sets of states representing answers *yes*, *no*, and *do not know*. Moreover, for every input word, at least one computation path must give either the answer *yes* or *no*, and the answers given must not be contradictory. In order to implement the three possible answers the state set is partitioned into three disjoint subsets $S = F_+ \dot\cup F_- \dot\cup F_0$, where F_+ is the set of accepting states, F_- is the set of rejecting states, and $F_0 = S \setminus (F_+ \cup F_-)$ is referred to as the set of neutral states. We specify F_+ and F_- in place of the set F. of SVCA and SVOCA. So, let $M = \langle S, \Sigma, F_+, F_-, \#, \delta_{nd}, \delta_d \rangle$ be an SVOCA. For each input $w \in \Sigma^+$, the set of states reachable by cell 1 is defined as $S_w = \{ s \in S \mid s \in (\Delta^{[t]}(w\#))(1) \text{ for some } t \geq 0 \}$, where $\Delta^{[t]}$ denotes the t-fold composition of Δ, that is, the set of configurations reachable in t time steps. For the "self-verifying property" it is required that for each $w \in \Sigma^+$, $S_w \cap F_+$ is empty if and only if $S_w \cap F_-$ is nonempty.

If all $w \in L(M)$ are accepted and all $w \notin L(M)$ are rejected after at most $t(|w|)$ time steps, then the self-verifying cellular automaton M is said to be of time complexity t. We illustrate the definitions with an example.

Example 1. The non-semilinear unary language $\{\, a^{2^n} \mid n \geq 0 \,\}$ is accepted by the SVOCA $M = \langle \{a, -, 1, X, \sim, <_1, <_2, \ominus, \otimes, \oplus, 0\}, \{a\}, F_+, F_-, \#, \delta_{nd}, \delta_d \rangle$ in realtime, where $F_+ = \{\oplus\}$, $F_- = \{\ominus, \otimes\}$, and the transition functions δ_{nd} and δ_d are defined as follows.

(1) $\delta_{nd}(a, a) = \{1, -\}$

(2) $\delta_{nd}(a, \#) = \{\oplus\}$

(3) $\delta_d(1, -) = X$

(4) $\delta_d(-, -) = -$

(5) $\delta_d(-, 1) = <_1$

(6) $\delta_d(-, <_1) = -$

(7) $\delta_d(-, <_2) = <_1$

(8) $\delta_d(X, -) = X$

(9) $\delta_d(X, <_1) = X$

(10) $\delta_d(<_1, X) = <_2$

(11) $\delta_d(<_1, \sim) = <_2$

(12) $\delta_d(<_2, X) = \sim$

(13) $\delta_d(<_2, \sim) = \sim$

(14) $\delta_d(\sim, \sim) = \sim$

(15) $\delta_d(1, \oplus) = \oplus$

(16) $\delta_d(X, \otimes) = \oplus$

(17) $\delta_d(<_1, \oplus) = \otimes$

(18) $\delta_d(<_1, \ominus) = \otimes$

(19) $\delta_d(<_2, \ominus) = \ominus$

(20) $\delta_d(\sim, \oplus) = \ominus$

(21) $\delta_d(\sim, \ominus) = \ominus$

In addition to these transitions, δ_d maps any state from $\{\ominus, \otimes, \oplus, 0\}$ to itself, regardless of its neighbor. And all still undefined transitions map to the state 0.

The idea of the construction is as follows (see Fig. 1). Assume that the cells are numbered from 1 to n from right to left. In the first step, each cell guesses whether its position is 2^i, for some $i \geq 1$ (1). Accordingly they enter state 1 or $-$. The rightmost cell can identify itself and always enters state $\oplus$ (2). Next, each cell in state 1 sends a signal with speed 1/2 to the left. The signal is realized by states $<_1$ and $<_2$ (5–7 and 10–13). Moreover, cells in state 1 change to state X (3) and each cell passed through by such a signal changes to state $\sim$ (12–14).

In addition, initially a signal s is sent by the rightmost cell to the left with speed 1. This signal is realized by the states $\{\ominus, \otimes, \oplus\}$ and possibly by state 0 if an initial guess is wrong. The states $\{\ominus, \otimes, \oplus\}$ represent accepting and rejecting decisions of the cells. Once such state is entered it is never left again. Therefore the decisions are not contradictory. Now the idea is that the initial guess is verified if and only if signal s meets a 1/2-speed signal in a cell that initially guessed to be at some position 2^i and, thus, is now in state X (16–21).

In order to evidence the correctness of the construction, let us first assume the initial guesses are correct. Then cells 1 and 2 behave as required by Transitions 2 and 15. Now let some cell 2^i enter the accepting state $\oplus$ at time 2^i (which is true for cells 1 and 2). Then the 1/2-speed signal sent by that cell has reached cell $2^i + 2^{i-1}$. This implies that the fast and slow signal will meet in cell 2^{i+1}, as required. Altogether, for the case of initially correct guesses, the decisions are never contradictory, they are correct, and the guesses are verified to be true.

For the cases where one of the initial guesses is wrong, the neutral state 0 is used. Whenever a slow and the fast signal do not meet in a cell being in state X, state 0 is entered. Moreover, it is entered whenever two neighboring cells are in state 1. In particular, since the state 0 is never left, the fast signal checks the correctness of the initial guesses from right to left. It is stopped by any cell in the neutral state 0. Again, no contradictory decisions are made and, no decision

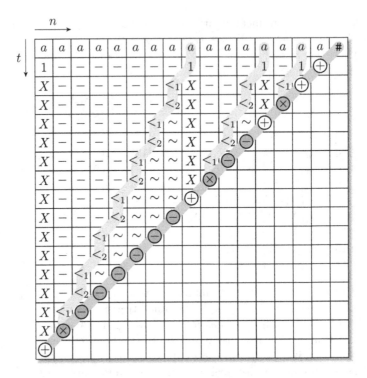

Fig. 1. Computation of a realtime SVOCA accepting the language $\{\, a^{2^n} \mid n \geq 0 \,\}$. Slow signals moving with speed $1/2$ are depicted in light gray, the fast signal with states $\ominus, \otimes, \oplus$ in a darker gray.

is made by the leftmost cell in case of wrong guesses. So, this realtime one-way cellular automaton accepts language $\{\, a^{2^n} \mid n \geq 0 \,\}$ and it is self-verifying. ∎

3   Characterization and Speed-Up

First we give evidence that self-verifying (one-way) cellular automata are in fact a generalization of deterministic (one-way) cellular automata. To this end, it is reasonable to consider only time complexities t that allow the leftmost cell to recognize the time step $t(n)$. Such functions are said to be *time-computable*. For example, the identity $t(n) = n$ is a time-computable time complexity for (O)CA. A signal which is initially emitted by the rightmost cell and moves with maximal speed, arrives at the leftmost cell exactly at time step n. By slowing down the signal to speed $\frac{x}{y}$ (that is, the signal moves x cells to the left and then stays in a cell for $y - x$ time steps), it is seen that the time complexities $\lfloor \frac{y}{x} \cdot n \rfloor$, for any positive integers $x < y$, are time-computable. More details can be found in [3].

Lemma 2. *Any (one-way) deterministic cellular automaton with a time-computable time complexity t can effectively be converted into an equivalent (one-way) self-verifying cellular automaton with the same time complexity t.*

For any time-computable time complexity t, the closures of the families $\mathscr{L}_t$(SVOCA) and $\mathscr{L}_t$(SVCA) under complementation are immediately seen. In order to construct an SVOCA that accepts the complement of the language accepted by a given SVOCA, it is sufficient to interchange the accepting and rejecting states while the neutral states remain as they are. On the other hand, Example 1 gives a witness for the strictness of the inclusion $\mathscr{L}_{rt}$(OCA) $\subset$ $\mathscr{L}_{rt}$(SVOCA) since all unary languages accepted by realtime OCA are regular. This observation raises the natural question whether every language accepted by some realtime NOCA, whose complement is again accepted by some realtime NOCA, is accepted by a realtime SVOCA.

Proposition 3. *Let t be a time-computable time complexity. Every language $L \in \mathscr{L}_t(NCA)$ whose complement $\overline{L}$ belongs to $\mathscr{L}_t(NCA)$ as well is accepted by some t-time SVCA. The same is true for one-way devices.*

Proof. Let M_1 be a device accepting L and M_2 be a device accepting $\overline{L}$ with time complexity t. Now a t-time self-verifying devices M simulates M_1 and M_2 on different tracks, that is, it uses the same two channel technique of [7,19].

Then it remains to define the set of accepting states as $F_+ = \{\, (s, s') \mid s \in F_1 \,\}$ and the set of rejecting states as $F_- = \{\, (s, s') \mid s' \in F_2 \,\}$, where F_1 is the set of accepting states of M_1 and F_2 is the set of accepting states of M_2.   □

Since it is straightforward to extract an NOCA accepting the complement of $L(M)$ from a given SVOCA M, the characterizations of the next theorem have been derived.

Theorem 4. *Let t be a time-computable time complexity. The family of languages $L \in \mathscr{L}_t(NCA)$ such that $\overline{L}$ belongs to $\mathscr{L}_t(NCA)$ as well coincides with the family $\mathscr{L}_t(SVCA)$. The same is true for one-way devices.*

Several types of cellular automata can be sped-up by a constant amount of time as long as the remaining time complexity does not fall below realtime. A proof in terms of trellis automata can be found in [4]. In [13] the speed-up results are shown for deterministic and nondeterministic cellular and iterative automata. The proofs are based on sequential machine characterizations of the parallel devices. In particular, deterministic CA and OCA can be sped-up from $(n + t(n))$-time to $(n + \frac{t(n)}{k})$-time [1,13]. Thus, lineartime is close to realtime. The question whether every lineartime CA can be sped-up to realtime is an open problem. The problem is solved for OCA. The realtime OCA languages are a proper subfamily of the lineartime OCA languages [4,20].

Next we are going to derive a stronger result for SVOCA from which follows that realtime is as powerful as lineartime. The result follows from the characterization of Theorem 4 and known results for NCA and NOCA [2], where the so-called *packing-and-checking* technique is introduced and used. The basic principle is to guess the input in a packed form on the left of the array. Then the verification of the guess can be done by a deterministic OCA in realtime.

Theorem 5. *Let $k \geq 1$ and t be a time-computable time complexity. Then $\mathscr{L}_{k \cdot t}(SVCA) = \mathscr{L}_t(SVCA)$. The same is true for one-way devices.*

Proof. Given a $(k \cdot t)$-time SVCA M, there are $(k \cdot t)$-time NCA M_1 and M_2 with $L(M_1) = L(M)$ and $L(M_1) = \overline{L(M)}$ by Theorem 4. Both can be sped-up to t-time as shown in [2]. Applying Theorem 4 again yields a t-time SVCA that accepts $L(M)$. The reasoning for one-way devices is similar.   □

In particular, we have:

Corollary 6. *The families $\mathscr{L}_{rt}(SVOCA)$ and $\mathscr{L}_{lt}(SVOCA)$ coincide and the families $\mathscr{L}_{rt}(SVCA)$ and $\mathscr{L}_{lt}(SVCA)$ coincide.*

4   Self-verifying One-Way Cellular Automata

4.1   Computational Capacity

First we recall that Example 1 gives a witness for the strictness of the following inclusion.

Theorem 7. *The family $\mathscr{L}_{rt}(OCA)$ is properly included in $\mathscr{L}_{rt}(SVOCA)$.*

The inclusion of the previous result can be pushed higher in the hierarchy of language families. However, the strictness of the inclusion gets lost. The question of the strictness is strongly related to the famous open problem whether or not the realtime CA languages are a proper subfamily of the CA languages.

Theorem 8. *The family $\mathscr{L}_{lt}(CA)$ is included in $\mathscr{L}_{rt}(SVOCA)$.*

Proof. Let $L \in \mathscr{L}_{lt}(CA)$. Since the family $\mathscr{L}_{lt}(CA)$ is closed under reversal [19], there exists a lineartime CA accepting L^R. This CA, in turn, can be sped-up by a multiplicative and additive constant [13]. Hence there is a CA $M = \langle S, \Sigma, F, \#, \delta \rangle$ that accepts L^R with time complexity $2n - 1$.

First a deterministic OCA $M' = \langle S', \Sigma', F, \#, \delta' \rangle$ is constructed such that M' accepts the language $\{ \sqcup^{|w|} w^R \mid w \in L(M) \}$ with time complexity $2n - 2$, (where $\sqcup \notin S$ and $n > 1$): Let $S' = (S \cup \{\sqcup\}) \cup (S \cup \{\sqcup\})^2$, $A' = A \cup \{\sqcup\}$, and $\forall s_1, s_2 \in S \cup \{\sqcup\}$: let $\delta'(s_1, \#) = (s_1, \sqcup)$ and $\delta'(s_1, s_2) = (s_1, s_2)$. Furthermore $\forall (s_1, s_2), (s_2, s_3) \in (S \cup \{\sqcup\})^2$:

$$\delta'((s_1, s_2), (s_2, s_3)) = \begin{cases} \delta(s_3, s_2, s_1) & \text{if } (s_1 \neq \sqcup \wedge s_2 \neq \sqcup \wedge s_3 \neq \sqcup) \\ \delta(\#, s_2, s_1) & \text{if } (s_1 \neq \sqcup \wedge s_2 \neq \sqcup \wedge s_3 = \sqcup) \\ \delta(s_3, s_2, \#) & \text{if } (s_1 = \sqcup \wedge s_2 \neq \sqcup \wedge s_3 \neq \sqcup) \\ \sqcup & \text{otherwise} \end{cases}.$$

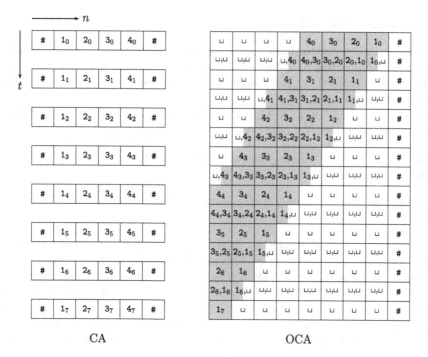

Fig. 2. Example for the proof of Theorem 8.

The basic idea is that during an intermediate step the cells of M' are collecting the information needed to simulate one step of the CA (see Fig. 2). Due to the one-way information flow a cell i thereby can collect information from the cells $i+1$ and $i+2$ and, thus, simulate one step of the CA cell $i+1$. Therefore, the relevant part of the configuration shifts in space to the left.

The cells of an SVOCA M'' that accepts the language $\{\, w^R \mid w \in L(M) \,\}$ are constructed such that they can store two input symbols. Under input w^R the SVOCA M'' guesses in its first step the configuration $\sqcup^{|w|} w^R$ whereby two adjacent symbols are stored in one cell, respectively. The subsequent verification of the guess can be done by a deterministic realtime OCA as shown by the packing-and-checking technique in [2]. In parallel to the verification M'' simulates the OCA M' with double speed on the compressed input. Therefore, M'' has time complexity $1 + \frac{2n-2}{2} = n$. Since $L(M'') = \{\, w^R \mid w \in L(M) \,\} = L^R(M) = (L^R)^R = L$ the theorem follows.

In order to make M'' self-verifying it enters accepting states if the guesses are correct and the simulation ends accepting, and enters rejecting states when the guesses are correct and the simulation does *not* end in an accepting state. All other states, in particular those entered in case of wrong guesses, are neutral. □

4.2   Closure Properties

This section is devoted to the closure properties of the family of realtime SVOCA languages, summarized in Table 1. From above we know already that the family of languages accepted by realtime SVOCA is closed under complementation, union, and intersection.

It is known that $\mathscr{L}_{rt}(OCA)$ is closed under reversal [4], which is a long-standing open problem for $\mathscr{L}_{rt}(CA)$.

Proposition 9. *The family of languages accepted by realtime SVOCA is closed under reversal.*

Proposition 10. *The family of languages accepted by realtime SVOCA is closed under concatenation.*

Proof. Let $L_1, L_2 \in \mathscr{L}_{rt}(SVOCA)$. If the empty word belongs to L_1 then language L_2 belongs to the concatenation and vice versa. Since the family of languages accepted by realtime SVOCA is closed under union, it remains to consider languages $L_1, L_2 \in \mathscr{L}_{rt}(SVOCA)$ that do not contain the empty word. Let M_1, M_2 be acceptors for L_1 and L_2. As an intermediate step, we construct a self-verifying cellular automaton M with two-way information flow, that is, each cell is connected to its both nearest neighbors and the leftmost cell receives a boundary symbol on its free input line.

Since the family $\mathscr{L}_{rt}(SVOCA)$ is closed under reversal, there is a realtime SVOCA M_1^R that accepts the reversal L_1^R of L_1. Now M has two tracks with identical inputs. On one track it simulates M_2, whereby each cell that enters an accepting or rejecting state is marked accordingly. On the second track, M simulates M_1^R from left to right. That is, the simulation is such that each cell receives the state from its left neighbor. So, the information flow is from left to right. Again, each cell that enters an accepting or rejecting state is marked accordingly.

Let the input be $x_1 x_2 \cdots x_n$. If a cell at position i is marked accepting by the simulation of M_2, the word $x_i x_{i+1} \cdots x_n$ belongs to the language L_2. If a cell at position i is marked accepting by the simulation of M_1^R, the word $x_i x_{i-1} \cdots x_1$ belongs to the language L_1^R and, thus, $x_1 x_2 \cdots x_i$ belongs to the language L_1. So, the input $x_1 x_2 \cdots x_n$ belongs to the concatenation $L_1 L_2$ if and only if M_1^R may mark a cell at position i and M_2 a cell at position $i+1$ accepting, for $1 \le i < n$.

In order to check this condition, M uses a signal that is emitted from the rightmost cell when the simulation of M_1^R reaches that cell at time step n. The signal moves to the left and informs the leftmost cell at time step $2n$.

When the signal arrives, the leftmost cell enters an accepting state if and only if the signal has found two adjacent cells marked accepting. So, M accepts any input from $L_1 L_2$ and only inputs from the concatenation $L_1 L_2$. If the signal found neither two adjacent cells marked accepting, nor two adjacent cells that are marked accepting and unmarked, nor two adjacent cells unmarked the leftmost cell enters a rejecting state. In this case, no matter between which two adjacent symbols one assumes the cut between first and second factor, M has explicitly rejected at least one of them. Clearly, in this case the input cannot belong to the concatenation. On the other hand, if some input does not belong to the concatenation, then there is always a computation of M that results in such a marking. So, M rejects any input that does not belong to $L_1 L_2$ and only inputs that do not belong to $L_1 L_2$. In any other case, the leftmost cell remains in a neutral state.

So far, we have constructed a two-way self-verifying cellular automaton with time complexity $2n$. The proof of Theorem 8 can almost literally be used to show that also a lineartime two-way self-verifying cellular automaton can be simulated by a realtime SVOCA. □

Next, we turn to the operations homomorphism and inverse homomorphism.

Proposition 11. *The family of languages accepted by realtime SVOCA is not closed under homomorphisms.*

Proof. It is well known that every recursively enumerable language is the homomorphic image of the intersection of two context-free languages [10]. Moreover, every context-free language is the homomorphic image of the intersection of a regular language and a Dyck language [5].

The Dyck languages as well as the regular languages are realtime OCA languages [7] and therefore realtime SVOCA languages. Additionally, the family of realtime SVOCA languages is closed under intersection. So, if the family $\mathscr{L}_{rt}(\text{SVOCA})$ would be closed under homomorphisms, it would contain every recursively enumerable language. Due to the time bound to realtime this is a contradiction. □

Proposition 12. *The family of languages accepted by realtime SVOCA is closed under inverse homomorphisms.*

The closure of $\mathscr{L}_{rt}(\text{SVOCA})$ with respect to Kleene star and non-erasing homomorphisms are not known. They are settled for nondeterministic devices since, basically, for iteration it is sufficient to guess the the positions in the array at which words are concatenated, and for non-erasing homomorphism it is sufficient to guess the pre-image of the input. However, self-verifying devices have to reject explicitly if the input does not belong to the language. It seems that they have to 'know' that all choices either do not lead to accepting computations or are 'wrong.'

Table 1. Closure properties of the language family $\mathscr{L}_{rt}(\text{SVOCA})$ in comparison with the family $\mathscr{L}_{rt}(\text{OCA})$, where h_λ denotes λ-free homomorphisms.

Family	$-$	$\cup$	$\cap$	R	$\cdot$	$*$	h_λ	h	h^{-1}
$\mathscr{L}_{rt}(\text{SVOCA})$	Yes	Yes	Yes	Yes	Yes	?	?	No	Yes
$\mathscr{L}_{rt}(\text{OCA})$		Yes	Yes	Yes	No	No	No	No	Yes

4.3 Decidability Questions

Now we turn to decidability questions. The membership problem is decidable for realtime SVOCA languages since the family is effectively included in the deterministic context-sensitive languages. However, even realtime OCA can accept the so-called valid computations of Turing machines. These are languages of encodings of accepting Turing machine computations (see [18] for details or [15] for a survey). Hence many of the not even semi-decidable problems for Turing machines can be reduced to realtime OCA (see [18] for details or [15] for a survey). The following theorem is from [15].

Theorem 13. *For any language family that effectively contains $\mathscr{L}_{rt}(OCA)$ the problems emptiness, universality, finiteness, infiniteness, context-freeness, and regularity are not semidecidable.*

So, we have the following consequences.

Corollary 14. *The problems emptiness, universality, finiteness, infiniteness, inclusion, equivalence, regularity, and context-freeness are not semidecidable for realtime SVOCA.*

Finally, we turn to the problem to decide whether a given realtime nondeterministic one-way cellular automaton is self-verifying or not.

Theorem 15. *Given a realtime deterministic one-way cellular automaton M, it is not semidecidable whether or not M is an SVOCA.*

Proof. Let M be a realtime OCA with accepting states F. An equivalent realtime SVOCA M' is constructed (Lemma 2). Next, M' is modified by adding a new input symbol (and neutral state) $\boxminus$ and new states $\ominus \in F_-$ and $\oplus \in F_+$. The transition functions are modified such that a cell in state $\boxminus$ in the first step nondeterministically can either change to $\ominus$ and remain in that state forever or to stay in $\boxminus$ unless its right neighbor is in an accepting state. In the latter case, the cell changes from state $\boxminus$ to $\oplus$ and stays in that state from then on.

We claim that M' is self-verifying if and only if $L(M')$ is empty. If $L(M')$ is empty, none of its cells will ever enter an accepting state. So, a cell that is in state $\ominus$ remains in $\ominus$ and, thus, will not give a contradictory answer. On the other hand, if there is $w \in L(M')$, then on input $\boxminus w$ by the choices of the leftmost cell there is a rejecting computation, but an accepting one as well. Therefore, in this case, M' is not self-verifying. If it were semidecidable whether a realtime OCA is self-verifying then one could semidecide emptiness contradicting Corollary 14. □

By Lemma 2 any deterministic CA with a time-computable time complexity can effectively be made self-verifying. But it is non-semidecidable whether it already *is* self-verifying. That generalizes immediately to nondeterministic cellular automata. However, Lemma 2 does not since an input may induce accepting as well as non-accepting computations, which would become rejecting. In fact, it is an open problem whether the family of realtime one-way nondeterministic cellular automata is closed under complementation or not.

References

1. Bucher, W., Čulik II, K.: On real time and linear time cellular automata. RAIRO Inform. Théor. **18**, 307–325 (1984)
2. Buchholz, T., Klein, A., Kutrib, M.: On interacting automata with limited nondeterminism. Fundam. Inform. **52**, 15–38 (2002)
3. Buchholz, T., Kutrib, M.: On time computability of functions in one-way cellular automata. Acta Inform. **35**, 329–352 (1998)
4. Choffrut, C., Čulik II, K.: On real-time cellular automata and trellis automata. Acta Inform. **21**, 393–407 (1984)
5. Chomsky, N.: Context-free grammars and pushdown storage. Tech report, QPR 65, Massachusetts Institute of Technology (1962)
6. Duriš, P., Hromkovič, J., Rolim, J.D.P., Schnitger, G.: Las Vegas versus determinism for one-way communication complexity, finite automata, and polynomial-time computations. In: Reischuk, R., Morvan, M. (eds.) STACS 1997. LNCS, vol. 1200, pp. 117–128. Springer, Heidelberg (1997). https://doi.org/10.1007/BFb0023453
7. Dyer, C.R.: One-way bounded cellular automata. Inf. Control **44**, 261–281 (1980)
8. Fernau, H., Kutrib, M., Wendlandt, M.: Self-verifying pushdown automata. In: Freund, R., Mráz, F., Průša, D. (eds.) Non-Classical Models of Automata and Applications (NCMA 2017), vol. 329, pp. 103–117. Austrian Computer Society, Vienna (2017). books@ocg.at
9. Fischer, P.C., Kintala, C.M.R.: Real-time computations with restricted nondeterminism. Math. Syst. Theory **12**, 219–231 (1979)
10. Ginsburg, S., Greibach, S.A., Harrison, M.A.: One-way stack automata. J. ACM **14**, 389–418 (1967)
11. Hromkovic, J., Schnitger, G.: On the power of Las Vegas for one-way communication complexity, OBDDs, and finite automata. Inf. Comput. **169**, 284–296 (2001)
12. Hromkovic, J., Schnitger, G.: Nondeterministic communication with a limited number of advice bits. SIAM J. Comput. **33**, 43–68 (2003)
13. Ibarra, O.H., Kim, S.M., Moran, S.: Sequential machine characterizations of trellis and cellular automata and applications. SIAM J. Comput. **14**, 426–447 (1985)
14. Jirásková, G., Pighizzini, G.: Optimal simulation of self-verifying automata by deterministic automata. Inf. Comput. **209**, 528–535 (2011)
15. Kutrib, M.: Cellular automata and language theory. In: Meyers, R. (ed.) Encyclopedia of Complexity and System Science, pp. 800–823. Springer, Heidelberg (2009). https://doi.org/10.1007/978-0-387-30440-3
16. Kutrib, M.: Non-deterministic cellular automata and languages. Int. J. Gen. Syst. **41**, 555–568 (2012)
17. Kutrib, M., Worsch, Th.: Self-verifying cellular automata. Technical report, 1803, Universität Gießen (2018). http://www.informatik.uni-giessen.de/reports/Report1803.pdf
18. Malcher, A.: Descriptional complexity of cellular automata and decidability questions. J. Autom. Lang. Comb. **7**, 549–560 (2002)
19. Smith III, A.R.: Real-time language recognition by one-dimensional cellular automata. J. Comput. Syst. Sci. **6**, 233–253 (1972)
20. Umeo, H., Morita, K., Sugata, K.: Deterministic one-way simulation of two-way real-time cellular automata and its related problems. Inf. Process. Lett. **14**, 158–161 (1982)

CARPenter: A Cellular Automata Based Resilient Pentavalent Stream Cipher

Rohit Lakra, Anita John, and Jimmy Jose$^{(\boxtimes)}$

Department of Computer Science and Engineering,
National Institute of Technology Calicut, Kozhikode, India
{rohit_m160263cs,anita_p170007cs,jimmy}@nitc.ac.in

Abstract. Cellular Automata (CA) are a self reproducing model widely accepted for their applications in pattern recognition, VLSI design, error correcting codes, cryptography etc. They have also been widely accepted as good random number generators. The pseudorandom properties of 3- and 4-neighbourhood CA have been studied and they show that the neighbourhood radii has an impact on pseudorandomness. This motivated us to perform the exploration of 5-neighbourhood 1-dimensional CA for better cryptographic properties. We construct a class of linear and nonlinear rules for 5-neighbourhood CA and also propose a new stream cipher design using 5-neighbourhood CA inspired from the Grain cipher.

Keywords: Cellular Automata (CA) · 3-neighbourhood CA
5-neighbourhood CA · Cryptography · Stream Cipher

1 Introduction

In cryptography, the encryption techniques can be classified as symmetric key encryption and asymmetric key encryption. Symmetric key encryption encrypts plaintext into ciphertext using a common key shared between the sender and the receiver. This encryption can be done either on blocks of plaintext or one bit at a time. A block cipher encrypts a fixed size of n-bits block of data at a time. A stream cipher encrypts 1 bit or byte of data at a time. It normally uses a long stream of pseudorandom bits as the key. In order to implement a secure stream cipher, its pseudorandom generator should be unpredictable and the reuse of key should never happen. Stream ciphers are faster and have a lower hardware complexity than block ciphers. They are also appropriate when buffering is limited. The eSTREAM project [1] which was started as part of ECRYPT [2] aimed to promote the design of efficient stream ciphers. The finalists in eSTREAM were classified under two profiles namely, profile-1 and profile-2.

The ciphers in profile-1 were intended to give excellent throughput when implemented in software whereas the ciphers in profile-2 were intended to be efficient in terms of the physical resources required when implemented in hardware. Two widely studied ciphers Grain [3] and Trivium [4] belong to profile-2.

© Springer Nature Switzerland AG 2018
G. Mauri et al. (Eds.): ACRI 2018, LNCS 11115, pp. 352–363, 2018.
https://doi.org/10.1007/978-3-319-99813-8_32

Recent studies and research in the field of stream ciphers and CA have shown the use of CA as a better cryptographic primitive. Parallel transformations of stream cipher can be achieved using CA and this provides high throughput which is beneficial in the case of stream ciphers. Work done in [5–9] clearly discusses the cryptographic suitability of CA as stream ciphers. They also give some light to the fact that as the neighborhood of CA increases, the cryptographic properties of the cipher also increases if proper CA rules are employed but with the cost of time needed for doing the computation. FresCA [7] and Cavium [5] were the designs that applied CA in the eSTREAM finalists GRAIN and TRIVIUM respectively.

CA based stream ciphers CASTREAM [10] and FResCA were proposed in ACRI 2012 and ACRI 2016 respectively. Here, we propose CARPenter as a stream cipher based on 5-neighbourhood CA. This paper is organized as follows. Section 2 discusses the terminologies and basics of CA. Section 3 gives a literature survey on CA based stream ciphers. Section 4 discusses 5-neighbourhood CA and the linear and nonlinear rules associated with it. Description of the proposed stream cipher design is provided in Sect. 5. The cryptographic suitability of the new design is discussed in the last section.

2   Preliminaries

2.1   Cellular Automata

A cellular automaton is a collection of cells and each cell is capable of storing a value and a next-state computation function which is also called CA rule. Rules determine the behaviour of a cellular automata [11]. The state of each cell of a CA together at any instant t defines the global state of the CA. The next state of the ith cell of a 3-neighbourhood CA at any instance t is given by

$$S_i^{t+1} = f(S_{i-1}^t, S_i^t, S_{i+1}^t).$$

The next state of ith cell of a 5-neighbourhood CA is given by

$$S_i^{t+1} = f(S_{i-2}^t, S_{i-1}^t, S_i^t, S_{i+1}^t, S_{i+2}^t).$$

where f is the next state function or rule, S_i^{t+1} denotes the next state of the ith cell, S_{i-2}^t is the current state of second left neighbour, S_{i-1}^t is the current state of first left neighbour, S_i^t is the current state of the cell to be updated, S_{i+1}^t is the current state of first right neighbour, S_{i+2}^t is the current state of second right neighbour. In general, the number of cells n that participate in a CA cell update is given by $n = 2a+1$ where a is the radius of the neighbourhood [11].

Cellular automata with null boundary is the one in which the left neighbour of the leftmost cell and the right neighbour of the rightmost cell are zero [12]. Hybrid CA is a cellular automata where more than one rule is involved in the generation of next state [12]. If a cellular automata of n bits (where n is an integer) evolves $2^n - 1$ different states before getting back to the initial state, then it is called as maximum length CA.

There are 256 (2^{2^3}) and 4294967296 (2^{2^5}) such Boolean functions or rules possible for 3-neighbourhood CA and 5-neighbourhood CA respectively. Rules are named as decimal equivalent of the binary number that is formed by applying that rule to all 2^n possibilities of the neighbourhood of a n-neighbourhood CA. Last combination with all ones becomes the most significant bit and first combination with all zeros becomes the least significant bit.

2.2   Cryptographic Properties of Boolean Functions

Cryptographically suitable Boolean functions should satisfy certain properties. Some important cryptographic properties are discussed below. A detailed description of cryptographic properties can be found in [13]. Some basic definitions are provided to better understand some of the cryptographic properties.

Affine Function: A Boolean function which can be expressed as the XOR of some or all of its inputs and a Boolean constant is called Affine function.

Hamming Weight: The number of 1's in the truth table representation of a Boolean function is called its Hamming weight.

Hamming Distance: Hamming distance between two given functions is the Hamming weight of the XOR of the two functions.

Balancedness. The balanced Boolean functions have equal number of zeros and ones in their truth table. Balancedness should be satisfied by all the Boolean functions used in cryptographic applications. There is a statistical bias present in unbalanced Boolean functions which can be exploited by differential and linear cryptanalysis.

Algebraic Degree. Algebraic degree is the maximum number of variables present in an AND term among all the AND terms of a given Boolean function. Higher algebraic degree is necessary in order to have high linear complexity.

Nonlinearity. Nonlinearity of a Boolean function is given as the minimum Hamming distance of the given Boolean function to all the affine functions.

Correlation Immunity. A Boolean function is k^{th} order correlation immune if the output of the given Boolean function is independent of atmost k input variables.

Resiliency. A Boolean function which is both balanced and k^{th} order correlation immune is called k-resilient. If a Boolean function is not k-resilient, then the output depends on at most k input variables which can be exploited to recover the initial state of k inputs.

3   Literature Survey on CA Based Stream Ciphers

CA have a natural tendency to resist fault attacks [9]. CASTREAM [10], CAR30 [6], CAvium [5] and FResCA [7] are some of the CA based stream ciphers. CAS-TREAM is a CA based stream cipher suitable for both hardware and software. It makes the nonlinearisation faster. In CASTREAM, each state bit is influenced by all key bits and IV bits after six iterations. CAR30 is a stream cipher based on CA Rule 30 and a maximum length linear hybrid CA with rule 90 and 150. It is efficient for both hardware and software and its generic design leads to its scaling up to any length of key and IV. This cipher is found to be faster than both Grain and Trivium. CAvium design is a modification of Trivium using CA which increases its strength against almost all the attacks against its reduced rounds. The design has faster startup as it has reduced the number of rounds from 1152 to 144 in the initialization phase and hence needs less clock cycles. It is more secure and faster than Trivium at the cost of more computations per iteration. FResCA (Fault Resistant Cellular Automata Based Stream Cipher) is a modification of Grain, another eSTREAM finalist. This is a 4-neighbourhood CA based Grain-like cipher whose initialization is 8 times faster than Grain since there are only 32 iterations in the initialization phase of FresCA whereas Grain has 256 iterations. FResCA eliminates fault attacks possible in Grain cipher and is also resistant to many other different attacks. Its cells are updated using linear and nonlinear rules and its output depends upon a nonlinear mixing function called NMix [14].

4   Five-Neighbourhood CA

In most of the applications, 1-dimensional 3-neighbourhood Cellular Automata are used. In [8], 4-neighbourhood nonlinear CA were studied and shown to provide good randomness and less correlation. In [11], Catell and Muzio have given a method to synthesize a 3-neighbourhood Linear Hybrid CA. Based on [11], Maiti and Roy Chowdhury in [15] have given an algorithm to synthesize 5-neighbourhood null boundary Linear Hybrid CA (LHCA) using two linear rules. The randomness and diffusion properties of 3-, 4- and 5-neighbourhood were studied and it was shown that the CA can be improved with increase in size of neighbourhood radius of the CA cell if appropriate CA rules are used. The diffusion rate of 5-neighbourhood CA is high and hence is found suitable for high speed application. The improvement comes at a cost of increased computation.

4.1   Five Neighborhood Linear Rules

Based on [15], we have found a 128-bit 5-neighbourhood Linear Hybrid CA rule vector. Out of the 2^{2^5} possible 5-neighbourhood rules, only $2^5 = 32$ rules are linear. Out of these 32 rules, only $2^3 = 8$ are of exactly 5-neighbourhood [15]. The combination of rule R0 and rule R1 given below gives the largest number of rule vectors (8) for 5-bit maximum length 5-neighbourhood CA [15]. Hence, these two rules are considered for finding 128-bit 5-neighbourhood maximum length CA. These two rules are given as

R0 : $S_i^{t+1} = S_{i-2}^t \oplus S_{i-1}^t \oplus S_{i+1}^t \oplus S_{i+2}^t$
R1 : $S_i^{t+1} = S_{i-2}^t \oplus S_{i-1}^t \oplus S_i^t \oplus S_{i+1}^t \oplus S_{i+2}^t$

R0 and R1 are in resemblance to linear rules 90 and 150 respectively of the 3-neighbourhood CA. Rules 90 and 150 are used in [11] to synthesize a maximum length 3-neighbourhood hybrid CA. The state transition function of the ith cell of 5-neighbourhood CA using the rules R0 and R1 can be expressed as

$$S_i^{t+1} = S_{i-2}^t \oplus S_{i-1}^t \oplus d_i.S_i^t \oplus S_{i+1}^t \oplus S_{i+2}^t$$

where $d_i = 0$ if R0 is used and $d_i = 1$ if rule R1 is used [15].

An n-cell 5-neighbourhood CA can be represented as a combination of these two rules as an n-tuple $[d_1, d_2, ..., d_n]$ called as rule vector. A 5-neighbourhood CA is represented by a characteristic matrix over GF(2) and the characteristic matrix has a characteristic polynomial [15]. A characteristic polynomial is a degree n polynomial, where n is the length of rule vector of CA. A CA is maximum length if and only if its characteristic polynomial is primitive [16]. Theorem 1 [15] has been used to derive the characteristic polynomial of CA.

Theorem 1: Let $\triangle_n$ be the characteristic polynomial of a n-cell null boundary 5-Neighbourhood CA with rule vector $[d_1, d_2, \ldots, d_n]$. $\triangle_n$ satisfies the following relation

$$\triangle_n = (x + d_n)\triangle_{n-1} + \triangle_{n-2} + (x + d_{n-1})\triangle_{n-3} + \triangle_{n-4}, n > 0$$

Initially $\triangle_{-3} = 0$, $\triangle_{-2} = 0$, $\triangle_{-1} = 0$, $\triangle_0 = 1$.

Theorem 1 provides an efficient algorithm to compute the characteristic polynomial of a CA. We found a 128-bit maximum length null boundary CA rule vector $[0, 0, \ldots, 0, 1, 0, 1, 0, 0, 0, 0, 0, 1, 0]$ and its primitive characteristic polynomial (CP) is

$CP = x^{128} + x^{127} + x^{125} + x^{122} + x^{120} + x^{119} + x^{117} + x^{115} + x^{113} + x^{112} +$
$x^{111} + x^{110} + x^{106} + x^{104} + x^{103} + x^{94} + x^{90} + x^{89} + x^{88} + x^{87} + x^{85} + x^{84} + x^{83} +$
$x^{82} + x^{79} + x^{78} + x^{76} + x^{75} + x^{72} + x^{71} + x^{69} + x^{67} + x^{65} + x^{64} + x^{62} + x^{58} + x^{57} +$
$x^{56} + x^{53} + x^{51} + x^{49} + x^{48} + x^{44} + x^{43} + x^{42} + x^{39} + x^{37} + x^{36} + x^{35} + x^{34} + x^{30} +$
$x^{26} + x^{25} + x^{24} + x^{23} + x^{21} + x^{20} + x^{19} + x^{18} + x^{15} + x^{14} + x^{10} + x^8 + x^4 + x^2 + x + 1.$

Proof:
Rule Vector:
$$[d_1, d_2, \ldots, d_{118}, d_{119}, d_{120}, d_{121}, d_{122}, d_{123}, d_{124}, d_{125}, d_{126}, d_{127}, d_{128}]$$
$$= [0, 0, \ldots, 0, 1, 0, 1, 0, 0, 0, 0, 0, 1, 0]$$

Derivation of the characteristic polynomial:-
Initially $\triangle_{-3}=0$, $\triangle_{-2}=0$, $\triangle_{-1}=0$, $\triangle_0 = 1$.

$$\triangle_1 = (x + d_1)\triangle_0 + \triangle_{-1} + (x + d_0)\triangle_{-2} + \triangle_{-3}$$
$$= x$$
$$\triangle_2 = (x + d_2)\triangle_1 + \triangle_0 + (x + d_1)\triangle_{-1} + \triangle_{-2}$$
$$= x^2 + 1$$

$$\vdots$$

$$\triangle_{128} = (x + d_{128})\triangle_{127} + \triangle_{126} + (x + d_{127})\triangle_{125} + \triangle_{124}$$
$$= x^{128} + x^{127} + x^{125} + x^{122} + x^{120} + x^{119} + x^{117} + x^{115} + x^{113} + x^{112} + x^{111} +$$
$$x^{110} + x^{106} + x^{104} + x^{103} + x^{94} + x^{90} + x^{89} + x^{88} + x^{87} + x^{85} + x^{84} + x^{83} + x^{82} +$$
$$x^{79} + x^{78} + x^{76} + x^{75} + x^{72} + x^{71} + x^{69} + x^{67} + x^{65} + x^{64} + x^{62} + x^{58} + x^{57} + x^{56} +$$
$$x^{53} + x^{51} + x^{49} + x^{48} + x^{44} + x^{43} + x^{42} + x^{39} + x^{37} + x^{36} + x^{35} + x^{34} + x^{30} +$$
$$x^{26} + x^{25} + x^{24} + x^{23} + x^{21} + x^{20} + x^{19} + x^{18} + x^{15} + x^{14} + x^{10} + x^8 + x^4 + x^2 + x^1 + 1$$

$\triangle_{128}$ represents a characteristic polynomial (CP). Test for primitivity of obtained CP is done by using a primitive polynomial search program(ppsearch256) given in [17].

4.2 Five Neighborhood Nonlinear Rule

In [18], Leporati and Mariot have investigated bipermutive rules of a given radius and studied a set of 5-neighbourhood nonlinear rules for their cryptographic suitability. All the rules have been studied taking Rule 30 as the benchmark. Based on the test results obtained from NIST [19] and ENT [20] tests, the following two rules have been found out to be better [18].

Rule $1452976485 : S_i^{t+1} = (\neg S_{i-2}^t \cdot \neg S_i^t \cdot \neg S_{i+1}^t \cdot \neg S_{i+2}^t) + (\neg S_{i-2}^t \cdot \neg S_{i-1}^t \cdot S_{i+1}^t \cdot \neg S_{i+2}^t)$
$+(\neg S_{i-2}^t \cdot S_i^t \cdot \neg S_{i+1}^t \cdot S_{i+2}^t) + (S_{i-2}^t \cdot \neg S_i^t \cdot \neg S_{i+1}^t \cdot S_{i+2}^t) + (S_{i-2}^t \cdot S_i^t \cdot \neg S_{i+1}^t \cdot \neg S_{i+2}^t)$
$+(\neg S_{i-2}^t \cdot S_{i-1}^t \cdot S_{i+1}^t \cdot S_{i+2}^t) + (S_{i-2}^t \cdot \neg S_{i-1}^t \cdot S_{i+1}^t \cdot S_{i+2}^t) + (S_{i-2}^t \cdot S_{i-1}^t \cdot S_{i+1}^t \cdot \neg S_{i+2}^t)$

Rule $1520018790 : S_i^{t+1} = (\neg S_{i-2}^t \cdot \neg S_{i-1}^t \cdot \neg S_{i+1}^t \cdot \neg S_{i+2}^t) + (\neg S_{i-2}^t \cdot \neg S_{i-1}^t \cdot S_{i+1}^t \cdot \neg S_{i+2}^t)$
$+(\neg S_{i-2}^t \cdot S_{i-1}^t \cdot \neg S_i^t \cdot \neg S_{i+2}^t) + (S_{i-2}^t \cdot \neg S_{i-1}^t \cdot \neg S_{i+1}^t \cdot \neg S_{i+2}^t) + (\neg S_{i-2}^t \cdot S_{i-1}^t \cdot S_i^t \cdot S_{i+2}^t)$
$+(S_{i-2}^t \cdot \neg S_{i-1}^t \cdot S_{i+1}^t \cdot S_{i+2}^t) + (S_{i-2}^t \cdot S_{i-1}^t \cdot \neg S_i^t \cdot S_{i+2}^t) + (S_{i-2}^t \cdot S_{i-1}^t \cdot S_i^t \cdot \neg S_{i+2}^t)$

where '+' and '.' and $\neg$ represents OR, AND and NOT Boolean operations respectively.

5   Description of CARPenter - Cellular Automata Based Resilient Pentavalent Stream Cipher

Our cipher model is inspired by the design of Grain, one of the eSTREAM finalists and FResCA, a CA based version of Grain. The design consists of three blocks, namely linear block (L block), nonlinear block (NL block) of lengths 128 bits each and a nonlinear mixing block (NMix). Figure 1 shows initialization of the cipher and Fig. 2 shows the generation of keystream bits. Both linear and nonlinear block use 5-neighbourhood rules and together form the 256-bit state of the cipher. Output stream is produced by NMix block after performing nonlinear mixing.

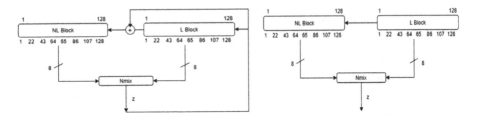

Fig. 1. Cipher initialization   **Fig. 2.** Keystream generation

5.1   Nonlinear Block

Cells of nonlinear block will be updated using one of the 5-neighbourhood nonlinear rules (Rule 1452976485, Rule 1520018790) given in Sect. 4.2.

5.2   Linear Block

Cells of linear block are updated using a 5-neighbourhood Linear Hybrid CA rule vector which has been realized using two linear rules R0 and R1 discussed in Sect. 4.1. The cell positions 2, 8 and 10 use rule R1 and all the remaining 125 positions use rule R0 to realize the maximum length CA.

5.3   Nonlinear Mixing Block

NMix is a Boolean function which is nonlinear, balanced and reversible [14]. It is used as good key mixing function in block ciphers and also resists differential attacks. The NMix function is defined for two n-bits inputs. If input bit sets are $X = x_1, x_2, \ldots, x_{n-1}, x_n$ and $Y = y_1, y_2, \ldots, y_{n-1}, y_n$ and output bit set is $Z = z_1, z_2, \ldots, z_{n-1}, z_n$, then NMix for i^{th} bit is defined as follows.

$$z_i = x_i \oplus y_i \oplus c_{i-1}$$
$$c_i = x_0.y_0 \oplus \cdots \oplus x_i.y_i \oplus x_{i-1}.x_i \oplus y_{i-1}.y_i$$

and $x_{-1} = y_{-1} = c_{-1} = 0, 0 \leq i \leq n - 1$

Input to the NMix is eight bits each from both the linear and nonlinear blocks and the Most Significant Bit (MSB) of NMix is the output of the cipher. All the input bits are present in the computation of MSB of nonlinear mixing block which provides good diffusion.

5.4   Working of CARPenter

CARPenter is a Grain-like **C**ellular **A**utomata Based **R**esilient **P**entavalent Stream Cipher. The cipher has two phases, namely initialization phase and keystream generation phase. The initialization phase consists of 16 iterations and the output is suppressed in this phase. Here, the number of iterations (16 iterations) is less when compared to Grain (256 iterations) and FresCA (32 iterations). The 128-bit key is loaded into the nonlinear block and the 128-bit IV is loaded into the linear block of the cipher. During this phase, the output is fed back to the linear and nonlinear blocks as shown in the Fig. 1. The output of the NMix function is XORed with the first bit in the linear block and this has dual role in nonlinear block. It acts as the second-right-neighbour of the 127th bit and as both first- and second-right-neighbour of the 128th bit in the nonlinear block. This is shown in Fig. 3.   The output of NMix also acts as the second-right-

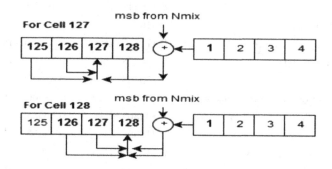

Fig. 3. Updation of cell 127 and cell 128 of nonlinear block

neighbour of the 127th bit and as both first- and second-right-neighbours of the 128th bit in the linear block. In each iteration, each bit in the nonlinear block changes its state according to the 5-neighbourhood nonlinear rule mentioned in Sect. 4.2. In the linear block, the state transition takes place according to the rules R0 and R1. We need to select taps in both linear and nonlinear blocks of the cipher. Taps are the bit positions that affect the output. Eight taps each are selected from both linear and nonlinear blocks so that the number of inputs to the NMix block are 16. The eight taps correspond to the bit positions 1, 22, 43, 64, 65, 86, 107, and 128 in both the blocks. In order to have influence of all the state bits in output in lesser number of iterations, the taps are positioned equally except the two middle ones. After initialization phase, the feed back lines are removed and the keystream bits are generated.

6   Security Analysis

6.1   NIST Statistical Test

National Institute of Standards and Technology (NIST) has developed a statistical test suite known as NIST-statistical test suite [19]. It is a package of 15 tests to test the randomness of pseudo-random binary sequence of arbitrary length. To test the randomness of CARPenter, a bit stream of length 0.1 billion bits has been generated and fed to the NIST test suite. Input bit stream is divided into

100 keystreams of 1 million bits each by the NIST test suite. All the tests passed with appropriate p-values as shown in Table 1.

Table 1. NIST test result

SI.No	Test name	Nonlinear rule - 1		Nonlinear rule - 2	
		P-value	Status	P-value	Status
1	Frequency test	0.955835	Pass	0.657933	Pass
2	Block frequency test	0.494392	Pass	0.289667	Pass
3	Cumulative sums test	0.595549	Pass	0.108791	Pass
4	Runs test	0.616305	Pass	0.955835	Pass
5	Longest runs test	0.171867	Pass	0.534146	Pass
6	Rank test	0.739918	Pass	0.191687	Pass
7	FFT test	0.153763	Pass	0.616305	Pass
8	Non overlapping template test	0.595549	Pass	0.289667	Pass
9	Overlapping template test	0.834308	Pass	0.595549	Pass
10	Universal	0.419021	Pass	0.334538	Pass
11	Approximate entropy	0.115387	Pass	0.419021	Pass
12	Random excursions	0.178278	Pass	0.026648	Pass
13	Random excursions variant	0.706149	Pass	0.723129	Pass
14	Serial	0.759756	Pass	0.319084	Pass
15	Linear complexity	0.994250	Pass	0.202268	Pass

6.2 Resiliency

The two bipermutive nonlinear rules used in the NL block of CARPenter are 2-resilient [18]. Since the rules are 2-resilient, they are both balanced and 2nd order correlation immune.

6.3 Algebraic Attack

If the number of different input variables available in the output Boolean function is high, then the immunity against the algebraic attack will be high. The output function of CARPenter contains 16 and 68 different input variables in first and second iteration respectively and will increase with each iteration. After 16 iterations, at the time of keystream generation the output Boolean function will be affected by all the 256 bits of the cipher. So output Boolean function of the cipher will have high algebraic degree at the time of key generation and this fact will prevent the algebraic attack on CARPenter.

6.4   Linear Attack

Nonlinearity of output Boolean function in the first iteration is 32256 and will increase with each iteration. At the time of key generation phase, nonlinearity will be much higher.

6.5   Meier-Staffelbach Attack

Meier and Staffelbach attacked the Rule-30 based stream cipher designed by Wolfram in [21]. The state of the ith cell from time t to $t + n$ (temporal sequence) is known to the attacker. This attack tries to guess the right half of initial state and then tries to generate the right adjacent neighbour of temporal sequence. Since there is a many-to-one mapping from the right side to the temporal sequence, a guessed right side value may give correct right adjacent sequence. Since there is a linear relation between the temporal sequence and the left half, the attack calculates the left half, by moving backward from $t + n$ to t. Then the calculated seed is used to generate the temporal sequence. Attack is successful if the generated temporal sequence matches with original temporal sequence.

This attack is not applicable to CARPenter. In order to compute the right adjacent neighbour of temporal sequence, knowledge of the state of left neighbour is required because of the use of 5-neighbourhood CA. Random value cannot be assigned to the left hand side of the temporal sequence because there is no many-to-one mapping from left hand side to the temporal sequence.

6.6   Time/Memory/Data Tradeoff Attack

If inner state of a stream cipher consists of n bits, then $O(2^{n/2})$ is the complexity of this attack on stream cipher. Inner state of the CARPenter consists of 256 bits which makes it difficult to perform Time/Memory/Data/tradeoff attack.

6.7   Fault Attack

In this attack, a fault can be introduced at any bit position. The attacker has partial control over the timing and the position of the fault. She can observe the behaviour of the cipher by resetting the cipher and reintroducing the fault at different positions. Because of the use of CA in CARPenter, the fault tracking becomes impossible. In NL block, the fault will dissipate nonlinearly and any fault introduced in linear block will reach the nonlinear block in initialization phase itself making it difficult to track the fault.

7   Conclusion

We have proposed a Grain-like, 5-neighbourhood CA based stream cipher called CARPenter. The cipher exhibits very good cryptographic properties. The use of 2-resilient nonlinear rule makes our cipher resilient. Initialization phase of CARPenter is faster than Grain and FResCA. Generated keystream has good pseudorandomness and is strong against different attacks.

References

1. The eSTREAM project. http://www.ecrypt.eu.org/stream/project.html. Accessed 12 May 2018
2. European network of excellence for cryptography. http://www.ecrypt.eu.org/. Accessed 12 May 2018
3. Hell, M., Johansson, T., Maximov, A., Meier, W.: A stream cipher proposal: grain-128. In: 2006 IEEE International Symposium on Information Theory, pp. 1614–1618, July 2006
4. De Canniere, C., Preneel, B.: Trivium specifications. In: eSTREAM, ECRYPT Stream Cipher Project (2006)
5. Karmakar, S., Mukhopadhyay, D., Roy Chowdhury, D.: Cavium - strengthening trivium stream cipher using cellular automata. J. Cell. Autom. **7**, 179–197 (2012)
6. Das, S., Roy Chowdhury, D.: CAR30: a new scalable stream cipher with rule 30. Cryptogr. Commun. **5**(2), 137–162 (2013)
7. Jose, J., Roy Chowdhury, D.: FResCA: a fault-resistant cellular automata based stream cipher. In: El Yacoubi, S., Was, J., Bandini, S. (eds.) ACRI 2016. LNCS, vol. 9863, pp. 24–33. Springer, Cham (2016). https://doi.org/10.1007/978-3-319-44365-2_3
8. Jose, J., Roy Chowdhury, D.: Investigating four neighbourhood cellular automata as better cryptographic primitives. J. Discrete Math. Sci. Cryptogr. **20**(8), 1675–1695 (2017)
9. Jose, J., Das, S., Roy Chowdhury, D.: Prevention of fault attacks in cellular automata based stream ciphers. J. Cell. Autom. **12**(1–2), 141–157 (2016)
10. Das, S., Roy Chowdhury, D.: *CASTREAM*: a new stream cipher suitable for both hardware and software. In: Sirakoulis, G.C., Bandini, S. (eds.) ACRI 2012. LNCS, vol. 7495, pp. 601–610. Springer, Heidelberg (2012). https://doi.org/10.1007/978-3-642-33350-7_62
11. Cattell, K., Muzio, J.C.: Synthesis of one-dimensional linear hybrid cellular automata. IEEE Trans. Comput. Aided Des. Integr. Circuits Syst. **15**(3), 325–335 (1996)
12. Chaudhuri, P.P., Roy Chowdhury, D., Nandi, S., Chattopadhyay, S.: Additive Cellular Automata Theory and Application, 1st edn. IEEE Computer Society Press, Washington, D.C. (1997)
13. Feng, D., Wu, C.-K.: Boolean Functions and Their Applications in Cryptography, 1st edn. Springer, Heidelberg (2016). https://doi.org/10.1007/978-3-662-48865-2
14. Bhaumik, J., Roy Chowdhury, D.: Nmix: an ideal candidate for key mixing. In: Proceedings of the International Conference on Security and Cryptography. SECRYPT 2009, 7–10 July 2009, Milan, Italy, pp. 285–288. INSTICC Press (2009). SECRYPT is part of ICETE - The International Joint Conference on e-Business and Telecommunications
15. Maiti, S., Roy Chowdhury, D.: Study of five-neighborhood linear hybrid cellular automata and their synthesis. In: Giri, D., Mohapatra, R.N., Begehr, H., Obaidat, M.S. (eds.) ICMC 2017. CCIS, vol. 655, pp. 68–83. Springer, Singapore (2017). https://doi.org/10.1007/978-981-10-4642-1_7
16. McEliece, R.J.: Finite Fields for Computer Scientists and Engineers, 1st edn. Springer, Boston (1987). https://doi.org/10.1007/978-1-4613-1983-2
17. A primitive polynomial search program. http://notabs.org/primitivepolynomials/primitivepolynomials.htm. Accessed 12 May 2018

18. Leporati, A., Mariot, L.: Cryptographic properties of bipermutive cellular automata rules. J. Cell. Autom. **9**, 437–475 (2014)
19. Nist statistical test suite. https://csrc.nist.gov/projects/random-bit-generation/documentation-and-software. Accessed 12 May 2018
20. ENT - a pseudorandom number sequence test program. http://www.fourmilab.ch/random/. Accessed 12 May 2018
21. Meier, W., Staffelbach, O.: Analysis of pseudo random sequences generated by cellular automata. In: Davies, D.W. (ed.) EUROCRYPT 1991. LNCS, vol. 547, pp. 186–199. Springer, Heidelberg (1991). https://doi.org/10.1007/3-540-46416-6_17

Inversion of Mutually Orthogonal Cellular Automata

Luca Mariot[✉] and Alberto Leporati

Dipartimento di Informatica, Sistemistica e Comunicazione,
Università degli Studi Milano-Bicocca, Viale Sarca 336, 20126 Milan, Italy
{luca.mariot,alberto.leporati}@unimib.it

Abstract. Mutually Orthogonal Cellular Automata (MOCA) are sets of bipermutive CA which can be used to construct pairwise orthogonal Latin squares. In this work, we consider the inversion problem of pairs of configurations in MOCA. In particular, we design an algorithm based on coupled de Bruijn graphs which solves this problem for generic MOCA, without assuming any linearity on the underlying bipermutive rules. Next, we analyze the computational complexity of this algorithm, remarking that it runs in exponential time with respect to the diameter of the CA rule, but that it can be straightforwardly parallelized to yield a linear time complexity. As a cryptographic application of this algorithm, we finally show how to design a $(2, n)$ threshold Secret Sharing Scheme (SSS) based on MOCA where any combination of two players can reconstruct the secret by applying our inversion algorithm.

Keywords: Cellular automata · Latin squares
Secret sharing schemes · de Bruijn graph

1 Introduction

The *inversion problem* is one of the oldest research questions investigated in the field of *Cellular Automata* (CA). Indeed, the first results in this aspect of CA theory dates back at least to Hedlund [4] and Richardson [14]. Stated informally, the inversion problem consists in determining a preimage of a given configuration under the action of a surjective CA. When dealing with the specific class of *reversible* CA, one can compute such unique preimage in parallel by applying an *inverse CA* to the desired configuration.

However, the general case of surjective CA usually requires the specification of an *inversion algorithm* which computes a preimage in a *sequential* way, starting from the knowledge of the states of some of its cells. Sutner [17] was among the first to describe this inversion algorithm using the *de Bruijn graph* representation of CA. More specifically, he showed that a preimage of a configuration corresponds to a *path* on the vertices of the de Bruijn graph associated to the CA, where the edges are labeled by the cells of the configuration. The existence of such a path is guaranteed under the assumption that the CA global rule is surjective.

© Springer Nature Switzerland AG 2018
G. Mauri et al. (Eds.): ACRI 2018, LNCS 11115, pp. 364–376, 2018.
https://doi.org/10.1007/978-3-319-99813-8_33

De Bruijn graphs turned out to be a very useful tool to address several interesting questions related to the inversion problem, such as studying the spatial periods of surjective CA preimages [10] and solving the parity problem through CA [2].

A recent research thread involving the inversion problem concerns *Mutually Orthogonal Latin Squares* (MOLS) generated by CA. In particular, it has been shown in [7] that CA with *bipermutive* local rules can be used to define Latin squares, and pairs of linear bipermutive rules whose associated polynomials are coprime generate orthogonal Latin squares. The idea of the construction is to split the CA initial configuration in two parts, in order to index the rows and the columns of the squares. Then, the final configurations obtained by applying two linear bipermutive rules with coprime polynomials are used to fill the two entries in the square at the coordinates specified by the initial configuration. In what follows we refer to a pair of bipermutive CA generating orthogonal Latin squares as *Orthogonal Cellular Automata* (OCA), and to a set of pairwise OCA as *Mutually Orthogonal Cellular Automata* (MOCA).

It can be remarked that any pair of OLS defines a permutation between the Cartesian product of the rows/columns sets and the overlapped entries. Hence, starting from a pair of final configurations generated by two OCA, an interesting problem is to reconstruct the unique preimage (i.e. the row and column coordinates) which generated them.

The aim of this paper is to investigate the inversion problem in MOCA, without assuming any linearity of the underlying local rules. As a matter of fact, the inversion of OCA defined by *linear* rules has already been settled in [7], and it basically amounts to inverting a *Sylvester matrix*. Consequently, in this work we focus on pairs of OCA defined by general bipermutive rules, whose exhaustive and heuristic constructions have already been addressed in [8,11].

We leverage on the de Bruijn graph representation to solve the inversion problem. In particular, we design an algorithm which, given as inputs the *coupled de Bruijn graph* of two nonlinear OCA and a pair of final configurations, computes their unique preimage by using a variant of *Depth-First Search* (DFS). We remark in particular that the computational complexity of this algorithm is exponential in the diameter of the OCA rules. Nonetheless, we also show that this algorithm can be straightforwardly parallelized with respect to the initial DFS calls, thus yielding an overall linear time complexity.

As an application of our inversion algorithm, we design a perfect *secret sharing scheme* based on MOCA where every pair of players can reconstruct the secret, while any single player cannot gain any information about it. More specifically, we show that the reconstruction phase consists in the application of the inversion algorithm on the two shares of the players, using the coupled de Bruijn graph of the OCA that the dealer used to compute such shares.

The rest of this paper is organized as follows. Section 2 covers all basic definitions and results concerning cellular automata, orthogonal Latin squares and secret sharing schemes used to prove the results of the paper, addressing the inversion problem in the case of MOCA defined by nonlinear bipermutive rules.

Section 4 describes the application of our inversion algorithm to the design of a $(2, n)$ threshold secret sharing scheme. Finally, Sect. 5 summarizes the key findings of the paper and puts them into perspective.

2   Preliminary Definitions

In this section, we recall the basic definitions and notions which we will use in the rest of the paper. In particular, Sect. 2.1 covers all necessary background about CA and their representation based on de Bruijn graphs. Section 2.2 gives the basic definitions regarding orthogonal Latin squares and how they can be used to construct perfect $(2, n)$ secret sharing schemes. Section 2.3 briefly reviews the construction of OLS by means of linear OCA and the exhaustive and heuristic search of OLS by nonlinear OCA.

2.1   Cellular Automata

Throughout this work, we focus on one-dimensional *No Boundary Cellular Automata* (NBCA), formally defined as follows:

Definition 1. *Let Σ be a finite alphabet and $n, d \in \mathbb{N}$ with $n \geq d$. Additionally, let the function $f : \Sigma^d \to \Sigma$ be a* local rule *of diameter d. The* No Boundary Cellular Automaton *(NBCA) $F : \Sigma^n \to \Sigma^{n-d+1}$ is the vectorial function defined for all $x \in \Sigma^n$ as*

$$F(x_1, \cdots, x_n) = (f(x_1, \cdots, x_d), f(x_2, \cdots, x_{d+1}), \cdots, f(x_{n-d+1}, \cdots, x_n)). \quad (1)$$

Function F is also called the CA global rule.

In other words, an NBCA can be viewed as an array of $n \geq d$ cells, where each of the leftmost $n - d + 1$ cells computes its next state by evaluating rule f on the neighborhood formed by itself and the $d - 1$ cells to its right. In particular, the rightmost $d - 1$ cells of the array are ignored, so that the size of the CA "shrinks" by $d - 1$ cells upon application of the global rule F.

In the rest of this paper, we assume that the state alphabet Σ is the *finite field* with two elements $\mathbb{F}_2 = \{0, 1\}$. In this case, a NBCA can be interpreted as a particular kind of *vectorial Boolean function* $F : \mathbb{F}_2^n \to \mathbb{F}_2^{n-d+1}$, where each *coordinate function* $f_i : \mathbb{F}_2^n \to \mathbb{F}_2$ defining the i-th output value corresponds to the local rule applied to the neighborhood of the i-th cell. Since in this case the local rule is a single-output d-variable Boolean function $f : \mathbb{F}_2^d \to \mathbb{F}_2$, it can be uniquely represented by the 2^d-bit output column of its *truth table*, which we denote by Ω_f. In the CA literature it is customary to identify a local rule f by its *Wolfram code*, which is the decimal encoding of its truth table Ω_f.

A local rule $f : \mathbb{F}_q^d \to \mathbb{F}_2$ is called *right* (respectively, *left*) *permutive* if, by fixing the values of the leftmost (respectively, rightmost) $d - 1$ cells to any value $\tilde{x} \in \Sigma^{d-1}$, the resulting restriction $f_{\tilde{x}} : \Sigma \to \Sigma$ is a permutation over Σ. Moreover, f is called *bipermutive* if it is both left and right permutive. When

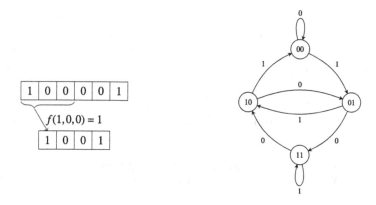

Fig. 1. Example of NBCA defined by rule 150, together with its de Bruijn graph.

$\Sigma = \mathbb{F}_2$, a bipermutive rule $f : \mathbb{F}_2^d \rightarrow \mathbb{F}_2$ is defined for all $x = (x_1, \cdots, x_d) \in \mathbb{F}_2^d$ as:

$$f(x_1, \cdots, x_d) = x_1 \oplus g(x_2, \cdots, x_{d-1}) \oplus x_d, \qquad (2)$$

where $g : \mathbb{F}_2^{d-2} \rightarrow \mathbb{F}_2$ is a $(d-2)$-variable Boolean function.

Another common way for representing a CA is through its *de Bruijn graph*. Let us assume that $u, v \in \Sigma^n$ are two strings over the alphabet Σ of length n such that $u = u_1 x$ and $v = x v_1$, where $u_1, v_1 \in \Sigma$ and $x \in \Sigma^{n-1}$ is a string of length $n-1$. In other words, u and v *overlap* respectively on the rightmost and leftmost $n-1$ symbols. The *fusion* between u and v is the string $z = u \odot v$ of length $n+1$ obtained by adding to u the last symbol of v [17]. Then, one can formally define the de Bruijn graph associated to a CA as follows:

Definition 2. *Let $F : \Sigma^{\mathbb{Z}} \rightarrow \Sigma^{\mathbb{Z}}$ be a CA defined by a local rule $f : \Sigma^d \rightarrow \Sigma$ of diameter d. The de Bruijn graph associated to F is the directed labeled graph $G_{DB}(f) = (V, E, l)$ where $V = \Sigma^{d-1}$ and such that for any $v_1, v_2 \in V$, one has $(v_1, v_2) \in E$ if and only if there exists $z \in \Sigma^d$ such that $z = v_1 \odot v_2$. The label function $l : E \rightarrow \Sigma$ on the edges is defined for all $(v_1, v_2) \in E$ as $l(v_1, v_2) = f(v_1 \odot v_2)$.*

Stated otherwise, the vertices of the de Bruijn graph correspond to all possible blocks of $d-1$ cells. Two vertices v_1 and v_2 are connected by an edge if and only if they overlap respectively on the rightmost and leftmost $d-1$ cells, and the label on this edge is obtained by computing the CA local rule on the fusion of v_1 and v_2. Figure 1 depicts an example of binary NBCA $F : \mathbb{F}_2^6 \rightarrow \mathbb{F}_2^4$ induced by the local rule $f(x_i, x_{i+1}, x_{i+2}) = x_i \oplus x_{i+1} \oplus x_{i+2}$, whose Wolfram code is 150, together with its de Bruijn graph.

2.2 Orthogonal Latin Squares and Secret Sharing Schemes

Given $N \in \mathbb{N}$, let us denote by $[N]$ the set $\{1, \cdots, N\}$. Then, one can formally define orthogonal Latin squares as follows:

Definition 3. *A* Latin square *L of order* $N \in \mathbb{N}$ *is a* $N \times N$ *matrix whose rows and columns are permutations of* $[N]$, *i.e. every element of* $[N]$ *occurs exactly once in each row and each column. Two Latin squares* L_1, L_2 *of order* N *are called* orthogonal *if for all distinct pairs of coordinates* $(i_1, j_1), (i_2, j_2) \in [N] \times [N]$ *one has*

$$(L_1(i_1, j_1), L_2(i_1, j_1)) \neq (L_1(i_2, j_2), L_2(i_2, j_2)), \tag{3}$$

that is, the *superposition of* L_1 *and* L_2 *yields all possible pairs in the Cartesian product* $[N] \times [N]$.

Remark 1. *Two orthogonal Latin squares* L_1, L_2 *of order* $N \in \mathbb{N}$ *induce a permutation* $\pi : [N] \times [N] \to [N] \times [N]$ *over the Cartesian product* $[N] \times [N]$, *which is defined as*

$$\pi(i, j) = (L_1(i, j), L_2(i, j)) \tag{4}$$

for all $(i, j) \in [N] \times [N]$.

A set n pairwise orthogonal Latin squares of order $[N]$ is denoted as $n-$ MOLS (*Mutually Orthogonal Latin Squares*). Figure 2 reports an example of orthogonal Latin squares of order $N = 4$, together with their superposition.

1	3	4	2
4	2	1	3
2	4	3	1
3	1	2	4

1	4	2	3
3	2	4	1
4	1	3	2
2	3	1	4

1,1	3,4	4,2	2,3
4,3	2,2	1,4	3,1
2,4	4,1	3,3	1,2
3,2	1,3	2,1	4,4

Fig. 2. Orthogonal Latin squares of order $N = 4$.

Orthogonal Latin squares turn out to have several applications in cryptography and coding theory [5,16], one of the most interesting being *secret sharing schemes* (SSS). Informally speaking, a SSS is a procedure which enables a trusted party (called the *dealer*) to share a *secret* S among a set of n players. In particular, the players receive *shares* of the secret from the dealer, and only certain *authorized subsets* of players specified in an *access structure* can reconstruct the secret by combining together their shares. A SSS is called *perfect* if any subset not belonging to the access structure cannot determine the secret (in an information-theoretic sense).

In this work we focus mainly on perfect $(k, n)-$ *threshold* SSS, where the authorized subsets are those having cardinality at least k. Hence, any combination of k shares is enough to uniquely determine the secret, while knowing $k - 1$ or less shares keeps any value of the secret equally likely.

The connection between perfect threshold SSS and orthogonal Latin squares is established by the following result [16]:

Theorem 1. *A perfect* $(2, n)-$ *threshold SSS exists if and only if there exists a set of* n *MOLS of order* N.

The *setup phase* of a $(2, n)-$ threshold SSS from a set of n MOLS $L_1, \cdots, L_n$ goes as follows. First, the secret S is represented as a row $i \in [N]$ of the squares, and the dealer randomly chooses a column $j \in [N]$. Then, for each $m \in \{1, \cdots, n\}$, the dealer secretly sends to the m-th player the share $B_m = L_m(i, j)$, i.e. the entry of the m-th Latin square at row i and column j. Finally, the dealer publishes the Latin squares $L_1, \cdots, L_n$.

In the recovery phase, any pair of players p, q respectively holding shares B_p, B_q can recover the secret simply by overlaying the two public Latin squares L_p, L_q. Since L_p and L_q are orthogonal, the pair of shares (B_p, B_q) occurs at a single pair of coordinates (i, j), the row of which is the secret S. Conversely, if p tries to determine the secret on her own without knowing the share B_q, there will be exactly N pairs $(B_p, \cdot)$ in the overlay of the two Latin squares, due to the fact that L_p and L_q are orthogonal. A symmetric argument holds when q tries to determine S by herself without knowing B_p. Hence, the knowledge of a single share leaves the value of the secret completely undetermined, which makes the scheme perfect.

2.3   Construction of OLS by CA

We now describe how CA can be employed to obtain orthogonal Latin squares, briefly recalling the construction reported in [7]. In what follows, given a binary vector $x \in \mathbb{F}_2^n$, we will denote by $\phi(x) \in \{1, \cdots, 2^n\}$ the integer number corresponding to the decimal representation of $x + 1$. On the contrary, for any integer number $i \in \{1, \cdots, 2^n\}$, $\psi(i) \in \mathbb{F}_2^n$ will stand for the n-bit binary representation of $i - 1$. Notice that $\phi = \psi^{-1}$ and $\psi = \phi^{-1}$.

Let $F : \mathbb{F}_2^{2(d-1)} \to \mathbb{F}_2^{d-1}$ be a CA based on a local rule $f : \mathbb{F}_2^d \to \mathbb{F}_2$ of d variables. This means that F is a vectorial Boolean function mapping binary strings of length $2(d-1)$ to strings of length $d - 1$. Setting $N = 2^{d-1}$, one can associate a $N \times N$ square matrix S_F to F as follows: for each $(i, j) \in [N] \times [N]$, the entry of S_F at row i and column j equals

$$S_F(i, j) = \phi(F(\psi(i) || \psi(j))), \tag{5}$$

where $||$ denotes the concatenation operator. Thus, the entry $S_F(i, j)$ is determined by computing the CA on the input vector where the first $d - 1$ bits corresponds to the binary representation of row i, while the last $d - 1$ are the binary representation of column j.

One may wonder under which conditions the matrix associated to a CA is a Latin square. As shown in the next result [7], this situation happens when the underlying local rule is bipermutive:

Lemma 1. *Let* $F : \mathbb{F}_2^{2(d-1)} \to \mathbb{F}_2^{d-1}$ *be a CA with bipermutive local rule* $f : \mathbb{F}_2^d \to \mathbb{F}_2$. *Then, the square* S_F *induced by* F *is a Latin square of order* $N = 2^{d-1}$.

As an example, Fig. 3 depicts the Latin square of order $N = 4$ associated to the CA $F : \mathbb{F}_2^4 \to \mathbb{F}_2^2$ with bipermutive local rule 150. A natural question immediately following from Lemma 1 is when the Latin squares associated to two bipermutive CA F, G are orthogonal. In this case, we call the pair F, G as *Orthogonal Cellular Automata* (OCA), and by analogy a family of bipermutive CA whose associated Latin squares are MOLS is called a set of *Mutually Orthogonal Cellular Automata* (MOCA).

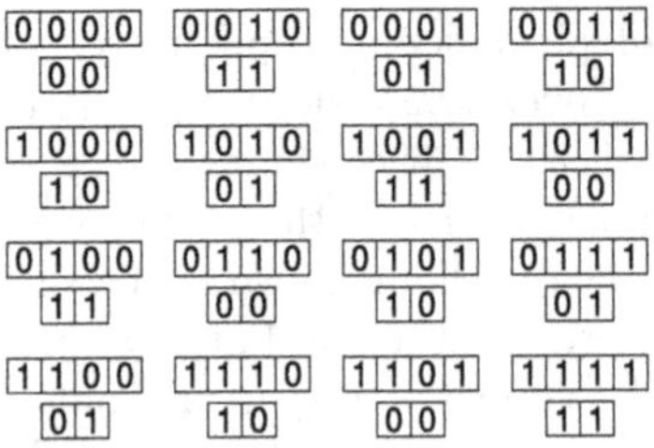

1	4	3	2
2	3	4	1
4	1	2	3
3	2	1	4

Fig. 3. Example of Latin square to the CA $F : \mathbb{F}_2^4 \to \mathbb{F}_2^2$ with local rule 150.

The question has been settled in [7] for *linear* rules. A local rule $f : \mathbb{F}_2^d \to \mathbb{F}_2$ is linear if there exists a vector $a = (a_1, \cdots, a_d) \in \mathbb{F}_2^d$ such that $f(x_1, \cdots, x_d) = a_1 x_1 \oplus \cdots \oplus a_d x_d$ for all $x = (x_1, \cdots, x_d) \in \mathbb{F}_2^d$. In this case, rule f is bipermutive if and only if $a_1 = a_d = 1$. Additionally, one can easily associate to f a *polynomial* $p_f(X) \in \mathbb{F}_2[X]$ of degree $d-1$ by defining it as $p_f(X) = a_1 + a_2 X + \cdots + a_d X^{d-1}$. Using this representation, the authors of [7] proved the following result:

Theorem 2. *Let $F, G : \mathbb{F}_2^{2(d-1)} \to \mathbb{F}_2^{d-1}$ be two CA respectively defined by two linear bipermutive rules $f, g : \mathbb{F}_2^d \to \mathbb{F}_2$. Further, let p_f, p_g denote the two polynomials respectively associated to f and g. Then, F and G are OCA if and only if $\gcd(p_f, p_g) = 1$, that is, if and only if f and g are coprime.*

In [8] the authors performed an exhaustive search for finding all OCA pairs equipped with nonlinear bipermutive rules of diameter up to $d = 6$. Further, the optimization problem of determining nonlinear OCA of diameter $d = 7, 8$ has been addressed in [11]. In particular, since exhaustive search is not feasible for any $d > 6$, the authors resorted to *genetic algorithms* (GA) and *genetic programming* (GP).

3   Computing Preimages of OCA

We can now formally state the *inversion problem for OCA* which we analyze in the rest of this paper:

Problem 1. *Let $F, G : \mathbb{F}_2^{2(d-1)} \to \mathbb{F}_2^{d-1}$ be a pair of OCA respectively defined by bipermutive local rules $f, g : \mathbb{F}_2^d \to \mathbb{F}_2$, and let $w, z \in \mathbb{F}_2^{d-1}$ be two $(d-1)-$bit vectors. Then, find the vector $c = x \parallel y$ with $x, y \in \mathbb{F}_2^{d-1}$ such that $(F(c), G(c)) = (w, z)$.*

Using the terminology of Latin squares, Problem 1 requires finding a pair of row/column coordinates $(\phi(x), \phi(y))$ such that the corresponding entry in the superposition of Latin squares S_F and S_G is the pair $(\phi(w), \phi(z))$. Since S_F and S_G are orthogonal, by Remark 1 such pair of coordinates is unique.

Notice that Problem 1 does not assume any linearity on the bipermutive local rules underlying the two OCA, so the inversion algorithm which we develop in this section works both for linear and nonlinear OCA. Before describing it, we first need to introduce some additional data structures and algorithms.

Let $G_{DB}(f) = (V, E, l_f)$ and $G_{DB}(g) = (V, E, l_g)$ be the de Bruijn graphs respectively associated to two CA $F, G : \Sigma^{2(d-1)} \to \Sigma^{d-1}$ equipped with local rules $f, g : \Sigma^d \to \Sigma$ of diameter d. Then, the *coupled de Bruijn graph* induced by F and G is the de Bruijn graph $G_{DB}(f, g) = (V, E, l_{f,g})$ whose edge labeling function $l : E \to \Sigma \times \Sigma$ is defined for all $(v_1, v_2) \in E$ as

$$l(v_1, v_2) = (l_f(v_1, v_2), l_g(v_1, v_2)). \tag{6}$$

Thus, the labeling on the coupled de Bruijn graph is formed setting side by side the edge labels of the de Bruijn graphs of the single CA.

In what follows, we will make use of the variant of *Depth First Search* originally introduced in [10] to compute the *unfolding* of de Bruijn graphs. Given a configuration y of length p and a vertex v of a de Bruijn graph $G_{DB}(f) = (V, E, l)$ associated to a CA, this algorithm visits $G_{DB}(f)$ starting from a single vertex v_1 and following the path on the edges labeled by y. In particular, contrary to the plain version of DFS, this variant does not mark the visited edges, so that in principle they can be visited multiple times. The fusion of the vertices $v_1, \cdots, v_p$ visited during this algorithm determines a preimage x of configuration y. In our case, we will denote by DFS-MOD(V, E, l, v, w, z) a call to this DFS variant on the coupled de Bruijn graph $G_{DB}(f, g) = (V, E, l)$ associated to f and g, starting from vertex v and reading the edge labels determined by juxtaposing the configurations $w, z \in \mathbb{F}_2^{d-1}$. In particular, it is not guaranteed that a preimage of w, z can be found, since for any $i \in \{1, \cdots, d-1\}$ there might be no edges labeled with (w_i, z_i) that exit from vertex v_i visited by the DFS on step $i - 1$. Thus, we will assume that DFS-MOD$(G_{DB}(f, g), l, v, w, z)$ either returns a preimage c of w, z or the value NIL when such preimage cannot be constructed starting from vertex v.

We can now describe the structure of our inversion procedure for OCA, whose pseudocode is reported in Algorithm 1. The procedure takes as input the coupled de Bruijn graph $G_{DB}(f, g)$ of two OCA $F, G : \mathbb{F}_2^{2(d-1)} \to \mathbb{F}_2^{d-1}$ defined by bipermutive rules $f, g : \mathbb{F}_2^d \to \mathbb{F}_2$ respectively, and two configurations $w, z \in \mathbb{F}_2^{d-1}$. The first three steps of the algorithm simply extract the vertex set, the edge set and the labeling function of the graph, while the fourth step initializes the configuration to be returned to NIL. Then, the `while` loop is performed until there are edges in E labeled with the first symbols of w and z, and c equals NIL. Inside the loop, the only instruction is the call to DFS-MOD starting from the first vertex of the edge. If the DFS visit successfully completes, then a preimage of (w, z) is returned and assigned to c, otherwise c remains NIL. As soon as a preimage is found or there are no other edges labeled with (w_1, z_1) in the coupled de Bruijn graph, the execution exits the *while* loop and the current value of c is returned.

Algorithm 1. INVERT-OCA($G_{DB}(f,g), w, z$)

$V := $ VERTEX($G_{DB}(f,g)$)
$E := $ EDGES($G_{DB}(f,g)$)
$l := $ LABELS($G_{DB}(f,g)$)
$c := NIL$
while $e \in \{(v_1, v_2) \in E : l(v_1, v_2) = (w_1, z_1)\}$ AND $c = NIL$ **do**
  $c := $ DFS-MOD(V, E, l, v_1, w, z)
end while
return c

We now prove the correctness and the time complexity of Algorithm 1, under the assumption that F and G are OCA.

Theorem 3. *Let* $F, G : \mathbb{F}_2^{2(d-1)} \to \mathbb{F}_2^{d-1}$ *be two OCA with bipermutive local rules* $f, g : \mathbb{F}_2^d \to \mathbb{F}_2$ *and let* $G_{DB}(f,g)$ *be the coupled de Bruijn graph of* F *and* G. *Then, for any pair of final configurations* $w, z \in \mathbb{F}_2^{d-1}$, *the procedure* INVERT-OCA *correctly returns the unique preimage* $c \in \mathbb{F}_2^{2(d-1)}$ *such that* $(F(c), G(c)) = (w, z)$ *in* $\mathcal{O}(d \cdot 2^d)$ *steps.*

Proof. Correctness. *Let* $w, z \in \mathbb{F}_2^{d-1}$ *be two configurations of* $d - 1$ *bits, and let* $\phi(w), \phi(z)$ *be their decimal representations ranging in* $[N]$, *where* $N = 2^{d-1}$. *Since the two Latin squares* S_F *and* S_G *are orthogonal, the pair* $(\phi(w), \phi(z))$ *appears exactly once in their superposition. Let* $i, j \in [N]$ *be respectively the row and column coordinates where such pair occurs. Given the binary representation* $\psi(i), \psi(j) \in \mathbb{F}_2^{d-1}$ *of* i, j *and denoting by* $c = \psi(i) \| \psi(j)$ *their concatenation, this means that*

$$(F(c), G(c)) = (w, z) \tag{7}$$

Algorithm 1 invokes DFS-MOD *on all vertices* $v \in V$ *which have an outgoing edge labeled by* (w_1, z_1). *In particular, due to the fact that* S_F *and* S_G *are orthogonal, there will be exactly one call which returns a value different from* NIL, *and this value corresponds to the only preimage* c *which satisfies Eq. (7).*

Complexity. *To determine the time complexity of* INVERT-OCA, *first remark that a single call to* DFS-MOD *requires at most* $d - 1$ *steps to complete, because the two configurations* w, z *have length* $d - 1$ *each, and their symbols are pairwise read during the DFS visit. In particular, a DFS visit could return before* $d - 1$ *steps, due to the fact that there are no outgoing edges labeled with the pairs of symbols of* w *and* z. *To conclude, we need to determine how many times* DFS-MOD *is invoked. Lemma 3 in [8] shows that the local rules of OCA are pairwise balanced, meaning that there are exactly* 2^{d-2} *edges on the coupled de Bruijn graph labeled with* (w_1, z_1). *Consequently,* DFS-MOD *is invoked* 2^{d-2} *times, thus the overall time complexity of* INVERT-OCA *is* $\mathcal{O}(d \cdot 2^d)$. $\qquad\square$

One may notice that the time complexity of Algorithm 1 is exponential with respect to the diameter of the CA. However, remark that Algorithm 1 can be straightforwardly parallelized by assigning a processor to each DFS call inside the `while` loop. Hence, by using 2^{d-2} processors in parallel, the time complexity of INVERT-OCA can be reduced down to $\mathcal{O}(d)$, which is the number of steps necessary to complete a DFS visit.

4 Application to Secret Sharing Schemes

On account of Theorem 2, a set $\{p_1, \cdots, p_n\}$ of n *pairwise coprime polynomials* of degree $d-1$ is equivalent to a family of n linear MOCA of order $N = 2^{d-1}$, and thus by Theorem 1 it is also equivalent to a perfect $(2, n)$-threshold SSS. However, publishing the whole set of n MOLS is not an efficient way to implement the recovery phase of a SSS, especially if the size of the squares is huge. Thus, one needs to find a compact way to describe the recovery phase of the secret starting from the knowledge of two shares.

In this concluding section, we show how our inversion algorithm INVERT-OCA can be used precisely for this purpose. To our knowledge, this is the first time that a full perfect $(2, n)$-threshold SSS based on CA is described in the literature. As a matter of fact, there have been other attempts at designing CA-based secret sharing schemes (such as [9,13]), but the resulting access structures suffered from an additional *adjacency constraint* on the shares, since they actually represent blocks of CA configurations.

Let the secret S be a vector of $\mathbb{F}_2^m$ where $m = d-1$, and assume that there are n players $P_1, \cdots, P_n$. Then, the setup phase of our $(2, n)$-threshold SSS is as follows:

SETUP PHASE
Initialization:
1. Find n local rules $f_1, \cdots, f_n : \mathbb{F}_2^d \to \mathbb{F}_2$ which give rise to a set of n MOCA of order $N = 2^{d-1}$. By Theorem 2, this can be done for example by picking n relatively prime polynomials $p_{f_1}(x), \cdots, p_{f_n}(x)$ over $\mathbb{F}_2$
2. Concatenate secret S with a random vector $R \in \mathbb{F}_2^m$, thus obtaining a configuration $C \in \mathbb{F}_2^{2m}$ of length $2(d-1)$
Loop: For all $i \in \{1, \cdots n\}$ do:
1. Given $F_i : \mathbb{F}_q^{2m} \to \mathbb{F}_2^m$ the NBCA defined by rule f_i, compute $B_i = F_i(C)$
2. Send share B_i to player P_i
Termination: Publish the n local rules $f_1, \cdots, f_n$ defining the MOCA.

For the recovery phase, suppose that two players P_i and P_j want to determine the secret. Let B_i and B_j respectively denote the share of P_i and P_j. Since the local rules of the MOCA are public, both P_i and P_j know the CA linear rules f_i and f_j used by the dealer to compute their shares. Hence, they adopt the following procedure to recover S:

RECOVERY PHASE

Initialization:
1. Find the CA linear rules f_i and f_j published by the dealer corresponding to players P_i and P_j
2. Compute the coupled de Bruijn graph $G_{DB}(f_i, f_j)$

Reconstruction:
1. Compute configuration C by calling INVERT-OCA($G_{DB}(f_i, f_j), B_i, B_j$)
2. Return the first half of C as the secret S

Hence, the recovery phase of this SSS simply consists in computing the preimage of the pair of configurations represented by the shares B_i, B_j under the action of the two OCA with local rules f_i, f_j. In particular, the whole preimage returned by INVERT-OCA contains both secret S in its left half and the random column chosen by the dealer in the second half.

5   Discussion, Conclusions and Directions for Future Work

In this paper, we described an algorithm to invert a pair of configurations under the action of two OCA. Specifically, starting from the coupled de Bruijn graph of the two OCA of diameter d, the algorithm applies a DFS-based search until a valid path labeled with the two configurations is found. The existence of such unique path is guaranteed by the fact that the two OCA define a pair of orthogonal Latin squares, and thus a bijection among pairs of $(d-1)$-bit vectors. Since there are 2^{d-1} vertices in the coupled de Bruijn graph, in the worse case the running time of our algorithm is exponential in the diameter of the CA. However, this algorithm is easily parallelizable, by assigning a DFS call to a separate processor. Hence, using $\mathcal{O}(2^d)$ processors in parallel yields a time complexity which is linear in the CA diameter. As an application of this algorithm, we showed how to implement the recovery phase of a $(2, n)$-threshold secret sharing scheme based on MOCA.

Taking a closer look at the computational complexity of Algorithm 1, one may notice that we did not consider the size of the input in our analysis. As a matter of fact, the de Bruijn graph of a CA is already exponential in the CA diameter, something which apparently hinders the applicability of our inversion algorithm. However, depending on the nature of the underlying local rules, one can find more efficient representations of this algorithm. For instance, if the local rules are linear, then it is possible to adapt the preimage construction procedure described in [9] as follows: first, the leftmost $(d-1)$-cell block of the preimage is randomly guessed. Then, one exploits the right permutivity property of the two local rules to compute the two values for the d-th cell of the preimage. If the two values are equal, then the preimage is consistent up to that point, and the next cell in position $d+1$ can be computed. This process is repeated rightwards, until either a mismatch is found between the two computed values (meaning that one has to start over with a new left block of $d-1$ cells), or the rightmost block is completed (i.e. the correct preimage mapping to the pair of configurations has been found). Under this procedure, one can compute the two values for the current preimage cell using the *Algebraic Normal Form* (ANF) [3] of the two CA local rules. If the rules are linear, then the size of their ANF is linear in the CA diameter d, since it just corresponds to an XOR of a subset of the input variables. Of course, in the general case of nonlinear bipermutive rules the size of the ANF can still be exponential in the diameter.

However, we remark that this issue is mainly a matter of trade-off between the required amount of nonlinearity of the CA local rules and their ANF sizes, which highly depends on the specific application domain of our inversion algorithm. Returning to our secret sharing scheme example, most of the existing protocols used in practice are actually linear. Thus, plugging linear rules into our example described in Sect. 4 would yield another linear threshold scheme with a recovery phase that can be performed in $\mathcal{O}(d)$ steps using $\mathcal{O}(2^d)$ processors in parallel. As a consequence, it would be interesting to compare the complexity of our scheme with those of other well-established linear SSS, such as Shamir's scheme [15]. Further, as pointed out in [7], the inversion problem of two linear OCA actually amounts to the inversion of a *Sylvester matrix*. Hence, another direction worth exploring for further research is to investigate the computational complexity of inverting this kind of matrices, in order to verify if a faster inversion algorithm can be designed.

Under a different perspective, for certain applications there is the need for *nonlinear* secret sharing schemes. An example are *cheater-immune secret sharing schemes* based on nonlinear constructions, which are robust towards dishonest players who submit fake shares during the reconstruction phase [18]. In this case, it would be interesting to analyze the trade-off between the amount of nonlinearity that the local rules must have to achieve cheater-immunity and the size of their ANF. A possible strategy could be to cast this question in terms of an optimization problem, and then solve it through heuristic techniques such as *Genetic Programming* (GP), which already proved to be successful in the design of S-boxes with good cryptographic properties and small implementation costs [12].

As a closing remark, we note that determining how large a family of MOCA can be is still an open problem, even in the linear case. As shown in [7], verifying whether a set of linear bipermutive CA of diameter d form a family of MOCA is equivalent to check that the polynomials associated to the local rules are pairwise coprime. However, despite the enumeration of coprime polynomials over finite fields is a well-developed research topic (see e.g. [1]), as far as we know there are no works in the literature addressing coprimality of monic polynomials with nonzero constant term, which is exactly the subclass corresponding to linear bipermutive local rules. Very recently, the first author showed a construction of a family of pairwise coprime polynomials of this kind in his PhD thesis [6], thus providing a first lower bound on its size. Nonetheless, optimality of this construction is still open.

References

1. Benjamin, A.T., Bennett, C.D.: The probability of relatively prime polynomials. Math. Mag. **80**(3), 196–202 (2007)
2. Betel, H., de Oliveira, P.P.B., Flocchini, P.: Solving the parity problem in one-dimensional cellular automata. Nat. Comput. **12**(3), 323–337 (2013)
3. Carlet, C.: Boolean functions for cryptography and error correcting codes. In: Crama, Y., Hammer, P.L. (eds.) Boolean Models and Methods in Mathematics, Computer Science, and Engineering, 1st edn, pp. 257–397. Cambridge University Press, New York. (2010)
4. Hedlund, G.A.: Endomorphisms and automorphisms of the shift dynamical systems. Math. Syst. Theory **3**(4), 320–375 (1969)
5. Keedwell, A.D., Dénes, J.: Latin Squares and Their Applications. Elsevier, New York City (2015)
6. Mariot, L.: Cellular automata, Boolean functions and combinatorial designs (2018). https://boa.unimib.it/bitstream/10281/199011/2/phd_unimib_701962.pdf
7. Mariot, L., Formenti, E., Leporati, A.: Constructing orthogonal Latin squares from linear cellular automata. CoRR abs/1610.00139 (2016)
8. Mariot, L., Formenti, E., Leporati, A.: Enumerating orthogonal Latin squares generated by bipermutive cellular automata. In: Dennunzio, A., Formenti, E., Manzoni, L., Porreca, A.E. (eds.) AUTOMATA 2017. LNCS, vol. 10248, pp. 151–164. Springer, Cham (2017). https://doi.org/10.1007/978-3-319-58631-1_12
9. Mariot, L., Leporati, A.: Sharing secrets by computing preimages of bipermutive cellular automata. In: Wąs, J., Sirakoulis, G.C., Bandini, S. (eds.) ACRI 2014. LNCS, vol. 8751, pp. 417–426. Springer, Cham (2014). https://doi.org/10.1007/978-3-319-11520-7_43
10. Mariot, L., Leporati, A., Dennunzio, A., Formenti, E.: Computing the periods of preimages in surjective cellular automata. Nat. Comput. **16**(3), 367–381 (2017)
11. Mariot, L., Picek, S., Jakobovic, D., Leporati, A.: Evolutionary algorithms for the design of orthogonal Latin squares based on cellular automata. In: Proceedings of the Genetic and Evolutionary Computation Conference. GECCO 2017, 15–19 July 2017, Berlin, Germany, pp. 306–313 (2017)
12. Mariot, L., Picek, S., Leporati, A., Jakobovic, D.: Cellular automata based s-boxes. Cryptogr. Commun. (2018). https://doi.org/10.1007/s12095-018-0311-8
13. del Rey, Á.M., Mateus, J.P., Sánchez, G.R.: A secret sharing scheme based on cellular automata. Appl. Math. Comput. **170**(2), 1356–1364 (2005)
14. Richardson, D.: Tessellations with local transformations. J. Comput. Syst. Sci. **6**(5), 373–388 (1972)
15. Shamir, A.: How to share a secret. Commun. ACM **22**(11), 612–613 (1979)
16. Stinson, D.R.: Combinatorial Designs - Constructions and Analysis. Springer, New York (2004). https://doi.org/10.1007/b97564
17. Sutner, K.: De Bruijn graphs and linear cellular automata. Complex Syst. **5**(1), 19–30 (1991)
18. Tompa, M., Woll, H.: How to share a secret with cheaters. J. Cryptol. **1**(2), 133–138 (1988)

Asynchronous Cellular Automata

Eroders and Proliferation: Repairing that Goes Wrong

Ilir Capuni[(✉)]

University of New York Tirana, Kodra e Diellit, 1001 Tirana, Albania
ilir@bu.edu

Abstract. We study a cellullar automata inspired asynchronous model of computation that models core features of the structure and functioning of living cells. We describe cell repair rules that ensure that the structure and the computation performed by a group of cells withstands occasional faults that may occur.

We observe that some self-organizing healing strategies of cells do admit that, under certain conditions, cells do exhibit massive proliferation of cells.

Keywords: Faults · Nubots · Eroders · Proliferation

1 Introduction

We consider a specific version of the Nubot model established in [4], which can be understood as asynchronous and non-deterministic cellular automata. The model allows the creation and destruction of cells, and most importantly, it admits exponential growth. We consider the dynamics of this model under noise that may cause that some cells alter their state to an arbitrary state, die completely, or create a cell on an empty site. The basic problem in the study of reliable computation is the storage problem: we want to save one bit of information – say bit 0 — forever, despite the faults caused by the noise mentioned above. A typical solution of this problem in plain vanilla two-dimensional CA in Von Neumann neighborhood is to encode this bit on a CA using the repetition code, and then apply the Toom's rule [3]. At each instance of time, a cell checks its current state, the neighboring square to the North and the neighboring square to the East. If the majority of these states is 1, then the state of the current square becomes 1; otherwise it becomes 0. This rule is applied synchronously.

We say that a CA is an *eroder* if it wipes all islands in a finite (but not necessarily uniform) number of steps. The Toom's rule is an eroder. Per [2], even when the updates are performed asynchronously, the CA is still an eroder (in a bit modified but still equivalent sense). In our model, Toom's rule is a good starting point but it is not enough.

The model facilitates reasoning about basic rules that guide the robustness of organized groups of cells (aka colonies) against random noise or decay that

© Springer Nature Switzerland AG 2018
G. Mauri et al. (Eds.): ACRI 2018, LNCS 11115, pp. 379–384, 2018.
https://doi.org/10.1007/978-3-319-99813-8_34

may cause that certain cells die, some get their state altered to an arbitrary state, or that a new cell is created at an empty site. We will present majority based rules that will wipe islands of We observe that under certain conditions, a massive proliferation of cells occurs. Alas, this proliferation is programmatically guided by the repair rules.

This paper is aimed to be a starting point for further study of proliferation phenomena and in particular, to study optimal rules that provably prevent it from occurring altogether.

2   The Model

The model uses a two-dimensional triangular grid with a coordinate system using x and y. A pair $p \in \mathbb{Z}^2$ is called a *site*, and it has 6 neighbors. A *cell* is the basic unit of the model defined as state-labeled disk of unit diameter centered on a site. Each site has at most one cell. A (finite) set of rules specifies how adjacent cells interact with each-other. This set is embedded in each cell. Cells have also a state – a finite amount of information from a fixed finite set called the *state space*. Cells are connected to each other through bonds. After applying a set of rules, they can change their state or the type of bond between them. These rules are applied asynchronously. Two adjacent cells can have a *rigid* (depicted as a solid disk) or a *flexible bond* (depicted as a small circle), or no bond at all between them.

Rules are written as follows:

$$r = (s1, s2, b, u) \rightarrow (s1', s2', b', u'),$$

where $s1, s2 \in \Sigma \cup \{\text{empty}\}$ are cell states from the finite set Σ, empty denotes the absence of a cell; $b \in \{\text{flexible, rigid, null}\}$ is the bond type between two cells, u is the relative position of the $s2$ cell to the $s1$ cell. The same applies for the right part of the arrow. If $s1$ or $s2$ is empty, the bond b between them is null, also if either or both $s1'$, $s2'$ is empty, then b' is null.

In Fig. 1 we give some examples that illustrate state and bond changes, cell creation and cell removal with the following respective rules: $r1 = (2, 4, \text{null}, x) \rightarrow (1, 5, \text{null}, x)$, $r2 = (0, 0, \text{null}, x) \rightarrow (0, 0, \text{flexible}, x)$, $r3 = (1, 1, \text{rigid}, x) \rightarrow (1, 1, \text{null}, x)$, $r4 = (5, 2, \text{rigid}, x) \rightarrow (1, 3, \text{flexible}, x)$, $r5 = (a, \text{empty}, \text{null}, x) \rightarrow (x, 1, \text{flexible}, x)$, $r6 = (b, 1, \text{rigid}, x) \rightarrow (1, \text{empty}, \text{null}, x)$.

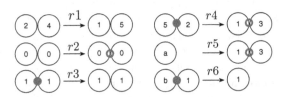

Fig. 1. Examples of cell interaction rules. Rule $r1$ change states. Rule $r2$ make a flexible bond. Rule $r3$ break a rigid bond. Rule $r4$ change a rigid bond to a flexible bond and change the states. Rule $r5$ appearance of a cell. Rule $r6$ disappearance of a cell.

3   Fault-Tolerance Step-by-Step

Clearly, having a single cell saving the information embedded within is impossible, since noise can change the state of the cell or remove the cell completely. For this, we need to split this task among a group of cells. This group of cells will have a specific size and certain geometric properties (see Fig. 2). We will call such a group of cells a *colony*.

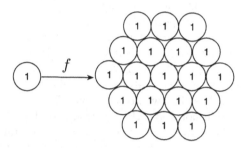

Fig. 2. Encoding one cell using redundancy on a colony

We focus our attention on the following problem: how one colony of cells with the same state (say, they display number 1) can live forever despite "occasional" flips of some cells' states. For the moment, we assume that the colony that we are observing is of infinite size. We cannot apply the idea of the Toom's rule directly, because our model is asynchronous, each cell in our model has 6 immediate neighbors, and our rules define the change of a pair of cells rather of a one single cell. However, its core idea — the majority voting — is a good starting point. Below we develop this idea precisely in several steps.

1. **Majority rule.** Let us consider one large enough colony of cells, all of them displaying the same state. Neighboring cells of a shape are connected via rigid bonds. Suppose that noise can only flip the state of some cells. To apply the Toom's rule, we need the following rules: $r1 = (1, 0, 1, E) \rightarrow (a, 0, 1, E)$, $r2 = (a, 0, 1, NE) \rightarrow (0, 0, 1, NE)$, and $r3 = (a, 1, 1, NE) \rightarrow (1, 1, 1, NE)$, where state a is an intermediate one that helps us to determine properly the state of the cell in the next step. When rule $r1$ is applied, the cell checks its own state and the neighbor in the east. Then by using $r2$ and $r3$ we take into consideration the two possible states of the neighbor cells in the northeast, which results in the majority of the states of itself, east and northeast neighbor. The above rules are given for state 1. Rules pertaining to the state 0 are written analogously.

2. **When a cell is deleted by noise.** If a cell is deleted by the noise, then a new cell with state X is added instead of it. State X represents a kind of an "undifferentiated state" of a cell. Such a cell is called a *generic*. To add a cell with state X in the interior part of the shape we

use $r7 = (1, \text{empty}, 0, E) \rightarrow (1, X, 1, E)$. We apply rules similar to $r7$ on any of the possible six directions in order to fill all the gaps that can be created in the shape. Then we change the bonds to rigid ones throughout the shape with the rules like $r8 = (X, 1, 0, SW) \rightarrow (X, 1, 0, SW)$. A cell with state X determines its new state according to the state of its neighbors. If it sees 0 in the East, it behaves like it was a cell with state 1 and sets its state to a; otherwise it sets it to b. We do this using $r9 = (X, 0, 1, E) \rightarrow (a, 0, 1, E)$ and $r10 = (X, 1, 1, E) \rightarrow (b, 1, 1, E)$, where states a and b are intermediate states in the process of "differentiation" of a newly created cell with the state X to a cell with a state 0 or 1 respectively.

3. **Preserving the shape through a liner.** Until now, we did not consider the size of a colony nor its shape. However, since we have added a rule that creates a cell on an empty site, we need to introduce a kind of a boundary that preserves the geometrical features of a colony and does not allow its uncontrolled growth. For this, we need to "wrap" a colony with a liner with a kind of cells that will not apply the creation rule. For this, we add a three layer shell around the shape made of cells with specific state for each layer of the shell, say with the state $a1$ for the first layer, $a2$ for the second, and $a3$ for the outermost layer. The cells of the outer layer cannot create a cell on an empty site. If a cell of this kind is killed, then it will be created by the cells of the other layers of the liner. To determine properly the state of the new cells, Toom's rule is applied by the cells comprising the liner, using $r16 = (V, A, 1, E) \rightarrow (V', A, 1, E)$, $r17 = (V', A, 1, SE) \rightarrow (A', A, 1, SE)$, $r18 = (D, V, 1, W) \rightarrow (D', V, 1, W)$, and $r19 = (D', V, 1, NW) \rightarrow (A', V, 1, NW)$
   If one of the cells of the liner is deleted, we add a new cell using $r11 = (A, \text{empty}, 0, NE) \rightarrow (A, D, 1, NE)$. If the state of a cell is D, and it has a neighboring cell with a state in $\{1, 0, a, b\}$, then, its state changes to X by $r12 = (D, 0, 1, W) \rightarrow (X, 0, 1, W)$. Further, if a cell with a state in $\{a, b, 1, 0\}$ has a neighbor with state A', its state switches to D, that is $r13 = (a, A', 1, NE) \rightarrow (D, A', 1, NE)$. If a cell whose state is V neighbors a cell with the state in $\{0, 1, a, b\}$, then it changes its state to X by rule $r14 = (V, b, 1, SW) \rightarrow (X, b, 1, SW)$. When it sees X, it becomes D by the application of $r15 = (V, X, 1, E) \rightarrow (D, X, 1, E)$.

4. **When a cell is created by mistake.** If the noise causes a cell to be created on an empty site with the empty neighborhood, that cell will die, after it has confirmed that it is surrounded by empty sites.

Assuming that the noise cannot kill or modify consecutive cells of the liner, in [1], the recovery power of the rules is demonstrated for various convex shapes with various degree of initial damages of the colony in terms of islands of cells with different state or holes of missing cells.

4 Uncontrolled Programatically Guided Proliferation of Cells

Let us assume that a colony has a shape of a regular hexagon and its interior is initially filled with number 1. We will show that some of the above repair rules, may lead to uncontrolled proliferation of cells under some conditions and circumstances that we will demonstrate below.

1. **Colony without a liner.** Trivially, if the liner is missing, then the rules that create cells on empty sites will fire, hence growing the shape constantly. Indeed, recall that the creation of the cells is performed in all directions.

2. **The case of one layer liner.** For simplicity, let us begin by considering a one layer liner. Suppose that two consecutive cells of the liner are removed as depicted in Fig. 3. The system in a noise-free setting will evolve as depicted in Fig. 4. Clearly, this would not happen if only one cell of the liner could have been removed since there is no majority which can allow this spread.

   We also point out that this kind of proliferation is much slower and rare (in probabilistic terms) or does not occur at all on the other sides of the colony. Indeed, recall that the majority rules are applied in N and NE direction.

3. **The case when the liner has three layers.** Let us consider a "wound" on the liner at the same side as before. The wound consists of three consecutive cells of the outermost liner, two cells of the second layer next to them, and two neighboring cells of these of the third layer. This is a sufficiently large wound in which, with probability 1/3, a proliferation will occur as in the case of the one layer liner.

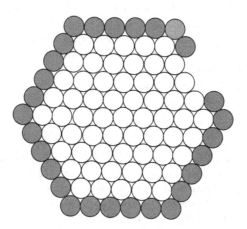

Fig. 3. A wound on a liner

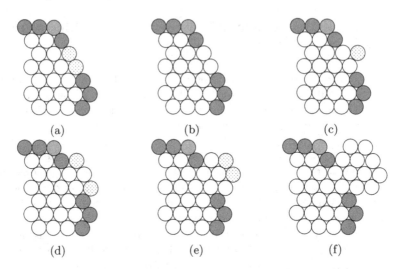

(a)   (b)   (c)

(d)   (e)   (f)

Fig. 4. In (a), two generic cells are created, which according to the majority rules will result in (b). Now these two cells, will create another generic cell as shown in (c). The evolution now continues by having a massive proliferation of cells.

5   Conclusions and Open Questions

In the paper, the focus is given to the problem of preserving the information and the shape of a group of cells referred to as a colony when automaton is subjected to noise. We proposed rules which do preserve information within the colony despite the noise. Alas, under certain conditions, the repair rules do admit massive proliferation of cells. As shown in the examples given, even majority computation does have some influence in these sequences of bad events. Finding repair rules that provably do not admit proliferation of cells is the most intriguing open question in this context. Furthermore, geometric properties of colonies appear to have some influence in the proliferation phenomena. Establishing this link formally, is also an interesting open question.

References

1. Capuni, I., Halimi, A., Hitaj, D.: Towards indestructible molecular robots. In: SOF-SEM (Student Research Forum Papers/Posters), pp. 112–119 (2015)
2. Gray, L.F.: Toom's stability theorem in continuous time. In: Bramson, M., Durrett, R. (eds.) Perplexing Problems in Probability, vol. 44, pp. 331–353. Springer, Boston (1999). https://doi.org/10.1007/978-1-4612-2168-5_18
3. Toom, A.L.: Stable and attractive trajectories in multicomponent systems. Adv. Probab. **6**, 549–575 (1980). 12
4. Woods, D.: Active self-assembly and molecular robotics with nubots. Change **1**(1), 2 (2015)

A Pedagogical Example: A Family of Stochastic Cellular Automata that Plays Alesia

Nazim Fatès[✉]

Université de Lorraine, CNRS, Inria, LORIA, 54000 Nancy, France
`nazim.fates@loria.fr`

Abstract. Alesia is a two-player zero-sum game which is quite similar to the rock-paper-scissors game: the two players simultaneously move and do not know what the opponent plays at a given round. The simultaneity of the moves implies that there is no deterministic good strategy in this game, otherwise one would anticipate the moves of the opponent and easily win the game. We explore how to build a family of one-dimensional stochastic cellular automata to play this game. The rules are built in an iterative way by progressively increasing the complexity of the transitions. We show the possibility to construct a family of rules with interesting results, including a good performance when confronted to the Nash-equilibrium strategy.

Keywords: Stochastic cellular automata
Probabilistic dynamical systems · Zero-sum markov strategy games

1 Introduction

The purpose of this note is to present a sketch on how stochastic cellular automata can be used to play a simple strategy game in which randomness has a central role. This game, named *Alesia* after the battle that opposed Gallic tribes and the army of J. Caesar 52 BC, has simple rules [4]: **(1)** The two players initially have the same number of soldiers, say 50. **(2)** Each round, the two players fight a *battle* by *simultaneously* engaging a given number of soldiers. The soldiers are then lost, whatever the outcome. Players must engage at least one soldier at each round (if they have not lost all their soldiers). **(3)** The winner of battle is simply the player who has engaged more troops; the front moves by one step in the direction of his opponent. **(4)** The winner of the game is the player who succeeds to reach his opponent's camp, that is, to make the front advance more than W steps, where W is fixed in advanced (here we take $W = 2$). **(5)** The game ends in a draw if none of the players reaches the opponent's camp.

To illustrate these rules, an example of game is given on Fig. 1-left.

After playing a few games, one discovers that any good strategy should find a balance between playing too much or too little soldiers at each battle.

© Springer Nature Switzerland AG 2018
G. Mauri et al. (Eds.): ACRI 2018, LNCS 11115, pp. 385–395, 2018.
https://doi.org/10.1007/978-3-319-99813-8_35

sA	pA								pB	sB
50	11	o	. . @ . .	o					14	50
39	12	o	. @ . . .	o					12	36
27	9	o	. @ . . .	o					1	24
18	5	o	. . @ . .	o					5	23
13	4	o	. . @ . .	o					3	18
9	3	o	. . . @ .	o					4	15
6	2	o	. . @ . .	o					3	11
4	2	o	. @ . . .	o					4	8
2	1	o	@	o					2	4
1	-	@	. . . . .	o					-	2

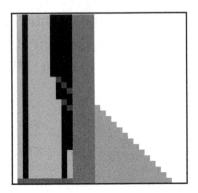

Fig. 1. (left) Example of an Alesia game: sA, sB, pA, and pB are the soldiers and the plays of player A and B, respectively. (right) Example of space-time diagram produced by the q2h2 player (see below). The cells in blue, brown, and green code the initial condition (states A, F, B); the result is given by the number of black cells (state V); other colours encode auxiliary states (see below for details). Time goes upward. (Color figure online)

Indeed, a large number of soldiers ensures victory but depletes the reserves for the next rounds. On the contrary, a small number of soldiers saves the reserves but increases the risks to loose the battle.

The other important point is that a good strategy is necessarily stochastic. Indeed, if for instance a player always plays 4 at the first round, the opponent can foresee this decision and decide to play 5 and thus win the first round. If the player always plays 20, the opponent's interest is to play only 1, and to deliberately loose the first round to gain an advantage in the number of soldiers. Of course, this argument can be recursively applied to the next rounds...

Our aim is to analyse whether simple cellular automata could calculate a good strategy for this game. Our motivation is to explore how "noisy" components with an elementary behaviour can cooperate to perform an interesting computation, as in a biological organisms. We are aware that cellular automata constitute a Turing-universal model of computation, and can thus compute any function that is computable by a classical machine, but our goal here is to make a decision emerge from *simple* non-deterministic mechanisms.

The links between cellular automata and game theory have been mainly explored with iterated two-player games on grids or graphs: these models distribute n players on a grid (or on a graph) and make the players interact by pairs with their neighbours. The players generally update their strategy according to the payoff received and the goal is to observe how the strategies dynamically evolve on the graph [6]. Interestingly enough, it can be observed that even small variations in the updating method (e.g., from synchronous to partially synchronous) may radically change the ultimate evolution of the system [3].

However, the use of cellular automata for the design of strategies is almost absent from the literature. Fraenkel has presented a pioneering work of how cellular automata may compute a particular strategy [2]. Cook, Larsson and Neary also made interesting connections between (deterministic) one-dimensional cellular automata and a generalisation of the game of Nim called the Blocking Wythoff Nim [1].

The purpose of this paper is to present some other simple examples by taking the Alesia game as a starting point. It can thus be considered as a *pedagogical* example in order to solve a problem in a distributed way. Our goal is not to reach optimality, but we will nevertheless compare our solutions to an optimal strategy in order to have a quantitative estimation of the quality of our cellular automata strategy.

2   Definitions

2.1   Formalisation of the Game

We now introduce the formal definitions of the game. We assume that the game starts with N soldiers and that the "arena" is such that a player needs to make W (cumulative) steps in the direction of his opponent to win.

For the sake of simplicity we model a game by an infinite sequence of moves. Let a_t, b_t be the number of soldiers of player A and B, respectively, at time t and α_t, β_t the number of soldiers that they respectively engage at time t. We have:

$\forall t \in \mathbb{N}, a_{t+1} = a_t - \alpha_t$ and $\forall t \in \mathbb{N}, b_{t+1} = b_t - \beta_t$.

The position of the front evolves according to $w_0 = 0$ and:

$$w_{t+1} = w_t + \begin{cases} 1 & \text{if } \alpha_t > \beta_t \\ -1 & \text{if } \alpha_t < \beta_t \\ 0 & \text{otherwise.} \end{cases}$$

The game stops when one of the players hits the camp of his adversary or when there are no more soldiers. As the outcome of the game depends on the sequence of moves $s = (a_t, b_t)_{t \in \mathbb{N}}$, we call this sequence the *game* for the sake of simplicity.

Since each player is forced to play at least one soldier at each time step, the number of rounds is finite; we denote it by $T(s)$.

The gain $G(s)$ that results from a game s is 1, -1 or 0, if player A wins, or if player B wins, or if there is a draw, respectively. Formally, we have:

$$T(s) = \min_{t \in \mathbb{N}} \{w_t = W + 1 \text{ or } w_t = -W - 1 \text{ or } (a_t, b_t) = (0, 0)\},$$

$$\text{and} : G(s) = \begin{cases} 1 & \text{if } w_T = W + 1, \\ -1 & \text{if } w_T = -W - 1, \\ 0 & \text{otherwise.} \end{cases}$$

The rules of the game impose $a_0 = b_0 = N$ and: $\forall t < T, a_t > 0 \implies 1 \le \alpha_t \le a_t$, and $b_t > 0 \implies 1 \le \beta_t \le b_t$ and, for $t \ge T$, we set $\alpha_t = \beta_t = 0$.

2.2 Stochastic Cellular Automata

For the sake of simplicity, we will use one-dimensional cellular automata with nearest-neighbours interaction. To describe our model, we simply take an infinite line of cells: $\mathbb{Z}$. Note however that for the simulations, it is more convenient to use periodic boundary conditions ($\mathbb{Z}/n\mathbb{Z}$ with a large value for n).

We denote by Q the set of states the cells can hold. A configuration represents the global state of the system; it is an element of $Q^{\mathbb{Z}}$.

A stochastic cellular automaton is defined with a local transition function $\varphi : Q^3 \times Q \rightarrow [0,1]$ and we write $\varphi((x,y,z),q) = p$ to express that a cell with a neighbourhood state (x, y, z) has a probability p to update to the state q. We require: $\forall (x, y, z) \in Q^3$, $\sum_{q \in Q} \varphi((x, y, z), q) = 1$.

The global transition function thus maps a configuration x^t to the configuration x^{t+1} such that:

$$\forall i \in \mathbb{Z}, \ \Pr[x_i^{t+1} = q] = \varphi\big((x_{i-1}^t, x_i^t, x_{i+1}^t), q\big),$$

and where all the probabilities are drawn independently for each cell.

In order to build a strategy that uses a cellular automaton, we will translate the state of the game into a configuration, make this configuration evolve, and then interpret the resulting configuration as an action of the player. Given two players A and B, we will measure their *relative strength* with the expected gain that player A has against player B. This statistical estimation is obtained by repeating N games opposing A and B. If N_A and N_B are the number of games that A or B won, respectively, then the expected gain of A against B is given by $(N_A - N_B)/N$.

We now present how we build a cellular automaton player by progressively improving the strategy players. This improvements are made by defining families of rules and making each new family compete against the previously found players. This method can be seen as a "bootstrapping" technique because each level of complexity emerges from a previously defined level of complexity.

3 Cellular Automata Players

All our players are Markovian: they base their decision on the current state of the game only. For the sake of readability, we will assume that the player we are describing is player A, while its opponent is player B. We recall our notations: a, b denote the number of soldiers of player A and B, respectively, and w denotes the position of the front at time t, the number of soldiers played by a given player Π is denoted by $\Pi(a, w, b)$. We also assume that the game is played in "standard" conditions, that is, with $W = 2$ and $N = 50$ [5].

3.1 Uniform Distribution Players

The first player we can consider, denoted by uniform, plays a uniform number between 1 and a. It will serve as the basis of our bootstrapping process. Formally:

uni-M$(a, w, b) = \mathcal{U}\{a\}$, where $\mathcal{U}\{0\} = 0$ and $\mathcal{U}\{k\}$ draws a random number uniformly in $\{1, \dots, k\}$ for $k > 0$.

This strategy is easy to defeat with the following opponent: beatUnif always plays 1 unless the front is in position $-W$ (danger of loosing the game), in which case it plays b (as many soldiers as the opponent has). Formally: beatUnif$(a, w, b) = b$ if $w = -W$ and beatUnif$(a, w, b) = 1$ otherwise.

Our simulations show that beatUnif has an expected gain of 0.93 against unif: it wins the game with a probability greater than 95%.

Table 1. Expected gains of uni-M players opposed to other uni-M player. The deviation from an antisymmetrical form are due to the statistical variations (10^5 samples).

	uni-10	uni-12	uni-14	uni-16	uni-18	uni-20	uni-22	uni-24
uni-10		−0.133	−0.178	−0.182	−0.170	−0.146	−0.109	−0.057
uni-12	0.130		−0.068	−0.076	−0.060	−0.027	0.016	0.075
uni-14	0.177	0.069		−0.030	−0.017	0.016	0.061	0.122
uni-16	0.180	0.071	0.027		−0.006	0.018	0.068	0.133
uni-18	0.171	0.058	0.013	0.003		0.016	0.049	0.105
uni-20	0.148	0.026	−0.017	−0.023	−0.015		0.030	0.075
uni-22	0.108	−0.019	−0.065	−0.068	−0.053	−0.033		0.042
uni-24	0.060	−0.072	−0.124	−0.126	−0.103	−0.076	−0.038	

3.2 Uniform Distribution Players with Saturation

The weakness of uniform comes from the fact that it is too "generous": it is easy to "exhaust" simply by using a defensive strategy. A straightforward improvement of this player is to limit the maximum number of soldiers engaged at each time step. We define uni-M as the player which draws a number uniformly between 1 and a and then plays this value if it is lower than a threshold value M, or plays M otherwise. Formally: uni-M$(a, w, b) = \max\{\mathcal{U}\{a\}, M\}$.

The question then comes to know what is the best setting for M. Again, as there is no "absolute" good player; we thus simply oppose players with various settings of M and observe how they perform one against the other.

The results are presented in Table 1. The data represents the expected gain of uni-M players with different settings of M. These experiments indicate that a good setting of M is in the interval 16–18. Indeed uni-16 and uni-18 have a positive expected gain defeat when opposed to the other players and when opposed to each other, the difference in expected gain is not significant.

We are now in position to continue our bootstrapping process: our next objective is to build a CA player that performs better than uni-18. Before going on, let us observe that "coding" the uniform or uni-M players with a one-dimensional cellular automaton is not that easy. Indeed, if the input is coded in the form of a configuration that has n cells in a given state, it is not clear how cells could interact *locally* in order to produce every possible output between 0 and $n - 1$ (or n) with an *equal* probability.

Table 2. Expected gains of `binomial` players against `uniform` players (10^5 samples).

	uni-8	uni-10	uni-12	uni-14	uni-16	uni-18	uni-20
bin-22	0.554	0.409	0.370	0.375	0.368	0.377	0.391
bin-24	0.589	0.428	0.400	0.411	0.430	0.441	0.463
bin-26	0.608	0.433	0.399	0.417	0.451	0.475	0.501
bin-28	0.622	0.428	0.380	0.405	0.448	0.485	0.513
bin-30	0.628	0.420	0.345	0.368	0.420	0.468	0.504
bin-32	0.627	0.398	0.314	0.319	0.374	0.431	0.480

3.3   Another Simple Player: The Binomial Player

If we have a set of cells which can hold a state with a given probability, the most intuitive "computation" is to draw a number according to a binomial distribution. We define the `binomial` players as the strategy where each soldier of the player has a probability ρ "to be played". For a given ρ, we set $R = 100 * \rho$ and denote by `bin-R` the `binomial` with parameter $\rho = R/100$.

To encode our player, we simply use the binary alphabet $Q = \{0, 1\}$ and map a game state (a, w, b), to the initial condition $x \in Q^{\mathbb{Z}}$ formed by a consecutive 1's on a background of 0's. Then each cell independently applies the rule where a 0 remains a 0 and a 1 remains a 1 with probability ρ and becomes a 0 with probability $1 - \rho$. We have: `binomial`$(a, f, b) = card\{i \in \mathbb{Z}, y_i = 1\}$, where y denotes the configuration obtained by a one-step transformation of x.

Table 3. Expected gains of `binomial` players against other `binomial` players (10^5 samples).

	bin-15	bin-20	bin-25	bin-30		bin-20	bin-22	bin-24	bin-26
bin-15		-0.182	-0.327	-0.417	bin-20		-0.004	-0.005	0.000
bin-20	0.180		-0.002	-0.021	bin-22	0.006		0.015	0.039
bin-25	0.328	0.003		0.098	bin-24	0.005	-0.018		0.035
bin-30	0.419	0.017	-0.099		bin-26	0.005	-0.030	-0.029	

Table 2 shows the expected gain of various `binomial` players against various `uniform-M` players. We observe that for each value of M, there is a different value of ρ which maximizes the expected gain. The player which has the *highest minimal* expected gain is `bin-24`. It is interesting to note that if we take $\rho = 0.28$, the "best" opponent of this `binomial` players is `uni-12` and *not* `uni-18`, as expected from what was seen by making `uniform-M` players together. This illustrates the fact that it is not possible to compare the expected gain of rules with a total order. Given three players A,B,C, we can observe that B performs better than C versus A, and nevertheless B is beaten by C.

When opposing the `binomial` players one against another, the best player is `bin-22` (Table 3). Our objective is now to find a player that beats this new challenger.

4   Taking into Account the Situation: The q2h2 Player

The previous model was not really a cellular automaton since there was no interaction between cells. The next improvement we can do is to take into account the position of the front and number of soldiers of the opponent.

We request that the initial state of the game to be translated in an initial condition of the cellular automaton with a simple method. Typically, the number of soldiers and the position of the front should be coded with a "unary" code, that is, each number of soldiers should correspond to the same number of cells in a given state, plus or minus some constants. Let us now present a player which respects these constraints, we name it q2h2.

The model employs 8 states: $Q = \{E, A, V, V*, R, F, F*, B\}$; its elements respectively represent the following states: empty, A-soldier, voluntary, voluntary-star, reluctant, front, front-star, B-soldier. The 'star' represents an information that travels from right to left in order to transmit an influence from the B-soldier cells to the different cells which represent the strength of player A. The following rules describe how this influence is transmitted.

We associate to a game position (a, w, b) an initial configuration x_{ini} built as follows : the a first cells are in state A. Next, we put δ cells in state F, where $\delta = W + w + 1$ represents the state of the front. The next following b cells are in state B. We thus have: $x_{\text{ini}}(a, w, b) = ..EE \underbrace{AAAAA}_{a\,\text{times}} \underbrace{FFF}_{\delta\,\text{times}} \underbrace{BBBBBBB}_{b\,\text{times}} EEE...$

The evolution of the cellular automaton can be described with the following scenario: soldiers of player A (state A) turn to the voluntary state (V) or to the reluctant state (R) in one step. After that, some reluctant soldiers of A may turn to voluntary according to the "danger" they feel. This danger is evaluated as a combination of b and w: (a) the more soldiers the opponent has, the greater the danger; (b) the smaller the front is, the greater the danger. In practice, each cell in state B has a given probability (p_T) to initiate a signal that will travel to the left until it eventually reaches a cell in state R; it then turns this cell to a V. This signal can also be absorbed with probability p_A.

As the information travels from the right to the left, we can define the local function $\varphi\big((x, y, z), q\big)$ with the use of the probabilistic function $\xi(q, q')$, which takes as an input the state of the cell itself q and the state of right neighbour q' and outputs a state in Q with a given probability. This function, which depends on three probabilities p_V, p_T and p_A, is defined as follows.

– An empty cell remains empty: $\xi(E, \cdot) = E$.

- Each A immediately decides if it turns to a voluntary state or to a reluctant state: $\xi(A, \cdot) = \begin{cases} V & \text{with probability } p_V, \\ R & \text{with probability } 1 - p_V. \end{cases}$

- The behaviour of front cells and front-star cells depend on what they see on their right: (a) a B cell: this corresponds to the case where the "stars" are initiated by the soldiers of the opponent. (b) another F or F* cell: this case corresponds to the transmission of the star to the left. We set a probability p_A to be absorbed, i.e., the star is not transmitted. This reads:

$$\xi(F, B) = \xi(F*, B) = \begin{cases} F* & \text{with probability } p_T, \\ F & \text{with probability } 1 - p_T, \end{cases} \quad \text{and:}$$

$$\xi(F, F*) = \xi(F*, F*) = \begin{cases} F* & \text{with probability } 1 - p_A, \\ F & \text{with probability } p_A. \end{cases}$$

In all other cases, the front cells remains stable, the front-star cells become front cells: $\xi(F, q) = F(F*, q) = F$ for $q \notin \{B, F, F*\}$. (Note that in a normal behaviour, the only useful case is $q = E$.)

- A voluntary cell or voluntary-star cell simply transmits the star from right to left. This reads: $\xi(V, q') = \xi(V*, q') = V*$ if $q' \in \{V*, F*\}$ and $\xi(V, q') = \xi(V*, q') = V$ otherwise.

- A refractory cell remains refractory unless it sees a star on its right. This is translated by: $\xi(R, V*) = \xi(R, F*) = V$ and $\xi(R, q') = R$ if $q' \notin \{V*, F*\}$.

- Cells in state B simply disappear at the rate of one cell per time step. This reads: $\xi(B, E) = E$ and $\xi(B, q') = B$ if $q' \neq B$.

An illustration of this behaviour can be seen on Fig. 1-right. (As it can be easily guessed, the front-star are drawn in red and the voluntary-star cells are in green.)

Table 4. Expected gains of q2h2 players with $p_A = 0$ against bin-22 (left) and bin-35 (right). The two parameters p_T (columns) and p_V (lines) are varied (2.10^4 samples).

p_V \ p_T	0.10	0.20	0.30	0.40	0.50
0.0	-0.986	-0.189	0.470	0.637	-0.240
0.5	-0.565	0.133	0.530	0.346	-0.656
0.10	-0.070	0.264	0.507	-0.076	-0.864
0.15	0.021	0.342	0.343	-0.500	-0.953
0.20	0.062	0.328	0.023	-0.774	-0.989

	0.10	0.20	0.30	0.40	0.50	0.60
0.0	-0.997	-0.870	-0.212	-0.026	-0.246	-0.844
0.10	-0.415	0.007	-0.111	-0.311	-0.776	-0.984
0.20	0.107	-0.171	-0.382	-0.753	-0.971	-0.999
0.30	-0.205	-0.436	-0.735	-0.960	-0.998	-1.000
0.40	-0.501	-0.743	-0.948	-0.996	-1.000	-1.000
0.50	-0.778	-0.949	-0.997	-1.000	-1.000	-1.000

To analyse this rule, first, let us simply set $p_A = 0$, in other words, we do not take into account the state of the front. We ask how we can tune p_V and p_T in order to beat the binomial players. Recall that so far our best binomial player is bin-22 ($\rho = 0.22$). Table 4-left shows the result of this player against bin-22 for different values of p_V and p_T. It can be seen that this player is easy to defeat: for example, for $p_V = 0.40$ and $p_T = 0$, one obtains an expected gain greater than 0. A zero value indicates that in fact, in this case it is sufficient to take into account only the strength of the opponent to obtain good results.

Note that the value of (p_V, p_T) which maximises the expected gain against binomial players varies greatly with ρ. For example, for bin-35, the best expected gain is obtained for $p_V = 0.20$ and $p_T = 0.10$, and this gain ($\sim$0.15) is much lower than for bin-22. This may seem paradoxical but remember that bin-22 is the player which has the best result against the other binomial players, and that we know nothing for the other rules. All we can say is that we are sure that even with $p_A = 0$ the family of q2h2 players *dominates* the family of binomial players: for every binomial player, there exists a q2h2 player which can defeat it. This is a direct consequence of the fact that the q2h2 players include all the binomial players simply by setting $p_T = 0$.

Table 5. Expected gains of binomial players (lines) against q2h2 players (columns) with $p_V = 0.22$, $p_A = 0$ and a varying value of p_T (10^4 samples).

p_T	0.0	0.5	0.10	0.15	0.20	0.25	0.30
bin-15	−0.330	−0.541	−0.650	−0.709	−0.607	−0.276	0.277
bin-20	0.007	−0.114	−0.269	−0.389	−0.376	−0.102	0.323
bin-25	−0.008	0.086	0.058	−0.020	−0.048	0.083	0.387
bin-30	−0.082	0.015	0.157	0.206	−0.203	0.286	0.478
bin-35	−0.192	−0.143	0.009	0.188	0.326	−0.408	0.554

Table 5 show how various binomial players can be defeated by fixing $p_V = 0.22$ and setting an appropriate value of p_T. Similar results can be obtained for other values of p_V, which confirms the great advantage of the q2h2 players against the binomial players.

Despite these encouraging results, we could not find any setting of (p_V, p_T) which would dominate all the other binomial players. Once again, the difficulty stems from the impossibility to establish a total order between rules. For example the rule with the setting $(p_V, p_T) = (0.5, 0.8)$ defeats bin-22 (with an expected gain of 0.60) and is defeated by bin-35 (with an expected gain of 0.67)... but, as seen above, bin-22 defeats bin-35!

In a second step, to demonstrate how setting a positive value of p_A can be useful, simply examine a precise situation and leave a more systematic study for future work. In the paragraph above we showed how setting $p_A = 0$ and varying p_V and p_T allows us to defeat every binomial player. However, against bin-30, only a small region of (p_V, p_T) has a positive expected gain, and the maximum positive gain one can obtain is around 0.1.

Table 6-left shows the expected gain of q2h2 against bin-30 when we set $p_T = 0.25$ and vary p_A and p_V. It can be seen that allowing $p_A > 0$ gives much better results: in particular for $p_V = 0.15$ and $p_A = 0.8$, the expected again is above 0.4, which is quite impressive.

Table 6. Expected gains of q2h2 players with $p_T = 0.25$ against bin-30 (left) and against Nash (right). The two parameters p_A (lines) and p_V (columns) are varied (10^5 samples).

	0.10	0.15	0.20	0.25
0.20	0.111	-0.065	-0.256	-0.370
0.40	0.254	0.208	-0.010	-0.213
0.60	0.280	0.348	0.178	-0.027
0.80	0.276	0.395	0.272	0.081
0.100	0.267	0.403	0.280	0.108

	0.0	0.2	0.4	0.6	0.8	0.10
0.20	-0.050	-0.058	-0.075	-0.095	-0.115	-0.148
0.40	-0.039	-0.033	-0.043	-0.056	-0.063	-0.088
0.60	-0.035	-0.029	-0.027	-0.029	-0.039	-0.048
0.80	-0.093	-0.051	-0.038	-0.029	-0.027	-0.038
0.100	-0.183	-0.139	-0.081	-0.046	-0.043	-0.033

We have seen that it is not possible to totally order the players according to their respective scores. There exists however a strategy which is never defeated (on average). We denote this player by Nash, as it corresponds to what is called the Nash equilibrium: Nash gives a guarantee to have a positive expected gain against any player P, but against a third player P', it may be that P performs better than Nash.

We have tested the performance of q2h2 against Nash, with a setting of $p_T = 0.25$ and different values of p_V and p_A. The results are displayed on Table 6-right: we see that in some cases, the average expected loss is close to zero and of the same amplitude as the noise on the measures. In practice, this implies that one can hardly distinguish between the Nash player and the q2h2 player with the proper settings.

These first results are rather encouraging and there are many directions in which they can be deepened. For example, it is interesting to examine the scaling properties of our cellular automata: while obtaining the optimal Nash-equilibrium player demands more time as the size of the game increases, our models can easily be applied to larger sizes, maybe with an adjustment of the three probabilities. Of course, the behaviour of this cellular automaton can also be obtained with classical mathematical functions but here we wanted to examine how simple interacting elements would play this game. Our goal was to show that a non-trivial behaviour can be obtained by progressively increasing the complexity of the rules. Another research direction would be to make the system evolve autonomously and see if it can discover new levels of complexity without an external aid.

Acknowledgements. We express our sincere gratitude to Bruno Scherrer for introducing us to the game of Alesia and for providing us with an optimal Nash player program. We thank Irène Marcovici for her valuable comments on the manuscript.

References

1. Cook, M., Larsson, U., Neary, T.: A cellular automaton for blocking queen games. Nat. Comput. **16**(3), 397–410 (2017)
2. Fraenkel, A.S.: Two-player games on cellular automata. More Games Chance **42**, 279–306 (2002)
3. Grilo, C., Correia, L.: Effects of asynchronism on evolutionary games. J. Theor. Biol. **269**(1), 109–122 (2011). https://doi.org/10.1016/j.jtbi.2010.10.022
4. Meyer, C., Ganascia, J.G., Zucker, J.D.: Learning strategies in games by anticipation. In: Proceedings of IJCAI (1), pp. 698–707 (1997)
5. Perolat, J., Scherrer, B., Piot, B., Pietquin, O.: Approximate dynamic programming for two-player zero-sum Markov games. In: Proceedings of International Conference on Machine Learning 2015, Lille, France, vol. 37, pp. 1321–1329 (2015)
6. Szabó, G., Fáth, G.: Evolutionary games on graphs. Phys. Rep. **446**(4–6), 97–216 (2007). https://doi.org/10.1016/j.physrep.2007.04.004

On Fixable Families of Boolean Networks

Maximilien Gadouleau[1]([✉]) and Adrien Richard[2]

[1] Department of Computer Science, Durham University, Durham, UK
m.r.gadouleau@durham.ac.uk
[2] Laboratoire I3S, UMR CNRS 7271 & Université Côte d'Azur,
Sophia Antipolis, France

Abstract. The asynchronous dynamics associated with a Boolean network $f : \{0,1\}^n \to \{0,1\}^n$ is a finite deterministic automaton considered in many applications. The set of states is $\{0,1\}^n$, the alphabet is $[n]$, and the action of letter i on a state x consists in either switching the ith component if $f_i(x) \neq x_i$ or doing nothing otherwise. This action is extended to words in the natural way. We then say that a word w *fixes* f if, for all states x, the result of the action of w on x is a fixed point of f. A whole family of networks is *fixable* if its members are all fixed by the same word, and the *fixing length* of the family is the minimum length of such a word. In this paper, which is building closely on [2] where these notions have been introduced, we are interested in families of Boolean networks with relatively small fixing lengths. Firstly, we prove that fixing length of the family of networks with acyclic asynchronous graphs is $\Theta(n2^n)$. Secondly, it is known that the fixing length of the whole family of monotone networks is $O(n^3)$. We then exhibit two families of monotone networks with fixing length $\Theta(n)$ and $\Theta(n^2)$ respectively, namely monotone networks with tree interaction graphs and conjunctive networks with symmetric interaction graphs.

Keywords: Boolean networks · Asynchronous dynamics
Fixed points · Asynchronous graph

1 Introduction

A **Boolean network** (**network** for short) is a finite dynamical system defined by a function

$$f : \{0,1\}^n \to \{0,1\}^n, \qquad x = (x_1, \ldots, x_n) \mapsto f(x) = (f_1(x), \ldots, f_n(x)).$$

The "network" terminology comes from the fact that these systems are typically used to model networks of interacting entities. For a list of applications of Boolean networks to gene networks, neural networks, and more, see [2] and references therein.

The **interaction graph** of f depicts the architecture of the network of interactions, and is often considered as the main parameter of f. Formally, it is the directed graph $G(f)$ with vertex set $[n] := \{1, \ldots, n\}$ and an arc from j to i

G. Mauri et al. (Eds.): ACRI 2018, LNCS 11115, pp. 396–405, 2018.
https://doi.org/10.1007/978-3-319-99813-8_36

if f_i depends on x_j, that is, if there exist $x, y \in \{0, 1\}^n$ that only differ in the component j such that $f_i(x) \neq f_i(y)$.

In many applications, the dynamics derived from f is the asynchronous dynamics [1]; it is represented by the directed graph $\Gamma(f)$, called **asynchronous graph** of f. This graph is defined as follows. For any $i \in [n]$, the result of the action of the letter i on x is given by

$$f^i(x) := (x_1, \ldots, f_i(x), \ldots, x_n). \tag{1}$$

The vertex set of $\Gamma(f)$ is $\{0, 1\}^n$, the set of all the possible **states**, and there is an arc from x to y if and only if $y \neq x$ and $y = f^i(x)$ for some i. See Fig. 1 for an illustration.

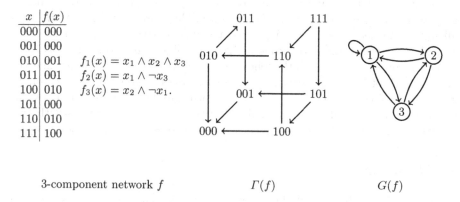

x	$f(x)$
000	000
001	000
010	001
011	001
100	010
101	000
110	010
111	100

$f_1(x) = x_1 \wedge x_2 \wedge x_3$
$f_2(x) = x_1 \wedge \neg x_3$
$f_3(x) = x_2 \wedge \neg x_1.$

3-component network f $\Gamma(f)$ $G(f)$

Fig. 1. A network f with its asynchronous graph $\Gamma(f)$ and its interaction graph $G(f)$.

The action in Eq. (1) is extended to any word $w = i_1 i_2 \ldots i_k$ on the alphabet $[n]$ as

$$f^w := f^{i_k} \circ f^{i_{k-1}} \circ \cdots \circ f^{i_1}.$$

A word w **fixes** f if $f^w(x)$ is a fixed point of f for every x [2]. If f admits a fixing word we say that f is **fixable**. For instance, the network in Fig. 1 is fixed by $w = 1231$, and it is hence fixable. It is rather easy to see that f is fixable if and only if there is a path in $\Gamma(f)$ from any initial state to a fixed point of f. We may think that the fixability is a strong property. However, for n sufficiently large, more than half of the n-component networks are fixable:

Theorem 1 (Bollobás, Gotsman and Shamir[4]). *Let $\phi(n)$ be the fraction of n-component networks that are fixable. Then $\lim_{n \to \infty} \phi(n) = 1 - \frac{1}{e}$.*

For any fixable network f, the **fixing length** of f is the minimum length of a word fixing f and is denoted as $\lambda(f)$. For instance, we have seen that $w = 1231$ fixes the network in Fig. 1, and it is easy to see that no word of length three fixes this network, thus it has fixing length exactly 4. For any fixable n-component network f, we have $\lambda(f) \leq 4^n$. Indeed, let $\{0, 1\}^n = \{x^1, \ldots, x^{2^n}\}$

and recursively define the word $W := w^1, \ldots, w^{2^n}$ such that $f^{w^1,\ldots,w^k}(x^k)$ is a fixed point for all $1 \le k \le 2^n$. Since every w^k can be chosen to be of length at most 2^n, we have $|W| \le 4^n$. By extension, we say a family $\mathcal{F}$ of n-component networks is fixable if there is a word w such that w fixes f for all $f \in \mathcal{F}$. The fixing length $\lambda(\mathcal{F})$ is defined naturally as the minimum length of a word fixing $\mathcal{F}$. By concatenating all the fixing words W for each member f of $\mathcal{F}$, we obtain $\lambda(\mathcal{F}) \le 4^n |\mathcal{F}|$.

We are then interested in families $\mathcal{F}$ which can be fixed "rapidly", i.e. far below the trivial upper bound above. In [2], the following families have been shown to have small fixing lengths: monotone networks (fixing length $O(n^3)$), networks with acyclic interaction graphs (fixing length $\Theta(n^2)$), and increasing networks (fixing length $\Theta(n^2)$). Studying the fixing length of an entire family allows us to identify some patterns common to the asynchronous dynamics of all the members of that family. For instance, the word of cubic length fixing all monotone networks given in [2] has a recursive structure, thus showing a recursive pattern in the asynchronous dynamics of any monotone network.

In this paper, we focus on the following two classes. Firstly, we prove that the fixing length of the family of n-component networks with acyclic asynchronous graphs is in $\Theta(n2^n)$. Secondly, we exhibit two families of monotone networks which have linear and quadratic fixing lengths: monotone networks with tree interaction graphs and conjunctive networks with symmetric interaction graphs.

2   Notation

Let $w = w_1 \ldots w_p$ be a word. Then length p of w is denoted $|w|$. We say that a word $u = u_1 \ldots u_q$ is a **subword** of w is there exits $1 \le i_1 < i_2 < \cdots < i_q \le p$ such that $u = w_{i_1} \ldots w_{i_q}$. The empty word is denoted ϵ. A word w is n-**universal** if every permutation of $[n]$ (word of length n without repetition) is a subword of w. The minimum length of an n-universal word is denoted $\lambda(n)$. We then have $\lambda(n) = n^2 - o(n^2)$ (see [2] and references therein):

Directed graphs have no parallel arcs, and may have loops (arcs from a vertex to itself). Paths and cycles are always without repeated vertices. Given a directed graph G, the **underlying undirected** graph H of G has the same vertex set, and two vertices i and j are adjacent in H if and only if $i \ne j$ and G has an arc from i to j or from j to i. We refer the reader to the authoritative book on graphs by Bang-Jensen and Gutin [3] for basic concepts, notation and terminology.

Given $x, y \in \{0, 1\}^n$, we write $x \le y$ to mean that $x_i \le y_i$ for all $i \in [n]$. Equipped with this partial order, $\{0, 1\}^n$ is the usual Boolean lattice. An n-component network f is **monotone** if it preserves this partial order, that is,

$$\forall x, y \in \{0, 1\}^n, \qquad x \le y \Rightarrow f(x) \le f(y).$$

We denote by $F_M(n)$ the family of n-component monotone networks and by $\lambda_M(n)$ the fixing length of $F_M(n)$. More generally, if $F_X(n)$ is any family of n-component fixable networks, then $\lambda_X(n)$ is the fixing length of $F_X(n)$. If G is a directed graph, then $F(G)$ denotes the set of n-component networks f such that the interaction graph of f is isomorphic to a subgraph of G. Then, $F_X(G) := F_X(n) \cap F(G)$ and $\lambda_X(G)$ is the fixing length of $F_X(G)$.

Let f be an n-component network. We set $f^\epsilon := \mathrm{id}$ and, for any integer i and $x \in \{0,1\}^n$, we define $f^i(x)$ as in Eq. (1) if $i \in [n]$, and $f^i(x) := x$ if $i \notin [n]$. This extends the action of letters in $[n]$ to letters in $\mathbb{N}$, and by extension, this also defines the action of a word over the alphabet $\mathbb{N}$.

Let G be a directed graph with vertex set $[n]$. The **conjunctive network on G** is the n-component network f defined as follows: for all $i \in [n]$ and $x \in \{0,1\}^n$,

$$f_i(x) = \bigwedge_{j \in N^-(i)} x_j,$$

where $N^-(i)$ is the in-neighbourhood of i in G (with $f_i(x) = 1$ if the in-neighbourhood of i is empty). As shown in [2], every conjunctive network on n vertices has a fixing length of at most $2n - 2$, and this is tight.

3 Asynchronous-Acyclic Networks

A network is **asynchronous-acyclic** if its asynchronous graph is acyclic. The family of all such networks is denoted as $F_{A\Gamma}(n)$. Clearly, any asynchronous-acyclic network is fixable. It is well known, and easy to prove, that if $G(f)$ is acyclic then so is $\Gamma(f)$ [8].

Let $P = x^1 x^2 \dots x^l$ be a path of the n-cube, and let i_k be the component that differs between x^k and x^{k+1}, $1 \le k < l$. The word $i_1 i_2 \dots i_{l-1}$ is the word **induced** by P, and a word is an **n-path-word** if it is induced by at least one path of the n-cube. A word w is an n-path-word if and only if, for all $i < j$, there exists $k \in [n]$ which occurs an odd number of times in $w_i \dots w_j$ [5]. Note that an n-path-word has no consecutive repetitions and is of length at most $2^n - 1$. A word W is **n-path-universal** if it contains all n-path-words as subwords. Let $\Lambda(n)$ denote the minimum length of an n-path-universal word. For instance, for $n = 2$, the maximal n-path-words are 121 and 212, hence the word 1212 is n-path-universal and $\Lambda(2) = 4$. In general, $\Lambda(n) = \Theta(n2^n)$:

Lemma 1. *For all $n \ge 1$, $n2^{n-1} \le \Lambda(n) \le (n-1)(2^n - 1) + 1$.*

Proof. We first show the lower bound. For that, we define inductively a Hamiltonian path P^n of the n-cube in the following way: $P^1 := x^1 x^2$ with $x^1 = 0$ and $x^2 = 1$ and, for $n > 1$, P^n is defined from $P^{n-1} = x^1 x^2 \dots x^{2^{n-1}}$ by setting

$$P^n := (0, x^1)(0, x^2) \dots (0, x^{2^{n-1}})(1, x^{2^{n-1}})(1, x^{2^{n-1}-1}) \dots (1, x^2)(1, x^1).$$

P^n then corresponds to the canonical Gray code. Let w^n be the word induced by P^n. It is easy to see that the letter n appears exactly 2^{n-1} times in w^n. Thus any n-path-universal word contains at least 2^{n-1} occurrences of the letter n. By symmetry, every letter appears at least 2^{n-1} times, thus $\Lambda(n) \ge n2^{n-1}$.

We now show the upper bound. Let

$$W := 1, u^1, u^2, \ldots, u^{2^n-1} \quad \text{with} \quad \begin{cases} u^k := 2, 3, \ldots, n & \text{if } k \text{ is odd} \\ u^k := n-1, n-2, \ldots, 1 & \text{if } k \text{ is even.} \end{cases}$$

Then W contains all words of length at most $2^n - 1$ without consecutive repetitions, and hence is n-path-universal. □

Theorem 2. *A word fixes $F_{A\Gamma}(n)$ if and only if it is n-path-universal, thus*

$$\lambda_{A\Gamma}(n) = \Lambda(n).$$

Moreover, $\max_{f \in F_{A\Gamma}(n)} \lambda(f) = 2^n - 1$.

Proof. Let P be any path of the n-cube, and let w be the word induced by P. Consider the n-component network f whose asynchronous graph only has the arcs contained in P. Then f is clearly asynchronous-acyclic and a word fixes f if and only if it contains w as a subword. We deduce the following three properties (the third is obtained from the second using the fact that the n-cube has a Hamiltonian path, e.g. the path P^n constructed above):

(1) Any word fixing $F_{A\Gamma}(n)$ is n-path-universal, thus $\lambda_{A\Gamma}(n) \geq \Lambda(n)$.
(2) For any n-path-word w, there exists $f \in F_{A\Gamma}(n)$ with $\lambda(f) \geq |w|$.
(3) There exists $f \in F_{A\Gamma}(n)$ with $\lambda(f) \geq 2^n - 1$.

Conversely, let us prove that $\lambda(f) \leq 2^n - r$ for any $f \in F_{A\Gamma}(n)$ with r fixed points. Since $r \geq 1$, together with the property *(3)*, this shows the second assertion of the statement. Let $x^1 x^2 \ldots x^{2^n}$ be a topological sort of $\Gamma(f)$: for all $1 \leq p \leq q \leq 2^n$, $\Gamma(f)$ has no arc from x^q to x^p. Then x^p is a fixed point if and only if $p > 2^n - r$. Furthermore, we have the following two properties: *(i)* for all $i \in [n]$ we have $f^i(x^p) = x^q$ for some $q \geq p$; and *(ii)* if $p \leq 2^n - r$ then there exists at least one component in $[n]$, say i_p, such that $f^{i_p}(x^p) = x^q$ for some $q > p$. We will prove that $w := i_1 i_2 \ldots i_{2^n - r}$ fixes f. Let $1 \leq p \leq 2^n$, and let us prove, by induction on k, that:

$$\forall 1 \leq k \leq 2^n - r, \qquad f^{i_1 i_2 \cdots i_k}(x^p) = x^q \text{ for some } q > k.$$

If $k = 1$, we deduce that $f^{i_1}(x^p) = x^q$ for some $q > 1$ from *(i)* if $p \geq 2$, and from *(ii)* if $p = 1$. Suppose now that $k > 1$. By induction, $f^{i_1 i_2 \cdots i_{k-1}}(x^p) = x^l$ for some $l > k - 1$. We then deduce that $f^{i_1 i_2 \cdots i_k}(x^p) = f^{i_k}(x^l) = x^q$ for some $q > k$ from *(i)* if $l > k$, and from *(ii)* if $l = k$. This completes the induction. The particular case $k = 2^n - r$ shows that $f^w(x^p) = x^q$ for some $q > 2^n - r$, and thus $f^w(x^p)$ is a fixed point.

It remains to prove that any n-path-universal word $W = j_1 j_2 \ldots j_s$ fixes f. Let $y^1 \in \{0,1\}^n$, and for all $1 \leq k \leq s$, let

$$y^{k+1} := f^{j_1 j_2 \cdots j_k}(y^1) \qquad (\text{or, equivalently, } y^{k+1} := f^{j_k}(y^k)).$$

Let us prove that $y^{s+1} = f^W(y^1)$ is a fixed point. This is clear if y^1 is a fixed point. Otherwise $y^1 \neq y^{s+1}$. Then, in the sequence $y^1 y^2 \ldots y^{s+1}$, let $a_1, \ldots a_t$

be the positions such that $y^{a_k} \neq y^{a_k+1}$. The states visited by the sequence then correspond to the path $P := y^{a_1} y^{a_2} \ldots y^{a_t} y^{a_t+1}$ of $\Gamma(f)$, where $a_{t+1} := s + 1$, and $w := j_{a_1} j_{a_2} \ldots j_{a_t}$ is the word induced by this path. Suppose, for a contradiction, that y^{a_t+1} is not a fixed point. Let y^{a_t+2} be an out-neighbor y^{a_t+1} in $\Gamma(f)$, and let i be the component that differs between these two states. Then $y^{a_1} y^{a_2} \ldots y^{a_t+1} y^{a_t+2}$ is a path of $\Gamma(f)$, and $w' := j_{a_1} j_{a_2} \ldots j_{a_t} i$ is the word induced by this path. Hence, w' is a subword of W. By construction, $a_1 a_2 \ldots a_t$ corresponds to the first occurrence of w in W. That is, setting $a_0 := 0$, we have the following: for all $1 \leq k \leq t$, a_k is the first position in W greater than a_{k-1} where the letter j_{a_k} appears. Since w' is a subword of W, we deduce that i appears after the position a_t, that is, there exists $a_t < b \leq s$ such that $j_b = i$. By the definition of the sequence $a_1, \ldots a_t$, we have $y^k = y^{s+1}$ for all $a_t < k \leq s+1$, and thus $y^b = y^{s+1} = y^{a_t+1}$. But then, $y^{b+1} = f^i(y^b) = f^i(y^{a_t+1}) = y^{a_t+2} \neq y^{a_t+1} = y^b$, a contradiction. Thus every n-path-universal word fixes $F_{A\Gamma}(n)$. Thus $\lambda_{A\Gamma}(n) \leq \Lambda(n)$, and with the property *(1)* we obtain an equality. $\square$

4   Monotone Networks

It is proved in [2] that the fixing length of the family of n-component monotone networks $F_M(n)$ is $O(n^3)$ and $\Omega(n^2)$; closing the gap is challenging. In this section, we introduce two classes of monotone networks with linear and quadratic fixing lengths respectively. The first family is based on trees. We say a directed graph is **loop-full** if every vertex has a loop.

Theorem 3. *Let G be a loop-full tree with n vertices and L leaves. Then*

$$\lambda_M(G) = 2n - L - 1.$$

Proof. The result is clear for $n \leq 2$, thus we assume $n \geq 3$ henceforth. Then G has a non-leaf, say r; we then root G at r. We order the non-leaf vertices of G in non-decreasing order of distance from the root (and hence $r = 1$ and $1, \ldots, N := n - L$ are non-leaves) and we denote the leaves as $N + 1, \ldots, n$ (in no particular order). Note that according to this order, $i \leq j$ if and only if the path from j to r goes through i.

We first prove that $\lambda_M(G) \leq 2n - L - 1 = 2N - 1 + L$. Let $W^1 := 1$ and $W^i := iW^{i-1}i$ for all $i \in [N]$; therefore,

$$W := W^N = N, N - 1, \ldots, 2, 1, 2, \ldots N$$

has length $2N - 1$. Let $f \in F_M(G)$ and $x \in \{0,1\}^n$. We say that x is fixed on $[i]$ if $f_j(x) = x_j$ for all $j \in [i]$.

Claim. For all $i \in [N]$, $f^{W^i}(x)$ is fixed on $[i]$.

Proof. This is obvious for $i = 1$, thus assume that $i > 1$. Let

$$x^1 := f^i(x), \quad x^2 := f^{W^{i-1}}(x^1), \quad x^3 := f^i(x^2).$$

By induction, x^2 is fixed on $[i-1]$, and we want to prove that $f^{W^i}(x) = x^3$ is fixed on $[i]$. Since we have have $f_i(x^3) = x_i^3$, if x^3 is not fixed on $[i]$ there exists $j \in [i-1]$ such that $f_j(x^3) \neq x_j^3 = x_j^2 = f_j(x^2)$. Thus $x^3 \neq x^2$, and this implies $x_i^3 \neq x_i^2$, and since i is the only component that differs between these two states, there is an arc from i to j in G. Assume that $x_i^3 > x_i^2$, the other case being similar. Then $f_i(x^2) = x_i^3 = 1$, and $x^3 \geq x^2$. Since f_j is monotone, we deduce that $f_j(x^3) > f_j(x^2) = x_j^2 = 0$. Thus $x_i^2 = x_j^2 = 0$. Since, i is a leaf in the subgraph of G induced by $[i]$, and since j is adjacent to i in G, we deduce that, in G, i has no in-neighbors in $[i] \setminus \{i, j\}$. Since $x_i^2 = x_j^2 = 0$, we deduce that, for all in-neighbors k of i in G, we have $x_k \geq x_k^2$, with an equality if $k \neq i, j$ (since then k does not appear in W^i). Since f_i is monotone, we deduce that $f_i(x) \geq f_i(x^2) = 1$. Thus $f_i(x) = 1$ and we deduce that $x_i^1 = 1$. Since $x_i^1 = x_i^2$ (because i does not appear in W^{i-1}), we obtain a contradiction. Thus $f^{W^i}(x)$ is fixed on $[i]$ for all $i \in [N]$. $\qquad\square$

In particular, $y := f^W(x)$ is fixed on $[N]$. Let $\Omega = W, N+1, \ldots, n$ and $z := f^{N+1,\ldots,n}(y) = f^{\Omega}(x)$. Then we claim that z is a fixed point of f. First, it is easy to check that $f_l(z) = z_l$ for any leaf l. Second, by the claim above, $f_p(z) = f_p(y) = y_p = z_p$ for any non-leaf p which is not adjacent to any leaf. All that is left to show is that non-leaves which are adjacent to some leaves are still fixed by f^{Ω}. Let $m \in N$ be a non-leaf, Λ be the set of leaves adjacent to m and P be the other neighbours of m. Then $z_P = y_P$, $z_m = y_m = f_m(y_P, y_\Lambda)$ (by the claim) and $z_l = f_l(y_m, y_l)$ for all $l \in \Lambda$. Suppose that $y_m = 0$ (the case $y_m = 1$ is similar). Then $z_l \leq y_l$, since otherwise we have $z_l = 1 = f_l(0, 0)$, which implies that f_l is either constant or non-monotonic. Thus $f_m(z_P, z_\Lambda) \leq f_m(y_P, y_\Lambda) = y_m = z_m = 0$ and m is indeed fixed.

We now prove that $\lambda_M(G) \geq 2N - 1 + L$. Let f be the conjunctive network on G and let w be a word fixing f. Firstly, every $i \in [n]$ appears in W. Indeed, let $j \neq i$ and $x \in \{0,1\}^n$ such that $x_j = 1$ and $x_k = 0$ for all $k \neq j$. Then the only fixed point reachable by x is the all-zero state and hence the value of x_i must be updated. This first claim is sufficient to prove the lower bound when $N = 1$, thus we assume $N \geq 2$ in the sequel. Secondly, W contains every sequence of the form ij as a subword for any distinct $i, j \in [N]$. Indeed, let $u, i, \ldots, j$ be a path in G. By considering the state $x \in \{0,1\}^n$ such that $x_u = 1$ and $x_k = 0$ for all $k \neq u$, we see that W must contain ij as a subword. Now consider the subword W' of W only containing the occurrences of letters from N. Let $k \in [N]$ be the letter whose first occurrence in W' happens last (thus the first occurrence of k is in position $q \geq N$). Since W' contains ki as a subword for all $i \in [N]$, we see that $|W'| \geq N + (N-1)$. By the first claim, $|W| \geq |W'| + L \geq 2N - 1 + L$. $\qquad\square$

The **circumference** of a directed graph G is the length of a longest cycle in G, and zero if G is acyclic. It is easy to verify that G has circumference at most two if and only if the underlying undirected graph of each strong component of G is a tree. An *l*-**feedback vertex set** is a set of vertices I such that $G \setminus I$ has circumference at most l. The *l*-**feedback number** of G, denoted as $\tau_l(G)$, is the minimum cardinality of an *l*-feedback vertex set of G. In [2], it is shown that, for every directed graph G with n vertices, $\lambda_M(G) \leq (2\tau_1(G)^2 + 1)n$. We now show that a bounded 2-transversal number in G implies that $F_M(G)$ has quadratic fixing length.

Corollary 1. *For every directed graph G with n vertices,*

$$\lambda_M(G) \leq \tau_2(G)n^2 + 3n.$$

Proof. Let $\tau := \tau_2(G)$, $\alpha := n - \tau$, and let us label the vertices of G from 1 to n in such a way that $I = \{\alpha + 1, \ldots, n\}$ is a minimum 2-feedback vertex set of G. Let $T_1, \ldots, T_k$ be the strong components of $G \setminus I$ in topological order. Note that $\alpha \geq 2$ and that the underlying undirected graph of every T_i is a tree, say with n_i vertices. Let w^i be a word of length at most $2n_i - 1$ fixing each $F_M(T_i)$, which exists in virtue of the previous theorem. It is then easy to see that the word $w = w^1, \ldots, w^k$ fixes $F_M(G \setminus I)$, and $|w| \leq 2\alpha - k \leq 2n$.

By adapting the proof of [2, Theorem 13], we can prove the following result. If w is a word fixing $F_M(G \setminus I)$ and if, for all $1 \leq k \leq \tau$, w^k is an $(\alpha + k)$-universal word, then $F_M(G)$ is fixed by the word

$$W := w, \alpha + 1, w^1, \alpha + 2, w^2, \ldots, n, w^\tau.$$

Applying this result to our problem yields a word W of length

$$|W| = |w| + \tau + \sum_{k=1}^{\tau} \lambda(\alpha + k) \leq 2n + n + \sum_{i=\alpha+1}^{n} i^2 \leq \tau n^2 + 3n.$$

$\square$

The second family is described as follows. A directed graph is **symmetric** if, for all distinct vertices i and j, if there is an arc from i to j then there is also an arc from j to i (thus a symmetric directed graph can be regarded as an undirected graph with possibly a loop on some vertices). We consider the family $F_{CS}(n)$ of conjunctive networks on symmetric directed graphs.

Say a word w over the alphabet $[n]$ is *(n,k)*-**universal** if it contains, as subwords, all the words of length $n - k$ without repetition (there are $(n-k)!\binom{n}{k}$ such words). Let $\lambda_k(n)$ denote the minimum length of an (n, k)-universal word. In particular, $\lambda_0(n) = \lambda(n)$ and $\lambda_k(n) = 0$ for $k \geq n$.

Lemma 2. *For all fixed k, $\lambda_k(n) = n^2 - o(n^2)$.*

Proof. Let $W^k := 1, w^1, w^2, \ldots, w^{n-k}$ with $w^r := 2, 3, \ldots, n$ if r is odd and $w^k := n - 1, n - 2, \ldots, 1$ otherwise. Then it is easy to check that W^k is (n, k)-universal. Thus

$$\lambda_k(n) \leq (n - 1)(n - k) + 1.$$

Furthermore, if ω^k and ω^{n-k} are any two words that are (n, k)-universal and $(n, n - k)$-universal respectively, then $\omega := \omega^k, \omega^{n-k}$ is n-universal. This shows that $\lambda(n) \leq \lambda_k(n) + \lambda_{n-k}(n)$, and from the upper bound above we obtain

$$\lambda_k(n) \geq \lambda(n) - (n - 1)k - 1.$$

Since $\lambda(n) = n^2 - o(n^2)$ as n tends to infinity, this proves the lemma. $\square$

By this lemma and the theorem below, the fixing length of $F_{CS}(n)$ is $\Theta(n^2)$.

Theorem 4. *For all $n \geq 1$,*

$$\lambda_1(n) \leq \lambda_{CS}(n) \leq \lambda_2(n) + n.$$

Proof. We first prove the lower bound. This is obvious for $n \geq 1$, so suppose that $n > 1$. Let $i_1 i_2 \ldots i_n$ be a permutation of $[n]$, and let f be the n-component conjunctive network defined by $f_{i_1}(x) = x_{i_1} \wedge x_{i_2}$, $f_{i_n}(x) = x_{i_n} \wedge x_{i_{n-1}}$ and $f_{i_k}(x) = x_{i_{k-1}} \wedge x_{i_{k+1}}$ for all $1 < k < n$. Then the interaction graph of f is symmetric, and the arguments in the proof of Theorem 3 shows that any word fixing f contains $i_2 \ldots i_n$ as subword (as well as $i_{n-1} i_{n-2} \ldots i_1$). Hence, any word fixing $F_{CS}(n)$ contains all the words of length $n-1$ without repetition, and is thus of length at least $\lambda_1(n)$.

We now prove the upper bound. Consider the word $W := w, \omega$, where $w := 12 \ldots n$ and ω is a shortest $(n, 2)$-universal word. Then $|W| = \lambda(n) + n$ and we will prove that W fixes $F_{CS}(n)$. Let G by any symmetric directed graph with vertex set $[n]$, and let f the conjunctive network on G. Let H be the underlying undirected graph of G. Let $H_1 \ldots H_p$ be the connected components of H, with vertices $V_1, \ldots, V_p$. Let any $x \in \{0,1\}^n$, $y := f^w(x)$, $z := f^\omega(y) = f^W(x)$ and $1 \leq q \leq p$.

Suppose first $|V_q| = 1$, say $V_q = \{i\}$. Then there are two possibilities: either i has no loop in G, and then $f_i = 1$ is constant, thus $y_i = z_i = f_i(z) = 1$; or i has a loop and then $x_i = y_i = z_i = f_i(z)$. Suppose now that $|V_q| \geq 2$.

Claim. Either $y_i = 1$ for all $i \in V_k$, or $y_i = y_j = 0$ for some edge of H_q.

Proof. For the sake of contradiction, suppose that the subgraph of H_q induced by $\{i \in V_q : y_i = 0\}$ contains an isolated vertex, say i. Let j be adjacent to i in H_k. If $i < j$ then $f^{1 \cdots j-1}(x)_i = y_i = 0$ and thus $y_j = f^{1 \cdots j}(x)_j = f_j(f^{1 \cdots j-1}(x)) = 0$, a contradiction. Thus $k < i$ for every vertex k adjacent to i in H_q. Then i has a loop, since otherwise $y_i = f_i(f^{1 \cdots i-1}(x)) = \bigwedge_{k \in N^-(i)} y_k = 1$. We deduce that

$$y_i = x_i \wedge \bigwedge_{k \in N^-(i) \setminus \{i\}} y_k = 0,$$

thus $x_i = 0$, but then we would have $y_k = 0$ for any neighbour k of i, a contradiction. This proves the claim. $\qquad\square$

If $y_i = 1$ for all $i \in V_q$, then we clearly have $y_i = z_i = f_i(z) = 1$ for all $i \in V_q$. Otherwise, $y_i = y_j = 0$ for some edge ij of H_k. It is easy to check that $f^u(y)_i = f^u(y)_j = 0$ for any word u. Thus the states of i and j are always blocked in zeroes when performing the updates in ω, which allows these two zeroes to be propagated to the whole component H_q. Since any vertex k in H_q is reachable from the edge ij by a path of length at most $n - 2$, it is easy to verify that $z_k = 0$ for all $k \in V_q$, and we deduce that $f_k(z) = 0 = z_k$ for all $k \in V_q$. Hence, in any case, $f_k(z) = z_k$ for all $k \in V_q$, and thus z is a fixed point of f as desired. $\qquad\square$

5 Perspectives

Asynchronous dynamics of monotone networks is the subject of some previous work, which seems to suggest some amount of structure and yet some richness. Let us mention some properties of the asynchronous dynamics of a n-component monotone network f. Firstly, [7] shows that the asynchronous graph of almost any n-component network can be embedded into the asynchronous graph of a $(2n)$-component monotone network. As a consequence, f can have a fixed point y and state x such that the shortest path from x to y in the asynchronous graph of f is of exponential length. Secondly, and despite the first property, any state can be individually fixed in linear time. More precisely, for any state x there exists a fixed point y of f such that $\Gamma(f)$ has a geodesic from x to y [6]. Thirdly, all the states can be concurrently fixed in cubic time [2].

From our work on the fixing length of monotone and conjunctive networks, four main quantities arise:

$$\lambda'_M(n) := \max_{f \in F_M(n)} \lambda(f), \qquad \lambda_M(n), \qquad \lambda'_C(n) := \max_{f \in F_C(n)} \lambda(f), \qquad \lambda_C(n).$$

We know that $\lambda'_C(n) = 2n - 2$, and that the other three quantities are $O(n^3)$ and $\Omega(n^2)$ [2]. The main problem is then to determine the asymptotic behaviour of those three quantities. In particular, is there an asymptotic gap between $\lambda'_M(n)$ and $\lambda_M(n)$, or between $\lambda_C(n)$ and $\lambda_M(n)$?

References

1. Abou-Jaoudé, W., et al.: Logical modeling and dynamical analysis of cellular networks. Front. Genet. **7**, 94 (2016)
2. Aracena, J., Gadouleau, M., Richard, A., Salinas, L.: Fixing monotone Boolean networks asynchronously (2018, submitted). https://arxiv.org/abs/1802.02068
3. Bang-Jensen, J., Gutin, G.Z.: Digraphs: Theory, Algorithms and Applications, 2nd edn. Springer, London (2008). https://doi.org/10.1007/978-1-84800-998-1
4. Bollobás, B., Gotsman, C., Shamir, E.: Connectivity and dynamics for random subgraphs of the directed cube. Isr. J. Math. **83**, 321–328 (1993)
5. Gilbert, E.N.: Gray codes and paths on the n-cube. Bell Labs Tech. J. **37**, 815–826 (1958)
6. Melliti, T., Regnault, D., Richard, A., Sené, S.: On the convergence of boolean automata networks without negative cycles. In: Kari, J., Kutrib, M., Malcher, A. (eds.) AUTOMATA 2013. LNCS, vol. 8155, pp. 124–138. Springer, Heidelberg (2013). https://doi.org/10.1007/978-3-642-40867-0_9
7. Melliti, T., Regnault, D., Richard, A., Sené, S.: Asynchronous simulation of boolean networks by monotone boolean networks. In: El Yacoubi, S., Wąs, J., Bandini, S. (eds.) ACRI 2016. LNCS, vol. 9863, pp. 182–191. Springer, Cham (2016). https://doi.org/10.1007/978-3-319-44365-2_18
8. Robert, F.: Iterations sur des ensembles finis et automates cellulaires contractants. Linear Algebra Appl. **29**, 393–412 (1980)

Fast-Parallel Algorithms for Freezing Totalistic Asynchronous Cellular Automata

Eric Goles[1,2,3], Diego Maldonado[2], Pedro Montealegre-Barba[1(✉)],
and Nicolas Ollinger[2]

[1] Facultad de Ingenieria y Ciencias, Universidad Adolfo Ibañez, Santiago, Chile
p.montealegre@uai.cl
[2] Univ. Orléans, LIFO EA 4022, 45067 Orléans, France
[3] LE STUDIUM, Loire Valley Institute for Advanced Studies, Orléans, France

Abstract. In this paper we study the family of two-state Totalistic Freezing Cellular Automata (FTCA) defined over the triangular grids with von Neumann neighborhoods. We say that a Cellular Automaton is Freezing and Totalistic if the active cells remain unchanged, and the new value of an inactive cell depends only of the sum of its active neighbors. We study the family of FTCA in the context of asynchronous updating schemes (calling them FTACA), meaning that at each time-step only one cell is updated. The sequence of updated sites is called a *sequential updating schemes*. Given configuration, we say that a site is *stable* if it remains in the same state over any sequential updating scheme.

In this context, we consider the ASYNCHRONOUS STABILITY problem, consisting in decide whether there is a sequential updating scheme such that an inactive cell becomes active. We show that in this family the problem is **NC**, i.e. it can be solved by fast-parallel algorithms.

1 Introduction

Introduced by von Neumann and Ulam in the 1950s, Cellular automata (CA) is a discrete complex system that has been used to model different real-world phenomena. A Cellular Automaton is defined over a regular grid divided in *cells*, each one having a *state* which evolves according to the states of their neighbors in the grid in synchronous time-steps. The hypothesis that each cell has a clock capable of synchronizing all the cells at the same time is somehow unrealistic. Looking for more realistic models is introduced the idea of studying *asynchronous cellular automata* (ACA), where cells evolve one by one, following a predefined order called *updating scheme*.

An active research topic in the context of the study of CAs, is the prediction problem, i.e. anticipate the future state of a cell given an initial configuration. In the context of ACA, this problem can be translated into find a sequential updating scheme that changes the state of a cell. Our objective is to study the prediction in the context of the *Computational Complexity Theory*. More

© Springer Nature Switzerland AG 2018
G. Mauri et al. (Eds.): ACRI 2018, LNCS 11115, pp. 406–415, 2018.
https://doi.org/10.1007/978-3-319-99813-8_37

precisely, our objective is to classify the prediction problem of a ACA (CA) in one of the following classes: **P** of problems solvable in polynomial time on a deterministic Turing machine; **NC** of problems that can be solved by a fast-parallel algorithm, and **NP** the problems that can be solved in polynomial time in a non-deterministic Turing machine. It is known that **NC** ⊆ **P** ⊆ **NP**, and it is a wide-believed conjecture that the inclusion is proper (for further details on this definition we refer to [1]).

Recently, in [2], is studied a particular family of CA, the *freezing* CA (FCA). These are CA where the state of a cell can only change to another bigger state. For example, if the states are *active* and *inactive*, the active cell remains active forever in a freezing CA. It is direct that, every initial configuration consisting on N cells reaches a fixed point in $\mathcal{O}(N^2)$ steps, on every updating scheme. However, there are cells that remain inactive regardless of the chosen updating scheme. These cells are called *stable*. We call ASYNCSTABILITY the problem of deciding, given an initial configuration, if a given cell is stable on any updating scheme.

In [3] it was studied the *freezing majority cellular automaton*, also known as *bootstrap percolation model*, in arbitrary undirected graph. In this case, an inactive cell becomes active if and only if the active cells are the most represented in its neighborhood. In this paper, it is shown that in these ACAs any updating scheme converges at the same fixed point and it was proved that ASYNCSTA-BILITY is **P**-Complete over graphs such that its maximum degree (number of neighbors) ≥ 5. Otherwise (graphs with maximum degree ≤ 4), the problem is in **NC**. This clearly includes the two-dimensional case with triangular grid.

In this paper, we consider a family of two-state two dimensional *Asynchronous Cellular Automaton* (ACA) defined in a triangular grid. The triangular grid consists of a regular toroidal two-dimensional grid of triangular cells, each one having two possible states, such as *active* and *inactive* or 1 and 0 (see Fig. 1). The family we present is the *Freezing Totalistic Asynchronous Cellular*

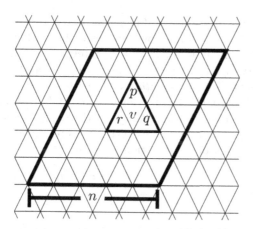

Fig. 1. Triangular grid, a cell u with its neighbors p, q and r.

Automata. The term *totalistic* means that the next state of a cell depends in the sum of the states of their neighbors.

We show that for every Freezing Totalistic Asynchronous Cellular Automata in this family the problem AsyncStability is in **NC**. We show this result following two approaches:

- Infiltration approach: FTACAs where there is a connected set S of inactive cells such that, if any set in the perimeter of S becomes active, then for every cell in the connected set there is an updating scheme that activates it (we say that the set was infiltrated).
- Monotone approach: We use a result of [3] that relates the behavior of monotone rules on asynchronous updating schemes with respect to the same rules in synchronous updating schemes.

The paper is structured as follows: First, in Sect. 2, we give the main definitions and notations. In Sect. 3, we study the complexity of FTACAs using the infiltration approach. In Sect. 4, we study the complexity of FTACAs using the monotone approach. Finally, in Sect. 5 we give some conclusions.

2　Preliminaries

We consider a finite configuration over the triangular grid with dimension $n \times n$, denote $T(n)$, as Fig. 1. Each triangle on the grid is called a *cell* and it has three adjacent cells. A cell that is adjacent to a cell u is called a *neighbor* of u. The set of neighbors of u is denoted by $N(u)$ and is called the *von Neumann Neighborhood*.

Each cell in the grid has two possible *states*, which are denoted 0 and 1. We say that a site in state 1 is *active* and a site in state 0 is *inactive*. A *configuration* of the grid is a function x that assigns values in $\{0,1\}$ to a rhomboid shaped area of $2n^2$ cells $T(n)$, see Fig. 1. The value of the cell u in the configuration x is denoted x_u.

Given a finite configuration x of dimension $n \times n$, the periodic configuration $c = c(x)$ is an infinite configuration over the grid, obtained by repetitions of x in all directions. The configuration $c(x)$ can be interpreted as a torus, where each cell in the boundary of x has a neighbor placed in the opposite boundary of x.

A *Asynchronous cellular automata* (ACA) with states $\{0,1\}$ and *local function* $f : \{0,1\}^{N(0,0)} \to \{0,1\}$, is a function $F : \{0,1\}^{T(n)} \to \{0,1\}^{T(n)}$, where the new state of the configuration x are defined by the *asynchronous* application cell by cell of the local function on $c(x)$ following the order given by $\sigma : \mathbb{N} \to T(n)$. Formally the t-th asynchronous iteration of c is given by,

$$F^{\sigma(0)}(c) = c; \qquad F^{\sigma(t)}(c)_z \quad = \begin{cases} f(F^{\sigma(t-1)}(c)_{N(z)}) & \text{if } z = \sigma(t) \\ c_z & \text{otherwise.} \end{cases}$$

Where $\sigma : \mathbb{N} \to T(n)$, called *asynchronous iteration mode*, is a function where each n^2 visit each cell of x.

This definition meaning that in each time t we iterate only the cell $\sigma(t)$.

An asynchronous cellular automaton is called *freezing*.

[2] (FACA) if the local rule f satisfies that the active cells always remain active. A cellular automaton is called *totalistic*.

[4] (TACA) if the local rule f satisfies $f(c_{N(u)}) = f(c_u, \sum_{v \in N(u)} c_v)$, i.e. it depends only in the sum of the states in the neighborhood of a cell.

We call FTACA the family of two-state freezing totalistic asynchronous cellular automata, over the triangular grids, with von Neumann neighborhood. In this family, the active cells remain active, because the rule is freezing, and the inactive cells become active depending only in the sum of their neighbors.

Let F be a FTACA. We can identify F with a set $\mathcal{I}_F \subseteq \{0, 1, 2, 3\}$ such that, for every configuration c and site u:

$$f(c_{N(u)}) = \begin{cases} 1 \text{ if } (c_u = 1) \vee (\sum_{v \in N(u)} c_v \in \mathcal{I}_F), \\ 0 \text{ otherwise.} \end{cases}$$

We will name the FTACAs according to the elements contained in $\mathcal{I}_F$, as the concatenation of the elements of $\mathcal{I}_F$ in increasing order (except when $\mathcal{I}_F = \emptyset$, that we call ϕ). For example, let Maj be the freezing majority vote CA, where an inactive cell becomes active if the majority of its neighbors is active. Note that $\mathcal{I}_{Maj} = \{2, 3\}$. We call then Maj the rule 23 in this notation.

We deduce that there are 2^4 different FTCA, each one of them represented by the corresponding set $\mathcal{I}_F$. We will focus our analysis in the FTACAs where the inactive state is a quiescent state, which means that the inactive sites where the sum of their neighborhoods is 0 remain inactive. Therefore, we will consider initially only 8 different FTACA.

Definition 1. *Given a configuration $c \in \{0,1\}^{\mathbb{Z}^2}$ and a FTACA F, we say that a site v is stable if and only if $c_v = 0$ and it remains inactive after any iterated application of the rule under any updating scheme, i.e., $F^{\sigma(t)}(c)_v = 0$ for all $t \geq 0$ and any updating scheme σ.*

From the previous definition, we consider the problem ASYNCSTABILITY, which consists in deciding if a cell on a periodic configuration c is stable. More formally, if F is a FTACA, then:

> Asynchronous Stability (ASYNCSTABILITY)
> **Input:** A finite configuration x of dimensions $n \times n$ and a site $u \in [n] \times [n]$ such that $x_u = 0$.
> **Question:** Does there exists an updating scheme σ and $T > 0$ such that $F^{\sigma(T)}(c(x))_u = 1$?

We will study this problem using two approaches:

The infiltration approach, we study rules where a cell with one active neighbor becomes active (i.e. FTACA with "1" in its rule number). The technique here is to find a connected component of cells that it needs exactly one active neighbor to activate. If we find an active cell outside it such that it can activate a cell in the connected component (infiltrate the set), then we can activate our decision cell following a path connecting the infiltrated cell with our decision cell.

Monotone approach, where we study the monotone freezing rules. In this rule any updating scheme reaches the same fixed point. We then use results of [5] for the synchronous updating scheme (usual CA) to study AsyncStability.

Since in rule 123 a cell is stable if and only if all the cells in the configuration are inactive and, in the rule, ϕ all the inactive cells are stable, then we will not study these rules, because trivially for these AsyncStability is in **NC**.

2.1   Some Graph Topics

For a set of cells $S \subseteq \mathbb{Z}^2$, we call $G[S] = (S, E)$ the graph defined with vertex set S, where two vertices are adjacent if the corresponding sites are neighbors for the von Neumann neighborhood.

For a graph $G = (V, E)$, a sequence of vertices $P = v_1, \ldots, v_k$ is called a v_1, v_k- path if $\{v_i, v_{i+1}\}$ is an edge of G, for each $i \in [k-1]$.

Definition 2. *A graph G is called* connected *if for every pair of vertices $u, v \in V(G)$, G contains a u, v-paths.*

A maximal set of vertices of a graph G that induces a connected subgraph is called a *connected component* of G.

This structure is quick to find using a parallel machine.

Proposition 1 ([6]). *There is an algorithm that computes the connected components of a graph with n vertices in time $\mathcal{O}(\log^2 n)$ with $\mathcal{O}(n^2)$ processors.*

2.2   Monotonicity

For two configurations c and c', denote by $\leq$ the partial order relation over configurations, where $c \leq c'$ if and only if $c_u \leq c'_u$ for every $u \in \mathbb{Z}^2$. A (A)CA $G : \{0,1\}^{\mathbb{Z}^2} \to \{0,1\}^{\mathbb{Z}^2}$ is called *monotone* if $c \leq c'$ implies that $G(c) \leq G(c')$. For example, the freezing majority automata is monotone. Some of our FCA are in a particular class of CA, the *monotone cellular automata*.

Definition 3. *A CA F is monotone if $\forall c, c' \in Q^{\mathbb{Z}^d} : c \leq c' \Rightarrow F(c) \leq F(c')$, where $\leq$ is induced by order in Q cell by cell.*

A fixed point of an ACA (resp. CA) F is a configuration that remains invariant on the application F on every updating scheme (resp. the synchronous updating scheme). In [3] it is shown that any configuration of a Monotone Freezing ACA reaches the same fixed point that it reaches on the synchronous version of the rule.

Proposition 2 ([3]). *Any configuration of a Monotone Freezing ACA reaches the same fixed point that it reaches on the synchronous version of the rule.*

We will call Stability the problem to decide if a cell becomes stable when every cell evolve synchronously. Proposition 2 implies that for Freezing Monotone rules, the Stability problem is equivalent to the AsyncStability problem.

3   The Infiltration Technique

In this section we study the rules where an inactive cell becomes active with one active neighbor. These cases include the rules 1, 12 and 13. For all this rules we define, for an initial configuration x, V_{+1} the set of all cells in $T(n)$ that *need exactly one active neighbor to be activated*, formally $V_{+1} = \{v \in [n] \times [n] : x_v = 0 \wedge \sum_{w \in N(v)} x_w + 1 \in \mathcal{I}_\mathcal{F}\}$

We define G_{+1} as the graph induced by V_{+1}. Also we define B_{+1}, called *boundary* of G_{+1}, as the cell in the complement of V_{+1} with at least one neighbor in V_{+1}, formally $B_{+1} = \{v \notin V_{+1} : V_{+1} \cap N(v) \neq \emptyset\}$ (Fig. 2).

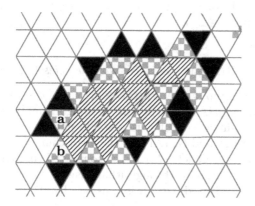

Fig. 2. ▨: Cell in V_{+1}. ◼: Cell in B_{+1}. Example of V_{+1} and B_{+1} for rule 1. The cell without number are in state 0. The cell (a) is not in V_{+1} cannot evolve. The cell (b) is not in V_{+1} because evolves immediately.

To decide if an initially inactive cell u will becomes active, note that if $u \neq G_+$ then u is stable. Without loss of generality, we suppose that G_{+1} is connected and containing u (otherwise, we restrict to the connected component of G_{+1} containing u). Also, we will use the next lemma easy to check. The following lemma explains what happens if a cell infiltrates the border.

Lemma 1. *If there is an updating scheme such that some cell in B_{+1} becomes activated, then there is an updating scheme activating u.*

Proof. Roughly, if a boundary cell v becomes active (it infiltrates V_{+1}), then, by connectivity, we choose a $v - u$ path of cells in V_+. Then, choosing an updating scheme activating the cells of the $v - u$ path one by one form v we activate u.

Now we will see that is enough check the information of the neighborhood of each border cell is enough to know if this cell is stable or it infiltrate to V_{+1}. We are not interested in the cells that become active with three active neighbors, because this cells can belong to B_{+1} and also they cannot affect its neighbors, because every one of this is already active.

Lemma 2. *To decide if a boundary cell $v \in B_{+1}$ will become active or it is stable depends only of $N(v)$.*

Proof. Let $v \in B_{+1}$. We will consider the following facts:

- By definition of B_{+1}, v has at least one inactive neighbor, the neighbor in V_{+1}.
- Given that $v \notin V_{+1}$, then it has at least one active neighbor, otherwise $v \in V_{+1}$.
- If v has exactly one active neighbor, then v evolves in one time-step and we are done.
- If v has exactly two active neighbor, then v evolves in one iteration and we decide (because 2 belongs to $\mathcal{I}_F$) or it does not evolve, then v is stable and we decide (because $2 \notin \mathcal{I}_F$).

We deduce the lemma.

Theorem 1. ASYNCSTABILITY *is in* **NC** *for the rules 1, 12 and 13.*

Proof. Let (x, u) be an input of ASYNCSTABILITY, i.e. x is a finite configuration of dimensions $n \times n$, and u is a site in $[n] \times [n]$. Our algorithm for ASYNCSTABILITY first check if the neighborhood of u is a stable pattern or can evolve in one step, then computes V_{+1} and G_{+1}. Then, the algorithm compute the connected components of G_{+1} and restricts G_{+1} to the connected component containing u and then compute B_{+1}. Finally, the algorithm answers *Reject* if there is a vertex $v \in B_{+1}$ that can be activated. Otherwise answer *Accept*.

This algorithm works too on the rules changing with three active neighbors, because to activate a boundary cells with three neighbors implies to have an active cell in V_{+}.

Algorithm 1. AsyncStability solving 1, 12 and 13

Input: $x \in \{0, 1\}^{T(n)}$ and $u \in T(n)$ such that $x_u = 0$.
1: **if** $N(u)$ is a stable pattern **then return** *Accept* **end if**
2: **if** $f(x_{N(u)}) = 1$ **then return** *Reject* **end if**
3: Compute the $V_{+1} = \{v \in \mathbb{Z}^2 : x_v = 0 \ \wedge \ |x_{N(v)}|_1 + 1 \in \mathcal{I}_F\}$.
4: Compute the graph $G_{+1} = G[V_{+1}]$.
5: Compute the connected components of G_{+1}, $\{C_i\}_{i=1}^M$.
6: Redefine $V_{+1} = C_i : u \in C_i$.
7: Compute the $B_{+1} = \{v \notin V_{+1} : V_{+1} \cap N(v) \neq \emptyset\}$.
8: **for all** $v \in B_{+1}$ **do in parallel**
9:    **if** $f(x_{N(v)}) = 1$ **then return** *Reject* **end if**
10: **end for**
11: **return** *Accept*

Let $N = n^2$ the size of the input. The **lines 1–6** are computed easily in time $\mathcal{O}(\log N)$ using $\mathcal{O}(N)$ processors. The **line 7** is computed in time $\mathcal{O}(\log N)$ using

$\mathcal{O}(N)$ processors, 1 processor by cell $v \in [n] \times [n]$ and it test that $|x_{N(v)}|_1 + 1 \in \mathcal{I}_F$. The **line 8** is computed in time $\mathcal{O}(\log N)$ using $\mathcal{O}(N)$ processors, 1 processor by edge (u, v) in the grid (there is $\mathcal{O}(N)$ edges) and it add (u, v) to the edges of G_{+1} if u and v are in V_{+1}. The **line 9** is computed in time $\mathcal{O}(\log N)$ using $\mathcal{O}(N)$ processors by Proposition 1. The **line 10** is computed in time $\mathcal{O}(\log N)$ using $\mathcal{O}(N)$ processors, 1 processor by cell v in each connected component, it test that $v = u$ and define i as the index of the connected component containing u. Each processor remove form V_+ its vertex is not in C_i. The **line 11** is computed in time $\mathcal{O}(\log N)$ using $\mathcal{O}(N)$ processors, 1 processor by cell $v \notin V_{+1}$ and it test that $V_{+1} \cap N(v) \neq \emptyset$. The **line 12–16** are computed in time $\mathcal{O}(\log N)$ using $\mathcal{O}(N)$ processors, 1 processor by cell $v \in B_{+1}$ and it test that $f(x_{N(v)}) = 1$. If there is a cell that verifies this condition return *Reject*.

4   Monotone Rules

Given that we know the complexity of STABILITY for 23 then ASYNCSTABILITY has at the most the same complexity.

Theorem 2. ASYNCSTABILITY *is in **NC** for the rule* 23.

Proof. In [3] is shown an algorithm solving STABILITY in time $\mathcal{O}(\log^2 n)$ with $\mathcal{O}(n^3 / \log n)$ processors. Roughly the stable cells are characterized as the cells in a bi-connected component (cycles) or a cell in a path between two cycles in the graph induced by inactive cells. The complexity of the algorithm is then given by the complexity of to compute bi-connected components. For more information about this can be found in [7] (Fig. 3).

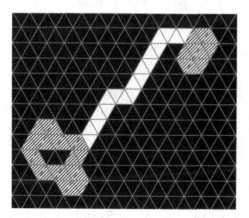

Fig. 3. Example of fix point for the rule 23. The north east lines cells are cells in the a bi-connected component of inactive cells. The white cells are in a path of inactive cells connecting two bi-connected components of inactive cells.

Moreover, we can use this fact to know the complexity of AsyncStability in its non-monotone versions, the ACA 2.

Lemma 3. *Let a configuration x. The cell u with at least one inactive neighbor. Then u is stable for the rule 23 if and only if u is stable for the rule 2.*

Proof. Note that a site u that is stable for rule 23 is directly stable for rule 2. Indeed, an updating scheme that activates u for rule 2 also activates u on rule 23. Suppose now that u is not stable for rule 23 and let σ be an updating scheme such that after t time-steps u becomes active. Moreover, we pick σ such that t is minimum. Since t is minimum, we can assume that every cell that is updated before u is initially inactive, and switches from inactive to active. Moreover, note that a cell with three active neighbors does not affect the dynamics of other cells, because active cells remain active. Therefore, we assume that every cell updated in σ before u had exactly two inactive neighbors. Finally, suppose that in $t - 1$ cell u had three active neighbors. Since we are assuming that u had at least one inactive neighbor, it means that there is a time step in $0, \ldots, t - 2$ in which u had two active neighbors. This contradicts the minimality of t. We deduce that u had exactly two active neighbors at time t. Therefore u becomes active on rule 2 updated according to σ.

The previous lemma show that it is possible to use the algorithm to solve AsyncStability for 23 to solve AsyncStability for the rule 2.

Theorem 3. AsyncStability *is in **NC** for the rule 2.*

Algorithm 2. AsyncStability solving 2

Proof. **Input:** $x \in \{0,1\}^{T(n)}$ and $u \in T(n)$ such that $x_u = 0$.
 1: **if** $N(u)$ has three active neighbors **then return** *Reject* **end if**
 2: To solve AsyncStability for the rule 23.
 3: **return** The same answer obtained in the previous line.

Let $N = n^2$ the size of the input. The **lines 1–3** are computed easily in time $\mathcal{O}(\log N)$ using $\mathcal{O}(N)$ processors, because is to compute the sum of three cell. The **lines 4** are computed in time $\mathcal{O}(\log^2 n)$ using $\mathcal{O}(n^3/\log n)$ processors., because is the complexity of AsyncStability for the rule 23, see Theorem 2.

5   Concluding Remarks and Perspectives

In this paper we proved that the AsyncStability problem is in **NC** for all Freezing Totalistic Asynchronous Cellular Automata (FTACA) in the triangular grid with the von Neumann Neighborhood. There are 16 FTACA. We focus our study on 8 rules, where the inactive state is quiescent. There are some rules that are trivial (ϕ and 3). Rules 1, 12 and 13 are in **NC** by the infiltration approach and the rules 2 and 23 are in **NC** by the monotone approach.

If we consider the rules where 0 is not quiescent the infiltration approach and monotone approach can be modified to compute ASYNCSTABILITY in **NC** too. For the infiltration approach is enough to remove the inactive cells with only inactive cell in its neighborhood to V_+, because now this cell can not 1 neighbor to active. For monotone approach note that for all configuration c and updating scheme σ we have $F^\sigma_{23}(c) \leq F^\sigma_{023}(c)$. Let C the set of cell initially with every neighbor inactive and S the set of cells stables for the rule 23, then is enough to check if is possible destroy the cycles of stable cells protecting u activating some cells of $C \cap S$. Further research consists in to study the FTACA two-dimensional squared grid $\mathbb{Z}^2$. Here each cell has four neighbors, the they are 32 FTACA in this family.

Acknowledgments. Research founded by CONICYT+PAI+CONVOCATORIA NACIONAL SUBVENCIÓN A INSTALACIÓN EN LA ACADEMIA CONVOCATORIA AÑO 2017 + PAI77170068 (P.M.)

References

1. Papadimitriou, C.M.: Computational Complexity. Addison-Wesley, Reading (1994)
2. Goles, E., Ollinger, N., Theyssier, G.: Introducing freezing cellular automata. In: Cellular Automata and Discrete Complex Systems, 21st International Workshop (AUTOMATA 2015). TUCS Lecture Notes, Turku, Finland, vol. 24, pp. 65–73 (2015)
3. Goles, E., Montealegre-Barba, P., Todinca, I.: The complexity of the bootstraping percolation and other problems. Theor. Comput. Sci. **504**, 73–82 (2013)
4. Wolfram, S.: Statistical mechanics of cellular automata. Rev. Mod. Phys. **55**(3), 601–644 (1983)
5. Goles, E., Montealegre, P.: A fast parallel algorithm for the robust prediction of the two-dimensional strict majority automaton. In: El Yacoubi, S., Wąs, J., Bandini, S. (eds.) ACRI 2016. LNCS, vol. 9863, pp. 166–175. Springer, Cham (2016). https://doi.org/10.1007/978-3-319-44365-2_16
6. JáJá, J.: An Introduction to Parallel Algorithms. Addison Wesley Longman Publishing Co. Inc., Redwood City (1992)
7. JáJá, J., Simon, J.: Parallel algorithms in graph theory: planarity testing. SIAM J. Comput. **11**(2), 314–328 (1982)

Stochastic Stability in Schelling's Segregation Model with Markovian Asynchronous Update

Gabriel Istrate[1,2(✉)]

[1] Department of Computer Science, West University of Timişoara,
Bd. V. Pârvan 4, Timişoara, Romania
gabrielistrate@acm.org
[2] e-Austria Research Institute, Bd. V. Pârvan 4, cam. 045 B, Timişoara, Romania

Abstract. We investigate the dependence of steady-state properties of Schelling's segregation model on the agents' activation order. Our basic formalism is the Pollicott-Weiss version of Schelling's segregation model. Our main result modifies this baseline scenario by incorporating *contagion* in the decision to move: (pairs of) agents are connected by a second, *agent influence* network. Pair activation is specified by a random walk on this network.

The considered schedulers choose the next pair *nonadaptively*. We can complement this result by an example of adaptive scheduler (even one that is quite fair) that is able to preclude maximal segregation. Thus scheduler nonadaptiveness seems to be required for the validity of the original result under arbitrary asynchronous scheduling. The analysis (and our result) are part of an *adversarial scheduling approach* we are advocating to evolutionary games and social simulations.

1 Introduction

Schelling's Segregation Model [1] is one of the fundamental dynamical systems of Agent-Based Computational Economics, perhaps one of the most convincing examples of Asynchronous Cellular Automata (ACA) [2] employed in the social sciences. It exhibits large-scale self-organizing neighborhoods, due to agents' desire to live close to their own kind. A remarkable feature of the model that has captured the attention of social scientists is the fact that segregation is an *emergent* phenomenon, that may appear even in the presence of just mild preferences (at the individual level) towards living with one's own kind. The model has sparked a significant interest and work, coming from various areas such as Statistical Physics [3], agent-based computational economics [4,5], game theory [6], theoretical computer science [7–9], or applied mathematics [10].

This work was supported by a grant of the Ministry of Research and Innovation, CNCS - UEFISCDI, project number PN-III-P4-ID-PCE-2016-0842, within PNCDI III.

© Springer Nature Switzerland AG 2018
G. Mauri et al. (Eds.): ACRI 2018, LNCS 11115, pp. 416–427, 2018.
https://doi.org/10.1007/978-3-319-99813-8_38

Schelling's segregation model is an asynchronous dynamical system on a graph (usually a finite portion of the one-dimensional or the two-dimensional lattice). It can be described, informally as follows: vertices in the graph are in one of three states: *unoccupied*, when no agent sits on the given node, or one of *red/blue* (± 1), corresponding to the color of the agent inhabiting the node. Agents have a (non-strict) preference towards living among agents of the same color. This is modeled by considering a *local neighborhood* around the agent. Depending on the density of like-colored agents in the neighborhood the agent may be in one of two states: *happy* and *unhappy*. An unhappy agent may seek to trade places with another agent in order to become happy. It was originally observed via "pen-and-paper simulations", and proved rigorously in a variety of settings, that segregated states may arise even when agent only have a weak preference for its own color, and are happy to live in a mixed neighborhood, as long as it contains "enough" of its own kind. Difference in the topology, activation order, specification of the update mechanism account for the dizzying variety of variants of the model that have been investigated so far (for the intellectual context of the model and a related one, due to Sakoda, see [11]).

Qualitative properties of asynchronous cellular automata are highly dependent on activation order [12,13]. In particular, when viewed as dynamical systems, ACA may exhibit a multitude of limit cycles, and the update dynamics "chooses" one of these limit cycle in a path dependent manner. The challenge then becomes to explain the selection of one particular limit cycle among many possible ones.

One particularly interesting class of techniques, brought to evolutionary games by Foster and Young [14] (see also [6]) uses the concept of *stochastic stability* to deal with this problem. It was the fundamental insight of Peyton-Young [6] that adding continuous small perturbations to a certain dynamics might help "steer"—the system towards a particular subset of equilibria, the so-called *stochastically stable states*. Indeed, in several versions of Schelling's segregation model [5,6,15] the most segregates states are identified as precisely the stochastically stable equilibria of the dynamics.

Though such results are interesting, they are still not realistic enough enough: results about stochastic stability in models on graphs may be sensitive to the precise specification of the update order, which in realistic scenarios need not be the random one. As noted in many papers, precise specification of an asynchronous schedule in social systems can arise from many factors, including geography or agent incentives [16]. It is thus important to study validity of baseline results under different scheduling models. A dramatic example of this type is that of the related model of *logit response dynamics*, another model analyzed via stochastic stability [17]. Going in this model from a random single-node update to parallel modes (the so-called *revision process* of [18]) may lead (in general games) to the selection (via stochastic stability) of states that are not even Nash equilbria. In contrast, for local interaction games the parallel *all-logit* rule has a Gibbs limiting distribution [9], similar to the random update case.

Neither random scheduling nor parallel update can accurately model *social contagion* phenomena, i.e., agents becoming active as a result of other agents' action, via communication or imitation. Thus it is of interest to study the robustness social models to variations in the update rule. Indeed, in [19, 20] we have proposed an *adversarial approach to social simulations*. Roughly speaking, this means that we consider the baseline dynamics under random scheduling, then modify the update order to arbitrary scheduling, and attempt to derive necessary and/or sufficient conditions on the scheduler that make the results from the random update case extend to the adversarial setting. We have accomplished this in [20] for Prisoners' Dilemma with Pavlov strategy, a Markov chain previously investigated in [21], and in [19] for the logit response dynamics.

The purpose of this paper is to introduce contagion in evolutionary versions of Schelling's segregation model, as studied by Pollicott and Weiss [10], and study the setting where the set of agents that becomes active is specified by a random walk on a second "communication" network. A similar model was investigated for the logit response dynamics in [19], and is apparently consistent with some real-life contagion phenomena in power networks [22]. In the most general setting this communication network works on *pairs of vertices*. The more natural case where agents influence each other is a special case of our setting. The feature of the Pollicott-Weiss model that is of special interest to our study is that, although Schelling's model might have multiple equilibria, it is only the most segregated states that are stochastically stable. Our result shows that this extends to a scenario with social contagion: we prove a result with a similar flavor under a more general nonadaptive model of activation.

Even though we use analytic rather than experimental techniques, our results are naturally related to a long line of research that investigates the robustness of discrete models under various scheduling models [13, 23]. On the other hand the notion we consider, that of stochastic stability, is highly related to the analysis of cellular automata using dynamical systems techniques [24]. In contrast to many such studies, though, that only perturb the initial system state, stochastic stability embodies the notion of stability under continuous (but vanishingly small) perturbations.

2   Preliminaries

We first review the notion of *stochastic stability* for perturbed dynamical systems described by Markov chains:

Definition 1. *Let the Markov chain P^0 be defined on a finite state set Ω. For every $\epsilon > 0$, we also define a Markov chain P^ϵ on Ω. Family $(P^\epsilon)_{\epsilon \geq 0}$ is called a* regular perturbed Markov process *if all of the following conditions hold:*

- *For every $\epsilon > 0$ Markov chain P^ϵ is irreducible and aperiodic.*
- *For each pair of states $x, y \in \Omega$, $\lim_{\epsilon > 0} P^\epsilon_{xy} = P^0_{xy}$.*
- *Whenever $P_{xy} = 0$ there exists a real number $r(m) > 0$, called the* resistance *of transition $m = (x \to y)$, such that as $\epsilon \to 0$, $P^\epsilon_{xy} = \Theta(\epsilon^{r(m)})$.*

Let μ^ϵ be the stationary distrib. of P^ϵ. State s is stochastically stable *if* $\lim_{\epsilon \to 0} \mu^\epsilon(s) > 0$.

We use a standard tool in this area: a result due to Young (Lemma 3.2 in [6]) that allows us to recognize stochastically stable states in a Markov Chain using *spanning trees of minimal resistance*:

Definition 2. *If $j \in S(G)$ is a state, a* tree rooted at node j *is a set T of edges so that for any state $w \neq j$ there exists an unique (directed) path from w to j. The* resistance *of a rooted tree T is defined as the sum of resistances of all edges in T.*

Proposition 3 (Young). *The stochastically stable states of a regular Markov process (P_ϵ) are precisely those states $z \in \Omega$ such that there exists a tree T rooted at z of minimal resistance (among all rooted trees).*

3 The Model

We consider an $N \times N$ two-dimensional lattice graph G with periodic boundary conditions (that is, a torus). Let V be the set of vertices of this graph. Each vertex of G hosts an agent, colored either red or blue. The neighborhood of a vertex v is the *four-point neighborhood*, consisting of the cell to the left, up, right, down of the cell holding v. An agent's utility is written as $\forall i \in V$, $u_i(x) = r \cdot w(x_i) + \epsilon_i$, where r is a positive constant, assumed similarly to [5] to be the same for all agents, and $w(x)$ is defined, similarly to [10], as the difference between the number of neighbors of x having the same color and the number of neighbors of x having the opposite color. Finally, ϵ_i are (possibly different) agent-specific constants.

Next we specify our scheduling model, defined as follows:

Definition 4. [Markovian contagion]: *To each pair of vertices e we associate a probability distribution D_e on $V \times V$ such that $e \in supp(D_e)^1$. We then choose the pair to be scheduled next as follows: Let p_i be the pair chosen at stage i. Select the next scheduled pair p_{i+1} by sampling from the set of pairs in D_{p_i}. We assume that for any two pairs e, e' the following condition holds:*

$$Pr[e \to e'] > 0 \Leftrightarrow Pr[e' \to e] > 0. \tag{1}$$

In other words: the next scheduled pair only depends on the last scheduled pair, succession relation $e \to e'$ specifies a *bidirected graph* $H(G)$ whose vertex set is $V \times V$, and the scheduled pair can be seen as performing a random walk (possibly a non-uniform one) on $H(G)$. In particular the next chosen pair is *not* guaranteed to have different labels on endpoints. Furthermore, graph $H(G)$ should be connected, otherwise the choice of a particular initial sequence of moves could preclude a given edge from ever being scheduled sometimes in the future.

---

[1] This translates, intuitively, to the following condition: we always give the participants in a swap the chance to immediately reevaluate their last move.

Observation 1. *A particular case of Definition 4, which justifies the name contagion is described informally as follows:* agents, *rather than pairs, are given the opportunity to switch. They randomly choose a swapping neighbor among those available to them. There exists a second, separate* influence network *I. The next scheduled agent is one of the neighbors (in I) of the previously scheduled agent. Indeed, to describe this scenario in the setting of the previous definition, define D_e to consist of pairs e' that share with e a vertex.*

Observation 2. *The random scheduler is a particular case of Definition 4, when D_e is the uniform distribution on $V \times V$.*

To complete the description of the dynamics, we only need to specify the probability that two agents inhabiting the different endpoints of a pair $e = (u, v)$ switch when pair e is scheduled. This is accomplished using the so-called *log-linear response rule* [6,18,25], specified as follows: let S be the state before the switch and T be the state obtained if the two agents at u, v switch. Then:

$$Pr[S \to T] = \frac{e^{\beta \cdot [u_1(T) + u_2(T)]}}{e^{\beta [u_1(S) + u_2(S)]} + e^{\beta [u_1(T) + u_2(T)]}}, \tag{2}$$

where u_1, u_2 are the corresponding utility functions of the two agents at the endpoints of the scheduled pair, and $\beta > 0$ is a constant. This is, of course, the noisy version of the best-response move, that would choose the move that maximizes the sum of utilities $u_1(\cdot) + u_2(\cdot)$.

The *state of the system* is defined by a vector $\overline{w} \in \{-1, +1\}^V$ is a vector encoding the labels of all vertices of the torus. To obtain a description of the dynamics as an aperiodic Markov chain we have to complete the description of the system state by a pair r of vertices, i.e., the last pair that had the opportunity to switch by being scheduled. Thus the state space of the Markov chain is $S(G) := \{\pm1\}^V \times (V \times V)$. When $H(G)$ is strongly connected, M_β is ergodic, so it has an unique stationary distribution Π_β. It is easy to see (and similar to previous results e.g. in [6]) that the family of chains $(M_\epsilon)_{\epsilon>0}$ is a regularly perturbed Markov process (where we define $\epsilon = e^{-\beta}$).

Definition 5. *A state $w \in \{\pm1\}^V$ is called* maximally segregated *if w realizes the minimum value of the number of red-blue edges (of the torus), across all possible states on G with a given number of red/blue agents.*

In [10] a complete characterization of a maximally segregated state was obtained (Theorem 2 in that paper). Roughly they are horizontal or vertical "bands", possibly with a "strip" attached, or a rectangle, possibly with at most two "strips" attached. We refer the reader to [10] for details, and don't discuss it any further.

4   Main Result and Its Interpretation

Our main result is:

Theorem 6. *The stochastically stable states for Schelling's segregation model with Markovian contagion form a subset of the set $Q \subseteq S(G)$,*

$$Q = \{(w, e) | w \text{ is maximally segregated and } e \in V \times V\} \qquad (3)$$

In other words: **the conclusion that stochastically stable states in Schelling's segregation model are maximally segregated is robust to extending the update model from a random one to those from the family from Definition 4, that incorporate Markovian contagion.**
    The defining feature of the class of schedulers in the previous result seems to be that they choose the next scheduled pair *nonadaptively*: the next pair only depends on the last scheduled pair, and **not** on other particulars of the system state. Indeed, in the full version of the paper we will complement the result above by another one (very easy to state and prove), that shows that some **adaptive** scheduler (despite being quite fair) can forever preclude the system from ever reaching maximal segregation (thus "breaking the baseline stylized result").

Proof. We will employ a fundamental property, noted for models of segregation such as the one in this paper e.g. in [5]: they are *potential games* [26], i.e., they admit a function $L : S(G) \to \mathbf{R}$ such that, for any player i, any strategy profile (i.e., vector of player strategies) $x_{-i} := (x_j)_{j \in V, j \neq i}$, and any two strategies z, t for player i

$$u_i(z; x_{-i}) - u_i(t; x_{-i}) = L(z; x_{-i}) - L(t; x_{-i}). \qquad (4)$$

    In other words, differences in utility of the i'th player as a result of using different strategies are equal to the differences in potential among the two corresponding profiles. The function L is defined simply as $L(s) = \sum_i u_i(s)$. Strictly speaking the potential above is defined for the original Policott-Weiss model i.e., defined on $\{\pm 1\}^V$, instead of $S(G)$. But it can be easily extended by simply applying it to any pair (s, e) (thus neglecting e). Moreover, the following property holds, which determines the resistance of moves:

Lemma 7. *Let $A \in \{\pm 1\}^V$ be a state of the system, and let $e = (i, j)$ be a pair in $V \times V$. Let B be a state obtained by making the move $m = A \to B$ (B is either A or is the state obtained from A by swapping the states A_i, A_j). Then the resistance $r(m)$ of move m is equal to:*

$$r(m) = [u_i(A) + u_j(A)] - [u_i(B) + u_j(B)] = 2(L(A) - L(B)) > 0 \qquad (5)$$

when $A \to B$ is a swap that diminishes potential, and to

$$[u_i(C) + u_j(C)] - [u_i(A) + u_j(A)] = 2(L(C) - L(A)) > 0 \qquad (6)$$

when $A = B$, but the corresponding swap $A \to C$ would be a potential improving one. In all other cases $r(m) = 0$ (that is m is a neutral move).

In other words, a move has positive resistance when one of the following two alternatives hold: (a) The move corresponds to a decrease in potential. The resistance of the move is, in this case, equal to the potential decrease. (b) The move corresponds to preserving the current state (as well as agents' utilities), but the other possible move would have led to a state of higher potential. The resistance of the move is, in this case, equal to the difference in potentials between this better state and the current one.

Proof. Follows directly from Eq. (2) and the definition of resistance.

We apply this result to prove the following lemma:

Lemma 8. *Consider a state $Y \in Q$ that is maximally segregated. Consider another state X, and a tree T rooted at X having minimal potential. Then there exists another tree $\overline{T}$ rooted at Y whose potential is at most that of tree T, strictly less in case when X is not a maximally segregated state.*

Proof. Note that, by the definition of utility functions, maximally segregated states are those that maximize the potential.

Since T is an oriented tree, there is an unique directed path

$$p : [Y = (s_0, e_0) \to \ldots \to (s_k, e_k) \to (s_{k+1}, e_{k+1}) \to \ldots \to (s_r, e_r) = X] \quad (7)$$

in T from Y to X. Here $s_0, s_r \in \{\pm 1\}^V$ are states, and e_0, e_r are pairs in $V \times V$. First, we decompose T into three subsets as follows:

1. The set of edges of p (see Fig. 1).
2. The set of edges of, W_Y the subtree rooted at y.
3. The edges of subtrees W_k rooted at nodes (s_k, e_k) of p, other than Y (but possibly including X).

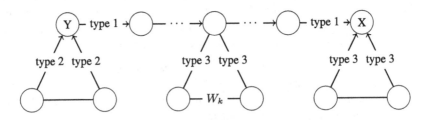

Fig. 1. Decomposition of edges of tree T. Path p is on top.

Lemma 9. *Without loss of generality we may assume that the path p contains no two consecutive vertices (s_k, e_k) and (s_r, e_r), $k < r$, with $s_k = \ldots = s_r$ and all the moves between s_k and s_r having zero resistance.*

Proof. Suppose there was such a pair k, r. Take one with maximal $k - r$. Define a tree T' by

- First connecting (s_k, e_k) directly to (s_{r+1}, e_{r+1}). This is legal since $s_k = s_r$. Indeed, since activating edge e_{r+1} move the system from s_r to s_{r+1}, activating the same edge moves the system from (s_k, e_k) to s_{r+1} as well.
- Also connecting $(s_{k+1}, e_{k+1}), \ldots, (s_r, e_r)$ directly to (s_{r+1}, e_{r+1}).

It is easy to see that T' is a tree with the same resistance as T, since the only removed edges have zero resistance.   □

In particular, applying iteratively Lemma 9, we may assume that all transitions on the path from p to q either change the system state or have positive resistance.

Now, to obtain tree $\overline{T}$ we will first obtain a graph $\overline{\overline{T}}$, in which every node has *at least one path* to node Y. "Thinning out" this directed graph to a tree yields a tree $\overline{T}$ of even lower resistance. To obtain directed graph $\overline{\overline{T}}$:

1. First, add to $\overline{\overline{T}}$ the edges of T_Y.
2. Next, define path q from X to Y as follows:

$$q : [(s_r, e_r) \to (s_{r-1}, e_r) \to (s_{r-2}, e_{r-1}) \to \ldots \to (s_0, e_1) \to (s_0, e_0)]. \quad (8)$$

In other words, q aims to "undo" the sequence of moves in path p from Eq. (7) from Y to X. However, since the states of the Markov chain also have as a second component a pair in $V \times V$, (corresponding to the last scheduled edge), we need to take a little extra care when defining q. Specifically q starts at X but **cannot** simply reverse the edges of p, since these do **not** correspond to legal moves. To define q, we first make a move at e_r by "undoing" the last move of p^2. This yields state (S_{r-1}, e_r) (since pair e_r is scheduled in this as well). We then continue to "undo moves of p" until the state becomes S_0. This is possible because of condition (1): since pair e_{r+1} can be scheduled after e_r, scheduling e_r can move the system from s_r to s_{r-1}, scheduling pair e_{r-1} can move the system from s_{r-1} to s_{r-2}, and so on, until state S_0 is reached. At this moment the last activated pair was e_1. q then moves to Y by making a move (with no effect) on e_0.
   Note that every such path will contain, for every $k = 1, r$, a vertex whose state is s_k.
3. For every tree component W_k obtained by removing path p from T, attached to p at (s_k, e_k) perform one of the following:

---

[2] This is where we use a property specific to our model of Schelling segregation, as opposed to proving a result valid for general potential game: the property that we employ is that in Schelling's model any move m "can be undone". This means that there is a move n using the same pair of vertices as m that brings the system back to where it was before. Move n simply "swaps back" the two agents if they were swapped by m, and leaves them in place otherwise.

- **Case 1:** $s_k = s_{k-1}$.
  In this case the point $(s_k, e_k) = (s_{k-1}, e_k)$ is on path q as well, therefore we also add the rooted tree W_k to $\overline{\overline{T}}$. This is possible since attaching a tree to a node depends only on the system state, but *not* on the last scheduled node. Moreover, *the resistance of W_k does not change* as a result of this attachment.

- **Case 2:** $s_k \neq s_{k-1}$ *and move* $(s_{k-1}, e_{k-1}) \rightarrow (s_k, e_k)$ *has resistance* > 0.
  In this case, since in configuration s_{k-1} and scheduled move e_k we have a choice between moving to s_k and staying in s_{k-1}, it follows that the transition $(s_{k-1}, e_{k-1}) \rightarrow (s_{k-1}, e_k)$ has zero resistance and $L(s_k) < L(s_{k-1})$. Hence transition $(s_k, e_k) \rightarrow (s_{k-1}, e_k)$ has zero resistance.
  We now add the tree $\overline{W_k} = W_k \cup \{(s_k, e_k) \rightarrow (s_{k-1}, e_k)\}$ (rooted at node (s_{k-1}, e_k), which is on q) to $\overline{\overline{T}}$. The tree $\overline{W_k}$ has the same total resistance as W_k. All nodes from W_k, including (s_k, e_k) can now reach Y via q.

- **Case 3:** $s_{k-1} \neq s_k$, *move* $(s_{k-1}, e_{k-1}) \rightarrow (s_k, e_k)$ *has zero resistance and all moves on p between s_k and X have zero resistance.*
  Then we add to $\overline{\overline{T}}$ this portion of p, together with W_k. This way we connect nodes in W_{k-1}, W_k to Y (via X and q). All added edges except those of one of the trees W_l have zero resistance.

- **Case 4:** $s_{k-1} \neq s_k$, *the move* $(s_{k-1}, e_{k-1}) \rightarrow (s_k, e_k)$ *has zero resistance, but some move on p, between s_k and X has positive resistance.*
  Let $(s_{k+l}, e_l) \rightarrow (s_{k+l+1}, e_{l+1})$ be the closest move (i.e., the one that minimizes l) with positive resistance.
  If $s_{k+l} = s_{k+l+1}$ then we have already connected (s_{k+l}, e_l) to Y, as it falls under Case 1. Now just add all the (zero resistance) edges of p between s_k, e_k and (s_{k+l}, e_{k+l}), together with edges of W_k, to connect all such nodes to Y.
  If $s_{k+l} = s_{k+l+1}$ then we have already connected (s_{k+l}, e_l) to Y, as it falls under Case 2. We proceed similarly.

The previous construction has ensured that any pair (s, e) is connected by *at least* one path to Y. Thinning out $\overline{\overline{T}}$ we get a rooted tree $\overline{T}$ having resistance less or equal to the resistance of $\overline{\overline{T}}$. Since the four outlined transformations only add, in addition to trees W_k, edges of zero resistance, to compare the total resistances of T and $\overline{T}$ one should simply compare the total resistances of paths p and q. We claim that this difference in resistances of these paths is equal to the difference in potentials:

Claim. $r(p) - r(q) = 2(L(Y) - L(X)) \geq 0$.

Proving Claim (4) would validate our conclusion, since $L(Y) - L(X) \geq 0$, and $L(X) = L(Y)$ iff X is a global minimum state for the potential function. We prove this by considering the correspondence between edges of paths p and q: to each edge e of p one can associate an unique edge e' of Q that "undoes e".

By the additivity of both resistance and potential, it is enough to prove that, for every edge e of p and its associated edge of q, e', $r(e') - r(e)$ is equal to twice the difference in potentials between S_{fin}, the final state for the forward transition and S_{init}, the initial state. The first thing to note is none of the two resistances can be infinite: the transition $e \to e'$ corresponds to a move of the perturbed Markov chain (optimal or not). Its inverse corresponds to "undoing" that move, which is a legal move (eventually perturbed) in itself. We employ Lemma 7 and identify several cases:

- *The move e corresponds to **not** switching, and its resistance is zero.* Let S_1 be the common state, and let S_2 be the state corresponding to a switch. Then $S_1 = S_{init} = S_{fin}$. Also, $L(S_1) \geq L(S_2)$. So the move e' also stays in state S_1 (when it could have gone to S_2), which is the optimal action, given that $L(S_1) \geq L(S_2)$. Thus in this case both the "forward" and the "backward" transition have resistance zero, and do not count towards the sum of resistances on the path.
- *The move e corresponds to **switching**, and its resistance is zero.* Then, $S_{fin} = S_2$, $S_{init} = S_1$. By Lemma 7 $L(S_2) > L(S_1)$. The backward move has positive resistance equal to $2(L(S_2) - L(S_1))$. The result is verified.
- *The move e corresponds to **not** switching, and its resistance is nonzero.* Then $S_{init} = S_{fin} = S_1$ and $L(S_1) < L(S_2)$ (since switching would be beneficial). Therefore in the backward move the state stays S_1 (when it could have gone to S_2). The resistance is equal to $2(L(S_2) - L(S_1))$, the same as the resistance of the forward move. Therefore $r(e') - r(e) = L(S_{fin}) - L(S_{init}) = 0$.
- *The move e corresponds to **switching**, and its resistance is nonzero.* Then, $S_{fin} = S_2$, $S_{init} = S_1$, by Lemma 7 $L(S_2) < L(S_1)$ and the resistance of the forward move is equal to $2(L(S_1) - L(S_2)) = 2(L(S_{init}) - L(S_{fin}))$. The resistance of the backward move is equal to zero, so the result is verified in this case as well.

Thus the claim is established and the proof of the theorem is complete.

5   Outlook and Further Work

Theorem 6 is only the main result in the adversarial analysis of Schelling's segregation model. It shows that stochastically segregated states are maximally segregated. Is the converse true? Namely, is every maximally segregated state stochastically stable? Such a result is indeed true in 1D versions of Schelling's segregation model (such as the one presented in [6]). We will discuss the 2D case with Markovian contagion in the journal version of the paper.

Other topics deserving research include studying conditions that preclude segregation, determining the convergence time of the segregation dynamics with Markovian contagion, models with Markovian contagion and concurrent updates [8,9], etc. We plan to address these and other issues in follow-up papers.

References

1. Schelling, T.C.: Dynamic models of segregation. J. Math. Sociol. **1**, 143–186 (1971)
2. Fatès, N.: A guided tour of asynchronous cellular automata. In: Kari, J., Kutrib, M., Malcher, A. (eds.) AUTOMATA 2013. LNCS, vol. 8155, pp. 15–30. Springer, Heidelberg (2013). https://doi.org/10.1007/978-3-642-40867-0_2
3. Vinković, D., Kirman, A.: A physical analogue of the Schelling model. Proc. Nat. Acad. Sci. **103**(51), 19261–19265 (2006)
4. Pancs, R., Vriend, N.J.: Schelling's spatial proximity model of segregation revisited. J. Public Econ. **91**(1–2), 1–24 (2007)
5. Zhang, J.: Residential segregation in an all-integrationist world. J. Econ. Behav. Organ. **24**(4), 533–550 (2004)
6. Young, H.P.: Individual Strategy and Social Structure: an Evolutionary Theory of Institutions. Princeton University Press, Princeton (1998)
7. Brandt, C., Immorlica, N., Kamath, G., Kleinberg, R.: An analysis of one-dimensional Schelling segregation. In: Proceedings of the 44th Annual ACM STOC, pp. 789–804 (2012)
8. Montanari, A., Saberi, A.: Convergence to equilibrium in local interaction games. In: Proceedings of 50th Annual IEEE FOCS, pp. 303–312. IEEE (2009)
9. Auletta, V., Ferraioli, D., Pasquale, F., Penna, P., Persiano, G.: Logit dynamics with concurrent updates for local interaction games. In: Bodlaender, H.L., Italiano, G.F. (eds.) ESA 2013. LNCS, vol. 8125, pp. 73–84. Springer, Heidelberg (2013). https://doi.org/10.1007/978-3-642-40450-4_7
10. Pollicott, M., Weiss, H.: The dynamics of Schelling-type segregation models. Adv. Appl. Math. **27**, 17–40 (2001)
11. Hegselmann, R.: Thomas C. Schelling and James M. Sakoda: the intellectual, technical, and social history of a model. J. Artif. Soc. Soc. Simul. **20**(3), 15 (2017)
12. Fates, N., Morvan, M.: An experimental study of robustness to asynchronism for elementary cellular automata. arXiv preprint nlin/0402016 (2004)
13. Bouré, O., Fates, N., Chevrier, V.: Probing robustness of cellular automata through variations of asynchronous updating. Nat. Comput. **11**(4), 553–564 (2012)
14. Foster, D., Young, H.P.: Stochastic evolutionary game dynamics. Theor. Popul. Biol. **38**(2), 219–232 (1990)
15. Young, H.P.: The dynamics of conformity. In: Social Dynamics, pp. 133–153 (2001)
16. Page, S.E.: On incentives and updating in agent based models. Comput. Econ. **10**(1), 67–87 (1997)
17. Kandori, M., Mailath, G.J., Rob, R.: Learning, mutation, and long run equilibria in games. Econometrica **61**, 29–56 (1993)
18. Alós-Ferrer, C., Netzer, N.: The logit-response dynamics. Games Econ. Behav. **68**(2), 413–427 (2010)
19. Istrate, G., Marathe, M.V., Ravi, S.S.: Adversarial scheduling analysis of game-theoretic models of norm diffusion. In: Beckmann, A., Dimitracopoulos, C., Löwe, B. (eds.) CiE 2008. LNCS, vol. 5028, pp. 273–282. Springer, Heidelberg (2008). https://doi.org/10.1007/978-3-540-69407-6_31
20. Istrate, G., Marathe, M.V., Ravi, S.S.: Adversarial scheduling analysis of discrete models of social dynamics. Math. Struct. Comput. Sci. **22**(5), 788–815 (2012)
21. Dyer, M., Greenhill, C., Goldberg, L.A., Istrate, G., Jerrum, M.: The convergence of iterated prisoner's dilemma game. Comb. Probab. Comput. **11**, 135–147 (2002)
22. Hines, P., Dobson, I., Rezaei, P.: Cascading power outages propagate locally in an influence graph that is not the actual grid topology. IEEE Trans. Power Syst. **32**(2), 958–967 (2017)

23. Fatès, N., Morvan, M.: Perturbing the topology of the game of life increases its robustness to asynchrony. In: Sloot, P.M.A., Chopard, B., Hoekstra, A.G. (eds.) ACRI 2004. LNCS, vol. 3305, pp. 111–120. Springer, Heidelberg (2004). https://doi.org/10.1007/978-3-540-30479-1_12

24. Dennunzio, A., Formenti, E., Kůrka, P.: Cellular automata dynamical systems. In: Rozenberg, G., Bäck, T., Kok, J.N. (eds.) Handbook of Natural Computing, pp. 25–75. Springer, Heidelberg (2012). https://doi.org/10.1007/978-3-540-92910-9_2

25. Blume, L.E.: Population games. In: Durlauf, S., Young, H.P. (eds.) Social Dynamics: Economic Learning and Social Evolution. MIT Press, Cambridge (2001)

26. Monderer, D., Shapley, L.S.: Potential games. Games Econ. Behav. **14**, 124–143 (1996)

Cellular Automata Pseudo-Random Number Generators and Their Resistance to Asynchrony

Luca Manzoni[✉] and Luca Mariot

Dipartimento di Informatica, Sistemistica e Comunicazione,
Università degli Studi di Milano-Bicocca, Viale Sarca 336, 20126 Milan, Italy
{luca.manzoni,luca.mariot}@disco.unimib.it

Abstract. Cellular Automata (CA) have a long history being employed as pseudo-random number generators (PRNG), especially for cryptographic applications such as keystream generation in stream ciphers. Initially starting from the study of rule 30 of elementary CA, multiple rules where the objects of investigation and were shown to be able to pass most of the rigorous statistical tests used to assess the quality of PRNG. In all cases, the CA employed where of the classical, synchronous kind. This assumes a global clock regulating all CA updates which can be a weakness if an attacker is able to tamper it. Here we study how much asynchrony is necessary to make a CA-based PRNG ineffective. We have found that elementary CA are subdivided into three class: (1) there is a "state transition" where, after a certain level of asynchrony, the CA loses the ability to generate strong random sequences, (2) the randomness of the sequences increases with a limited level of asynchrony, or (3) CA normally unable to be used as PRNG exhibit a much stronger ability to generate random sequences when asynchrony is introduced.

1 Introduction

Cellular Automata (CA) are one of the oldest nature-inspired computational models in computer science [25,26]. Defined informally, CA are composed of a lattice of identical finite state automata (or *cells*) all updating at the same time according to their state and the state of their neighbours. CA have been successfully employed in multiple fields, like for instance the modelling of physical systems [5] such as fluids [4], natural ecosystems [1], traffic flows [13], and of pedestrians in crowds [2]. Here, we mainly deal with the cryptographic applications of CA. In particular, we consider the well-known problem of generating *pseudo-random sequences* by exploiting the dynamical behaviour of CA. Pseudo-random sequences play a fundamental role in cryptography, for example in keystream generation for stream ciphers [14]. Differently from other studies,

Luca Manzoni was partially supported by "Premio giovani talenti 2017" of Università degli Studi di Milano-Bicocca and Accademia dei Lincei.

G. Mauri et al. (Eds.): ACRI 2018, LNCS 11115, pp. 428–437, 2018.
https://doi.org/10.1007/978-3-319-99813-8_39

we do not try to find new CA that works well as PRNG; instead, we study how asynchrony influences the ability of a CA to produce pseudo-random sequences.

In classical CA, all cells update at the same time (i.e., *synchronously*), the underlying assumption being that there is a single, global clock regulating all cells. This is, however, a strong assumption since real-world systems are usually not synchronous. Once this assumption is dropped, there are multiple ways to introduce asynchronous behaviours in CA. For example by using a probabilistic activation [9–11], updating a cell at a time according to a given sequence [18], having different areas of the CA update with different speeds [17,19], or even more general updating schemes [8,28]. Here we deal with a simplified model of asynchrony where the CA is partitioned in separate, contiguous sequences of cells, all cells inside the same sequence update in parallel, but the sequences update sequentially.

Our goal is to study what happens when the aforementioned assumption of a global clock is broken not by design, but by a malicious actor who wants to tamper with the PRNG. Since PRNG are used in cryptographic applications, limiting the amount of damage that can be carried on by damaging them (or, at least, the global clock governing their updates) is paramount. Here, in particular we experimentally study how different levels of asynchrony impacts the generation of pseudo-random sequences generated by *elementary CA*.

The paper is organised as follows: some necessary basic notions are recalled in Sect. 2. Section 3 briefly reviews the state of the art in CA-based PRNG, mostly focusing on the synchronous approach. Section 4 describes in the detail experiments we performed. In particular, Sect. 4.1 explains all the experimental settings used, while a general discussion of the experimental results is carried out in Sect. 4.2. The discussion of the results, particularly the classification of the observed behaviours in three broad classes, is given in Sects. 4.3, 4.4 and 4.5. Some further considerations and directions for future works are presented in Sect. 5.

2   Basic Notions

In this section we recall some basic notions on CA, their properties, and how they can be employed as PRNG.

Definition 1. *A cellular automaton (CA) is a tuple (Σ, f, r) where Σ is a finite alphabet, $r \in \mathbb{N}$ is the radius, and $f : \Sigma^{2r+1} \to \Sigma$ is the local function of the CA. If the CA only has a finite number $n \in \mathbb{N}$ of cell, i.e., it is a finite CA, we say that it is a CA of size n.*

A CA is said to be an *elementary CA* (ECA) when its alphabet is $\{0, 1\}$ and it has radius 1. There are exactly 256 ECA, each one numbered with its Wolfram code, a number between 0 and 255 whose binary expansion represents the output column of the truth table defining the local function of the CA.

Here we only deal with CA of finite size with *periodic boundary conditions*, that is, the cell adjacent to the n-th one is the first one and vice versa. In the following we assume that the subscript denoting the cell position is to be interpreted modulo n, the size of the CA.

The *configuration* of a cellular automaton (Σ, f, r) of size n is a vector $c = c_0, \ldots, c_{n-1} \in \Sigma^n$. The CA updates its state using a global rule $F \colon \Sigma^n \to \Sigma^n$ where each cell updates its state at the same time using the local rule, thus giving the following global rule:

$$F(c)_i = f(c_{i-r}, \ldots, c_i, \ldots, c_{i+r}), \text{ for } 0 \leq i < n$$

Finite CA of length n with alphabet $\{0, 1\}$ are usually employed as PRNG in the following way [27]:

- A *random seed* of n bits is the initial configuration of the CA;
- To obtain an new pseudo-random bit the entire CA is updated and one cell (usually the central one) is sampled.

Since CA update all cells in parallel and each cell requires only access to local information, they can be easily parallelized and/or implemented in hardware [23].

2.1   The Asynchronous Model

While classical CA are inherently synchronous, in recent years multiple variations of CA were defined with the addition of some kind of asynchronous behaviour. In our work we deal with a very specific kind of asynchrony, where a finite CA of length n has its set of cells $\{0, \ldots, n-1\}$ partitioned into k contiguous segments $I_0, \ldots, I_{n-1}$ with $I_i = \{i\frac{n}{k}, \ldots, (i+1)\frac{n}{k} - 1\}$, where k is a divisor of n. At time 0 only the cells in the segment I_0 are updated; at the successive time step only the cells in the segment I_1 are updated, and so on. In general, at the t-th time step only the cells in the segment $t \bmod k$ are updated. This kind of asynchrony can be tuned by using the parameter k: when $k = 1$ there is only one segment and the update is synchronous, like in classical CA. When $k = n$ only one cell updates at each time step, mimicking the behaviour of fully asynchronous CA [18]. It is also possible to obtain intermediate levels of asynchrony: for example, with $k = 2$ the CA is effectively split into two parts which update alternately.

In this paper we empirically study how increasing the value of k influences the ability of a CA to produce robust pseudo-random sequences (i.e., which pass rigorous statistical tests). To avoid the risk of sampling multiple times a cell that still has not updated, we perform the sampling every k steps. In this case for $k = 1$ the behaviour is the same as in classical CA and in all other cases we ensure that the sampled cell has always been updated between two samplings.

3   Related Work

In this section, we give a brief historical overview of the literature concerning pseudo-random sequence generation by means of cellular automata.

Wolfram [27] was the first to propose a PRNG based on a chaotic CA to be employed in cryptographic applications. Specifically, he suggested to use a periodic CA equipped with rule 30, and to sample the value of a certain cell as a pseudo-random sequence. Some years later, Damgård [7] showed a concrete construction of iterated hash function based on Wolfram's PRNG.

Unfortunately, Wolfram's PRNG later turned out to be very weak from a cryptographic standpoint: Meier and Staffelbach [22] proved that it is vulnerable to a known plaintext attack, unless the CA is composed of at least 1000 cells. The attack exploits the *quasi-linearity* of rule 30, which allows to rewrite it in an equivalent way where the initial seeds are not equiprobable. Analogously, Daemen et al. [6] cryptanalysed Damgård's hash function, proving that it is computationally feasible to generate collisions in it.

Sipper and Tomassini [24] proposed a *cellular programming approach* based on a non-uniform CA, where the rule vector specifying which rule is applied in each cell is evolved by a *Genetic Algorithm* (GA). The fitness of each cell is evaluated by computing the entropy of the pseudo-random sequence generated by its current rule for 4096 time steps, averaging the results over 300 initial random configurations. The final rule vectors evolved through the cellular programming algorithm were then further investigated by testing longer sequences with the ENT statistical test suite.

A common trend that can be noticed in the CA-based PRNG literature is that the cryptographic quality of the pseudo-random sequences is usually assessed by means of statistical tests. A more refined approach which emerged in the last years consists in analysing the *cryptographic properties* of the local rules underlying the CA, by interpreting them as *Boolean functions*. Considering Wolfram's PRNG, it turns out that rule 30 is both *balanced* and *nonlinear*, but it is not *first order correlation-immune* [21]. This is the reason why Meier and Staffelbach's attack proved to be successful. As a consequence, recent works like Formenti et al. [12] and Leporati and Mariot [15,16] focused on the search of local functions of radius 2 and 3 in order to find new rules with a better trade-off of balancedness, nonlinearity and correlation-immunity, and which can also pass stringent statistical tests (such as the NIST suite [3]) when plugged into Wolfram's PRNG model.

4   Experiments

4.1   Experimental Settings

For performing the experiments we considered only *balanced ECA*, meaning that the truth table of the local rules is composed of an equal number of zeros and ones. The reason behind this choice is that balancedness is a fundamental cryptographic criterion, and CA with unbalanced rules have an inherent statistical bias in their dynamics [16]. Hence, since our aim in this work is to investigate the resilience against asynchrony of local rules which already yield good pseudo-random sequences in the classical synchronous update scheme, we focused only on the subset of balanced rules.

The initial random seed was chosen using https://random.org to obtain a 64 bit initial configuration for the CA. For each CA 1000 runs with different initial configurations were performed and 10^6 bits were generated in each run, thus producing sequences of 10^9 bits. The values k governing the asynchrony of the CA were all divisors of 64, the length of the CA configuration: 1 (synchronous behaviour), 2, 4, 8, 16, 32, and 64 (fully asynchronous behaviour).

The randomness of each sequence was assessed using the NIST test suite [3], consisting of 188 statistical tests. The quality of the pseudo-random sequences generated is thus expressed using a value from 0 (no test passed) to 188 (all tests passed). It is important to remember that, while not passing a large enough number of statistical tests indicates a weakness, even passing them all does not ensure that the PRNG employed is robust.

4.2   Experimental Results

We have experimentally observed three main behaviours depending on the level of asynchrony in CA:

1. A "phase transition" happens when enough asynchrony is present. Before the cutoff value the CA retains its ability to generate strong pseudo-random sequences. After the cutoff value most of the statistical tests fail (Sect. 4.3).
2. The CA ability to generate strong pseudo-random sequences increases with a limited amount of asynchrony and decreases with a large amount of it (Sect. 4.4).
3. A CA that is usually unsuitable to be used as a PRNG generates sequences with better pseudo-randomness once a limited amount of asynchrony is added (Sect. 4.5).

We are excluding from this classification the CA that did not pass a high enough level of statistical tests with any level of asynchrony. The subdivision of the remaining balanced ECA rules in the three classes is presented in Table 1. In the following we discuss the results obtained for each one of these classes.

Table 1. The subdivision in classes of balanced ECA.

Type 1	30, 45, 75, 86, 89, 101, 135, 149
Type 2	106, 120, 169, 225
Type 3	60, 90, 105, 150, 154, 165, 166, 180, 195, 210

4.3   Type 1 Rules

Type 1 rules includes rule 30, which as remarked in Sect. 3 was among the first employed as a PRNG, even if later it was found to have some weaknesses [22]. The results for this class of rules is shown in Fig. 1.

It is possible to observe that most of the rules pass all or almost all the tests when the parameter k is below 32, with 188 or 187 tests passed by each rule. The first difference can be observed when $k = 32$:

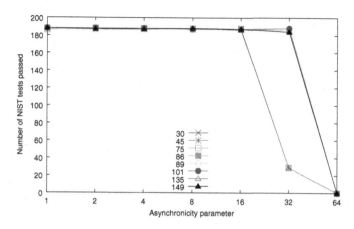

Fig. 1. The number of NIST test passed by type 1 rules with the change in asynchrony

- rules 86, 89, 101, and 149 still pass most of the tests (from a maximum of 188 for rule 101 to a minimum of 184 for rule 149);
- rules 30, 45, 75, and 135 have a sharp decrease in the number of tests passed, which is 29.

In all cases, when full asynchrony is present, none of the rules in this class can pass even one of the tests, showing that full asynchrony completely changes the behaviour of the CA.

4.4 Type 2 Rules

Type 2 rules are, in some sense, similar to the ones of type 1, as it can be observed in Fig. 2. With a high enough level of asynchrony (i.e., $k = 32$ or $k = 64$), they are unable to pass any statistical test of the NIST suite. It is for small levels of asynchrony that their behaviour differ. In fact, when updates happen synchronously the rules of this class are not as good as the ones of type 1, with the number of tests passed ranging from 167 (rule 169) to 172 (rules 106 and 120). When a small amount of asynchrony is added (k between 2 and 16) their ability to generate strong pseudo-random sequences increases. This is a quite interesting behaviour since it shows that asynchrony is not always an hindering factor for using CA as PRNG, but can be also employed to strengthen them.

4.5 Type 3 Rules

Possibly the most interesting class of rules is the one where asynchrony is an essential factor in enabling the generation of strong pseudo-random sequences, as it can be observed in Fig. 3.

All of these rules have in common the fact that they pass none of the NIST tests when the updates are synchronous. Once asynchrony is added the behaviour

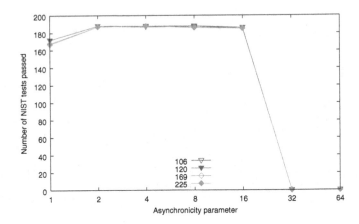

Fig. 2. The number of NIST test passed by type 2 rules with the change in asynchrony

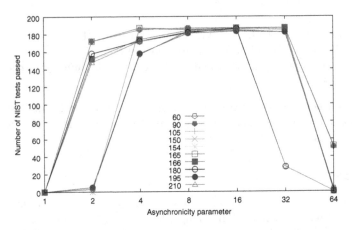

Fig. 3. The number of NIST test passed by type 3 rules with the change in asynchrony

changes drastically. As it is possible to observe in Table 2, the maximum number of NIST statistical tests passed is, for most of the rules neat the maximum (188). Among the rules considered, there are simple ones, like rule 90, the "traffic rule", whose behaviour is, in the synchronous case, extremely predictable since, after n steps (in our case $n = 64$) an attacker has enough information on the CA to predict exactly its dynamics. When asynchrony is introduced this ceases to be true and, while there is no assurance that similar predictions are not possible, the statistical tests are unable to expose any clear regularity in the resulting data.

An observation of the results, however, shows that not all rules in this class share exactly the same behaviour, even if, in the general trend, they are all quite similar. Therefore, we can further subdivide the rules of this class into four distinct sub-classes:

1. rules 154 and 166 already show increased scores in the tests with $k = 2$, showing that even a limited amount of asynchrony is sufficient;
2. rules 180 and 210 perform similarly to 154 and 166, but they show a decrease for $k = 32$ that is not present in the latter two rules;
3. rules 60, 105, 150, and 195 require more asynchrony ($k = 4$) before reaching high enough scores in the statistical tests;
4. rules 90 and 165 are able to pass more tests than any other rule for full asynchrony (51 and 52 tests, respectively).

In particular, the last case is of particular interest, since it seems to highlight that the two considered rules have some characteristic that is able to counteract, in a limited way, the effect of full asynchrony. It could be interesting to understand what this characteristic is in order to take it into account in the design of new CA-based PRNG.

Table 2. The maximum number of tests passed by the rules of type 3 together with the value of the asynchrony parameter where the maximum was reached.

Rule	60	90	105	150	154	165	166	180	195	210
Max score	184	187	186	187	186	187	187	186	183	187
k		16	8, 16, 32	4	4	16	4, 16, 32	32	16	16	16

5 Conclusions

In this paper we have explored the effect of increasing levels of asynchrony in ECA used as PRNG. Since they can be employed in cryptographic applications, it is important to understand what is the edge that an attacker can gain by disturbing the global clock regulating the update of the cells. Three different interesting behaviours were found. The least unexpected one is the type 1 behaviour, where there is an abrupt decrease in the pseudo-randomness quality of the sequences generated when asynchrony increases. Similar to the first class, type 2 CA exhibit a more complex behaviour, where a limited amount of asynchrony produces an increase in the pseudo-randomness quality of the generated sequences, while a further increase greatly reduces it. Finally, CA of type 3 are usually unsuited to be used as PRNG, but a limited amount of asynchrony make them competitive with the traditional rules employed for pseudo-random number generation. It is noticeable the fact that there are no CA where the decrease in quality is smoother; it appears as if the qualities necessary for obtaining a good PRNG are "binary": they are either almost all present or almost all absent.

This preliminary study opens many different possibilities for exploring the relationship between pseudo-randomness and asynchrony. It is currently unknown if the same behaviours can also be found in CA with radius grater than 1 or if new behaviours will appear. The results found for CA of type 3 open a lot of questions on why such CA need asynchrony to generate pseudo-random sequences: what are the factors that make them predictable when synchronous and unpredictable when asynchronous? Moreover, the way asynchrony has been introduced in this study is quite limited: the updates are always performed in contiguous blocks of the same size. It would be interesting to study if different updating patterns produce different behaviours or if the observed ones are all the possible ones.

Finally, another direction for further research is to relate the results presented in this paper with the cryptographic properties of the considered local rules. An interesting starting point could be to compare the three classes of rules observed in our experiments with respect to the property of *asynchrony immunity*, recently introduced in [20]. Of course, this line of research could also be generalised to rules of higher radius.

References

1. Balzter, H., Braun, P.W., Köhler, W.: Cellular automata models for vegetation dynamics. Ecol. Model. **107**(2), 113–125 (1998)
2. Bandini, S., Rubagotti, F., Vizzari, G., Shimura, K.: A cellular automata based model for pedestrian and group dynamics: motivations and first experiments. In: Malyshkin, V. (ed.) PaCT 2011. LNCS, vol. 6873, pp. 125–139. Springer, Heidelberg (2011). https://doi.org/10.1007/978-3-642-23178-0_11
3. Bassham III, L.E., et al.: SP 800–22 Rev. 1a. A statistical test suite for random and pseudorandom number generators for cryptographic applications (2010)
4. Cappuccio, R., Cattaneo, G., Erbacci, G., Jocher, U.: A parallel implementation of a cellular automata based model for coffee percolation. Parallel Comput. **27**(5), 685–717 (2001)
5. Chopard, B.: Cellular automata modeling of physical systems. In: Meyers, R. (ed.) Encyclopedia of Complexity and Systems Science, pp. 865–892. Springer, New York (2009). https://doi.org/10.1007/978-1-4614-1800-9
6. Daemen, J., Govaerts, R., Vandewalle, J.: A framework for the design of one-way hash functions including cryptanalysis of Damgård's one-way function based on a cellular automaton. In: Imai, H., Rivest, R.L., Matsumoto, T. (eds.) ASIACRYPT 1991. LNCS, vol. 739, pp. 82–96. Springer, Heidelberg (1993). https://doi.org/10.1007/3-540-57332-1_7
7. Damgård, I.B.: A design principle for hash functions. In: Brassard, G. (ed.) CRYPTO 1989. LNCS, vol. 435, pp. 416–427. Springer, New York (1990). https://doi.org/10.1007/0-387-34805-0_39
8. Dennunzio, A., Formenti, E., Manzoni, L., Mauri, G.: *m*-Asynchronous cellular automata: from fairness to quasi-fairness. Nat. Comput. **12**(4), 561–572 (2013)
9. Fatès, N., Morvan, M.: An experimental study of robustness to asynchronism for elementary cellular automata. Complex Syst. **16**(1), 1–27 (2005)
10. Fatès, N., Morvan, M., Schabanel, N., Thierry, E.: Fully asynchronous behaviour of double-quiescent elementary cellular automata. Theor. Comput. Sci. **362**, 1–16 (2006)
11. Fatès, N., Regnault, D., Schabanel, N., Thierry, É.: Asynchronous behavior of double-quiescent elementary cellular automata. In: Correa, J.R., Hevia, A., Kiwi, M. (eds.) LATIN 2006. LNCS, vol. 3887, pp. 455–466. Springer, Heidelberg (2006). https://doi.org/10.1007/11682462_43

12. Formenti, E., Imai, K., Martin, B., Yunès, J.-B.: Advances on random sequence generation by uniform cellular automata. In: Calude, C.S., Freivalds, R., Kazuo, I. (eds.) Computing with New Resources. LNCS, vol. 8808, pp. 56–70. Springer, Cham (2014). https://doi.org/10.1007/978-3-319-13350-8_5
13. Kanai, M., Nishinari, K., Tokihiro, T.: Stochastic cellular-automaton model for traffic flow. In: El Yacoubi, S., Chopard, B., Bandini, S. (eds.) ACRI 2006. LNCS, vol. 4173, pp. 538–547. Springer, Heidelberg (2006). https://doi.org/10. 1007/11861201_62
14. Klein, A.: Stream Ciphers. Springer, London (2013). https://doi.org/10.1007/978-1-4471-5079-4
15. Leporati, A., Mariot, L.: 1-resiliency of bipermutive cellular automata rules. In: Kari, J., Kutrib, M., Malcher, A. (eds.) AUTOMATA 2013. LNCS, vol. 8155, pp. 110–123. Springer, Heidelberg (2013). https://doi.org/10.1007/978-3-642-40867-0_8
16. Leporati, A., Mariot, L.: Cryptographic properties of bipermutive cellular automata rules. J. Cell. Automata 9(5–6), 437–475 (2014)
17. Manzoni, L., Umeo, H.: The firing squad synchronization problem on CA with multiple updating cycles. Theor. Comput. Sci. 559, 108–117 (2014)
18. Manzoni, L.: Asynchronous cellular automata and dynamical properties. Nat. Comput. 11(2), 269–276 (2012)
19. Manzoni, L., Porreca, A.E., Umeo, H.: The firing squad synchronization problem on higher-dimensional CA with multiple updating cycles. In: 4th International Workshop on Applications and Fundamentals of Cellular Automata - AFCA 2016, Hiroshima, Japan, November 2016
20. Mariot, L.: Asynchrony immune cellular automata. In: El Yacoubi, S., Wąs, J., Bandini, S. (eds.) ACRI 2016. LNCS, vol. 9863, pp. 176–181. Springer, Cham (2016). https://doi.org/10.1007/978-3-319-44365-2_17
21. Martin, B.: A walsh exploration of elementary CA rules. J. Cell. Automata 3(2), 145–156 (2008)
22. Meier, W., Staffelbach, O.: Analysis of pseudo random sequences generated by cellular automata. In: Davies, D.W. (ed.) EUROCRYPT 1991. LNCS, vol. 547, pp. 186–199. Springer, Heidelberg (1991). https://doi.org/10.1007/3-540-46416-6_17
23. Shackleford, B., Tanaka, M., Carter, R.J., Snider, G.: FPGA implementation of neighborhood-of-four cellular automata random number generators. In: Proceedings of the ACM/SIGDA International Symposium on Field Programmable Gate Arrays, FPGA 2002, Monterey, CA, USA, 24–26 February 2002, pp. 106–112 (2002)
24. Sipper, M., Tomassini, M.: Computation in artificially evolved, non-uniform cellular automata. Theor. Comput. Sci. 217(1), 81–98 (1999)
25. Ulam, S.: Random processes and transformations. In: Proceedings of the International Congress on Mathematics, vol. 2, pp. 264–275 (1952)
26. Von Neumann, J.: Theory of self-reproducing automata. University of Illinois Press (1966). Edited by A.W. Burks
27. Wolfram, S.: Cryptography with cellular automata. In: Williams, H.C. (ed.) CRYPTO 1985. LNCS, vol. 218, pp. 429–432. Springer, Heidelberg (1986). https://doi.org/10.1007/3-540-39799-X_32
28. Worsch, T.: A note on (intrinsically?) universal asynchronous cellular automata. In: Proceedings of Automata 2010, Nancy, France, 14–16 June 2010, pp. 339–350 (2010)

Crowds, Traffic and Cellular Automata

Drivers' Behavior Effects in the Occurrence of Dangerous Situations Which May Lead to Accidents

I. M. Almeida[1], R. C. P. Leal-Toledo[1(✉)], E. M. Toledo[2], D. C. Cacau[1], and G. V. P. Magalhães[1]

[1] Federal Fluminense University, Niteroi, Brazil
leal@ic.uff.br
[2] LNCC, UFJF, Petropolis, Brazil

Abstract. This paper presents an analysis how different acceleration policies to reach the maximum speed of the road, considered as a heterogeneity unobserved in usual measurements, influence the probability of occurrence of Dangerous Situations (DS) that can lead to accidents between vehicles. For this, a modified version of the NaSch model is proposed. The probability Density Function (PDF) Beta is used to describe these distinct behaviors. The effect of these policies on the traffic dynamics was also analyzed. A new metric is presented so that we can analyze results where real deceleration rates data are used to evaluate accident probability.

Keywords: Accidents · Traffic · Cellular automata
Dangerous Situations · Computer simulation

1 Introduction

In densely populated areas the frequent traffic jams cause significant economic and social damages. In order to make effective planning, traffic flow simulations can be of fundamental importance to better understand traffic flow behavior, in different situations, helping to improve traffic networks design and of the definition of more efficient transportation systems. For this purpose, microscopic numerical models, as those based on Cellular Automata (CA), have emerged as an alternative to model traffic flow helping to understand its behavior. Microscopic models typically focus their attention on the behavior of individual vehicles, the road topology and on the influence coming from neighborhood vehicles.

The fundamental traffic model proposed by Nagel and Schreckenberg [1], is a stochastic Cellular Automata model of vehicular traffic, known as the NaSch model. It reproduces the basic features of traffic flow. Many others CA models were proposed trying more realistic traffic representation. Among these we find the so called "slow to start" rules [2–4] to model the meta-stable traffic flows. Some others models embody anticipation rules in order to take into account

© Springer Nature Switzerland AG 2018
G. Mauri et al. (Eds.): ACRI 2018, LNCS 11115, pp. 441–450, 2018.
https://doi.org/10.1007/978-3-319-99813-8_40

drivers' movement at next time step. By including anticipation and the brake lights concept [5–9] in the modeling, the vehicles do not solely determine their velocities based on the distance to the next vehicle in front of it, but they also consider the speed and the deceleration of the ahead vehicle. Others models try to include characteristics of driver's behavior at the moment of the definition of its new speed [6,10,11].

The dense road traffic has increased the number of accidents. The absence of observations of behaviors that can potentially cause modifications in traditional analyses, may lead to erroneous inferences or erroneous accident predictions. To carry out simulations that can bring information about the effects of distinct acceleration policies behavior is fundamental to understand occurrence of roads Dangerous Situations (DS) that can lead accidents.

Recently, cellular automata models have been extended to investigate car accidents probabilities. Boccara et al. [12] were the first authors to propose conditions for car accidents occurrences in the deterministic NaSch model. Huang et al. [13] presented analytical expressions for car accidents in this model with lower maximum velocity, $V_{max} = 1$, and Fukui et al. [14] for high velocities. In Jiang et al. [15], car accidents probabilities are obtained for the so called velocity effect (VE) model. Moussa [16] analyzes car accidents occurrence based on delayed reaction time of the successor car. More recently, Bentaleb et al. [17] presents car accidents occurrence probability in the extended Nagel-Schreckenberg (NaSch) model considering fast and slow vehicles. It also analyzes the effect of damaged vehicles evacuation from the road. Results of car accidents probabilities for the non deterministic NaSch model were obtained [18–20] and also for two-lane CA model [21]. The influence of speed limit zone in roads [22] and intersections [23] were also analyzed for open boundary conditions and Speed Limit Zone. Madani and Moussa [24] present results for NaSch Model and NaSch model with the "slow-to-stop" rule.

In this work we present a modified version of the NaSch model that proposes to evaluate numerically how distinct acceleration policies, to reach the same maximum speed of the road, can influence the traffic dynamics and the Dangerous Situations (DS) evaluation that can result in traffic accidents. Simulating these behaviors, unobserved in usual measurements, can contribute to improve the procedures that evaluate the probability of accidents on roads, actual deceleration data were used to evaluate the accidents probability and the results were compared to those obtained when the road maximum velocity changes. The paper is structured as follows: Sect. 2 presents the NaSch modified model, with heterogeneity in acceleration and deceleration policies and its influence in the traffic flow. Section 3 describes conditions for the occurrence of Dangerous Situations and analyzes results for distinct acceleration policies. In Sect. 4 we show results when actual deceleration data were used to evaluate the probability of accidents. Discussions and conclusions are presented in Sect. 5.

2   Modified Nagel-Schreckenberg Model

The Nagel-Schreckenberg (NaSch) model is a one-dimensional probabilistic cellular automata traffic model, that represents the lane as a lattice of cells, where a vehicle occupies one cell and each cell is either empty or occupied by one vehicle. At any instant of time t, a vehicle occupies the cell $x(i,t)$ and has the velocity $v(i,t)$, which tells how many cells it will move at that instant of time. The number of unoccupied cells in front of each vehicle, generally called as gap, is denoted by $d(i,t) = x(i+1,t) - x(i,t-1) - L$, where $L = 1$ is the vehicles' length, and the vehicle $i+1$ is considered to be in front of the vehicle i. A periodic boundary condition is considered. The four distinct rules applied in parallel for all vehicles are given by *Algorithm 1* (Table 1):

Table 1. Algorithm 1.

(1) Acceleration	$v(i, t+1) = min[v(i,t) + A, V_{max}]$
(2) Deceleration	$v(i, t+1) = min[v(i, t+1), d(i,t)]$
(3) Random deceleration	$v(i, t+1) = max[v(i, t+1) - A, 0]$, with a probability p
(4) Movement	$x(i, t+1) = x(i,t) + v(i, t+1)$

The model uses parameters such as: V_{max}, the maximum velocity that a vehicle can reach; A, the acceleration rate of the vehicles; p, the stochastic parameter that represents the probability through which a vehicle randomly slows down, aiming to model the uncertainty about the drivers' behavior.

The traditional NaSch model sets $A = 1\,\text{cell/s}^2$. The typical length of a cell is $7.5\,\text{m}$. Each time step corresponds to one second, resulting vehicles' speed multiples of $1\,\text{cell/s}$, which is equivalent to $27\,\text{km/h}$. Also, V_{max} is typically set as $5\,\text{cell/s}$, corresponding to $135\,\text{km/h}$.

Although being a simple model, the NaSch model is able to represent traffic's main characteristics such as the spontaneous occurrence of traffic jams and to show the relation between traffic flow and density, representing two different phases (free and congested flow) and a transition stage between them [25].

2.1   The Proposed Modification in the NaSch Model

Despite the random deceleration rule in the NaSch model, the parameter A is a constant. We investigate whether different acceleration policies influence in traffic dynamics or not. A more refined lattice discretization is proposed to allow the representation of these different policies and each driver's profile tends to accelerate in a characteristic way: abruptly (aggressive profile) or more smoothly (non aggressive profile). A non-uniform Probability Density Function (PDF) is used to describe trends in the drivers' acceleration policy. The new acceleration parameter is stochastic and is calculated as $A = int[(1 - \alpha)A_{max}]$, where α is a random value between 0 and 1 and *int* is the function that returns the nearest integer of its argument. Therefore, the probability p models the drivers' intention to accelerate while α models how they will accelerate. In this work, α is modeled by a continuous Beta Function (PDF), defined as $B(a,b) = \Gamma(a+b)/[\Gamma(a)\Gamma(b)x^{a-1}(1-x)^{b-1}]$, where $0 \le x \le 1$ and $\Gamma(n+1) = n!$, n is a positive integer. Depending on the values of the parameters a and b, majority of α values will tend to different values between 0 a 1 and those closer to 0 will produce accelerations A closer to A_{max}, while those closer to 1 will produce accelerations A closer to 0. In fact, the α values float around the Beta mean value, which are given by $\mu = \frac{a}{a+b}$. Thus, it is possible to predict each profile acceleration trend based on the average of the Beta function used to model it. Therefore, each profile is defined by a different pair (a,b) of parameters, that defines a Beta function, and the different mean values of these distributions model the desired acceleration tendencies.

2.2   Numerical Results

For all results presented in this paper, the parameters of the model are set as: size of the cell equal to 1.5 m; $V_{max} = 25$ cell/s $= 135$ km/h; $A_{max} = 5$ cell/s$^2 = 7.5$ m/s^2; $p = 0.30$. To maintain analogy with the traditional NaSch model, a vehicle in our model occupies 5 cells $= 7.5$ m. Beta functions were chosen to represent the different acceleration policies, with distinct averages and similar variance. Besides the results from traditional NaSch model, four different profiles were considered in this work, the Beta functions that describe their acceleration are: $B(10,30)$, Aggressive profile, with an average acceleration of $\mu = 4$ cells/s^2; $B(20,28)$, called Intermediary I, with $\mu = 3$ cells/s^2; $B(28,20)$, Intermediary II, with $\mu = 2$ cells/s^2 and $B(30,10)$, Non-Aggressive profile, with $\mu = 1$ cells/s^2.

All the simulations were performed with a lane composed of 10,000 cells, with density varying from 1 to 100 (given in percentage of occupied cells). An usual simulation varies the density ρ, while keeping constant the parameters V_{max}, A, and p. A total of 15,000 time units were simulated, but only the data from the last 5,000 units were taken into consideration since transient effects were not the target. The modified model was configured, to every profile, with $A_{max} = 5$ cell/s^2, $V_{max} = 25$ cell/s, $p = 0.30$. The simulation starts with vehicles at random positions and $V = 0$.

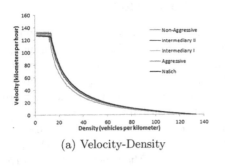   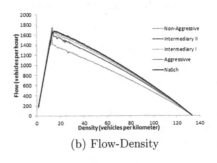

(a) Velocity-Density   (b) Flow-Density

Fig. 1. Diagrams

Traffic Flow, $Vmax = 25$ cell/s. In this section, we present in Fig. 1, fundamental (flow-density) and velocity-density diagrams for traditional and modified NaSch model. Since $V_{max} = 135$ km/h in all simulations, Fig. 1(a) and (b) show the impact of the different acceleration policies on traffic dynamics. In the free flow region of the diagram presented in Fig. 1(a), the mean velocity of the *Aggressive* driver is lower than the *Non-Aggressive* one, under the same speed limit. However, the inverse happens when the interaction between vehicles begins. Even though the modified model takes the NaSch as base, the *Non-Aggressive* profile starts to represent the meta-stability region in Fig. 1(b).

3   Conditions for the Occurrence of Dangerous Situations

In this work we analyzed the impact the consideration of different drivers profiles has in the occurrence of situations that can lead to traffic accidents, which is a heterogeneity unobserved in usual measurements in a usual scenario. It should be noted, in rule (2) of *Algorithm*1, that the models prevent collisions between vehicles. Thus, we analyze the occurrence of dangerous situations (DS) which could lead to collisions between vehicles in a real scenario. As usual, we consider the DS caused by sudden deceleration and sudden stop and adapt the conditions utilized by Moussa [12,16,24].

3.1   Dangerous Situations Caused by Sudden Deceleration

Real accidents frequently happen when vehicles are at high speeds and a sudden deceleration occurs. If the vehicle i, that is behind the $i+1$, is near enough, this situation may lead to an accident. Hence, we consider a Dangerous Situation (DS) due to sudden deceleration when the following conditions are satisfied:

Condition 1: $\tau \cdot v(i,t) > d(i,t) + v(i+1,t+1)$
Condition 2: $v(i+1,t) - v(i+1,t+1) \geq V_d$

τ is a reaction time and the parameter V_d is the deceleration limit, beyond which the risk of an accident exists. In Condition 1, the vehicle i has a velocity v greater than the space d it has to move at the current time. The Condition 2 indicates when the front car has decelerated more than a limit V_d, previously defined.

3.2   Dangerous Situations Caused by Sudden Stop

In this definition of DS, the vehicle $i+1$ will stop at the next instant of time and, since the vehicle i, that is behind it, is close enough, this situation might lead to an accident. In this context, the following conditions are satisfied:

Condition 1: $\tau \cdot v(i,t) > d(i,t)$
Condition 2: $v(i+1,t) \geq V_{min}$
Condition 3: $v(i+1,t+1) = 0$

where V_{min} is a velocity limit, beyond which the risk of an accident exists. In Condition 1, the vehicle i is close enough to the vehicle ahead, i.e. it is at a speed v greater than the space it has to move at the current time. In Condition 2, the vehicle ahead $i+1$ is moving with a velocity higher than or equal to V_{min} at the current instant of time. The Condition 3 indicates that the vehicle ahead $i+1$ will stop at the next instant of time $t+1$. Moussa [16] and Madani and Moussa [24], in their work with the NaSch model, consider $V_{min} = 1\,cel/s$, what corresponds to 27 km/h in their discretization. In this work we can represent velocities smaller than 27 km/h.

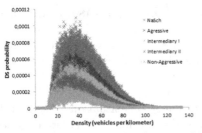

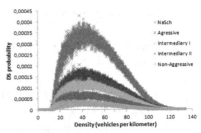

(a) DS due to sudden deceleration, $V_d = 10\,m/s^2$

(b) DS due to sudden stop, with $V_{min} = 5\,cell/s$

Fig. 2. Analysis of Dangerous Situations (DS)

3.3 Numerical Results

The probability per vehicle and per time step for a DS to occur is denoted by Pds. Figure 2(a) presents the results for the probability of Dangerous Situations (Pds) due to sudden deceleration, using $V_d = 10\,cell/s = 15\,m/s^2$, while Fig. 2(b) presents results for the Pds due to sudden stop, using $V_{min} = 5\,cell/s = 27\,km/h$, to compare with results presented in Madani and Moussa [24] for the NaSch model. In all simulations we consider $\tau = 1\,s$. We can observe that in the free flow region, since vehicles do not stop, there are no vehicle accidents. The value of the critical density where DS is maximum appears to remain unchanged with respect to the four different Beta functions.

Note that in the NaSch model, drivers have a constant acceleration rate A and, for the discretization used in this work, $A = 5\,cell/s^2$. The most aggressive driver considered in the modified NaSch model here proposed, accelerates $A = 4\,cell/s^2 = 6.0\,m/s^2$ in average. For comparison reasons, the results presented for the NaSch model were obtained following the propositions of Madani and Moussa [24]. It is noticeable in Fig. 2(b) that, even under the same speed limit, the more aggressive the profile is, the higher is the probability of occurrence of DS.

4   Conditions for the Occurrence of Accidents

In the previous section we presented conditions that analyzed the occurrence of dangerous situations (DS) that can cause traffic accidents. However, in some cases an attentive driver would be able to avoid the accident. In this section we propose a new metric to evaluate the existence of DS that are highly probable to lead to accidents in a real scenario.

4.1   Accidents Probability

We intended to evaluate if a considered vehicle would be able to brake and avoid collision, given a maximum deceleration rate parameter being counted as an accident wich does not occur. The metric is similar to the case of sudden stop, but now it is taken into account the maximum deceleration rate MDR a real vehicle is capable of performing. Thus, the conditions are defined as:

Condition 1: $v(i,t) - d(i,t) \geq MDR$
Condition 2: $v(i+1,t) > 0$
Condition 3: $v(i+1,t+1) = 0$

Condition 1 indicates whether the vehicle i would have sufficient distance to brake or not. If $v(i,t) - d(i,t) \geq MDR$, then the vehicle i needs to perform a deceleration higher than MDR, what would be impossible in a real scenario. Conditions 2 and 3 represent the sudden stop.

4.2   Numerical Results

Accident Probability. Figure 3(a) presents the result obtained for $MDR = 5\,\text{cell/s}^2 = 7.5\,\text{m/s}^2$ as the maximum deceleration rate that a vehicle could perform in a real scenario. Thus, we consider a real accident when a vehicle needs to decelerate more than $7.5\,\text{m/s}^2$.

We considered that the Maximum Deceleration Rate (MDR) of a normal vehicle is between 6.0 and $9.0\,\text{m/s}^2$. Figure 3(b) presents the result of accident probability for the *Aggressive* driver, where the parameter MDR is varied.

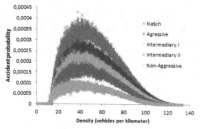 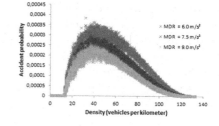

(a) Accident probability, for different drivers profile, $MDR = 5$ cell/s^2

(b) Aggressive driver for different MDR

Fig. 3. Relations of the accident analysis with maximum deceleration rate (MDR)

The Influence of the Speed Limit and the Drivers' Behavior. Results presented in the previous sections indicate that the acceleration policies impact decisively on the number of accidents in the road. Thus, in order to compare the influence of the speed limit of the road with the impact of the acceleration policy of the drivers in the accident probability, we present a comparative result in Fig. 4(a). Five different driver profiles, with different speed limits, were considered: (1) Aggressive drivers with the speed limit of $V_{max} = 25$ cell/s; with $V_{max} = 20$ cell/s; with $V_{max} = 15$ cell/s; and with $V_{max} = 10$ cell/s; (2) Non-Aggressive drivers with the speed limit of $V_{max} = 25$ cell/s. It can be observed in Fig. 4(a) that, for the used metric, even with the decrease of the speed limit for the Aggressive profile, its curve remains well above the curve for the Non-Aggressive profile with a much higher speed limit. This indicates that the vehicle acceleration policy has greater impact on the number of accidents due to collision between vehicles than the speed limit, except in Region 1 (Fig. 4), where in profiles using $V_{max} = 135$ km/h there is already interaction between vehicles, earlier than the curves using $V_{max} < 135$ km/h with Agressive profile.

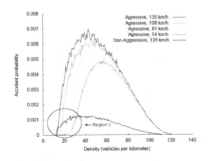 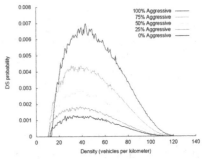

(a) Influence of V_{max} against the acceleration profile.

(b) Sudden stop, with $V_{min} = 5\,cell/s$, for different profile ratios.

Fig. 4. Accident analysis

The situation in which the road is filled with drivers of different acceleration profiles is also analyzed. Aggressive and Non-Aggressive profiles, with the same speed limit of $V_{max} = 25$ cell/s, are used to simulate that situation. Figure 4(b) presents results obtained due to sudden stop with $V_{min} = 5$ cell/s, where different ratios for the Aggressive profile were considered. These results suggest that the probability of Dangerous Situations increases as the road's ratio of drivers with aggressive acceleration policies increases.

5   Conclusions

In this article we presented a modified version of the NaSch model that proposes to numerically analyze the influence of heterogeneity due to different acceleration policies for vehicles under the same speed limit, that usually is an unobserved situation in usual traffic flow measuring. To enable this analysis, the lane discretization was refined and heterogeneity was introduced in the drivers' acceleration, using a continuous probability density function, the Beta function, to model it. The usage of functions with different mean values made possible the consideration of drivers with different steering behaviours, given by their acceleration profile. Dangerous Situations on roads, which can cause collisions between vehicles, were also analyzed for this modified NaSch model. Actual deceleration rates data was used to evaluate the probability of accidents and the obtained results were compared to those obtained when varying the road's maximum velocity.

Having distinct drivers' behaviors allowed us to capture its effects on traffic dynamics and evaluate the most important features of the traffic flow phenomena. It was shown, for instance, how the fundamental diagram are affected by these behaviors. We observed that, even under the same maximum velocities, different policies influences the flow, improving the average speed in free flow regimes and altering the region of bottled flow, depending on the considered profile.

Using the Dangerous Situation definition [12,16,24], adapted for our proposed modified NaSch model, we noted that DS decreased with more cautious acceleration policies. We also observed that these behaviors have fundamental importance on avoiding collisions between vehicles and may be more relevant than the maximum speed of the road.

Acknowledgement. Authors thank CNPq/PIBIC/PIBIT (UFF, LNCC) scholarship.

References

1. Nagel, K., Schreckenberg, M.: A cellular automaton model for freeway traffic. Journal de physique I **2**(12), 2221–2229 (1992)
2. Takayasu, M., Takayasu, H.: 1/f noise in a traffic model. In: Fractals in Natural Sciences, pp. 486–492 (1994)
3. Barlovic, R., Huisinga, T., Schadschneider, A., Schreckenberg, M.: Open boundaries in a cellular automaton model for traffic flow with metastable states. Phys. Rev. E **66**(4), 046113 (2002)
4. Kuang, H., Zhang, G.X., Li, X.L., Lo, S.M.: Effect of slow-to-start in the extended BML model with four-directional traffic. Phys. Lett. A **378**(21), 1455–1460 (2014)
5. Larraga, M.E., del Río, J.A., Schadschneider, A.: New kind of phase separation in a CA traffic model with anticipation. J. Phys. A: Math. General **37**(12), 3769 (2004)
6. Larraga, M.E., Alvarez-Icaza, L.: Cellular automaton model for traffic flow based on safe driving policies and human reactions. Physica A: Stat. Mech. Appl. **389**(23), 5425–5438 (2010)
7. Knospe, W., Santen, L., Schadschneider, A., Schreckenberg, M.: Towards a realistic microscopic description of highway traffic. J. Phys. A: Math. General **33**(48), L477 (2000)
8. Knospe, W., Santen, L., Schadschneider, A., Schreckenberg, M.: A realistic two-lane traffic model for highway traffic. J. Phys. A: Math. General **35**(15), 3369 (2002)

9. Tian, J.F., Jia, N., Zhu, N., Jia, B., Yuan, Z.Z.: Brake light cellular automaton model with advanced randomization for traffic breakdown. Transp. Res. Part C: Emerg. Technol. **44**, 282–298 (2014)
10. Zamith, M., Leal-Toledo, R.C.P., Clua, E.: A novel cellular automaton model for traffic freeway simulation. In: Sirakoulis, G.C., Bandini, S. (eds.) ACRI 2012. LNCS, vol. 7495, pp. 524–533. Springer, Heidelberg (2012). https://doi.org/10.1007/978-3-642-33350-7_54
11. Zamith, M., Leal-Toledo, R.C.P., Clua, E., Toledo, E.M., de Magalhães, G.V.: A new stochastic cellular automata model for traffic flow simulation with drivers' behavior prediction. J. Comput. Sci. **9**, 51–56 (2015)
12. Boccara, N., Fuks, H., Zeng, Q.: Car accidents and number of stopped cars due to road blockage on a one-lane highway. J. Phys. A: Math. General **30**(10), 3329 (1997)
13. Huang, D.W.: Exact results for car accidents in a traffic model. J. Phys. A: Math. General **31**(29), 6167 (1998)
14. Fukui, M., Ishibashi, Y.: Traffic flow in 1D cellular automaton model including cars moving with high speed. J. Phys. Soc. Jpn. **65**(6), 1868–1870 (1996)
15. Jiang, R., Jia, B., Wang, X.L., Wu, Q.S.: Dangerous situations in the velocity effect model. J. Phys. A: Math. General **37**(22), 5777 (2004)
16. Moussa, N.: Car accidents in cellular automata models for one-lane traffic flow. Phys. Rev. E **68**(3), 036127 (2003)
17. Bentaleb, K., Lakouari, N., Marzoug, R., Ez-Zahraouy, H., Benyoussef, A.: Simulation study of traffic car accidents in single-lane highway. Phys. A: Stat. Mech. Appl. **413**, 473–480 (2014)
18. Huang, D.W., Wu, Y.P.: Car accidents on a single-lane highway. Phys. Rev. E **63**(2), 022301 (2001)
19. Yang, X.Q., Ma, Y.Q.: Car accidents in the deterministic and nondeterministic Nagel-Schreckenberg models. Modern Phys. Lett. B **16**(09), 333–344 (2002)
20. Jiang, R., Wang, X.L., Wu, Q.S.: Dangerous situations within the framework of the Nagel-Schreckenberg model. J. Phys. A: Math. General **36**(17), 4763 (2003)
21. Moussa, N.: Simulation study of traffic accidents in bidirectional traffic models. Int. J. Modern Phys. C **21**(12), 1501–1515 (2010)
22. Zhang, W., Yang, X.Q., Sun, D.P., Qiu, K., Xia, H.: Traffic accidents in a cellular automaton model with a speed limit zone. J. Phys. A: Math. General **39**(29), 9127 (2006)
23. Marzoug, R., Echab, H., Lakouari, N., Ez-Zahraouy, H.: Car accidents at the intersection with speed limit zone and open boundary conditions. In: El Yacoubi, S., Was, J., Bandini, S. (eds.) ACRI 2016. LNCS, vol. 9863, pp. 303–311. Springer, Cham (2016). https://doi.org/10.1007/978-3-319-44365-2_30
24. Madani, A., Moussa, N.: ICS: an interactive control system for simulating the probability of car accidents with object oriented paradigm and cellular automaton. Int. J. Comput. Sci. Eng. **3**(8), 2965 (2011)
25. Gerwinski, M.: Krug: analytic approach to the critical density in cellular automata for traffic flow. Phys. Rev. E **60**(1), 188 (1999)

Cellular Automata Based Modeling of Competitive Evacuation

Grzegorz Bazior$^{(\boxtimes)}$, Dariusz Pałka, and Jarosław Wąs

Faculty of Electrical Engineering, Automatics, Computer Science and Biomedical Engineering, Department of Applied Computer Science, AGH University of Science and Technology, Mickiewicza 30, 30-059 Krakow, Poland
{bazior,dpalka,jarek}@agh.edu.pl

Abstract. In the paper we present a model using Cellular Automata dedicated for competitive evacuation. Floor field models of pedestrian dynamics are the starting point. We have observed that during competitive evacuation, the dynamics of particular pedestrians is similar to the dynamics of particles in granular flow when viscosity is taken into account. In order to address this issue we have prepared real experiments and have proposed and implemented a Cellular Automata model using an idea of viscosity.

Keywords: CA-based models · Pedestrian dynamics
Competitive evacuation · Crowd dynamics · Evacuation · Viscosity

1 Introduction

The rules of behavior of people in different situations are of interest to architects, engineers and security managers. Competitive evacuation is one of the greatest challenges, in particular when it occurs in a situation of high density of pedestrians [7]. Generally, simulation of such situations is not a trivial task, especially if we take into account a discrete framework. However, discrete models are generally much more efficient and useful for simulations of large scenarios. It should be stressed that in classical CA-based models like [2,10] different physical analogies, namely: floor fields, bosons, transition functions, etc. are applied. There are no direct calculations of superposition of forces for particular pedestrians like in molecular dynamics models of granular flow [6,9], however, one can point out hybrid algorithms [3,15] when some forces influence the movement of pedestrians in terms of CA lattices.

The main concept in many CA based models is the static floor field [2,5, 16], which points out attractors – pedestrians' aims [13], and dynamic floor field which provide mechanisms analogous to chemo-taxis. Sample mechanisms regulating pedestrians' speeds in CA models, are discussed in [1,8].

In this paper our starting point is a classical CA-based model of floor field and we propose additional rules which mimic movement in high densities when pedestrians become competitive. Idea of friction in pedestrian dynamics was proposed in [11,12]. We propose extension of this idea taking into account analysis

© Springer Nature Switzerland AG 2018
G. Mauri et al. (Eds.): ACRI 2018, LNCS 11115, pp. 451–459, 2018.
https://doi.org/10.1007/978-3-319-99813-8_41

of viscosity in high densities. In our approach friction is dependent on the pressure force (precisely - crowd pressure) and we take into consideration pressure from different directions. In order to address this issue we performed some real experiments which illustrate viscosity in high densities.

2   Motivation and Observations

When a group of people relocates in the conditions of high density, apart from social forces, additional direct physical forces caused by mutual pressure appear. These forces result in jams in narrow passages, that is the speed of movement of particular persons decreases. In case of pressure, people from the back pass the narrow passage much more slowly than in a situation when there is no crowd. While describing human traffic, most discrete models based on Cellular Automata do not take into account physical effects between people in high density, which happen e.g. during competitive evacuations. It might considerably influence the accuracy of simulation results, e.g. while setting the time required for the evacuation of a building.

In one of Cracow's universities we have carried out a set of experiments with competitive (Fig. 1) and non-competitive evacuation (Fig. 2).

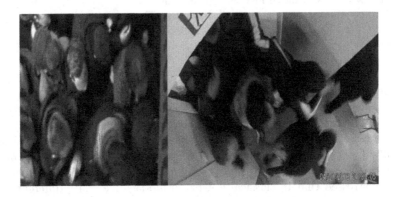

Fig. 1. Experiments with competitive evacuation. Blockages are visible.

A group of 68 students took part in the experiments and their task was to pass the door following two scenarios. We have divided experiments for two parts: during the first one they had to obtain the best individual time and during the second one they had to obtain the best time for the whole group [14]). The door width was 1 m.

During competitive evacuation we observed high local densities and congestions. We also observed stopping of particular participants (Fig. 1).

During non-competitive evacuation we observed no rivalry between pedestrians and lower densities of pedestrians. Due to much less pressure between

Fig. 2. Experiments with non-competitive evacuation.

students in this situation blockades in the narrow passage were not observed (Fig. 2).

One can distinguish different flow characteristics during the experiments. In Fig. 3 we present pedestrians' flow through the door per second.

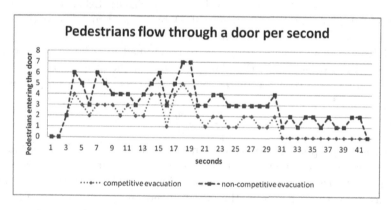

Fig. 3. Flow per second in various experiment scenarios per 1 m of door width. As we can see competitive evacuation has lower maximum flow, but it takes shorter for entire group.

Analogously, we present density of participants (students) in the analyzed scene (Fig. 4).

3 Proposed Model

3.1 Basic Issues

In order to map the dependence between the speed of moving through narrow passages and the crowd's pressure, the movement of a group of people will be

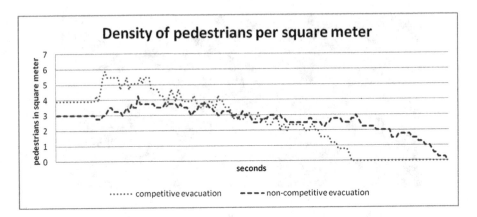

Fig. 4. Density of pedestrians per 1 square meter during competitive evacuation.

compared to fluid flow. In describing fluid flow with the use of equations of motion, viscosity is an important factor. Adopting the approach from classic physics textbooks (e.g. [4]), the impact of viscosity on the fluid motion can be illustrated with the following experiment (see Fig. 5). Let us assume that we have two flat plates and liquid (e.g. water) between them. The bottom plate is fixed, and the top plate is moving horizontally with speed v_0, as a result of applied force F. The force which needs to be applied in order to keep speed v_0 is proportional to the area of the plates (A) and to the proportion v_0/d, where d is the distance between the plates. So, shear stress (F/A) is proportional to v_0/d:

$$\frac{F}{A} = \mu \frac{v_0}{d} \tag{1}$$

Viscosity is the proportionality factor μ in this formula. If force F, area A and the distance d between the plates are the same, when viscosity increases, the speed with which the top plate moves decreases. Analogously, if we treat a group of people as fluid, the decrease in the speed of motion which happens in narrow passages for high densities (in case of the crowd pressure) can be explained as the increase of liquid viscosity. So, for high densities the crowds behave as non-Newtonian fluid, for which - when the pressure grows (caused by the increase of the forces operating between persons) - viscosity grows (shear thickening fluid).

3.2   The Details of the Model

The model presented in this paper is an extended version of standard models of Cellular Automata, which are based on static and dynamic fields. The extension is achieved by introducing additional interactions between persons representing physical forces occurring in situation with high density of crowds (e.g. in case of competitive evacuation). These interactions can increase the pressure affecting particular persons and, by doing this, increase viscosity in a given area. A classic

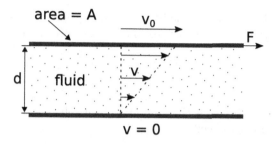

Fig. 5. Velocity of fluid layers between two plates. Based on [4].

CA model [2] has been applied in the study as the base model. Following this model, physical interactions have been introduced as additional bosons transferred between cells occupied by individuals - we call them 'p-bosons' (physical forces bosons). These bosons propagate between consecutive time steps of the simulation (we assume that the speed of propagation of interactions is much higher that the speed with which these individuals move). Individuals whose preferred direction of movement is directed at the cell occupied by another individual (one person presses another) are the source of p-bosons creation. A p-boson also carries information about the direction of this interaction (it is the same as the direction of pressure exerted by one person on another) - it can assume one of 8 values (consistent with the Moore neighborhood). Bosons are propagated along the direction of the impact till the moment when cells are occupied by other individuals; at the moment when an empty cell appears, a boson cascade is no longer propagated. It corresponds to a situation occurring in real life: physical interactions between persons are propagated only for a crowd with high density; when density is low, the interaction is no longer propagated. When p-bosons reach a person who faces an obstacle (a wall or people pressing him from this direction) on his other side (looking from the direction of a given boson), they increase viscosity in the cell occupied by this person. In case of a wall, i.e. a fixed obstacle, all p-bosons coming from the opposite direction increase viscosity - let us call them compensated bosons. When bosons reach a person pressed by other people from the opposite direction (bosons have an opposite direction), the number of compensated bosons is the smaller value of the number of bosons coming from two opposite directions.

3.3   The Impact of Viscosity on People's Movement

As it was shown above, the consequence of the increase of viscosity is the decrease of the maximum speed $v0$ with which a layer of liquid moves. Analogously, when people move, the increase of viscosity should lead to the decrease of the speed with which they move. Because in the base model [2] the speed of moving is constant and equals 40 cm (the length of the side of the cell) divided by 1 time step (that is 1/3 of a second), the introduction of slowing down must be expressed as the lack of movement (remaining in the same cell) in a given time step. In the proposed model it was assumed that the probability of a blockade (lack of movement of a given person) is proportional to viscosity in a given cell:

$$P_{blockade} \sim \mu \tag{2}$$

where:

- $P_{blockade}$ is probability of a blockade in a given cell
- μ is viscosity in a given cell

The proportionality factor can be introduced to the equation above:

$$P_{blockade} = c \cdot \mu \tag{3}$$

where:

- c is proportionality factor

The higher physical pressure is exerted on a person by other people (the number of compensated p-bosons), the more slowed down the person will be, and the greater viscosity will appear in the cell occupied by this person. The c factor's value can be estimated empirically by comparing with data from real life experiments.

4   Implementation and Results

We have implemented the above mentioned floor field model using $C++$ programming language. Our starting point was a classical floor field model [2].

In order to compare the results of the simulation with experimental data, we prepared a simulation with analogous geometry and allocation of pedestrians. The initial allocation of pedestrians visualised as 3D figures is visible in Fig. 6:

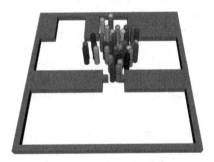

Fig. 6. Initial allocation of participants (before opening the door).

Next we compared two versions of the application. Firstly, we implemented a traditional floor field model without the viscosity mechanism. A sample screenshot from the simulation is visible in Fig. 7.

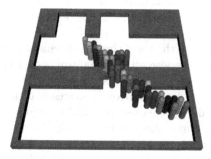

Fig. 7. Simulation of the competitive scenario without viscosity after 4.7 s since the simulation started.

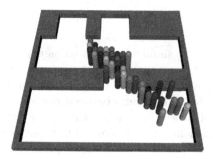

Fig. 8. Simulation of the competitive scenario with viscosity after 4.7 s since the simulation started.

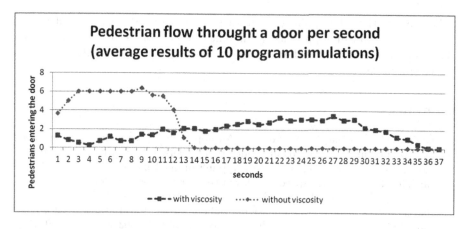

Fig. 9. Flow per second in our program with and without considering viscosity (flow through 1 m of door width).

Next we implemented a floor field model with the viscosity mechanisms. As we can see, it reflects a situation of local congestions caused by a competitive behavior of pedestrians.

As can be seen in Fig. 9, the total time of evacuation in case of a traditional floor field model without the viscosity mechanism is over two times shorter then when this mechanism is present. Such fast movement of people is possible when density is low, that is there are no narrow passages or other obstacles which slow the crowd down and make people exert physical pressure on one another. In case of high density such fast movement is impossible due to a frequent occurrence of blockades. The proposed viscosity mechanism can improve the model in such situations - as can bee seen in Figs. 9 and 3 the total time of evacuation (that is a time step during which flow through the door continues) estimated by the model with the viscosity mechanism and time obtained in real life experiments are similar (Fig. 8).

5   Conclusions

We have performed a set of simulations as well as experiments regarding non-competitive and competitive evacuation. We have noticed that the great pressure between participants particularly influences flow in the bottleneck. The pressure is more clearly visible in blockages between participants in the door. Thus, competitive behavior of pedestrians, when the exit is narrow (1 m) makes the evacuation process inefficient - we observe the faster-is-slower effect.

In the simulation part of our study we have proposed applying the concept of viscosity, which is responsible for the transition function in high densities, to competitive behavior of pedestrians. We compared classical floor field models with a model including the viscosity mechanism. We have confirmed that such a mechanism can reflect the faster-is-slower effect [17] during competitive evacuation.

We believe that the application of idea of viscosity for pedestrian flow is a convenient mechanism of presenting different levels of competitive evacuation or even panic. Discrete modes like CA are efficient, thus such an implementations can be profitable.

References

1. Bandini, S., Crociani, L., Vizzari, G.: An approach for managing heterogeneous speed profiles in cellular automata pedestrian models. J. Cell. Autom. **12**, 401–421 (2017). https://www.researchgate.net/publication/316583613_An_approach_for_managing_heterogeneous_speed_profiles_in_cellular_automata_pedestrian_models
2. Burstedde, C., Klauck, K., Schadschneider, A., Zittartz, J.: Simulation of pedestrian dynamics using a two-dimensional cellular automaton. Phys. A: Stat. Mech. Appl. **295**(3–4), 507–525 (2001). https://doi.org/10.1016/S0378-4371(01)00141-8
3. Dietrich, F., Koester, G., Seitz, M., von Sivers, I.: Bridging the Gap: from cellular automata to differential equation models for pedestrian dynamics. J. Comput. Sci. **5**(5), 841–846 (2014)

4. Feynman, R., Leighton, R., Sands, M.: The Feynman Lectures on Physics, The Definitive: Feynman Lectures on Physics, vol. 2, 2nd edn. California Institute of Technology, California (2005)
5. Gwizdałła, T.M.: The evacuation process study with the cellular automaton floor field on fine grid. In: El Yacoubi, S., Wąs, J., Bandini, S. (eds.) ACRI 2016. LNCS, vol. 9863, pp. 248–257. Springer, Cham (2016). https://doi.org/10.1007/978-3-319-44365-2_25
6. Helbing, D., Molnár, P.: Social force model for pedestrian dynamics. Phys. Rev. E 51(5), 4282–4286 (1995). https://doi.org/10.1103/PhysRevE.51.4282
7. Kirchner, A., Klüpfel, H., Nishinari, K., Schadschneider, A., Schreckenberg, M.: Simulation of competitive egress behavior: comparison with aircraft evacuation data. Phys. A: Stat. Mech. Appl. 324(3), 689–697 (2003). http://www.sciencedirect.com/science/article/pii/S0378437103000761
8. Kirchner, A., Klüpfel, H., Nishinari, K., Schadschneider, A., Schreckenberg, M.: Discretization effects and the influence of walking speed in cellular automata models for pedestrian dynamics. J. Stat. Mech.: Theory Exp. 2004(20), P10011 (2004). http://stacks.iop.org/1742-5468/2004/i=10/a=P10011
9. Korecki, T., Pałka, D., Wąs, J.: Adaptation of social force model for simulation of downhill skiing. J. Comput.l Sci. 16, 29–42 (2016). https://doi.org/10.1016/j.jocs.2016.02.006
10. Nishinari, K., Kirchner, A., Namazi, A., Schadschneider, A.: Extended floor field ca model for evacuation dynamics. IEICE Trans. Inf. Syst. E87–D, 726–732 (2004)
11. Schadschneider, A.: Conflicts and friction in pedestrian dynamics. In: Umeo, H., Morishita, S., Nishinari, K., Komatsuzaki, T., Bandini, S. (eds.) ACRI 2008. LNCS, vol. 5191, pp. 559–562. Springer, Heidelberg (2008). https://doi.org/10.1007/978-3-540-79992-4_76
12. Schadschneider, A., Seyfried, A.: Validation of ca models of pedestrian dynamics with fundamental diagrams. Cybern. Syst. 40, 367–389 (2009). https://www.researchgate.net/publication/220231745_Validation_of_CA_Models_of_Pedestrian_Dynamics_with_Fundamental_Diagrams
13. Vizzari, G., Manenti, L., Ohtsuka, K., Shimura, K.: An agent-based pedestrian and group dynamics model applied to experimental and real-world scenarios. J. Intell. Transp. Syst. 19(1), 32–45 (2015). https://doi.org/10.1080/15472450.2013.856718
14. Wąs, J.: Experiments on evacuation dynamics for different classes of situations. In: Klingsch, W.W.F., Rogsch, C., Schadschneider, A., Schreckenberg, M. (eds.) Pedestrian and Evacuation Dynamics 2008, pp. 225–232. Springer, Berlin Heidelberg, Berlin, Heidelberg (2010). https://doi.org/10.1007/978-3-642-04504-2_17
15. Wąs, J., Gudowski, B., Matuszyk, P.J.: Social distances model of pedestrian dynamics. In: El Yacoubi, S., Chopard, B., Bandini, S. (eds.) ACRI 2006. LNCS, vol. 4173, pp. 492–501. Springer, Heidelberg (2006). https://doi.org/10.1007/11861201_57
16. Wei, X., Song, W., Lv, W., Liu, X., Fu, L.: Defining static floor field of evacuation model in large exit scenario. Simul. Model. Pract. Theory 40, 122–131 (2014). https://doi.org/10.1016/j.simpat.2013.09.007
17. Wei-Guo, S., Yan-Fei, Y., Bing-Hong, W., Wei-Cheng, F.: Evacuation behaviors at exit in ca model with force essentials: a comparison with social force model. Phys. A: Stat. Mech. Appl. 371, 658–666 (2006). https://www.sciencedirect.com/science/article/pii/S0378437106003633

Simulating Pedestrian Dynamics in Corners and Bends: A Floor Field Approach

Luca Crociani[1][(✉)], Kenichiro Shimura[2], Giuseppe Vizzari[1],
and Stefania Bandini[1,2]

[1] Complex Systems and Artificial Intelligence research center,
University of Milano-Bicocca, Viale Sarca, 336 - U14, 20126 Milan, Italy
{luca.crociani,giuseppe.vizzari,stefania.bandini}@disco.unimib.it
[2] Research Center for Advanced Science and Technology, The University of Tokyo,
4-6-1, Komaba, Meguro-Ku, Tokyo 153-8904, Japan

Abstract. Computer simulation for the study of pedestrian dynamics is an active and lively area in which contributions from different disciplines still produce advancements on the state of the art. Discrete modelling of pedestrian dynamics represents a more computationally efficient approach than the continuous one, despite the potential loss of precision in the reproduced trajectories or modelling artefacts. To overcome these issues and reducing the intrinsic effects of employing a discrete environment, several works have been proposed focusing on distinct objectives within this framework. This paper proposes a general approach to reproduce smooth and rounded trajectories of pedestrians in presence of bends and corners, by means of a so-called angular floor field. The proposed algorithm works with arbitrary settings and it is tested on benchmark situations to evaluate its effects from both a quantitative and qualitative perspective.

Keywords: Cellular automata · Pedestrian dynamics
Angular floor field

1 Introduction and Related Works

Computer simulation systems for the study of pedestrian dynamics is at the same time an application area in which research has completed its cycle, producing technological transfer, and an active and lively area in which contributions from different disciplines still produce advancements on the state of the art. Discrete pedestrian simulation models are viable alternatives to particle based models, based on a continuous spatial representation (see, e.g., [13]) and they are able to reproduce realistic pedestrian dynamics from the point of view of a number of observable properties. The well-known *floor-field* [3] model represents the most successful representative of Cellular Automata approaches to pedestrian simulation, with numerous extensions and improvements over the initial definition.

ⓒ Springer Nature Switzerland AG 2018
G. Mauri et al. (Eds.): ACRI 2018, LNCS 11115, pp. 460–469, 2018.
https://doi.org/10.1007/978-3-319-99813-8_42

While models adopting a continuous spatial representation can present issues in generating smooth but also plausible trajectories in particular situations (see, e.g., [12] for conceptual issues in even relatively simple situations, but also [8] for technical issues in the numerical implementation of force-based continuous models), the intrinsic limits in generating clean trajectories with discrete models are well-known, and they show up particularly in geometries where the effective trajectories of pedestrians become less linear (e.g., a corner). On the other hand, several works aimed at quantifying and, if possible, reducing the effects and errors provided by the discretization can be found in the literature: for example, the works [9,16] study the influence of rotation of the rectangular grid on the simulated space utilization. Moreover, a set of verification and validation tests particularly tailored for discrete models and for the quantification of the influence of discretization errors on the simulated pedestrian dynamics has been proposed in [11].

In this line of work, this paper presents an approach to improve the plausibility of trajectories crossing corners and bends, with the definition of a particular floor field describing values of *angular distance* towards the target. It must be noted that the idea of angular fields to induce circular trajectories of pedestrian is not completely new in the literature: [14] introduced a static field in polar coordinates to simulate the circumnavigation around the Kaaba during the ritual of the Tawaf. The problem of simulating plausible trajectories at corners is also discussed by Dias and Lovreglio [5], who propose two versions of static field – a discrete and a continuous one – both empirically estimated (although just with a dataset describing trajectories of individual pedestrians walking in a 90-degree corner setting).

In this paper we aim at providing a more general approach, defining an algorithm to generate potential fields from targets in arbitrary geometries and considering the possible presence of obstacles. The algorithm for the computation of the field makes use of a mapping function that translates the coordinates of cells. The algorithm is completely general but it has been tested with a discrete simulation model made by the authors [1], which is briefly introduced in Sect. 2. The approach for the calculation of angular fields is described in Sect. 3 and analysed in the next section with benchmark tests for a quantitative evaluation, considering the fundamental diagram in a corner scenario, and a qualitative one by checking the simulated trajectories of pedestrians. Conclusions will end the paper.

2   A Discrete Model for Pedestrian and Group Dynamics

The model here described and used to test the algorithm for the generation of the angular floor field is the one firstly introduced in [15], and later extended and improved with many works by the authors (e.g. [1]) allowing the reproduction of heterogeneous speeds and group behaviour.

The model is an extension of the classic floor field model [3] and it employs the same space discretization by means of a rectangular grid of 0.4×0.4 m^2 cells.

Positions of obstacles and the configuration of the environment is allowed by means of *spatial markers*, defining: (*i*) areas where pedestrians will be generated; (*ii*) obstacles; (*iii*) final destinations; (*iv*) intermediate destinations, used to divide the environment in smaller components and to allow the computation of higher-level paths for pedestrians to their final destination; (*v*) labels describing the name and typology of environment the cell belongs to (e.g. staircase, ramp, flat floor, etc.).

Space annotation allows the definition of additional grids to the one representing the environment, as containers of information for pedestrians and their movement. This describes the well-known *floor field* approach [3]. These discrete potentials are used to support pedestrians in the navigation of the environment, representing their interactions with static objects or with other pedestrians. Three kinds of floor fields are defined in our model:

- *path field* (static), which indicates distances from one destination;
- *obstacles field* (static), which indicates distances from neighbour obstacles or walls;
- *proxemics field* (dynamic), which provides information to identify crowded areas at a given time-step.

The behaviour of simulated pedestrians at a locomotion layer is defined with probabilistic mechanisms. According to their *desired speed* and to the assumed duration of the time-step of the model, pedestrians are activated for the movement at each turn, and they can move in the Moore neighbourhood of their position. The choice of movement is modelled in a probabilistic fashion by means of a utility function $U(c)$:

$$U(c) = \frac{\kappa_g G(c) + \kappa_{ob} Ob(c) + \kappa_s S(c) + \kappa_c C(c) + \kappa_d D(c) + \kappa_{ov} Ov(c)}{d} \quad (1)$$

$$P(c) = N \cdot e^{U(c)} \quad (2)$$

Parameters κ are the calibration weights allowing to configure a pedestrian-like behaviour and N of Eq. 2 is a normalization factor. Individual functions of Eq. 1 model respectively: (i) attraction towards the current target; (ii) obstacle repulsion; (iii) keeping distance from other pedestrians; (iv) cohesion with other group members; (v) direction inertia; (vi) moving in a cell occupied by another pedestrian (overlapping) to avoid gridlock in counter-flow situations. Details about how these functions are defined will not be provided since they are considered out of the scope of this paper (for a thorough discussion on this aspect, see [1, 15]).

3 A General Algorithm for Angular Fields

The computation of static floor fields can be performed by using several existing methodologies and metrics, as discussed by [10], which lead to very different results and behaviours of simulated pedestrians. Floor fields are generally computed using the Dijkstra's algorithm [6] on the grid of the environment, considering cells as nodes of a graph with edges reflecting the Moore Neighbourhood. The weight of each edge –information used to compute the distance from each cell to the destination– is assigned as the Euclidean distance between the linked cells, so that horizontally or vertically aligned neighbours have distance 1 and other ones have $\sqrt{2}$. Figure 1(a) shows an example computation in a 90° turning, with the destination positioned in the bottom right.

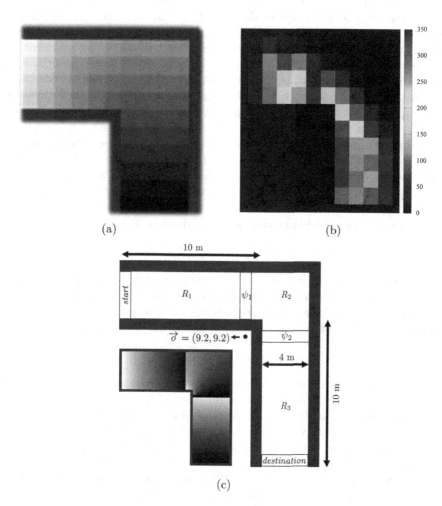

Fig. 1. (a) Gray-scale representation of field values after the computation. (b) Space utilisation of a simulation run (number of time-steps each cell has been occupied). (c) L-shaped scenario used to calculate the fundamental diagram and gray scale representation of floor fields leading towards the destination.

This technique works with arbitrary settings, providing proper paths for pedestrians from any cell of the walkable space and allowing them to avoid obstacles. On the other hand, it can also provide implausible space utilizations of pedestrians with geometries like the example bend, where in the real world pedestrians tend to assume smoothly curved trajectory. In such settings, this field diffusion from a unique destination leads pedestrians to flatten their trajectories close to the wall much before the turning, differently from what is observed in the reality (see, e.g., [5]). Moreover, a pattern of mostly used cells is clearly visible in the direct surrounding of the corner, as shown in Fig. 1(b).

The issue can be addressed by dividing the setting in more *regions*, annotating intermediate destinations (see the test environment in Fig. 1(c)), each one spreading its own floor field in the connected regions of the environment (as discussed by the authors in [4]). This relevantly improves the space utilization in the area before the bend, but it still generates narrow turnings of pedestrians after reaching the first target: once they start following the gradient spread by the target after the bend, their much probably move towards the south direction and this is again a modelling artefact.

In order to generally achieve smooth trajectories when pedestrians have to rotate around corners or obstacles, we introduce an algorithm employing a mapping function $\phi(\vec{x})$ applied to each coordinate $\vec{x}$ of cells, which deforms the geometry by translating the cells of the bend in a "linear" environment where the Dijkstra algorithm with the Euclidean metric will be used. The distance metric between two neighbour cells with coordinates $\vec{i}$ and $\vec{j}$ is, thus, firstly defined as:

$$\delta(\vec{i}, \vec{j}) = ||\phi(\vec{i}) - \phi(\vec{j})|| \tag{3}$$

Regarding the mapping function, we are interested in outcoming a floor field that encodes the *angular distance* between neighbour cells. Hence, we use a function ϕ that transforms the coordinate of cells into polar ones, according to a reference vector $\vec{o}$ and a unit vector $\vec{m}$, as the following function:

$$\phi_{\vec{o},\vec{m}}(\vec{x}) = (\angle(\vec{m}, \vec{x} - \vec{o}), ||\vec{x}||) \tag{4}$$

where $\angle$ is a function returning the counter-clockwise angle between the first and second vector, $\vec{o}$ describes the origin point of the turning (i.e. the corner of the bend) and $\vec{m}$ the direction of the marked intermediate destination, which is calculated as the difference between its farthest cell from $\vec{o}$ and its closest. An example result of the mapping is graphically shown in Fig. 2(a) and (b), considering $\vec{o} = (0,0)$ and $\vec{m} = (1,0)$.

As shown in Fig. 2(c), the usage of the mapping makes the approach robust and generally working with obstacles inside the turning area.

4   Experimental Results

In this section we propose two simulation campaigns aimed at testing the proposed approach for the simulation of bends in benchmark environments. The first

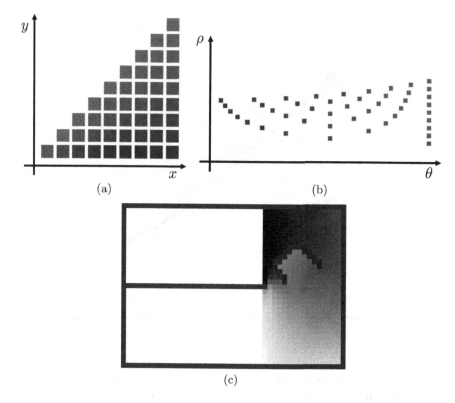

Fig. 2. Mapping cells positions (a) to polar coordinates (b). (c) Computed angular field with an irregular obstacle at the turning.

experiment analyses the dynamics generated in a 90-degree turning at aggregated level with the fundamental diagram, while the second one focuses on the space utilization in a slightly different environment describing a u-turn. For both experiments we configure the same calibration parameters of the model, which have been found to fit well empirical datasets of pedestrian dynamics in other benchmark settings and allowing to reproduce plausible behaviour in low density situations (see [1]).

4.1   Fundamental Diagram in a 90-Degrees Turn

We analyse the fundamental diagram in a L-shaped environment with a 1-directional flow configured as shown in Fig. 1(c). Standard floor fields are generated from the final destination and from the intermediate ψ_1, while the target ψ_2 generates an angular field in the cells of the region R_2. Note that the intermediate destinations have not been placed at the very borders of the corner, but slightly moved "backward", and the origin of the angular field has been assigned to $\overrightarrow{o} = (9.2\,\text{m}, 9.2\,\text{m})$. This is motivated by the fact that pedestrians tend to

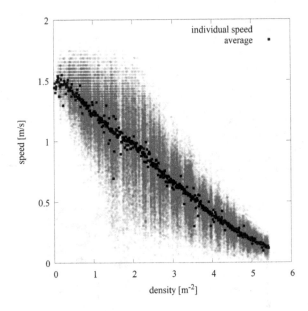

Fig. 3. Results of the simulation campaign in the form density–speed.

start the turning slightly before the border of the bend (see, e.g., in [5]) and, in addition, they usually do not use all the space available inside this geometry.

A unique long simulation of about 50000 time-steps (3.5 h) was run with a very low frequency of generation of pedestrians (about 1 every 100 time-steps) and with their re-introduction in the start area once they arrive at the destination. In this way the whole fundamental diagram is calculated with a unique long run, guaranteeing a sufficiently large number of samples for each density point to achieve a stable average.

In order to compute the fundamental diagram, travel times τ_i of every travel of pedestrians are collected and used to compute the average speed $\nu(\tau_i) = 24/\tau_i$ m/s (24 m represents the length of the central path in the L environment). Results of the density–speed relation are presented in Fig. 3. Overall the results do not show a relevant difference with the simulated fundamental diagram for the 1-directional flow in a corridor, and the data are in good agreement with literature datasets.

4.2   Analysis of Space Utilisation in a U-Turn

For a qualitative evaluation of the behaviour generated in environments with the proposed angular fields, it is now analysed the space utilization on a u-turn environment. To allow the comparison with real world data, we simulated the setting of the controlled experiment discussed in [2]. The experiment studied a 1-directional flow of pedestrians climbing down two short runs of stairs (2.8 m each) linked by a semicircular landing and composing a u-turn. The size of the

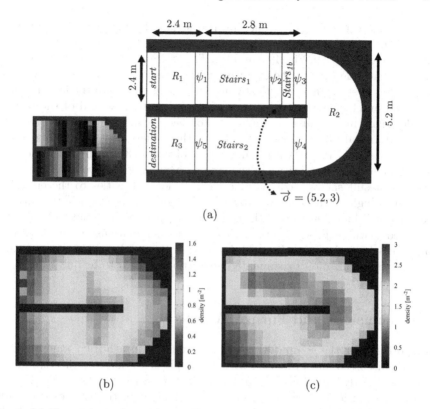

(a)

(b)   (c)

Fig. 4. (a) U-turn scenario used to evaluate the space utilization generated with the proposed angular field, together with a grey scale representation of the path fields followed by simulated pedestrians. (b–c) Cumulative mean density map related to 10 simulation runs for the simulation of the low (b) and high (c) density scenario.

scenario and its annotation are described in Fig. 4(a). Note how the first run of stairs has been divided into two regions: this was done to reproduce the tendency to approach the bend in an inner zone by pedestrian slightly before the end of the staircase –at ψ_2 instead of the target ψ_3 (analogously as in [17]). For both targets ψ_3 and ψ_4, the origin point $\overrightarrow{o}$ is assigned to (5.2 m, 3 m) to reproduce trajectories at the bend closer to the central wall, as it is observed in [2].

Two configurations of the simulation scenario are proposed to analyse the effect of a growing density in the dynamics of the system. A low density scenario is configured with a light incoming flow of about 2.5 ped/s, for a total of 300 pedestrian in a single simulation run. For the high density situation, the experimental procedure S1 of [2] is reproduced, describing a higher incoming flow to the setting with an arrival rate of about 4.4 ped/s (a plausible approximation of the initial bottleneck of 2.4 m of the experiment). To gather a reliable result, 10 iterations of simulation have been run for both scenario and statistics have been averaged accordingly.

We evaluate the usage of space by pedestrians by means of the results of local densities, with a comparison between the cumulative mean density map. The results are shown in Fig. 4(b) and (c). The low density scenario characterizes a free-flow situation where the two areas with higher values in the heat map are the two runs of stairs, and practically no congestion appears in the landing zone. The situation changes at the increase of the incoming flow and of the density of pedestrians inside this environment. For the second scenario, in fact, the configured arrival rate of pedestrians led to the achievement of a similar range of values observed in [2], with a maximum of about $3\,\mathrm{ped/m^2}$, and the heat map highlights higher densities in the landing instead of the two staircases. The simulation result shows a comparable trend of local densities to the empirical data, whose higher values are distributed before and at the center of the turning. The pattern of high densities at the center of the turning turns out to be slightly translated towards the second run of stairs in the simulations and it also seems a bit wider than what was observed, but overall the result is in good agreement and the space utilization by simulated pedestrians appear to be quite similar to the observation.

5   Conclusions and Future Works

An algorithm for the computation of angular fields in arbitrary environments has been discussed and evaluated with the implementation in a discrete model for pedestrian dynamics coming from previous works by the authors [1]. The evaluation tests have shown a good agreement between trajectories simulated with the angular field and empirical ones from a controlled experiments, highlighting that the proposed approach effectively reduces the artefacts generated by the discrete environment. From a more quantitative perspective, the fundamental diagram generated on a L-shaped setting crossed by a 1-directional flow showed a quite similar trend to the standard uni-directional flow in the corridor. While the data are in agreement with literature datasets, the lack of a significant difference between the flow generated in a corridor setting and in the L-shaped environment (as instead is highlighted in, e.g., [7]) suggests that the behaviour of pedestrians at the bend needs further investigation. Our conjecture is that the desired walking speed should decrease due to the fact that the pedestrian cannot anticipate the presence of obstacles or other pedestrians around the corner, and ignoring this actually causes an overestimation of the flow.

References

1. Bandini, S., Crociani, L., Vizzari, G.: An approach for managing heterogeneous speed profiles in cellular automata pedestrian models. J. Cell. Automata **12**(5), 401–421 (2017)
2. Burghardt, S., Seyfried, A., Klingsch, W.: Fundamental diagram of stairs: critical review and topographical measurements. In: Weidmann, U., Kirsch, U., Schreckenberg, M. (eds.) Pedestrian and Evacuation Dynamics 2012, pp. 329–344. Springer, Cham (2014). https://doi.org/10.1007/978-3-319-02447-9_27

3. Burstedde, C., Klauck, K., Schadschneider, A., Zittartz, J.: Simulation of pedestrian dynamics using a two-dimensional cellular automaton. Phys. A: Stat. Mech. Appl. **295**(3–4), 507–525 (2001)
4. Crociani, L., Invernizzi, A., Vizzari, G.: A hybrid agent architecture for enabling tactical level decisions in floor field approaches. Transp. Res. Procedia **2**, 618–623 (2014)
5. Dias, C., Lovreglio, R.: Calibrating cellular automaton models for pedestrians walking through corners. Phys. Lett. A **382**(19), 1255–1261 (2018)
6. Dijkstra, E.W.: A note on two problems in connexion with graphs. Numerische Mathematik **1**(1), 269–271 (1959)
7. Gorrini, A., Bandini, S., Sarvi, M., Dias, C., Shiwakoti, N.: An empirical study of crowd and pedestrian dynamics: the impact of different angle paths and grouping. Transp. Res. Rec. **41**(42), 10 (2013)
8. Köster, G., Treml, F., Gödel, M.: Avoiding numerical pitfalls in social force models. Phys. Rev. E **87**, 063305 (2013)
9. Koyama, S., Shinozaki, N., Morishita, S.: Pedestrian flow modeling using cellular automata based on the Japanese public guideline and application to evacuation simulation. J. Cell. Automata **8**, 361–382 (2013)
10. Kretz, T., Bönisch, C., Vortisch, P.: Comparison of various methods for the calculation of the distance potential field. In: Klingsch, W.W.F., Rogsch, C., Schadschneider, A., Schreckenberg, M. (eds.) Pedestrian and Evacuation Dynamics 2008, pp. 335–346. Springer, Berlin Heidelberg (2010). https://doi.org/10.1007/978-3-642-04504-2_29
11. Lubas, R., Porzycki, J., Was, J., Mycek, M.: Validation and verification of CA-based pedestrian dynamics models. J. Cell. Automata **11**(4), 285–298 (2016)
12. Pettré, J., Ondrej, J., Olivier, A., Crétual, A., Donikian, S.: Experiment-based modeling, simulation and validation of interactions between virtual walkers. In: Proceedings of the 2009 ACM SIGGRAPH/Eurographics Symposium on Computer Animation, SCA 2009, New Orleans, Louisiana, USA, 1–2 August 2009, pp. 189–198 (2009)
13. Schadschneider, A., Klingsch, W., Klüpfel, H., Kretz, T., Rogsch, C., Seyfried, A.: Evacuation dynamics: empirical results, modeling and applications. In: Meyers, R.A. (ed.) Encyclopedia of Complexity and Systems Science, pp. 3142–3176. Springer, New York (2009). https://doi.org/10.1007/978-0-387-30440-3_187
14. Shimura, K., Khan, S.D., Bandini, S., Nishinari, K.: Simulation and evaluation of spiral movement of pedestrians: towards the Tawaf simulator. J. Cell. Automata **11**(4), 275–284 (2016)
15. Vizzari, G., Manenti, L., Crociani, L.: Adaptive pedestrian behaviour for the preservation of group cohesion. Complex Adapt. Syst. Model. **1**(7) (2013)
16. Zawidzki, M.: The influence of grid rotation in von Neumann and Moore neighborhoods on agent behavior in pedestrian simulation. Complex Syst. **23**, 343–354 (2014)
17. Zeng, Y., Song, W., Huo, F., Vizzari, G.: Modeling evacuation dynamics on stairs by an extended optimal steps model. Simul. Model. Pract. Theory **84**, 177–189 (2018)

Study on the Efficacy of Crowd Control and Information Provision Through a Simple Cellular Automata Model

Claudio Feliciani[1]([✉]), Kenichiro Shimura[1], Daichi Yanagisawa[1,2], and Katsuhiro Nishinari[1,2]

[1] Research Center for Advanced Science and Technology, The University of Tokyo, Tokyo 153-8904, Japan
`feliciani@jamology.rcast.u-tokyo.ac.jp`
[2] Department of Aeronautics and Astronautics, Graduate School of Engineering, The University of Tokyo, Tokyo 113-8656, Japan

Abstract. This study presents a simple Cellular Automata model which allows to estimate the combined effect of crowd control and information provision on pedestrian dynamics. We assume the case of a closed loop consisting of two lanes connected in only two points where pedestrians are allowed to move from the inner to the outer loop and in the opposite direction. Both lanes are virtually divided by a wall which does not allow to visually inspect the other side except on the locations connecting them. To investigate the effect of information provision we assume that a given number of pedestrians have information on the speed in both lanes. In addition, we assume that lane changing locations are guarded by security staff which can give orders to the crowd on which lane to choose. However, only a given number of pedestrians are compliant and will obey to the orders. Initial settings for the simulation have been set so that free flow in both lanes is obtained only when the number of lane changes is limited and density is equal in both inner and outer loops. Results show that crowd control strategy, compliance ratio and information provision have a clear impact on the overall group speed. The combined analysis of all variables showed that efficient information provision is the most reliable method to ensure an adequate speed (and flow) even when crowd control fails or when compliance is low.

1 Introduction

The urbanization trend of the last decades has led to an increasing interest to topics related to pedestrian traffic, with crowd management and (real time) information provision taking an important role in this context. A large number of simulation models have been created to allow predicting the motion of pedestrians inside buildings during normal operation and in case of evacuation. Although early simulation models considered pedestrian crowds in a very homogeneous way and were designed for very specific situations [1], modern simulation

© Springer Nature Switzerland AG 2018
G. Mauri et al. (Eds.): ACRI 2018, LNCS 11115, pp. 470–480, 2018.
https://doi.org/10.1007/978-3-319-99813-8_43

tools allow to consider very diverse crowds and to take into account architectural features such as stairs or escalators [2], thus making results more accurate.

It is therefore now possible to design buildings such as transportation hubs or events' venues already considering pedestrian traffic at the early stages of the planning process. This represents a considerable advantage in making those structures more safe and comfortable in regard to pedestrian traffic, since modifications for finished structures are hard to make and very costly.

However, even the most accurate and complex simulation models are still not able to account for psychological features, which represent an important aspect in pedestrian motion [7]. Although research is showing an increasing interest in this direction, it will take a long time until mechanisms of collective psychology will be completely understood and numerical models developed. Even then, very peculiar behavior for a specific type of crowd (football fans, protesters...) may be not exactly modeled as the outbreak of some behaviors is mostly random and dependent on the surrounding events (a goal scored, arrival of the police...). In addition, it is always possible that a mass event taking place in a carefully designed location may deteriorate into a chaotic situation due to poor event planning, thus vanishing the effort made in the design phase for that building.

A consequence of the above discussion is that active crowd control (or guidance) will always play a central role even with the increase in accuracy of simulation models. Having an efficient crowd control strategy (i.e. having a system or staff providing guidance to the crowd) is therefore fundamental to ensure safe and comfortable mass events. While this aspect may be straightforward in theory, practical aspects are much more complex and very specific for the environment and the crowd to be controlled. In addition, while accurate data are not available, it is known that some people (sometimes most of the crowd) tend to not follow suggestions from guidance personnel and under those conditions crowd control is therefore ineffective.

To ensure smoother pedestrian motion, information provision may also help, thus allowing the crowd itself to take decisions based on accurate facts rather than their own perception. With this said, it is not always possible (or easy) to inform everyone (for example in the case of people with hearing/visual disabilities) and some people may ignore information surrounding them.

In this study we consider a simple scenario and investigate how the different aspects discussed above relate to each other's and which strategy is the most effective to increase pedestrian flow and speed in a specific situation.

2   Selected Case Study

The scenario presented here has been inspired by the "fork case" often considered in vehicular traffic; a situation which occurs when a large road connecting two locations get divided into two smaller roads for most of its length. When all the cars take one road, traffic jams occur and average travel time between both locations increases. To ensure that both roads are used equally, optimal information provision is required at the time drivers decide which road to use.

A number of studies [4,5,8–10] have focused their attention on these optimal strategies and the type of information which is required to avoid traffic jam.

To adapt it to pedestrian traffic and also account for the effect of crowd control, we will consider a partially different design. The general idea is to recreate a situation where a structure generating a large amount of pedestrian flow is connected to another point attracting it (like a train station and a stadium for example). It is often the case that different direct paths are connected each other's by smaller transverse routes which allow to change path in case of congestion.

In simulations, it is convenient to consider a loop, which allows to recreate an infinite path. We can therefore assume a loop consisting of two paths: an inner route and an outer route. Both paths get connected in two opposite locations where pedestrians may move from one path to the other in case of need. A schematic representation of the scenario considered for this study is given in Fig. 1(a).

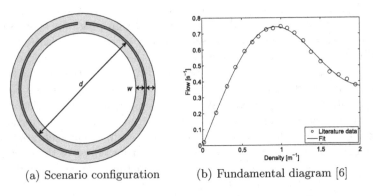

(a) Scenario configuration   (b) Fundamental diagram [6]

Fig. 1. Scenario considered for the simulation and fundamental diagram for pedestrian unidirectional motion. Chosen values are: $d = 10\,$m and $w = 0.8\,$m.

Now, in order to enforce the need for crowd control it is necessary to choose initial conditions which will either require an action from the crowd to avoid congestion or an external intervention. We can further assume that in the locations where lane change is allowed, pedestrians either decide to change by themselves or are forced by guidance personnel present on-site (supervisors).

To choose the best initial configuration it is necessary to consider the fundamental diagram for pedestrians, which is presented in Fig. 1(b) using data from the literature by Jelić et al. [6]. Given the diameter of the loop, the width of both paths and the number of pedestrians for each route in the initial setup it is possible to compute the flow. By selecting a very different number of pedestrians between the inner and outer loop the total flow will be lower than the optimal flow reached when density is uniform everywhere (given in Fig. 2(b)).

To create a realistic scenario which could possibly be reproduced experimentally in the future, a crowd of 60 people is chosen. Figure 2(a) shows the ratio

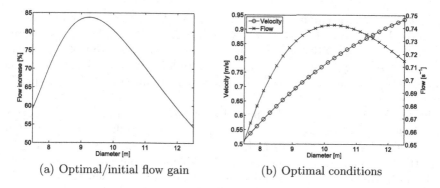

(a) Optimal/initial flow gain   (b) Optimal conditions

Fig. 2. Optimal conditions (right) and increase in flow relative to the initial configuration (left) for different values of mid-diameter. Both graphs are created using the
fitting of the experimental data by Jelic et al. given in Fig. 1(b).

between the total initial flow and the optimal flow for a starting configuration
having 50 people in the inner loop and 10 people in the outer one (both values
are chosen to create a large optimal/initial difference). The maximum gain in
Fig. 2(a) is found for a diameter of about 9.2 m and consequently we decided
to use a mid-diameter (between inner and outer loop) of 10 m. Under these
circumstances the optimal speed is about 0.78 m/s (see Fig. 2(b)).

3   Cellular Automata Model

The hypothetical scenario presented above has been written into a Cellular
Automata simulation model whose characteristics are described in this section.
To simplify the computational algorithm, instead of two loops two horizontal
parallel paths have been used. The end of each path is connected with its start
so that the endless characteristic of the loops is recreated. Path width was chosen
equal 0.8 m with a cell size of 0.4 m. Considering those dimensions and the mid-
diameter chosen earlier, the internal and external loops had a length of 73 and
85 cells respectively. Lane change locations have been set at a uniform distance
along the mid-path[1] (see Fig. 3).

Fig. 3. Computational grid used in the model. Positions for lane change are given in
dark gray and pedestrians as dots.

---

[1] Since inner and outer loop have different lengths, lane change location is not exactly
uniformly distributed in the linear representation. On average there is a 6 cells
difference between both lane change positions in both loops.

Motion inside each loop is computed based on the Fukui–Ishibashi model [3]. This model was chosen because it allows to reproduce the fundamental diagram of pedestrian motion with good accuracy and account for its asymmetry in regard to density (see Fig. 1(b)). In addition, its rules for position update are rather simple, thus allowing more flexibility in adding more important aspects specific for this study.

In the Fukui–Ishibashi model, particles (or pedestrians in this case) can proceed for a maximum of u_{max} cells with a hopping probability $p = (0, 1]$ if they have at least u_{max} empty cells in front. If the empty space is less than u_{max} cells, they will proceed as many cells as possible with the same hopping probability p. In this study $u_{max} = 2$ and $p = 0.85$ have been taken to fit with the experimental fundamental diagram found in the literature.

In our analysis we will always consider long time intervals (several hours) to generate results. Under this assumption, it is possible to use the following equation to get a velocity expressed in physical units which can be useful to quickly evaluate the results:

$$V = \frac{X}{S \cdot N} \cdot \frac{v_{free}}{p \cdot u_{max}} \tag{1}$$

In (1) X is the total distance traveled by all pedestrians (in cells), N is the number of pedestrians (60 here), S is the total number of simulation time steps and v_{free} is the free walking speed (set at $1.20\,\mathrm{m/s}$ here).

The time step has been chosen considering that the maximum distance traveled by one person in one time step is stochastically given by $\Delta x \cdot u_{max} \cdot p$ with Δx being the mesh length. Considering the free walking speed and the numerical values provided earlier, the time step can be computed as:

$$\Delta t = \frac{\Delta x \cdot u_{max} \cdot p}{v_{free}} = 0.57 \text{ s} \tag{2}$$

Parallel update is used for computing positions at each iteration, i.e. pedestrians reserve their position before actually moving and conflicts (which occur only when changing loop) are resolved with equal probability among contenders.

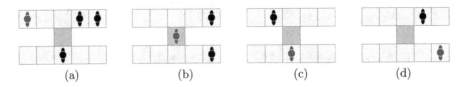

Fig. 4. Example for a lane change from outer to inner loop. Pedestrian considered is given in blue (dark gray). Images from (a) to (d) are in sequential order. (Color figure online)

An additional important aspect in the dynamics of the model are the rules used for lane change. A pedestrian is allowed to change lane when he/she is at a distance of one or two cells from the lane change position (remember that pedestrians are allowed to move a maximum of two cells per iteration). If the cell used for lane change is empty he/she is allowed to move to that location and later enter the opposite loop. If the central cell is occupied he/she will have to keep moving and may have a chance to change loop at the next location. Figure 4 shows an example for a pedestrian moving from the outer to the inner loop. In all the cases, lane change results in a slowdown (in particular when entering the new loop) as it should be in the real case.

In our model, we assume that each lane change position is supervised, i.e. switching direction (move to inner or outer loop) is given by the corresponding supervisor. We further assume that pedestrians can be compliant (i.e. will follow any order given) or non-compliant (ignore orders). Compliant ratio is the ratio of compliant pedestrians over the total number. Finally, we assume that a variable portion of pedestrians have access to reliable information (informed pedestrians), i.e. they know the walking speed for each loop. In practical terms, we can consider those people as having access to navigation systems or paying attention to information given in monitors along the path. Informed ratio is the number of informed pedestrians over the total.

Under those assumptions lane change for a given pedestrian may occur under the following conditions:

- *The pedestrian is compliant.* If a lane change is ordered he/she will move to the loop indicated by the corresponding supervisor. Non-compliant pedestrians can ignore those orders and follow their own intuition as given below.
- *The pedestrian is non-compliant.* If that pedestrian has information on the speed in both loops (informed pedestrian), he/she can decide to move based on a rational decision (i.e. he/she will choose the fastest one if the difference is larger than $0.1\,\mathrm{m/s}$). All pedestrians are able to remember the walking speed for the last $10\,\mathrm{s}$. Consequently, non-informed pedestrians can decide to change loop by comparing their recent walking speed with the one of the opposite loop when the lane change position is reached. If the other lane is faster they will move in it.

To account for the effects of crowd control, different strategies has been used to determine how supervisors give information to pedestrians in each lane change location. The three scenarios considered here are listed as follow:

- *Worst-case scenario:* each supervisor has a limited field of view (90°) and take decisions by his/her own. Order for lane change will be issued so that both lanes have the same number of pedestrians. This quickly leads into a long lane taking half of the inner and half of the outer loop (see Fig. 5(a)).
- *Best-case scenario:* each supervisor has a complete overview (360°) of the area and knows the density in each loop. In addition, both will work together until the density difference between both loops is below $0.05\,\mathrm{m^{-1}}$. The final outcome will be something like the case shown in Fig. 5(b).
- *Realistic scenario:* each supervisor has a limited view (again 90°) but both are communicating with each other's considering a communication delay of

2 s and a reaction time before acting of 3 s (this "reaction time" also includes the decision making process, hence the relative long time used).

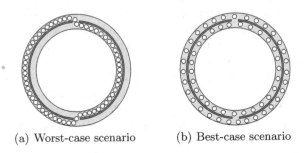

(a) Worst-case scenario   (b) Best-case scenario

Fig. 5. Typical results for different crowd control strategies.

4   Results

Using the model presented above a number of simulations have been run by changing the compliant ratio, the number of people informed and the crowd control strategy. Starting condition for each simulation has been of 50 people in the inner loop and 10 in the outer loop, mid-diameter has been chosen of 10 m. Average overall speed has been used as a parameter to calibrate and validate the model and to measure the efficacy of crowd control strategies and information provision.

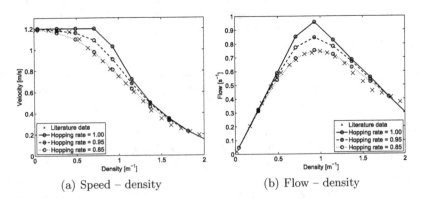

(a) Speed – density   (b) Flow – density

Fig. 6. Comparison between experimental fundamental diagram from literature [6] and numerical results obtained using the Fukui–Ishibashi model.

4.1 Validation of Fundamental Dynamics

First of all, in order to find the most appropriate parameters and check the validity of the Fukui–Ishibashi model used for the dynamics of pedestrians, we run a number of simulations for the simplest case, i.e. without loop change and with the same density in both loops. Results for different values of hopping probability are given in Fig. 6. Each simulation has been run for a corresponding time of one hour. In general, a fairly good agreement is found for a hopping probability of 0.85 for the whole range of densities considered in this study (a maximum of $1.76\,\mathrm{m^{-1}}$ is found when all the 60 people are in the inner loop).

4.2 Effect of Information Provision and Compliance

We can now consider the case where it is possible to change lane and those locations are supervised by crowd control personnel. Results for simple situations considering information provision and compliance *separately* are given in Fig. 7. To study information provision, we assumed that pedestrians are free to choose (in other words all are non-compliant and crowd control strategy is irrelevant), while for compliance we assumed a completely non-informed crowd.

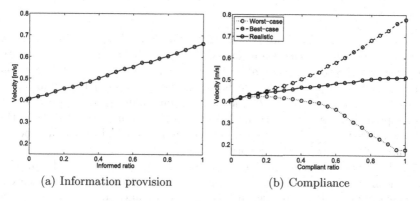

(a) Information provision   (b) Compliance

Fig. 7. Simple effect of information provision and compliance on the speed of the crowd for different crowd control strategies.

From Fig. 7(a) it is seen that information provision has a linear effect on the overall speed of the group. The more people are informed the faster the crowd moves. The relation with compliance (given in Fig. 7(b)) clearly depends on the strategy used for crowd control, with the realistic case lying between both extreme scenarios. In general, compliance has a slightly non-linear relationship, which becomes more evident for high level of compliance.

4.3 Combined Effect and Relation with Crowd Control

Finally, we wish to consider the effect of compliance and information provision *together* and see how this may affect the overall speed of the group in regard to the different crowd control strategies presented earlier. In this regard, both the compliant and the informed people ratio have been varied for the three crowd control strategies generating the three diagrams shown in Fig. 8. A variable number of 10 to 40 one-hour simulations were run to generate each dot.

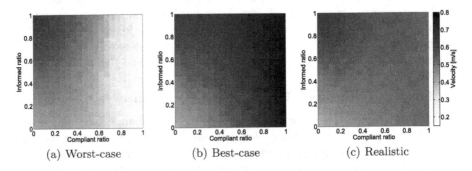

(a) Worst-case   (b) Best-case   (c) Realistic

Fig. 8. Influence of compliance and information provision on the overall speed of the group considering three different crowd control strategies. Color scale is the same for the three cases and is given on the right. (Color figure online)

In the worst-case scenario it is clearly seen that when compliance is high pedestrians are at the mercy of supervisors, who, by failing in their control strategies, contribute to considerably slowing down the whole crowd. When compliance is low (and pedestrians are basically free to choose) then information provision plays a more important role and the maximum speed is found for the non-compliant case where everyone is informed. It is important to notice that in the worst-case scenario difference between minimum and maximum speed is large (around 0.50 m/s) and the optimal speed is never reached.

The best-case scenario shows the opposite result compared to the previous case. The maximum speed, which is equal to the optimal one in this case, is found for fully compliant crowds. In this case, compliance seems to play a minor role when all people are informed, making the upper part of Fig. 8(b) almost constant. In the best-case scenario speed difference is lower than the previous case (0.37 m/s), showing that optimal crowd control strategies benefit in all conditions.

Finally, we can consider the realistic case, whose result is a sort of average between the worst-case and best-case scenario. As for the previous cases, speed is obviously constant along the full-compliant line. In this case, it is however interesting to notice that the non-compliant informed case has an higher speed (0.72 m/s) than the compliant uninformed case (0.55 m/s). Overall, the three cases show that having an informed crowd is more important than focusing on crowd control and compliance. While only a small improvement is found in the best-case scenario, differences get easily larger as the crowd control strategy fails.

5   Conclusions

In this study, a hypothetical scenario where both pedestrians' compliance and information provision have an impact on the overall performance of the system has been presented and studied through a Cellular Automata simulation model. Results clearly showed that when compliance is high, the crowd control strategy has a dramatic effect on the overall system and the advantages of having an informed crowd are nullified. On the other hand, having an informed crowd represents the best tradeoff, guaranteeing that even when crowd control is not optimal, good results in terms of crowd dynamics are obtained. Results also show that in case of a complete failure of crowd control an informed not-compliant crowd may still represent the best outcome given the worst-case condition.

Although the case studied here is very simple and more research need to be done on the subject by also considering more in detail decision making for large crowds, results may suggest that, when a choice is needed, informing a crowd should be prioritized on enforcing organizers' decision, especially when the outcome of crowd control is uncertain.

Acknowledgments. This work was partially supported by JST-Mirai Program Grant Number JPMJMI17D4, Japan.

References

1. Blue, V., Adler, J.: Cellular automata microsimulation of bidirectional pedestrian flows. Transp. Res. Rec.: J. Transp. Res. Board **1678**, 135–141 (1999). https://doi. org/10.3141/1678-17
2. Daamen, W.: SimPed: a pedestrian simulation tool for large pedestrian areas. In: Conference Proceedings EuroSIW, pp. 24–26 (2002)
3. Fukui, M., Ishibashi, Y.: Traffic flow in 1D cellular automaton model including cars moving with high speed. J. Phys. Soc. Jpn. **65**(6), 1868–1870 (1996). https:// doi.org/10.1143/JPSJ.65.1868
4. Hino, Y., Nagatani, T.: Effect of bottleneck on route choice in two-route traffic system with real-time information. Phys. A: Stat. Mech. Appl. **395**, 425–433 (2014). https://doi.org/10.1016/j.physa.2013.10.044
5. Imai, T., Nishinari, K.: Optimal information provision for maximizing flow in a forked lattice. Phys. Rev. E **91**(6), 062818 (2015). https://doi.org/10.1103/ PhysRevE.91.062818
6. Jelić, A., Appert-Rolland, C., Lemercier, S., Pettré, J.: Properties of pedestrians walking in line: fundamental diagrams. Phys. Rev. E **85**(3), 036111 (2012). https:// doi.org/10.1103/PhysRevE.85.036111
7. Templeton, A., Drury, J., Philippides, A.: From mindless masses to small groups: conceptualizing collective behavior in crowd modeling. Rev. Gen. Psychol. **19**(3), 215 (2015). https://doi.org/10.1037/gpr0000032
8. Wahle, J., Bazzan, A.L.C., Klügl, F., Schreckenberg, M.: The impact of real-time information in a two-route scenario using agent-based simulation. Transp. Res. Part C: Emerg. Technol. **10**(5–6), 399–417 (2002). https://doi.org/10.1016/S0968-090X(02)00031-1

9. Wang, W.X., Wang, B.H., Zheng, W.C., Yin, C.Y., Zhou, T.: Advanced information feedback in intelligent traffic systems. Phys. Rev. E **72**(6), 066702 (2005). https://doi.org/10.1016/S0968-090X(02)00031-1

10. Yokoya, Y.: Dynamics of traffic flow with real-time traffic information. Phys. Rev. E **69**(1), 016121 (2004). https://doi.org/10.1103/PhysRevE.69.016121

Cumulative Mean Crowding and Pedestrian Crowds: A Cellular Automata Model

Andrea Gorrini[1($\boxtimes$)], Luca Crociani[1], Giuseppe Vizzari[1],
and Stefania Bandini[1,2]

[1] Department of Computer Science, Complex Systems and Artificial Intelligence
research center, University of Milano-Bicocca, Milan, Italy
{andrea.gorrini,luca.crociani,giuseppe.vizzari,
stefania.bandini}@disco.unimib.it
[2] Research Center for Advanced Science and Technology, The University of Tokyo,
Tokyo, Japan

Abstract. Cellular Automata simulations of crowd dynamics can support the design of transportation facilities in terms of efficiency, comfort and safety. The development of realistic CA models requires the acquisition of empirical evidences about human individual and collective behavior. The paper reports the results of controlled experiments of personal space in static and dynamic situations: the area surrounding human body, linked to crowding due to spatial intrusion/restriction. We propose a discrete representation of personal space through discrete potentials and an innovative crowding estimation method (i.e. Cumulative Mean Crowding). Simulation results are focused on the parametric evaluation of pedestrians' psychological stress reaction to density.

Keywords: Modeling and simulations · Pedestrian crowds
Personal space · Crowding

1 Introduction

The use of advanced computer-based systems for the simulation of pedestrian crowd dynamics is a consolidated and successful domain, thanks to its capability to support the design of mass gathering and transportation facilities (including large stadiums, railway stations, subways and other venues where effective positioning of entry and exit points is required), offering optimized architectural solutions in terms of efficiency, comfort and safety. Although there are some objections about the simplified level of correspondence between computer-based simulations and crowd phenomena [19], the use of advanced simulation systems offer a sufficient level of expressiveness allowing to envision those phenomena that are difficult to be directly observed in real scenarios, testing alternative conditions and courses of action (i.e. *what-if scenarios*).

© Springer Nature Switzerland AG 2018
G. Mauri et al. (Eds.): ACRI 2018, LNCS 11115, pp. 481–491, 2018.
https://doi.org/10.1007/978-3-319-99813-8_44

In order to finalize pedestrian crowd simulations into operational steps it is necessary the acquisition of empirical evidences about human behavior, considering both individual and collective behavioral dynamics. This is aimed at defining descriptive sets of metrics and parameters for characterizing crowd phenomena, supporting the development of computational models against real data. In line with other Cellular Automata models present in the literature [1,16,23,24], the current work is aimed at applying the general framework of the Proxemic Theory [11], coming from anthropology and environmental psychology, to define a microscopic CA model focused on spatial interpersonal distances among pedestrians and psychological stress reaction in situation of variable density.

The condition of inappropriate proximity with others or spatial restriction in crowded situations represents, in fact, a stressful factor among human beings. Pedestrian crowd dynamics are characterized by turbulences and reciprocal competition, due to the low degree of freedom for spatial positioning. Continuous and sudden detouring maneuvers are needed to adjust trajectories and to avoid collision with oncoming pedestrians. However, the condition of density is not sufficient by itself to elicit a psychological stress reaction. This is related to the spatial invasion of personal space [20]: the area surrounding human body, linked to *crowding* in case of spatial intrusion/restriction.

The proposed CA model is based on the results achieved through of a series of experiments focused on measuring the size and shape of personal space in static and dynamic situations. In particular, we focused on the front zone of *static personal space* (from now denoted as *SPS*) and *pedestrian personal space* (from now denoted as *PPS*). The results achieved by means of a simulation campaign execution allowed to define an innovative crowing estimation method based on the invasion of personal space among the simulated pedestrians (i.e. *Cumulative Mean Crowding*, from now denoted as *CMC*). This represents a novel contribution for the estimation of psychological stress reaction among pedestrians, comparing traditional approaches devoted to the merely estimation of density in the environment (e.g., flow rate [13], Level of Service [9]).

The general framework of the Proxemic Theory is presented in Sect. 2. Section 3 presents the results of an experimental study focused on *SPS* and *PPS*. The description of the model and the novel discrete representation of *PPS* are presented in Sect. 4. Simulation results and the metric for the analysis of the *CMC* are presented in Sect. 5. The paper ends with final remarks about the achieved results and future works.

2   Personal Space and Crowding

In analogy with territorial behavior in animals, proxemics [11] is a type of non-verbal communication among human beings based on the dynamic regulation of interpersonal distances: intimate, personal, social and public distances. Proxemics is based on the notion of *SPS* [20]: a boundary regulation mechanism around the human body, intended to protect themselves from physical and psychological threats [6]. The condition of inappropriate proximity with others or the

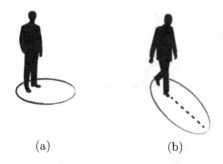

(a)   (b)

Fig. 1. The spatial configuration of *SPS* (a) and *PPS* (b). The latter is characterized by an additional margins in the front zone to avoid intrusion while walking.

condition of spatial restriction in situation of high density represents a stressful factor strictly linked to *crowding* [2]: a physiological and psychological response of arousal and stress mediated by the endocrine system and associated with some after-effects, including reducing tolerance for frustration and aggressive behavior.

The shape of *SPS* is commonly represented as a circular area surrounding individuals, but this configuration does not adequately characterize the flexibility of this body buffer zone in relation to human distance receptors (including visual, auditory, olfactory and thermal receptors). In particular, the asymmetrical and flexible shape of *SPS* is related to the subject's head orientation and visual mechanisms [12]: the front and lateral zones of *SPS* are slightly larger than the rear zone (see Fig. 1/a). In case of dynamic situations while walking (see Fig. 1/b), the front zone of *PPS* is composed of a pacing zone for foot placement and an additional margins in the front zone to avoid spatial intrusion or collision with oncoming pedestrians [9,22].

Crowding stress reaction to density depend on several factors related to social, cultural and environmental factors. For instance, the size of personal space is influenced by cultural preference in spatial positioning [11]. Male exhibit more aggressive responses under crowded conditions than female [8]. Crowding in primary environment (e.g., home, classroom) has more significant effects than relatively unimportant environments (e.g., shopping center) [21]. Lastly, the intensity of sensory inputs and physical contact in high density situations can be labeled either positively (e.g., concert, sport event) or negatively (e.g., transportation facility), depending on contexts of social interaction [18].

3 Experimental Data

A series of experiments have been performed by the authors [10] in 2013 at The University of Tokyo (Tokyo, Japan) to measure the size of *SPS* and *PPS*, taking into account also the impact of walking speed. In particular, the front zone of *PPS* was assumed to be larger than the one in static situations and

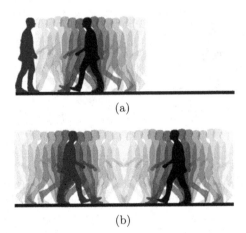

(a)

(b)

Fig. 2. A schematic representation of stop-distance procedure (a) and locomotion-distance procedure (b), which have been used to respectively measure *SPS* and *PPS*. The participant (experimental subject) is highlighted in red color, while the confederate of the experimenter is highlighted in black color. (Color figure online)

linearly speed-dependent, due to the need of an additional margin projected towards the direction of movement to anticipate the spatial intrusion of oncoming pedestrians.

3.1   Experimental Procedures

The experiments were participated by a sample of 20 Asiatic male students, aged from 18 to 25 years old and with sufficient visual capacity (if necessary fitted with glasses or contact lenses). The size of *SPS* was measured by means of the *stop-distance* procedure [12] (see Fig. 2/a), which consisted of asking the confederate to approach the participant walking straight ahead from a distance of 5 m (neutral facial expression, no speaking, no eye contact). The experimental subject was asked to stop the approach when he felt uncomfortable about spatial nearness. The spatial distance between the confederate and the participant is measured as the size of the front zone of *SPS*.

To measure the size of *PPS* we used the *ad hoc* designed *locomotion-distance* procedure (see Fig. 2/b), which consists of asking participant and confederate to approach the each other walking straight ahead from a distance of 5 m (neutral facial expression, no speaking, no eye contact). Participant was asked to stop when he felt uncomfortable about the closeness of the confederate, who immediately stops after. The distance between them is measured as the size of the front zone of *PPS*.

To test the impact of *walking speed* on personal space, the procedure was repeated at low speed (0.93 m/s), medium speed (1.23 m/s) and high speed (1.46 m/s). To control and maintain the speed of the participant and of the

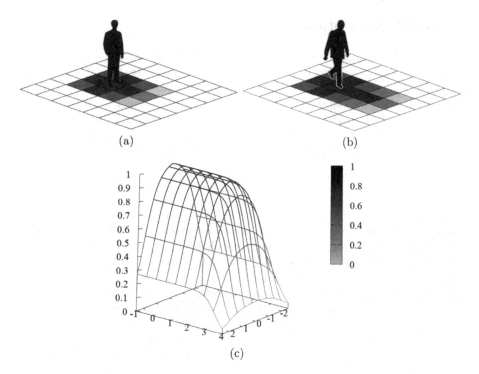

(a)   (b)

(c)

Fig. 3. The modeled spatial configuration of *SPS* (a) and *PPS*(b). Numerical values of the potential of *PPS* considering axis origin as the position and (0,1) as direction of the agent (c).

confederate constant while approaching, they were asked to walk following trajectories and foot markers drawn on the floor and to synchronize their gait to digital-metronome background sounds.

3.2   Experimental Results

Results showed a significant effect of walking speed on the size of *PPS* (ANOVA, $p < 0.05$). In particular, the size of the front zone of *PPS* in case of a reciprocal approach at low speed (0.9 m/s), medium speed (1.23 m/s) and high speed (1.46 m/s) were respectively 71.45 cm (sd 21.78), 68.9 cm (sd 24.02) and 91.1 cm (sd 30.3). Further analyses showed that the size of the front zone of *PPS*(high speed procedure) is significantly larger than the one of *SPS* (72.15 cm, sd 25.71, t-test, $p < 0.05$). Results confirmed the asymmetrical and flexible shape of *PPS* which is affected by the need of an additional margin projected ahead towards the direction of movement to anticipate the spatial intrusion of oncoming pedestrians. This allowed to model a discrete representation of the measured elliptical shape of *PPS* and to define a crowding estimation method based on spatial intrusion/restriction in situations of variable density.

4   Model Description

The proposed CA model for the microscopic simulation of crowd dynamics is based on the representation of pedestrians as occupied states of the cells, while pedestrian interactions are represented through the *floor field* method [3,7]: a virtual traces that influence pedestrian transitions and movements. At each time-step of the simulation, agents evaluate cells c of the Moore neighborhood with the utility function $U(c)$. This aggregates the components associated to the reproduction of a particular behavior by means of a weighted sum:

$$U(c) = \frac{\kappa_g G(c) + \kappa_{ob}Ob(c) + \kappa_s S(c) + \kappa_d D(c) + \kappa_{ov}Ov(c)}{d} \tag{1}$$

Individual functions model respectively: (i) goal attraction; (ii) obstacle repulsion; (iii) keeping distance from other pedestrians; (iv) direction inertia; (v) overlapping to avoid gridlock in counter-flow situations. The first three elements are modeled with the usage of *floor-field* approach [7,17] to model the base behavior of pedestrians: movement towards a target, obstacle avoidance, proxemics with other pedestrians in a repulsive sense. After the utility evaluation for all the cells of the neighborhood, the choice of action is decided by the probability to move in each cell c as (N is the normalization factor): $P(c) = N \cdot e^{U(c)}$.

In line with other works present in the literature [23,24], the proposed CA model is devoted to the explicit representation of the asymmetrical shapes of personal space in static and locomotion situations (see Fig. 1). In particular, on the basis of the achieved experimental results we introduced a discrete representation of the shape of *SPS* and *PPS* into the simulated environment (see Fig. 3). Moreover, we introduced a potential considering positions and directions of each pedestrian, and providing a value $\in [0,1]$ that describes whether a cell in the surrounding of the agent position belongs to its *SPS* or *PPS* (see Fig. 3/c). The potential is designed with functions that aim at reproducing the flexible spatial configuration of personal space in relation to human distance receptors:

$$\phi_r(x) = \frac{1}{1 + e^{r \cdot (x-r)}} \tag{2}$$

$$\psi(x,y) = \phi_2(|x|) \cdot \phi_{3.5}(|y|) \tag{3}$$

Function ϕ_r is a customized sigmoid used to represent the spatial boundaries of *SPS* and *PPS* into the two axis in a smooth way, with parameter r describing the length of the area considered inside it. Function ϕ_r is based on considering the pedestrian centered in the origin and moving along the y-axis (during the simulation the potential is then rotated and translated accordingly). $\psi(x,y)$ thus provides a value $\in [0,1]$ describing whether the cell with coordinates x,y belongs to the personal space of a pedestrian (numerical values assigned to r are expressed in cells).

For the representation of *SPS* in the discrete space, values of the function are cut and discretized in the rectangle of width 3 cells and height 4, as in Fig. 4(a). In case of diagonal movement, the potential of *SPS* is rotated as shown in Fig. 4(b).

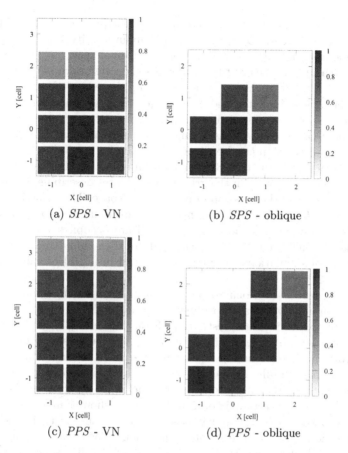

(a) *SPS* - VN

(b) *SPS* - oblique

(c) *PPS* - VN

(d) *PPS* - oblique

Fig. 4. The representation of *SPS* and *PPS* in case of agent's orientation (the last movement of the agents), belonging to the Von Neumann (VN) neighborhood (a, c) and in case of diagonal orientation (b, d).

According to the experimental results presented in Sect. 3, the discrete representation of *PPS* is based instead on a rectangle of width 3 cells and height 5, as in Fig. 4(c). In case of diagonal movement, the potential of *PPS* is rotated as shown in Fig. 4(d).

It must be noted that in this work we did not integrate the notions of denoted in the Eqs. 2 and 3 into the model, yet. Future works presented in Sect. 6 will be focused on integrating the notion of *SPS* and *PPS* into the model for a more expressive representation of proxemic-based behavioral rules among each agent.

5   Crowding Estimation Through Simulations

A simulation campaign of pedestrian crowd dynamics has been executed starting from the configuration of a counter flow situation in a corridor-like scenario (fully balanced bi-directional flow), characterized by the presence of No. 54 agents in total. The objective was to compare results about density and crowding stress reaction among agents due to the invasion of personal space.

In particular, the novelty of this work is based on an innovative crowding estimation method (i.e. Cumulative Mean Crowding) based on the invasion of *SPS* and *PPS* among the simulated pedestrians. According to other works focused on the empirical estimation of crowding among animal entities [4, 15], the proposed *CMC* has been calculated by considering the discretized shape of *SPS* and *PPS* for each agent in the simulated environment, and the possibility to be invaded by other agents due to the contextual condition of density. For each step of the simulation, each agent store in the grid, in coordinates describing its position, a value $\in 0, 1$ related to the invasion of its personal space. The value is calculated with respect to the gradients shown in Fig. 4, considering only occupied cells of the agent's surrounding. If more than one cell are occupied, the maximum of those values is considered. Values of the grid are then cumulated and averaged over the time of simulations, resulting in the end in a grid of values in range $[0, 1]$ (see Fig. 5/b).

Simulation results are focused on comparing data about cumulative mean density and cumulative mean crowding, to estimate the stress reaction among agents due to spatial invasion/restriction. Results (see Fig. 5) highlight fruitful insights regarding the evident difference among the mere estimation of density and the crowding stress reaction among agents due to the invasion of *SPS* and *PPS*. In particular, results about density show a situation of slight congestion only at the center of the simulated scenarios being an accurate method for the recognition of the pedestrian jam. *CMC*, instead, show a more homogeneous distribution of values, but it makes possible to recognize situations of spatial invasion/restriction also at the agents' generation areas. Starting from the consideration that highlighting that the condition of density is not sufficient by itself to elicit crowding [2], the proposed *CMC* represents a novel contribution for the assessment of pedestrian crowd dynamics focusing on the level of comfort experienced by pedestrians in situations of variable density.

6   Conclusions

The paper presents a novel CA model of pedestrian crowd dynamics focused on the general framework of proxemics and on the discrete representation of personal space among pedestrians. This is based on the experimental results achieved by the authors [10] about the asymmetrical and flexible shape of personal space in static and motion situations. Starting from the results of a simulation campaign execution, the paper proposes an innovative method (i.e. Cumulative Mean Crowding) for estimating the psychological stress reaction among pedestrians due to spatial invasion of personal space in situations of variable density.

Simulations were focused on comparing data about cumulative mean density and cumulative mean crowding. Simulations results highlighted that the pro-

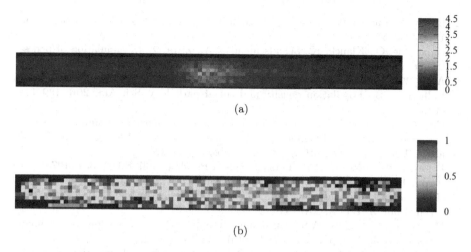

Fig. 5. Simulation results about cumulative mean density (a) and cumulative mean crowding (b) of the simulated scenario.

posed *CMC* method could be successfully combined to the use of more consolidated approaches devoted to the merely estimation of density in the environment (e.g., flow rate [13], Level of Service [9]) to consider also pedestrians' comfort while walking through mass gathering/transportation facilities.

It must be noted that in this work we did not integrate the notions of *SPS* and *PPS* into the model for a more expressive representation of proxemic-based behavioral rules among each agent. Future works will be focused on integrating this aspect, and on introducing the notion of shared personal space among group members. Previous studies performed by the authors have highlighted, in facts, the importance to consider pedestrian crowd dynamics as characterized by the presence of groups [5]. Moreover, since proxemic behavior depends on several socio-psychological factors related to the variability among culture [14], the achieved simulation results definitely encourages future cross-cultural experimental investigations about personal space and tolerance for spatial intrusion, testing also the impact of participants' culture on *CMC*.

Acknowledgement. The experimental studied were performed within the authorization of the Ethics Committee of The University of Tokyo, and they were funded by the Japan Society for the Promotion of Science. The authors thank Prof. Katsuhiro Nishinari, Kenichiro Shimura and Claudio Feliciani for their fruitful contribution.

References

1. Bandini, S., Rubagotti, F., Vizzari, G., Shimura, K.: A cellular automata based model for pedestrian and group dynamics: motivations and first experiments. In: Malyshkin, V. (ed.) PaCT 2011. LNCS, vol. 6873, pp. 125–139. Springer, Heidelberg (2011). https://doi.org/10.1007/978-3-642-23178-0_11

2. Baum, A., Paulus, P.: Crowding. In: Handbook of Environmental Psychology, vol. 1, pp. 533–570 (1987)

3. Burstedde, C., Klauck, K., Schadschneider, A., Zittartz, J.: Simulation of pedestrian dynamics using a two-dimensional cellular automaton. Physica A: Stat. Mech. Appl. **295**(3–4), 507–525 (2001)

4. Calhoun, J.B.: Population density and social pathology. Sci. Am. **206**, 139–149 (1962)

5. Crociani, L., Gorrini, A., Feliciani, C., Vizzari, G., Nishinari, K., Bandini, S.: Micro and macro pedestrian dynamics in counterflow: the impact of social groups. CoRR abs/1711.08225 (2017). http://arxiv.org/abs/1711.08225

6. Evans, G.W., Howard, R.B.: Personal space. Psychol. Bull. **80**(4), 334 (1973)

7. Ezaki, T., Yanagisawa, D., Ohtsuka, K., Nishinari, K.: Simulation of space acquisition process of pedestrians using proxemic floor field model. Physica A: Stat. Mech. Appl. **391**(1–2), 291–299 (2012)

8. Freedman, J.L., Levy, A.S., Buchanan, R.W., Price, J.: Crowding and human aggressiveness. J. Exp. Soc. Psychol. **8**(6), 528–548 (1972)

9. Fruin, J.J.: Pedestrian Planning and Design. Metropolitan Association of Urban Designers and Environmental Planners, New York (1971)

10. Gorrini, A., Shimura, K., Bandini, S., Ohtsuka, K., Nishinari, K.: Experimental investigation of pedestrian personal space: toward modeling and simulation of pedestrian crowd dynamics. Transp. Res. Rec.: J. Transp. Res. Board **2421**, 57–63 (2014)

11. Hall, E.: The Hidden Dimension. Doubleday, New York (1966)

12. Hayduk, L.A.: Personal space: where we now stand? Psychol. Bull. **94**(2), 293–335 (1983)

13. HCM: Highway Capacity Manual. Transportation Research Board, National Research Council, Washington, DC (2010)

14. Iwata, O.: Crowding and behavior in Japanese public spaces: some observations and speculations. Soc. Behav. Personal.: Int. J. **20**(1), 57–70 (1992)

15. Lloyd, M.: Mean crowding. J. Anim. Ecol. **36**, 1–30 (1967)

16. Manzoni, S., Vizzari, G., Ohtsuka, K., Shimura, K.: Towards an agent-based proxemic model for pedestrian and group dynamics: motivations and first experiments. In: The 10th International Conference on Autonomous Agents and Multiagent Systems, vol. 3, pp. 1223–1224. International Foundation for Autonomous Agents and Multiagent Systems (2011)

17. Nishinari, K., Kirchner, A., Namazi, A., Schadschneider, A.: Extended floor field CA model for evacuation dynamics. IEICE Trans. Inf. Syst. **87**(3), 726–732 (2004)

18. Patterson, M.L.: An arousal model of interpersonal intimacy. Psychol. Rev. **83**(3), 235–45 (1976)

19. Seitz, M.J., Templeton, A., Drury, J., Köster, G., Philippides, A.: Parsimony versus reductionism: how can crowd psychology be introduced into computer simulation? Rev. Gen. Psychol. **21**(1), 95 (2017)

20. Sommer, R.: Personal Space. Prentice-Hall, Upper Saddle River (1969)

21. Stokols, D.: On the distinction between density and crowding: some implications for future research. Psychol. Rev. **79**(3), 275–277 (1972)

22. Suma, Y., Yanagisawa, D., Nishinari, K.: Anticipation effect in pedestrian dynamics: modeling and experiments. Physica A: Stat. Mech. Appl. **391**(1–2), 248–263 (2012)

23. Wąs, J., Gudowski, B., Matuszyk, P.J.: Social distances model of pedestrian dynamics. In: El Yacoubi, S., Chopard, B., Bandini, S. (eds.) ACRI 2006. LNCS, vol. 4173, pp. 492–501. Springer, Heidelberg (2006). https://doi.org/10.1007/11861201_57

24. Wąs, J., Lubaś, R., Myśliwiec, W.: Proxemics in discrete simulation of evacuation. In: Sirakoulis, G.C., Bandini, S. (eds.) ACRI 2012. LNCS, vol. 7495, pp. 768–775. Springer, Heidelberg (2012). https://doi.org/10.1007/978-3-642-33350-7_80

Cellular Automata Based Evacuation Process Triggered by Indoors Wi-Fi and GPS Established Detection

N. Kartalidis, I. G. Georgoudas, and G. Ch. Sirakoulis[✉]

Laboratory of Electronics, Department of Electrical and Computer Engineering,
Democritus University of Thrace, 671 00 Xanthi, Greece
{nkarta, igeorg, gsirak}@ee.duth.gr

Abstract. This study presents the principles of an application that is designed to facilitate customized evacuation from indoor spaces. The proposed approach combines in-doors detection using existing wireless networks based on trilateration technique and proper evacuation estimation based on cellular automata (CA). An efficient application has been developed that can be installed in smartphones under Android operation system and technically fulfills the scopes of the aforementioned evacuation model. More specifically, it offers the user the option to view her/his location at any time and to find the closest possible route to an exit in case of an emergency. The efficiency of the application to provide reliable guidance towards an exit is also evaluated. Preliminary results are reasonably encouraging; provided that the application is properly customized then a reliable, real-time evacuation guidance could be realized.

Keywords: Cellular automata · Evacuation · Modelling · Trilateration Smartphones · Wireless · Android

1 Introduction

Indoor Positioning System (IPS) is a new scientific research area that has already offered a wide region of applications, although its realization has not been fully standardized yet [1]. Till today there are quite a few commercial systems found on the market; however no standard for an IPS system exists. The proposed so far IPSs utilize diverse technologies, namely distance measurement to neighboring anchor nodes (nodes with known positions, for example Wi-Fi access points), magnetic positioning, dead reckoning, etc. As such, these systems either actively locate mobile devices and tags or provide ambient location or environmental context for devices to get sensed [2].

One of the key issues arising from navigating in large public venues is the identification of the location of an individual at any time. Indeed, areas such as stadiums, shopping malls, museums and many public spaces are often occupied by many people that make the move to these areas even more difficult. On the other hand, applications have been already developed that employ the knowledge of the exact location of an individual, in order to display the appropriate content in one of the electronic devices that she/he possesses. An example of such an embodiment is the ability to

© Springer Nature Switzerland AG 2018
G. Mauri et al. (Eds.): ACRI 2018, LNCS 11115, pp. 492–502, 2018.
https://doi.org/10.1007/978-3-319-99813-8_45

automatically open an e-wallet application when the user approaches the cashier of a store and/or to activate her/his mobile phone. Such applications that belong to the so-called aware applications are incorporated into the Internet of Things (IoT).

The proposed approach combines in-doors detection using existing wireless networks and proper evacuation estimation based on Cellular Automata (CA). Wi-Fi – based detection is realized using the trilateration technique. The study focuses on the convenient application of pre-established equipment. The feasibility of available methods to be realized with the use of commercial devices already widespread on the market forms a key criterion for the selection of an identification method because it is easy to be adopted by users. Currently, most people who visit public areas carry a smart mobile phone (smartphone) and almost all areas are already equipped with access points of Wi-Fi wireless networks. Furthermore, it would be valuable that IPSes could also provide effective guidance towards an exit, especially in case of emergency. In such conditions, it is important for individuals to be guided towards exits in a swiftly and safe manner. Thus, the main objective of this study is the implementation and evaluation of an active and dynamic guidance method.

According to the structure of this paper, Sect. 2 presents a short review of research, whereas in Sect. 3, the theoretical principles of the model are described. In Sect. 4, the CA-based active route leading method is developed. The corresponding smartphones'-oriented application is described, discussed and evaluated in Sect. 5. Conclusions are drawn, and future perspectives are proposed in the last section of the paper.

2   Related Work

In the framework of this study, various works on the navigation using wireless networks were studied. More particularly, different approaches have been utilized so far to achieve localization. The most popular and simplest approach is to calculate the distance from some access points and then apply a method such as triangulation or triple positioning to determine the specific position [3]. In such approaches, the appropriate placement of the necessary number of access points is considered as a prerequisite. Another approach allows navigation without the knowledge of access points in the room, with the aid of the sensors of the device that are used to calculate the direction and speed of the user's movement. However, this method falls relatively short in accuracy and requires several improvements mainly related to the limitation of errors [4]. In several studies, a method is used, which employs a modified centroid approach with or without weights that offers quite good accuracy and reliability [5]. In some methods, the compass is used to improve accuracy [4, 5], whereas in others, the device is calibrated by successive fixed signal strength measurements, before starting the detection process [3]. In some more complex detection techniques, fluctuations in signal strength are exploited to identify the location of access points so that they can be applied even in unknown locations [3]. Another almost common and relatively easy practice is fingerprinting [6, 7], whereby certain combinations in the signal power levels obtained from the access points are assigned to certain locations within the area of interest by making use of a suitable database that has been previously created.

A relevant idea is to create databases that help improve the accuracy of detection methods using crowdsourcing [8], where data collected by the devices of different users are uploaded to a network for sharing. Several attempts focus on developing robust navigation methods against fluctuations in the received signal. Yet another object that several studies deal with, even if their main objective is not the creation of a navigation system, is to estimate the distance between the user and an obstacle, as well as the existence of noise sources [7, 9].

As far as it regards the estimation of an exit route, the use of CA has been preferred. In most works, they are used in order to predict and study crowds in building evacuation situations, but they can also serve as an excellent basis of instructing platforms in indoor navigation systems; especially since they can emulate the movement of many individuals within an area [10, 11]. More recent studies apply distributed techniques to succeed real-time evacuation guidance [12] and pave the way of more standardized and well developed techniques for real-time applications referring to pedestrian and crowd evacuation issues.

In this work, we focused on the study, application, realization and possible improvement of detection methods without the use of databases, in order to draw conclusions about their suitability under various scenarios. More particularly, the main aim of this study is the development of an application that enables real-time indoors detection using exclusively smartphones as well as wireless network access points already in place. Extended use of smartphone devices and Wi-Fi wireless networks, along with ease of implementation and low cost of installation constitute the main reasons of that choice.

3   The Theoretical Principles of the Model

3.1   Detection Using Trilateration Method

Trilateration is a geometric technique that determines the location of a point [13, 14] and extensively used on tracking systems such as GPS. In two-dimensional geometry, in case that a point lies on two circles, then the centers and the two radii of the circles provide sufficient information to limit the possible locations down to two. Additional information may limit possible options to one unique location (see Fig. 1).

In the localization method that has been developed in this study, the position of an unknown object is determined with the use of two known points. The reason is that the availability of two instead of three access points within the range of the user's device is closer to realistic scenarios. It should be considered that wireless access points are located within an area to provide access to networks rather than being used for navigation purposes. Thus, the number of existing access points in most locations is not so large as to allow detection with trilateration of three points, and it is unreasonable to place additional access points just for that purpose. In addition, two-point calculations are simpler and less costly.

The trilateration method allows the user to be identified by only two access points, making it perhaps the most cost-effective method when using hardware. Moreover, the fact that detection at any time does not require knowledge of the prior position means

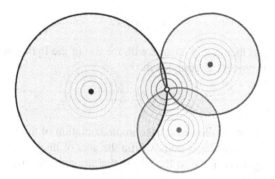

Fig. 1. Trilateration method. The positions of circle centers and their radii are known. The desired point is the intersection of the three circles.

that the error does not accumulate over time and that there are no prerequisites for the initial position of the user at the beginning of the navigation. This method needs only the knowledge of the received signal strength indication (RSSI) to be realized and does not use any kind of sensor, such as a compass or accelerometer, making it less energy-demanding for the mobile device. RSSI is a measurement of the power of a radio wave and it represents the weakening of its power along its path in space. However, this method also has some drawbacks. The fact that it is necessary to know in advance the location and identity of the access points as well as that these points should be placed within the area of interest in a specific way means that the method cannot be used in unknown areas, especially in case that the placement of access points is beforehand inappropriate. Moreover, the method is impossible to be applied in case that the contact with an access point is lost. Additionally, in locations that are very close to the imaginary line joining the two access points, it is possible the trilateration method to fail, in the event of an error in the distance calculation.

Assuming that the access points have been appropriately positioned and that their identity and coordinates are known, the trilateration method is implemented in two main steps: the calculation of the user's distance from each access point and the application of the trilateration method itself. The procedure applied is as follows. Given the coordinates of the access points, hence the distance between them and the knowledge of the user's distance from the access points, the dimensions of the triangle formed by the user's device and the two access points is known. Then, applying properly a system of Cartesian coordinates and trigonometric formulas, the coordinates of the user's position can be calculated. First, we use the type of Heron to find the surface of the triangle formed by the user's device and the two access points:

$$A = \sqrt{p(p-a)(p-b)(p-c)} \tag{1}$$

where a, b, c the sides of the triangle formed, with a representing the side that joins the two access points and p the semi-perimeter of the triangle. Then the height h of the triangle is calculated, which corresponds to the y coordinate of the position:

$$h = 2A/a \tag{2}$$

The x coordinate is then easily located with the use of the Pythagorean theorem and thus, the positioning process is completed:

$$x = \sqrt{b^2 - y^2} \tag{3}$$

Overall, the exact steps followed for the implementation of the trilateration method are: (1) The location of any access point within the area of interest is searched and it is detected whether they correspond to the points that are used for the application of the trilateration method, (2) in case that both necessary access points are found, the user's device distance from each of them is calculated, (3) the trilateration method is applied and from the resulting coordinates, the location of the user is defined in the area of interest, and (4) the procedure is repeated at regular intervals to calculate the user's new location.

3.2   The Route Estimation Model

A key element in each navigation system is its ability to find the shortest possible route to a desired point. In addition, the fact that other users are also trying to find an exit means that their presence should be taken into account in the process of estimating the route, otherwise it may cause accidents during the evacuation process. In order to meet the needs described above, a method of finding a route to the shortest exit is implemented in the context of this work. This method is based on the use of two-dimensional CA. The main reason for the selection of CA is that they enable the estimation of an effective route in near real time. In addition, by appropriately implementing a system of CA, it is possible to take into account the presence of other users within the same area, or even the sudden appearance of obstacles or a passage that is not accessible [11, 15–17]. But there is also another factor that may be of decisive importance to the use of CA. In crowded areas, a CA-based route estimation system could act anticipatively and prevent congestion in front of exits, provided that detected positions of the users could update the initial configuration of the CA grid [18].

In this model, the space is represented by a grid of identical square cells, each representing a predetermined surface with side a. The grid of the CA is considered homogeneous and isotropic. A variable is assigned to each cell, the value of which corresponds to the state of the cell. The possible states are: (1) free, which corresponds to a free area, (2) occupied, which corresponds to an area that is occupied by a user, (3) obstacle, which corresponds to a static obstacle or a wall, (4) a passage, which corresponds to a door through which the user goes from one part of the venue to another, (5) exit, which corresponds to the exit of the area of interest. For each step of the exit path exploring process, the state of each cell is refreshed. Thus, the movement of all people is taken into account. It is assumed that individuals move at a fixed and specific speed. In addition, each user can move one cell at a time. Acceleration and deceleration times of the user are considered negligible. According to the rule that applies to route calculation, at each step, each individual is selected to move one cell in one of the eight possible different directions corresponding to adjacent cells and form the so-called Moore neighborhood. The choice of the cell depends on whether it meets the shortest route criterion and whether it is occupied or not by another person or an obstacle. As far as the shortest route selection is concerned, this is based on the minimum number of cells to be covered from any position to the exit moving only horizontally or vertically. Thus, in the CA plane, the distance D, between a cell located at position (p_1, p_2) and another one positioned at (q_1, q_2) is defined by Eq. (4). The main advantage of such an adoption is that calculations with irrational numbers such as $\sqrt{2}$ or π are technically avoided, thus the process becomes simpler and faster.

$$D = |p_1 - q_1| - |p_2 - q_2| \tag{4}$$

The cell corresponding to the smallest number of steps is the one selected as the next person's location. The process is repeated until the individual reaches the exit. The length of the side a of the cell corresponds to a good compromise between accuracy and computational cost. A very small value (and therefore many cells) means more accuracy but greater cost and therefore increased time to calculate the route. Obviously, the CA grid is adapted to the needs and layout of the area of interest. The fundamental flowchart of the CA model is presented in Fig. 2.

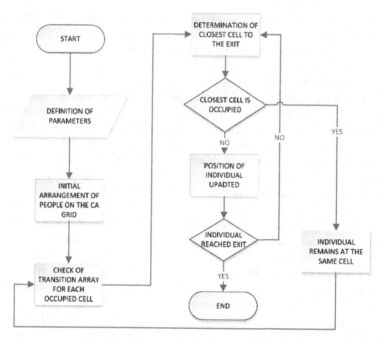

Fig. 2. The fundamental flowchart of the CA-based evacuation model.

4   The Application and the Experimental Process

In order to test the effectiveness of the model, an application is developed running on a smart mobile phone device. There are two prerequisites that should be satisfied in order this application to be operational. First, an appropriate sensor (compass) should be installed on the mobile device and data from this sensor should be accessible. Second, access to information about the Wi-Fi networks to which the device can be connected should also be available.

The dominant platforms for such devices are three; Apple iOS, Microsoft Windows Phone and Google Android. As far as Windows Phone is concerned, the development of such an application is not an option, because Wi-Fi network information is not available. The same restriction applies for iOS. Finally, the platform in which the application is developed is Google Android. There are a couple of reasons that led to such a decision, and, more specifically, that all necessary tools that someone needs to access the information for navigation are available. Furthermore, it is an open platform with a large community and good support from developers. It also supports developing of applications in Java programming language. Finally, the corresponding integrated developing environment (IDE), i.e. Android Studio is highly regarded as an efficient choice. The application that is developed can operate on devices running Android 4.4 and more recent versions. All implemented methods are written in Java. The application enables parameterization by the user in order for the corresponding results to match the equipment that is used.

Figure 3 shows the operation of the application. The user initially chooses the desired tracking method (here trilateration), and then selects the map of the space to which she/he wants to navigate. The location of the user in space is marked with a red mark.

In addition, for the needs of the tests, a message is displayed on the device at regular intervals, indicating information about the position and inclination of the device, as well as details of surrounding access points (identity, transmission frequency, power signal, distance). At any time during the tracking process, the user can enable the output path finder option. Once the option is enabled, the application activates the CA-based evacuation method. As soon as the process is completed, the route that the user has to follow in the space is displayed on the screen of the device. This process can be repeated at any time for any user's location.

Measurements for position detection took place indoors, in a venue without walls but surrounded with various furniture. A Linksys and a Netgear rooter devices were considered for the realization of the trilateration tracking method. First, the signal strength was measured for each router at different distances. The purpose of this process is to calculate the values of the constants to be used in the formula for calculating the distance. Theoretically, the application of various router devices would downgrade the accuracy of this method because it does not take into account the differences among the devices. In practice, however, it was proven that the corresponding differences in the received signal value were negligible. Tests were then performed to determine the accuracy of the detection methods. A common problem in all methods is the generation of fluctuations in the signal level even if the mobile device

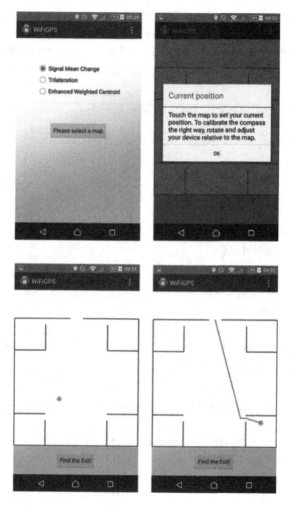

Fig. 3. A snapshot of the CA-based application that defines the evacuation route. (Color figure online)

is at a fixed location. There are many factors that affect the signal, such as the operation of other devices, the shape of the space, interference from other networks, etc.

According to the trilateration method the user's position is recalculated each time (see Fig. 4). As shown in Table 1, which shows the mean deviation from the actual position for 10 consecutive measurements at different positions, the method achieves relatively good accuracy in position calculation. However, it was empirically proven that this method requires fairly high accuracy in calculating the distance of the device from the access points, otherwise it may not be able even to detect the position of the user. A study of the efficiency of the route estimation method using CA took place. In particular, the ability of the proposed CA-based method to find the exit form different starting positions was studied, as well as the ability of the method to find the optimum path and the corresponding response time. A grid that simulates a venue with 4 rooms and one exit was constructed for testing purposes. Then the response of the model was tested for different initial locations. During simulations, we assumed no other persons in the area.

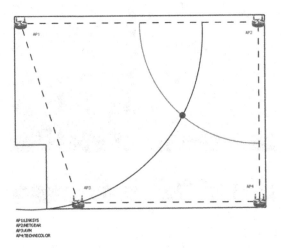

Fig. 4. Example of application of the trilateration method. The user's calculated position is marked in red. (Color figure online)

Table 1. Deviation of the calculated position from the actual when performing the trilateration method.

Number of measurement	Deviation (m)
1	0.1
2	0.3
3	NA
4	0.8
5	NA
6	1.5
7	0.7
8	1.2
9	1.5
10	1.3

In all cases studied, the method was able to provide a route to the exit. In addition, all routes proposed by the method were reasonable and short. The time response of the model depends on the required number of iterations. In case that the number of iterations can be defined dynamically, the method is terminated as soon as the exit route is determined.

5 Conclusions and Future Perspectives

The main conclusion is that it is indeed possible to navigate indoors using Wi-Fi networks and without the use of specialized equipment. Trilateration method provides in most cases acceptable results and it is executed quickly and with relatively small cost. Regarding the route estimation method, experimental results are very encouraging. Indeed, the use of CA is suitable for finding a real-time exit route, providing short and reliable routes in any case.

Based on our early observations during the experimental process, we can propose some future improvements. Initially, other detection methods such as compass-based and weighted centroid should also be tested. Moreover, the CA-based route estimation method could run centrally on a system stronger than a smartphone and then sending the application to the device concerned. Last but not least, a major challenge is the application of the proposed method to larger environments, where the tool will be definitely proved more useful, especially in correspondence with very interesting recent research results that indicate that individuals do not tend to optimize their paths [19].

References

1. Curran, K., Furey, E., Lunney, T., Santos, J., Woods, D., McCaughey, A.: An evaluation of indoor location determination technologies. J. Locat. Based Serv. 5(2), 61–78 (2011)
2. Furey, E., Curran, K., Mc Kevitt, P.: HABITS: a Bayesian filter approach to indoor tracking and location. Int. J. Bio-Inspired Comput. (IJBIC) 4(2), 79–88 (2012)
3. Mazuelas, S., et al.: Robust indoor positioning provided by real-time RSSI values in unmodified WLAN networks. IEEE J. Sel. Topics Sig. Process. 3(5), 821–831 (2009)
4. Han, D., Jung, S., Lee, M., Yoon, G.: Building a practical Wi-Fi-based indoor navigation system. IEEE Pervasive Comput. 13(2), 72–79 (2013)
5. Nižetić Kosović, I., Jagušt, T.: Enhanced weighted centroid localization algorithm for indoor environments. Int. J. Electron. Commun. Eng. 8(7), 1219–1223 (2014)
6. Cheng, Y.-C., Chawathe, Y., LaMarca, A., Krumm, J.: Accuracy characterization for metropolitan-scale Wi-Fi localization. In: Proceedings of the 3rd International Conference on Mobile Systems, Applications, and Services, pp. 233–245. IEEE (2005)
7. Chrysikos, T., Georgopoulos, G., Kotsopoulos, S.: Empirical calculation of shadowing deviation for complex indoor propagation topologies at 2.4 GHz. In: Proceedings of 2009 International Conference on Ultra Modern Telecommunications & Workshops, pp. 1–6. IEEE (2009)
8. Zhuang, Y., Li, Y., Lan, H., Syed, Z., El-Sheimy, N.: Smartphone-based WiFi access point localisation and propagation parameter estimation using crowdsourcing. IET Electron. Lett. 51(17), 1380–1382 (2015)
9. Chrysikos, T., Georgopoulos, G., Kotsopoulos, S.: Attenuation over distance for indoor propagation topologies at 2.4 GHz. In: Proceedings of 2011 IEEE Symposium on Computers and Communications, pp. 329–334. IEEE (2011)
10. Georgoudas, I.G., Sirakoulis, G.Ch., Andreadis, I.Th.: An anticipative crowd management system preventing clogging in exits during pedestrian evacuation processes. IEEE Syst. J. 5 (1), 129–141 (2011)
11. Bandini, S., Mauri, G., Serra, R.: Cellular automata: from a theoretical parallel computational model to its application to complex systems. Parallel Comput. 27(5), 539–553 (2001)

12. Lujak, M., Billhardt, H., Dunkel, J., Fernández, A., Hermoso, R., Ossowski, S.: A distributed architecture for real-time evacuation guidance in large smart buildings. Comput. Sci. Inf. Syst. **14**(1), 257–282 (2017)
13. https://en.wikipedia.org/wiki/Trilateration
14. https://www.britannica.com/science/trilateration
15. Georgoudas, I.G., Koltsidas, G., Sirakoulis, G.Ch., Andreadis, I.Th.: A cellular automaton model for crowd evacuation and its auto-defined obstacle avoidance attribute. In: Bandini, S., Manzoni, S., Umeo, H., Vizzari, G. (eds.) ACRI 2010. LNCS, vol. 6350, pp. 455–464. Springer, Heidelberg (2010). https://doi.org/10.1007/978-3-642-15979-4_48
16. Lubaś, R., Wąs, J., Porzycki, J.: Cellular automata as the basis of effective and realistic agent-based models of crowd behavior. J. Supercomput. **72**(6), 2170–2196 (2016)
17. Tsompanas, M.-A.I., Sirakoulis, G.Ch., Adamatzky, A.I.: Evolving transport networks with cellular automata models inspired by slime mould. IEEE Trans. Cybern. **45**(9), 1887–1899 (2015)
18. Tsiftsis, A., Georgoudas, I.G., Sirakoulis, G.Ch.: Real data evaluation of a crowd supervising system for stadium evacuation and its hardware implementation. IEEE Syst. J. **10**(2), 649–660 (2016)
19. Crociani, L., Vizzari, G., Yanagisawa, D., Nishinari, K., Bandini, S.: Route choice in pedestrian simulation: design and evaluation of a model based on empirical observations. Intelligenza Artificiale **10**(2), 163–182 (2016)

Parallel Implementations of Cellular Automata for Traffic Models

Moreno Marzolla$^{(\boxtimes)}$ (iD)

Department of Computer Science and Engineering,
University of Bologna, Bologna, Italy
`moreno.marzolla@unibo.it`

Abstract. The Biham-Middleton-Levine (BML) traffic model is a simple two-dimensional discrete Cellular Automaton (CA) that has been used to study self-organization and phase transitions in traffic flows. From the computational point of view, the BML model exhibits the usual features of discrete CA, where the new state of each cell is computed according to simple rules involving its current state and that of the immediate neighbors. In this paper we evaluate the impact of various optimizations for speeding up CA computations on shared-memory parallel architectures using the BML model as a case study. In particular, we analyze parallel implementations of the BML automaton for multicore CPUs and GPUs. Experimental evaluation provides quantitative measures of the payoff of different optimization techniques. Contrary to popular claims of "double-digit speedups" of GPU versus CPU implementations, our findings show that the performance gap between CPU and GPU implementations of the BML traffic model can be greatly reduced by clever exploitation of all available CPU features.

Keywords: Biham-Middleton-Levine model · Cellular automata
Parallel computing

1 Introduction

Cellular Automata (CA) are a simple computational model of many natural phenomena, such as virus infections in biological systems, turbulence in fluids, chemical reactions [4] and traffic flows [7]. In its simplest form, a discrete CA consists of a finite lattice of cells (domain), where each cell can be in any of a finite number of states. The cells evolve synchronously at discrete points in time; the new value of a cell depends on its current value and on that of its neighbors according to some fixed rule.

Simulating the evolution of CA models can be computationally challenging, especially for large domains and/or complex update rules. However, many CA models belong to the class of *embarrassingly parallel computations*, meaning that new states can be computed in parallel if multiple execution units are available. This is indeed the case, since virtually every desktop- or server-class

© Springer Nature Switzerland AG 2018
G. Mauri et al. (Eds.): ACRI 2018, LNCS 11115, pp. 503–512, 2018.
https://doi.org/10.1007/978-3-319-99813-8_46

processor on the market provides parallel capabilities, such as multiple execution cores and Single Instruction Multiple Data (SIMD) instructions. Moreover, programmable Graphics Processing Units (GPUs) are ubiquitous and affordable, and are particularly suited for this kind of applications since they provide a large number of execution units that can operate in parallel.

Unfortunately, exploiting the computational power of modern parallel architectures requires programming techniques and specialized knowledge that are not as diffuse as they should be. Additionally, there is considerable misunderstanding about which programming technique and/or parallel architecture is the most effective in a given situation. This results in many exaggerated claims that later proved to be unsubstantiated [6].

In this paper we study the impact of various optimizations for speeding up CA computations on parallel architectures by using the Biham-Middleton-Levine (BML) model as a case study. We focus on two common computing architectures: (*i*) multicore CPUs, i.e., processors with multiple independent execution units, and (*ii*) general-purpose GPUs that include hundreds of simple execution units that can be programmed for any kind of computation. Starting with an unoptimized CPU implementation of the BML model, we develop incremental refinements that incorporate more advanced features: shared-memory programming, SIMD instructions, and a full GPU implementation. We compare the various implementations on two machines to study the impact of each optimization. Our findings show that, for the BML model, CPUs can be extremely effective if all their features are correctly exploited. We believe that the findings reported in this paper can be useful for improving the simulation of other, more realistic, traffic models based on Cellular Automata.

This paper is organized as follows: in Sect. 2 we briefly describe the main features of the BML model. Then, we illustrate a simple serial implementation of the model (Sect. 3), that is later improved to take advantage of multicore parallelism on the CPU (Sect. 4), of Single Instruction Multiple Data extensions (Sect. 5), and of GPUs parallelism (Sect. 6). In Sect. 7 we compare the performance of the implementations above. Finally, the conclusions of this work are reported in Sect. 8.

2   The Biham-Middleton-Levine Traffic Model

The BML model [1] is a simple CA that describes traffic flows in two dimensions. In its simplest form, the model consists of a periodic square lattice of $N \times N$ cells. Each cell can be either empty, or occupied by a vehicle moving from top to bottom (TB) or from left to right (LR). The model evolves by alternating horizontal and vertical phases. During a horizontal phase, all LR vehicles move one cell right, provided that the destination cell is empty. Similarly, during a vertical phase all TB vehicles move one cell down the grid if possible. A vehicle exiting the grid from one side reappears on the opposite side.

Despite its simplicity, the BML model undergoes a phase transition when the density ρ of vehicles exceeds a critical value that depends on the grid size N [1,3].

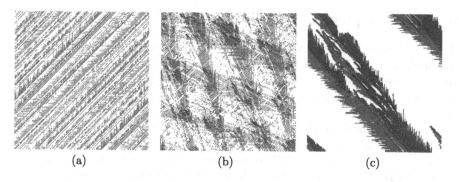

(a)   (b)   (c)

Fig. 1. BML model on a 256 × 256 lattice after 4096 steps. (a) Free-flowing phase, $\rho = 0.25$; (b) Intermediate phase, $\rho = 0.32$; (c) Globally jammed phase, $\rho = 0.38$. Red dots represent LR vehicles, while blue dots represent TB vehicles. (Color figure online)

When ρ is below the critical threshold, the system stabilizes in a *free-flowing state* where vehicles arrange themselves in a non-interfering pattern to achieve maximum average speed. If the density is just above the critical threshold, a global jam eventually develops and no further movement is possible.

Figure 1 shows three configurations of the BML model after 4096 steps (each step includes a horizontal and vertical phase) on a grid of size 256 × 256 for different values of the vehicle density ρ. There are approximately $\rho N/2$ vehicles of each type that are initially placed randomly on the grid. Figure 1(a) shows the free-flowing state that arises when $\rho = 0.25$. Increasing the vehicle density $\rho = 0.32$ Fig. 1(b) shows the intermediate phase that can be observed if the value of ρ is increased, but is still below the critical threshold. When the density ρ reaches the critical threshold, all vehicles are eventually stuck in a global traffic jam as shown in Fig. 1(c), and the average speed drops to zero. In fact, the free-flowing and jammed states might coexist, i.e., have non-zero probability to occur, when ρ lies within some interval around the critical point [3].

The following rule can be used during a horizontal phase to compute the new state center' of a cell, given its current state center and the current state of its left and right neighbors:

$$
\text{center}' = \begin{cases} \text{LR} & \text{if left} = \text{LR} \land \text{center} = \text{EMPTY} \\ \text{EMPTY} & \text{if center} = \text{LR} \land \text{right} = \text{EMPTY} \\ \text{center} & \text{otherwise} \end{cases}
$$

Similarly, the following rule can be used to compute the new state of a cell during a vertical phase, given its current state and the state of its neighbors locate at the top and bottom:

$$
\text{center}' = \begin{cases} \text{TB} & \text{if top} = \text{TB} \land \text{center} = \text{EMPTY} \\ \text{EMPTY} & \text{if center} = \text{TB} \land \text{bottom} = \text{EMPTY} \\ \text{center} & \text{otherwise} \end{cases}
$$

3   Serial Implementation

The BML model is a *synchronous* CA, since it requires that all cells are updated at the same time. To achieve this it is possible to use two grids, say `cur` and `next`, holding the current and next CA configuration, respectively. Cell states are read from `cur` and new states are written to `next`. When all the new states have been computed, `cur` and `next` are exchanged.

Since the C language lays out 2D arrays row-wise in memory, it is easier to treat `cur` and `next` as 1D arrays, and use a function (or macro) `IDX(i,j)` to compute the mapping of the 2D coordinates (i, j) to a linear index. Therefore, we write `cur[IDX(i,j)]` to denote the cell at coordinates (i, j) of `cur`. In case of a $N \times N$ grid, the function `IDX(i,j)` will return $(i \times N + j)$.

Since the BML model is a three-state CA, two bits would be sufficient to encode each cell. However, to simplify memory accesses we use one byte per cell. The following code defines all necessary data types, and shows how the horizontal phase can be realized (the vertical phase is very similar, and is therefore omitted).

```
typedef unsigned char cell_t;
enum {EMPTY = 0, LR, TB};
cell_t *cur, *next;

void horizontal_step(cell_t *cur, cell_t *next, int N) {
  int i, j;
  for (i=0; i<N; i++) {
    for (j=0; j<N; j++) {
      const cell_t left = cur[IDX(i,(j-1+N)%N)];
      const cell_T center = cur[IDX(i,j)];
      const cell_t right = cur[IDX(i,(j+1)%N)];
      cell_t *out = &next[IDX(i,j)];
      *out = (left == LR && center == EMPTY ? LR :
             (center == LR && right == EMPTY ? EMPTY :
             center)));
    }
  }
}

void vertical_step(cell_t *cur, cell_t *next, int N) { ... }
```

A direct implementation of the BML morel uses grids of $N \times N$ elements. However, care must be taken when accessing the neighbors of cell (i, j) to avoid out-of-bound accesses. A common optimization is to surround the domain with additional rows and columns, called *ghost cells* [5]. The domain becomes a grid of size $(N + 2) \times (N + 2)$, where the true domain consists of the cells (i, j) for all $1 \leq i \leq N + 1, 1 \leq j \leq N + 1$, while those on the border contain a copy of the cells at the opposite side (see Fig. 2).

The top and bottom ghost rows must be filled before each vertical update phase (Fig. 2(a)), while the ghost columns on the left and right must be filled before each horizontal phase (Fig. 2(b)). Ghost cells simplify the indexing of neighbors and provide a significant speedup as will be shown in Sect. 7.

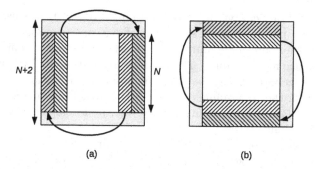

Fig. 2. An $N \times N$ domain (white) augmented with ghost cells (gray). The corners of the extended domain are ignored, since they are not used by the BML update rules.

4   OpenMP Implementation

OpenMP [2] is an open standard that supports parallel programming on shared-memory architectures; bindings for the C, C++ and FORTRAN languages are available. OpenMP allows the programmer to annotate portions of the code as parallel regions; the compiler generates the appropriate code to dispatch those regions to the processor cores.

In the C and C++ languages, OpenMP annotations are specified using `#pragma` preprocessor directives. One such directives is `#pragma omp parallel for`, that can be used to automatically distribute the iterations of a "for" loop to multiple cores, provided that the iterations are independent (this requirement must be verified by the programmer). The update loop(s) of the BML model can then be parallelized very easily as follows (we are assuming the presence of ghost cells, so that the indexed i and j assume the values $1, \ldots, N$).

```
. . .
#pragma omp parallel for
for (i=1; i<N-1; i++) {
  for (j=1; j<N-1; j++) {
    /* update cell (i,j) */
  }
}
. . .
```

5   SIMD Implementation

Modern processors provide SIMD instructions that can apply the same mathematical or logical operation to multiple data items stored in a register. A SIMD register is a small vector of fixed length (usually, 128 or 256 bits). Depending on the processor capabilities, a 128-bit wide SIMD register might contain two 64-bit doubles, four 32-bit floats, four 32-bit integers, and so on.

Some applications can greatly benefit from SIMD instructions, since they execute multiple operations in the same time of one corresponding scalar instruction. However, there are some limitations: (*i*) SIMD instructions are processor-specific, and hence not portable; (*ii*) automatic generation of SIMD instructions from scalar code is beyond the capabilities of most compilers and requires manual intervention from the programmer; (*iii*) SIMD instructions might impose constraints on how data is laid out in memory, e.g., by forcing specific alignments for memory loads and stores.

The SSE2 instruction set of Intel processors provides instructions that can operate on 16 chars packed into a 128-bit SIMD register. This allows us to compute the new states of 16 adjacent cells at the time. The SIMD version of the BML model has been realized using *vector data types* provided by the GNU C Compiler (GCC). Vector data types are a proprietary extension of GCC that allow users to use SIMD vectors as if they were scalars: the compiler emits the appropriate instructions to apply the desired arithmetic or logical operator to all elements of the SIMD vector.

The conditional branches required to compute the next state of the BML model pose a challenge. The reason is that a branch may cause a different execution path to be taken for different elements of the same SIMD register, which contrasts with the SIMD paradigm that requires that the same sequence of operations is applied to all data items. To overcome this problem it is possible to compute the new states using a technique called *selection and masking*, that makes use of bit-wise operations only. The idea is to replace a statement like a = (C ? x : y), where C is 0 or -1 (0xffffffff in two's complement, hexadecimal notation), with the functionally equivalent statement a = (C & x) | (~C & y), where no branch appears.

The code below defines a vector datatype v16i of 16 chars and uses it to compute the new state out of 16 adjacent cells at the time.

```
typedef char v16i __attribute__((vector_size(16)));
void horizontal_step(cell_t *cur, cell_t *next, int N) {
  int i, j;
  for (i=1; i<N+1; i++) {
    for (j=1; j<(N+1)-15; j += 16) {
      const v16i left = __builtin_ia32_loaddqu((char*)&cur[IDX(i,j-1)]);
      const v16i center = __builtin_ia32_loaddqu((char*)&cur[IDX(i,j)]);
      const v16i right = __builtin_ia32_loaddqu((char*)&cur[IDX(i,j+1)]);
      const v16i mask_lr = ((left == LR) & (center == EMPTY));
      const v16i mask_empty = ((center == LR) & (right == EMPTY));
      const v16i mask_center = ~(mask_lr | mask_empty);
      const v16i out = ((mask_lr & LR) | (mask_empty & EMPTY) | \
                        (mask_center & center));
      __builtin_ia32_storedqu((char*)&next[IDX(i,j)], out);
    }
  }
}
```

left, center and right can be thought as arrays of length 16 holding the values of the left, center, and right neighbors of 16 adjacent cells. Their contents are fetched from memory using the __builtin_ia32_loaddqu (*Load Double Quad-*

word Unaligned) intrinsic; we are assuming that the domain is extended with ghost cells.

The `mask_lr`, `mask_empty` and `mask_center` vector variables contain the value -1 in the positions where `LR`, `EMPTY` and `center` should be stored, respectively. Note that the compiler automatically converts scalars to vectors in order to handle mixed comparisons like (`left == LR`). Conveniently, SSE2 comparison instructions generate the value -1 for *true* instead of 1. The new states out of the 16 cells can then be computed using bit-wise operators that the compiler translates into a sequence of SIMD instructions. The result is stored back in memory using the `__builtin_ia32_storedqu` (Store Double Quadword Unaligned) intrinsic.

6   CUDA Implementation

A modern GPU contains a large number of programmable processing cores that can be used for general-purpose computations. The first widely used framework for GPU programming has been the CUDA toolkit by NVidia corporation. A CUDA program consists of a part that runs on the CPU and one that runs on the GPU. The source code is annotated using proprietary extensions to the C, C++ or FORTRAN programming languages that are understood by the `nvcc` compiler. Recently, CUDA has evolved into an open standard called OpenCL that is supported by other vendors; however, in the following we consider CUDA since it is currently more robust and efficient than OpenCL.

The basic unit of work that can be executed on a CUDA-capable GPU is the *CUDA thread*. Threads can be arranged in one-, two-, or three-dimensional *blocks*, that can be further assembled into a one-, two-, or three-dimensional *grid*. Each thread has unique coordinates describing its position in a block or grid. The CUDA paradigm favors decomposition of a problem into very small tasks that are assigned to threads (*fine-grained parallelism*). The CUDA runtime schedules threads to cores for execution; the hardware supports multitasking with almost no overhead, so that the number of threads can (and usually does) exceed the number of cores.

Implementation of the BML model with CUDA is quite simple, and consists of transforming the `horizontal_step` and `vertical_step` functions to *CUDA kernels*, i.e., blocks of code that can be executed by a thread. CUDA kernels are designated with the `__global__` specifier. Using two-dimensional blocks of threads it is possible to assign one thread to each cell of the automaton; this requires launching $N \times N$ threads to handle the whole domain. The `horizontal_step` function becomes a CUDA kernel as follows:

```
__global__
void horizontal_step(cell_t *cur, cell_t *next, int N) {
    const int i = 1 + threadIdx.y + blockIdx.y * blockDim.y;
    const int j = 1 + threadIdx.x + blockIdx.x * blockDim.x;
    if (i < N+1 && j < N+1) { /* update cell (i,j) */ }
}
```

CUDA cores have no direct access to system RAM; instead, they can only use the GPU memory, called *device RAM*. Therefore, input data must be transferred from system RAM to device RAM before the CUDA threads are activated. Once computation on the GPU is completed, the output data is transferred back to system RAM. The parameters cur and next above point to device RAM.

Table 1. Hardware used for the experimental evaluation

	Machine A	Machine B
CPU	Intel Xeon E3-1220	Intel Xeon E5-2603
Max clock rate	3.50 GHz	1.70 GHz
Cores	4	12
HyperThreading	No	No
RAM	16 GB	64 GB
L2 Cache	256 KB	256 KB
L3 Cache	8192 KB	15360 KB
GPU	Quadro K620	GeForce GTX 1070
Max clock rate	1.12 GHz	1.80 GHz
CUDA cores	384	1920
Device RAM	1993 MB	8114 MB

7   Performance Evaluation

In this section we compare the following implementations of the BML model described so far: the scalar version *without* ghost cells from Sect. 3 (**serial**); the scalar version *with* ghost cells (**Serial+halo**); the OpenMP version from Sect. 4 (**OpenMP**); the SIMD version from Sect. 5 (**SIMD**); a combined OpenMP+SIMD version, where cells are updated using SIMD instructions and the outer loops are parallelized with OpenMP directives (**OpenMP+SIMD**); and finally, the CUDA version from Sect. 6 (**CUDA**). In the cases where OpenMP is used, we make use of all processor cores available in the machine.

All implementations have been realized under Ubuntu Linux version 16.04.4 using GCC 5.4.0 with the flags -O3 -march=native to enable various optimizations; the CUDA version has been compiled with the proprietary nvcc compiler from the CUDA Toolkit version 9.1. We run the programs on two multi-core machines equipped with CUDA capable GPUs, whose specifications are shown in Table 1. Machine A has a fast, four-core processor but includes a low-end GPU. Machine B has a more powerful GPU and a processor with twelve cores; however, each core runs at a lower clock rate than those on machine A.

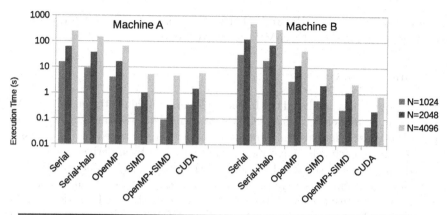

| | Machine A | | | Machine B | | |
N	1024	2048	4096	1024	2048	4096
Serial	15.446	61.957	249.026	31.554	126.298	508.046
Serial+halo	9.091	36.545	148.266	18.725	75.046	304.818
OpenMP	4.080	16.256	65.366	2.988	12.184	44.763
SIMD	0.294	1.021	5.252	0.524	2.044	9.652
OpenMP+SIMD	0.090	0.339	4.730	0.228	1.079	2.292
CUDA	0.351	1.482	5.970	0.052	0.202	0.768

Fig. 3. Mean execution time of BML model implementations ($\rho = 0.3$, 1024 steps)

The BML model has been simulated with a vehicle density $\rho = 0.3$ on a domain of size $N \times N$, $N = 1024, 2048, 4096$ for 1024 steps. Figure 3 shows the execution time of each implementation, computed as the average of five executions. Note the logarithmic scale of the vertical axis, that is necessary since the execution times vary more than two orders of magnitude.

The use of ghost cells provides a significant reduction of the execution time (about 40%) compared to the use of the modulo operator. The OpenMP version using all available processor cores provides an additional speedup of about 2× for machine A and about 6× for machine B (recall that machine B has more cores). These speedups come very cheaply: the OpenMP version differs from the scalar implementation with ghost cells by a couple of `#pragma omp parallel for` directives that have been added to the functions computing the horizontal and vertical steps.

The SIMD implementation provides perhaps the most surprising results, especially on machine A. A single CPU core delivers more computing power than the mid-range GPU installed on the machine; by combining OpenMP and SIMD instructions it is possible to further reduce the execution time on the CPU. The OpenMP+SIMD version is more than four times faster than the GPU for $N = 1024, 2048$; however, the gap closes for the larger domain size $N = 4096$.

Machine B has a slower CPU and a better GPU, so the GPU version is four to five times faster than the OpenMP+SIMD version.

8   Conclusions

In this paper we have analyzed the impact of several implementations of the BML traffic model on modern CPUs and GPUs. Starting with a scalar version, we have applied the *ghost cells* pattern to reduced the overhead caused by the access to the neighbors of each cell. A parallel version has then been derived by applying OpenMP directives to the serial implementation, to take advantage of multicore processors. More effort is required to restructure the code to take advantage of SIMD instructions; the payoff is however surprising: the SIMD version running on a single CPU core proved to be faster than a GPU implementation running on a mid-range graphic card.

The results suggest that traffic models can greatly benefit from accurately tuned CPU implementations, especially considering that a fast CPU can execute this type of workload faster than an average GPU. However, the most useful optimization, namely, the use of SIMD instructions, requires technical knowledge that the average user is unlikely to possess. It is therefore advised that traffic simulators and other CA modeling tools make these features available to the scientific community.

We are extending the work described in this paper by considering more complex and realistic traffic models based on CA. We expect that the findings reported above will still apply to a certain extent to any discrete CA.

References

1. Biham, O., Middleton, A.A., Levine, D.: Self-organization and a dynamical transition in traffic-flow models. Phys. Rev. A **46**(10), R6124–R6127 (1992). https://doi.org/10.1103/PhysRevA.46.R6124
2. Dagum, L., Menon, R.: OpenMP: an industry-standard API for shared-memory programming. IEEE Comput. Sci. Eng. **5**, 46–55 (1998). https://doi.org/10.1109/99.660313
3. D'Souza, R.M.: Coexisting phases and lattice dependence of a cellular automaton model for traffic flow. Phys. Rev. E **71**, 066112 (2005). https://doi.org/10.1103/PhysRevE.71.066112
4. Gutowitz, H. (ed.): Cellular Automata: Theory and Experiment. MIT Press, Cambridge (1991)
5. Kjolstad, F.B., Snir, M.: Ghost cell pattern. In: Proceedings of the 2010 Workshop on Parallel Programming Patterns, ParaPLoP 2010, pp. 4:1–4:9. ACM, New York (2010). https://doi.org/10.1145/1953611.1953615
6. Lee, V.W., et al.: Debunking the 100× GPU vs. CPU myth: an evaluation of throughput computing on CPU and GPU. In: Proceedings of the 37th Annual International Symposium on Computer Architecture, ISCA 2010, pp. 451–460. ACM, New York (2010). https://doi.org/10.1145/1815961.1816021
7. Maerivoet, S., Moor, B.D.: Cellular automata models of road traffic. Phys. Rep. **419**(1), 1–64 (2005). https://doi.org/10.1016/j.physrep.2005.08.005

Holonification of Road Traffic Based on Graph Theory

Igor Haman Tchappi[1,2]($\boxtimes$), Stéphane Galland[1], Vivient Corneille Kamla[3], and Jean Claude Kamgang[3]

[1] LE2I, Univ. Bourgogne Franche-Comté, UTBM, 90010 Belfort, France
igortchappi@gmail.com
[2] Faculty of Sciences, University of Ngaoundere, BP: 454, Ngaoundere, Cameroon
[3] ENSAI, University of Ngaoundere, BP: 454, Ngaoundere, Cameroon

Abstract. Organizational models and holonic multiagent systems are growing as a powerful tool for modeling and developing large-scale complex system. The main issue in deploying holonic multiagent systems is the building of the holonic model called holarchy. This paper presents a novel top down approach based on graph theory in order to build recursively the initial holarchy of road traffic. Moreover, multilevel indicators based on standard deviation is proposed to evaluate the consistency of the holonification process.

Keywords: Graph theory · Holonic multiagent systems
Road traffic · Multilevel model

1 Introduction

In the last decades, there has been several research on agent organization in multiagent System (MAS) field. Organizational approach could improve the overall performance and effectiveness of multiagent systems and allows to model successfully complex systems [9] by defining several abstractions levels of system. Road traffic is a complex system because interactions between vehicles are non-linear, the collective behavior of vehicles is non-trivial and traffic exhibits hierarchical self-organization behavior under selective constraints. Modeling and simulation of traffic is one of the effective solution in order to understand the relationship between level exhibited by traffic and to manage and improve traffic flow. Three main approaches are presented to model road traffic in literature [12]: microscopic, intermediate (mesoscopic and hybrid or multilevel) and macroscopic approach. Macroscopic approach is unable to manage destination of drivers and generally is applied on highway while microscopic level requires a high computational cost and generally is applied on small urban area scale with a high degree of accuracy. Both of macroscopic and microscopic models are not suitable to deal with large scale traffic, particularly in developing countries, e.g. Cameroon where there is few clusters to run efficiently microscopic model or there is none

© Springer Nature Switzerland AG 2018
G. Mauri et al. (Eds.): ACRI 2018, LNCS 11115, pp. 513–525, 2018.
https://doi.org/10.1007/978-3-319-99813-8_47

highway to apply macroscopic models. To model and simulate large scale traffic in these countries, we argue that an intermediate approach like mesoscopic or multilevel is needed. Multilevel or hybrid models [14, 16] integrate different levels of detail in the same model (micro-meso, meso-macro, micro-macro) with the advantages of the models integrated. This motivation leads the paper to focus on multilevel modeling of large scale road traffic.

The principle generally applied in the creating of a multilevel model for traffic is to divide the road network into several parts. Each part is associated to an abstraction level. The goal of hybridization is therefore to deals with the transition between the different abstraction levels at the border [3]. Consequently, most of the existing hybrid models are static and define a priori the different abstraction levels [18]. However, to be able to observe congestion formation or to find the exact location of a jam in a macro section, a dynamic hybrid modeling approach is needed [2]. There are a very few works dedicated to the dynamic multilevel of traffic flow [2]. The paper takes a step towards a dynamic multilevel agent-based model by using holonic multiagent systems (HMAS).

HMAS have been studied on various large-scale applications successfully. Holonic organizations are among the successful organizational models that have been introduced in MAS [10]. HMAS allows to dynamically switch between levels of detail according to the simulation's objectives or available computational resources [9]. HMAS is a recursive structure of holons. A holon is a natural or artificial structure that is stable and coherent and that consists of several holons as sub-structures. In the context of MAS, a holon is assimilated to an agent that could be composed by other agents.

In general, the life-cycle of HMAS consists of two primary stages: *building the initial holarchy* and controlling its structure against internal and external stimuli during its lifetime [7]. The initial holarchy represents the system structure in term of composition at time $t = 0$. While, the control structure of the system against internal and external stimuli represents the life of system structure at time $t > 0$. The contribution of this paper is on **building the initial holarchy** of a large-scale road traffic with a descending approach using a graph for supporting the decomposition process. To this end, our model considers the road traffic as a recursive system and the recursive decomposition of traffic is presented within this paper.

The paper presents a holonification method based on graph theory. Graph theory is used to model and solve various problems [1] and contains many well established algorithms like graph bisection. In the proposed method, vehicles are represented by the graph's vertices and the follower $\rightarrow$ leader relationship by the graph's edges. The method is a top-down recursive bisection of graph in order to build the initial holarchy of road traffic. The validation of our multilevel approach is based on a standard deviation indicators.

The rest of this paper is organized as follows: in Sect. 2, a brief description of several HMAS and related works are presented. Section 3 explains our graph-based holonification road traffic algorithm in detail. Experimentation and results is presented in Sect. 4. Finally, Sect. 5 gives a conclusion and future works.

2   Holonic Multiagent Systems and Related Works

Holonic modeling is used to model the intrinsic hierarchical nature of the systems. A holon, according to Koestler [13] is defined as simultaneously a whole and a part of the whole, thus it can be made up of other holons, strictly meeting three conditions: being stable, having a capacity for autonomy and being able to cooperate. One of the most interesting properties of holonic systems, which is the essence of their complexity, is that a holon can be both an entity and an organization. The holons are therefore stable and self-similar or recursive structures. The hierarchic structure of HMAS allows to simulate a system at several abstraction levels according to the simulation objectives or available computational resources. A holarchy, i.e. a hierarchy of holons is shown on Fig. 1. HMAS can allows to switch into different level of holarchy dynamically [9]. To design HMAS, the generic Capacity-Role-Interaction-Organization (CRIO) metamodel [4,11] could be used.

As stated before, the life-cycle of HMAS consists of two stages: building the initial holarchy (holonification) and controlling the system structure over time. The initial holarchy of HMAS depicts the overall composition of all holons at each level at time $t = 0$. The control structure against internal and external stimuli depicts the self-organization of HMAS over time.

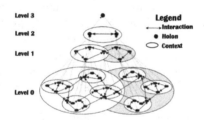

Fig. 1. A nested holarchy of four holarchical level [9]

Among the works on building the initial holarchy of HMAS, Esmaeili et al. [6] propose a method, inspired from social networks, to build the initial holonic structure of multiagent network with a bottom-up approach. The prerequisite of their method is an un-weighted undirected multiagent network model. They use urban traffic signal control to evaluate the quality of the holons constructed. The main limit of this work is they assume that importance of their agents is based on eigenvector centrality. In fact, this assumption is restrictive and not compatible with several complex system.

Abdoos et al. [1] propose a method to construct the initial holarchy for a multiagent urban area network based on graph theory. In their method, agents are modeled using an undirected and weighted graph in which the weights denote the degrees of the dependencies between the agents. Authors propose a quality measure to evaluate the consistency of their method. The main drawback of this algorithm is the rebuilding of the graph after each choice of best candidates to form or to join a holon. Another shortcoming is that they build only the first level of holarchy. Our approach can build more than one hierarchical levels.

In order to solve the above issues, we consider the graph partitioning in graph theory [5]. Let a graph G a pair of sets $G = (V, E)$. The set V is the set of vertices and the set E contains the edges of the graph. The partitioning problem is defined as follows: given a graph $G = (V, E)$, partition V into subsets such that: (i) no subset is empty, (ii) the union of subsets is equal to V, (iii) all the subsets are disjoint two by two. Bisection is the partition of graph in two subsets. In application, in general, bisection of graph is recursive that's means first partition the graph in two partitions, then partition each of these two partitions in two sub-partitions and so on. For some important classes of graphs, recursive bisection works quite well and if the goal does not insist on partitions of exactly equal size, it is possible to use recursive bisection to find good partitions [5]. Holonification is therefore very similar to partitioning in graph theory [1].

3   Graph-Based Model for the Holonification of Road Traffic

In highway or urban areas, vehicles follow one another on a line and tend to regroup in convoys when approaching a heavy vehicle or when the road becomes winding [19]. These groups of spontaneous vehicles are called convoy in this paper. Whenever a spontaneous grouping of entities is possible, organizational and holonic approaches are interesting [18]. The partitioning approaches are well adapted to road traffic because the dynamics of road traffic triggers the formation of "natural" clusters at the intersections, or convoys on the highways [19].

Vèque et al. [19] assert that *"the geographical position of vehicles is one of the important criteria in clustering "* In the same paper, they also assert that: *"since vehicles move in a space constrained by routes, other criteria are also significant such as speed and direction"*. According to these assertions, in our model the criterion used to model vehicles are speed, position, length of vehicle and direction (lane).

3.1   Organizational Model of Road Traffic

One approach concerning the design of a multilevel agent based model is to observe, detect and possibly reify (or more precisely agentify) phenomena emerging from agents interactions [15]. According to this assertion, in order to build our multilevel road traffic model, we can observe the emergent phenomena in traffic and reify it. In traffic simulation, congestion—the queue of tighter vehicles—is an emergent phenomenon due to the interaction between the vehicles. In this paper, this queue is called "convoy". The paper uses the CRIO metamodel [4,11] and Fig. 2 presents the organizational model of road traffic. There a three organizations:

(i) **Free Driver**: In this organization, the role **Free** is defined. It is played by an agent, which is moving with its desired speed.

(ii) **Car Following**: In this organization, the role **Leader** and **Follower** are defined. The **Leader** is the vehicle located just in front of the **Follower**.

(iii) **Convoy**: In this organization, the roles **Head** and **Member** are defined. The agent which plays **Head** is the vehicle on the top of convoy; the others agents vehicles which belongs to a convoy play **Member**. The **Head** role is the representative of the convoy and imposes his speed to all the convoy.

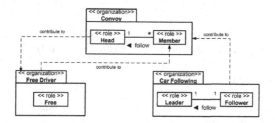

Fig. 2. Road traffic organizational model according to the ASPECS [4] methodology's formalism. Each organization is representing by a box with the stereotype "**organization**". Each role is defined within an organization and represented by a box with the "**role**" stereotype. Links between roles boxes represent the interaction between the agents which are playing these roles.

An organization is made up of sub-organizations, so we can recursively define road traffic organization as follows:

$$Organization ::= \langle Convoys, Free\_Drivers \rangle \tag{1}$$

$$Convoys ::= \{Convoy\} \tag{2}$$

$$Convoy ::= \langle Head, Members \rangle \tag{3}$$

$$Members ::= \{Car\_Following\} \tag{4}$$

$$Car\_Following ::= \langle Leader, Follower \rangle \tag{5}$$

$$Free\_Drivers ::= \{Free\} \tag{6}$$

$$Free ::= \langle Agent \rangle \tag{7}$$

$$Leader ::= \langle Agent \rangle \tag{8}$$

$$Follower ::= \langle Agent \rangle \tag{9}$$

$$Agent ::= \langle Vehicle, Driver \rangle \tag{10}$$

3.2 Holonic Model of Road Traffic

In order to represent car following interaction among vehicles, concepts from graph theory is useful to model relationships and interactions in complex systems. In this paper, a directed and weighted graph is used in which, the agents (couple vehicle–driver) are represented by the vertices. A directed edge represents the car following interaction among two vehicles (a follower and a leader). Road traffic could be represented by a graph as in Eq. 11.

$$G = ((V, E),\ \mathcal{W}_E, \mathcal{W}_V),\ \mathcal{W}_E : E \rightarrow \mathbb{R}_+,\ \mathcal{W}_V : V \rightarrow \mathbb{R}_+^4 \qquad (11)$$

V represents the set of vertices (vehicles); E represents the set of edges (car following interactions among follower and leader); $\mathcal{W}_E$ is the weight of edges (inter-distances between leader and follower); and $\mathcal{W}_V$ is the weight of vertices (features of vehicles).

$\forall v \in \mathcal{W}_V,\quad \mathcal{W}_V(v) = (x, y, l, L)$, x is position, y is speed, l is length and L is lane where agent vehicle moves.

$\forall e = (v_1, v_2) \in E$, v_2 is the leader of v_1 or v_1 is the follower of v_2. The weight of each edge is inter-distance between vehicles and is given by Eq. 12.

$$\forall e = (v_1, v_2) \in E, \mathcal{W}_E(e) = x(v_2) - x(v_1) - l(v_2) \qquad (12)$$

Numerous approaches exist depending on the problem to partition a graph. If the geometric layout of the graph is known, an appropriate recursive bisection could be used [5]. In our case, we have the geometric information about the road traffic graph, consequently, application of recursive bisection in order to build the top-down holarchy of traffic is possible. Figures 3 and 4 present an example of geometric layout of traffic with two lanes and a few vehicles and his corresponding graph according to our method. In this example, $G = (V, E)$ is defined such that $V = (v_1, v_2, v_3, v_4, v_5, v_6, v_7, v_8, v_9, v_{10}, v_{11}, v_{12})$ and $E = ((v_1, v_2), (v_2, v_3),$ $(v_3, v_4), (v_4, v_5), (v_5, v_6), (v_6, v_7), (v_8, v_9), (v_9, v_{10}), (v_{10}, v_{11}), (v_{11}, v_{12}))$.

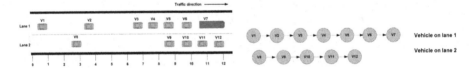

Fig. 3. Example of a traffic situation. It is a road composed by two lanes. Car are in yellow color and truck in blue color (Color figure online)

Fig. 4. Traffic graph that corresponds to the traffic situation in Fig. 3.

The road traffic graph have the following properties: (i) simple directed graph (oriented and without loops or multiple edges), (ii) planar graph (can draw in a plane without crossing two edges), (iii) acyclic graph (graph without cycle).

Let be $G_1 = (V_1, E_1)$, $G_2 = (V_2, E_2)$ two partitions of G. A cut is a partition of the vertices of a graph into two disjoint subsets. A cut [5] of G is defined by Eq. 13.

$$cut(G_1, G_2) = \sum_{v_1 \in V_1, v_2 \in V_2} \mathcal{W}_E(v_1, v_2) \qquad (13)$$

3.3 Holon Formation

The holonic model partitions and hierarchizes agents into group or holons in such that the most related group of agents belong to the same holon. The proposed holonification algorithm to extract the holarchy for a given graph $G = \langle (V, E), \mathcal{W}_V, \mathcal{W}_E \rangle$, is given by Algorithm 1. In this algorithm, vehicles are vertices and interactions follower $\rightarrow$ leader between vehicles are edges. Algorithm 1 begins with a graph of the set of agents' vehicles with their own internal state described by four variables characteristics: speed, length, position and lane. The algorithm starts at level 0 with an empty set of holons and build the upper level (the holarchy). Decomposition of the graph is based on bisection on the edge with a maximum weight (line 7) if the graph is connected (road traffic on a single lane). Nevertheless, if the graph is not connected (road traffic on several lanes), the recursive bisection firstly makes a connected graph (line 9) in order to build single lanes. During the recursive bisection of the graph, new holons are created at each abstraction level. We have assumed that holons can't overlap, i.e. at each abstraction level, holons are disjoints.

Algorithm 1. Extract all the holarchy

1: **procedure** HOLARCHY($G = (V, E), level = 0$)
2:     Create an empty holon H at level $level$
3:     $H^{level} \leftarrow V$
4:     **if** $|V| \geq 2$ **then**
5:         for each $e \in E$, compute $\mathcal{W}_E(e)$ as in Eq. 12
6:         **if** G is a connected graph **then**
7:             $G_1, G_2 = maxCut(G)$ ▷ Not traditionally max cut; but on the maximum edge weight
8:         **else**
9:             $G_1, G_2 = minCut(G)$ ▷ Not traditionally min cut; but on the minimum edge weight
10:         **end if**
11:         HOLARCHY($G_1 = (V_1, E_1), level + 1$)
12:         HOLARCHY($G_2 = (V_2, E_2), level + 1$)
13:     **else**
14:         HOLARCHY($G = (V, E), level + 1$) if level $level + 1$ exist   ▷ Stopping condition
15:     **end if**
16: **end procedure**

3.4 Multilevel Indicators

The holonic model reduces the complexity of the system's model. Holons with complex objectives are decomposed into sub-holons such that holon behavior approximates the behavior of his sub-holons. To this end, the behavior of a holon is obtained by finding the mean of the behavior (mean of speed, unweighted barycenter of position) of his sub-holons.

Multilevel indicators helps to ensure the consistency of the decomposition process [9]. In other words, multilevel indicators is a tool for validating that an aggregated behavior of a given holon is an acceptable approximation of his holons members. In order to ensure the consistency of this approximation, standard deviation σ is used. Standard deviation is a statistical concept used to measure the dispersion of a data-set. It measures the dispersion of a set of vehicles inter-distance as defined by Eq. (14), and the dispersion of a set of vehicles speed, as described by Eq. (15).

$$\sigma_{\mathcal{W}_E} = \sqrt{\frac{1}{|E|} \sum_{e \in E} (\mathcal{W}_E(e) - \overline{\mathcal{W}_E(e)})^2} \quad \text{where} \quad \overline{\mathcal{W}_E} = \frac{1}{|E|} \sum_{e \in E} \mathcal{W}_E(e) \quad (14)$$

$$\sigma_{y(V)} = \sqrt{\frac{1}{|V|} \sum_{v \in V} (y(v) - \overline{y(V)})^2} \quad \text{where} \quad \overline{y(V)} = \frac{1}{|V|} \sum_{v \in V} y(v) \quad (15)$$

4   Case Study and Experimental Results

In this section, the application of our model on a case study is presented and discussed.

4.1   Description of the Case Study

Generally, in traffic simulation, vehicles are generated and distributed on a road network according to an Origin/Destination matrix. Let Fig. 5 represents vehicles on a lane at time $t = 0$ of the system life. The initial characteristics of vehicles are recorded in Table 1. For case study simplification, all vehicles are on the same lane, and the length of the vehicles are not considered, i.e. vehicles are points. Application of our recursive bisection algorithm gives the holarchy shown in Fig. 6.

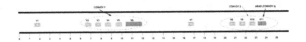

Fig. 5. A view of the road traffic state for the case study.

Table 1. Pair (position, velocity) of each vehicle in the case study

	v_1	v_2	v_3	v_4	v_5	v_6	v_7	v_8	v_9	v_{10}	v_{11}
X (position)	2	7	8	9	10	12	17	21	22	23	24
Y (velocity)	45.0	20.1	20.5	20.3	19.9	20.8	40.0	31.1	31.5	31.2	31.7

Holons composition are given by Table 2. As the standard deviation of a group consisting of a single member is zero, we did not insert these values in order to not saturate Table 2.

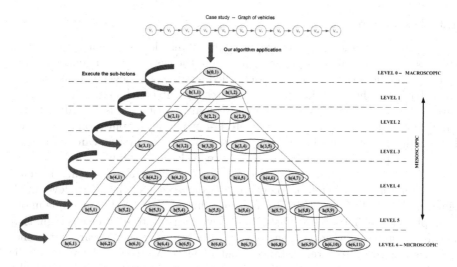

Fig. 6. Initial holarchy of vehicles built with the recursive bisection algorithm on the case study.

Table 2. Holons composition in holarchy presented in Fig. 6

Level	Holons	σ_{W_E}	$\sigma_{y(V)}$
0	$h(0,1) = \{v_1, v_2, v_3, v_4, v_5, v_6, v_7, v_8, v_9, v_{10}, v_{11}\}$	$\sigma_x^{h(0,1)} = 1.66$	$\sigma_y^{h(0,1)} = 8.38$
1	$h(1,1) = \{v_1\};$ $h(1,2) = \{v_2, v_3, v_4, v_5, v_6, v_7, v_8, v_9, v_{10}, v_{11}\}$	$\sigma_x^{h(1,2)} = 1.44$	$\sigma_y^{h(1,2)} = 6.84$
2	$h(2,1) = \{v_1\}; h(2,2) = \{v_2, v_3, v_4, v_5, v_6\};$ $h(2,3) = \{v_7, v_8, v_9, v_{10}, v_{11}\}$	$\sigma_x^{h(2,2)} = 0.43$ $\sigma_x^{h(2,3)} = 1.29$	$\sigma_y^{h(2,2)} = 0.31$ $\sigma_y^{h(2,3)} = 3.45$
3	$h(3,1) = \{v_1\}; h(3,2) = \{v_2, v_3, v_4, v_5\};$ $h(3,3) = \{v_6\}; h(3,4) = \{v_7\};$ $h(3,5) = \{v_8, v_9, v_{10}, v_{11}\}$	$\sigma_x^{h(3,2)} = 0$ $\sigma_x^{h(3,5)} = 0$	$\sigma_y^{h(3,2)} = 0.22$ $\sigma_y^{h(3,5)} = 0.23$
4	$h(4,1) = \{v_1\}; h(4,2) = \{v_2\};$ $h(4,3) = \{v_3, v_4, v_5\}; h(4,4) = \{v_6\};$ $h(4,5) = \{v_7\}; h(4,6) = \{v_8\};$ $h(4,7) = \{v_9, v_{10}, v_{11}\}$	$\sigma_x^{h(4,3)} = 0$ $\sigma_x^{h(4,7)} = 0$	$\sigma_y^{h(4,3)} = 0.24$ $\sigma_y^{h(4,7)} = 0.20$
5	$h(5,1) = \{v_1\}; h(5,2) = \{v_2\}; h(5,3) = \{v_3\};$ $h(5,4) = \{v_4, v_5\}; h(5,5) = \{v_6\}; h(5,6) = \{v_7\};$ $h(5,7) = \{v_8\}; h(5,8) = \{v_9\}; h(5,9) = \{v_{10}, v_{11}\}$	$\sigma_x^{h(5,4)} = 0$ $\sigma_x^{h(5,9)} = 0$	$\sigma_y^{h(5,4)} = 0.20$ $\sigma_y^{h(5,9)} = 0.25$
6	$h(6,1) = \{v_1\}; h(6,2) = \{v_2\}; h(6,3) = \{v_3\};$ $h(6,4) = \{v_4\}; h(6,5) = \{v_5\}; h(6,6) = \{v_6\};$ $h(6,7) = \{v_7\}; h(6,8) = \{v_8\}; h(6,9) = \{v_9\};$ $h(6,10) = \{v_{10}\}; h(6,11) = \{v_{11}\}$		

4.2 Discussion

Several abstraction levels are considered for the vehicles. The more precise level corresponds to the microscopic level (level 6 in the case study): a vehicle is associated with a holon. At the upper level called macroscopic (level 0 of case study), the behavior of the super-holon approximates a group of vehicles. The interest of this work (the holarchy) is to switch between abstraction levels according to the simulation's objectives (visualization, etc.) or available computational resources. For example, if computational resources is available, the system can be modeled at the most precise level (microscopic). Nevertheless, if computational resources is insufficient, system can be modeled at a higher level of abstraction. The main research question is therefore to ensure the consistency of the upper level modeling. Standard deviation helps us to ensure this consistency. For example in our example, at level 0, the value of standard deviation of inter-distance is high: that means the gaps between vehicles is very dispersed, i.e. vehicles are not homogeneous according to inter-distance point of view. Moreover, the value of the standard deviation of speed vehicles is high: that means the values of vehicles speeds are very dispersed, i.e. the vehicles are therefore not homogeneous according to speed point of view. In this case, we conclude that a holon $h(0,1)$ seems not to be a good approximation of its sub-holons. Nevertheless, at the level 3 of the holarchy in Fig. 6, the values of the standard deviation tend to zero: vehicles have sensibly the same speed, and the gap between them is approximately equal. These groups of vehicles are called convoy. We argue that if computational resources is not available, this system can be modeled with an acceptable approximation at level 3, level 4 etc.

Convoy is a group of "similar" vehicles, i.e., in a convoy, vehicles seem to have approximately the same speed and approximately the same inter-distance. Formally, convoy can be define as simple directed, planar, connected and acyclic weighted sub-graph on vertices and edges as in Eq. 16. In contrary with road traffic graph which is not necessarily connected convoy is always a connected graph.

$$G' \subseteq G \quad \text{such that} \quad G' = ((V', E'), \mathcal{W}_{E'}, \mathcal{W}_{V'}), \quad \sigma_{\mathcal{W}_{E'}} \leq \epsilon_1, \quad \sigma_{y(V')} \leq \epsilon_2 \tag{16}$$

$\epsilon_1 \to 0$ is the maximum standard deviation of inter-distance. $\epsilon_2 \to 0$ is the maximum standard deviation of speed. These values can be studied through observations of real convoys. An agent which plays the role Head of convoy is a vertex $v \in V$ such that output degree equals zero.

Since traffic is open and highly dynamic, our model can be apply in situation when traffic is low dynamic like peak hour, congested traffic, platoon, convoy in order to deal with the dynamicity of lane changing strategy.

4.3 Experimental Results

In order to validate the relevance of our top down decomposition algorithm, an evaluation of the algorithm's execution cost is realized. SARL [17] agent programming language and the Janus agent framework [8] are used for implementing

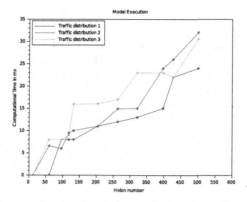

Fig. 7. Evaluation of the run-time performance of the holonification algorithm.

our algorithm. SARL is a general-purpose agent-oriented programming language which focus on holonic modeling and simulation. Tests were performed on a desktop computer, Pentium III, 800 MHz, 512 MB of RAM. Figure 7 presents the performances of our algorithm's execution with three traffic conditions. The corresponding linear regression line, which approximates the average traffic distribution has the following equation: $y = 0.057747x + 0.809038$. We assert that the execution of our algorithm has a good performance because the slope of the linear regression tends to zero.

It should be noted that the internal states of the agents are generated for running the model. They should be replaced by internal states issued from field interviews.

5   Conclusion and Future Works

Holonic multiagent systems are an effective tool to model traffic [9]. The first issue concerning holonic systems is the way how holarchy is structured (presentation of the whole containing/contained element of system) at time $t = 0$. This papers presents a top-down decomposition approach of road traffic system based on HMAS and graph theory. Multilevel indicators are proposed, based on the standard deviation, in order to evaluate the consistency of the created holons.

Road traffic is a open system and need to manage the holarchy that is builded over time. The main research questions to this end are how to manage a new holon in system? How can a sub-holon can be leave his super-holon if it's not meets the criteria of the group any more? How a holon can join a new group of holons? Future works include dynamic self-organization of the holons over time, and proposition of others multilevel indicators that will take into account the spatio-temporal properties of the system and the driver behaviors. Since the paper discuss only on the numerical results under virtual situation, a future work include also numerical results on real situation in one developing country.

References

1. Abdoos, M., Esmaeili, A., Mozayani, N.: Holonification of a network of agents based on graph theory. In: Jezic, G., Kusek, M., Nguyen, N.-T., Howlett, R.J., Jain, L.C. (eds.) KES-AMSTA 2012. LNCS (LNAI), vol. 7327, pp. 379–388. Springer, Heidelberg (2012). https://doi.org/10.1007/978-3-642-30947-2_42
2. Bouha, N., Morvan, G., Hassane, A., Kubera, Y.: A first step towards dynamic hybrid traffic modelling. In: Proceedings of the 29th European Conference on Modelling and Simulation (ECMS), pp. 64–70 (2015)
3. Bourrel, E., Lesort, J.: Mixing micro and macro representations of traffic flow: a hybrid model based on the LWR theory. In: 82th Annual Meeting of the Transportation Research Board (2003)
4. Cossentino, M., Gaud, N., Hilaire, V., Galland, S., Koukam, A.: ASPECS: an agent-oriented software process for engineering complex systems. Auton. Agents Multi-Agent Syst. 20(2), 260–304 (2010)
5. Elsner, U.: Graph partitioning a survey. Numerische Simulation auf massiv parallelen Rechnern SFB 393 (1997)
6. Esmaeili, A., Mozayani, N., Jahed Motlagh, M.R.: Multi-level holonification of multi-agent networks. In: 2014 Iranian Conference on Intelligent Systems (ICIS), pp. 1–5. IEEE, February 2014
7. Esmaeili, A., Mozayani, N., Motlagh, M.R.J., Matson, E.T.: A socially-based distributed self-organizing algorithm for holonic multi-agent systems: Case study in a task environment. Cogn. Syst. Res. 43, 21–44 (2017)
8. Galland, S., Gaud, N., Rodriguez, S., Hilaire, V.: Janus: another yet general-purpose multiagent platform. In: The 7th Agent-Oriented Software Engineering Technical Forum (TFGAOSE-2010), Paris, France. IEEE Computer Society Press (2010)
9. Gaud, N., Galland, S., Gechter, F., Hilaire, V., Koukam, A.: Holonic multilevel simulation of complex systems: application to real-time pedestrians simulation in virtual urban environment. Simul. Modell. Pract. Theory 16, 1659–1676 (2008)
10. Gerber, C., Siekmann, J., Vierke, G.: Holonic multi-agent systems. Research Center for Artificial Intelligence (DFKI) Technical report 681, German (1999)
11. Hilaire, V., Koukam, A., Gruer, P., Müller, J.-P.: Formal specification and prototyping of multi-agent systems. In: Omicini, A., Tolksdorf, R., Zambonelli, F. (eds.) ESAW 2000. LNCS (LNAI), vol. 1972, pp. 114–127. Springer, Heidelberg (2000). https://doi.org/10.1007/3-540-44539-0_9
12. Jaume, B.: Fundamentals of Traffic Simulation. Springer, New York (2010). https://doi.org/10.1007/978-1-4419-6142-6
13. Koestler, A.: The Ghost in the Machine. Hutchinson, Paris (1967)
14. Mammar, S., Mammar, S., Lebacque, J.: Highway traffic hybrid macro-micro simulation model. In: 11th IFAC Symposium on Control in Transportation System (2006)
15. Morvan, G.: Multi-level agent-based modeling. A literature survey. arXiv:1205.0561v7 (2013)
16. Poschinger, A., Kates, R., Keller, H.: Coupling of concurrent macroscopic and microscopic traffic flow models using hybrid stochastic and deterministic disaggregation. In: Transportation and Traffic Theory for the 21st Century (2002)
17. Rodriguez, S., Gaud, N., Galland, S.: SARL: a general-purpose agent-oriented programming language. In: The 2014 IEEE/WIC/ACM International Conference on Intelligent Agent Technology, Warsaw, Poland. IEEE Computer Society Press (2014)

18. Tchappi, I.H., Kamla, V.C., Galland, S., Kamgang, J.C.: Towards an multilevel agent-based model for traffic simulation. Procedia Comput. Sci. **109**, 887–892 (2017)
19. Vèque, V., Kaisser, F., Johnen, C., Busson, A.: CONVOY: a new cluster-based routing protocol for vehicular networks. In: Vehicular Networks Models and Algorithms. ISTE Publishing Knowledge/John Wiley and Sons Inc. (2013)

Author Index

Printed in the United States
By Bookmasters